HANDBOOK ON SMART GROWTH

Handbook on Smart Growth

Promise, Principles, and Prospects for Planning

Gerrit-Jan Knaap

Professor, Urban Studies and Planning, Director, National Center for Smart Growth, Associate Dean, School of Architecture, Planning and Preservation, University of Maryland, USA

Rebecca Lewis

Associate Professor, Planning, Public Policy and Management, Co-Director, Institute for Policy Research and Engagement, University of Oregon, USA

Arnab Chakraborty

Professor of Urban and Regional Planning, University of Illinois at Urbana-Champaign, USA

Katy June-Friesen

Ph.D. Candidate, Philip Merrill College of Journalism, Editor, National Center for Smart Growth, University of Maryland, USA

EE Edward Elgar
PUBLISHING

Cheltenham, UK • Northampton, MA, USA

Cover image: Montgomery Planning (M-NCPPC)

Published by
Edward Elgar Publishing Limited
The Lypiatts
15 Lansdown Road
Cheltenham
Glos GL50 2JA
UK

Edward Elgar Publishing, Inc.
William Pratt House
9 Dewey Court
Northampton
Massachusetts 01060
USA

Paperback edition 2024

A catalogue record for this book
is available from the British Library

Library of Congress Control Number: 2022937601

This book is available electronically in the **Elgar**online
Geography, Planning and Tourism subject collection
http://dx.doi.org/10.4337/9781789904697

ISBN 978 1 78990 468 0 (cased)
ISBN 978 1 78990 469 7 (eBook)
ISBN 978 1 0353 3732 3 (paperback)

Printed and bound by CPI Group (UK) Ltd, Croydon, CR0 4YY

Contents

Figures

Tables

Contributors

Jacob Becker
Jacob Becker is an Associate on the Carbon Free Electricity team at the Rocky Mountain Institute. His current work includes developing a financial modeling tool to quantify the impacts of utility planning scenarios and facilitating utility public engagement activities centered on equity. He received his Masters in both Environmental Science and City and Regional Planning at the University of North Carolina at Chapel Hill.

Philip R. Berke
Philip R. Berke is Research Professor, Department of City & Regional Planning; and Director of the Center for Resilient Communities and Environment, Institute for the Environment of the University of North Carolina. His research focuses on understanding interactions among networks of policy institutions, networks of land and development plans produced by such institutions, and social and physical vulnerability to hazards and climate change. He is senior editor for the *Oxford University Encyclopedia of Water Resources Management and Climate Policy*.

Ariel H. Bierbaum
Ariel H. Bierbaum is Assistant Professor of Urban Studies and Planning at the University of Maryland. Drawing on interdisciplinary perspectives, her research centers schools as a space of inquiry to achieve deep insights on planning practice and theory and the place of schools and school districts, as organizations, public assets, and core sites of realizing spatial justice. She previously served as Program Director and Senior Researcher at the Center for Cities + Schools at the University of California-Berkeley.

Martin A. Bierbaum
Martin A. Bierbaum is the former Associate Director of the National Center for Smart Growth at the University of Maryland. He was a leader in New Jersey state government planning for more than 15 years, including as Deputy Director for Smart Growth/Sustainability in the Governor's Policy Office, and was founding director of the Land Use Center at The College of New Jersey. He is now semi-retired and continues to write on planning issues and work as a planning consultant.

John I. Carruthers
John I. Carruthers is Associate Professor in the Department of City and Regional Planning and Director of the Graduate Program in Regional Science, at Cornell University. He was previously the founding Director of the Sustainable Urban Planning Program, at the George Washington University. Prior to that, Dr Carruthers served as a Research Economist at the Department of Housing and Urban

Development, and, during this time, was affiliated with the University of Maryland's National Center for Smart Growth.

Arnab Chakraborty

Arnab Chakraborty, AICP, is Professor of Urban and Regional Planning at the University of Illinois at Urbana Champaign. His research concerns land use regulations, housing and transportation equity, and scenario planning techniques. Chakraborty is an affiliate of the Center for Global Studies at UIUC and the National Center for Smart Growth at the University of Maryland. He is an associate editor of the *Journal of American Planning Association* and is a site visitor for the Planning Accreditation Board.

Timothy S. Chapin

Timothy S. Chapin is Dean of the College of Social Sciences and Public Policy and a professor of Urban and Regional Planning at Florida State University. Chapin's areas of expertise include growth management and comprehensive planning, urban redevelopment and revitalization, and urban economic development. He has published over 20 peer-reviewed articles, 10 book chapters, and 25 reports for planning clients, and secured over $3 million in outside funding to support his work.

Kelly J. Clifton

Kelly J. Clifton is the J. Armand Bombardier Chair of Regional Transportation Planning in the School of Community and Regional Planning at the University of British Columbia. Her work examines the interactions between human activities, transportation, technology, and the environment with the aim of improving public health and wellbeing. She sustains a research program in understanding and modeling pedestrian behaviors that was initiated during her time as a faculty member at the University of Maryland in the National Center for Smart Growth.

Casey Dawkins

Casey Dawkins is Professor of Urban Studies and Planning and an Affiliate of the National Center for Smart Growth at the University of Maryland, College Park. His current research addresses housing justice; US housing policy; the causes, consequences, and measurement of residential segregation by race and income; and the link between land use regulations and housing affordability. He has written two books and over 50 refereed journal articles and book chapters on these topics.

Reid Ewing

Reid Ewing is Distinguished Professor of City and Metropolitan Planning at the University of Utah, He directs the Metropolitan Research Center at the University. He holds master's degrees in Engineering and City Planning from Harvard University, and a PhD in Urban Planning and Transportation Systems from the Massachusetts Institute of Technology. A recent citation analysis found that Ewing, with more than 25,000 citations, is the sixth most highly cited among 1,100 academic planners in North America.

Nicholas Finio

Nicholas Finio, PhD, is Associate Director of the National Center for Smart Growth at the University of Maryland, College Park. His research is focused on the measurement, causes, and consequences of neighborhood change and the links between social inequality and land use policy and regional planning.

Andrea Garfinkel-Castro

Andrea Garfinkel-Castro is a doctoral candidate at the University of Utah. Her dissertation looks at the impacts of Black Lives Matter protests on local planning culture to address the dissonance between planning's longstanding goals for equity and actual outcomes. Her research interests include creative and affordable pedestrian safety in low-income settings, and culturally relevant and 'smart' landscapes and urbanisms. She is a proponent of radical planning as an approach to democratizing planning knowledge and to empower and engage communities in planning.

Steven R. Gehrke

Steven R. Gehrke is Assistant Professor in the Department of Geography, Planning, and Recreation at Northern Arizona University. His research interests include sustainable transportation planning and travel behavior modeling, with a focus on walking, cycling, and emerging mobility services.

Robert Goodspeed

Robert Goodspeed is Associate Professor of Urban and Regional Planning at the Taubman College of Architecture and Urban Planning at the University of Michigan. He teaches and conducts research in the areas of collaborative planning, urban informatics, and scenario planning theory and methods. He is the author of the book *Scenario Planning for Cities and Regions: Managing and Envisioning Uncertain Futures*. He is a member of the American Institute of Certified Planners and serves as a board member of the Lincoln Institute of Land Policy's Consortium for Scenario Planning.

Bernadette Hanlon

Bernadette Hanlon is Associate Professor of City and Regional Planning at Ohio State University. She specializes in the study of suburban transformation and community development. She has written two books, *Once the American Dream: Inner-ring Suburbs in the Metropolitan United States*, and *Cities and Suburbs: New Metropolitan Realities in the US* (with John Rennie Short and Thomas J. Vicino), and also co-edited (with Thomas J. Vicino) *The Routledge Companion to the Suburbs*. She has written several articles in leading journals in urban studies.

Marccus D. Hendricks

Marccus D. Hendricks is Assiociate Professor of Urban Studies and Planning and the Director of the Stormwater Infrastructure Resilience and Justice (SIRJ) Lab at the University of Maryland. His research explores how social processes and development patterns create hazardous human-built environments, vulnerable infrastructure, and the related risks in urban stormwater management and flooding. Recently, he was appointed to the US EPA's Science Advisory Board and as an author on the Human Social Systems chapter of the *Fifth National Climate Assessment.*

Katy June-Friesen

Katy June-Friesen is a PhD candidate at the Philip Merrill College of Journalism, University of Maryland, and a writer/editor for the National Center for Smart Growth and the Small Business Anti-Displacement Project. Her dissertation examines the public discourse and journalism about (re)development, neighborhood change, and spatial inequality in the Washington, DC, suburbs. She has worked in media for 15 years, and her journalism has appeared in national outlets. She edits nonprofit and scholarly publications and writes and researches for documentary media and public history projects.

Jonathan P. Katz

Jonathan P. Katz is a recent Master of Community Planning graduate from the University of Maryland, College Park and is now a civil servant. In his graduate work, he focused on aging and disability and planning. He has prior work experience with New York City's workforce development and small business assistance agency. He also holds degrees from the University of Chicago and University of Oxford.

Nikhil Kaza

Nikhil Kaza is Professor of City and Regional Planning and an adjunct in the Ecology, Environment and Energy Program at the University of North Carolina at Chapel Hill. His work is at the intersection of urbanization patterns, local energy policy and equity. In particular, he is interested in the role of local governments to influence energy production and consumption through urban form and patterns.

Jinyhup Kim

Jinyhup Kim is Assistant Professor in the Department of Urban Planning and Design at the Keimyung University, Daegu, Korea. Prior to joining the Keimyung University, Dr. Kim was a research fellow of Lee Kuan Yew Centre for Innovative Cities at the Singapore University of Technology and Design. His current research focuses on U.S. and Korea housing policy for baby boomers and millennials; housing pricing and market dynamics through machine learning; housing discrimination in peer-to-peer platforms. He has published articles in leading journals like Housing Policy Debate, Housing Studies, Journal of Real Estate Literature, and Journal of Urbanism.

Elijah Knaap

Elijah Knaap, PhD, is the Associate Director of the Center for Geospatial Sciences at the University of California, Riverside. His research investigates the relationships between spatial structure, social inequality, and public policy using computational and quantitative methods. In addition to his academic work, he is a core software developer for the Python Spatial Analysis Library (PySAL).

Gerrit-Jan Knaap

Gerrit-Jan Knaap is Executive Director of the National Center for Smart Growth, Professor of Urban Studies and Planning, and Associate Dean of the School of Architecture, Planning and Preservation at the University of Maryland. His research interests include the interactions between housing markets and policy, the economics and politics of land use planning, the efficacy of economic development instruments, and the impacts of environmental policy. Knaap has authored or co-authored over 65 articles in peer-refereed journals, and co-authored or co-edited nine books.

John D. Landis

John D. Landis is Professor Emeritus of City and Regional Planning at the Weitzman School of Design at the University of Pennsylvania. He previously held faculty positions at the University of California, Berkeley, the Georgia Institute of Technology, and the University of Rhode Island. John's current research is focused on the mechanisms, forms and equity impacts of urban and suburban growth; and on how entrepreneurial innovations are reshaping global cities. He holds a PhD from UC Berkeley and a Bachelor's of Science degree from MIT.

Rebecca Lewis

Rebecca Lewis is Associate Professor in Planning, Public Policy and Management at the University of Oregon and the Co-Director of the Institute of Policy Research and Engagement. She is an affiliate of the National Center for Smart Growth. She studies land use policy, transportation finance, and the nexus of land use, transportation, housing and climate change. Her work has been funded by the National Institute for Transportation and Communities, National Science Foundation, and the Department of Land Conservation and Development.

Willow Lung-Amam

Willow Lung-Amam is Associate Professor of Urban Studies and Planning at the University of Maryland, College Park, where she also serves as Director of Community Development at the National Center for Smart Growth Research and Education and Director of the Small Business Anti-Displacement Network. Her research focuses on issues of urban and suburban inequality, particularly related to issues of redevelopment, gentrification, racial segregation, immigration, and neighborhood opportunity. She is the author of *Trespassers? Asian American and the Battle for Suburbia*, and a forthcoming book on redevelopment politics and equitable development organizing in the Washington, DC, suburbs.

Lori Lynch

Lori Lynch is Professor and Chair of the Department of Agricultural and Resource Economics at the University of Maryland. She examines various issues related to farmland preservation and land conservation as well as providing advice to farmland program managers and legislative bodies. Her PhD was from the University of California, Berkeley and her MS from University of California, Davis.

David A. Newburn

David Newburn is Associate Professor in the Department of Agricultural and Resource Economics and a research affiliate of the National Center for Smart Growth Research and Education at the University of Maryland. He has worked extensively on spatial models of land-use change for managing residential development and has examined the effectiveness of land-use policies to protect forest and farmland. He received his doctoral degree from the University of California, Berkeley.

Yan Song

Dr Yan Song is Professor in the Department of City and Regional Planning at the University of North Carolina at Chapel Hill. Dr Song's research interests include spatial analysis of urban spatial structure and urban form, green cities, land use development and regulations, land use and transportation integration, and how to accommodate research in the above fields by using planning supporting systems, such as GIS, urban analytics, and other computer-aided planning tools.

Emily Talen

Emily Talen is Professor of Urbanism at the University of Chicago, where she teaches urban design and directs the Urbanism Lab. She holds a PhD in urban geography from the University of California, Santa Barbara. She is a Fellow of the American Institute of Certified Planners, and the recipient of a Guggenheim Fellowship. Talen has written extensively on the topics of urban design and social equity. Her latest book is *Neighborhood* (Oxford University Press, 2018).

Jeffrey M. Vincent

Jeffrey M. Vincent is co-founder and director at the Center for Cities and Schools at the University of California, Berkeley. He has a PhD in City and Regional Planning from Berkeley. His research sits at the intersection of land use planning, community development, and educational improvement, with a particular focus on how school facilities serve as educational and neighborhood assets. He has studied issues of public school facility planning, financing, and equity for nearly two decades.

Haoluan Wang

Haoluan Wang is a doctoral student in the Department of Agricultural and Resource Economics at the University of Maryland. His research interests include agri-environmental policies that subsidize farmers' adoption of conservation practices on working farmland and land conservation with a focus on spatial spillovers. He received his MSc in Agricultural and Resource Economics from the University of Alberta and a BA in International Economics and Trade from Zhejiang University.

Hanxue Wei

Hanxue Wei is a doctoral student in the field of Regional Science in the Department of City and Regional Planning, at Cornell University. She previously worked as an urban planner at East China Architectural Design & Research Institute and China Intelligent Urbanization Co-creation Center for High Density Region in Shanghai,

China. She has a Master of Science in Urban Design from Georgia Institute of Technology and a Masters in Urban Planning from Tongji University.

Timothy F. Welch
Timothy F. Welch is a Senior Lecturer in Urban Planning in the School of Architecture and Planning at the University of Auckland. His research is in the area of transportation, infrastructure and urban modeling with a focus on the use of big data, analytical methods and technology and reference to equity and climate change.

Lucien Wostenholme
Lucien Wostenholme is a junior at the College of Architecture, Art, and Planning at Cornell University pursuing a BS in Urban and Regional Studies. His research interests lie at the intersection of planning, economics, and policy, particularly the arena of sustainable growth. Outside of academia, he holds positions within two student-run consulting organizations, with experience conducting impact analyses for Sierra Club and Ithaca's public bus system.

Preface

In 1997, Governor Parris Glendening signed into law Maryland's nationally renowned Smart Growth and Neighborhood Conservation Act. It was immediately lauded as a bold new approach to land use planning and management and described by the Kennedy School as "one of the most innovative programs in the country" and by the World Wildlife Fund as "a gift to the earth." It included five components: the Priority Funding Act, the Rural Legacy Program, the Live Near Your Work Program, the Brownfields Redevelopment program, and the Job Creation Tax Credit. The Act did not usurp local land use authority but used the power of state funding to encourage development in places planned for growth.

The passage of the Maryland Smart Growth Act is widely recognized as one of the key milestones in the progression of smart growth as a concept and national movement. The Act not only established the principle that incentives are preferred over regulations, but also the notion that government approaches to land use should involve multiple government agencies, that transportation and land use policy must be closely integrated, and that policy should be informed by the best available data and scientific expertise. In Maryland, the establishment of the National Center for Smart Growth was an important element of this strategy.

In 2000, the University of Maryland (UMD) launched an internal competition for new research initiatives that would raise its profile as one of the leading research universities in the nation. Proposals for new initiatives had to be interdisciplinary and involve at least two colleges or schools on the College Park campus. After some internal conversations, we submitted a proposal to establish a Center for Growth Management Studies. The proposal included support from the College of Agriculture, College of Engineering, and School of Public Policy. The proposal was one of four funded that year, out of 11 submissions.

When the governor's office learned of the growth management initiative at UMD, there was immediate interest in collaboration. We met with Governor Glendening to discuss how the new research initiative could help support the exciting but nascent new smart growth program led by the state. Senator Ron Young joined the conversation and suggested the research center adopt a new name: The National Center for Smart Growth Research and Education (NCSGRE). All agreed this was a bold title and a good way to marry these two initiatives. Subsequently, Governor Glendening added funding for the center from the supplemental state budget. In the fall of 2000, NCSGRE was launched.

Like many other centers at research universities, the NCSGRE engages students and faculty in research and educational programs. Unlike most other research centers, however, the NCSGRE is deeply embedded in state policymaking with an explicit mission of providing knowledge of direct benefit to the state. By statute, the

NCSGRE director sits on the governor's Smart Growth Subcabinet and the state's Sustainable Growth Commission. And by statute, the NCSGRE must work with the Maryland Department of Planning to collect and report measures of smart growth failure and success.

Over the last 20 years, NCSGRE graduate students, faculty, and staff have written countless technical papers and reports, books, and peer-refereed journal articles. Many of these publications are cited in the chapters that follow. Perhaps most importantly, and most lastingly, the NCSGRE assembled a highly productive group of scholars and helped train graduate students who now hold leadership positions at premier universities, nonprofit organizations, and government agencies around the world. These NCSGRE affiliates and alumni, who have authored or co-authored 14 of the 18 chapters in this volume, represent the next generation of smart growth advocates and scholars.

This volume was intended to be the focus of NCSGRE's 20th anniversary celebrations in College Park, Maryland. The COVID-19 pandemic unfortunately made that impossible. But work on this volume continued, and what would have been said at that celebration is proudly conveyed in the pages that follow. Twenty-plus years ago we proposed to create a center that would establish the University of Maryland as a national leader in research and education about this new idea called smart growth. Today we are pleased to see that the NCSGRE has delivered on this promise.

James Cohen and Steve Hurtt
Emeritus Lecturer and Emeritus Dean, School of Architecture, Planning, and
Preservation

Introduction

The birth date of smart growth is difficult to identify. In the late 1980s, intolerance for urban sprawl had reached a high point in many parts of the country. Growth management had evolved from the practice of a few bold municipalities to a widespread topic of interest among planning practitioners, policymakers, advocates, and researchers. Pioneering state land use programs in Oregon, Florida, and elsewhere were rising in influence and catching the attention of states looking for an appropriate role in the battle against sprawl. And discussions were beginning at the federal level about how to integrate land use into decision-making about transportation funding.

Then, in 1991, at a meeting in central California, a group of architects, planners, and policy advocates pronounced the Ahwahnee Principles, articulating what would evolve into the principles of smart growth. Now widely known, these smart growth principles proposed a development pattern that is compact with mixed uses, a sense of place, a range of transportation and housing options, laced with public open spaces, and surrounded by farms, forests, and natural resources. Proponents of these development patterns claimed they would provide multiple and widespread benefits, including less time in cars and improved physical health, more affordable housing in high-quality neighborhoods, and more pristine air, water, and wildlife habitat. A network of influential organizations supported by the Clinton–Gore Environmental Protection Agency quickly spread the word, and by the late 1990s "smart growth" had arguably become the dominant planning paradigm in the United States.

To advance this new paradigm, the American Planning Association in 1997 published *The Growing Smart Legislative Guidebook,* and Maryland Governor Parris Glendening signed the Maryland Smart Growth and Neighborhood Conservation Act; both drew widespread attention and acclaim. In the 25–30 years since, countless academic and professional meetings, interactive websites, professional reports, and scholarly articles have both promoted and pilloried smart growth principles. Yet it is difficult to find a source that answers basic questions, such as:

- How have the principles of smart growth evolved over time?
- How and to what extent have the principles of smart growth become embedded in the plans, regulations, and policies of state, local, and federal government agencies?
- What has academic research revealed about the validity of smart growth principles?
- Have we made significant progress toward addressing the problems that smart growth was intended to address?
- What challenges did the original smart growth principles fail to address?

To answer these questions, we commissioned leading scholars from across the nation to write chapters on particular aspects of smart growth. We organized their contributions into seven parts.

Part I contains two chapters that provide an introduction to smart growth, the history of the concept, and an overview of its evolution over time. They also address issues of governance, including how local, state, regional, and national governments pursued smart growth at various points in time.

The birth of smart growth was a reflection of its times. Incomes, housing values, and gas prices grew steadily throughout most of the 1990s. Unemployment remained low while housing starts climbed. The US economy flourished, but urban sprawl was rampant. The consumption of farm and forest land far outpaced population growth. The number of vehicle miles traveled grew at rates that outpaced the capacity of existing road networks and created widespread traffic delays. The demand for schools, parks, and other public services strained the budgets of state and local governments. Previous attempts to stop or control growth had failed, both in the courts and on the ground. In this environment, smart growth was conceived. Proponents promised that urban growth could be sustained, but its form and location would be better managed with tools that favored incentives over regulations and with governance structures that favored intergovernmental cooperation over top-down mandates.

Against this backdrop, John Landis in Chapter 1 presents an introduction to, history of, and new agenda for smart growth. He begins by describing the 10 smart growth principles and how the piecemeal planning approaches of the past gave rise to these principles. He then reviews the history of smart growth implementation, highlighting the pioneering efforts of metropolitan Portland, Oregon, and the state of Maryland. He notes that implementation proceeded in fits and starts over the course of political cycles and concludes with a "smart growth 2.0" agenda, a topic we revisit in Chapter 18.

In Chapter 2, Martin Bierbaum, Rebecca Lewis, and Timothy Chapin explore the governance challenges of smart growth. Unlike past efforts at growth management, the smart growth attack on sprawl was launched at multiple levels in what they describe as the marble cake of land use governance. The authors pay particular attention to the role of states, in part because of Maryland's outsized role in defining an incentive-based and intergovernmental approach. They then describe a fourth wave of land use governance in which the language of smart growth is superseded by the language of sustainable development, and regional approaches ascend over state intervention. They conclude with thoughts on the future governance of smart growth in these times of growing political division, but they refrain from offering a universal approach for all times and places.

Combined, these two chapters portray a movement that captured the imagination of planners, policymakers, and land use advocates across the nation with the notion that urban growth itself was not bad, but its location and form needed shaping. By relying on incentives instead of regulations and by integrating efforts among and within government agencies, there was hope that smart growth could overcome some of the implementation challenges of the past. That didn't happen. While smart growth concepts became widely accepted within the planning community, and smarter growth projects and communities now sprinkle the nation, the incentives and the new government strategies have not overcome the entrenched preferences, political forces, and physical challenges that stymie implementation. Thus, while there is some evidence that smart growth concepts have become embedded in state and local plans and policies, many states have moved beyond smart growth, and the extent to which urban development today or in the recent past now reflects the principles of smart growth remains highly uncertain.

The prescription for smart growth was presented in 10 principles, supported by a broad network of mostly Washington-based organizations and promoted nationwide using modern public relations strategies. The chapters in Parts II, III, and IV examine these smart growth principles, as pronounced by the Smart Growth Network.[1] The US Environmental Protection Agency continues to lead the Smart Growth Network, which includes many of the nation's premier planning, development, environmental, and local government organizations. The 10 principles prescribe where urban growth should occur, what characteristics growth should exhibit, how growth should be integrated with transportation systems, and the process through which growth should be accommodated.

The principles are familiar to students of planning. As discussed in several of the chapters, some principles reflect pre-1990s growth management and growth control concepts, while others were novel at the time. As listed by the Smart Growth Network, they are:

1. Mix land uses
2. Take advantage of compact building design
3. Create a wide range of housing opportunities and choices
4. Create walkable neighborhoods
5. Foster distinctive, attractive communities with a strong sense of place
6. Preserve open space, farmland, natural beauty, and critical environmental areas
7. Strengthen and direct development toward existing communities
8. Provide a variety of transportation choices
9. Make development decisions predictable, fair, and cost effective
10. Encourage community and stakeholder collaboration in development decisions

To explore what planners, policymakers, and researchers have learned about these principles over the last three decades, we commissioned leading national scholars to write chapters on the first eight outcome-driven principles of smart growth. We do not assert that the last two process-focused principles are unimportant; we felt that the criteria for their evaluation were fundamentally different from those of the first eight, and there was less information on which to draw. We recognize this was a judgment call.

Each chapter addresses the logic of a smart growth principle and its historical antecedents. Authors also examine the goal of the principle and detail the urban development and land use planning challenges that the principle was designed to address. In addition, each chapter describes the implementation tools and strategies that local and state governments adopted to implement the principle. Authors reflect on which tools have worked best and which were ineffective. Finally, they consider the pertinence of smart growth principles under current conditions and offer recommendations for moving forward.

First, Part II addresses principles that prescribe the location of urban development. Authors define the concept of urban containment and the challenges of promoting compact building design; explore the struggle to preserve natural resources, with a focus on farm and forest lands; and consider the challenge of redevelopment, and the means and extent to which smart growth can direct growth to existing urban areas.

In Chapter 3, John Carruthers, Hanxue Wei, and Lucien Wostenholme provide a review of urban containment, a term that captures the principle of promoting compact building design. They introduce and contextualize the concept as a pragmatic response to urban sprawl, which is a pattern of development that poses a number of objective problems smart growth seeks to address. They suggest that containment grew as a matter of public policy in the 1970s and has since evolved into a wider landscape of policies, ranging from large-scale frameworks in the form of regional urban growth boundaries to small-scale frameworks in the form of local design standards. They conclude by suggesting that a "smart growth 2.0" should adopt a more market-oriented perspective on containment, include fewer regulations and policy incentives, and aim to channel the positive externalities of urbanization and overcome the negative externalities.

In Chapter 4, David Newburn, Lori Lynch, and Haoluan Wang explore the preservation of open space, farmland, and critical environmental areas. Although most Americans reside in urban and suburban areas, the authors argue that exurban development on large lots has caused the greatest loss of farm and forest land in the United States. They discuss four policy approaches to manage growth and promote land conservation: regulatory instruments, incentive-based policies, participatory preservation programs, and transfer-of-development rights programs. They then reframe the urban–rural planning dichotomy and describe synergistic policies for improving land preservation. The authors conclude by examining challenges to policy evaluation and offer recommendations for future research and new approaches to land preservation.

In Chapter 5, Bernadette Hanlon describes three types of infill development—development on underutilized land, demolition and replacement, and building renovation—and the potential barriers and challenges to each. These barriers include community opposition, poorly suited infrastructure, and prohibitive redevelopment costs. She then describes the consequences of infill development—some favorable, such as rising density, diversity, and infrastructure cost savings; some less favorable, such as gentrification and displacement. She concludes with a discussion of the ways in which suburban poverty, changing automobile technology, and the COVID-19 pandemic might affect the future of infill development in the United States.

Next, Part III addresses principles that prescribe the form and character of urban development. Authors explore the challenge of mixed-use development and the benefits, measurement, and implementation of mixed land uses; discuss issues of urban design and how to create vibrant communities with a sense of place; and address the struggle to provide housing choices, with a focus on housing affordability and diversity.

In Chapter 6, Yan Song summarizes recent research on land use mix and examines the effects of mixing uses on outcomes of interest to planners and policymakers. These include commuting behavior and health, environmental quality, housing markets, and urban vibrancy. She presents alternative approaches to categorizing, developing, and implementing use-mix measures and discusses the strengths and weaknesses of each measure. Finally, she provides an overview of land use mix policies and practices, reflects on needs for future research, and concludes with recommendations for research, policy, and practice to advance the growth of mixed-use development.

In Chapter 7, Emily Talen lays out the urban design principles of smart growth and the challenge of fostering distinctive, attractive communities with a strong sense of place. Normatively, she suggests, this often translates into an emphasis on walkability, compactness, and diversity. She argues, however, that the application of design principles requires sensitivity to locational context, a realistic time frame, attention to social goals, and process-oriented concerns. She shows how urban design principles that are conducive to smart growth offer tangible benefits, provides a review of progress to date, and concludes with thoughts about the future of urban design, particularly as it relates to the COVID-19 pandemic and social justice movements.

In Chapter 8, Casey Dawkins and Jinyhup Kim review recent empirical evidence to assess the effects of smart growth regulatory reforms on two dimensions of housing choice: affordability and diversity. They find that traditional land use regulations have been shown to inflate the price of housing and limit the diversity of housing options, but they maintain that it is difficult to draw definitive conclusions about the housing market impacts of comprehensive smart growth policy. This is because restrictive regulations are often adopted in concert with other compensatory policies that mediate their impact. Furthermore, they suggest, policies designed to promote a diversity of housing options may or may not foster local population diversity or inclusion. They conclude that land use regulatory reform is a promising tool, but not the only one, for expanding housing choice.

Finally, Part IV addresses principles that prescribe the relationship between transportation and land use. The transportation–land use connection is a key concept in the promotion of smart growth. Authors explore the concept of walkability, with a focus on what makes a neighborhood walkable and how travel behavior responds, and investigate the challenge of providing transportation choices while reducing reliance on the automobile.

In Chapter 9, Kelly Clifton critically reviews the progress that has been made promoting walking in cities over the last 25 years. She argues that improvements in data on pedestrian behavior and urban form characteristics have deepened our understanding of walking for utilitarian and recreational purposes, the relationship between walking and the built environment, and the link between walking and health outcomes. Although she suggests walking as a mode of transportation is on the rise, Clifton raises concerns about the unequal benefits of walkable places, the persistence of pedestrian fatalities and injuries, and the continued dominance of the automobile in suburban areas. Looking ahead, she describes how technology will likely automate the mobility of people and goods, as well as generate new modes of urban mobility. She concludes with a prescriptive agenda for walking and other forms of sustainable transport as part of a "smart growth 2.0."

In Chapter 10, Timothy Welch and Steve Gehrke address how automobility has long shaped the transportation–land use connection and review the determinants and consequences of the nation's reliance on the automobile. Using a review of the literature and specific case studies, they highlight four smart growth tools that can mitigate the ill effects of the automobile: non-auto infrastructure, transit-oriented development, complete streets, and parking management. They conclude with thoughts on how emerging transportation technologies might impact the future of smart growth.

Together, the chapters in Parts II, III, and IV reveal that we have learned a great deal about smart growth principles over the last 25–30 years. None of the principles are without continuing controversy and debate, but research confirms that smart growth principles can produce the environmental benefits they were established to promote. The principles have merit, and we have made some progress toward implementing them, but the challenges that smart growth was originally conceived to address remain far from resolved. The devil, of course, is in the details. Compact growth can reduce energy consumption without raising housing costs if there is upzoning to relieve development pressures. Mixed uses can reduce automobile travel if the right uses are mixed in the right locations. Strategic investment in urban design can enhance sense of place, but it matters whose sense of place. Farm and forest conservation can enhance water quality, but it matters a great deal what land uses are preserved.

Further, every principle faces substantial challenges to implementation: a fragmented structure of land use governance, deference to property rights, a continuing preference for cars and single-family homes, and the difficulty of changing the form of cities that are over two centuries old. And because the implementation of nearly every smart growth principle can produce more desirable places to live and work, they can all increase home prices and rents and exacerbate social inequities. This does not suggest smart growth principles are invalid, or that efforts should not continue to mitigate urban sprawl; it does suggest, however, that there is no set of urban development principles that will always and everywhere further both environmental and social objectives.

Some critical issues that were not addressed by the original smart growth principles have risen in salience over the last 25–30 years, including health, equity, climate, energy, and technology issues. Parts V and VI include seven chapters about these issues and suggest that the scope of smart growth must expand if it is to confront the pressing social and environmental challenges of today.

All social movements are products and reflections of the times when they arose. Smart growth is no different. The attack on sprawl came at a time of relative prosperity and social harmony in the United States, conditions few would argue prevail today. While systemic racism remained pervasive after the 1960s civil rights era, Black Lives Matter wasn't launched until 2013, after George Zimmerman was acquitted for killing Trayvon Martin. Obesity rates in the United States had been rising for decades, but the Robert Wood Johnson Foundation didn't launch the Active Living by Design campaign until 2002. Al Gore as Vice President was a vocal warrior in the fight against climate change, but the Paris Agreement wasn't signed until 2015. Gasoline prices peaked in 2012, but the cost of solar energy fell 70 percent between 2010 and 2020. Finally, Amsterdam pioneered the digital city in 1994, but IBM didn't launch its $50 million Smarter Cities campaign until 2009. Thus, while the principles of smart growth have not changed since the early 1990s, the social, environmental, and political context in which smart growth must now operate has changed a great deal.

While the issues in Part V and VI were not directly addressed by the original 10 smart growth principles, it is not the case that smart growth advocates were not aware of them or failed to consider them in their advocacy for smart growth. Certainly, some issues were aligned more closely than others. The empirical evidence that obesity and its adverse health consequences was related to urban form, for example, became rapidly imbedded in smart growth messaging. Similarly, smart growth was quickly promoted as a strategy for addressing climate change as the awareness of that issue became more prevalent. And smart growth advocates were certainly supportive of calls for social equity, even though it took time for them to become active in this arena. Still, these and other issues were not central to the smart growth agenda when smart growth was first conceived. They cannot be ignored if smart growth is to remain relevant in the future.

Part V addresses health and equity issues, including a chapter on education and workforce development, now widely understood as closely related to urban development patterns. Authors also examine the relationship between development patterns and public health, an issue the recent COVID-19 pandemic has made even more evident; discuss gentrification and ask if there can be smart growth without displacement of existing businesses and residents; and address the broader relationship between smart growth and social equity and how the two objectives have merged over time.

In Chapter 11, Ariel Bierbaum, Jeffrey Vincent, and Jonathan Katz argue that individual and community success requires that all people have realistic opportunities to access high quality public education and workforce training options. Without such opportunities, cycles of poverty and disenfranchisement continue. They contend, however, that smart growth advocates have largely neglected education and workforce training and should foreground interconnections between smart growth and education, schools, and workforce development. These interconnections are not some aspirational or normative ideal, they suggest, but rather a principle upon which smart growth advocates and planning professionals can and should build a much-needed body of knowledge.

As described by Andrea Garfinkel-Castro and Reid Ewing in Chapter 12, the fields of urban planning and public health were both conceived in the early 1900s in response to the need for clean drinking water, adequately lit and ventilated housing, access to parks and open spaces, and public spaces for social interaction. Over time, however, the two fields grew apart as most cities in the developed world built the basic infrastructure to assure healthy environments and adequate living standards. But in the last two decades, scholars and practitioners again realized that rising issues of public health—physical activity and obesity, traffic accidents, air quality, and mental health—are closely linked to the built environment. The authors examine the relationship between these newer public health concerns and urban development patterns at multiple scales, showing that urban form and public health are closely related, but often in complex and indirect ways. They conclude with suggestions for how public health could be more directly included in a "smart growth 2.0."

In Chapter 13, Nicholas Finio and Elijah Knaap investigate the relationship between smart growth and gentrification. They begin with a review of empirical literature on the movement of higher-class individuals into disinvested urban areas in US cities—a pervasive phenomenon over the last 30 years, despite population decline in major central cities. They argue that smart growth advocates, in their zeal to stop urban sprawl, historically failed to consider the negative social impacts of redevelopment. By limiting suburban growth, smart growth policies can cause the loss of affordable housing and accelerate gentrification and displacement. The authors conclude by detailing how a "smart growth 2.0" can more equitably mitigate the consequences of gentrification.

In Chapter 14, Willow Lung-Amam and Katy June-Friesen examine equity issues in smart growth efforts. They first examine the forces that brought smart growth and equitable development movements closer together in recent decades, as well as the critical questions and tensions that continue to push them apart. They then trace the slow but critical turn in the smart growth movement—from a time when the concerns facing low-income communities of color and other marginalized groups were largely divorced from questions of smart growth—to today, when equity concerns are more in the foreground. They highlight three key tensions and challenges: building regional coalitions and scaling up equitable development policies; prioritizing policies to deconcentrate or invest in poor neighborhoods; and the limits of infill, mixed-use development strategies.

Part VI details climate, energy, and technology issues not addressed by the original smart growth principles. Authors explore the potential of smart growth to address the challenges of climate change mitigation and adaptation, a nexus with yet unexploited potential; address energy sourcing and supply, noting that the spatial demands of renewable energy can conflict with the principles of smart growth; and examine smart cities technologies and identify how smart technologies can both serve to mitigate and exacerbate the challenges of smart growth.

In Chapter 15, Marccus Hendricks and Philip Berke explore the relationship between smart growth and climate change, including smart growth's potential to both mitigate greenhouse gas emissions and adapt to a changing climate. They begin with a conceptual framing of how specific smart growth principles might serve to advance both mitigation and adaptation. They then review the empirical evidence and find that smart growth can serve as an effective, though limited, strategy for addressing climate change. They also find that many smart growth developments have missed the opportunity to mitigate climate risks. They conclude with thoughts about the future of smart growth as an approach to climate change.

In Chapter 16, Jacob Becker and Nikhil Kaza explore ways to decrease energy consumption and increase renewable generation while upholding the goals of smart growth. Specifically, they suggest, smart growth policies that promote compact development can lessen energy uses in both the transportation and building sectors. The decarbonization of the energy systems, however, has the potential to create sprawl due to low energy density of renewable energy sources. To address the challenges and opportunities of integrating energy planning principles into smart growth, they argue that land use guidelines can be used to lessen the institutional and physical barriers to reducing fossil fuel consumption and energy sprawl.

In Chapter 17, Robert Goodspeed discusses the rise and logic of the "smart city" idea, arguing it often takes the form of managerial innovations that are less politically controversial than smart growth. As a consequence, smart city and smart growth ideas are largely separate debates. But he suggests that smart growth proponents engage with digital technologies in two areas related to traditional smart growth policy goals: ensure that new technologies such as automated vehicles reinforce smart growth, and upgrade professional tools to better monitor and respond to urban change. Such integration of smart cities and smart growth, he concludes, can form the basis for a "smart growth 2.0."

In sum, the chapters in Parts V and VI foreground important issues that were not as pressing when smart growth was born, or at least not for smart growth's target demographic. The principles of smart growth were conceived in large to address White, middle-class concerns about traffic congestion, water and air pollution, property taxes, and the banality of urban sprawl. They were not designed to address the social and environmental issues of today, such as equitable access to jobs and quality education, human physical and mental health, climate change, and housing affordability.

In some cases, the principles of smart growth are easily adapted and well suited to tackle these additional challenges. Promoting transportation choices, for example, can help address climate change, promote healthy physical activity, and enhance access to opportunity. In other cases, the smart growth principles of compact development and resource preservation may contribute to gentrification and housing unaffordability, as well as slow the transition to renewable energy. And in yet other cases, the goals of smart growth might be more easily addressed with smarter technologies than smarter development patterns. Three decades ago, it was not possible to address the ill effects of urban sprawl directly with better use of data and data science, time-varying congestion tolls, shared electric vehicles, and other less carbon-intensive forms of heat and transportation. It is now.

Finally, Part VII takes stock of the previous chapters and summarizes what we have learned about the penetration of smart growth principles, the validity of those principles, and the extent to which we have made progress toward the goals these principles established. In Chapter 18, we attempt to summarize and synthesize the previous chapters and consider smart growth as an integrated concept.

Toward that end, we first address the extent to which smart growth has become embedded in the national conversation about urban growth and development and, with the limited information available, the extent to which smart growth has become embedded in state and local land use plans and policies. Then, with reference to national environmental and social trend data, we explore the extent to which smart growth has "bent the curve" on the social and environmental issues it was intended to address. We then discuss the challenges of implementation, with a reconsideration of why smart growth is more difficult to implement than discuss.

Finally, we conclude with a policy agenda for a "smart growth 2.0." Here we make the case that for smart growth to continue to shape urban policy and urban development patterns, it must not only redouble its crusade against urban sprawl but address critical contemporary technological and social issues that are most salient with policymakers today.Smart growth advocates must redouble their efforts to advance the existing principles of smart growth. They must address urban sprawl but expand their scope to address new and critical challenges that are inextricably entwined with the location and character of urban growth.

Gerrit Knaap, Rebecca Lewis, Arnab Chakraborty, and Katy June-Friesen

NOTE

1.   https://smartgrowth.org/smart-growth-principles/

PART I

SMART GROWTH HISTORY, PERFORMANCE, AND GOVERNANCE

1. Smart growth: introduction, history, and an agenda for the future

John D. Landis

Smart growth tries to steer urban growth to locations where it creates positive land use synergies and community quality-of-life benefits while minimizing adverse environmental, public service, and fiscal impacts. Unlike some prior urban planning paradigms, smart growth isn't explicitly pro-growth or anti-growth. Rather, it acknowledges that the complex forces of population and economic growth are beyond any single municipality's control, and that the choice confronting local elected officials is not *whether* to accommodate growth but *how* to accommodate it. This is the growth half of the smart growth label. The smart half lies in using incentives to direct growth to places where it *is* wanted rather than using regulations to prevent growth from occurring where it is not wanted. Smart growth also tries to give people more choices about where and how they live, including choices among neighborhoods, housing types, densities, travel modes, and urban and cultural amenities. The term smart growth came into widespread use in the mid-1990s (Daniels, 2001; Knaap, 2006), but its underlying principles are much older, some dating all the way back to the early twentieth century. More recently, smart growth has been overtaken by other buzzword planning approaches, notably sustainability and resilience, but 10 years after the Great Recession, as the nation gears up for another round of suburban population growth, the ideas at the core of the smart growth movement remain both relevant and important.

This introductory chapter does four things. First, by way of context, I briefly review smart growth principles and the extent to which smart growth programs are currently in use in American cities, counties, and states. Next, I summarize the origins of the smart growth idea and explain how and why the idea has changed. Third, I connect smart growth ideas to the history and evolution of urban planning practice; starting with the rise of zoning in the 1920s; the emergence of the environmental and growth management movements in the early 1970s; and then finally, into the 1990s, when, along with the new urbanism (and other urban-related "isms"), smart growth began enjoying broad popularity. Lastly, building on smart growth's successes and disappointments during its first 25 years, I pose a series of smart growth challenges and opportunities for the next 25.

WHAT IS SMART GROWTH?

Beyond a preference for incentives and choice, the smart growth paradigm includes a series of normative principles and practices intended to promote resource-conserving urban and suburban development forms. Ten such smart growth principles were first identified by the US Environmental Protection Agency (EPA) and the Smart Growth Network in 1996. They are:

- Mix land uses.
- Take advantage of compact building design.
- Create a range of housing opportunities and choices.
- Create walkable neighborhoods.
- Foster distinctive, attractive communities with a strong sense of place.
- Preserve open space, farmland, natural beauty, and critical environmental areas.
- Strengthen and direct development toward existing communities.
- Provide a variety of transportation choices.
- Make development decisions predictable, fair, and cost effective.
- Encourage community and stakeholder collaboration in development decisions.

In practice, some smart growth ideas soon emerged as more central than others. In his 10-year anniversary review of smart growth, Anthony Downs (2005, p. 368)[1] summarized the new movement's core ideas and preferred practices as:

- **"Limiting outward extension of new development in order to make set-tlements more compact and preserve open spaces."** This could be accomplished in multiple ways, including through the use of urban growth bound-aries, by limiting suburban highway construction, through the establishment of transfer-of-development-rights (TDR) programs, by subsidizing infill develop-ment, and through the creation of agricultural and rural land conservancies.
- **"Raising residential densities in both new-growth areas and existing neigh-borhoods."** This is best done through up-zoning and by extending high-quality public transit service.
- **"Providing for more mixed land uses and pedestrian-friendly layouts to minimize the use of cars on short trips."** This too is best done via zoning—in particular, the establishment of mixed-use zoning districts—and by pedestrian-supporting infrastructure investments.
- **"Loading the public costs of new development onto its consumers via impact fees rather than having those costs paid by the community in general."**
- **"Emphasizing public transit to reduce the use of private vehicles."** This can be done by making public transit service more convenient, and/or by making car use more expensive.
- **"Revitalizing older existing neighborhoods."** This can be done via redevel-opment and/or by encouraging the owners of existing properties to upgrade or densify them.

Over time, the original list of smart growth planning ideas has expanded to include more process and equity principles. These include:

- Practices to expand the supply of affordable and/or assisted housing.
- Practices that make the development entitlement process simpler and less expensive.
- Practices that encourage pedestrian-oriented street layouts and recreation spaces.
- Practices that promote a greater variety of housing types and designs to accommodate more diverse families and households.

Smart growth arrived on the American scene in the early 1990s following years of growing frustration that existing land use regulatory regimes were either too feeble or too partial to properly manage development in America's rapidly growing urban areas (Chapin, 2012). Smart growth made its formal debut in 1997 with the publication by the American Planning Association (APA) of *The Growing Smart Legislative Guidebook: Model Statutes for Planning and the Management of Change* (Klein & Meck, 1998). That same year, the Natural Resources Defense Council (NRDC) and the Surface Transportation Policy Project (STPP) collaborated on publishing *The Tool Kit for Smart Growth*, which promoted compact growth, mixed land uses, and transit-oriented development.

The two documents had different but complementary purposes. Echoing the purpose of the 1922 Standard Zoning Enabling Act (SZEA), which had been written to introduce municipalities to the proper practice of zoning, the *Growing Smart Legislative Guidebook* was designed as a comprehensive, one-stop, how-to manual for states interested in bringing their planning and zoning laws into the twenty-first century. As such, it was focused on the administrative and legal procedures of creating a planning process friendly to smart growth. By contrast, the NRDC/STPP's *Toolkit* volume was designed to help local governments navigate different smart growth approaches, choose the ones that were best for them, and then pursue appropriate implementation programs. To the APA, the smart part of smart growth meant a land use planning regime that was up-to-date, purposeful, and legally defensible. To the NRDC and STPP, it meant having the right day-to-day tools for the job of promoting compact growth, mixed land uses, and transit-oriented development. (See Table 1A.1 in Appendix for a glossary of who's who in smart growth.)

Nobody who advocated for smart growth claimed the idea was fundamentally new. In a 2000 article that tried to put the smart growth movement into a proper legislative and historical context, Robert W. Burchell, David Listokin, and Catherine C. Galley connected smart growth back to the US Department of Commerce's creation of the Standard Zoning Enabling Act in 1922; the 1954 Housing Act, which shifted federal urban renewal activities from slum clearance to neighborhood revitalization; the mainstreaming of community planning under Section 701 of the 1954 Housing Act; the early emergence of (limited) state control over sensitive resource areas in the 1960s; the National Environmental Policy Act of 1969; and President Carter's 1978 Urban Conservation Order. In terms of physical antecedents, they connected smart growth's focus on balanced densities and diverse land uses back to Ebenezer Howard, Barry Parker, and Raymond Unwin's creation of Letchworth Garden City in 1903, and the work of Clarence Stein and Henry Wright in Radburn, New Jersey, during the 1920s. Their main conclusion regarding smart growth, taken from the title of their article, was that it was "more than a ghost of urban policy past, [but] less than a bold new horizon."

WHERE HAS SMART GROWTH BEEN TRIED?

To the degree that smart growth may be regarded as a movement, it did not attract all that many adherents. Of the 50 states, only Maryland adopted a comprehensive program[2] around what is smart growth's principal tenant: the creation (and funding) of incentives to redirect low-density suburban growth into higher-density urban neighborhoods. As Patricia Salkin noted in her 1999 *Urban Lawyer* article summarizing the then-contemporary state of smart growth initiatives, the common path for state smart growth legislation typically started with an expression of grassroots concern over rising sprawl levels, declining farmland supplies, and increasing public service costs and tax rates. In response, state legislatures, often with the backing of a new governor, would usually then form a task force or legislative committee to study the problem and propose workable solutions. The task force/subcommittee's interim report would recommend some combination of strengthened farmland and resource protection laws, that state growth management goals be inserted into local plans, that local zoning ordinances be amended to facilitate higher-density residential and mixed-use development, and that state agencies take on a bigger role in providing planning information and technical assistance and coordinating growth and conservation policies across municipal boundaries.

These recommendations would then go into the legislation-writing process. What would typically emerge from this sausage-making process was closer coordination between state planning and resource agencies, a slight streamlining of state planning laws, some small increase in funding for innovative growth management initiatives, and a renewed commitment to upholding private property rights. Stronger land conservation regulations, mandatory urban growth boundaries, and sharp increases in state funding for mixed-use and higher residential densities would all invariably fall by the legislative wayside (Table 1A.2). Legislators would then declare their state to be on the forefront of smart growth planning efforts and move on to other concerns. Planners were often equally fickle, quickly moving on to the next major planning fad, be it sustainability, livability, or resilience.[3]

This story of thwarted ambition notwithstanding, it would be a mistake to conclude that the smart growth movement has not had a significant impact. Even if the APA's goal of using smart growth as a lever to reform state planning laws never panned out, numerous local governments have embraced smart growth as a framework within which to update and modify their comprehensive plans (Godschalk, 2000). Tables 1A.3 and 1A.4 in the Appendix summarize the core planning principles animating the current comprehensive plans of the nation's 20 fastest growing counties and cities[4]—precisely the places smart growth is designed to help. Of the nation's 10 fastest-growing urban counties between 2010 and 2018, smart growth planning principles are present to one degree or another in nine of them, and central in five. The presence of smart growth principles is especially notable in three fast-growing Texas counties, a state not known for promoting forward-thinking land use planning practices. Smart growth planning principles are not quite so evident in the comprehensive plans of the nation's 10 fastest-growing large and medium-sized cities: just two—Macon, Georgia, and Meridian, Idaho—have incorporated more than a handful of smart growth principles or provisions into their local comprehensive plans. This difference in smart growth emphasis between counties and cities is likely due to the fact that counties tend to have much more undeveloped land than cities. This is especially evident in Texas, where the plans produced in fast-growing counties are more oriented around smart growth planning principles than the plans produced in fast-growing cities.

The smart growth provisions present in local plans typically focus more on results than on particular policies or regulations. They include discussions of the need to contain sprawl and redirect future population growth to established neighborhoods, of the potential for transit-oriented development, of the importance of encouraging more housing and transportation choices, and of the need to better coordinate future population growth allocations and infrastructure investments on a community-wide level. They are less explicit about how these goals are to be achieved. A few refer to the use of incentives and trading schemes (e.g., transfer of development rights), but most fall back on the need to make existing regulations more outcome-oriented and less process-oriented—a direction that stands at odds with the commonly-articulated desire to make community planning more participatory and inclusive. This tension is at the heart of Downs' 2005 critique of smart growth, entitled "Smart growth: Why we discuss it more than we do it."

Smart growth has also made an impact abroad. In Canada, the adoption of smart growth planning principles designed to densify residential development in existing neighborhoods is reported to have had a noticeable effect in Halifax, Toronto, Vancouver, and Montreal (Tomalty & Alexander, 2005; Grant, 2009; Hess & Sorenson, 2015). In Australia, the locus of residential growth in the post-1980 period has gradually shifted from suburban communities to a mix of suburbs and urban neighborhoods (Coffee et al., 2016). This trend, which is especially notable in Melbourne, predates smart growth's early-2000s Australian arrival, but it has no doubt been helped by it. In Britain, discussions about smart growth have taken two paths. In the Greater London area, the debate has been how to incentivize higher-density residential development as a means of expanding housing supplies (and restoring housing affordability), and whether and how much to relax the London Greenbelt, which was established in 1952 to contain London's imminent sprawl. Outside London, the discussion has centered on whether and how smart growth practices can be used to regenerate long-disinvested neighborhoods and industrial districts. In Europe, smart growth is viewed as providing potentially useful tools for promoting more sustainable urban development forms as well as for reinforcing urban agglomeration economies to promote increased innovation and business productivity (European Union Commission, 2010; Cooke & De Propris, 2011). In China, the pursuit of smart growth planning principles is viewed as having some potential for dealing with Chinese cities' worsening environmental and traffic congestion problems, while at the same time being at odds with the prevailing local government practice of assembling large development sites and then leasing them to private developers in exchange for payments, which helps fund needed infrastructure investments (Knaap & Zhao, 2009).

OLD WINE, NEW WINE, OR BOTH?

Smart growth has been criticized as just "old wine in new bottles." This isn't quite fair. Even if much of smart growth's substance wasn't particularly new, what made it seem fresh and newly relevant was its emphasis on incentives, choice, and regulatory certainty; and its de-emphasis, at least rhetorically, on blunt and imprecise regulations (Downs, 2005). How and why did this change in emphasis come to be?

Conceptually, smart growth can be seen as a sort of 3.0 version of American land use regulation (Chapin, 2012). Version 1.0, which emerged during the first three decades of the twentieth century, consisted of local zoning and subdivision regulations as authorized under enabling legislation passed by each state.[5] Zoning and subdivision ordinances are profoundly regulatory. They work by setting forth allowable lot sizes and configurations, land uses, building and massing envelopes, and public service requirements for every legal parcel. Property owners and developers who wish to do something different than what is prescribed on the zoning map must go through a cumbersome re-zoning or variance process. This adds time, money, and complexity to the development process.[6]

Zoning's rapid diffusion owed much to three US Supreme Court cases which established its legitimacy as well as its limits: *Hadacheck v. Sebastian* (1915), *Buchanan v. Wharley* (1917), and *Village of Euclid v. Ambler Realty Co.* (1926). *Euclid* was particularly relevant because it specifically dealt with a question then coming to the fore throughout the nation's new and growing suburbs: should apartment buildings be allowed in single-family neighborhoods? In addition to establishing the constitutionality of zoning, *Euclid* established that communities did not need to have an adopted comprehensive plan in order implement a zoning ordinance. This meant that communities could specify the land uses and densities they *didn't want* but did not have to specify those they *did want*. Under *Euclid*, local land use regulations could be used to prohibit *public bads* without also having to promote *public goods* via planning. This convenient cleaving of zoning from planning was American land use planning's original sin. It made it difficult to use zoning regulations and subdivision ordinances to encourage the types of land use and public facilities synergies that characterize good communities.

Different state and local governments pursued multiple strategies to remedy this disconnect. Some required local zoning codes to be consistent with adopted comprehensive plans. Others required that large swaths of suburban land be master-planned before being approved for development. Still others used their redevelopment and eminent domain powers to require private developers to include public-oriented facilities and land uses in their projects.

With returning World War II and Korean War veterans (and then Baby Boomers) flooding the housing market, these efforts to organize suburban growth proved mostly inadequate. Everybody, it seemed, wanted a single-family home with an attached garage (later, a two-car garage) on a quarter-acre lot within easy driving distance of a supermarket with convenient and visible parking. The fact that this home came with a federally-subsidized mortgage and was in a Whites-only neighborhood made the package all the more attractive. Long Island's Levittown, the mass-produced subdivision model on which most post-war suburbs would be based, wasn't popular just because it responded to pent-up demand. It was popular because it gave White, middle-class homeowners exactly the home, yard, and single-use neighborhood they most desired (Jackson, 1987).

There is a saying that goes, "having is not so pleasing as wanting."[7] Once the regulatory infrastructure designed to mass-produce suburban subdivisions was locked in place, its many limitations quickly became apparent. Under a zoning-based regulatory regime, builders and developers, not residents, have the lead in determining the rate at which development occurs and which farmlands are to be replaced by subdivisions. Further, a zoning-based regulatory system does not require that homebuilders and developers consider the cumulative environmental impacts of their projects, or their effects on public facility congestion. In much the same way, zoning-based systems encourage neighboring communities to compete with each other for high-revenue, low-cost land uses such as car dealerships and shopping centers, with the cumulative result being an unbalanced, auto-dependent land use mix. By the late 1960s, suburban communities that had initially been marketed to potential homebuyers as bucolic family retreats were beginning to experience the traffic jams and over-crowded parks and schools commonly associated with cities.

Unhappy with zoning's limited ability to deal with these issues, residents began pushing back by using new types of regulatory tools (Landis, 2021). Known collectively as growth management (or in some cases, growth control), these new tools included tempo controls, which put annual limits on how many building permits could be issued; urban containment regulations,[8] which limited the outward extent of urban services and land uses; and adequate public facilities ordinances (APFOs), which required that there be sufficient sewer, road, school, or park capacity before additional new development would be approved.

The first municipality to try out this new "version 2.0" of land use regulation was Ramapo, New York, in 1969 (Meck & Retzlaff, 2008). Despite the best efforts of developers to kill growth management in the courts—arguing that it constituted an illegal taking of private property rights—it repeatedly passed constitutional muster. This added to its grassroots attraction. From Ramapo, growth management quickly jumped westward to Boulder, Colorado, and to the communities of Livermore and Petaluma in the San Francisco Bay Area. In 1973, Montgomery County, Maryland, became the nation's first county to adopt a growth-management ordinance. By the early 1980s, more than 300 municipalities in California alone had adopted some form of local growth-management ordinance. These local growth management efforts were abetted by new state laws in California, which required all non-exempt projects to go through an environmental impact assessment process,[9] and in Florida, which subjected large development projects with regional impacts (known as DRIs) to a much more demanding development review process.

Ultimately, growth management did little better than zoning at managing runaway suburban development. Fueled by continuing population growth, low mortgage interest rates, popular preferences for more residential floor space, fiscal incentives for developers to move ever outward in search of cheaper land, and overly pliant city councils, new houses grew bigger, development densities fell further, and more and more farms were converted to subdivisions and shopping centers. Paradoxically, those municipalities that did the most to limit their own growth often ended up pushing successive rounds of development outward to less-regulated communities (Landis, 2006).

Unable to control when and where growth could occur, many communities enacted development impact fees to shift the incremental costs of growth-related infrastructure back to developers and new residents (Nelson, 1988). In another example of the law-of-unintended-consequences, this served to make communities even more dependent on unwanted development to finance their public facility needs. Planners argued that coordinating local growth policy across neighboring municipalities was the obvious answer to this dilemma, but except in Portland, this recommendation failed to gain traction in a neo-liberal political world that saw government as already too constraining of private property rights. As urbanist William H. Whyte had first warned in 1957, sprawl was voraciously consuming America's metropolitan landscapes. Everyone had their favorite critique of American urban development patterns and practices, but no one had an alternate vision that didn't rely on ratcheting up local land use regulations.

A NEW DESIGN MODEL FOR THE SUBURBS

Innovators find a way. In 1980, Florida businessman Robert S. Davis hired Miami-based architects Andrés Duany and Elizabeth Plater-Zyberk to help him plan a new community on 80 acres of Florida panhandle land that Davis had inherited from his grandfather. With fond childhood memories of Florida's pre-war beach cottage communities, Davis wanted his new town to actively promote the sense of identity and neighborliness that was missing from most subdivision communities. Davis named his new community Seaside, and although not an immediate commercial success, it attracted widespread popular attention and catapulted Davis, Duany, and Plater-Zyberk into the national spotlight. In an era where the car and almighty dollar spoke loudest, it was still possible, it turned out, to build a new community based on traditional neighborhood design principles such as walking and mixing land uses (Davis, 1989).

Meanwhile, in California, developer (and later California State Treasurer) Philip Angelides and planner and architect Peter Calthorpe were putting the finishing touches on plans for a much larger new community in Sacramento County, to be called Laguna West. In contrast to Seaside, which was accessible only by car, there were plans to connect Laguna West by light rail to downtown Sacramento. This being California, most Laguna West residents would still own cars, but if Calthorpe and Angelides had their way, they would need to use them a lot less. As in Seaside, garages were moved from the front of the house to back alleys, opening up space for porches. Laguna West's street system was designed as a radial and regular grid centered on its downtown core, which included a mixture of public as well as retail uses (Calthorpe, 1993). Most residents lived within 1/3 mile of Laguna West's planned light-rail station.[10]

Seaside and Laguna West attracted huge international attention and together served as focal points for architects, designers, planners and government officials to coalesce around a set of community planning principles that promoted pedestrian travel over car use. Known as both traditional neighborhood development (TND) and the new urbanism, this new approach emphasized maximizing multi-modal mobility by using a street grid; using building forms and materials to delineate neighborhoods; combining residences, shops, and public buildings in mixed-use districts; and reviving the use of alleys to move garages from the front of the house, where they had come to dominate residential facades, to the rear. Surveys and marketing studies found many potential homebuyers strongly preferred new urbanist designs to more commonplace residential subdivisions. One study comparing home values in the Duany-designed new urbanist community The Kentlands outside of Washington, DC, with those in neighboring Herndon, Virginia, found Kentlands homes selling at significant price premiums (Tu & Eppli, 1999). Even hardcore single-family homebuilders began admitting that the new urbanists were on to something.

There was just one problem: new urbanist projects were not immediately profitable for their sponsors. This meant that scaling up the new urbanism would either require finding developers happy to lose money—never a large group—or securing local political support for the highly-prescriptive (and expensive) design and development controls that were part and parcel of new urbanist designs. New urbanist communities could make money for their residents over time, but, within the prevailing framework of traditional single-use zoning and growth management, were not financially feasible as speculative ventures. What was needed for new urbanist communities to succeed in the marketplace was a planning model that combined a metropolitan-level perspective on resource protection and multi-modal transportation planning, a community-level perspective on everyday quality of life issues, and a business-based perspective that recognized the importance of regulatory clarity and certainty.

PORTLAND POINTS THE WAY

Fortunately, this model already existed in Portland, Oregon. In 1975, Portland Mayor Neil Goldschmidt took the unprecedented step of turning down federal transportation dollars because the US Department of Transportation (DOT) would not allow them to be used to build a new light-rail system in place of new highways. When DOT finally relented a few years later, Portland began building its MAX system, and the first line opened for service in 1986. Thirteen years earlier, at the urging of Governor Tom McCall, the Oregon state legislature had enacted Senate Bill 100 (Oregon State Senate Bill 100, 1973), which required the state's largest metropolitan areas to create urban growth boundaries (UGBs) to protect farm and forest lands from suburban sprawl. In 1979, Portland area voters approved the establishment of Metro, the nation's first limited metropolitan government, and gave it the job of delineating and periodically updating Portland's UGB. From their inception, Portland's UGB and MAX system were intended to work together: the UGB would redirect some amount of low-density suburban growth from Portland's fringe municipalities back into its older residential neighborhoods where it could be developed at higher densities and served by new MAX light rail lines. To make this growth redirection process smoother, the Portland City Council began up-zoning older neighborhoods to accommodate additional development. They also simplified the development permitting process, making it faster and more predictable.

In keeping with this market-friendly orientation, Portland's UGB is designed to be periodically expanded. In response to building industry complaints that an overly-restrictive UGB would cause housing prices to surge, Metro is required every six years to assess whether the UGB includes sufficient serviceable land to meet anticipated housing demand.[11] If it does not, the UGB must be extended outward. Since it was approved in 1979, Portland's UGB has been expanded some three dozen times, adding almost 30,000 acres of developable land. Portland area housing prices have risen faster than elsewhere in Oregon, but nowhere near as quickly as in other large West Coast cities.

As projected, Portland's existing urban neighborhoods have boomed. Property rights advocates continue to complain about the UGB's restrictiveness, but the development community has largely come to terms with it, having since found a way to make infill profitable. In his 1997 assessment of the UGB experience, urban historian and planner Carl Abbott characterized Portland as a place "where city and suburbs talk to each other—and often agree."

Helping to coordinate these various efforts was the Land Use, Transportation, Air Quality Connection project, better known as LUTRAQ. Initiated in 1988 by the environmental advocacy group 1000 Friends of Oregon to pre-empt state construction of a new freeway, LUTRAQ combined robust economic and transportation modeling with detailed geographic information system (GIS) data to enable planners to interactively identify and evaluate coordinated land use, transportation, and air quality scenarios. (Previous modeling efforts took land use patterns as a one-way input into regional transportation models.) With LUTRAQ in hand, planners could work together with environmentalists to identify alternative growth allocations and densities, evaluate the implications for land consumption, travel behavior, and air quality, and then interactively tweak the results to reduce drive-alone auto activities and air pollution emissions. With tools such as LUTRAQ, planners could move from pie-in-the-sky smart growth principles to on-the-ground smart growth plans (1000 Friends of Oregon, 1996).

Meanwhile, the local growth management movement that began in Ramapo in 1969 was coming to be seen as something which was, if not quite a failure, certainly much less than a success. Instead of constraining development at the fringe and promoting infill, it has had the opposite effect, redirecting growth from somewhat-restrictive first- and second-ring suburbs outward to less-restrictive unincorporated areas (Levine, 1999).

Planners have a tendency when confronted with a problem they cannot solve at the local level to take it to the metropolitan or state level, where it is assumed that parochial opposition will miraculously give way to broad-based support. This "bigger is always better" mentality gave rise to the state growth management movement during the mid-1980s. Beginning with Florida in 1985 and 1986, a succession of eight states[12] adopted state-level growth management guidelines or requirements intended to protect farmland, limit suburban sprawl, promote infill development, and reduce the fiscal cost of accommodating growth (see Table 1A.5 for a smart growth pocket timeline). None succeeded, because, as in Florida's case, they were designed in a fiscally unsustainable manner; or as in the case in New Jersey and Georgia, it was easier for neighboring communities to talk about jointly restricting developing than to actually do it.

INTO THE MAINSTREAM

The difficulties of bringing Seaside and Laguna West to scale and the successes of Portland's UGB/infill experiment were much on the minds of an invited group of mayors, city council members, and country supervisors who came together at the Ahwahnee Hotel in Yosemite Valley in 1991, at the invitation of California's Local Government Commission, to hear about alternatives to sprawl from six nationally recognized architects. The meeting culminated in the adoption of a set of 15 principles, henceforth known as the Ahwahnee Principles (Table 1A.6), to guide the planning of resource-efficient communities (Corbett & Velasquez, 1994). Following these principles, leaders hoped, would gradually transform the dominant commodity-based model of suburban development into a new model that emphasized livability, diversity, resource conservation, and expanded opportunities for social interaction.

Agreeing on a set of principles was the easy part. Converting those principles into widespread practice would be harder. Two groups soon formed to spread the word. The first, spearheaded by Seaside and Kentlands designer Andrés Duany, was the Congress for the New Urbanism, or CNU. The CNU focused its efforts on publicizing new urbanist projects, building a membership organization of urban designers, planners, and architects, and developing a formal set of planning and design practices which, if followed, would incrementally transform soulless subdivisions into vital urban communities. The other, more ad hoc, group, including planners, land use lawyers, policy researchers, and a few developers would go on to create the smart growth movement.

The major differences between the two groups centered on how growth was to be best accommodated and on the appropriate role of regulation. To members of the CNU, ensuring that growth occurred in resource-conserving forms trumped the question of whether growth was desirable and how much growth should be accommodated.[13] Accordingly, CNU members had few qualms about excluding development from places deemed inappropriate or employing strong design, environmental, and development regulations—regardless of their effects on housing prices or affordability levels.[14]

These priorities were reversed for members of the nascent smart growth movement. For them, ensuring that housing remained affordable could only be accomplished by making it easier for developers to accommodate projected market demand. This meant accommodating as much growth as realistic, and over the widest possible range of housing types and densities. Both groups agreed on the importance of protecting critical environmental resources, containing sprawl, expanding housing and transportation choices, and on reforming the local entitlements process to make it less process-oriented and more outcome-oriented. For smart-growthers, the best way to do this was to mix regulations and incentives in a manner that demonstrably achieved particular planning goals. This approach would reach its apogee in Maryland, where a combination of environmental regulations and increased funding for infill development was designed both to limit sprawl and to promote more compact development forms. It was this link between goals, the use of appropriate tools, and measurable outcomes that made smart growth smart. CNU members took a narrower view of the problem; to them, reforming the entitlements process meant strengthening design and development controls.

With no organization of their own, smart-growthers gravitated toward the American Planning Association (APA) and, in a few cases, the Urban Land Institute. All agreed that the situation was urgent. With the mild national recession of 1991 fully in the rearview mirror, suburban development was accelerating nationwide. Long-standing pejoratives like "sprawl" no longer seemed adequate to describe what was happening to America's suburbs, and new and more graphic terms such as "McMansions" and "big box centers" took their place.[15] In 1994, seeing an opportunity to lead the emerging national conversation over sprawl and smart growth, the American Planning Association, with funding from the US Department of Housing and Urban Development (HUD), the Henry Jackson Foundation, and the Annie E. Casey Foundation, began a three-year project to develop a set of model codes and statutes that state and local governments could use to update their planning processes and regulations to better incorporate smart growth principles. Guided by a large directorate of representatives from many national interest groups and organizations,[16]

APA's efforts culminated in the 1997 publication of the *Growing Smart Legislative Guidebook: Model Statutes for Planning and the Management of Change* (Meck, 2002).

In contrast to prior model statutes, most notably the Standard Zoning Enabling Act published in 1922 and the American Law Institute's Model Land Development Code published in 1976, both of which presented a single regulatory model for all states, the *Guidebook* offered a series of alternative statutes, strategies, and implementation paths from which state legislators and local officials (including regional planning agencies) could choose. These included provisions for state-level protection of critical resources and facility siting; templates for regional planning and coordination efforts; a more comprehensive and standardized format for municipal comprehensive plans; stronger subdivision ordinances; the expanded use of exactions, impact fees, and tempo controls; the wider use of transfer- and purchase-of-development-rights programs and other incentives; better integration of environmental assessment and management practices into local planning; and a whole spate of property tax and fiscal reforms intended to lessen the incidence of fiscally-motivated zoning.

Issues of sprawl and smart growth had also captured the attention of the National Resources Defense Council (NRDC), which, in collaboration with another anti-sprawl/pro-public transportation interest group, the Surface Transportation Policy Project (STPP), published its own smart growth resource manual in 1997.

The smart growth movement grew largely out of planning practice, but it also had important scholarly and research roots. Among the influential books that animated early smart growth advocates were Jane Jacobs' 1961 manifesto, *The Death and Life of the Great American City*, which stressed the values of fine-scale development keyed to city streets over highway-based growth forms; Ian McHarg's 1969 book *Design with Nature*, which demonstrated a practical technique for balancing suburban development and resource conservation; and The Real Estate Research Corporation's 1974 report, *The Costs of Sprawl*, which compared the fiscal costs and benefits of different forms and densities of suburban development and gave birth to the term "compact growth." Other influential works that had planners and elected officials alike questioning the standard suburban model of development included Ernest Shumacher's *Small is Beautiful* (1973), Allan Jacobs and Donald Appleyard's *Toward an Urban Design Manifesto* (1987), and Andrés Duany, Elizabeth Plater-Zyberk, and Jeff Speck's *Suburban Nation* (2001).

MARYLAND MAKES IT REAL

Smart growth would likely have been just another short-lived planning paradigm had it not been for Maryland's full-throated embrace of the idea in 1997 (Knaap, 2006). Maryland, and particularly Montgomery County, had long been among the nation's planning leaders. Maryland had established the nation's first State Planning Commission in 1933, converted it to a state Planning Department in 1959, and given it cabinet-level status in 1969. A steady stream of progressive planning legislation followed, including the Maryland State Planning Act of 1974, the Chesapeake Bay Critical Areas Act of 1984, and the Economic Growth, Resource Protection and Planning Act of 1992. At the county level, Montgomery County was the nation's first county to adopt an adequate public facilities ordinance in 1973 and an inclusionary housing requirement in 1974.

Following the forward-leaning examples of Washington and Oregon on the West Coast, and New Jersey on the East Coast, the Maryland Economic Growth, Resource Protection, and Planning Act (1992) required all the state's local governments to prepare comprehensive land use plans, incorporate six spatial development and resource conservation goals as well as a sensitive-areas element in their plans, encourage economic growth and regulatory streamlining, and review their plans every six years. Unusual for a state growth-management plan, Maryland's also included some teeth: once a local plan was adopted, a municipality's use of state transportation, environmental, economic development, and community development funding was to be limited to projects determined to be consistent with the plan.

The problem with this approach, or so it seemed to Parris Glendening, the former Prince George's County executive who was elected governor of Maryland in 1995, was that it was too oriented around sticks instead of carrots. Governor Glendening wanted Maryland to take a more forceful and incentive-oriented approach to smart growth, so rather than delegating the task of developing new smart growth laws and programs to the Maryland General Assembly or the state planning department, Glendening brought the job into the governor's office. The legislation that came out of Glendening's office in 1997 as the Maryland Smart Growth Act (also known as the Priority Funding Areas Act) had a number of new and innovative features (Cohen, 2002; Knaap & Frece, 2006). Most importantly, it limited incremental state funding for new road, water, and other infrastructure projects to areas within designated Priority Funding Areas, or PFAs. These included infill locations within existing urban municipalities, areas within the I-495 beltway around Washington, DC, and the I-695 beltway around Baltimore, and other locally-designated areas that met certain state-specified criteria.

Maryland's Smart Growth Act also funded four smaller smart growth initiatives, including a program to purchase rural resource lands threatened by urban development, a program to clean up and redevelop vacant and contaminated industrial properties, a subsidy program to enable workers to buy homes near their jobs, and a state income tax credit for employers adding 25 or more new jobs within PFA boundaries (Knaap & Frece, 2006). As important as what the Smart Growth Act included was what it omitted: no new state or local land use planning goals or mandates, no new state regulatory agencies, and no threats to withhold funding to which Maryland's communities were otherwise entitled. Not surprisingly, Glendening's Smart Growth Act was greeted warmly by planners and developers alike. Even so, the question on everyone's mind was: Would incentives alone would be enough to move the sprawl needle?

UPS AND DOWNS

Government officials in Washington, DC, watched Glendening's efforts with great interest. Maryland's subsidy and incentive-based programs aligned with President Bill Clinton's efforts to streamline government and make it more results-oriented, and with Vice President Al Gore's interests in innovation, sustainability, and climate change. Following the example of Portland's LUTRAQ simulation modeling, the US Congress, as a requirement of the Intermodal Surface Transportation Efficiency Act (ISTEA) of 1991, stipulated that regional transportation funding be contingent on meeting Clean Air Act targets. ISTEA was the first national policy statement in which state and metropolitan multi-modal transportation planning was explicitly connected to supportive land use policies (and vice versa), and, for many Metropolitan Planning Organizations, the ability to use ISTEA funds to directly connect transportation modeling with multi-jurisdictional land use planning represented a technical step forward which would undergird later efforts to identify smart growth strategies and programs. ISTEA also led to the creation of the Urban Economic Development Division (UEDD) within the US Environmental Protection Agency's Office of Policy, Economics and Innovation. Under the leadership of Harriet Tregoning, who would later become Maryland's secretary of planning and Governor Glendening's special secretary for smart growth, the UEDD created the Smart Growth Network, a cluster of national advocacy and interest groups committed to identifying and disseminating best-practice approaches to smart growth. Prohibited from actively lobbying by its bylaws, the Smart Growth Network sponsored the creation of another best-practice dissemination group, Smart Growth America, in 2000.

Aided by these networking and capacity-building groups, the smart growth word gradually began to get out. A 2002 survey by the APA of smart growth activity between 1999 and 2001 (American Planning Association, 2002) found that:

- More than 2,000 smart growth planning bills had been introduced in state legislatures;
- Eight states issued legislative task force reports on smart growth;
- Twenty-seven governors (including 15 Republicans, 10 Democrats, and two independents) made specific smart-growth related proposals and 17 had issued executive orders supportive of smart growth initiatives; and,
- Approximately one-quarter of states reported implementing moderate to substantial statewide planning reforms. (p. 6)

Sadly, these initiatives didn't have a lot of staying power at the state level. Fewer than one in five state smart growth legislative bills were actually enacted, and few executive orders were backed by new funding initiatives. The arrival of the George W. Bush administration in Washington, DC, in 2001 and increases in defense and homeland security funding after 9/11 led to a gradual scaling back of smart growth programs. Former Vice President Gore soon found a new passion, climate change.

Mild as it was, the 2001 national recession reminded many local officials that they couldn't and shouldn't take continued growth for granted. Concern that record housing price increases were the result of a speculative bubble gradually took root, leading everyone to wonder when the bubble would finally pop. By 2005, housing prices in the nation's 20 most active markets were an astonishing 90 percent higher than they had been just five years earlier, according to the Case-Schiller repeat housing sales price index.[17] The times were more anxious than bad, but no one seemed to want to rock the housing-price boat. Sure, McMansions were over the top, but their values would never decline, would they?

The Bush administration's massive response failure in the days after Hurricane Katrina that year put an effective end to all new domestic policy initiatives. From September 2005 until the collapse of Lehman Brothers three years later, the federal government was just marking time. After being termed out of office in 2003, Parris Glendening went to work for Smart Growth America, where, in 2005, he founded the Governors' Institute on Community Design. By 2008, smart growth was yesterday's news; the urban planning cognoscenti were now all talking about livability, sustainability, and climate change.

Smart growth enjoyed a temporary resurgence with the 2008 election of President Barack Obama. With no new federal money to spend—first because of the lingering effects of the Great Recession and later, in 2011, when Republicans took back control of the US House of Representatives—the Obama administration had to find economical ways to achieve its limited urban agenda. In terms of affordable housing and community development, it revived the prior HOPE VI public housing replacement program in a more community-centric form under the banner of Choice Neighborhoods. On the smart growth front, it brought together multi-modal transportation initiatives at DOT, community development and equity initiatives at HUD, and smart growth and environmental justice initiatives at the EPA via a single coordinating group called the Partnership for Sustainable Communities (PSC). Between 2009 and 2014, the PSC allocated just over $4 billion in grants and technical assistance to more than 1,000 communities to undertake plans and projects that combined investments in new transit systems, brownfields remediation, and affordable housing and community development. This was not new funding, per se, but rather, an effort to bring together existing planning and funding programs in different agencies with complementary goals to see if a more coordinated project selection process could generate additional synergies. This effort at cross-agency coordination and streamlined grant administration was welcomed by recipient municipalities (US Department of Housing and Urban Development, 2014) but how much it changed the final choice of funded projects is anyone's guess. Like most domestic programs, the PSC saw its funding cut in the aftermath of the 2012 budget agreement between Congress and President Obama, but soldiered on nonetheless, until being terminated by the Trump administration in 2017. As of this writing, the EPA maintains a smart growth website (www.epa.gov/smartgrowth) but is no longer actively administering funding programs.

What remains of smart growth policy leadership is headquartered in Smart Growth America, a partnership organization that brings together urban and transportation planners, real estate developers and investors, local economic development agencies, and municipal officials to exchange best practice approaches for promoting urban livability.

AGENDA FOR A "SMART GROWTH 2.0"

So, does smart growth work? Has it protected farmland, curbed sprawl, reduced private auto use, and increased housing choice in the ways its advocates had hoped? Thoughtful answers to these questions and more can be found in succeeding chapters in this volume.

What of the future? According to the US Census Bureau's most recent projections, the nation's population is expected to grow by nearly 100 million people by 2060. Almost all this increase will occur in metropolitan areas. Assuming that 25 percent of this growth takes the form of infill development—up from roughly ten percent during the 1990–2015 period (Ramsey, 2012)—America's suburban and exurban communities will have to accommodate an additional 75 million people by 2060. Presuming that the average metropolitan density continues at 2,500 persons per square mile, this will require an additional 30,000 square miles (or 19.2 million acres) of land currently in resource or open space use. This is a little less than the combined land area of the New York City, Los Angeles, Chicago, Miami, Philadelphia, Dallas-Ft. Worth, Houston, and Washington, DC.

Accommodating this amount of growth while protecting valuable resource land and maintaining the physical and economic integrity of existing communities will require the next generation of smart growth policies and programs to be more outcome-oriented than the first. Whereas the first generation of smart growth was principally concerned with mitigating the problems associated with sprawl, the next generation will have to take on additional challenges, including the following.

Facilitating Graceful and Community-appropriate Density

The core dilemma confronting smart growth advocates can be summed up in the old saying, "the only thing people dislike more than sprawl is density." Planners perceive density neutrally, in terms of zoning maps, massing diagrams, and additional housing units. Neighbors perceive density pejoratively, as lost daylight, crowded public services, increased traffic congestion and less street parking, higher tax assessments, and groups of different people moving in. Simply adopting smart growth programs does little to bridge this point-of-view gap. Instead, what's needed is for developers and their architects to create better and more locally-appropriate models of residential density. Not the 60-plus dwelling units-per-acre density appropriate for cities, but rather densities in the 15 to 40 dwelling units-per-acre range that make sense for residential neighborhoods. Properly designed projects in this density range can include sufficient off-street parking and still be dense enough to support bus or light-rail transit services. They can offer residents a modicum of privacy via private entrances, decks and courtyards while including bedrooms and bathrooms that don't feel like they were shoehorned in to make the pro forma work. It is this graceful housing density that the "Missing Middle" movement[18] seeks to popularize. Promoting graceful and locally appropriate density will require government regulators to work hand in hand with innovative private developers, much as the City of Los Angeles did in 1999 when it passed its Adaptive Reuse Ordinance (ARO), which provided developers with "as-of-right" permission to convert obsolete industrial buildings in downtown Los Angeles into new forms of infill housing.

Building Affordable Housing and Mitigating Gentrification Pressures

To the degree that builders can't supply enough mid-market housing to accommodate the increased demand for urban living, smart growth will exacerbate gentrification pressures. Whereas first-generation smart growth programs emphasized expanding housing choices as a way of attracting suburbanites to older urban neighborhoods, next generation programs must also emphasize expanding the supply of affordable housing. This can be done in a number of ways. Cities with hot housing markets can consider some form of inclusionary housing policy, which requires market-rate developers to set aside a fixed proportion of their new units for moderate- and low-income households. Cities can grant density bonuses or provide other forms of regulatory relief to developers who build mixed-income projects. Tax increment financing and transfer tax revenues, both of which benefit from rising property values, can be tapped to help fund new affordable housing or to enable low-income renters to remain in their units. Municipalities can systematically up-zone areas that are served well by transit and other public services to affordably accommodate the population growth that occurs with higher densities. This is the path Minneapolis embarked on in 2018 when it announced that duplexes and multi-family buildings would henceforth be allowed by right in many prior single-family districts. Truly smart growth does not require cities to aggressively build out every acre of available land, but it does require cities to make sure that the zoning and housing production pipeline has enough capacity to accommodate planned-for population and housing growth.

Smarter Suburban Redevelopment

Many of America's post-war suburbs are now middle-aged and in need of significant reinvestment. To the degree that new equity and financing infusions can promote pedestrian and mixed-use development forms, they offer great potential to achieve smart growth benefits and synergies (Newton et al., 2012). A 2017 study by the real estate brokerage firm CoStar estimated that nearly a quarter of the nation's 1,300 sub-urban shopping malls were at risk of losing their anchors and closing.[19] The growth in online shopping and delivery that has accompanied the 2020 COVID-19 pandemic has further accelerated this trend. For the communities in which these closed or at-risk shopping centers are located, these changes will present both challenges and opportunities. The challenges lie in the immediate loss of sales tax revenue. The opportunities lie in the potential to reuse former mall sites for housing and mixed-use development.[20] Beyond converting failing shopping centers to other uses, many suburbs present other significant infill and reuse opportunities. Whether it's called suburban smart growth or something else, future smart growth initiatives should pay as much attention to suburbs as future growth-receiving areas as they do to cities. June Williamson and Ellen Dunham-Jones' *Retrofitting Suburbia* (Dunham-Jones & Williamson, 2008) and *Case Studies in Retrofitting Suburbia* (Williamson & Dunham-Jones, 2021), and Alan Berger and Joel Kotkin's anthology *Infinite Suburbia* (2018) are two good jumping-off points for this much-needed rethinking.

Smarter Multi-modal Mobility Planning

Promoting higher-density and mixed-use development does little to get people out of their cars if there are few destinations to which they can conveniently walk or take public transportation. To overcome this problem, metropolitan transportation planners need to work much harder to identify specific origin-destination combinations that can be effectively served by non-driving modes, then collaborate with local land use planners to link redevelopment with improved transit service and non-motorized travel opportunities.

Ensuring Equitable Access to Improved Health Care and Schools

As the COVID-19 pandemic made clear, the public service benefits of urban living are not shared equally. This is particularly true for public health and schools. Despite suffering disproportionately from COVID-19, minorities living in cities were less able than Whites to avail themselves of needed health care, even when it was located nearby (Alcendor, 2020). Urban public schools are becoming more segregated by race and income, even in cities where residential segregation is on the wane (Orfield, Frankenberg & Lee, 2003). Smart growth planners and advocates cannot champion population growth in existing urban and suburban neighborhoods without also addressing the additional health care and school inequities generated by that growth. In terms of health access, smart growth planners should play a much greater role in ensuring that low-income and minority families have economic as well as physical access to preventive health services, not just urgent care. In terms of schools, smart growth advocates should work with city and public school officials to ensure that larger shares of the property value dividend that typically results from infill development and gentrification are directed to local public schools.

Green Infrastructure and Heat Island Programs

Smart growth and compact growth forms can help reduce greenhouse gas emissions (Ewing et al., 2009) but they may actually exacerbate stormwater runoff and heat island effect problems (Jacob & Lopez, 2009; Debbage & Shepherd, 2015). Future smart growth policies and programs must address the full spectrum of environmental issues, not just climate change. In the case of stormwater, they should mandate the use of green infrastructure in infill and high runoff locations. In the case of increased urban heating, they should require the use of more reflective building materials and the careful planting of additional trees and vegetation.

Smarter UGB and TDR Programs

Given the impressive success of Portland's extensible urban growth boundary in limiting sprawl and promoting infill development (Landis, 2021), it is a bit of mystery why more metropolitan areas have not adopted similar measures. The same is also true for transfer of development rights, which are being used successfully for similar purposes in several fast-growing Florida counties (Linkous & Chapin, 2014). Part of the problem is the prevalence of a "not invented here" mentality, the mistaken belief that smart growth models can only work in the places where they originated. The other problem with UGBs and TDRs is that they are perceived as useful solely for shifting growth from exurban locations to downtown neighborhoods. Unfortunately, the market for this type of diversion is extremely limited. To make UGB and TDR programs more useful, interested municipalities should focus instead on facilitating exurban-to-suburban transfers in which the housing forms in sending and receiving areas are similar. In the UGB case, this can be done through the careful up-zoning and densification of selected transit-accessible, single-family suburban neighborhoods. In the case of TDR, this can be done by designating appropriate receiving zones in suburban communities that are interested in bolstering their downtown areas, and by establishing a series of floor prices for different receiving areas, depending on how much density can be transferred.[21] The effect of these changes will be to move away from a "one-size-fits-all" UGB and TDR model and toward an approach that emphasizes local market conditions and preferences.

NOTES

1. Other notable overviews of smart growth include Daniels (2001); Porter et al. (2002); and Tregoning et al. (2002).
2. Connecticut, like Maryland, adopted funding programs incentivizing infill development, but did not adopt comparable programs protecting natural and resource areas. Tennessee adopted some smart growth programs but was careful not to label them as "smart growth."
3. Over time, Smart Growth America has broadened its agenda to focus more on transportation planning, redevelopment, and form-based codes.

4. The list of fastest-growing counties and cities is limited to places with a 2018 population of 100,000 or more.
5. The guidance for this enabling legislation was provided by the US Department of Commerce, which in 1922 published A Standard State Zoning Enabling Act (SZEA) as a model law to help make zoning practice more consistent within and between states.
6. Smart developers understand that the best way to make money is to find parcels that are under-zoned for the current real estate market, and then up-zone them to a more intense use. This strategy loses its appeal the more approvals that are needed, or costly mitigations that are required.
7. Although it sounds like something Shakespeare would have written, this line is actually spoken by *Star Trek*'s logical Mister Spock in the 1967 second season episode, "The Amok Time."
8. Urban Growth Boundaries (UGBs) and Urban Service Boundaries (USBs) are somewhat different. Owners of properties outside UGBs are precluded from rezoning them to more intense urban uses. Owners of properties outside USBs can develop their properties more intensely but must arrange for their own urban services (e.g., water and sewer, public safety) to be provided.
9. The most notable statutory exemption from the California Environmental Quality Act (CEQA) is for residential projects of four units or less.
10. Sacramento's light rail system was not ultimately extended to Laguna West.
11. As reported on Metro's UGB website (https://www.oregonmetro.gov/urban-growth -boundary).
12. Florida, Georgia, Maine, Maryland, New Jersey, Rhode Island, Tennessee, and Washington.
13. These principles are clearly articulated in the Congress for the New Urbanism's charter (https://www.cnu.org/who-we-are/charter-new-urbanism).
14. New urbanists have always been a little unclear about how the job of providing affordable housing should be divided between the federal government, state government, local government, and private and non-profit developers.
15. A later analysis of news media stories about sprawl by Fan et al. (2005) found that the number of stories increased steadily from fewer than 500 per quarter in the early 1990s to more than 2,200 per quarter in 1999.
16. Including representatives of the American Planning Association, Council of Governors' Policy Advisors, Council of State Community Development Agencies, National Conference of State Legislatures, National Association of Counties, National Association of Regional Councils, National Association of Towns and Townships, National Governors Association, National League of Cities, US Conference of Mayors, Member-at-Large for the Built Environment, Member-at-Large for Local Government Law, Member-at-Large for the Natural Environment.
17. https://us.spindices.com/indices/real-estate/sp-corelogic-case-shiller-us-national-home -price-nsa-index
18. https://missingmiddlehousing.com/
19. https://www.businessinsider.com/dying-shopping-malls-are-wreaking-havoc-on -suburban-america-2017-2
20. A best-practice example of this type of redevelopment is the Belmar Shopping Center in Lakewood, Colorado (https://www.denverpost.com/2014/05/06/10-years-later-belmar -exceeds-expectations-for-lakewood-growth-identity/).
21. The prices at which development rights are sold is determined in the TDR marketplace as the result of individual transactions. In asset markets where transactions are rare, or where the assets are extremely heterogeneous, prices tend to be idiosyncratic and uneven. This makes it difficult to consistently value the development rights being bought or sold.

REFERENCES

1000 Friends of Oregon. (1996). Analysis of alternatives: LUTRAQ report.

Abbott, C. (1997). The Portland region: Where city and suburbs talk to each other—and often agree. *Housing Policy Debate*, 8(1), 11–51.

Alcendor, D. J. (2020). Racial disparities-associated COVID-19 mortality among minority populations in the US. *Journal of Clinical Medicine*, 9(8), 2442.

American Planning Association. (2002). *Planning for Smart Growth: 2002 State of the States.* Chicago, IL: APA.

Berger, A., & Kotkin, J. (Eds.). (2018). *Infinite Suburbia*. Chronicle Books.

Buchanan v. Wharley citation: 245 U.S. 60, 38 S. Ct. 16 (1917).

Burchell, R. W., Listokin, D., & Galley, C. C. (2000). Smart growth: More than a ghost of urban policy past, less than a bold new horizon. *Housing Policy Debate*, 11(4), 821–879.

Calthorpe, P. (1993). *The Next American Metropolis: Ecology, Community, and the American Dream*. Princeton Architectural Press.

Chapin, T. S. (2012). Introduction: From growth controls, to comprehensive planning, to smart growth: Planning's emerging fourth wave. *Journal of the American Planning Association*, 78(1), 5–15.

Coffee, N., Baker, E., and Lange, J. (2016). Density, sprawl, growth: How Australian cities have changed in the last 30 years. *The Conversation:* September 28, 2016 (https://theconversation.com/density-sprawl-growth-how-australian-cities-have-changed-in-the-last-30-years-65870)

Cohen, J. R. (2002). Maryland's "smart growth": Using incentives to combat sprawl. *Urban Sprawl: Causes, Consequences and Policy Responses*. Urban Institute, 293–324.

Cooke, P., & De Propris, L. (2011). A policy agenda for EU smart growth: The role of creative and cultural industries. *Policy Studies*, 32(4), 365–375.

Corbett, J., & Velasquez, J. (1994). The Ahwahnee Principles: Toward more livable communities. *Western City*, 4–9.

Daniels, T. (2001). Smart growth: A new American approach to regional planning. *Planning Practice and Research*, 16(3-4), 271–279.

Davis, R. (1989). The Seaside Story. *Oz*, 11(1), 14.

Debbage, N., & Shepherd, J. M. (2015). The urban heat island effect and city contiguity. *Computers, Environment and Urban Systems*, 54, 181–194.

Downs, A. (2005). Smart growth: Why we discuss it more than we do it. *Journal of the American Planning Association*, 71(4), 367–378.

Dunham-Jones, E., & Williamson, J. (2008). *Retrofitting Suburbia: Urban Design Solutions for Redesigning Suburbs*. John Wiley & Sons.

EU Commission, (2010) *EUROPE 2020. A Strategy for Smart, Sustainable and Inclusive Growth*. Brussels, COM.

Ewing, R., Bartholomew, K., Winkelman, S., Walters, J., & Chen, D. (2009). Growing cooler: The evidence on urban development and climate change. *Renewable Resources Journal*, 25(4), 6–13.

Fan, D. P., Bengston, D. N., Potts, R. S., & Goetz, E. G. (2005). The rise and fall of concern about urban sprawl in the United States: An updated analysis. In D. N. Bengston (ed.), *Policies for Managing Urban Growth and Landscape Change*. US Department of Agriculture, Forest Service, North Central Research Station, 1–7, 265.

Godschalk, D. R. (2000). Smart growth efforts around the nation. *Popular Government*, 66(1), 12–20.

Grant, J. (2009) Theory and practice in planning the suburbs: Challenges to implementing new urbanism, smart growth, and sustainability principles. *Planning Theory & Practice*, 10(1), 11–33.

Hadacheck v. Sebastian citation: 239 U.S. 394, 36 S. Ct. 143 (1915).

Hess, P. M., & Sorensen, A. (2015). Compact, concurrent, and contiguous: Smart growth and 50 years of residential planning in the Toronto region. *Urban Geography*, 36(1), 127–151.

Intermodal Surface Transportation Efficiency Act (ISTEA) (Pub. L. No. 102-240, 105 Stat. 1914 (1991). https://www.govinfo.gov/content/pkg/STATUTE-105/pdf/STATUTE-105 -Pg1914.pdf

Jackson, K. T. (1987). *Crabgrass Frontier: The Suburbanization of the United States*. Oxford University Press.

Jacob, J.S., & Lopez, R. (2009). Is denser greener? An evaluation of higher density development as an urban stormwater-quality best management practice. *JAWRA, Journal of the American Water Resources Association*, 45(3), 687–701.

Klein, W., & Meck, S. (1998). *Growing Smart Legislative Guidebook: Model Statutes for Planning and the Management of Change*. Diane Publishing.

Knaap, G. (2006). A requiem for smart growth? In D.R. Mandelker (ed.), Planning Reform in the New Century. Chicago: American Planning Association, 103–128.

Knaap, G. J., & Frece, J. W. (2006). Smart growth in Maryland: Looking forward and looking back. *Idaho Law Review*, 43, 445.

Knaap, G., & Zhou, X. (2009). Smart growth and urbanization in China: Can an American tonic treat the growing pains of Asia? In Y. Song & C. Ding (eds), *Smart Urban Growth for China*. Cambridge: Lincoln Institute of Land Policy.

Landis, J. D. (2006). Growth management revisited: Efficacy, price effects, and displacement. *Journal of the American Planning Association*, 72(4), 411–430.

Landis, J. D. (2021). Fifty years of growth management in America. *Progress in Planning*, 145, 1–23.

Levine, N. (1999). The effects of local growth controls on regional housing production and population redistribution in California. *Urban Studies*, 36(12), 2047–2068.

Linkous, E. R., & Chapin, T. S. (2014). TDR program performance in Florida. *Journal of the American Planning Association*, 80(3), 253–267.

Local Government Commission (1991). *The Ahwahnee Principles for Resource-efficient Communities*. https://civicwell.org/civic-resources/ahwahnee-principles-for-resource -efficient-communities/

Meck, S. (2002). Growing smart legislative guidebook: Model statutes for planning and the management of change. *Natural Resources & the Environment*, 17, 175.

Meck, S., & Retzlaff, R. (2008). The emergence of growth management planning in the United States: The case of Golden v. Planning Board of Town of Ramapo and its aftermath. *Journal of Planning History*, 7(2), 113–157.

Natural Resources Defense Council, and the Surface Transportation Policy Project (1997) *The Tool Kit for Smart Growth*.

Nelson, A. C. (1988). Development impact fees. *Journal of the American Planning Association*, 54(1), 3–6.

Newton, P., Newman, P., Glackin, S., & Trubka, R. (2012). Greening the greyfields: Unlocking the redevelopment potential of the middle suburbs in Australian cities. *World Academy of Science, Engineering and Technology* 71, 138–157.

Oregon State Senate Bill 100 (Oregon Land Conservation and Development Act of 1973), https://www.oregon.gov/lcd/OP/Documents/sb100.pdf

Orfield, G., Frankenberg, E. D., & Lee, C. (2003). The Resurgence of School Segregation. *Educational Leadership*, 60(4), 16–20.

Porter, D. R., Dunphy, R. T., & Salvesen, D. (2002). *Making Smart Growth Work*. Urban Land Institute.

Real Estate Research Corporation. (1974). *The Costs of Sprawl*. Real Estate Research Corporation.

Ramsey, K. (2012). *Residential Construction Trends in America's Metropolitan Regions: 2012 Edition*. United States Environmental Protection Agency, Office of Sustainable Communities.

Salkin, P. E. (1999). Smart growth at century's end: The state of the states. *The Urban Lawyer*, 601–648.

Tomalty, R., & Alexander, D. (2005). *Smart Growth in Canada: Implementation of a Planning Concept*. Canada Mortgage and Housing Corporation/Société canadienne d'hypothèques et de logement.

Tregoning, H., Agyeman, J., & Shenot, C. (2002). Sprawl, smart growth and sustainability. *Local Environment*, 7(4), 341–347.

Tu, C. C., & Eppli, M. J. (1999). Valuing new urbanism: The case of Kentlands. *Real Estate Economics*, 27(3), 425–451.

US Department of Housing and Urban Development (2014). *Partnership for Sustainable Communities: Five Years of Learning from Communities and Coordinating Federal Investments*. US Department of Housing and Urban Development.

Village of Euclid v. Ambler Realty Co. citation: 272 U.S. 365, 47 S. Ct. 114 (1926).

Williamson, J., and Dunham-Jones, E. (2021). *Case Studies in Retrofitting Suburbia: Urban Design Strategies for Urgent Challenges*. New York: Wiley.

APPENDIX

Table 1A.1   *A who's who and what's what of smart growth planning practice*

The Ahwahnee Principles	A set of suburban design and development guidelines incorporating mixed-use, walkable, compact, and transit-oriented elements. Published by the California-based Local Government Commission in 1991.
Congress for the New Urbanism	A 2,600-member organization of architects, planners, developers, and local officials established in 1993 to research and advocate for place-based, mixed-use and walkable urbanism. (https://www.cnu.org/)
Funders Network for Smart Growth and Livable Communities	A partnership organization of 160 government agencies and nonprofits founded in 2003 to advocate for greater philanthropic involvement in promoting environmentally sustainable, socially equitable, and economically prosperous regions and communities. (https://www.fundersnetwork.org/)
Growing Smarter Guidebook	A guidebook published by the American Planning Association (APA) in 1997 to help state and local governments update their land use planning and regulatory procedures to better manage urban growth.
Growth Management	A precursor movement to smart growth focused on the adoption of state and municipal regulatory tools to better manage the pace and ameliorate the adverse impacts of excessive urban growth.
LUTRAQ	Land Use-Transportation-Air Quality Project: A research and modeling project undertaken in the Portland metropolitan area in the late 1980s and early 1990s to develop realistic smart growth planning scenarios.
National Center for Smart Growth Research and Education	A non-partisan research center at the University of Maryland that conducts research and provides training and technical assistance on smart growth and related land use issues. (www.umdsmartgrowth.org/)
Partnership for Sustainable Communities	A cooperative arrangement between the US Department of Housing and Urban Development, the US Department of Transportation, and the US Environmental Protection Agency to administer federal urban development, transportation, and environmental program grants in a coordinated and synergistic manner (currently inactive).
Priority Funding Areas (PFAs)	Existing Maryland communities and places where Maryland state agencies will provide additional investments in growth-supporting infrastructure.
Smart Growth America	A partnership organization of planning and environmental nonprofits and agencies, founded in 2000, that provides technical assistance, shares best practices, and advocates for smart growth planning principles. (https://smartgrowthamerica.org/)
Smart Growth Network	A partnership organization founded by the US Environmental Protection Agency in 1996 to disseminate and share best practices about smart growth. (Currently accessible as Smart Growth Online: https://smartgrowth.org/)
Transfer of Development Rights (TDR)	A smart growth implementation tool in which development rights in "sending zones" at the urban edge are sold to property owners in "receiving zones" in existing developed areas.
Transit-oriented Development (TOD)	The use of local regulations and incentives to direct mixed-use and higher-density residential development to areas adjacent to transit stations and stops as a means of reducing auto-dependence and increasing transit ridership and pedestrian activity.
Urban Growth Boundaries (UGBs)	A smart growth implementation tool that designates an extendable multi-county boundary beyond which new suburban development projects will not be permitted.

Table 1A.2   *1990s state smart growth and planning reform initiatives (as extracted from Salkin, 1999)*

State	Initial Smart Growth Actions	Follow-up Actions and Initiatives
Arizona	1998: The Arizona Legislature establishes a Growing Smarter Commission to study growth related issues in the state.	2000: Following the issuance of the Commission's final report, legislation is enacted requiring all Arizona counties, cities, and towns to adopt a general or comprehensive plan, dealing expressly with land and water conservation.
Colorado	1994: Following the release of a nine-step plan for Smart Growth in Colorado, Governor Roy Romer convenes a statewide summit to deal with projected population growth.	1995: An Interregional Coordinating Council is formed with representatives from Colorado's 11 regions to address growth and environmental issues. 1998: The Responsible Growth Act, which would provide grants to communities to implement innovative smart growth measures, is defeated by the Colorado Legislature.
Delaware	1994–95: The Delaware Cabinet Committee on State Planning Issues sponsors a series of statewide conferences on how to accommodate the state's projected population growth.	A 1997 Delaware Land Use Planning Summit results in the introduction of 11 bills overhauling land use planning practices in the state. The three bills that pass introduce new coordinating bodies and structures, but do not otherwise change established land use regulations and planning practices.
Hawaii	1997: A joint legislative committee is established to examine Hawaii's current land use planning laws and procedures and recommend improvements.	1998: Legislation reforming Hawaii's land use planning laws (which draws heavily on the approaches identified in the APA's Growing Smarter Project) is introduced and defeated.
Iowa	1997: The Iowa Legislature establishes a Commission on Urban Planning, Growth Management of Cities, and the Protection of Farmland to inventory and evaluate current land use patterns and planning policies.	1998: Following the issuance of the committee's draft report, legislation is introduced calling for improved land use inventorying and planning coordination between neighboring municipalities.
Maryland	1992: The Maryland Legislature enacts the Economic Growth, Resource Protection and Planning Act requiring municipalities to streamline development regulations in areas designated for growth.	1997: At the urging of Governor Parris Glendening, the Maryland Legislature enacts the Smart Growth Act, authorizing the awarding of tax credits and subsidies to development projects in designated Priority Funding Areas.
Massachusetts	1996: Governor Paul Celluci issues an executive order establishing a framework within which state agencies can better coordinate their urban growth planning and resource protection efforts	2000: The Massachusetts Legislature adopts the Community Preservation Act (CPA) enabling cities and towns to tax themselves and receive state matching funds to achieve a limited set of smart growth objectives, notably open space and historic resource protection.

State	Initial Smart Growth Actions	Follow-up Actions and Initiatives
Michigan	1994: The Michigan Natural Resources Commission establishes a Task Force on Integrated Land Use to recommend measures strengthening local planning laws and requirements.	1997: Two land use planning bills are introduced in the legislature. The first mandates the creation of Town Planning Commissions; it does not pass. The second, which expands funding for city, village, and municipal planning activities, does pass.
Minnesota	1997: The Minnesota Legislature passes the (voluntary) Community-Based Planning Act identifying 11 statewide planning goals and providing additional funds for improved local planning.	1997: The Legislature authorizes the voluntary creation of Metropolitan Urban Service Area (MUSA) boundaries, based on the MUSA boundary in place in the Minneapolis-St. Paul region since the 1970s.
New Mexico	1996: The New Mexico Legislature requests the state's Local Government Division to study the costs and benefits of growth and evaluate competing growth management alternatives.	1997: A series of follow-up bills mandating strengthened regional and local planning are defeated.
New York	1995: The Legislative Commission on Rural Resources continues its long-standing efforts to modernize state and local planning laws.	1998 & 1999: The Legislature fails to take action on a series of anti-sprawl and smart growth bills.
Ohio	1997: The Ohio Farmland Preservation Task Force is established to explore alternative sprawl reduction strategies.	2002: The Farmland Preservation Office in the Ohio Department of Agriculture creates a statewide farmland conservatrion easement program.
Pennsylvania	1997: Governor Tom Ridge convenes the 21st Century Environmental Commission to identify sprawl-reduction and farmland preservation approaches.	1999: Governor Ridge designates the Center for Local Government Services as the state's lead agency to provide improved planning services to local governments.
Tennessee	1997: Lieutenant Governor Wilder forms an Ad Hoc Study Committee on Annexation to reform county annexation practices, leading to Public Chapter 1101 being enacted in 1998.	1998: As part of a new state growth management law, Tennessee empowers counties and large cities to designate urban growth boundaries around planned growth areas.
Utah	1990: The Utah Legislature forms the Utah Tomorrow Strategic Planning Committee to take a more proactive and coordinated approach to land use and resource issues.	1997: Although willing to authorize funding for local smart growth planning assistance, the legislature refuses to authorize stronger resource protection and mandatory planning laws.
Virginia	1996: The Virginia General Assembly enacts the Regional Competitiveness Act, intended to encourage voluntary inter-municipal cooperation on growth and development issues.	1998: A joint resolution to create a 15-member smart growth subcommittee to study measures to reduce sprawl fails to pass.
Wisconsin	1994: Wisconsin Governor Tommy Thompson establishes the State Interagency Land Use Council to coordinate growth planning responsibilities between state agencies and recommend local planning reforms.	1998: After reviewing the Land Use Council's final report, the Legislature's Joint Special Committee on Land Use Policies declines to enact legislation that goes beyond improving state inter-agency coordination.

Table 1A.3   Inclusion of smart growth planning principles in the current comprehensive plans of the country's 10 fastest-growing urban counties

County & State	2018 population	2010–2018 population growth rate	Most recent plan update year	Smart Growth Planning Principles as articulated in Current Comprehensive Plans and Planning Documents	Author's smart growth rating (out of 5)*
Fort Bend County, Texas	788,000	35%	n/a	Fort Bend County has a community development department but no planning department. Significant planning activities are undertaken in its major cities, which include Katy, Sugarland, and Pearlman.	0
Denton County, Texas	859,000	30%	2015	Planning activities in Denton County are undertaken by the City of Denton, whose principal planning goals include promoting "a compact development pattern which includes expanded areas of mixed use, a broad array of housing and retail choices responding to changing demographics and market preferences, and reinvestment and infill in underutilized areas of the city."	4
Collin County, Texas	1,005,100	29%	2015	Collin County does not have a comprehensive plan. Plano, the largest city in Collin County, has an award-winning plan that emphasizes transit-oriented development, expanded housing and workplace choices, and master-planned development in currently undeveloped areas.	3
Lee County, Florida	754,600	22%	2019	The Lee County plan follows no overarching principles but is based instead on the land use decisions made in each of its 22 planning districts.	1
Travis County, Texas	1,248,743	22%	2014	Travis County's Land, Water, and Transportation Plan is guided by a central Development Concept that "encourages and supports new growth in the county's unincorporated [areas] to be more compact and connected; and to encourage housing and transportation choices by encouraging alternatives to single-family only land development patterns and mobility options for all ages beyond the automobile."	4
Wake County, N. Carolina	1,092,300	21%	1997	Wake County is currently modifying its comprehensive plan. The prior version, adopted in 1997, included two goals (out of 11) that referenced smart growth principles.	2
Denver City & County, Colorado	716,500	19%	2019	Five of the Denver Comprehensive Plan 2040's 55 goals explicitly reference smart growth planning principles. Most of them involve expanding transportation and housing opportunities.	2

County & State	2018 population	2010–2018 population growth rate	Most recent plan update year	Smart Growth Planning Principles as articulated in Current Comprehensive Plans and Planning Documents	Author's smart growth rating (out of 5)*
Charlotte-Mecklenburg County, N. Carolina	1,093,900	19%	2007	The Charlotte-Mecklenburg Planning Department is currently revising its comprehensive plan. Two of the eight goals and four of 14 objectives in the prior version were based on smart growth principles.	2
Orange County, Florida	1,348,900	18%	2009	Smart growth principles (direct future urban growth into existing neighborhoods while enhancing housing and transportation choices) form the core of the Orange County Comprehensive Plan's goals and strategies.	5
Polk County, Florida	708,000	18%	1992	The first and foremost of Polk County's "Basic Planning Principles" states that "Polk County shall manage future growth and development through a growth-management system which will direct urban-intensity development to areas where urban services are provided or are programmed to be provided."	4

Note: *Based on the overlap between smart growth planning principles and plan goals, principles, strategies, and implementation tools.

Table 1A.4   Inclusion of smart growth planning principles in the current comprehensive plans of the country's 10 fastest-growing middle-sized and large cities

City & State	2018 population	2010–2018 population growth rate	Most recent plan update year	Smart Growth Planning Principles as articulated in Current Comprehensive Plans and Planning Documents	Author's smart growth rating (out of 5)*
Macon, Georgia	153,000	68%	2017	Macon's comprehensive plan covers Bibb County as well. Roughly half a dozen of Macon's 90 planning objectives, mostly having to do with transportation, are based on smart growth planning principles.	4
Frisco, Texas	188,000	61%	2015	Only one of Frisco's 12 planning core principles, promoting more pedestrian-oriented development patterns, is based in smart growth.	1
Sugarland, Texas	118,000	50%	2009	Just three of Sugarland's 75 planning objectives (listed as the "means" to accomplishing the plan's goals) involve promoting balanced, mixed-use, and pedestrian-friendly land use patterns.	1
McKinney, Texas	192,000	46%	2018	McKinney's plan is organized around a preferred 2040 land use scenario that builds on 13 "place types" in 17 community planning districts. Transit-ready and mixed-use districts are two of the 13 place types.	2
Meridian, Idaho	107,000	42%	2008	Meridian is currently updating its comprehensive plan. About half of the 22 planning "policies" listed in the previous plan have a smart growth orientation.	4
Kent, Washington	130,000	40%	2015	Two of the plan's core principles are to (1) foster a growth pattern that accommodates 20 years of projected population and employment growth in compact, safe and vibrant neighborhoods and jobs centers; and (2) provide a safe, reliable and balanced multimodal transportation system for all users that will support current and projected growth using context-sensitive design.	2
Pearland, Texas	122,000	34%	2015	Pearland's plan is oriented around providing sufficient infrastructure to accommodate projected population growth, but also includes provisions for a "smart growth audit."	1
Irvine, California	283,000	33%	2015	Irvine does not mention of smart growth issues or principles in its land use element. The city's transportation element includes mild support for more pedestrian and bicycle facilities.	1

City & State	2018 population	2010–2018 population growth rate	Most recent plan update year	Smart Growth Planning Principles as articulated in Current Comprehensive Plans and Planning Documents	Author's smart growth rating (out of 5)*
Murfreesboro, Tennessee	141,000	30%	2017	Murfreesboro's growth policy is organized around a growth management approach which "involves a combination of techniques to proactively direct the pattern of growth with infrastructure provision, leading to better, long-term, economic sustainability."	2
Round Rock, Texas	129,000	29%	2019	Round Rock is currently updating its comprehensive plan. The results of a 2019 citizen survey found the least support for mixed-use development and expanded transportation options among 12 priority areas.	n/a

Note: *Based on the overlap between smart growth planning principles and plan goals, principles, strategies, and implementation tools.

Table 1A.5   A smart growth pocket timeline

1979	Portland Metro adopts the nation's first metropolitan urban growth boundary (UGB).
1979	Businessman and developer Robert S. Davis hires the Miami-based firm of Duany Plater-Zyberg to design Seaside, Florida, the nation's first new urbanist community.
1986	Florida Legislature enacts state Growth Management Act requiring "concurrency" between public infrastructure investments and private development.
1988	1000 Friends of Oregon undertakes the Land Use Transportation Air Quality (LUTRAQ) project.
1991	California-based Local Government Commission publishes the Ahwahnee Principles.
1991	US Congress passes the Intermodal Surface Transportation Efficiency Act (ISTEA) giving metropolitan planning organizations (MPOs) additional powers and responsibilities to coordinate land use and multi-modal transportation planning and funding.
1993	Congress for the New Urbanism (CNU) founded.
1994	American Planning Association (APA) authorizes effort to prepare The Smart Growth Legislative Guidebook (published in 1997).
1996	US Environmental Protection Agency forms Smart Growth Network.
1996– 2000	Seventeen states form task forces and legislative commissions to study potential smart growth reforms. Except for Maryland and Tennessee, most result in little substantive change beyond expanded technical assistance.
1997	At the urging of Governor Parris Glendening, Maryland enacts Maryland Smart Growth Act creating Priority Funding Areas (PFA) program.
2000	Smart Growth America is established.
2000	National Center for Smart Growth Education and Research is established at the University of Maryland.
2004	Sacramento Area Council of Governments (SACOG) publishes its first Blueprint Plan closely integrating metropolitan land use and transportation planning around smart growth principles.
2007	Smart growth gives way to sustainability with New York City's publication of its masterful PlaNYC sustainable development plan.
2009	The US Department of Transportation and US Department of Housing and Urban Development, together with the Environmental Protection Agency, jointly form the Partnership for Sustainable Communities to coordinate grant and project funding around smart growth principles.
2009	The Lincoln Institute of Land Policy publishes first comprehensive evaluation of statewide growth management and smart growth initiatives.
2017	The Trump Administration lets the Partnership for Sustainable Communities lapse.

Table 1A.6   The original Ahwahnee principles

1	All planning should be in the form of complete and integrated communities containing housing, shops, workplaces, schools, parks and civic facilities essential to the daily life of the resident.
2	Community size should be designed so that housing, jobs, daily needs and other activities are within easy walking distance of each other.
3	As many activities as possible should be located within easy walking distance of transit stops.
4	A community should contain a diversity of housing types to enable citizens from a wide range of economic levels and age groups to live within its boundaries.
5	Businesses within the community should provide a range of job types for the community's residents.
6	The location and character of the community should be consistent with a larger transit network.
7	The community should have a center focus that combines commercial, civic, cultural and recreational uses.

8	The community should contain an ample supply of specialized open space in the form of squares, greens and parks whose frequent use is encouraged through placement and design.
9	Public spaces should be designed to encourage the attention and presence of people at all hours of the day and night.
10	Each community or cluster of communities should have a well-defined edge, such as agricultural greenbelts or wildlife corridors, permanently protected from development.
11	Streets, pedestrian paths and bike paths should contribute to a system of fully connected and interesting routes to all destinations. Their design should encourage pedestrian and bicycle use by being small and spatially defined by buildings, trees and lighting; and by discouraging high-speed traffic.
12	Wherever possible, the natural terrain, drainage, and vegetation of the community should be preserved with superior examples contained within parks or greenbelts.
13	The community design should help conserve resources and minimize waste.
14	Communities should provide for the efficient use of water through the use of natural drainage, drought tolerant landscaping and recycling.
15	The street orientation, the placement of buildings and the use of shading should contribute to the energy efficiency of the community.

Source: The Local Government Commission (1991)

2. Smart growth governance in historical context: the rise and fall of states

Martin A. Bierbaum, Rebecca Lewis, and Timothy S. Chapin

INTRODUCTION

In the 1990s, the smart growth concept emerged as a model to encourage compact development, mixed use, housing choice, and multi-modal transportation alternatives. In large measure, its purpose was to reduce sprawl as the predominant metropolitan settlement pattern. This chapter examines the governance aspects of smart growth by state, local, regional, and federal agencies, but with a particular emphasis on the role of states within the wider context of American federalism.

While Maryland was the first state to adopt legislation and label it "smart growth," eight other states followed Maryland's lead with similar programs called "smart growth." Each achieved only modest success. As described in this chapter, smart growth, as a set of policies or a program at the state level, has waned over a relatively short period of time. Significant policy changes that were initially proposed have been disrupted by successive gubernatorial regimes pursuing different priorities, and also impeded by weakened legislative support, external social forces, and shifting political ideologies.

Two fundamental concerns frequently shape state planning in general and smart growth more specifically. The first is which government functions are better performed at which government level. According to American tradition, this concern is frequently framed in terms of "home rule." Local jurisdictions typically view state planning, even its less threatening smart growth variant, as an erosion of traditional home rule. A second difficult issue has to do with private property rights protections. Legal scholars and practitioners generally agree that carefully crafted land use controls embedded within a framework of plans supported by relevant and accurate data should not be interpreted as a threat to private property rights. Nevertheless, both these issues occasionally erupt and, in fact, have become more contentious over the past two decades.

This chapter is also about the difficulties encountered by political and legal reform movements. Reformers often learn that fresh starts are difficult, if not impossible. Some of the past may be broken with, but never all of it. Then, too, reform rarely moves in a single direction as the future is fraught with uncertainty and surprise. Resistance to change may be dismissed as resulting from popular ignorance or institutional inertia. Such assessments, however, too often over-simplify, with the devil often deeply embedded in the details.

The smart growth notion refers not to just its latest incarnation, but rather to a loosely bound movement connected to land use controls that gradually evolved from a renewed interest in state planning and growth management since 1970. The movement accelerated in the 1990s, and continued into the twenty-first century (Ingram et al., 2009). Although different states joined or exited this movement over time, core principles persisted. Experiences varied in different states, reflecting disparate pre-existing conditions, the nature of proposed changes, implementation effectiveness, and the impact of external forces. As Supreme Court Justice Louis D. Brandeis previously observed, American federalism encourages experimentation and innovation, and smart growth brought just that (Brandeis, 1932).

In 1997, when Maryland's Governor Parris Glendening urged the enactment of an amendment to Maryland's Economic Growth, Resource Protection, and Planning Act of 1992 to launch his administration's smart growth program, it was viewed as ground-breaking. As Landis described in the previous chapter, smart growth was more about encouraging growth where it is wanted than using government regulation to prevent growth from occurring where it is unwanted. Smart growth also implied changes in governance through modifications in intergovernmental relations that included an elevated, less coercive state role (DeGrove, 1984, 1992, 1993, 2005).

Comprehending smart growth through a state government lens is fitting. States occupy a preferred position within the American federal system to undertake essential land use control reforms if they choose to exercise it. Local jurisdictions that have been delegated land use controls are the creatures of the state. States retain necessary constitutional and statutory authority to make the essential legal adjustments. Second, while the federal government may be more legally potent with vastly more revenue raising capacity than states, it often works from a distance trying to impose uniform ways to address issues that simply defy national uniformity.

Yet, despite these advantages, states present their own challenges. Each state reflects its characteristic culture, social composition, and contending political factions. They tend to have limited revenue raising capacities. Their policies typically mirror implicit partnerships among government's multiple levels. When the federal government changes its priorities, states usually find it necessary to reshuffle their own priorities.

In interfacing with their respective local jurisdictions, state governments are impeded by home rule considerations often codified by law. This tradition relies upon a conviction that small political units represent the purest expression of popular rule. Government closest to its people is presumed best (Cohen, 2002). Local governments are viewed as citizen training grounds where rights and responsibilities are instilled. While such localism may be rooted in an idyllic view of Jeffersonian democracy, in the modern context localism easily degenerates into dysfunctional fragmentation (Weiher, 1991). Since local jurisdictions bear responsibility for the provision of a wide range of essential public services, they have significant impacts on the citizenry's quality of life (Danielson, 1976).

State governments may impede rational land use decision-making in other ways. For example, while states are presumed to centralize decision-making authority, the situation is often complicated. State bureaucracies are vertically structured and divided along functional lines. As state governments have expanded in size and become more specialized, lateral communication across bureaucracies along with inter-department coordination and integration has grown difficult. In addition, these bureaucracies may be taking cues from the federal initiatives, making coordination across state agencies more burdensome. John DeGrove, an astute observer of this scene, once wryly wrote that, "The notion that state agencies will actually move in the direction of coordinated behavior to further a clear and well understood set of state goals and policies is no less than revolutionary" (DeGrove, 1984).

We found that despite a compelling case for exercising state-level oversight, political support for comprehensive, mandatory, state-directed smart growth-oriented planning declined over time. Given recent shifts in state policy, we consider whether we have moved beyond the high-water mark for state-led smart growth efforts. State strategic advantages that may have previously been given significant weight have fallen far short of early expectations. The political pressures that impelled the momentum behind state land use controls in the 1970s through the 1990s are no longer present. Instead, the current support for those controls has waned, and in some states turned hostile. We discuss the likelihood of future governance roles at various sub-state jurisdictional levels in light of that history, and we briefly attempt to take into account new substantive policy priorities that will likely influence future policy concerns.

This chapter is organized as follows: in the next section, we describe the nature of American federalism and its relevance to understanding a complex land use governance "non-system" in the United States. Then, we discuss the short-lived "quiet revolution in state land use control." We follow by describing the re-engagement with state planning that occurred in the 1970s and eventually led to the emergence of smart growth in the 1990s. Next, we discuss smart growth and the challenges that it faced. The following section concentrates on a new paradigm for managing growth, a "fourth wave," marking a shift to "sustainable development" that incorporated nods to global climate change, social equity, inter-generational stewardship, and community resiliency. We then briefly discuss the "unquiet devolution" or governance during the disruptive Trump administration. Finally, we conclude our description of this half-century journey with a summary and modest set of portending premonitions for a future that remains murky.

MARBLE CAKE FEDERALISM AND LAND USE GOVERNANCE

Federalism is generally defined as a system of political organization with a central government exercising a level of control over the whole, with smaller government units exercising control over their limited geographical and subject matter jurisdiction (Salkin, 2012). The constitutional authority for land use regulation stems from the 10th Amendment of the US Constitution, as all powers not designated to the federal government are reserved to the states.

For the most part, before the twentieth century, with a few notable exceptions, local land use planning as it is now known did not exist. If planning occurred at all, it was haphazard. Urban settlers and real estate interests employed restrictive covenants, common-law nuisance provisions, and narrowly prescribed municipal actions to promote public safety (Salkin, 2012, 2015). Yet, a shift to local authority over land use was cemented in the early twentieth century when several cities adopted zoning ordinances. After New York City adopted a zoning ordinance in 1916, 20 states enabled local planning and zoning within 10 years (Wolf, 2008).

The US Department of Commerce drafted model codes for land use planning which facilitated a degree of national uniformity while allowing for variation among states and localities. These model acts were called the Standard State Zoning Enabling Act (SZEA), drafted in 1926, and the Standard City Planning Enabling Act (SCPEA), drafted in 1928. By 1930, 47 states had adopted zoning enabling legislation based on these model acts (Salkin, 2015). Through the widespread application of these model acts, most authority for land use controls was delegated by states to local jurisdictions.

The traditional view of American federalism was that there were three distinct layers – federal, state, and local – each performing distinctive functions and activities, operating as a three-tiered "layer cake." According to this view, national and state governments operated under a system of "dual federalism," one that relied upon three principles: (1) federal and state governments operated exclusively from one another with no overlapping or concurrent jurisdiction; (2) exclusive jurisdiction was based on distinct subject matters; and (3) the courts played an important role in ensuring that both, state and federal governments did not overstep their bounds (Salkin, 2012).

With the onset of the Great Depression and the New Deal, federal proliferation of grants-in-aid complicated this former understanding. The "layer cake" metaphor no longer fit. Instead, American federalism was re-interpreted as a more complicated "marble-cake" pattern, characterized by its less predictable swirls. American federal relations acquired a more intricate caste. This novel approach was dubbed "cooperative federalism."

According to cooperative federalism, no important government activity or function was still the exclusive province of any one of the government levels. Instead, functions were "shared" in hybridized ways. Local governments were no longer responsible for all "local" services. To the contrary, it was difficult to find any particular government service performed or regulation imposed that did not involve sharing among different government levels (Elazar, 1966).

Through cooperative federalism, state governments were viewed as early instruments of an expanded federal role, implementing federal policies and programs in cooperative ways. Under this approach, the federal government provided resources to states, usually distributed with federal conditions and matching fund requirements. States were invited to superintend federal law. In return, they and their local jurisdictions were afforded limited discretion to tailor programs to address their needs (Salkin, 2012).

A good example of cooperative federalism in the post-World War II era was the Section 701 program of the Housing Act of 1954. It provided federal funds for local land use planning. The program authorized planning assistance to state and local jurisdictions. To qualify for federal funding, local governments were required to adopt comprehensive land use plans. State governments administered the program for local jurisdictions that fell below specified population thresholds. Over three decades, thousands of local jurisdictions participated in this program, resulting in significant federal influence as well as state participation in local land use planning (Salkin, 2012).

Significant cooperative federalism initiatives at this time included the National Environmental Policy Act (NEPA), the Coastal Zone Management Act (CZMA), the Clean Water and Clean Air Acts, and the Endangered Species Act. Federal involvement in local land use controls was extended further through pragmatic means to address wide-ranging concerns under additional Congressional enactments through the start of the twenty-first century. This approach is consistent with liberal progressive ideology that continued to reflect its New Deal origins (Salkin, 2012).

Federal Planning

NEPA was enacted in 1969 and emanated from a concern that the environment had not been given sufficient weight in public decision-making. The Act established a Council on Environmental Quality (CEQ), effectively placing an environmental advisor in close proximity to the president. NEPA also declared encouraging productive and enjoyable harmony with the natural environment to be a national policy and required public agencies to assess the environmental impacts of their proposed actions. This federal Act subsequently spawned numerous "mini-NEPAs" on the state government level.

In 1970, following NEPA's enactment, the National Land Use Policy Act (NLUPA) was introduced in the US Congress, initially with support from the administration of President Richard Nixon. Its intent was to have the federal government encourage government coordination on the state level. If it had become law, NLUPA would have created a federal agency to encourage consistency among federal agencies with state plans; sponsored the development of a national land use database for state and local government use; and improved coordination and integration among land use authorities on multiple government levels. NLUPA, however, was not enacted, in part a casualty of Nixon's early resignation (Fishman & Weir, 2000; Kayden, 2000; Salkin, 2012, 2015).

Instead, a more piecemeal federal approach emerged. For example, in 1972, the Coastal Zone Management Act (CZMA) was enacted to establish a national Coastal Zone Management Program (CZMP) to address concerns that arose from the absence of a coherent national coastal strategy. It provides for pass-through grants from the federal government to states to local jurisdictions to devise land use plans within the coastal zone. Underscoring its extensive reach and significant impacts, the CZMP currently operates in 35 of the 50 states.

Also enacted in 1972, the Clean Water Act was intended to restore and maintain the chemical, physical, and biological integrity of the nation's waters. It indirectly affected local land use controls through its regulation of point and non-point sources of pollution. The Endangered Species Act signed into law in 1973 promoted cooperation among federal, state, and local government authorities. It provided financial incentives for cooperative agreements affecting habitat protection with obvious land use impacts.

In addition, the federal government owns an estimated 28 percent of all land in the United States, which falls within the jurisdictions of federal agencies such as the Bureau of Land Management, US Fish and Wildlife Service, National Park Service, and the US Forest Service. The largest share of federal lands is in 11 western states, where approximately 46 percent of land is federally owned and managed (Vincent et al., 2020). The high concentration of federally owned lands in that region means that the federal government is a major player in local government land use decision-making throughout the western United States (Salkin, 2012, 2015).

The federal government has taken notice of the importance of multiple federal agencies exercising land use controls to achieve its own policy goals. Federal agencies provide funds, technical assistance, and promulgate regulations that impact local land uses. Nevertheless, although some federal agencies have begun to collaborate to promote inter-governmental partnerships with respect to land use controls, for the most part, they engage through independent relationships with local governments in ways that are relevant only to the individual agency's mission (Salkin, 2012).

State Planning

State planning emerged in the 1920s almost simultaneously with enabling legislation for local government planning. For a decade during the New Deal, the federal government encouraged state planning by providing financial support and technical assistance to state planning boards (Salkin, 2015). The National Planning Board was established in 1933 but was subsequently renamed the National Resources Planning Board (NRPB) in 1939. Incipient state efforts, operating under its aegis, conducted state natural resource inventories and planned for major capital facilities. Under federal government tutelage, state planning boards proliferated from 14 in 1933 to 47 by 1938 (Brinkley, 2000; Meck, 2002). However, these early state planning efforts were disrupted during World War II.

State planning resumed in the post-World War II period, usually prompted by federal funding (Salkin, 2015). Hawaii was an early adopter in 1958, even before attaining statehood. California prepared a state plan in 1962. New York followed two years later. Grants-in-aid proliferated with respect to planning, urban redevelopment, and housing with the establishment of the US Department of Housing and Urban Development (HUD) in 1965. By 1968, state planning legislation was adopted in 14 additional states (Meck, 2002).

Regional Planning

Regional planning emerged to address issues that extended beyond local juris-dictional boundaries (Seltzer & Carbonell, 2011). It was encouraged by federal requirements at times due to the scale of issues, either environmental, transportation, or housing, and/or disaster impacts. For example, the Federal Housing Act in 1954 provided the impetus for regional planning by including grants to regional agencies that led to the establishment of regional "councils of governments" (COGs). The COGs consisted of representatives from local jurisdictions that were convened regu-larly for planning purposes.

The enactment of the federal Intergovernmental Cooperation Act in 1968 was additionally instrumental in encouraging regional planning reviews. A provision of that Act, as implemented by the federal Office of Management and Budget (OMB), required regional reviews of federal activities. Its purpose was to encourage improved coordination of federal programs with each other and with state and local plans and programs (Meck, 2002).

In other instances, the federal government supported the establishment of interstate entities to address concerns that transcended state boundaries. Planning agencies for Lake Tahoe, the Columbia River Gorge, and the Delaware River Basin Commission are examples of these initiatives. Sub-state regional entities, such as the Cape Cod Commission, Adirondack Park Agency, and New Jersey Pinelands Commission, provided additional examples of sub-state regional planning agencies that emerged during this period.

Among the better known and more visible regional initiatives on the sub-state juris-dictional level was the regional government formed in the twin cities Minneapolis–St. Paul region in 1967. The Met Council was created to address local concerns that resulted from fragmented planning among 300 separate local government units. In 1969, New Jersey created the Hackensack Meadowlands Development Commission (HMDC) that was empowered to regionally plan, zone, and regulate to protect the delicate balance of nature, provide for orderly development, and manage solid waste activities within the 31 square mile district located 13 miles from lower Manhattan. In 1971, the Atlanta Regional Commission (ARC) was created for the greater Atlanta region. It is governed by a 36-member planning board representing both public and private sectors. The agency is charged with planning related to transportation, the environment, and human services for the aging. In 1979, Portland, Oregon, estab-lished the Portland Metropolitan Service District. Its directors are elected from the region's dozen council districts. It provides a variety of regional services including solid waste management, transportation planning, and technical assistance to local governments. It also operates a metro zoo and convention center, and is responsible for the implementation of and revision to the region's urban growth boundary (UGB).

The federal government also provided impetus for the establishment of Metropolitan Planning Organizations (MPOs) with the Federal Highway Act of 1962. MPOs were required in urbanized areas of more than 50,000 people. Their purpose is to ensure enhanced regional cooperation with respect to transportation planning. Many COGs were subsequently designated as MPOs. These regional entities were strengthened by additional federal transportation funding in the 1990s. More than 400 MPOs currently operate in the United States. Federal requirements for MPOs require coordination with local governments and the public-at-large. The scope of MPO planning has been expanded gradually to include transportation planning's land use implications.

Yet despite scholarly interest and a modicum of federal support for regional land use planning, regional governance has been hampered by practical and political constraints. Regional entities require novel approaches to coordinate and integrate with existing land use control regimes.

Local Planning

Although there is ample evidence of the expansion of land use activities at higher jurisdictional levels, local jurisdictions continue to play the predominant role in land use decision-making. States ceded authority for planning and zoning to local governments early in this history. With rare exceptions, cities and counties in the United States are still mainly responsible for adopting comprehensive plans and enacting zoning ordinances. In some regions of the United States, authority rests with municipalities, while in others counties are primarily responsible for land use planning and decision-making.

Local government elected bodies (councils/commissions) adopt comprehensive plans and zoning ordinances. Professional planners, usually working within government planning or community development departments, coordinate plans and support administrative functions by implementing comprehensive plans. Planning departments author reports and implement the policies authorized by elected public officials. Planning commissions, often appointed by elected officials, serve as an intermediate step between professional planners and elected officials. These commissions interpret and apply zoning ordinances, make land use decisions and recommendations, and often serve as an interim step in the approval process. Because they represent constituents, elected officials tend to be accountable to local political pressures. Consequently, adopted local plans and enacted zoning ordinances often mirror local political realities.

Zoning became the main instrument of local land use controls prior to World War II. In 1926, the US Supreme Court approved the ability of local governments to regulate land use as a legitimate exercise of local police power by designating land use zones, which provided for different levels and kinds of development opportunities (*Village of Euclid v. Ambler Realty*, 1926). Zoning, as exercised by local jurisdictions, was viewed as a reasonable means to tame largely market-driven urbanization by regulating private property rights through application of the state's delegated police powers.

Euclidean zoning contributed to the American metropolitan landscape in, at first, barely noticeable ways. A distinctive metropolitan settlement style only gradually evolved, accelerating in the post-war era of rapid suburban expansion. That settlement pattern was typified by its relative low-density and bias for detached single-family dwellings with accompanying large private yards. As development centrifugally spread along improved transportation corridors, beyond older urban cores and aging suburbs, zoning provided a potent tool wielded by proliferating suburban jurisdictions. Its main purpose was to provide protection for single-family home values, located in neighborhoods characterized not only by their striking spatial generosity, but also by their legally protected social and functional purity (Hirt, 2014).

Richard Babcock cited these concerns in his classic, *The Zoning Game* in 1966. Babcock argued that municipal zoning produced a flawed metropolitan settlement pattern because its primary outcome was to protect homogeneous, single-family suburbs from urban, mixed-use development. He believed that the metropolitan development process was neither random nor entirely market-driven, but rather the result of a politically structured process. Zoning's dark side was its use as an exclusionary tool to facilitate population sorting (Weiher, 1991; Rothstein, 2018). Its fundamental flaw was that it served primarily local aims, imposing externalities on its neighbors, while underrepresenting legitimate regional and state concerns (Babcock, 1966). This basic flaw created the need for an alternative to local land use controls. It impelled a quest for state and regional remedies to address the deficiencies of local land use controls – only a half century after they were sanctioned by the Supreme Court.

THE QUIET REVOLUTION

Long before smart growth became part of the planning lexicon, those frustrated by local land use controls sought to more fully engage regions and states in this public policy conversation. In 1971, Fred Bosselman and David Callies pointed to this situation in their seminal report authorized by the Council on Environmental Quality, *The Quiet Revolution in Land Use Control* (1971). They found that local land use controls had become a "feudal-like system" in which municipalities decided land use issues for their own benefit to enhance their tax bases and to reduce anticipated social expenses.

Consequently, after decades of ceding land use controls to local governments, Bosselman and Callies urged states to claw back a portion of their authority. They explained that local land use controls provided municipal officials with at best paltry incentives to consider the needs of adjacent or nearby municipalities, or those of regions or states of which municipalities were only a small part (Salkin, 2015). The environmental movement in the 1960s and 1970s energized and enriched this planning momentum. Bosselman and Callies pointed to a growing trend of slow, but steady encroachment on traditional local land use authority that they expected to move in a single direction (Bosselman & Callies, 1971; Salkin, 2015).

According to Bosselman and Callies, the quiet revolution operated in the absence of any centralized leadership. It was unlikely to result in pitched battles between state and local governments. Instead, they expected a peaceful resolution to stem from a transforming consensus. Stakeholders would acknowledge that states and regions, not local governments, were the appropriate vehicles to make decisions about land use issues. Local governments, property owners, and development interests would gradually adjust to what they would learn was a preferable and more reasonable jurisdictional arrangement.

A year after their report was released, a judicial decision affecting municipal growth management further elevated the importance of the recommendations contained in *The Quiet Revolution*. The growth management movement ostensibly emerged with the 1972 decision of the New York Court of Appeals, that state's highest court, in a case involving the Ramapo Town Planning Board (*Golden v. Planning Board of Town of Ramapo*, 1972). In its decision, the New York court upheld a phased development ordinance in which the approval of a special permit for residential development was linked to provisions contained in an 18-year capital improvement plan. The capital improvement plan included five categories of infrastructure investments. The effort advanced the view that development should be phased and coordinated with the provision of capital facilities and community services.

The importance of shifting land use controls to greater than local authorities was further underscored by at least two milestones that soon followed. In 1975, the New Jersey Supreme Court delivered its first Mount Laurel decision (known as *Mount Laurel I*) regarding the case *South Burlington County NAACP v. Township of Mount Laurel*, in which plaintiffs challenged the township's zoning ordinance on the grounds that it excluded housing affordable to lower-income residents. In its landmark decision, which was reaffirmed and extended in *Mount Laurel II* in 1983, the court sided with the plaintiffs and interpreted the general welfare provisions of the state's constitution to require that municipalities enact land use policies that made "realistically possible the opportunity for an appropriate variety and choice of housing" that would address regional rather than just local housing needs. That principle became known as the "Mount Laurel Doctrine" (*South Burlington County NAACP v. Township of Mount Laurel,* 1975).

Unlike other states where an ascendant environmental movement emerged as the primary impetus for reform, New Jersey's state planning effort emanated from intervention by its supreme court in what it considered to be state and municipal policy failures with respect to the exclusion of suburban affordable housing choices. In 1985, in response to *Mount Laurel II*, the state legislature enacted the Fair Housing Act that was followed in 1986 by the New Jersey State Planning Act. The latter established a State Planning Commission charged with devising a State Development and Redevelopment Plan through a legislatively mandated planning process.

In 1975, the same year as the *Mount Laurel I* decision, the American Law Institute (ALI) published its Model Land Development Code (1975). That code's provisions called for state review and override of local land use decisions in specified situations. It included consideration of large-scale developments (developments of regional impact), which focused on land development that – because of its character, magnitude, or location – had substantial impact beyond local government boundaries.

The code also addressed the protection of resources of state or regional significance (areas of critical concern), concentrating on discrete geographical areas that possessed unique characteristics of significant interest to the state and region or containing land use interdependencies requiring comprehensive area-wide planning and regulation. States were expected to represent a view wider than just local jurisdictions and to intervene on behalf of that wider view (Pelham, 1979; DeGrove, 2005).

State growth management approaches promised improvement to local government planning and zoning practices. States could bolster local planning capacities by providing data, technical and financial assistance, and regulatory support. Planning could be reformulated as a continuous process with monitoring and evaluation and periodic adjustments. Local planning aligned with state or regionally determined goals, and subject to review by higher authority would be more effective (Pizor, 1982). State planning would meanwhile extend local planning approaches that were already in use (Porter, 2007). Newly introduced state and regional protocols were expected to enhance predictability about where, when, and the amount of development that was likely to occur and the ways that development could be coordinated with the provision of public infrastructure investments (Daniels, 1999).

The environmental movement energized planning momentum (Chapin, 2012). Regional and state planning provided potential for more effective means to strike an appropriate balance between real estate development and natural systems protection. Even if local land use controls were improved, there were still legitimate interests that could be neglected. Casting a wider planning net could better address the effects of state infrastructure investment impacts, tax policies, inter-jurisdictional conflicts, and externalized costs. In these ways, the case for state and regional land use controls during this period was strengthened (Healy & Rosenberg, 1979).

Nevertheless, by the end of the 1970s, this land use reform movement seemed to sputter. Tom Pelham, land use attorney and Florida Department of Community Affairs commissioner, wondered if the quiet revolution was dead or, if not dead, at least quiescent (Pelham, 1979). Echoing Justice Brandeis, Pelham lamented that Florida was truly the nation's chief land use laboratory given its extraordinary growth, and therefore merited microscopic scrutiny. He compiled a lengthy litany of hurdles impeding Florida's progress. It included, but was not limited to, the previous generation's heavy investment in local zoning (Pelham, 1979).

RE-ENGAGEMENT WITH STATE PLANNING

Nevertheless, the quiet revolution continued to spur innovation in a select group of states. John DeGrove took on dual responsibilities as both chronicler and advocate for state growth management, optimistically forecasting state planning's future (DeGrove, 1984, 1992, 2005). These changes were additionally documented by Weitz (1999) and Chapin (2012).

DeGrove described state planning in terms of successive waves. The first wave was mainly influenced by the environmental movement, a reasonable response to the rapid metropolitan growth during the post-war era. Seven states enacted state-level growth management programs. Their means were primarily regulatory. Only Oregon and Hawaii were comprehensive. North Carolina and California concentrated on coastal areas. Florida, Colorado, and Vermont focused on regional impacts and areas of critical state concern (DeGrove, 1984, 2005; Ingram et al., 2009).

Stakeholder opposition to this "first wave" stemmed mainly from the development community, local governments, and interest groups that feared growth management's dampening impacts. Environmental advocates and civic groups lined up against the opposition. Oregon epitomized this wave's approach whereby cities were required to create urban growth boundaries (UGBs) into which urban uses were directed and from which rural areas would be protected (Knaap & Nelson, 1992). Oregon provided a prototype of state government regulatory intervention yielding beneficial environmental results. The emphasis was on growth control, the preferred tool was state regulation, and the objective was to influence the location and amount of growth. Strong, sustained gubernatorial leadership was essential to these efforts (Chapin, 2012).

Throughout the 1970s, many state and local jurisdictions that had previously marginalized planning efforts began to acknowledge their importance. An increasing number of professional planners played significant roles. The approaches varied from strict controls to more professional approaches that addressed multiple aspects of growth management. The proliferation of professional planning programs at higher educational institutions throughout the country helped. The focus on planning was also strengthened by the ALI Model Land Development Code that helped to establish concepts, standards, and best practices with respect to land use planning and regulation. Eligibility requirements written into federal and state grants and permit applications also enhanced this trend.

The "second wave" of state planning moved beyond the environmental focus to wider concerns that included improving coordination between real estate development and public infrastructure investments. During this second wave, responsibilities were reallocated among multiple government levels. Public infrastructure investments attained increased importance as land use planning tools. Public–private partnerships to fund those infrastructure improvements became more prevalent (DeGrove, 1992, 2005; Ingram et al., 2009).

Growth management shed its earlier, more restrictive emphasis on growth control/ no growth/slow growth to a broadened understanding, as evidenced by policies in Florida in 1985, Washington State in 1990–1991, and Maryland in 1992. This second wave concentrated on consistency, infrastructure concurrency, compact urban forms, natural systems, housing, and economic development as the defining components of state planning systems (DeGrove, 1992, 2005; Ingram et al., 2009).

Florida's approach with its 1985 legislative package, dubbed its "Growth Management Act," marked the transition from first to second wave (Chapin, Connerly & Higgins, 2007). It featured comprehensive plans as the centerpiece of local, regional, and state planning activities and linked plans to development decisions and state infrastructure investments. Unlike other states that identified concepts such as compact development, affordable housing, or farmland protection and open space preservation, Florida relied heavily upon planning processes and legally enforced comprehensive plans to implement its growth management strategy (Chapin, 2012).

While environmental concerns continued to influence land use decision-making in some places, public infrastructure investments emerged as the major driver in others. Congested roads, stretched water supply and wastewater treatment systems, and overcrowded schools provided impetus for these infrastructure investments. As the fiscal impacts of sprawling development became more conspicuous, demand for dwindling federal funds led states to become more creative and cost-effective (Frank, 1989; Chapin, 2012). Heightened fiscal pressures induced a growing number of states to turn inward through improved planning techniques to more carefully assess and contain their costs.

The public infrastructure investment focus of this second wave included public debates related to "adequate facilities requirements," or in Florida, "concurrency" as a planning tool. In other states the designation of "urban service areas" (USAs) or "urban service boundaries (USBs) were employed to limit the spatial extent of new development. In New Jersey, the Office of State Planning (OSP) relied on previously drawn Department of Environmental Protection sewer service maps to delineate boundaries between growth and limited growth areas.

Economic growth and real estate development were now less skeptically viewed. Instead, they were frequently deemed essential, but in need of professional planning treatment. While some plans were visionary and added value to development outcomes, others reinforced the status quo of low-density, sprawling development. Still others became too technical and bureaucratic, impeding innovative planning by adding to delays and expense (Chapin, 2012).

DeGrove proposed a state planning template that included state-established goals followed by mandated plans on state, regional, and local levels that were consistent with those goals. In DeGrove's template, active engagement through a reiterative planning process would lead to consistency across departments on each jurisdictional level. Mandated goals required plans, and an effective planning process was expected to transform intergovernmental relations as growth management was strengthened under state tutelage (DeGrove, 1984, 1992; Bierbaum, 2015).

But others questioned whether such a state comprehensive model uniformly implemented could comfortably fit with underlying American values and the diversity encouraged by its federal system. At least one alternative view skeptically raised questions about the ways that such a tidy template could be reconciled with diverse interests operating opportunistically throughout the country. That perceived world was more diverse, erratic, and noisy: too unpredictable to allow for the imposition of a state planning template. According to this view, "No principle of administrative rationality, constitutional entitlement, economic efficiency, or even ideological predisposition truly determines the government locus of decisions" (Popper, 1988).

Aside from this apparently contrarian view, potent political forces were already stirring that would eventually affect state planning and smart growth. Drawing on a historically deep well of government mistrust, President Ronald Reagan, elected in 1980, invoked "traditional American values." He asserted that government, and especially the federal government, was less a solution to problems than the problem itself. Reagan was determined to set a new direction.

An important aspect of Reagan's thinking was federalism's redefinition, a return to pre-New Deal "dual federalism." The Reagan administration tried to restore a more traditional division of responsibilities among federal, state, and local jurisdictions. Each government level was expected to be responsible for financing its own services, a relationship that the administration viewed as essential to restoring public account-ability (Beam, 1984).

This "Reagan Experiment" encouraged relinquishing program responsibilities to allow states to assume these responsibilities at their own discretion. It also reduced federal mandates and funding and induced states to recalculate their own priorities. It was a strategy that yielded fiscal stress for states that had pursued successive years of tax cutting (Palmer & Sawhill, 1982).

Concurrent with this "Reagan Experiment," a grassroots private property rights movement emerged. From this incipient movement's perspective, the US Constitution's intent of protecting private property rights was being undermined; property rights were being eroded by ever-expanding government authority, espe-cially at the federal level. To counteract the perceived threats to private property from the modern environmental movement and planning profession via state planning, endangered species and wetlands protection, and later smart growth initiatives, a national coalition was formed that operated on multiple government levels. Called the Tea Party in the east and the Wise Use movement in the west, this movement proved to be an immense challenge to state planning and smart growth.

THE EMERGENCE OF SMART GROWTH

Maryland Governor Parris Glendening introduced the idea of smart growth at the state level in 1997 as a means to strengthen the state's capacity to influence growth, preservation, and revitalization (Cohen, 2002). Thus began the "third wave" in state growth management. Glendening advanced the idea that the state would no longer subsidize sprawl, but instead direct state resources to areas with existing infrastruc-ture (Cohen, 2002). He stressed the importance of inter-department collaboration to direct future economic growth to established communities, rather than have develop-ment spill out into the countryside (Frece, 2008).

Glendening was frustrated by weak results regarding development patterns and water quality following the enactment of Maryland's Economic Growth, Resource Protection and Planning Act of 1992. That Act created an advisory commission to monitor progress made in implementing the new land use law, explore new solu-tions, and report annually to the governor and General Assembly. It left land use decision-making largely to local authority discretion.

Glendening, attempting to be more proactive, proposed a smart growth initi-ative that included a five-part legislative package: (1) Smart Growth Areas Act, which established Priority Funding Areas (PFAs); (2) Rural Legacy Program; (3)

Brownfields Voluntary Clean-up and Revitalization Program; (4) Job Creation Tax Credits; and (5) "Live Near Your Work" Program. It relied upon a combination of program incentives and infrastructure investments to redirect development to PFAs that surrounded urban areas and existing towns.

Glendening viewed himself as a liberal but believed that his smart growth program would appeal to fiscal conservatives. After all, it sought to conserve natural resources, save land, and protect taxpayers from the high cost of often redundant public infrastructure. Significantly, Glendening also promised local public officials that the state would not usurp local land use authority (Knaap & Frece, 2007; Frece, 2008).

To broaden the support for smart growth, Glendening also relied upon broader design and sustainability initiatives that were emerging in the 1990s. For example, Maryland's smart growth program drew inspiration from both "new urbanism" and the US Green Building Council's "green building" initiative, both of which garnered national interest. These national efforts brought new design and sustainability concepts to local jurisdictions and the development community. Traditional neighborhood developments (TNDs) and "LEED" (Leadership in Energy and Environmental Design) certification, with respect to buildings and eventually to neighborhoods, would become valuable additions to the smart growth toolkit.

In 1994, the American Planning Association (APA) launched its "Growing Smart" initiative. That initiative concentrated on assisting states in modernizing their planning statutes. However, it also popularized the idea of "growing smart" (APA, n.d; Meck, 2002). The APA's *Growing Smart Legislative Guidebook* was emblematic of the shift to new smart growth model codes. APA characterized the publication as an effort to draft the next generation of model planning and zoning legislation (Meck, 2002).

In addition, the Smart Growth Network formed in 1996. It represented local and nonprofit organizations and was supported by the US Environmental Protection Agency (EPA). The Smart Growth Network published the 10 principles of smart growth and became a clearinghouse of information. A separate nonprofit organization was created to advocate for smart growth nationally and influence local planning.

Inspired and buttressed by these external supports, Glendening pursued a smart growth approach that relied on financial and development incentives rather than regulations, which reduced conflict with local government authorities. The approach was marketed as a way to save state taxpayers money, while building upon partnerships with the private for-profit and non-profit sectors. Maryland's efforts were supported by the establishment of the National Center for Smart Growth Research and Education (NCSGRE) at the University of Maryland, which aimed to learn from other states while adding intellectual depth to this growing movement (Frece, 2008).

As designed, Maryland's smart growth approach provided an incentive-based, pro-development, low regulation, and low-cost means of promoting sustainable development, one which proved attractive to other states that were previously hesitant to tackle growth management issues. Connecticut, Massachusetts, Minnesota, Utah, Pennsylvania, and Tennessee followed with similar legislation. When New

Table 2.1   Smart growth state initiatives (1997–present)

State	Year adopted	Description	Emblematic policies/programs	Current status
Maryland	1997	Five programs used to encourage development, redevelopment, and conservation in targeted locations.	Priority Funding Areas (PFAs) and Rural Legacy Areas (RLAs).	Programs are still in place, but efficacy is questionable and emphasis has varied over time.
New Jersey	2001–2004	Promoted local plan consistency with the state plan via interactive cross-acceptance process; promoted plan implementation through plan endorsement process that included $3 million in smart growth grants to local jurisdictions for 3 years (1998–2001).	Smart growth grants; Coastal Zone Management Program regulations used to encourage urban centers-based development in coastal zone; Urban Rehab Code supplemented by educational and training institutes for local public officials; bureaucratic change management process to improve state agency horizontal consistency with state plan goals.	Grant programs exhausted; Coastal Zone Management Program regulations are still being implemented; some bureaucratic change was institutionalized.
Maine	2000–2002	Smart Growth Taskforce recommendations legislatively adopted; planning grants (2000); local funding via Municipal Investment Trust Fund (2001); consistency requirements for local planning, zoning, impact fees, school siting.	Several legislative bills (2001–2004); required review of local plans for consistency with State Growth Management Act.	Maine State Planning Office was eliminated in 2012.
Rhode Island	2001	Building rehab code; brownfields program; Neighborhood Opportunities Program; open space preservation program.	Increased state investments in urban communities; targeted growth support for local planning processes.	State Planning Council ongoing; three key programs still exist.
Vermont	2001–2005	Governor's executive order (EO) to manage land use policy and regulations along interstates combined with EPA challenge grants; created Development Cabinet (2000); Act 183 (2006) encouraged development where infrastructure exists; incentivized local governments to strengthen local plans to be eligible for federal/state funds.	Governor's EO related to highway interchanges; 2006 growth centers legislation (Act 183).	EO was scheduled to sunset in 2010, but 2007 report card indicated that state departments were largely ignoring EO.

State	Year adopted	Description	Emblematic policies/programs	Current status
Connecticut	2005	Required Priority Funding Areas (PFAs); state conservation and development plan; requirement that state spending for projects over $200k be in accordance with state plan; requirement that growth-related projects be in PFAs.	State conservation and development plan with a spending threshold for project reviews.	PFAs and state plan still intact, last revised in 2018.
Georgia	2000	Georgia Quality Growth Partnership (GQGP); requirement that state funding be spent in local governments that meet standards for planning (Qualified Local Governments); Atlanta metropolitan level transportation and land use; Georgia Community Greenspace Initiative.	Quality Growth Partnership; public/private partnership to share best practices.	Programs faded with successive gubernatorial administrations, but state planning and DCA continues; funding for greenspace program ended in 2004; website for GQGP came down in 2012.
Minnesota	1999	Smart growth criteria used to evaluate capital bonding; Governor Jesse Ventura's Smart Growth Initiative with smart growth goals and indicators.	Governor's Smart Growth Initiative.	Governor's Smart Growth Initiative faded once Ventura left office in 2003.
Tennessee	1998	Growth Policy Act required counties to work together to shape growth policies through plans; instituted state approval of local plans (no requirement for regular update); tied incentives for completing plans to provision of state funding for highways, community development and tourism.	Growth Policy Act (PC 1101).	Act is still in place but has been revised since 1998; cities/counties eluded compliance.

Jersey's gubernatorial administration changed in 2001, the state changed the name of its Office of State Planning (OSP) to the Office of Smart Growth (OSG).

Table 2.1 summarizes the various state smart growth programs adopted in the wake of Maryland's 1997 smart growth legislation. Though not exhaustive, the table captures many of the policies adopted by states in the 1990s and provides the current status of various initiatives.

Compared with efforts from earlier waves, most notably in Oregon and Florida, the shelf-life of this third wave was relatively short. Many smart growth programs ebbed with new governorships or were discarded in times of financial distress. Maryland and Connecticut demonstrated the most stability, but even their experiences reveal the implementation challenges they faced and long-run disruptions due to transitions in gubernatorial administrations. Interestingly, many of the subcabinets, commissions, and grant and award programs created under the name "smart growth" have retained the moniker even though the programs have faded. For example, Maryland's Smart Growth Subcabinet still exists after 25 years, even though its influence has diminished and most cabinet secretaries no longer attend.

The likely reality is that the smart growth policies contained in the Smart Growth Network's 2002 primer *Getting to Smart Growth: 100 Policies for Implementation* had more staying power at local jurisdictional levels than did the state level initiatives summarized in Table 2.1. Given the short lifespan and lackluster results of almost all state-level smart growth programs, it is unsurprising that a new paradigm of growth management began to emerge in the 2010s.

Given previous and largely unsuccessful efforts at regional governance, it is somewhat surprising how regional land use planning began to assume new importance in the last decade, especially with respect to transportation, water quality, water supply, and economic development issues in some parts of the country. Most notably, a shift to regional planning occurred within some states. For example, California and Oregon employed metropolitan planning organizations (MPOs) to develop and implement state climate change policies. Similarly, regional water supply entities that existed in many states, including Florida, and in the Mountain West and western states began to plan regionally. Even in New Jersey, watershed-based planning and management was resurrected in the 1990s. Despite this return to regional governance, regional land use planning in the United States remains relatively weak, aside from the exceptions of approaches in places such as Portland and Minneapolis.

A PARADIGM SHIFT: SUSTAINABLE DEVELOPMENT, THE FOURTH WAVE

After only a decade and a half, smart growth largely lost its luster at the state level. New governors pursued new priorities and state legislatures turned their attention to different matters. On the federal level, the Obama administration changed focus, identifying and prioritizing novel global challenges. The combination resulted in smart growth being displaced by "sustainable development," the emergent "fourth wave" of growth management's policy evolution over the decades (Chapin, 2012).

This fourth wave drew more heavily upon collaboration from public, private, and non-profit sectors to promote desirable development outcomes. Attention was increasingly given to climate change, energy issues, hazard mitigation, and community resiliency. With clear connections between automobile travel and greenhouse gas emissions, it still made sense to promote more compact development, protect the environment, and encourage multi-modal transportation alternatives. In this emergent wave, policy initiatives moved away from top-down, state-driven planning to local and regional market-driven approaches.

"Sustainable development" could draw upon its own history. In 1987, the United Nations published the Brundtland Commission Report, *Our Common Future*, which included a definition of the term: development that meets the needs of the present without compromising the ability of future generations to meet their own needs. International discussions ensued to elaborate on the concept, ultimately yielding the adoption of the resolution "Agenda 21," a statement of basic principles intended to guide nations in twenty-first century development. Also emerging from these discussions was the idea of the "triple bottom line," a recommendation that economic activity ought to be weighed against environmental and social equity concerns. Sustainable development also required understanding human impacts not only in terms of current consumption but also their impact on future generations.

Similar to smart growth initiatives, sustainable development relied less on comprehensive planning and more on targeting policies and investment to promote growth on a smaller scale in innovative ways. One example that emerged in New Jersey was Sustainable Jersey, a non-governmental organization that rewarded municipalities and school districts for engaging in sustainable practices in ways that local authorities long resisted when they were part of New Jersey's State Development and Redevelopment Plan. Addressing climate change, reducing greenhouse gas emissions, encouraging renewable energy sources, and devising more energy efficient strategies became the defining public policy issues associated with this fourth wave.

At the federal level, the Obama administration's Partnership for Sustainable Communities encouraged collaboration across functional departments at federal and regional levels. The partnership included the US Department of Transportation (DOT), HUD, and the EPA. Rather than targeting funding to state or local governments, regions were required to form teams with nonprofit, civic, public, and private for-profit groups to apply for federal funding. This program was innovative in mandating that federal agencies collaborate while distributing funding to regional-level, cross-sector partnerships through regional planning grants. While this program was relatively short-lived, its encouragement to collaborate across stakeholder groups had positive effects, and it increased attention to regional equity issues throughout the nation (Finio et al., 2021).

In the absence of more robust affirmative federal policy, state and local programs began to address aspects of climate change (Wheeler, 2008; Lewis et al., 2018). The primary concern of these policies has varied from clean energy to mitigation of greenhouse gas emissions to adaptation in coastal areas. Some states, such as Florida and Texas, focused on adaptation in coastal areas. Others, such as California, Oregon, and Washington, employed MPOs to regulate efforts to mitigate greenhouse gas emissions from transportation while pursuing clean energy at the state level. Local climate plans have proliferated, with several cities enacting local climate action plans (Deetjen et al., 2018).

For the most part, these recent planning initiatives were disconnected from earlier comprehensive and smart growth planning efforts. In addition, state climate programs are usually completely separate from contemporary land use and transportation plans (Lewis et al., 2018). At the state level, California pioneered ways to address land use and transportation to reach greenhouse gas reduction targets by region. The approach involved scenario planning and regional level modeling with an emphasis on achieving reduction targets (Barbour, 2016). Oregon, too, engaged in scenario planning to devise climate change strategies. These programs offered a different way forward – voluntary incentives for local governments to alter land use regulations to be consistent with regional transportation planning.

THE UNQUIET DEVOLUTION

What has happened to the quiet revolution? Has it been transformed into the "unquiet devolution"? A review of the last decade finds that Maryland and New Jersey saw program rollbacks due to a backlash against state planning. In Florida, the Community Planning Act of 2011 eliminated many of the key provisions of the 1985 Growth Management Act. In Oregon, planning efforts were attacked and undermined by citizen-led ballot initiatives. In most states where smart growth gained an early foothold, attention gradually dissipated with successive gubernatorial administrations.

The seeds of this unquiet devolution can be traced back at least to the "Reagan Experiment" during the 1980s, and the devolution has significantly expanded amidst the contemporary disruptive public mood, instigated in part by the Trump administration. Is this likely to be long-lasting, or just a temporary bump on the path to reform? The contemporary devolution coincided with the ascendancy of the Tea Party and Wise Use movements in the 1990s and accelerated with the rise of Anti-Agenda 21 advocacy groups during the Great Recession near the beginning of the twenty-first century.

The Tea Party and Wise Use movements attacked planning efforts that they presumed to be linked to globalism and Agenda 21. This political ideological turn altered the public policy debate significantly, disrupting the land use control reform landscape. The property rights movement has pursued a protean strategy – judicial, legislative, policy, and public relations – on multiple government levels. It has attained considerable public visibility, framing its major concern as oppressive government that has infringed on constitutionally protected private property rights.

After three decades since the "Reagan Experiment," this nascent anti-government and anti-regulation movement has become an entrenched political force, exemplified by the election of Donald Trump as President. During the Trump administration, the federal government significantly rolled back environmental protections and fair housing regulations, as well as dismantling the Office of Sustainable Communities and eliminating the Partnership for Sustainable Communities program. Comparable actions have occurred at state and local levels throughout the country. The impact of this broader movement upon land planning efforts, intergovernmental relations, and private property rights – especially with respect to state planning, smart growth, and sustainable development – are unknown. What is clear is that any future efforts to pursue smart growth, sustainable development, and progressive land planning will bring immediate outrage and pushback from a sizable percentage of the electorate.

FUTURE GOVERNANCE

What insights does the last half-century provide in terms of understanding future governance with respect to land use controls? At minimum, an improved understanding of this history should reduce future surprise. It may also help avoid the types of miscalculations made by Bosselman and Callies in defining *The Quiet Revolution* (1971) and by DeGrove as he charted a path for state growth management over several decades.

Much has changed since the 1970s, and progress has been made. Planning has grown, evolved, and become more professionalized, yielding ever more sophisticated practices and policy initiatives. It has at its disposal a more complete set of tools and techniques that can be applied on multiple government levels (see Goodspeed, Chapter 17). The range of issues that planners address has also significantly expanded. Despite the challenges and pushback to land planning as a concept, considerable activity related to land use controls on regional, state, and federal government levels is evident, and many states embrace land planning as a core element of their environmental *and* economic development agendas. These efforts are buttressed by robust and diverse local land use policies and programs. Even as federal, state, and regional land policy have expanded and contracted, local land use controls have not withered away, but remain prominent and essential.

The peaceful, logical, law reform envisioned by Bosselman and Callies seems sadly out of step with the current disruptive public mood; DeGrove's tidy state template and Glendening's "Gift to the Earth" fare no better. State growth management and smart growth have entered a wave of retrenchment, demise, and in some cases abandonment (Weitz, 2020). In some states, the remnants of once innovative approaches to smart growth governance – targeted growth and conservation areas, fiscal incentives, intergovernmental and interagency coordination – remain, despite their limited efficacy. But even at its zenith, state planning and smart growth only attracted a relatively small number of states. Further, the momentum provided by a robust and broadly held environment movement has long since given way to localism and anti-government sentiment.

To what extent will the current mood persist? While the way that these contending forces will eventually play out is unclear, it is likely that a persistent private property rights movement and continued calls for local control will remain. Their relative strength will vary among states. As Justice Brandeis foresaw, the states will continue to serve as laboratories for such experimentation. A judicious balance will have to be restruck. The general welfare will have to be redefined. The respective roles of different government levels will require additional tuning, as they always have and always will.

Furthermore, future public policy controversy will be affected by the contemporary issues currently confronting the nation. A pandemic-induced health crisis has ignited an economic predicament that reveals persistent social inequalities and a long delayed racial reckoning. Global climate change with its pervasive implications still looms. Global competition poses additional challenges requiring public investment. Questions of stewardship and impacts on future generations need to be taken into account. To what extent will these multiple and overlapping issues raise land use implications? Will addressing those implications require not just leveling the playing field, but tilting it in ways that will foster fundamental institutional change?

To better understand the effects of proposed political and legal reforms, perhaps the most important lesson learned from recounting this half-century's history of land use controls is that it is insufficient and impossible to fully anticipate the impacts of proposed reforms on existing values and institutions. Rather, the best that can be done is to actively and purposefully consider the impacts of existing values and institutions on any proposed reforms. Recognizing this history and managing expectations can reduce surprises in the decades to come.

If the past is prologue, future policy and program changes will be incremental, not dramatic, with fits and starts, sometimes forward and sometimes in reverse, while embedded within a complicated and contentious dialectic. Smart growth and what came after were not a phoenix dramatically rising from the ashes. As history has shown, there is no phoenix and there are no ashes. Land use planning is an ever evolving (and devolving) endeavor, buffeted by the leaders and the issues of the moment, as well as the history that affected those leaders and shaped those issues.

REFERENCES

American Planning Association. (n.d.). *Growing Smart*. American Planning Association. https://www.planning.org/growingsmart/

Babcock, R. F. (1966). *The Zoning Game: Municipal Practices and Policies*. University of Wisconsin Press.

Barbour, E. (2016). Evaluating sustainability planning under California's Senate Bill 375. *Transportation Research Record*, 2568(1), 17–25. https://doi.org/10.3141/2568-04

Beam, D. R. (1984). "New federalism, old realities: The Reagan administration and intergovernmental reform." In L. M. Salamon & M. S. Lund (Eds), *The Reagan Presidency and the Governing of America* (pp. 415–442). Washington, DC: Urban Institute Press.

Bierbaum, M. (2015). "The New Jersey State planning experience: From ambitious vision to implementation quagmire to goal redefinition." In G-J. Knaap, Z. Nedović-Budić & A. Carbonell (Eds), Planning for States and Nation-States in the U.S. and Europe. Cambridge, MA: Lincoln Institute for Land Policy.

Bosselman, F., & Callies, D. (1971). *The Quiet Revolution in Land Use Control.* Superintendent of Documents, Government Printing Office, Washington, DC. https://eric.ed.gov/?id= ED067272

Brandeis, Louis D. (1932). In *New State Ice Company v. Liebmann*, 285 U.S. 262 (1932).

Brinkley, A. (2000). "The National Resources Planning Board and the Reconstruction of Planning". In R. Fishman (Ed.), *The American Planning Tradition: Culture and Policy* (pp. 173–192). Essay, Woodrow Wilson Centre Press.

Chapin, T. S. (2012). Introduction: From growth controls, to comprehensive planning, to smart growth: Planning's emerging fourth wave. *Journal of the American Planning Association*, 78(1), 5–15. https://doi.org/10.1080/01944363.2011.645273

Chapin, T. S., Connerly, C. E., & Higgins, H. T. (2007). *Growth Management in Florida: Planning for Paradise*. London UK: Routledge.

Cohen, J. R. (2002). "Maryland's smart growth: Using incentives to combat sprawl." In G.D. Squires (Ed.), *Urban Sprawl: Causes, Consequences and Policy Responses*. Urban Institute.

Daniels, T. (1999). *When City and Country Collide: Managing Growth In The Metropolitan Fringe*. Washington, DC: Island Press.

Danielson, M. N. (1976). *The Politics of Exclusion*. Columbia University Press.

Deetjen, T. A., Conger, J. P., Leibowicz, B. D., & Webber, M. E. (2018). Review of climate action plans in 29 major U.S. cities: Comparing current policies to research recommendations. *Sustainable Cities and Society*, 41, 711–727. https://doi.org/10.1016/j.scs.2018.06 .023

DeGrove, J. M. (1984). *Land Growth & Politics*. Planners Press, American Planning Association.

DeGrove, J. M. (1992). *The New Frontier for Land Policy: Planning and Growth Management in the States*. Lincoln Institute of Land Policy.

DeGrove, J. M. (1993). "The emergence of state planning and growth management systems: An overview". In P. A. Buchsbaum & L. J. Smith (Eds), *State & Regional Comprehensive Planning: Implementing New Methods for Growth Management* (pp. 3–38). Essay, The American Bar Association.

DeGrove, J. M. (2005). *Planning Policy and Politics*. Lincoln Institute of Land Policy.

Elazar, D. J. (1966). *American Federalism: A View from the States*. New York: Thomas Y. Crowell Company.

Finio, N., Lung-Amam, W., Knaap, G.-J., Dawkins, C., & Knaap, E. (2021). Metropolitan planning in a vacuum: Lessons on regional equity planning from Baltimore's Sustainable Communities Initiative. *Journal of Urban Affairs*, 43(3), 467–485.

Fishman, R., & Weir, M. (2000). "Planning, environmentalism and urban poverty: The political failure of national land-use planning legislation 1970-1975." In *The American Planning Tradition: Culture and Policy* (pp. 192–215). Essay, Woodrow Wilson Centre Press.

Frank, J. (1989). *Pricing Strategies in the Promotion of Less Costly Development Patterns*. Florida Governor's Task Force on Urban Growth Patterns, Office of the Governor.

Frece, J. (2008). *Sprawl and Politics: The Inside Story of Smart Growth in Maryland*. Albany, NY: SUNY Press.

Golden v. Planning Board of the Town of Ramapo. 285 N.E. 2d (N.Y. 1972).

Healy, R. G., & Rosenberg, J. S. (1979). *Land Use and the States*. Washington, DC: RFF Press.

Hirt, S. (2014). *Zoned in the USA: The Origins and Implications of American Land-Use Regulation.* Ithaca, NY: Cornell University Press.

Ingram, G., Carbonell, A., Hong, Y-H., and Flint, A. (2009). *Smart Growth Policies: An Evaluation of Programs and Outcomes.* Cambridge, MA: Lincoln Institute of Land Policy.

Kayden, J. S. (2000). "National land-use planning in America: Something whose time has never come," *Washington University Journal of Law and Policy,* 3, 445.

Knaap, G. J., & Frece, J. (2007). Smart growth in Maryland: Looking forward and looking back. *Idaho Law Review,* 43.

Knaap, G. J., & Nelson, A. C. (1992). *The Regulated Landscape: Lessons on State Land Use Planning from Oregon.* Lincoln Institute of Land Policy.

Lewis, R., Zako, R., Biddle, A., & Isbell, R. (2018). Reducing greenhouse gas emissions from transportation and land use: Lessons from West Coast states. *Journal of Transport and Land Use,* 11(1), Article 1. https://doi.org/10.5198/jtlu.2018.1173

Meck, S. (2002). *Growing Smart Legislative Guidebook.* Washington, DC: American Planning Association.

Palmer, J. L., & Sawhill, I. (1982). "Perspectives on the Reagan experiment." In *The Reagan Experiment* (pp. 1–28). Essay, The Urban Institute Press.

Pelham, T. (1979). *State Land-use Planning and Regulation.* Lexington, MA, Toronto, Canada: Lincoln Institute of Land Policy, Lexington Books, D.C. Heath and Company.

Pizor, P. J. (1982). Managing growth in developing communities: A capacity-based approach and case study in applied growth management planning. Rutgers University.

Popper, F. (1988). Understanding American land use regulation since 1970: A revisionist interpretation. *Journal of the American Planning Association,* 54(3), 291–301.

Porter, D. R. (2007). *Managing Growth in America's Communities* (Second edition). Island Press.

Rothstein, R. (2018). *The Color of Law: A Forgotten History of How Our Government Segregated America.* Liveright.

Salkin, P. E. (2012). *The Quiet Revolution and Federalism: Into the Future.* John Marshall Law School.

Salkin, P. (2015). "*Land Use Regulation in the United States: An Intergovernmental Framework.*" In Planning for States and Nation-States in the U.S. and Europe. Lincoln Institute of Land Policy.

Seltzer, E., & Carbonell, A. (Eds.) (2011). *Regional Planning in America: Practice and Prospect* (Illustrated edition). Lincoln Institute of Land Policy.

South Burlington County NAACP v. Township of Mount Laurel, 67 N.J. 151, 336 A.2d 713, 1975 N.J.

Village of Euclid v. Ambler Realty Co., 272 U.S. 365 (1926).

Vincent, C. H., Bermejo, L. F., & Hanson, L. A. (2020). *Federal Land Ownership: Overview and Data* (p. 28). Congressional Research Service.

Weiher, G. (1991). *The Fractured Metropolis: Political Fragmentation and Metropolitan Segregation.* State University of New York Press.

Weitz, J. (1999). From quiet revolution to smart growth: State growth management programs, 1960 to 1999. *Journal of Planning Literature,* 14(2), 266–337. https://doi.org/10.1177/08854129922092694

Weitz, J. (2020). Retrenchment and demise of state growth management programs. *Journal of Comparative Urban Law and Policy,* 4(1), 45–55.

Wheeler, S. (2008). State and municipal climate change plans: The first generation. *Journal of the American Planning Association,* 74(4), 481–496.

Wolf, M. A. (2008). *The Zoning of America.* University of Kansas Press. https://kansaspress.ku.edu/978-0-7006-1620-6.html

PART II

SMART GROWTH PRINCIPLES: THE LOCATION OF URBAN DEVELOPMENT

3. Urban containment as smart growth

John I. Carruthers, Hanxue Wei, and Lucien Wostenholme

PROMOTING COMPACT URBAN FORM

Urban containment is an approach to smart growth aimed at promoting density in development, via various policy and planning strategies. While the meaning and tools of containment have evolved over time, one way or another, it has always been about finding ways, large and small, to take advantage of compact building design. Like so many other smart growth or growth management concepts, containment is rooted in the practice of land use planning and emerged along with the environmental movement of the 1960s. The concept began taking hold, initially as a form of local growth control, during the early 1970s when, for the first time in national history, the decennial census registered a significant population shift away from high-density urban centers toward low-density exurban hinterlands (Beale, 1975). Today, in between core and edge areas are a diversity of communities, which grew out of the post-World War II housing boom and have continued to expand ever since. This new order of development, which came to typify the American way of settlement, inspired widespread adoption of new planning strategies, with containment—in the form of greenbelts, concurrency requirements, urban growth boundaries, priority funding areas, and more—being central among them and implemented at the local and state levels of government.

It is impossible to discuss urban containment, which we define as the goal of promoting compact, mixed use development, without also discussing urban sprawl. Sprawl, the opposite of contained growth, has been the dominant mode of urbanization in the United States since at least the 1950s (Glaeser & Kahn, 2004). Sprawl is explained by many economists as the outcome of rising wealth plus falling commuting costs, accelerated by preferences for suburban living environments and small, easily-accessible local governments (Duranton & Puga, 2013, 2015). These and a host of other, more nuanced forces—some of which are discussed below— reshaped the disposition of development nationwide over the course of several decades, as growth shifted from the older manufacturing belt to the newer sunbelt, in an increasingly prosperous, automobile-oriented, and parochially-settled country. By the 1980s, urban sprawl was the norm and, by the mid-1990s, debate over its causes and consequences had reached something of a fever pitch in the planning literature (see, for example, the 1997 "point-counterpoint" debate between Gordon & Richardson and Ewing, featured in the *Journal of the American Planning Association*). By the early 2000s, sprawl remained as divisive as ever and evidence suggested that there was no foreseeable return to the massive urban environments of the past, meaning that, in most areas of the country, the suburban pattern was here to stay.

Nonetheless, the smart growth movement and the "quiet revolution" in land use control that began reshaping planning around environmental issues of extra-local concern more than 50 years ago—including open space conservation, farmland preservation, and resource protection—have changed much within American cities over the past two decades. As this chapter argues, containment has had some success conceptually in promoting compact urban form and, by extension, advancing various complementary objectives. At the same time, a combination of powerful demographic trends and market forces have proved to be key catalysts, making containment more tenable than it was in its early years. Many of today's urbanites are younger, educated individuals who have not only internalized the sentiments of yesteryear's revolution, but amplified them because of broader concerns for sustainable development, climate change, ecological resilience, social justice, and other issues. Moreover, in our view, this demographic has helped to reshape urban design by demanding compact, mixed-use redevelopment in cities nationwide. Further, a preference for adult, as opposed to child-related amenities is an important driver that planners should not overlook (Black et al., 2002). Purveyors of containment would therefore do well to recognize that it is not only the brute force of land use regulation that has made it an enduring policy concept, but also a set of motivating ideals and evolving preferences (Lewis & Baldassare, 2010).

What is urban containment, and what is its contemporary utility as a means of smart growth? This chapter provides an overview of containment policy, beginning with a summary of its evolution, followed by a review of empirical evidence on its impacts. We close by highlighting changes currently occurring within cities, with an eye toward how the rise of "consumer cities" (Glaeser et al., 2001; Glaeser & Gottlieb, 2006) might inform a new vision for smart growth—or a smart growth 2.0—going forward. Overall, we conclude that the concept of urban containment is viable in both principle and practice, however, we argue that planning policy should adopt a softer touch, aimed at overcoming the negative externalities of density (Glaeser, 2020).

CONTAINMENT AND URBAN GROWTH BOUNDARIES

The idea of urban containment dates at least to the vision set out by the British lay urbanist Ebenezer Howard in his 1898 book, *Garden Cities of Tomorrow*. Howard's vision called for a decentralized system of new towns, built at high densities and contained by greenbelts; each was to be a company town, specialized in a particular industry. The greenbelts would ensure that growth occurred at interior locations, thereby preventing development from tarnishing the countryside. Though Howard was certainly influenced by his observations of American cities—he had traveled among them—his main goal was to find a remedy for the adverse conditions found in London and other Victorian-era British cities by bringing together the best of both "town" and "country." That Howard's diagram, *The Three Magnets*, which details the draw of town, country, and a combination of the two, remains one of the most prominent ideas in urban planning more than a century after it was put forward testifies to the power of his vision. Also new at the time was Howard's explicitly regional perspective on planning for development.

In the United States, containment has evolved in fits and starts, initiated by both local and state governments. The earliest policies materialized in places that now seem obscure: Lexington, Kentucky, is typically cited as the first city to implement an urban growth boundary (in 1959) and it is notable because its boundary was based on an agreement with surrounding Fayette County (Kelly, 2004). The intergovernmental dimension is key because it is what distinguishes contemporary smart growth frameworks—and the growth management frameworks that preceded them, as discussed by Landis in Chapter 1 of this book—from purely local growth control efforts. Still, it is necessary to recognize that the comprehensive approach of today, generally organized at the state level, originates from various go-it-alone interventions. Another early experiment with containment occurred in Boulder, Colorado, which voted in 1967 for a 0.4 percent sales tax that was used to acquire surrounding land and piece together a publicly-held greenbelt (Porter, 1997). This boundary was further enforced by a blue line, so-called because it limited (by elevation) the areas to which Boulder would supply water. These and other early local efforts gave rise to the state-led efforts coordinating the practice of containment.

Along the way, there have been numerous obstacles, especially in the form of legal challenges to localities' right to limit the amount and nature of growth. A watershed event, in the context of smart growth, was the 1972 New York Supreme Court case, *Golden v. The Planning Board of the Town of Ramapo* (Nolon, 2003). Among other things, the case concerned the city's use of concurrency requirements to contain spatial expansion to areas that had the infrastructure to accommodate that expansion. Ramapo is situated in Rockland County in the Hudson Valley, just outside New York City, and lay squarely in the growth path of the already sprawling metropolitan region. Like other early adopters of growth controls—in particular, Petaluma and Santa Rosa, California, in the northern exurbs of San Francisco, which implemented development permitting cap programs (which Ramapo also had)—Ramapo's action is, with hindsight, a pragmatic response to a surge of development that the small community was ill-equipped to accommodate. While it is always possible to point to exclusionary motivations, the haphazard approach of the growth control movement was largely a byproduct of the fact that most state governments had yet to engage in any real oversight of local land use planning and related activity (see Porter, 1986 for a collection of essays on this period of local growth policy).

Thus, it was a year later, in 1973, with the passage of Oregon's Senate Bill 100, that urban containment made the leap from a growth control concept to a growth management concept. The Oregon Land Use Act created the state-based Land Conservation and Development Commission and Department of Land Conservation and Development, which resulted in locally-established urban growth boundaries (UGBs) around all of the state's urbanized areas. While the devil is in the details

(Knaap & Nelson, 1992), the means by which UGBs contain growth is straightforward, at least in principle: urbanization is allowed inside, but not outside, of UGBs, which separates urban from rural land. While theoretical analysis of UGBs can be complex (see, for example, Ding et al., 1999) the underlying concept is that limiting the supply of urban land makes it scarce, raising its price. Since land is the first ingredient of development, when builders face high land prices, the rationale goes, they will construct vertically rather than horizontally. Containment therefore needs to be complemented by design standards oriented around compact development, where site-scale codes reinforce regional-scale policy. (For particulars on form-based codes, see Talen, Chapter 7 in this book.) While containment may dictate smaller, high-density units, it does not dictate higher prices for finished housing and/or other construction.

Still, UGBs are controversial, and they are not perfectly effective—even in Oregon, whose actions have been emulated by, among others, Washington State, via its 1990 Growth Management Act. As Knaap & Nelson (1992) detail, UGBs and, by extension, many other forms of containment, do their work first and foremost by acting as supply constraints, but also as timing constraints, because they keep growth in place until they are expanded (Knaap, 1985), and as location constraints, because they preserve outlying greenbelt-like amenities (Nelson, 1985, 1986). Empirical work by Knaap and Nelson during the 1980s also helped distinguish the broader, intergovernmental approach of state growth management from the narrower, local approach of growth control. More recent work has further established the effectiveness of state-based UGB frameworks (Woo & Guldmann, 2011).

By the end of the 1990s, the urban economics literature, had, rather understandably, manifested a veritable cottage industry of consternation over land use policies aimed at growth control (Fischel, 1990), but few authors bothered to separate parochial policy from more inclusive intergovernmental attempts at growth management (Carruthers, 2002). Empirical work since then (see Kline & Alig, 1999; Song & Knaap, 2003, 2008; Song, 2005, 2012; Carruthers & Clark, 2010; Carruthers et al., 2010; Dempsey & Plantinga, 2013; Mathur, 2014, 2019) has generally upheld the intraregional findings by showing that UGBs are effective—and an interregional analysis, though now dated, suggests that Oregon's UGB-based approach is the one and only growth management framework in the United States that has managed to constrain urban sprawl without simultaneously disrupting property values (Carruthers, 2002). The key to Oregon's success in avoiding price distortions is the state's requirement that its UGBs hold a 20-year supply of developable land, and look even further into the future, toward a 30–50 year reserve (see Lewis et al., 2018 for an overview of urban expansion, including annexation and timing).

OTHER CONTAINMENT TOOLS

Although not a panacea, UGBs appear to be more effective than alternative measures; in particular, concurrency requirements of the sort used in Florida; priority funding areas of the sort used in Maryland; and farmland preservation policies of the sort used in Pennsylvania. While Florida's Growth Management Act is one of the first (and most rigid) statewide frameworks implemented in the United States (Ben-Zadok, 2005; DeGrove, 2005; Howell-Moroney, 2007) it has also proved to be one of the most vexing because of conflicting evidence about its impacts (Carruthers, 2002; Wassmer, 2006). In an analysis of compliance among Florida jurisdictions, Boarnet et al. (2011) found that the mechanisms of concurrency—which allow development to proceed when required infrastructure is in place, often at the urban fringe—are not particularly conducive to containment. (For a comprehensive review of Florida's approach, see Connerly & Chapin, 2007.)

Maryland's system of priority funding areas, implemented in 1997, was a new approach to containment that channeled state spending into areas identified by *both* the state and local governments as targets for growth (Lewis et al., 2009). This quintessential smart growth tool has probably not been in place long enough for it to have had far-reaching effects, and about 15 years after its implementation, evidence on its impact was mixed (Hanlon et al., 2012; Lewis & Knaap, 2012).

Development impact fees, a price-based mechanism that is favored by many economists, are another tool used by local governments across the United States (Altshuler & Gomez-Ibañez, 1993; Brueckner, 2007). The goal of impact fees is to make development "pay for itself" in terms of the demands it places on local public finance. To the extent that compact development is less expensive to support, as we discuss below, impact fees may also encourage containment, especially if growth is forced to internalize the costs that it incurs (Brueckner, 2000).

Lastly, various farmland preservation policies, including transfer of development rights (TDRs), purchase of development rights (PDRs), and other market-based instruments used in Pennsylvania and elsewhere (Daniels & Lapping, 2005) have often proven effective, yet there is less systematic evidence about their efficacy across the nation. Still, these and other resource-oriented approaches belong among the class of containment policies, particularly given their utility in rural settings, as Newburn, Lynch, and Wang describe in Chapter 4.

It bears emphasizing that these broader, regional policies work best when implemented via intergovernmental coordination because, ultimately, they are about focusing the distribution of growth not only *within*, but *among* jurisdictions. Moreover, it should be clear that, locally, none of the density (and/or other outcomes) that urban containment seeks to achieve is possible without local design standards aimed at delivering compact, mixed-use development, the implementation of which Song discusses in Chapter 6. As the smart growth principle about compact building design states:

> Compact building design is necessary to support wider transportation choices and provides cost savings for localities. Communities seeking to encourage transit use to reduce air pollution and congestion recognize that minimum levels of density are required to make public transit networks viable. In addition, local governments find that, on a per-unit basis, it is cheaper to provide and maintain services like water, sewer, electricity, phone service and other utilities in more-compact neighborhoods than in dispersed communities.

We discuss several of these assertions further below, including whether containment delivers on its intended objectives and whether it can continue to be useful going forward.

In sum, over the course of several decades, urban containment has emerged as a well-established element of smart growth in the United States. Evidence on the impacts of the various containment tools that localities have employed shows UGBs are most effective—however, it may be that other approaches, such as Maryland's priority funding areas, have not been in place long enough to deliver on their promise; time will tell. What is known is that containment works best as a coordinated, intergovernmental endeavor. Fragmented land use regulation inevitably shifts growth from one place to another, without doing anything to manage the overall tide of development (Carruthers & Úlfarsson, 2002). In Chapter 2, M. Bierbaum, Lewis, and Chapin discuss the intricacies and effectiveness of intergovernmental smart growth coordination.

CONTAINMENT VERSUS SPRAWL

The benefits of containment and compact development, as opposed to sprawl, are believed by many to be less costly to support, from the perspective of public finance; more inclusive, from the perspective of community justice; beneficial to fitness, from the perspective of public health; environmentally friendly, from the perspective of urban ecology; more efficient, from the perspective of transit; vibrant, from the perspective of decline; and less isolating, from the perspective of social capital. The trouble is that while urban sprawl is blamed for many problems, evidence of its alleged pathologies in the scholarly literature has, until recently, been in short supply. For many years, scholars argued that sprawl delivered the housing, lifestyle, and amenities people wanted. But a sea change arose in the late 1990s and early 2000s across the planning, economics, and other literature as researchers began to systematically (and objectively) evaluate the costs and benefits of alternative land use patterns. A recent meta-analysis, which synthesized nearly 350 measures of density, concluded that though "there are [both] sizeable benefits and costs associated with increases in density, the former exceed the latter for a typical large city in the developed world" (Ahlfeldt & Pietrostefani, 2019, p. 106).

So has containment been successful, and, if so, how and in what ways? The answer is decidedly mixed. While there is evidence, outlined in the introduction and discussed further below, that the rise of consumer cities has driven redevelopment and densification within cities, it is not at all clear how much of this is owed to containment policy vs. market demand. Nor is it clear, as discussed above, that containment policies have offset sprawl to a degree meaningful at the national scale. Indeed, a report by Lewis et al. (2013) documents that the spatial structure of cities in the United States continues to be dominated by growth at the fringe (Carruthers, 2003) and that population density gradients nationwide have continued to flatten over time. As Carruthers et al. (2010, 2012) illustrate, recent patterns of change within cities are variegated, making it problematic to generalize across them, yet it does appear that UGBs are comparatively effective tools.

Several key questions in the pool of literature on urban containment can help evaluate what smart growth has achieved: the extent to which containment has helped to reinvigorate central cities and the extent to which compact development lowers the cost of public services. A third element is the extent to which containment policies mediate housing bubbles by increasing pressure on core areas. These questions are also key to judging smart growth success going forward.

Since the World War II housing boom, the waves of suburbanization in the United States have been both driven by and responsible for urban blight. Central city decline is nothing if not a self-reinforcing process. The same market failures responsible for sprawl—namely, the social costs of traffic congestion, greenfield development, and infrastructure investment (Brueckner, 2000)—may also be responsible for urban blight (Brueckner & Helsley, 2011). Automobile ownership has enabled people to live in suburban communities (Glaeser et al., 2008), and suburban communities' heavy reliance on property taxes may also contribute to the kind of sprawl that necessitates their use. The contemporary built environment is the product of mutually reinforcing mechanisms, many of which—including traditional land use planning—have spurred suburbanization.

As noted previously, decreased commuting costs have contributed to residential sprawl, but also job sprawl, as people commute farther for employment throughout the United States (Baum-Snow, 2007), Europe (Garcia-López, 2019), and China (Zheng et al., 2017), among other places. Rising wealth, perhaps even more than decreased commuting costs, has enabled households to consume more space and relocate away from already declining areas (Wassmer, 2008). Containment policies have aimed to reverse these trends. One of containment's main objectives is central city revitalization; it is intended to stop the outward expansion of growth by turning it toward the core. An analysis by Dawkins & Nelson (2003) suggests that state growth management programs in general, and containment policies in particular, do promote central city redevelopment. Likewise, Hortas-Rico (2015) finds evidence from metropolitan areas nationwide that containment reduces blight by pushing growth toward the interior. These and related findings are consistent with the argument that market pressures can produce desirable outcomes. However, as noted, complementary design standards should be used as a release valve for this pressure (Aurand, 2010). There is also extensive evidence that amenity-rich urban environments are increasingly vital, as reflected in land rents, labor productivity, and more (Albouy, 2016). Urban containment can further fuel this vitality.

Another key argument for urban containment has long been that "denser is cheaper" (Frank, 1989; Juntunen et al., 2011; Carruthers, 2012). In his review of the causes of sprawl, for instance, Brueckner (2000) makes the case that sprawl is in part caused by the underpricing of urban infrastructure and recommends using impact fees as yet another tool for containment (Altshuler & Gomez-Ibañez, 1993; Brueckner, 2007).[1] Early on, the main evidence on the cost of public services came from work by Ladd and Yinger (1991) and Ladd (1992, 1994, 1998), which suggested that public services follow U-shaped cost curves, associated with the economies and diseconomies of scale in the production process.[2] However, these studies did not measure urban form; due to data limitations of the time, they measured density as population divided by county land area—a meaningless ratio, given that the geographic size of counties has nothing to do with how many people live in them. Next, Carruthers (2002) and Carruthers and Úlfarsson (2002, 2003, 2008) measured development patterns and found that density, gauged as people and jobs per acre of urbanized land, does bring down the cost of most public services. Carruthers and Úlfarsson (2008) calculated elasticities and (albeit coarsely) estimated the financial impacts. These analyses are rough, yielding only qualified evidence in support of this argument for containment. More recently, evidence from Spanish municipalities (Solé-Ollé & Bosch, 2005; Solé-Ollé, 2006; Hortas-Rico & Solé-Ollé, 2010; Hortas-Rico, 2015) has further reinforced the relationship between density and cost but the evidence, while compelling, is still rough. To the extent that there are economies of scale in public services, urban containment has likely helped deliver savings; certainly, the "harshness" of urban environments noted by Ladd and Yinger (1991) also produces diseconomies—poorly performing school districts are often the costliest to operate. Remarkably, the work cited here represents the sum total of what is known about the costs of alternative development patterns to sprawl. As a practical matter, it seems both important and possible, in an era of big data, to know how compact, contiguous growth affects public finance with greater precision.

Finally, given the market pressure that many containment policies, such as UGBs, are intended to exert, housing bubbles are another concern (Paciorek, 2013). Like bubbles for any commodity, housing bubbles are caused by speculators anticipating future price increases (Glaeser & Nathanson, 2015), but they also materialize as a result of regulatory limits on housing, which can, and do, raise prices (Gyourko & Molloy, 2015). In economic terms, constraints shift the market supply curve for housing backward, raising prices in the face of static (or increasing) demand; policies that make it more cumbersome for developers to deliver housing steepen the supply curve, making it less elastic. As pointed out above, historically, a primary objection to land use planning (in general) and growth controls (in particular) is that they are known to be redistributive (Fischel, 2015). Thus, care must be taken to manage land supplies in ways that contain growth but don't distort land and housing prices.

As discussed above, there is nothing about urban containment per se that inflates the level of housing prices. Indeed, some have argued that, when implemented via interjurisdictional cooperation, containment does not produce bubbles and can even ameliorate segregation (Nelson et al., 2004). On the other hand, building height restrictions and other forms of regulation that explicitly limit the supply of residential and/or commercial development in places that are attractive to people and/or firms are objectively problematic when it comes to prices, because they reduce choice (Glaeser, 2008). Such policies become even more troublesome when applied to the interior of a region that is subject to some exogenous form of containment, such as Manhattan Island or San Francisco Peninsula. Getting such restrictions out of the way may be the key to opening a new era of compact urban form that relies more on the attractiveness of mixed land uses (Koster & Rouwendal, 2012) and the rich tapestry of urban life—in addition to demand for environmental quality (Kahn & Walsh, 2015) in an era of anthropogenic climate change—than the brute force of land use regulation.

Containment has many goals, and a national (as opposed to a particular state or local) view shows its successes are best characterized as modest in terms of land use outcomes. It does appear that containment has had an impact on two of its key policy concerns, reinvigorating central cities and lowering the cost of public services. Continued attention should be focused on how it mediates (interacts with) housing bubbles. For all of the focus on large-scale containment policies in the form of UGBs and other regional policies, going forward, equal focus should be placed on small-scale codes in the form of compact, mixed-use design standards.

THE RISE OF CONSUMER CITIES

As Glaeser (2007, p. 4) notes, in the most basic sense, "cities are the absence of physical space between people and firms" and it is this organic (Jacobs, 1961) absence of space, or density, that containment seeks to achieve. The preceding section reviewed some reasons why density may be preferable to sprawl. What has yet to be addressed is the fact that most urbanization of the sort that containment seeks to achieve happened with little or no planning at all (Bertaud, 2018). Indeed, containment policies emerged only after decades of planning that actively channeled urbanization in the opposite direction; in this sense, the traditions of planning itself are a part of the landscape of problems that smart growth seeks to address. So, it is only fair to ask: What lies beyond regulation?

One answer to this question lies in the fact that cities are complex, unpredictable systems that renew themselves on an ongoing basis (Batty, 2018). Weber (1921) was apparently the first to coin the term "consumer city" in a taxonomy of urbanization that distinguished between consumer and producer cities, according to their economic base. A paper by Glaeser et al. (2001) made the term colloquial[3] and argued that modern cities function as centers of consumption as much as they do production. In many advanced economies, urban rents have risen faster than urban wages, indicating that demand for housing in cities outpaces demand for labor. People and firms locate in dense, amenity-rich urban areas in numbers that exceed the amount of space (i.e., available real estate) within them. The exurban tide that caught the attention of Beale (1975) has turned and the outcome is a new spatial order, in which real wages, or wages adjusted for prices, have fallen in many cities in the United States and around the world (Glaeser, 2008). What does this mean for smart growth? That markets are helping with the objective of containment: densifying core areas.

Long ago, Tiebout (1956) famously declared that people vote with their feet. While Tiebout was referring to local politics and public expenditure, the idea has broader, more powerful implications. In the wide-open, footloose labor markets of post-industrial economies, people and firms alike are free to locate where they choose, meaning that all geographic space—urban, suburban, exurban, and rural—is rationed by markets. Thus, even as the post-World War II housing boom and the so-called nonmetropolitan turnaround are readily explained by market forces (Duranton & Puga, 2013, 2015) and market failures, that explanation is incomplete, because it does not account for the failure of many central cities to deal with the many negative externalities found within them. If a place is undesirable to live, people will not want to locate there, which was the case in many American cities during the latter half of the twentieth century. By failing to contain the market failures associated with their high densities and large population sizes, many cities may have underwritten their own downfall during the latter half of the 1900s, however unwittingly.

Cities, compared with their sprawling surroundings, bring people together in ways that they cannot predict or prevent. This mixing has been shown to be an economic advantage (Ottaviano & Peri, 2005, 2006) and, however slowly, people also overcome differences by exposure to one another (Glaeser, 2005). Dense urban environments force this exposure and, one hopes, the kind of inclusiveness necessary for confronting the debilitating societal ailments that movements such as *Black Lives Matter* seek to address. In terms of containment, the general lesson is straightforward: tend to these rich urban environments in ways that people value (Koster & Rouwendal, 2012) and cities will densify, perhaps in a fashion more desirable than any land use policy could ever aspire to achieve.

THOUGHTS ON THE FUTURE OF CONTAINMENT

This chapter began by introducing the concept of urban containment, explaining its origins and objectives, then asking: What is the contemporary utility of urban containment as a means of smart growth? We conclude with some thoughts on a "smart growth 2.0."

The concept of urban containment endures, but it should be broadened from a regulatory concept of urban form to an organic concept of urban life. Containment policies have been effective as land use planning tools, but their utility as a tool for forcing growth into counterfactually desired locations and/or configurations may be reaching diminishing returns. Going forward, planners would be well-advised to cast containment as an organizing principle as much as a desired outcome. Second, the central concerns that containment has sought to address are generally worthwhile, though research remains lacking in many areas. The public health dimension briefly mentioned is a good example: researchers have found conflicting evidence that development patterns are relevant to obesity and other ailments, so advocates need to be mindful of overreach (Garfinkel-Castro and Ewing address the public health–built environment relationship in detail in Chapter 12). Third, we have noted the rise of consumer cities (Glaeser et al., 2001) and pointed out that one reason central cities in the United States suffered so much during the twentieth century is because they did not contain the market failures of dense urban environments. So, while the concept of containment is enduring, it is probably best achieved by policies aimed at channeling the positive externalities of urbanization and overcoming its inevitable negative externalities. In other words, by encouraging people to *choose* urban environments over the alternatives.

Last, this chapter would be remiss if it failed to say at least a few words about containment in an era of anthropogenic climate change. As discussed by Hendricks and Berke in Chapter 15, cities are a chief source of greenhouse gas emissions and evidence suggests that urban form is a mediating factor. Economists are optimistic about the ability of society to adapt via technological innovation and migration, but this adaptation cannot happen in a vacuum, meaning that there is an important role for planning (Calthorpe, 2013). As noted in the introduction, many of today's urbanites are younger, educated individuals who are concerned with sustainable development, ecological resilience, social justice, and other motivations. The perspectives, ideas, and energy of these individuals should not be overlooked, nor should their ability act as a unifying force for a vision that addresses the dominant challenge of the twenty-first century. After all, planning is about the future, and the future of all places grows more urgent as the world continues to warm.

NOTES

1. The very first study to address the question was apparently by Elis-Williams (1987) who looked at school expenditures in the United Kingdom and found evidence that the cost of education per student decreases with the size of the school and increases with the distance students live from the schools.
2. In microeconomics, the marginal and average costs of production are U-shaped functions; profit-maximizing firms cease production once the two become equivalent.
3. Cited, as of this writing, nearly 2,500 times, according to Google Scholar.

REFERENCES

Ahlfeldt, G. M. & Pietrostefani, E. (2019). The economic effects of density: A synthesis. *Journal of Urban Economics, 111*, 93–107.

Albouy, D. (2016). What are cities worth? Land rents, local productivity, and the total value of amenities. *Review of Economics and Statistics, 98*, 477–487.

Altshuler, A. & Gomez-Ibañez, J. (1993). *Regulation for revenue: The political economy of land use exactions.* Cambridge, MA: Lincoln Institute of Land Policy.

Aurand, A. (2010). Density, housing types and mixed land use: Smart tools for affordable housing? *Urban Studies, 47*, 1015–1036.

Batty, M. (2018). *Inventing future cities.* Cambridge, MA: The MIT Press.

Baum-Snow, N. (2007). Did highways cause suburbanization? *The Quarterly Journal of Economics, 122*, 775–805.

Beale, C. L. (1975). *The revival of population growth in nonmetropolitan America (ERS-606).* Washington, DC: Economic Research Service, US Department of Agriculture.

Ben-Zadok, E. (2005). Consistency, concurrency and compact development: Three faces of growth management in Florida. *Urban Studies, 42*, 2167–2190.

Bertaud, A. (2018). *Order without design: How markets shape cities.* Cambridge, MA: The MIT Press.

Black, D., Gates, G., Sander, S. & Taylor, L. (2002). Why do gay men live in San Francisco? *Journal of Urban Economics*, *51*, 54–76.

Boarnet, M. G., McLaughlin, R. B. & Carruthers, J. I. (2011). Does state growth management change the pattern of urban growth? Evidence from Florida. *Regional Science and Urban Economics*, *41*, 236–252.

Brueckner, J. K. (2000). Urban sprawl: Diagnosis and remedies. *International Regional Science Review*, *23*, 160–171.

Brueckner, J. K. (2007). Urban growth boundaries: An effective second-best remedy for unpriced traffic congestion? *Journal of Housing Economics*, *16*, 263–273.

Brueckner, J. K. & Helsley, R. W. (2011). Sprawl and blight. *Journal of Urban Economics*, *69*, 205–213.

Calthorpe, P. (2013). *Urbanism in the age of climate change*. Washington, DC: Island Press.

Carruthers, J. I. (2002). The impacts of state growth management programs: A comparative analysis. *Urban Studies*, *39*, 1959–1982.

Carruthers, J. I. (2003). Growth at the fringe: The influence of political fragmentation in United States metropolitan areas. *Papers in Regional Science*, *82*, 472–499.

Carruthers, J. I. (2012). The public finance of urban form. In R. Weber & R. Crane (Eds), *The Oxford handbook of urban planning*. New York, NY: Oxford University Press.

Carruthers, J. I. & Clark, D. E. (2010). Valuing environmental quality: A space-based strategy. *Journal of Regional Science*, *50*, 801–832.

Carruthers J. I. & Úlfarsson, G. F. (2002). Fragmentation and sprawl: Evidence from interregional analysis. *Growth and Change*, *33*, 312–340.

Carruthers, J. I. & Úlfarsson, G. F. (2003). Urban sprawl and the cost of public services. *Environment and Planning B*, *30*, 503–522.

Carruthers, J. I. & Úlfarsson, G. F. (2008). Does smart growth matter to public finance? *Urban Studies*, *45*, 1791–1823.

Carruthers J. I., Hepp, S., Knaap, G.-J. & Renner, R. N. (2010). Coming undone: A spatial hazard analysis of urban form. *Papers in Regional Science*, *89*, 65–88.

Carruthers J. I., Hepp, S., Knaap, G.-J. & Renner, R. N. (2012). The American way of land use: A spatial hazard analysis of changes through time. *International Regional Science Review*, *35*, 267–302.

Connerly, C. E. & Chapin, T. S. (Eds) (2007). *Evaluating Florida's growth management approach*. Aldershot: Ashgate.

Daniels, T. L. & Lapping, M. (2005). Land preservation: An essential ingredient in smart growth. *Journal of Planning Literature*, *19*, 316–329.

Dawkins, C. J. & Nelson, A. C. (2003). State growth management programs and central-city revitalization. *Journal of the American Planning Association*, *69*, 381–396.

DeGrove, J. M. (2005). *Planning policy and politics: Smart growth and the States*. Cambridge, MA: Lincoln Institute of Land Policy.

Dempsey, J. A. & Plantinga, A. J. (2013). How well do urban growth boundaries contain development? Results for Oregon using a difference-in-difference estimator. *Regional Science and Urban Economics*, *43*, 996–1007.

Ding, C., Knaap, G.-J. & Hopkins, L. D. (1999). Managing urban growth with urban growth boundaries: A theoretical analysis. *Journal of Urban Economics*, *46*, 53–68.

Duranton, G. & Puga, D. (2013). The growth of cities. In P. Aghion & S. Durlauf (Eds), *Handbook of economic growth, volume 2*. The Netherlands: North-Holland.

Duranton, G. & Puga, D. (2015). Urban land use. In G. Duranton, J. V. Henderson & W. Strange (Eds), *Handbook of regional and urban economics, volume 5A*. The Netherlands: North-Holland.

Elis-Williams, D. G. (1987). The effect of spatial population distribution on the cost of delivering local services. *Journal of the Royal Statistical Society, Series A*, *150*, 152–166.

Ewing, R. (1997). Is Los Angeles-style sprawl desirable? *Journal of the American Planning Association, 63*, 107–126.

Fischel, W. A. (1990). *Do growth controls matter? A review of empirical evidence on the effectiveness and efficiency of local government land use regulation.* Cambridge: Lincoln Institute of Land Policy.

Fischel, W. A. (2015). *Zoning rules! The economics of land use regulation.* Cambridge, MA: The Lincoln Institute of Land Policy.

Frank, J. (1989). *The costs of alternative development patterns: A review of the literature.* Washington, DC: The Urban Land Institute.

Garcia-López, M. A. (2019). All roads lead to Rome... and to sprawl? Evidence from European cities. *Regional Science and Urban Economics, 79*, 103–467.

Glaeser, E. L. (2005). The political economy of hatred. *Quarterly Journal of Economics, 120*, 46–86.

Glaeser, E. L. (2007). The economics approach to cities. National Bureau of Economic Research (Working Paper #13696).

Glaeser, E. L. (2008). *Cities, agglomeration, and spatial equilibrium.* New York, NY: Oxford University Press.

Glaeser, E. L. (2020). Urbanization and its discontents. National Bureau of Economic Research (Working Paper #26839).

Glaeser, E. L. & Gottlieb, J. D. (2006). Urban resurgence and the consumer city. *Urban Studies, 43*, 1275–1299.

Glaeser, E. L. & Kahn, M. E. (2004). Sprawl and urban growth. In J. V. Henderson and J. F. Thisse (Eds), *Handbook of regional and urban economics, Volume 4.* The Netherlands: North-Holland.

Glaeser, E. L. & Nathanson, C. G. (2015). Housing bubbles. In G. Duranton, J. V. Henderson & W. Strange (Eds), *Handbook of regional and urban economics, volume 5B.* The Netherlands: North-Holland.

Glaeser, E. L., Kahn, M. E. & Rappaport, J. (2008). Why do the poor live in cities? The role of public transportation. *Journal of Urban Economics, 63*, 1–24.

Glaeser, E. L., Kolko, J. & Saiz, A. (2001). Consumer city. *Journal of Economic Geography, 1*, 27–50.

Gordon, P. & Richardson, H. W. (1997). Are compact cities a desirable planning goal? *Journal of the American Planning Association, 63*, 95–106.

Gyourko, J. & Molloy, R. (2015). Regulation and housing supply. In G. Duranton, J. V. Henderson & W. Strange (Eds), *Handbook of regional and urban economics, volume 5B.* The Netherlands: North-Holland.

Hanlon, B., Howland, M. & McGuire, M. P. (2012). Hotspots for growth: Does Maryland's priority funding area program reduce sprawl? *Journal of the American Planning Association, 78*, 256–268.

Hortas-Rico, M. (2015). Sprawl, blight, and the role of urban containment policies: Evidence from US cities. *Journal of Regional Science, 55*, 298–323.

Hortas-Rico, M. & Solé-Ollé, A. (2010). Does urban sprawl increase the costs of providing local public services? Evidence from Spanish municipalities. *Urban Studies, 47*, 1513–1530.

Howard, E. (1898). *Garden cities of tomorrow.* Cambridge, MA: The MIT Press.

Howell-Moroney, M. (2007). Studying the effects of the intensity of U.S. state growth management approaches on land development outcomes. *Urban Studies, 44*, 2163–2178.

Jacobs, J. (1961). *The death and life of great American cities.* New York, NY: Random House.

Juntunen, L., Knaap, G.-J. & Moore, T. (2011). Fiscal impact analysis and the costs of alternative development patterns. In N. Brooks, K. P. Donaghy & G.-J. Knaap (Eds), *Oxford handbook of urban economics and planning.* New York, NY: Oxford University Press.

Kahn, M. E. & Walsh, R. (2015). Cities and the environment. In G. Duranton, J. V. Henderson & W. Strange (Eds), *Handbook of regional and urban economics, volume 5B.* The Netherlands: North-Holland.

Kelly, E. D. (2004). *Managing community growth.* Westport, CT: Praeger Publishers.

Kline, J. D. & Alig, R. J. (1999). Does land use planning slow the conversion of forest and farmlands? *Growth and Change, 30,* 3–22.

Knaap, G.-J. (1985). The price effects of urban growth boundaries in metropolitan Portland, Oregon. *Land Economics, 61,* 26–35.

Knaap, G.-J. & Nelson, A. (1992). *The regulated landscape: Lessons on state land use planning from Oregon.* Cambridge, MA: Lincoln Institute of Land Policy.

Koster, H. R. A. & Rouwendal, J. (2012). The impact of mixed land use on residential property values. *Journal of Regional Science, 52,* 733–761.

Ladd, H. F. (1992). Population growth, density, and the costs of providing public services. *Urban Studies, 29,* 273–295.

Ladd, H. F. (1994). Fiscal impacts of local population growth: A conceptual and empirical analysis. *Regional Science and Urban Economics, 24,* 661–686.

Ladd, H. F. (1998). Land use regulation as a fiscal tool. In H. F Ladd (Ed.), *Local government tax and land use policies in the United States: Understanding the links.* Cambridge, MA: Lincoln Institute of Land Policy.

Ladd, H. F. & Yinger, J. (1991). *America's ailing cities: Fiscal health and the design of urban policy.* Baltimore, MD: Johns Hopkins University Press.

Lewis, P. G. & Baldassare, M. (2010). The complexity of public attitudes toward compact development: Survey evidence from five states. *Journal of the American Planning Association, 76*(2), 219–237.

Lewis, R. & Knaap, G.-J. (2012). Targeting spending for land conservation: An evaluation of Maryland's rural legacy program. *Journal of the American Planning Association, 78,* 34– 52.

Lewis, R., Knaap, G.-J. & Sohn, J. (2009). Managing growth with priority funding areas: A good idea whose time has yet to come. *Journal of the American Planning Association, 75,* 457–478.

Lewis, R., Knaap, G.-J. & Schindewolf, J. (2013). The spatial structure of cities in the United States. Cambridge, MA: The Lincoln Institute of Land Policy.

Lewis, R., Parker, R., Zou, Z., Hovekamo, W., McGowen, M. & Sherrard, R. (2018). Voter-approved annexations in and urban growth boundary regime: The impacts of housing values, density, and economic equity. *Growth and Change, 49,* 286–313.

Mathur, S. (2014). Impact of urban growth boundary on land and housing prices. *Housing Studies, 29,* 128–148.

Mathur, S. (2019). Impact of an urban growth boundary across the entire house price spectrum: The two-stage quantile spatial regression approach. *Land Use Policy, 80,* 88–94.

Nelson, A. C. (1985). A unifying overview of greenbelt influences on regional land values. *Growth and Change, 2,* 43–48.

Nelson, A. C. (1986). Using land markets to evaluate urban containment programs. *Journal of the American Planning Association, 52,* 156–171.

Nelson, A. C., Dawkins, C. J. & Sanchez, T. W. (2004). Urban containment and residential segregation: A preliminary investigation. *Urban Studies, 2,* 423–439.

Nolon, J. R. (2003). Golden and its emanations: The surprising origins of smart growth. *The Urban Lawyer, 35,* 15–73.

Ottaviano, G. & Peri, G. (2005). Cities and cultures. *Journal of Urban Economics, 58,* 304–337.

Ottaviano, G. & Peri, G. (2006). The economic value of cultural diversity: Evidence from U.S. cities. *Journal of Economic Geography, 6,* 9–44.

Paciorek, A. (2013). Supply constraints and housing market dynamics. *Journal of Urban Economics, 77*, 11–26.

Porter, D. (Ed.) (1986). *Growth management: Keeping on target?* Washington, DC: Urban Land Institute with the Lincoln Institute of Land Use Policy.

Porter, D. (1997). *Managing growth in America's communities.* Washington, DC: Island Press.

Solé-Ollé, A. (2006). Expenditure spillovers and fiscal interactions: Empirical evidence from local governments in Spain. *Journal of Urban Economics, 59*, 32–54.

Solé-Ollé, A. & Bosch, N. (2005). On the relationship between authority size and the costs of providing local services: Lessons for the design of intergovernmental transfers in Spain. *Public Finance Review, 33*, 343–384.

Song, Y. (2005). Smart growth and urban development patterns: A comparative study. *International Regional Science Review, 28*, 239–265.

Song, Y. (2012). Suburban sprawl and smart growth. In R. Weber & R. Crane (Eds), *The Oxford handbook of urban planning.* New York, NY: Oxford University Press.

Song, Y. & Knaap, G.-J. (2003). New urbanism and housing values: A disaggregate assessment. *Journal of Urban Economics, 54*, 218–238.

Song, Y. & Knaap, G.-J. (2008). Quantitative classification of neighborhoods: The neighborhoods of new single-family homes in the Portland metropolitan area. *Journal of Urban Design, 12*, 1–24.

Tiebout, C. M. (1956). A pure theory of local expenditures. *Journal of Political Economy, 64*, 416–424.

Wassmer, R. W. (2006). The influence of local urban containment policies and statewide growth management on the size of United States urban areas. *Journal of Regional Science, 46*, 25–65.

Wassmer, R. W. (2008). Causes of urban sprawl in the United States: Auto reliance as compared to natural evolution, flight from blight, and local revenue reliance. *Journal of Policy Analysis and Management, 27*, 536–555.

Weber, M. (1921). *The City.* Free Press.

Woo, M. & Guldmann, J. M. (2011). Policies on the spatial structure of U.S. metropolitan areas. *Urban Studies, 46*, 2311–3536.

Zheng, S., Sun, W., Wu, J. & Kahn, M. E. (2017). The birth of edge cities in China: Measuring the effects of industrial parks policy. *Journal of Urban Economics, 100*, 80–103.

4. Farmland and forest conservation: evaluation of smart growth policies and tools

David A. Newburn, Lori Lynch, and Haoluan Wang

INTRODUCTION

The preservation of open space, farmland, and critical environmental areas is one of the main smart growth principles. Land preservation efforts often use limited resources to target high priority areas to protect prime farmland, contiguous forests, and environmentally sensitive areas (e.g., wetlands). Open-space protection provides amenities to nearby residents that increase local property values and creates recreational opportunities that improve community quality of life. Additionally, farmland and forests provide myriad environmental benefits that are public goods, such as habitat for species, watershed protection for clean drinking water and reduced flooding, carbon sequestration, and reductions in air pollution and urban heat island effects. Yet these public goods are often underprovided from a societal perspective. These market failures motivate the need for land use policies and programs to manage development in rural regions to preserve open space, farmland, and forest resources.

Land preservation efforts predate the smart growth movement. At the federal level, the United States started creating national parks in the late nineteenth century and now has amassed 84 million acres under the National Park Service. The US Fish and Wildlife Service manages over 89 million acres, primarily to conserve plants and animals in wildlife refuges and other areas. Additionally, the US Forest Service and Bureau of Land Management manage about 193 million and 248 million acres, respectively, on federal lands that allow multiple uses such as recreation, grazing, timber harvesting, wildlife habitat, and other uses. These four federal agencies acquired the vast majority of their land holdings prior to 1990, with a substantial portion of this land concentrated in the 11 coterminous western states and Alaska (Vincent et al., 2017).

Meanwhile, local and state governments and land trusts have focused recent smart growth preservation efforts closer to cities and towns, emphasizing farmland and open space protection. In recent elections, voters have demonstrated strong support to fund open space protection. Between 1988 and 2019, 2,096 ballot initiatives passed at the local or state level that raised more than $80 billion for public land conservation. Land trusts in the non-governmental sector play a substantial role in land conservation, with 1,363 active land trusts in 2015 nationwide, up from 535 in 1984 (Chang, 2016). Land trusts have turned increasingly toward conservation easements, which permanently limit uses of land, due in part to lower acquisition costs compared with outright purchase (fee simple title). The impressive growth in conservation easements acquired by land trusts nationwide increased to 13.3 million acres in 2010 from about 0.8 million acres in 1990 (see Table 1 in Parker & Thurman, 2019). Additionally, land trusts purchased 7.6 million acres of land outright in 2010, representing more than a threefold increase from the 2.2 million acres held in 1990. Since the late 1970s, state and local government programs have also increased land conservation, with 28 state-level programs protecting almost three million acres and 95 local programs protecting more than one million acres (Farmland Information Center, 2018). Yet, despite the goal of smart growth advocates and planners to protect rural areas, sufficient funding does not exist to preserve all rural lands from development.

While the majority of people reside in urban and suburban areas (Nechyba & Walsh, 2004), exurban large-lot development (one acre or more per house) in particular has caused substantially more farmland and forest loss in the United States. According to Brown et al. (2005), the total amount of land area developed nationwide at urban densities (more than one house per acre) increased from less than 1 percent to about 2 percent between 1950 and 2000. During the same period, the total amount of exurban land (rural residential development between 1 and 40 acres per house) increased from approximately 5 percent to 25 percent. Approximately 31 million acres of farmland was lost to development between 1992 and 2012 nationwide, including 11 million acres of prime farmland (American Farmland Trust, 2018). Heimlich and Anderson (2001) characterize two distinct types of residential development that impact agricultural and rural lands. Urban and suburban development typically require municipal sewer service for higher density (more than one house per acre). Meanwhile, exurban development (less than one house per acre) is typically serviced by individual private septic systems, thereby allowing this large-lot development to leapfrog into rural regions well beyond sewer service areas and create noncontiguous areas of fragmented forest and farmland. Heimlich and Anderson (2001) demonstrate that almost 80 percent of acreage converted to residential development occurs outside urban areas, and 94 percent of this acreage is large-lot development at one acre or more. For this reason, it is imperative to understand the effectiveness of various land use policies and programs to manage both types of development, particularly approaches that address the more challenging and pervasive impacts from exurban large-lot development.

LAND PRESERVATION MECHANISMS AND OUTCOMES

In this section, we discuss four policy approaches used to achieve smart growth goals for land conservation—regulatory techniques, incentive-based policies, participatory preservation programs, and transfer of development rights (TDR) programs (Duke & Lynch, 2006). Regulatory techniques alter the location and density of allowable development within designated areas. Incentive-based policies adjust the price in the existing market structure to encourage certain land uses through tax or subsidy mechanisms. In participatory preservation programs, government agencies and land trusts may purchase land parcels outright or create easements to retire the development rights from willing landowners. Lastly, TDR programs have developers purchase and retire development rights from willing rural landowners, in exchange for the right to develop elsewhere at higher density than allowed under current zoning. To provide a framework for improving future policy implementation, we summarize recent research findings on the prevalence and effectiveness of these policies and their indirect and unintended consequences below. We focus on the rural impacts of such tools; Carruthers, Wei, and Wostenholme (Chapter 3) and Hanlon (Chapter 5) focus on the urban impacts.

Regulatory Approaches

Regulatory approaches have been used to meet smart growth objectives for land conservation because they have low budgetary costs to governments and allow for a higher degree of spatial contiguity of land preservation than voluntary programs alone. Since regulatory approaches apply to all landowners in a given designated area, these techniques can be used for reducing development and protecting productive farmland or forest resources in contiguous areas. Yet it can sometimes be difficult to gain adequate support in the political process because of rural landowner opposition to placing new restrictions on property rights.

Zoning regulations have been one of the primary land use policies implemented to reduce farmland and forest conversion. Local governments implement zoning ordinances that specify allowable land uses and maximum density restrictions (housing units per acre). A major challenge when evaluating the effectiveness of zoning in reducing farmland conversion is that these regulations are not randomly assigned across the landscape. Empirical analysis often has factors unobserved by the researcher that affect the location of zoning designations and the probability of development. Failure to account for this relationship (known as endogeneity) can introduce bias into resulting estimations. Recent parcel-level models of residential land conversion have used quasi-experimental methods, including propensity score matching and difference-in-differences, to control for endogeneity in the evaluation of zoning policies. Butsic et al. (2011) analyzed the impact of agricultural zoning on residential land conversion in Columbia County, Wisconsin. If they assumed agricultural zoning is exogenous, they found zoning significantly reduced the probability of subdivision development. However, after correcting for the endogeneity of zoning using propensity score matching methods, they found zoning did not affect the probability of development. Similarly, after addressing the endogeneity of zoning using a difference-in-differences approach, Newburn and Ferris (2016) found that downzoning in Baltimore County, Maryland, did not significantly affect the probability of development. However, this rural downzoning did substantially reduce the density of development in areas designated for agricultural preservation. Other studies have similarly found that zoning regulations have significantly reduced the density of development in rural regions (McConnell et al., 2006b; Newburn & Berck, 2006).

Urban growth boundaries (UGBs) have been established in more than a hundred cities and counties in the United States (Staley et al., 1999). UGBs are spatially designated to control the expansion of urban development, while often aiming to preserve farmland and forest outside the boundary. Given that UGBs are also non-randomly designated, quasi-experimental methods are helpful to evaluate their effectiveness. Using a difference-in-differences hazard model, Cunningham (2007) found that the UGB adopted in the greater Seattle area lowered the likelihood of new housing outside the boundary by 28 to 39 percent. Applying similar methods, Dempsey and Plantinga (2013) focus on Oregon's UGBs and reveal that in many cities the effect of UGBs did constrain some, but not all, of the urban development with considerable variation across different cities. For more on Oregon UGBs, see Carruthers et al., Chapter 3 of this book.

An important issue is that UGBs may have different effects on different residential densities. However, residential land use change models are often specified using a binary dependent variable—develop or remain undeveloped (e.g., Cunningham, 2007; Dempsey & Plantinga, 2013). This binary specification implicitly assumes that growth management policies, such as UGBs, have the same effect on all residential density types. Allowing for multiple density classes, Newburn and Berck (2006) analyzed residential development in Sonoma County, California, where eight out of nine cities adopted UGBs. They found that suburban development (more than one house per acre) is largely constrained within UGBs. Basically, the UGBs primarily limit the extension of the municipal sewer service, which is required to develop at suburban densities. Meanwhile, exurban development (less than one house per acre) that relies on private septic systems is able to leapfrog into the rural region outside the UGBs. Newburn and Berck (2011) conducted policy simulations to further investigate the effect of UGBs versus expansion of municipal sewer service infrastructure in the same region, showing that UGBs are highly effective for managing suburban development but not exurban development.

UGBs may be viewed as an urban (but not exurban) containment strategy. Yet while the conventional view is that UGBs create a sharp perimeter between urban and rural lands, in which residential subdivision development is not allowed outside the boundary, exurban development is commonly found in rural areas outside of UGBs. For instance, Baltimore County, Maryland, established a UGB in 1967, which was highly effective in containing suburban development within the boundary. However, exurban large-lot development on septic systems continued unabated until Baltimore County enacted rural downzoning regulations a decade later in 1976 (Newburn & Ferris, 2016). Exurban development outside the UGB was only curtailed after the designation of agricultural zoning (one house per 50 acres). Similarly in Sonoma County, California, agricultural zoning was found to be the most effective approach to reduce exurban development (Newburn & Berck, 2006, 2011). It is important to consider effective tools for managing the threat of exurban development, which has been the leading cause of forest and farmland conversion in the United States (Brown et al., 2005; Heimlich & Anderson, 2001).

Incentive-based Approaches

Unlike regulatory methods that restrict allowable land uses or density, incentive-based policies utilize tax or subsidy mechanisms to alter the relative returns that landowners receive in order to encourage certain land uses. Some incentive-based approaches use the property tax system to decrease the tax burden for rural land uses, aiming to preserve agricultural and other rural resource uses in the face of increasing development pressures. As one of the oldest and most common incentive-based techniques, use-value assessment (UVA) determines the landowner property tax based on the existing use value in agriculture or forestry rather than the full market value. During the 1960s and 1970s, many state governments across the United States implemented UVA programs to preserve rural land uses; now almost every state has some form of UVA program for their resource lands.

According to Anderson and England (2015), this tax differential program amounts to tens of billions of dollars annually in foregone taxes and has been a poorly targeted policy instrument that often has a limited impact on the number of acres developed. These authors provide a detailed review with several criticisms of existing UVA programs nationwide and policy recommendations. First, many state programs have lax eligibility criteria for minimum parcel size or gross farm income, which may have the unintended consequence of lowering the cost for the formation of hobby farms and ranchettes. Land preservation efforts would be more efficient when using stricter size or income criteria targeted for operations primarily in agricultural or forestry use. Second, low penalties for early withdrawal may actually lower the cost for land speculators to hold land for future development. Third, voluntary enrollment is often poorly targeted, such that properties farther away from development pressures are more likely to participate. Despite being a pervasive strategy for land preservation, quasi-experimental analysis assessing the causal impact of UVA programs on farmland preservation has been limited to date. An exception is Butsic et al. (2011) who exploit the lotsize threshold in program eligibility using a regression discontinuity design. They found that the UVA program had a weak but significant effect on lowering the probability of subdivision development.

As a novel incentive-based smart growth policy initiative, Maryland's designated priority funding areas (PFAs) are intended to encourage growth in existing urban areas while indirectly reducing sprawl in rural areas. Carruthers et al. (Chapter 3) describe PFAs as the quintessential smart growth instrument. Unlike UGBs' regulatory approach, PFAs aim to restrict state spending on growth-related infrastructure (e.g., sewer, water, roads) to areas designated for urban growth. In practice, local governments have established PFAs based on existing or planned municipal sewer and water service, as well as areas with buildout densities greater than 3.5 housing units per acre. Lewis et al. (2009) analyzed every parcel developed to single-family housing on less than 20 acres in size after development, including time periods before PFAs and after. They found that PFAs have had no significant effect on the trends in development patterns. Several reasons have been put forth, including: (1) state government spending represents a minor portion of the infrastructure spending compared with local government spending; (2) the state has not restricted spending to PFAs since as much as 29 percent of state funds went to projects outside PFAs; and (3) PFAs are not required to be integrated with the local comprehensive planning process (Howland & Sohn, 2007; Lewis et al., 2009).

Another important reason for the limited effectiveness is that PFAs are designated primarily based on existing and planned sewer service infrastructure, so while they may be helpful for containing suburban and urban development, similar to UGBs, PFAs do not directly inhibit exurban development on septic systems. Lewis et al. (2009) found that about three-quarters of the acreage converted in Maryland occurred outside the PFAs as exurban large-lot development. Specifically, the average lot size was approximately 0.25 acres inside PFAs and 2 acres outside PFAs, both of which exhibited similar trends over time before and after PFA implementation (see Figure 7 and Table 4 in Lewis et al., 2009). Additionally, residential land-use change models have used a binary logit model specification to analyze the effect of PFAs (Hanlon et al., 2012; Shen & Zhang, 2007). Although these studies found that residential development is more likely to occur inside PFAs, this binary model is prone to aggregation bias because it implicitly assumes that PFAs have the same effect on a wide range of residential densities. As discussed earlier, a multinomial logit model that can accommodate multiple development types is needed to understand whether growth management policies, such as PFAs or UGBs, have different effects on different types of residential densities (Newburn & Berck, 2006, 2011). The trends in Lewis et al. (2009) clearly demonstrate that PFAs have had a limited effect on exurban development after PFAs were adopted in 1998. For more on Maryland's statewide program, see M. Bierbaum, Lewis, and Chapin's discussion in Chapter 2.

Participatory Approaches for Land Preservation

Participatory approaches for land preservation include when governments or non-governmental organizations enter the land market, either purchasing land outright or the development rights to land from willing landowners. The latter approach, often referred to as purchase of development rights (PDR) or purchase of agricultural conservation easements (PACE) programs, have gained in popularity because regulatory approaches have become more difficult to pass in some regions, and landowners seek compensation for restrictions to their land uses. Under PDR/PACE programs, the rights to convert a parcel up to its allowable zoned density are restricted, often in perpetuity, in exchange for a monetary payment or tax deduction benefits.

Evaluating these types of programs can be challenging because participation is voluntary, thereby leading to potential sample selection and endogeneity concerns. Moreover, PDR/PACE programs are often used in regions that have more development pressures and higher probability of farmland conversion. Quasi-experimental methods have allowed researchers to estimate causal impacts of these programs controlling for these challenges. Propensity score matching, for example, attempts to identify an appropriate control group with similar characteristics to compare to land use outcomes in the treatment group. Using this approach, Liu and Lynch (2011) found evidence in six Mid-Atlantic states that counties having a PDR program, on average, decreased the rate of farmland loss by 40 to 55 percent and decreased farmland acres lost by 375 to 550 acres per year. Nolte et al. (2019) similarly used propensity score matching to analyze the effectiveness of conservation easements in Massachusetts, finding that protected parcels had lower rates of forest loss and conversion to developed uses relative to counterfactual parcels without protection in the control group.

Land conservation programs often report their success based primarily on the number of acres protected, but other factors also matter. Programs that target additional factors can achieve greater benefits for the same budget. To improve targeting efficiency, Newburn et al. (2005) argue that land costs, environmental benefits, and the likelihood of future land-use conversion should be integrated into conservation planning when setting targeting priorities. As an example of this framework, Newburn et al. (2006) provide a spatially explicit parcel-level model to forecast the probability of future development and acquisition costs in Sonoma County, California, where the local government has operated a land acquisition program since 1990. To lower program costs, several PDR programs have implemented an auction mechanism to determine the compensation a landowner may receive for selling their development rights. Horowitz et al. (2009) found that, while an auction mechanism allows a PDR program to enroll more acres, it chooses the parcels as those "most on sale" rather than those with the highest benefits.

Federal and state tax credits have increased over time to incentivize landowners to place land under easements or sell their property outright. Parker and Thurman (2018) found that tax incentives for donating conservation easements have dramatically increased the amount of protected land. They argue, however, that these tax incentives often target the parcels with the highest tax deductions, instead of those with the highest benefit-cost ratios that would provide the most efficient outcomes for the public. Vercammen (2019) provided a theoretical model of a tax credit program for conservation easements and similarly found that the land with high environment value may have a smaller probability of being donated for an easement. The policy implication is that land trusts need to be discriminating when selecting donated parcels for conservation easements and should reject some parcels that provide low social or environmental benefits. But this is not always the case in practice, because land trusts often want to protect as much land as possible, particularly since taxpayers in general, not the land trusts, are those affected by the foregone taxes collected from donated easements.

Spatial contiguity of conserved land is a desirable goal and one to be targeted for several reasons. First, there are additional environmental and ecological benefits when land parcels are conserved in spatially contiguous patterns (Fooks et al., 2016). Second, conserving large contiguous tracts of land generally requires lower average conservation costs for acquisition and operation costs (Lynch & Lovell, 2003). Third, a critical mass of contiguous farms may be needed when economies of scale exist in support industries (Lynch & Carpenter, 2003) and to avoid conflicts with non-farm neighbors.

In practice, research has shown mixed results regarding the spatial contiguity of land through conservation programs. Many programs accept landowners voluntarily and do not have strong mechanisms nor the budget to enroll a large number of contiguous acres. Lynch and Musser (2001) found that preservation programs were less likely to enroll contiguous parcels and those most threatened by development pressure. Stoms et al. (2009) found little evidence of easements linking with other open spaces to achieve large contiguous blocks of protected areas in the San Francisco Bay Area. In an effort to avoid the scattershot of noncontiguous protected parcels in some prior programs, Maryland created the Rural Legacy Program as part of its smart growth legislation passed in 1997. Rural Legacy Areas (RLAs) strategically restricted program spending solely to designated priority areas so to protect rural land in a contiguous area (Lewis & Knaap, 2012). Lynch and Liu (2007) found that RLAs positively impacted preserved acres as well as increasing the probability of preservation within them.

Land preservation programs may interact at a regional scale with one another through strategic spatial behaviors (Albers et al., 2008; Parker & Thurman, 2011), such as free-riding on another program's conservation efforts or working together (i.e., crowding in/out conservation effort). For example, Albers et al. (2008) explored spatial interactions of private land trusts and public conservation programs in California, Illinois, and Massachusetts and found some evidence that private land conservation is attracted to government open-space protection. Liu and Lynch (2009) found that parcels in designated RLAs were more attractive to other preservation programs; more preservation from other programs occurs in RLAs, thereby increasing contiguity of protected land.

Even if the land has been conserved, farmland owners may not find it viable to continue agricultural activities unless they are profitable. Most easements are negative in that they typically restrict certain developed uses rather than require the continuation of agricultural or other resource uses. Therefore, what types of farms are enrolled in preservation programs and the degree to which they remain active in farming remains an important question that deserves further attention. One benefit of PDR/PACE programs is the cash payments they provide farmland owners. If farmers use this money to invest in their business, it may boost their profits and sustain their farm activities especially if they are credit-constrained. In several states, numerous farmland owners said they sold their development rights in part to improve their business viability (Esseks et al., 2013). Lynch (2007) found that landowners of preserved farms were more likely to invest than those of unpreserved farms. Lynch and Lovell (2003) also found that preserved farms were more likely to grow crops, earn a higher percentage of family income from farming, have more acres, and have a child to take over the farm business. Gottlieb et al. (2015) found that owner-operators of preserved farmland tend to be more actively engaged in their farm businesses. Operators with higher farm sales had an increased probability of investing the easement money in their farm operations, which can increase the likelihood they will remain in business and thus enhance the preservation of farmland.

Transfers of Development Rights

TDR programs are a market-based approach for land preservation. Local zoning rules provide the basis for the development rights granted to each property. TDR programs set up a market between landowners and developers, whereby willing landowners sell their development rights for properties to be preserved (sending areas) and developers buy these rights to develop elsewhere (receiving areas) at higher density than current zoning. The TDR mechanism shares elements of two other approaches—the regulatory approach of zoning, which defines the number of allowable development rights, and the participatory approach of conservation easements. The attractiveness of TDR programs within smart growth planning is that developers pay the cost of land conservation instead of taxpayers via government expenditures. Pruetz and Standridge (2008) have identified 191 TDR programs that have preserved over 350,000 acres nationwide. However, most of these TDR programs have limited or no trading activity, and the largest five TDR programs represent about three quarters of this preserved acreage. TDR programs clearly have yet to deliver substantial land conservation, particularly compared with land trusts, which have preserved over 13.3 million acres in conservation easements in the United States (Parker & Thurman, 2019).

Although several factors explain the limited success of TDRs in various case studies, the lack of demand is perhaps the most critical issue in many TDR programs (Pruetz & Standridge, 2008; Walls & McConnell, 2007). The optimal density has to be constrained under the current baseline zoning in receiving areas so that developers will see a benefit from using TDRs. In other words, using TDRs reduces the average lot size in a residential subdivision, so developers need to believe that they can make higher profits selling the higher density project while covering the additional costs incurred for purchasing TDRs.

The location of receiving areas has been a key aspect of creating demand for TDR programs. Conventional TDR programs, aiming to transfer development from rural sending areas to urban receiving areas, have been the least successful (Linkous & Chapin, 2014). Despite the goal of many planners and smart-growth advocates to channel TDR use into higher density development within cities, towns, and other urban areas that have existing infrastructure, most of the TDR activity has occurred when receiving areas are designated in some portion of the rural region (Linkous & Chapin, 2014; Walls & McConnell, 2007).

McConnell et al. (2006a), for example, provide a detailed review of the TDR program in Calvert County, Maryland, that allowed flexibility for both urban and rural receiving areas. In this evaluation, the vast majority of TDR usage occurred in rural receiving areas, which had a baseline zoned density at one unit per five acres and allowable density with TDRs at one unit per two acres. A fundamental reason for higher TDR demand relates to the marginal value of additional yard space. When more than doubling the density with TDRs in rural areas, many residents are likely to find two-acre or five-acre lots to be a similar housing product. Hence, the willingness to pay for a larger lot without TDRs is not high enough to outbid the higher density project with TDRs. This is often not the case when doubling density within urban receiving areas, which may substantially impinge on the available yard space when comparing development options—single-family detached without TDRs versus single-family attached or multifamily dwellings with TDRs. Another important consideration, as explained by McConnell et al. (2006a), is that the receiving areas in Calvert County are only designated in a portion of the rural region. These rural community districts already had substantial rural residential development and limited potential for contiguous agricultural and forest lands. Sending areas were mainly prime farmland and resource areas, representing the county's designated priority preservation areas. This is essentially a mechanism to create clustered development at a landscape scale in the rural region. Sending areas had substantial farmland preservation. Meanwhile, rural receiving areas had a baseline zoning at one house per five acres with limited agricultural activity, and they were allowed to be denser rural residential areas than they would have been otherwise.

POLICY IMPLICATIONS FOR IMPROVING PROGRAM PERFORMANCE

Reframing Urban–Rural Planning

Smart growth programs often consider urban and rural areas, where urban areas are targeted for growth and rural areas are to be protected. Despite the goal of smart growth advocates to protect rural areas, there is typically not enough political will to downzone or allocate sufficient funding for the preservation of the entire rural area. Exurban large-lot development typically causes greater loss and fragmentation of farmland and forests than the expansion of urban and suburban areas. Policymakers need to recognize that rural areas are heterogeneous and to better understand how to manage exurban large-lot development on septic systems, which is more footloose than suburban development on contiguously expanding municipal sewer service lines.

We propose that future smart growth programs designate three main planning regions. The first region is comprised of existing and planned sewer service areas that are the locally designated growth areas for suburban and urban development. Infrastructure planning and growth management policies, such as UGBs, are effective for managing this type of growth. The second region is the designated priority preservation areas that are rural regions outside planned sewer service areas and dominated by contiguous prime farmland and environmentally sensitive forest lands and wetlands. Within these areas, policymakers can implement agricultural zoning as a primary tool, as well as targeting high benefit parcels with conservation easements and differential farmland taxation with stricter requirements for eligibility. Daniels

(1997) argues that, when politically feasible, agricultural zoning at a maximum of one housing unit per 25 acres is typically recommended to maintain intact farming and resource areas. The third region is the "sacrifice zones" in the rural regions outside planned sewer service zones that already have substantial existing large-lot development on septic systems or have been zoned for rural residential development allowing one to five acres per housing unit. The reality is that rural residential development rights have been granted historically for large swathes of the rural region due to prior zoning plans and existing large-lot development patterns. Land preservation is challenging in this region because it requires buying out these expensive development rights using participatory easement programs and often faces political opposition to further downzoning.

As a new generation of smart-growth legislation, Maryland's Sustainable Growth and Agricultural Preservation Act of 2012 reflects the three main planning regions outlined above (Maryland Department of Planning, 2012). This statewide legislation, also known as the septic law, directly aims to tackle the major threat of exurban large-lot development—in contrast to previous smart-growth tools such as PFAs that had limited effects on managing this type of rural land conversion (Lewis et al., 2009). Maryland's septic law specifies that existing and planned sewer service areas are the designated growth tiers for urban development. The rural region is divided into two categories. Priority preservation areas, designated by local county governments, are no longer allowed to have new major residential subdivisions on septic systems. Essentially, this is a new regulatory approach that restricts the number of development rights to a minor subdivision in designated priority preservation areas. The remainder of the rural region is not affected by the septic law (i.e., business as usual). That is, major residential subdivisions are allowed in accordance with existing zoning and other land-use regulations.

Planning in this latter rural region can be difficult because the default option is the continuation of low-density rural residential development filling in the historically granted development rights. Clustering requirements are an alternative option because this has the advantage of preserving a large parcel for farmland or open space, while forcing the allowable development rights onto smaller housing lots. Clustered subdivision development may nonetheless result in conflicts due to the close proximity of agricultural activities and new rural residential neighbors (e.g., drift from agricultural chemicals, nuisance smells from spreading manure, heavy farm machinery sharing rural roads). Depending on community goals, another option is to allow areas zoned for rural residential to become denser as sacrifice zones, in exchange for land preservation elsewhere. Rural residential zoned areas, for example, acted as receiving areas with the most TDR activity in Calvert County, Maryland, while the priority preservation areas were designated as sending areas to significantly preserve the agricultural and rural landscape (McConnell et al., 2006a).

Synergistic Policy Efforts for Land Preservation

Coordinating a variety of planning tools is helpful for achieving land preservation goals, especially through the collaboration between state and local governments. Attention should be paid to both direct and indirect interactions when multiple policies are adopted.

First, rural downzoning regulations can improve the effectiveness of participatory PDR programs. With rural downzoning, the government or land trusts will likely incur a lower cost to purchase land or conservation easements, such that more acreage can be preserved. Rural downzoning can also improve PDR program effectiveness to achieve spatial contiguity. Conservation easements create open-space amenities that may attract neighboring residential development, thereby potentially resulting in fragmented conservation and development outcomes. Agricultural zoning reduces this unintended spatial spillover effect since it lowers the development potential across the designated agricultural zoned areas. At the same time, PDR programs can improve the performance of rural agricultural zoning plans, particularly when the funding is targeted and restricted solely to priority areas. Lewis and Knaap (2012) indicate that RLAs are mainly designated in areas with agricultural protective zoning (less than one housing unit per 20 acres); therefore buying out the remaining development rights is more feasible in these priority areas with intact farmland, forests, and environmentally sensitive lands.

Second, multiple preservation programs that focus funding in the same targeted areas can have synergistic effects. Combining TDR and PDR programs, for instance, may have subtle and indirect interaction effects that may achieve better outcomes. One of the challenges in developing active markets for TDR programs is the uncertainty in prices for development rights, as well as high transaction costs for buyers and sellers to negotiate prices. McConnell et al. (2006a) show that TDR activity was initially limited at program inception and only increased after the county government introduced a PDR program. Basically, the PDR program set a floor price for selling development rights that was publicly shared. This price signal substantially reduced price uncertainty, spurring TDR activity between private developers and rural landowners. Local governments may also facilitate TDR activity through the establishment of a TDR bank. The bank can purchase TDRs from willing rural landowners in sending areas who cannot find private developers. This government purchase can help establish the stability of prices for TDRs and then inform potential developers of this option to purchase TDRs. The TDR bank creates an ongoing preservation revolving fund by buying TDRs, later selling them to private developers, and then using the proceeds to buy more TDRs. While uncommon to date, some of the most successful TDR programs in the United States have used them as a fundamental aspect to facilitate this market, including King County, Washington, and Palm Beach County, Florida (Pruetz & Standridge, 2008).

Third, the creation of a TDR program can make rural downzoning more politically feasible. Rural landowners often resist the designation of agricultural downzoning plans. This regulatory approach basically places new restrictions on private property owners without compensation that may invite political opposition or even legal chal-lenges. The establishment of TDRs to sell can partially compensate rural landowners for the loss of land value that may result from agricultural downzoning, as was done for the rural downzoning and TDR program in Montgomery County, Maryland (Pruetz & Standridge, 2008; Walls & McConnell, 2007).

CONCLUSIONS AND FUTURE DIRECTIONS

Exurban large-lot development has been a greater cause of farmland and forest loss than the combined footprint of urban and suburban development in the United States (Heimlich & Anderson, 2001). Environmental impacts from exurban development on biodiversity are substantial due to the large extent and noncontiguous form of development, resulting in habitat loss and fragmentation and the introduction of inva-sive species (Hansen et al, 2005). Combating wildfire exacerbated by climate change is also made more difficult because of the widely dispersed low-density exurban development, particularly in the rural–urban interface across the western United States (Mann et al., 2014; Radeloff et al., 2018). Exurban homes in rural areas create challenges for forest management intervention strategies to mitigate wildfire risk, such as prescribed burns or letting natural fires burn to restore ecological processes to the landscape.

An empirical challenge in accurately estimating program effectiveness is that most land-use policy interventions are not randomly assigned across the landscape, and are thus subject to endogeneity that confounds estimation. Angrist and Pischke (2009) provide a thorough explanation of quasi-experimental techniques that can be used to address the endogeneity issue in program evaluation. As an example, propensity score matching attempts to emulate an experimental setup from observational data by comparing land-use outcomes in the treated group and outcomes for matched observations in the control group that are as similar as possible in terms of observ-able characteristics (Liu & Lynch, 2011; Nolte et al., 2019). The synthetic control method similarly generates a weighted average of untreated group outcomes to form a "synthetic" control unit that is similar to the treated group (Fang et al., 2019). The difference-in-differences approach accounts for the baseline differences in character-istics between the treated and untreated groups prior to the implementation of policy interventions (Cunningham, 2007; Newburn & Ferris, 2016). Regression discontinu-ity design aims to elicit the causal effects of interventions by comparing observations lying closely above and below a threshold in the program design (Butsic et al., 2011). These quasi-experimental techniques will hopefully become more widely used in the future to provide rigorous program evaluation for land use policies that aim to manage development and preserve rural areas.

While recent research has made significant advances in identifying issues and evaluating the effectiveness of smart growth programs aimed at land conservation, many challenges still exist and future research is needed. We identify several areas in particular where researchers should put further attention. First, more empirical analysis is needed on the effectiveness of UVAs to reduce the rate of farmland conversion. Many states have an agricultural property tax differential program that has enrolled a large portion of the existing farmland across the United States. Nonetheless, it is challenging to assess the effectiveness given the voluntary enrollment of landowners, and because states often implemented this tax program decades ago. Second, impact fee programs place charges on developers during the permit approval process for residential development. Prior studies have analyzed the effect of impact fees on the spatial location of housing in urban areas (Burge & Ihlanfeldt 2006; Burge et al., 2013). This research shows that impact fees can be used as an effective urban containment strategy, with the potential to limit development at the urban fringe and encourage development in the urban core. However, we could find no empirical analysis regarding the effect of impact fees on land conversion in rural areas. Third, analysis of post-preservation land use activities has received limited attention in the land preservation literature to date. A common critique is that land preservation programs should be judged not solely on the number of acres preserved since activities on protected land are heterogeneous. For instance, the degree to which landowners remain active in farming after preservation remains an important question that merits further investigation. Survey data asking farmers about post-preservation activities generally suffers from sample selection, and the analysis is often limited to cross-sectional data when longitudinal panel data would be more helpful to understand land-use dynamics (Gottlieb et al., 2015). With the increasing availability of high-resolution remote sensing data, researchers can take advantage of these technological advances in combination with survey data to monitor and evaluate land use activities on preserved land (see Goodspeed, Chapter 17).

Lastly, we argue that multiple policies may help create synergistic efforts for achieving smart growth goals for land preservation. Indeed many regions that are most active in land preservation are highly regulated landscapes with multiple intervention strategies. Yet these multiple policy approaches may interact in unexpected ways. Spatial spillovers and interdependencies of policies are important to consider. It has been challenging to identify the direct effect of policies using existing program evaluation techniques, let alone the indirect and unintended consequences of multiple interacting policies. Further theoretical modeling and careful empirical analysis is needed to advance our understanding on how the design of multiple policies can be improved to create more effective land preservation outcomes within smart growth programs.

REFERENCES

Albers, H. J., Ando, A. W., & Chen, X. (2008). Spatial-econometric analysis of attraction and repulsion of private conservation by public reserves. *Journal of Environmental Economics and Management*, 56, 33–49.
American Farmland Trust. (2018). *Farms under Threat: The State of America's Farmland.* Washington, DC: American Farmland Trust.

Anderson, J. E., & England, E. W. (2015). *Use-value Assessment of Rural Lands: Time for Reform?* Cambridge, MA: Lincoln Institute of Land Policy.

Angrist, J., & Pischke, J. (2009). *Mostly Harmless Econometrics: An Empiricist's Companion.* Princeton, New Jersey. Princeton University Press.

Brown, D. G., Johnson, K. M., Loveland, T. R., & Theobald, D. M. (2005). Rural land use trends in the contemporaneous United States 1950–2000. *Ecological Applications*, 15(6), 1851–1863.

Burge, G., & Ihlanfeldt, K. (2006). Impact fees and single-family home construction. *Journal of Urban Economics*, 60, 284–306.

Burge, G. S., Trosper, T. L., Nelson, A. C., Juergensmeyer, J. C., & Nicholas, J. C. (2013). Can development impact fees help mitigate urban sprawl? *Journal of the American Planning Association*, 79(3), 235–248.

Butsic, V., Lewis, D. J., & Ludwig, L. (2011). An econometric analysis of land development with endogenous zoning. *Land Economics*, 87(3), 412–432.

Chang, K. (2016). *National Land Trust Census.* Washington, DC: Land Trust Alliance.

Cunningham, C. R. (2007). Growth controls, real options, and land development. *The Review of Economics and Statistics*, 89(2), 343–358.

Daniels, T. L. (1997). Where does cluster zoning fit in farmland protection? *Journal of the American Planning Association*, 63, 129–137.

Dempsey, J. A., & Plantinga, A. J. (2013). How well do urban growth boundaries contain development? Results for Oregon using a difference-in-difference estimator. *Regional Science and Urban* Economics, 43, 996–1007.

Duke, J. M., & Lynch, L. (2006). Four classes of farmland retention techniques: Comparative evaluation and property rights implications. *Land Economics*, 82(2), 189–213.

Esseks, J. D., Schilling, B. J., & Hahn, A. (2013). *Impacts of the Federal Farm and Ranch Lands Protection Program: An Assessment Based on Interviews with Participating Landowners.* Lincoln, NE: Center for Great Plains Studies, University of Nebraska, Lincoln.

Fang, L., Howland, M., Kim, J., Peng, Q., & Wu, J. (2019). Can transfer of development rights programs save farmland in metropolitan counties? *Growth and Change*, 50, 926–946.

Farmland Information Center. (2018). *2018 Status of State Purchase of Agricultural Conservation Easement Programs.* Northampton, MA: American Farmland Trust.

Fooks, J. R., Higgins, N., Messer, K. D., Duke, J. M., Hellerstein, D., & Lynch, L. (2016). Conserving spatially explicit benefits in ecosystem service markets: Experimental tests of network bonuses and spatial targeting. *American Journal of Agricultural Economics*, 98(2), 468–488.

Gottlieb, P. D., Schilling, B. J., Sullivan, K., Esseks, J. D., Lynch, L., & Duke, J. M. (2015). Are preserved farms actively engaged in agriculture and conservation? *Land Use Policy*, 45, 103–116.

Hanlon, B., Howland, M., & McGuire, M. P. (2012). Hotspots for growth: Does Maryland's Priority Funding Area program reduce sprawl? *Journal of the American Planning Association*, 78(3), 256–268.

Hansen, A., Knight, J., Marzluff, J. Powell, S., Brown, K., Gude, P. & Jones, K. (2005). Effects of exurban development on biodiversity: Patterns, mechanisms, and research needs. *Ecological Applications*, 15(6), 1893–1905.

Heimlich, R. E., & Anderson, W. D. (2001). *Development at the Urban Fringe and Beyond: Impacts on Agriculture and Rural Land.* Agricultural Economic Report No. 803. Washington, D.C.: U. S. Department of Agriculture, Economic Research Service.

Horowitz, J. K., Lynch, L., & Stocking, A. (2009). Competition-based environmental policy: An analysis of farmland preservation in Maryland. *Land Economics*, 85(4), 555–575.

Howland, M., & Sohn, J. (2007). Has Maryland's priority funding areas initiative constrained the expansion of water and sewer investments? *Land Use Policy*, 24(1), 175–186.

Lewis, R., & Knaap, G. (2012). Targeting spending for land conservation: An evaluation of Maryland's Rural Legacy Program. *Journal of the American Planning Association*, 78(1), 34–52.

Lewis, R., Knaap, G., & Sohn, J. (2009). Managing growth with Priority Funding Areas: A good idea whose time has yet to come. *Journal of the American Planning Association*, 75(4), 457–478.

Linkous, E. R., & Chapin, T. S. (2014). TDR program performance in Florida. *Journal of the American Planning Association*, 80(3), 253–267.

Liu, X., & Lynch, L. (2009). *Does Targeting a Designated Area Crowd Out the Other Preservation Programs' Efforts?* Agricultural and Applied Economics Association Annual Meeting, July 26–28, 2009, Milwaukee, Wisconsin.

Liu, X., & Lynch, L. (2011). Do agricultural land preservation programs reduce farmland loss? Evidence from a propensity score matching estimator. *Land Economics*, 87(2), 183–201.

Lynch, L. (2007). Economic benefits of farmland preservation. In C. T. F. de Brun (Ed.), *The Economic Benefits of Land Conservation* (pp. 13–23). The Trust for Public Land.

Lynch, L., & Carpenter, J. (2003). Is there evidence of a critical mass in the Mid-Atlantic agriculture sector between 1949 and 1997? *Agricultural and Resource Economics Review*, 32(1), 116–128.

Lynch, L., & Liu, X. (2007). Impact of designated preservation areas on rate of preservation and rate of conversion: Preliminary evidence. *American Journal of Agricultural Economics*, 89(5), 1205–1210.

Lynch, L., & Lovell, S. J. (2003). Combining spatial and survey data to explain participation in agricultural land preservation programs. *Land Economics*, 79(2), 259–276.

Lynch, L., & Musser, W. N. (2001). A relative efficiency analysis of farmland preservation programs. *Land Economics*, 77(4), 577–594.

Mann, M., Berck, P., Moritz, M., Batllori, E., Baldwin, J., Gately, C. & Cameron, D. (2014). Modeling residential development in California from 2000 to 2050: Integrating wildfire risk, wildland and agricultural encroachment. *Land Use Policy*, 41, 438–452.

Maryland Department of Planning. (2012). *Implementation Guidance for the Sustainable Growth and Agricultural Preservation Act of 2012*. Baltimore, MD: Maryland Department of Planning.

McConnell, V., Kopits, E., & Walls, M. (2006a). Using markets for land preservation: Results of a TDR program. *Journal of Environmental Planning and Management*, 49(5), 631–651.

McConnell, V., Walls, M., & Kopits, E. (2006b). Zoning, TDRs, and the density of development. *Journal of Urban Economics*, 59, 440–457.

Nechyba, T., & Walsh. R. (2004). Urban sprawl. *Journal of Economic Perspectives*, 18(4), 177–200.

Newburn, D. A., & Berck, P. (2006). Modeling suburban and rural-residential development beyond the urban fringe. *Land Economics*, 82(4), 481–499.

Newburn, D. A., & Berck, P. (2011). Growth management policies for exurban and suburban development: Theory and an application to Sonoma County, California. *Agricultural and Resource Economics Review*, 40(3), 375–392.

Newburn, D. A., Berck, P., & Merenlender, A. M. (2006). Habitat and open space at risk of land-use conversion: Targeting strategies for land conservation. *American Journal of Agricultural Economics*, 88(1), 28–42.

Newburn, D. A., & Ferris, J. S. (2016). The effect of downzoning for managing residential development and density. *Land Economics*, 92(2), 220–236.

Newburn, D. A., Reed, S., Berck, P., & Merenlender, A. M. (2005). Economics and land-use change in prioritizing private land conservation. *Conservation Biology*, 19, 1411–1420.

Nolte, C., Meyer, S. R., Sims, K. R. E., & Thompson, J. R. (2019). Voluntary, permanent land protection reduces forest loss and development in a rural-urban landscape. *Conservation Letters*, 12(6), e12649. https://conbio.onlinelibrary.wiley.com/doi/10.1111/conl.12649

Parker, D. P., & Thurman, W. N. (2011). Crowding out open space: the effects of federal land programs on private land trust conservation. *Land Economics*, 87(2), 202–222.

Parker, D. P., & Thurman, W. N. (2018). Tax incentives and the price of conservation. *Journal of the Association of Environmental and Resource Economists*, 5, 331–369.

Parker, D. P., & Thurman, W. N. (2019). Private land conservation and public policy: Land trusts, land owners, and conservation easements. *Annual Review of Resource Economics*, 11, 337–354.

Pruetz, R., & Standridge, N. (2008). What makes transfer of development rights work?: Success factors from research and practice. *Journal of the American Planning Association*, 75(1), 78–87.

Radeloff, V., Helmers, D., Kramer, A., Mockrin, M., Alexandre, P., Bar-Massada, A., Butsic, V., Hawbaker, T., Martinuzzi, S., Syphard, A., & Stewart, S. (2018). Rapid growth of the US wildland-urban interface raises wildfire risk. *Proceedings of the National Academy of Sciences*, 115(13), 3314–3319.

Shen, Q., & Zhang, F. (2007). Land-use changes in a pro-smart-growth state: Maryland, USA. *Environment and Planning A*, 39, 1457–1477.

Staley, S. R., Edgens, J. D., & Mildner, G. C. S. (1999). *A Line in the Land: Urban-growth Boundaries, Smart Growth, and Housing Affordability*. Policy Study No. 263, Reason Public Policy Institute.

Stoms, D. M., Jantz, P. A., Davis, F. W., & DeAngelo, G. (2009). Strategic targeting of agricultural conservation easements as a growth management tool. *Land Use Policy*, 26, 1149–1161.

Vercammen, J. (2019). A welfare analysis of conservation easement tax credits. *Journal of the Association of Environmental and Resource Economists*, 6(1), 43–71.

Vincent, C., Hanson, L., & Argueta, C. (2017). *Federal Land Ownership: Overview and Data*. Report R42346, Congressional Research Service.

Walls, M. & McConnell, V. (2007). *Transfer of Development Rights in U.S. Communities: Evaluating Program Design, Implementation and Outcomes*. Washington, DC. Resources for the Future.

5. Redevelopment and the smart growth movement: definitions, consequences, and future considerations

Bernadette Hanlon

INTRODUCTION

Low-density, auto-centric suburban expansion is prevalent in the United States and other nations (Keil, 2018). Characterized as urban sprawl, this form of development is disparaged by planners, environmentalists, policymakers, and others for its negative effects on the environment (Ewing, 2008), public health (Frumkin et al., 2004), and a sense of community and belonging (Bressi, 1994; Calthorpe, 1993). In the 1990s, smart growth emerged with the expressed aim of reducing sprawl by seeking to limit new development in greenfield areas on the urban fringe and, at the same time, to strengthen and direct growth to locations where there is existing infrastructure, housing, and employment.

The targeting of growth to existing communities should ideally lead to the creation of mixed-use, dense, and walkable development where residents have more housing and transportation choices, including the ability to use public transit for commuting purposes. Smart growth policies typically utilize market-based tactics and state government incentives to encourage development in certain areas and to increase density (Benfield et al., 2001; Ewing, 1997; Knaap & Frece, 2007). Yet, the smart growth movement influence goes beyond specific state laws to include regional and local planning efforts, design interventions, and advocacy aimed at the revitalization of suburban and urban neighborhoods close to core places in the region. These efforts seek to not just limit sprawl, but also to retrofit this form of development to create more density.

In this chapter, I focus on the principle of smart growth that aims to "strengthen and direct development toward existing communities." This kind of development is often referred to as infill development, and it takes on different forms. I describe what this looks like and what the literature identifies as the barriers and challenges to this type of growth, then follow up with an examination of its consequences. I conclude with future considerations related to infill development for the smart growth movement going forward.

INFILL DEVELOPMENT AND ITS MECHANISMS

In this chapter, I focus on targeted development in the form of infill. We can describe infill development as the practice of constructing on "vacant, abandoned, passed over or underutilized land within built-up areas of existing communities" (Maryland Department of Planning, 2001, p. 49). For the purposes of this chapter, I include in this definition the demolition and replacement—as well as the renovation and rehabilitation of—existing structures within existing communities. For advocates of smart growth, infill development is beneficial because, for one, it can reduce the need for new development on the metropolitan fringe. It also conserves community resources by taking advantage of existing infrastructure, and it has the benefit of increasing walkability and providing the opportunity for more mixed-use development. I begin with an examination of the nature and extent of infill in the United States and then describe the different forms this infill can take.

Extent and Nature of Infill Development

Studies measure and define infill in different ways. Landis et al. (2006) defined potential infill sites as vacant and underutilized parcels within incorporated cities or in unincorporated areas with a residential density of at least 2.4 dwellings per acre. In this study, the authors found nearly 500,000 potential infill sites in California. In the case of Steinacker (2003) and Farris (2001), infill is defined as new residential development that occurs inside the central city. In a study of 22 metro regions using housing permits to identify residential construction, Farris (2001) found that very little residential development is infill; only 5.2 percent of permits went toward infill development in central cities during the 1990s. Central cities received only 2.2 percent of permits for single-family housing, and 14.9 percent of permits for multifamily housing across the regions. Steinacker (2003) found that 20 percent of total development from 1996 to 2000 was infill development. Most development, therefore, occurs as non-infill.

For both Steinacker and Farris, any residential construction taking place outside the city is not infill. There are criticisms of this definition since certainly infill occurs in, for example, older suburbs (McConnell & Wiley, 2010; Hanlon & Airgood-Obrycki, 2018). An important finding from Steinacker's work is that infill development tends to be at higher densities than new development outside the city. Economic theory would suggest that infill development is higher density because of higher land prices in infill areas (McConnell & Wiley, 2010). Ottensmann (1977), based on a series of regression models, found land value increases led to a decline in single-family residential development. In this sense, multifamily housing is more likely than single-family development in high land value areas. In a study of suburban infill development in Montgomery County, Maryland, Wiley (2007) found that infill does include more condominiums and town home development than non-fill development. Between 1990 and 2004, infill represented 80 percent of residential development in the county but only 30 percent of the residential land. However, one of the findings from Wiley's study is that infill residential development, while denser than non-fill, was greater in lot and structure size than existing development around the new infill. In other words, while infill is denser than non-fill development it is not necessarily denser than existing development nearby.

The aforementioned studies were conducted some time back, but there are more recent investigations using different measures. In a study of urban spatial structure in 35 metropolitan areas in the United States, Lewis et al. (2013) investigated the distribution of population growth and densities in urbanized areas to determine the extent of infill and urban sprawl. They found that in most metropolitan areas, the urbanized areas and principal cities experienced population and population density increases, an indication of infill development. For instance, in metropolitan areas such as Portland, the urbanized area became much denser in terms of population growth. The authors found that the fastest growing metropolitan areas had growth both in the urban core as well as in the periphery, indicating the simultaneous occurrence of both infill development and sprawl regionally.

Certainly, infill development is desirable from a smart growth perspective since the assumption is that without development in existing areas, more urban growth will occur in the metropolitan fringe. What is interesting about the Lewis et al. (2013) study, is that population growth gets distributed across the metropolitan landscape, causing densities to rise in existing communities while at the same time expanding the metropolitan periphery. Heris's (2017) study of density and growth rates across several metropolitan areas in the United States produced somewhat similar findings. Using high-resolution impervious surface coverage data from the US Geological Survey along with data on housing density from the US Census, Heris (2017) identified different density settlement types (high, medium, and low density) across 50 metropolitan areas and examined the extent of housing construction in these areas between 2000 and 2010. For example, he found that 47 percent of new dwellings construction in the metropolitan areas of New York occurred in high-density areas, indicating significant infill and increased density. This was similar to Lewis et al.'s findings for New York. Heris found similar patterns in Los Angeles, San Francisco, and Boston, although new housing was also built in medium- and low-density areas and, in the case of Boston, in medium- and low-density suburbs. Some metropolitan areas, in contrast, experienced lots of new housing development in undeveloped areas but little infill development. To summarize, it appears some metropolitan areas are better than others at encouraging infill. Heris's methodology may be useful for those who want to determine the effects of different policy and planning strategies on sprawl and infill.

Various smart growth-oriented planning tools are available to ensure infill development occurs and at high densities. Lewis et al. (2013) suggest that Portland, because of its urban growth boundary, encourages infill development. A revolution in zoning and building codes is happening in city and suburban planning departments across the country, including introducing more flexibility and allowing for dense, mixed-use development as infill (Talen, 2013 and Talen, Chapter 7 of this volume). Examples include the introduction of mixed-use zoning (e.g., planned unit development or form-based codes) and overlay districts that encourage dense development in existing communities. A great example is the creation of the Bridge Street District in Dublin, Ohio, a suburb outside Columbus. Dublin's city council adopted the district in 2013, using form-based codes to ensure the vision for an urban, mixed-use development would become a reality. In Dublin, there is little evidence that growth management policy influenced this urban-like development. Neither the Columbus metropolitan region nor the State of Ohio have the type of urban containment policies discussed in Chapter 3 by Carruthers, Wei, and Wostenholme, who along with Talen (Chapter 7) highlight the importance of local design standards for creating compact mixed-use development.

Different Forms of Infill Development

There are different forms of infill and various policies and planning strategies aimed at encouraging each type. As Table 5.1 shows, one type is suburban retrofitting. This includes the kind of infill that occurred in Bridge Street District in Dublin, Ohio. It is highly intentional and involves large-scale infill construction such as the building of new mixed-use, compact communities in existing suburbs. A new urbanism approach to planning, originating in the fields of architecture and urban design, influences this kind of redevelopment (Knaap & Talen, 2005).

In their book *Retrofitting Suburbia*, Ellen Dunham-Jones and June Williamson (2011) document hundreds of examples of suburban retrofit projects throughout the United States. These projects involved large-scale redevelopment that increases density, encourages walking and mixed land uses, and makes more accessible public spaces with pedestrian and bike-friendly interconnected streets, all of which are characteristics of new urbanism (Ellis, 2002; Squires, 2002; Talen, 2015).

Changes to zoning aim to encourage these kinds of retrofit projects. This might involve the creation of a new zoning code such as Planned United Development (PUD), which allows for mixed-use development, and/or the establishment of an overlay district to allow for building at higher than typical densities, for instance in certain sections of a city or suburb.

Local governments can also implement adaptive reuse ordinances (AROs) to encourage the adaptive reuse of existing development. These ordinances typically simplify and facilitate the permitting process and offer incentives that enable developers to exceed maximum densities and building heights when they reuse a certain site or building. An example is Los Angeles's ARO first passed in 1999, then modified in the early 2000s. Studies confirm that the program has encouraged the adaptive reuse of buildings close to transit stops and may have even increased redevelopment during the 2008 to 2012 recession (Riggs & Chamberlain, 2018). Los Angeles's program includes incentives that reduce the costs of renovation.

In addition, local governments offer tax incentives to property owners and developers to redevelop in specific locations. For example, Baltimore County, a suburban county outside Baltimore city, offers a Revitalization Tax Credit for qualified

Table 5.1   *Examples of different forms of infill development*

Infill type	Characteristics	Policy and planning strategies
(Sub)urban Retrofit	New urbanist-style development; regreening of parking lots; adaptive reuse of big-box stores and dead malls.	Adaptive reuse ordinances (AROs); overlay districts, planned unit development (PUD) and mixed-use zoning; tax increment financing (TIF).
Brownfield Redevelopment	Remediation of contaminated industrial sites; likely to occur in high-value areas; sustainable building practices and green remediation are important.	Tax incentives, government grants and loans.
Transit-Oriented Development	Dense development at certain sites along transit lines.	Master planning; infrastructure funding; land acquisition financing; affordable housing financing.
Teardown and Rebuild	McMansion infill in high-value areas; close to downtown areas; along transit lines; homes with small lots.	Zoning, design review, historic districts.
Accessory Dwelling Units (ADUs)	Increased affordable housing.	ADU ordinances.
Residential Rehabilitation and Reinvestment	Revitalized neighborhoods and new mixed-use districts, with potential for gentrification and displacement.	Historic districts, tax incentives.

improvements to senior housing or commercially zoned properties that are inside designated commercial revitalization districts.

Brownfield redevelopment, another form of infill, is important in this regard. Brownfields are abandoned or underutilized properties that are environmentally contaminated or perceived to be contaminated because of previous uses. These sites are mostly in urban areas and older suburbs where there was once heavy industry (Davis & Sherman, 2010). The redevelopment of brownfields involves the remediation of the site to eliminate the negatives effects of any environmental toxins on public health and the environment. This redevelopment can revitalize urban areas both economically and environmentally.

In a recent evaluation of brownfield redevelopment, Green (2018) found that it is more likely when the project includes green innovation and sustainable building practices, and when it is located in a high-value area. While he found that tax incentives did not predict brownfield redevelopment, he suggests that tax incentives can help bring a brownfield redevelopment project to completion. Cleanup of brownfield sites for redevelopment often receives public funding, either directly in the form of grants or loans or indirectly through tax incentives (Eckerd & Keeler, 2012).

Infill through transit-oriented development (TOD) is a key smart growth effort to reduce automobile use and encourage dense development. Peter Calthorpe was instrumental in codifying the TOD concept, outlined in his 1993 book, *The Next American Metropolis*, although the idea of TOD has a long history in the United States (Carlton, 2009). After all, streetcar suburbs at the end of the nineteenth century were peripheral communities built along the streetcar lines (Warner, 1978). Calthorpe's work, however, energized the planning community around linking regional transit systems and land use, although the number and nature of TOD projects has not materialized as he envisioned. Calthorpe anticipated that TOD would occur along new transit lines, when in fact TOD has been more likely as infill development along existing transit infrastructure. Welch and Gehrke further detail in Chapter 10 how more sustainable modes of transportation can facilitate compact and smarter growth.

Ideally, there is a concentration of services, retail, and entertainment activities in areas immediately around transit stations that provide employment opportunities to the local community. These transit stops are situated within a 5- to 10-minute walk from the nearby neighborhood. TOD recognizes that a certain level of density is needed to make transit viable (Cervero & Guerra, 2011), and master plans to determine the zoning around transit stops are necessary. So are infrastructure investment support and technical assistance from metropolitan planning organizations (MPOs), as well as funding from government sources in such key program areas of land acquisition and redevelopment financing, tax credits, and affordable housing financing.

Manipulation of tax revenues is a longstanding strategy to encourage developers to build in cities. One of the most popular ways to finance redevelopment in the United States is Tax Increment Financing (TIF) (Briffault, 1997). TIFs work by creating a special taxing district around an area targeted for reinvestment and allotting future property tax revenue to fund redevelopment projects there. The area in question must be defined as "blighted," typically measured by the presence of obsolete buildings and land uses and as designated by state enabling legislation (Weber, 2002). TIF is a complex mechanism that requires city council and school board approval and, in some cases, a local referendum (Dunham-Jones & Williamson, 2011). Because of the requirement of school board approval, TIFs in the suburban context can be extra challenging. As Dunham-Jones and Williamson (2011) note in their documentation of suburban redevelopment, retrofit projects in Georgia halted because of a successful lawsuit challenging the legality of utilizing school-based tax revenue for non-school-based development. "Whether school revenue is being held hostage to support redevelopment remains a thorny issue for many municipalities," write the authors (p. 77).

Thus far, evaluations of TIFs focus on the effect on property value growth (Byrne, 2006; Dye & Merriman, 2000) and employment or job creation (Byrne, 2010). Study results suggest that TIFs tend to concentrate in areas with rapidly growing property values, counter to the rule that requires TIFs to be the cause of property value growth rather than vice versa (Briffault, 2010; Dye & Sundberg, 1998; Gordon, 2003).

What is the goal of TIFs in the context of smart growth? Studies suggest that TIFs produce greater property value growth for mixed-use development (Bhatta et al., 2003), which can bolster smart growth efforts to encourage denser development. Yet results also indicate that TIFs do not bring redevelopment to the most blighted and disadvantaged areas of the city, raising equity concerns. More studies are necessary to fully understand the impact of TIF and other tax incentive strategies specifically for the smart growth goal of encouraging redevelopment in existing communities.

A third form of infill development includes the teardown and demolition of existing homes in existing communities. In the suburban context, this process is referred to as mansionization or McMansion infill (Nasar et al., 2007), because torn down homes are typically small and replacement homes are much larger. In Australian suburbs, "knockdown rebuild" (Pinnegar et al., 2010) is the term used.

Demolition is more likely to occur among older properties with frame structures and small lots (Weber et al., 2006). Teardowns occur in older, wealthy suburbs (Charles, 2013a, 2013b), in communities close to transit (Dye & McMillen, 2007), in more modest income suburbs with amenities and low taxes, in high performing school districts, and near downtowns (Charles, 2013a, 2013b). In the case of Sydney, Australia, 'knockdown rebuild' occurs in disadvantaged middle-ring suburbs but it is not necessarily a form of gentrification. Rather, it is the result of upwardly mobile residents of these communities choosing to redevelop and upgrade into bigger houses while also remaining in the neighborhood (Pinnegar et al., 2010). Charles (2013a) found evidence of this pattern in Chicago, noting that residents in modest income suburbs who accumulate wealth or gain access to finance capital remain in these communities after rebuilding larger houses for themselves. In some communities, there have been planning efforts to prevent teardowns, as the replacement of small post-war homes with "monster homes" disrupts the visual symmetry of the street, blocks light in neighboring homes, and can mean the loss of historic structures (Nasar et al., 2007). Regulatory interventions related to building mass, design, and siting of structures have attempted to limit mansionization construction activity (Szold, 2005).

Adding more units to lots within existing subdivisions also increases infill. Infilling single-family residential neighborhoods with secondary units or accessory dwelling units (ADUs) increases residential density and has the potential to provide affordable housing choices for singles, seniors, and single-parent households. In some cases, ADUs or secondary units are detached from the primary residence but on the same lot. In other instances, the secondary unit is attached, as in the case of a garage conversion.

In a recent study of ADUs in East Bay in the San Francisco region, Wegmann and Chapple (2012) found that about 16 percent of single-family residences in the area had at least one secondary unit. Some of these units are detached, rear yard structures; others are garage conversions. They found a potential market for ADUs among homeowners in the study area who currently do not have ADUs. There is also strong evidence that many illegal secondary units are prevalent in jurisdictions across the United States and provide housing options for low-income renters (Wegmann & Nemirow, 2011).

Despite this "shadow housing market," jurisdictions do attempt to regulate ADUs. This is especially the case for those built on the same lot but separate from the primary residence. Most jurisdictions limit the size of the ADU. For example, Nashville and Ann Arbor limit the size to 25 percent of the primary unit. In the case of Fort Lauderdale, ADUs must be smaller than 600 square feet. Planning regulations also utilize design guidelines to ensure the ADU is similar in style and visual appearance to the primary unit. Communities that allow ADUs often require parking availability for the residents of these units, and many require that the same person who owns the primary residence also owns the ADU.

More and more jurisdictions are expressing interest in ADU development as an affordable housing strategy. For example, California recently passed legislation to streamline the ADU approval process across the state. This law aims to alleviate the burden of strict local planning regulations and exorbitant fees for permits to build ADUs. The overarching goal of the law is not necessarily to increase density or create a smart growth community, but rather to incentivize the development of affordable housing. Smarter growth may be an unintended consequence.

Lastly, infill redevelopment can take the form of reinvestment in, and renovation of, existing structures. Owners of older housing, for example, often contemplate whether to reinvest in their existing homes or move to newer structures, which are typically in locations farther out. Theoretically, homeowners with capital will invest in upgrading older housing when there is certainty in the market, if their neighbors reinvest, and if growth controls limit the development of newer structures on the suburban fringe. Lewis (2012) identified the positive effects of certain smart growth policies on urban rehabilitation in Baltimore. She found that property renovation in the city was more likely in national historic districts, heritage areas, and community legacy areas, the latter of which are neighborhoods located inside targeted growth areas where funding is available to help local governments and community development organizations encourage homeownership and commercial revitalization. Lewis's work shows that using funding to encourage smart growth goals of historic preservation and revitalization positively effects renovation and rehabilitation in the community.

BARRIERS AND CHALLENGES TO INFILL DEVELOPMENT

Despite efforts to redevelop existing communities, there are significant barriers and challenges to successful implementation.

Even though many local planning departments may embrace the new urbanist and smart growth paradigms, residents can oppose infill development because they think it will create negative externalities such as increased traffic congestion and parking problems (Wheeler, 2001). For instance, in a study of ADUs in East Bay, Wegmann and Chapple (2012) found that homeowners in neighborhoods with secondary units cite pressure on parking as the most negative reaction to this form of infill development. There was similar reaction in Montgomery County, Maryland, to its ADU ordinance.

Certainly, infrastructure capacity such as parking is relevant to the success of infill projects. Public services can degrade if any resulting population growth is not supported with increased infrastructure capacity (Knaap et al., 2001). Investments in utility infrastructure including water, sewer, electricity, and communications conduits, as well as transportation infrastructure such as roads, streets, trails, and bike paths, are necessary for successful redevelopment. The infrastructure investment necessary for compact infill development may not, however, be any less costly than infrastructure for suburban expansion. In addition, adequate public facilities ordinances (APFOs), designed to manage urban growth by ensuring that adequate facilities are available at the time of development, can potentially be an impediment to infill development. Successful projects need to be proactive in planning for the infrastructure needs ahead of any large-scale retrofitting project.

Another potential barrier to infill redevelopment is not-in-my-back-yard (NIMBY) activities. The community can oppose redevelopment, especially if it involves the introduction of new subsidized or affordable housing in their neighborhoods. NIMBY complaints often center on fears that such redevelopment might lower property values (Nguyen, 2005) or lead to increased crime and a reduction in school performance (Tighe, 2010). More broadly, residents often believe that increased density and the added population that comes with this type of redevelopment will put surplus pressure on local services and amenities (Cinyabuguma & McConnell, 2013). Community and environmental groups can oppose redevelopment because of the appearance, design, and scale of the project (Goldstein et al., 2001). All of these negative reactions make it difficult to reform zoning codes and ensure the implementation of successful redevelopment projects.

There are also significant financial barriers to redevelopment. Unlike greenfield sites, redevelopment sites have existing structures that require demolition before any redevelopment occurs, which adds to the costs. Developers might also encounter costs for dealing with property tax liens, mortgage liens, and utility liens on an infill site (Goldstein et al., 2001). Essentially, the costs associated with redevelopment in existing communities are less predictable than in greenfield areas. While the infrastructure exists in these communities, it can be challenging to expand it when necessary, especially for high-density, large-scale projects. In addition, the condition of the infrastructure is problematic in older parts of the metropolitan area. In some cases, there is a need to update and repair aging sewer and water pipes, poorly conditioned sidewalks and roads, and outdated telecommunications infrastructure.

In addition to the potential for higher costs, conservative lending practices mean financial institutions are less likely to support mixed-use redevelopment, making it difficult for developers to obtain the necessary financing. This is even more challenging if the redevelopment project is slated for a distressed community, which prompts added scrutiny by investors and lenders who perceive greater risk. Perceptions about crime, poorly performing schools, and neighborhood attractiveness all affect the ability of developers to acquire financing for projects in certain neighborhoods.

Finally, assembling parcels for larger-scale infill and mixed-use development is far more challenging than for the typical single-family residential suburban subdivision in a greenfield site. Parcels shaped in awkward ways make it difficult to assemble a contiguous set for significant redevelopment. Small vacant lots scattered across different areas in the community are challenging to redevelop on a meaningful scale.

Dunham-Jones and Williamson (2011) note the benefits to "scraping" large parking lots and conveniently-sized dead malls to fill with new construction over time. These large parcels make redevelopment easier from a developer perspective.

As "brick and mortar" stores in the retail industry struggle to compete with online retailers, large-scale regional shopping malls are vulnerable to closure. These malls, because of their large footprint, have great potential. Ideally, large-scale retrofitting of older urban and suburban strip malls and regional shopping centers should be linked in what Williamson refers to as "incremental metropolitanism," which will encourage "the gradual emergence of a robust, efficient, multicentered network of infilled centers and corridors within existing and already urbanized North American metropolitan regions to replace the past pattern of ever-outward sprawl" (Williamson, 2013, p. 39). In practice, this is a challenge when there is no regional strategy for identifying large-scale sites for redevelopment. The fragmented political landscape across metropolitan regions makes coordinating and linking major retrofitting projects across jurisdictional boundaries difficult.

Overall, challenges to redevelopment are significant, including infrastructure challenges, NIMBYism, financing issues, physical barriers, and problems of political fragmentation that prevent coordination of redevelopment projects on a regional scale.

CONSEQUENCES OF INFILL DEVELOPMENT

By absorbing growth in existing communities, infill development lessens urban expansion into rural areas. In addition, infill can enhance the viability of existing communities, encouraging the revitalization of neighborhoods experiencing disinvestment and increasing the quality of life for residents in these areas. Infill also capitalizes on existing infrastructure and has the potential to reduce costs associated with building new infrastructure in fringe areas of the region.

In addition, infill in the form of mixed-use development is a good response to current and future market demand. In recent years the emerging discourse around the future of suburbia has stressed the importance of demographic shifts, including the projected dearth of traditional married couples with children and the growth of the 65-years-and-older population (Nelson, 2009). Such shifts reduce the demand for the typical single-family home in the suburbs (Grant et al., 2013), and these trends are projected to continue (Nelson, 2012). Redesigning urban and suburban areas with denser development will make them more appealing to changing households.

While changing demographics affect demand, so do changing consumer preferences. Recent market surveys suggest that seniors and young professionals are interested in living in more compact and walkable communities, and that future development ought to better align with this new demand (Myers & Gearin, 2001). In addition, the Center for Transit-Oriented Development (2004, 2007) projects that the demand for housing near transit will double between 2000 and 2030. Suburban governments are responding to perceived demand for denser, mixed- use development, especially as they try to compete with other suburbs and with gentrifying neighborhoods in the city.

For example, in 2007, Montgomery County, Maryland, began the process of comprehensive zoning reform. One of the major reforms involved the addition of commercial-residential (CR) zones. This zoning category was first employed in the county to create transit-oriented, mixed-use development in the White Flint area, where the CR zones relied on density bonuses to developers in return for provision of public benefits and amenities (Hanson, 2017). The White Flint redevelopment also included establishment of a special tax district to finance infrastructure projects. Once the CR zone and infrastructure financing was in place, developers began initiating significant redevelopment projects. Hanson suggests the White Flint plan and the new CR zone accommodated the "urban sensibilities" of the different populations moving into the area, including young professionals, non-traditional households, immigrant groups, and empty nesters. "The experience of Montgomery's mixed-use centers demonstrates that plans without markets cannot succeed," Hanson argues (2017, p. 128).

There are also environmental benefits to infill development composed of mixed use, walkable, transit-proximate or transit-oriented communities in accessible locations, particularly the benefit of reduced automobile use and automobile trip lengths. There is much debate in the academic literature around the relationship between urban form and travel behavior. Some suggest that land use patterns have insignificant or little impact on the way people move around (e.g., Boarnet & Crane, 2001). Others argue a combination of built environment features can influence travel behavior, including mode choice, trip generation, trip length, and vehicle miles traveled (VMT) (e.g., Ewing & Cervero, 2001, 2010; Frank et al., 2008; Rajamani et al., 2003; Zhang et al., 2012).

Within the context of infill development, what has emerged from meta-analyses of major studies is that destination accessibility—measured either as jobs reachable in a given time period or as the distance to downtown—is the variable most strongly correlated with a reduction in VMT (Ewing & Cervero, 2010). In this sense, building mixed-use, walkable neighborhoods far away from employment and job centers will not reduce the miles people drive in their cars. In the context of infill development, reinvestment in locations close to employment is important.

The second most relevant variable that is closely associated with a reduction in VMT is design, especially street connectivity and intersection density that reduces driving (Ewing & Cervero, 2010). Combining destination accessibility and design with redevelopment has the potential to change travel behavior in ways that have positive environmental effects. As studies on urban form and travel behavior show, increasing density alone is not enough to reduce driving. To encourage transit, it will be necessary to prioritize redevelopment close to transit stops, including bus stops and light rail stations. Coordinating infill projects to maximize any significant reduction in driving will be essential in light of climate change. Overall, sustainable redevelopment relies on the creation of walkable, mixed-use developments in locations central to the region that are connected to job centers and important destinations.

Despite the potential benefits of this type of growth, it is important to point out challenges and concerns. One specific area of concern is the potential for infill development to lead to gentrification. Research shows that McMansion infill, for instance, leads to increased property values and makes those neighborhoods unaffordable (Nasar et al., 2007). Charles (2013a) notes that McMansion infill began in high-property-value suburban neighborhoods but toward the end of the 2000s began to spread into adjacent, more modest-income neighborhoods. In a study in Baltimore County, Hanlon and Airgood-Obrycki (2018) found that McMansion infill occurred in working class, formerly industrial suburbs. Studies such as these warn that this kind of redevelopment could lead to the indirect displacement of lower-income households from suburbs as property values rise and they can no longer afford to live there.

As Finio and Knaap discuss in Chapter 13 of this book, smart growth efforts can fuel the gentrification process. Gentrification sometimes means the direct displacement of existing low-income residents who can no longer afford housing in the neighborhood, a process often difficult to measure (Freeman, 2005). In addition, gentrification can lead to indirect displacement when low-income populations are unable to afford to move in to gentrified neighborhoods (Marcuse, 1985), also referred to as exclusionary gentrification (Slater, 2009). Gentrification affects city neighborhoods and, while less discussed, older suburbs. In a recent study of Atlanta, Markley (2018) found new urbanist development led to gentrification in communities of color in the inner suburbs. Hanlon and Airgood-Obrycki (2018) also note the displacement of low-income groups because of the redevelopment of subsidized housing into a mix of market rate and senior housing in older suburbs outside Baltimore city.

There is some debate in the literature about the relationship between gentrification and transit-oriented development (TOD). Dong (2017) finds little evidence of gentrification along rail rapid transit lines in Portland, Oregon. Deka (2017), in his study of the effects of TOD in New Jersey, finds that homes near transit stations experienced an increase in home values but rent remained stable. He did not find any undesirable changes in population characteristics (e.g., race or ethnicity) near stations. Brown (2016) also showed little change in racial and ethnic composition along a bus rapid transit (BRT) corridor in Los Angeles but did note a rise in median home values, rents, and resident education levels that suggests gentrification within adjacent communities. The relationship between TOD and gentrification may depend on the city. Baker and Lee (2019), in a study of light rail transit (LRT) and changes in neighborhood conditions in 14 urbanized areas, found a strong connection between gentrification and the location of LRT stations in some cities but not others. In the case of San Francisco, for instance, gentrification was prevalent around LRT stations, but this was not the case in Portland, Oregon. The authors point to the role that local and regional planning efforts have in these outcomes.

When redeveloping urban and suburban communities with smart growth goals, it is important for planners and policymakers to creatively think of ways to ensure low-income and minority populations can remain and enjoy the benefits of revitalization. One important consideration is the preservation of existing affordable units in neighborhoods. The federal government has several programs to help with this including, the US Department of Housing and Urban Development's Rental

Assistance Demonstration (RAD) program that enables public housing authorities (PHA) to privatize and convert public housing to project-based Section 8 contracts, which is intended to redevelop aging housing but keep it affordable long term. This ensures a more stable source of funding and enables PHAs to leverage additional sources of funding for preservation. Encouraging redevelopment in areas near project-based Section 8 housing can be challenging, but when successful, can bring benefits to those living in these projects and help them remain.

States also preserve affordable units using the Low-Income Housing Tax Credit (LIHTC), which provides credits to developers and owners of long-term affordable housing. Some cities and municipalities use TIFs, as described above, for land acquisition and the rehabilitation of affordable housing. Community land trusts (CLT) permanently maintain affordable housing despite surrounding gentrification. Utilizing different affordable housing strategies alongside any redevelopment ensures low-income populations get to remain in revitalized neighborhoods.

Smart growth seeks the creation of sustainable communities through the infill process. An important third pillar of sustainability, in addition to environmental and economic aspects, is equitable development. As Lung-Amam and June-Friesen note in Chapter 14, equity concerns have not historically been at the forefront of smart growth efforts. Preventing the loss of affordable housing units is paramount and is likely most important in distressed inner-city neighborhoods. In other neighborhoods, especially in the suburbs, new redevelopment projects ought to include affordable housing units so that low-income populations can move into these new developments. Retrofitting the suburbs provides the opportunity to introduce affordable units into areas of opportunity. Encouraging accessory dwelling unit development has the potential to do the same.

FUTURE CONSIDERATIONS

There are three broad areas to consider when we think about the future of infill development within the context of the smart growth movement. The first concerns growing suburban poverty and the problem of decline among certain suburbs. Future redevelopment projects in the suburbs will have to seriously consider the needs of lower-income populations. TOD, mixed-used development, and apartment construction do not necessarily cater to all socioeconomic groups; despite the potential positive environmental or travel-related effects, there are serious equity concerns. As mentioned, there will need to be a concerted effort by planners, policymakers and smart growth advocates to ensure housing affordability and prevent displacement of low-income groups in urban and suburban redevelopment areas. In addition, as older suburbs struggle with an aging housing stock, programs to enable the renovation and reinvestment necessary to maintain these residential properties, especially for more moderate-income homeowners, are paramount.

Another future consideration relates to transformations in transportation technologies, including connected and automated vehicles (CAVs, a.k.a. self-driving cars) and on-demand ride hailing, such as Uber and Lyft. Because CAVs may reduce the time spent on driving, households may choose to live farther out in the metropolitan fringe. In this scenario, CAVs may lead to more suburban sprawl because owners of these private systems will have the ability to work in these vehicles during longer-distance commutes.

However, there are a variety of potential ways in which urban planning and policy can minimize or eliminate these effects. It is possible that CAVs could include public vehicles (Folsom, 2011). In this scenario, land use patterns could in fact become more compact as public CAV systems become more competitive than private transportation, including the private car. This is a good scenario for infill redevelopment. There is also the real potential that CAVs could reduce the need for large parking lots, many of which are underutilized at different times during the day and at night. The self-driving car can rearrange itself within a parking lot as space becomes available or can return to its trip origin. This would reduce the need for so much parking space that already exists in the city and suburbs. The redevelopment of these parking lots into walkable, denser housing or mixed-use environments has the potential to create more viable and sustainable neighborhoods.

In addition, there is currently little understanding about the possible impacts that CAV systems have on other modes of transportation including, for example, public transit, walking, and biking. As yet, we do not understand how pedestrian or cyclist behavior might be altered in a driverless environment (Blau et al., 2018). Finally, driverless cars, if heavily utilized, could negatively affect public transit use, and thus the desirability of transit-oriented development. Overall, it is unclear what effect driverless cars will have on future redevelopment and commuting patterns more broadly.

Such is the case with many new technologies as human mobility undergoes a revolution. According to a 2017 study, 21 percent of adults in major cities in the United States use on-demand services such as Uber and Lyft, with about a quarter of them using these services at least once a week (Clewlow & Mishri, 2017). One of the top reasons for using ride hailing services is to avoid parking. In addition, the study found these on-demand services have an overall negative impact on public transit use; the effect on light rail is positive, while the effect on bus ridership is negative. On-demand services, then, might be good for transit-oriented developments.

Last, as of this writing, we are in the midst of a global pandemic. During the COVID-19 pandemic, many people have lost their jobs, small businesses have had to close, and lucky employees are able to work from home. Young adults are engaged in remote learning in schools and universities across the country. The economic and financial fallout from the pandemic has already been significant, and universities, local governments, and states have implemented budget cuts. Certainly, the fiscal capacity of local and state governments to invest in new development in existing communities will likely be limited going forward, and remote work may impact office development that would be part of future mixed-use infill projects.

Suburban poverty, new automobile technologies, and the effects of the COVID-19 global pandemic—separately and combined—will affect future redevelopment and, as a consequence, smart growth efforts. Planners and policymakers who embrace infill development can work to address these dynamics in ways that ensure a socially and environmentally sustainable future metropolis.

REFERENCES

Baker, D. M., & Lee, B. (2019). How does light rail transit (LRT) impact gentrification? Evidence from fourteen US urbanized areas. *Journal of Planning Education and Research*, *39*(1), 35–49.

Benfield, K., Terris, J., & Vorsanger, N. (2001). *Solving sprawl: Models of smart growth in communities across America*. Washington, DC: Natural Resources Defense Council.

Bhatta, S. D., Merriman, D., & Weber, R. (2003). Does tax increment financing raise urban industrial property values? *Urban Studies*, *40*(10), 2001–2021.

Blau, M., Akar, G., & Nasar, J. (2018). Driverless vehicles' potential influence on bicyclist facility preferences. *International Journal of Sustainable Transportation*, *12*(9), 665–674.

Boarnet, M. G., & Crane, R. (2001). The influence of land use on travel behavior: Specification and estimation strategies. *Transportation Research Part A: Policy and Practice*, *35*(9), 823–845.

Bressi, T. W. (1994). Planning the American dream. In P. Katz (Ed.), *The new urbanism: Toward an architecture of community* (pp.15–28). New York: McGraw-Hill.

Briffault, R. (1997). The law and economics of federalism: The rise of sublocal structures in urban governance. *Minnesota Law Review*, *82*, 503–534.

Briffault, R. (2010). The most popular tool: Tax increment financing and the political economy of local government. *The University of Chicago Law Review*, *4*(1), 65–95.

Brown, A. E. (2016). Rubber tires for residents: Bus rapid transit and changing neighborhoods in Los Angeles. *Transportation Research Board: Journal of the Transportation Research Board*, *2539*(1), 1–10.

Byrne, P. (2006). Determinants of property value growth for tax increment financing districts. *Economic Development Quarterly*, *20*(4), 317–329.

Byrne, P. (2010). Does tax increment financing deliver on its promise of jobs? The impact of tax increment financing on municipal employment growth. *Economic Development Quarterly*, *24*(1), 13–22.

Calthorpe, P. G. (1993). *The next American metropolis: Ecology, community and the American dream*. Princeton: Princeton University Press.

Carlton, I. (2009). *Histories of transit-oriented development: Perspectives on the development of the TOD concept* (Working Paper, No. 2009, 02). University of California, Institute of Urban and Regional Development (IURD), Berkeley, CA.

Center for Transit-Oriented Development. (2004). *Hidden in plain sight: Capturing the demand for housing near transit*. Oakland, CA: Center for Transit-Oriented Development.

Center for Transit-Oriented Development. (2007). *2007 Demand estimate update*. Oakland, CA: Center for Transit-Oriented Development.

Cervero, R., & Guerra, E. (2011). *Urban densities and transit: A multi-dimensional perspective*. (Working Paper UCB-ITS-VWP-2011-6). Institute of Transportation Studies, University of California, Berkeley, Retrieved from https:// escholarship .org/ content/ qt3mb598qr/qt3mb598qr.pdf

Charles, S. L. (2013a). The spatio-temporal pattern of housing redevelopment in suburban Chicago, 2000–2010. *Urban Studies*, *51*(12), 2646–2664.

Charles, S. L. (2013b). Understanding the determinants of single-family residential redevelopment in the inner-ring suburbs of Chicago. *Urban Studies*, *50*(8), 1505–1522.

Cinyabuguma, M., & McConnell, V. (2013). Urban growth externalities and neighborhood incentives: another cause of urban sprawl? *Journal of Regional Science*, 53(2), 332–348.

Clewlow, R. R., & Mishra, G. S. (2017). *Disruptive transportation: The adoption, utilization, and impacts of ride-hailing in the United States*. UC Davis: Institute of Transportation Studies. Retrieved from https://escholarship.org/uc/item/82w2z91j

Davis, T. S., & Sherman, S. A. (2010). *Brownfields: A comprehensive guide to redeveloping contaminated properties*. Chicago, IL: American Bar Association.

Deka, D. (2017). Benchmarking gentrification near commuter rail stations in New Jersey. *Urban Studies*, 54(13), 2955–2972.

Dong, H. (2017). Rail-transit-induced gentrification and the affordability paradox of TOD. *Journal of Transport Geography*, 63, 1–10.

Dunham-Jones, E. & Williamson, J. (2011). *Retrofitting suburbia*. Hoboken, NJ: Wiley.

Dye, R. F., & McMillen, D. P. (2007). Teardowns and land values in the Chicago metropolitan area. *Journal of Urban Economics*, 61(1), 45–63.

Dye, R. F., & Merriman, D. (2000). The effects of tax increment financing on economic development. *Journal of Urban Economics*, 47(2), 306–328.

Dye, R. F., & Sundberg, J. O. (1998). A model of tax increment financing adoption incentives. *Growth and Change*, 29(1), 90–110.

Eckerd, A., & Keeler, A. G. (2012). Going green together? Brownfield remediation and environmental justice. *Policy Sciences*, 45, 293–314.

Ellis, C. (2002). The new urbanism: Critiques and rebuttals. *Journal of Urban Design*, 7(3), 261–291.

Ewing, R. (1997). Is Los Angeles-style sprawl desirable? *Journal of the American Planning Association*, 63(1), 107–126.

Ewing, R. (2008). Characteristics, causes, and effects of sprawl: A literature review. In J. M. Marzluff, E. Schulenberger, W. Endlicher, M. Alberti, G. Bradley, C. Ryan, U. Simon, & C. ZumBrunnen (Eds), *Urban ecology: An international perspective on the interaction between humans and nature* (pp. 519–535) Boston, MA: Springer.

Ewing, R., & Cervero, R. (2001). Travel and the built environment: A synthesis. *Transportation Research Record*, 1780, 87–113.

Ewing, R., & Cervero, R. (2010). Travel and the built environment. *Journal of the American Planning Association*, 76(3). 265–294.

Farris, T. J. (2001). The barriers to using urban infill development to achieve smart growth. *Housing Policy Debate*, 12(1), 1–30.

Folsom, T. C. (2011, May). Social ramifications of autonomous urban land vehicles. Paper presented at the *Institute of Electrical and Electronics Engineers (IEEE) International Symposium on Technology and Society*, Chicago: IL.

Frank, L., Bradley, M., Kavage, S., Chapman J., & Lawton, T. K. (2008). Urban form, travel time, and cost relationships with tour complexity and mode choice. *Transportation*, 35(1), 37–54.

Freeman, L. (2005). Displacement or succession? Residential mobility in gentrified neighborhoods. *Urban Affairs Review*, 40(4): 463–491.

Frumkin, H., Frank, L., & Jackson, R. J. (2004). *Urban sprawl and public health: Designing, planning, and building for healthy communities*. Washington, DC: Island Press.

Goldstein, J., Jensen, M., & Reiskin, E. (2001). *Urban vacant land redevelopment: Challenges and progress*. Cambridge, MA: Lincoln Institute of Land Policy.

Gordon, C. (2003). Blighting the way: Urban renewal, economic development, and the elusive definition of blight. *Fordham Urban Law Journal*, 31(2), 305–337.

Grant, J., Nelson, A. C., Forsyth, A., Thompson-Fawcett, M., Blais, P., & Filion, P. (2013). The future of suburbs. *Planning Theory and Practice*, 14(3), 391–415.

Green, T. L. (2018). Evaluating predictors for brownfield redevelopment. *Land Use Policy*, 73(C), 299–319.

Hanlon, B., & Airgood-Obrycki, W. (2018). Suburban revalorization: Residential infill and rehabilitation in Baltimore County's older suburbs. *Environment and Planning A, 50*(4), 895–921.

Hanson, R. (2017). *Suburb: Planning politics and the public interest.* Ithaca, NY: Cornell University Press.

Heris, M. P. (2017). Evaluating metropolitan spatial development: A method for identifying settlement types and depicting growth patterns. *Regional Studies, Regional Science, 4*(1), 7–25.

Keil, R. (2018). *Suburban planet: Making the world urban from the outside in.* Cambridge: Polity Press.

Knaap, G.-J., & Frece, J. (2007). Smart growth in Maryland: Looking forward and looking back. *Idaho Law Review, 43*(2), 445–473.

Knaap, G.-J., & Talen, E. (2005). New urbanism and smart growth: A few words from the academy. *International Regional Science Review, 28*(2), 107–118.

Knaap, G.-J., Ding, C., & Hopkins, L. D. (2001). Managing urban growth for the efficient use of public infrastructure: Toward a theory of concurrency. *International Regional Science Review, 24*(3), 328–343.

Landis, J., Hood, H., Li, G., Rodgers, T., & Warren, C. (2006). The future of infill housing in California: Opportunities, potential, and feasibility. *Housing Policy Debate, 17*(4), 681–726.

Lewis, R. (2012). The determinants of rehabilitation and redevelopment in Baltimore City. *Regional Science Practice and Policy, 4*(4), 335–354.

Lewis, R., Knaap, G.-J., & Schindewolf, J. (2013). *The spatial structure of cities in the United States.* The Lincoln Institute of Land Policy (Working Paper). Cambridge, MA.

Marcuse, P. (1985). Gentrification, abandonment and displacement: connections, causes and policy responses in New York City. *Journal of Urban and Contemporary Law, 28,* 195–240.

Markley, S. (2018). Suburban gentrification? Examining the geographies of new urbanism in Atlanta's inner suburbs. *Urban Geography, 39*(4), 606–630.

Maryland Department of Planning. (2001). *Models and guidelines for infill development.* Maryland Department of Planning, Baltimore, MD.

McConnell, V. D., & Wiley, K. (2010). *Infill development: Perspectives and evidence from economics and planning* (RFF Discussion Paper 10-13). Resources for the Future. Washington, DC.

Myers, D., & Gearin, E. (2001). Current preferences and future demand for denser residential environments. *Housing Policy Debate, 12*(4), 633–659.

Nasar, J. L., Evans-Cowley, J. S., & Mantero, V. (2007). McMansions: The extent and regulation of super-sized houses. *Journal of Urban Design, 12*(3), 339–358.

Nelson, A. C. (2009). The new urbanity: The rise of a new America. *The Annals of the American Academy of Political and Social Science, 626*(1), 192–208.

Nelson, A. C. (2012). The mass market for suburban low-density development is over. *The Urban Lawyer, 44*(4), 811–826.

Nguyen, M. T. (2005). Does affordable housing detrimentally affect property values? A review of the literature. *Journal of Planning Literature, 20*(1), 15–26.

Ottensmann, J. R. (1977). Urban sprawl, land values and the density of development. *Land Economics, 53*(4), 389–400.

Pinnegar S., Freestone R., & Randolph B. (2010). Suburban reinvestment through 'knockdown rebuild' in Sydney. In M. Clapson, & R. Hutchinson (Eds), *Suburbanization in a global society* (pp. 205–229). Bingley: Emerald Insight.

Rajamani, J., Bhat, C. R., Handy, S., Knaap, G.-J., & Song, Y. (2003). Assessing the impact of urban form measures in nonwork trip mode choice after controlling for demographic and level-of-service effects. *Transportation Research Record, 1831,* 158–165.

Riggs, W., & Chamberlain, F. (2018). The TOD and smart growth implications of the LA adaptive reuse ordinance. *Sustainable Cities and Society, 38*(April), 594–606.

Slater, T. (2009). Missing Marcuse: On gentrification and displacement. *City, 13*(2-3), 292–311.

Squires, G. D. (2002). *Urban sprawl: Causes, consequences, & policy responses*. Washington, DC: The Urban Institute.

Steinacker, A. (2003). Infill development and affordable housing: Patterns from 1996–2000. *Urban Affairs Review, 38*(4), 492–509.

Szold, T. S. (2005). Mansionization and its discontents: Planners and the challenge of regulating monster homes, *Journal of the American Planning Association, 71*(2), 189–202.

Talen, E. (2013). Zoning for and against sprawl: The case for form-based codes. *Journal of Urban Design, 18*(2), 175–200.

Talen, E. (2015). *Retrofitting sprawl: Addressing seventy years of failed urban form*. Athens, GA: University of Georgia Press.

Tighe, J. R. (2010). Public opinion and affordable housing: A review of the literature. *Journal of Planning Literature, 25*(1), 3–17.

Warner, S. B. (1978). *Streetcar suburbs*. Cambridge, MA: Harvard University Press.

Weber, R. (2002). Extracting value from the city: Neoliberalism and urban redevelopment. *Antipode, 34*(3), 519–540.

Weber R., Doussard M., Bhatta S. D., & McGrath, D. (2006). Tearing the city down: Understanding demolition activity in gentrifying neighborhoods. *Journal of Urban Affairs, 28*, 19–41.

Wegmann, J., & Chapple, K. (2012). *Understanding the market for secondary units in the East Bay*. (IURD Working Paper WP-2012-03). Berkeley Institute of Urban and Regional Development. Retrieved from https://escholarship.org/uc/item/9932417c.

Wegmann, J., & Nemirow, A. (2011). *Secondary units and urban infill: A literature review*. (Working Paper, No. 2011-02), University of California, Institute of Urban and Regional Development (IURD), Berkeley, CA.

Wheeler, S. (2001, November). Infill development in the San Francisco Bay Area: Current obstacles and responses. Paper presented at the *Annual Conference of the Association of Collegiate Schools of Planning*, Cleveland, Ohio.

Wiley, K. (2007). An exploration of suburban infill. Paper presented at the Smart Growth Conference, University of Maryland, College Park.

Williamson, J. (2013). *Designing suburban futures: New models from build a better burb*. Washington, DC: Island Press.

Zhang, L., Hong, J., Nasri, A., & Shen, Q. (2012). How built environment affects travel behavior: A comparative analysis of the connections between land use and vehicle miles traveled in US cities. *Journal of Transport and Land Use, 5*(3), 40–52.

PART III

SMART GROWTH PRINCIPLES: THE FORM AND FUNCTION OF URBAN DEVELOPMENT

6. Promoting mixed land uses for smart growth: implications and recommendations for research and practice

Yan Song

INTRODUCTION

Since the mid-twentieth century, the separation of land uses has been the cornerstone of conventional land use planning in the United States. Zoning ordinances throughout the country have had the effect of isolating employment, shopping, and services from residential housing. Partly motivated by exclusionary practices and by the need to mitigate perceived negative externalities, residential neighborhoods have been developed separate from jobs and services. Many have argued that the practice of separating land uses has led to excessive commuting times, traffic congestion, air pollution, inefficient energy consumption, loss of open space and habitat, inequitable distribution of economic resources, job/housing imbalance, and loss of sense of community.

Jacobs (1961) first raised the importance of land use mix in urban planning; since then, diversity in land use has been a critical target of research and practice regarding urban planning and design, transportation planning, health and preventive medicine, and property valuation (Ewing & Cervero, 2010; Frank et al., 2005; Song & Knaap, 2004). The interest in mixing certain land uses stems from emerging empirical evidence suggesting that a greater mix of complementary land use types, which may include housing, retail, offices, commercial services, light industrial and civic uses, is associated with benefits, most notably in transportation, public health, environment, urban economics, and placemaking. From a transportation point of view, the benefits of mixed uses emerge primarily from bringing a variety of origins and destinations closer together, enabling shifts to non-motorized travel modes and shorter travel distances. From a public health point of view, bringing a variety of interesting destinations closer to residential areas is a means of encouraging active travel modes. From an environmental point of view, bringing destinations together can shorten vehicle miles traveled and thereby improve air quality in urban areas. From an urban economics perspective, the appropriate mix of complementary urban land uses has the potential to increase land value and encourage higher density development through the provision of urban amenities. Furthermore, from a placemaking point of view, putting urban functions together can bring people together and make places more vibrant.

Therefore, in practice, mixed land use has become one of the central concepts in the urban planning field, a response to a set of complex problems, brought on by urban sprawl, that have beset most US metropolitan areas. Planners and researchers have begun advocating for mixing certain types of land uses. For example, Calthorpe (1993) emphasized that all transit-oriented developments (TODs) must be mixed use and contain a minimum amount of public, core commercial, and residential use. Aside from TODs, mixed land use has been mentioned in possibly every planning idea in recent years, including smart growth (Downs, 2005), new urbanism (Congress for the New Urbanism, 2000), and complete neighborhood (Pivo, 2005). The Smart Growth Network, established under the auspices of the US Environmental Protection Agency, promotes the mixing of residential and commercial uses as one of the ten principles of smart growth. The Congress for the New Urbanism (CNU) also calls for neighborhoods that are "compact, pedestrian friendly, and mixed-use," with "concentrations of civic, institutional, and commercial activity ... embedded in neighborhoods and districts, not isolated in remote, single-use complexes" (Congress for the New Urbanism, 1996). In addition, the Centers for Disease Control and Prevention (CDC) has identified mixing land uses as a strategy to promote active community environments (2005).

Despite the practical interest and mushrooming empirical research, there is still a need to enrich land use mix research to fill several gaps. In this chapter I seek to provide a synthetic examination of three areas of research. In the next section, I present our approach to categorizing, developing, and implementing land use mix measures; assessing various land use mix measures used in prior research; and discussing the strengths and weaknesses of these measures. Next, I summarize prior research on land use mix and outcomes of interest to planners and policymakers. In the third section, I summarize current policy instruments that promote land use mix. The final section draws conclusions and provides recommendations for researchers and practitioners interested in mixed land uses.

MEASURES OF LAND USE MIX

Before getting into measurement issues, it is helpful to note that mixing land use is an ambiguous recommendation and can be interpreted in many ways. Issues include what uses should be mixed, should they be mixed horizontally or vertically, at what geographic scale should they be mixed, and others. Given this ambiguity, researchers have taken a variety of approaches to measuring land use mix to assess the efficacy of this strategy.

Knowing the usual ways by which researchers have operationalized land use mix helps assess the efficacy of mixing land uses and enables comparative studies of land use mix and individual and social outcomes. In what follows, I review measures of land use mix in existing studies. I categorize various measures based on their different approaches to conceptualizing land use mix: appraising mix based on the concepts of accessibility (or proximity), intensity (or magnitude), and distribution pattern.

Accessibility is the degree to which mixed land activities are easy for residents to reach; intensity is the volume or magnitude of mixed land uses present in an area; and distribution pattern is the way in which different types of land uses are organized in an area. This chapter's discussion on measures of land use mix revolves around these three concepts. For each of the measures I also include a detailed example of at least one implementation of each measure, including references to studies that have used such measures.

Accessibility-based Land Use Mix Measures

Accessibility measures how far different land use activities are in relation to each other in geographic distances. When mixed land activities are in proximity, it is easier for residents to reach destinations. I include three measures in this category: one distance-based and two gravity-based measures.

Distance. The simplest measure of land use mix is the linear or street network distance between a residential land use (e.g., individual housing units) and the *nearest* non-residential land use such as the nearest commercial store, multi-family residential unit, public institutional use, light industrial site, or public park (see, for example, Song & Knaap, 2004). This measure takes adjacent non-residential land uses into consideration by calculating the nearest distances between pairs of observations. It also accounts for individual variances in proximity to other land uses. However, the measure offers little information on the broader context of the proximity because it pays no heed to land uses other than the closest one. In addition, the measure takes no notice of the size of the nearest non-residential land use.

Gravity. A slightly more complex measure is based on the gravity concept. The simplest gravity-based measure of land use mix can be defined as the sum of accessibility of residential land use to all other given types of non-residential land uses, discounted by the distance decay function between these two points.[1] This approach generates a relatively comprehensive measure of accessibility from a residential land use to a given type of non-residential land use by including distances to all other non-residential units. A major challenge with this straightforward approach is to fine-tune the impedance function to reflect the true impedance at that point, since as urban structures change, the distance decay or impedance function also changes. Another limitation of this measure is that it overlooks the scale or the size of non-residential land use activities.

Gravity with competition. Gravity with competition can be defined as the sum of accessibility of residential land use to all other given types of non-residential land uses, discounted by the distance decay function between these two points, and extended by considering both the supply side of non-residential land uses (i.e., the attractiveness of the non-residential land use) and the demand side of non-residential land uses (i.e., the competition for consuming the functions provided by the non-residential land use). This measure considers both the supply and demand for certain services (e.g., Shen, 1998; Song & Sohn, 2007 ;Weibull, 1976) and provides information on accessibility to non-residential land use in a more thorough way than the previous measures by considering both the scale (the attraction) of, and the competition for, the services. However, it assumes that accessibility is based only on the distance between various competitors and the destinations, and the destinations' relative attractiveness, for example as dictated by floorspace or number of employees.

Intensity-based Land Use Mix Measures

Intensity measures the magnitude of mixed land uses. I include two measures in this category: counts and area proportions of mixed land uses.

Counts. Counts can be defined as the number of non-residential activities in the neighborhood. I provide the following three examples of land use mix measures using counts. The first measure is the number of different types of land uses such as residential, commercial, light industrial (office), public institutional, and parks and recreational per acre in the user-defined neighborhoods (Cervero & Kockelman, 1997). The second is the number of employees by different sector in a user-defined neighborhood divided by gross land area in that neighborhood (Krizek, 2003). The third is the number of street blocks containing retail uses within a user-defined neighborhood as a measure of retail density (Cervero & Kockelman, 1997).

Area proportions. A second intensity measure is the proportion of different types of land uses within a user-defined neighborhood. I provide the following examples of land use mix measures using counts. The first is the percentage of different types of land uses within a user-defined neighborhood. The neighborhood can be defined, for example, by transportation analysis zones (TAZs), census tracts, or quarter-mile buffers around residential units (Song & Knaap, 2004). The second is the area of a particular land use type per parcel, calculated by dividing the area of parcels of a particular land use (e.g., residential, commercial, light industrial (office), public institutional, or parks and recreational) by the total number of land parcels in a user-defined neighborhood (McNally & Kulkarni, 1997). The third is the percentage of residential parcels with another land use. This measure is used to capture vertical mix where there is more than one land use category within one land parcel (Cervero & Kockelman, 1997).

The measures in this and the previous category are easy to compute and offer practical information on the intensity of a particular type of land use in a user-defined neighborhood. Unfortunately, there are several limitations of analyses based at the neighborhood level. First, as the counts or proportion of land uses are conventionally aggregated by areal units such as census boundaries and TAZs, fine variations at smaller-unit levels are averaged out and smoothed over during successive levels of aggregation, effectively disappearing with each higher level of aggregation (the modifiable areal unit problem, MAUP). Second, it is well understood that results are determined by the oftentimes *arbitrary* location of neighborhood boundaries and therefore might be misleading. It is also necessary to consider how different levels of aggregation can affect results. For example, a larger neighborhood is simply prone to more land use types. If the results change with the selection of different sizes of areal units, the reliability of results is called into question. Third, using larger neighborhoods (e.g., census tracts) raises concerns that the units of analysis are too large to have an intrinsic meaning with respect to the underlying land use distribution. The issue—the non-uniformity of space—has to do with the fact that the physical environmental conditions need to be taken into account as contexts to confirm or refute calculated distribution patterns. For example, the observed concentration of residential and non-residential uses can be less significant than originally thought because the other part of the city has a large lake.

Land Use Mix Pattern Measures

Compositional patterns of land use mix, as manifest through spatial distribution of land development, is another useful aspect to measure land use mix because the patterns can demonstrate how various land uses are spatially in relation to each other. Measures of land use patterns can be further classified into three dimensions: evenness, exposure, and clustering. First, evenness and diversity measures of land use mix compare the distributions of different land uses. Measures in this category include the Balance index, the Herfindahl-Hirschman index, the Dissimilarity index, the Gini coefficient, entropy, and the Atkinson index (Song et al., 2013). Second, exposure measures, which originate in the field of residential segregation, assess "the degree of potential contact or possibility of interaction" between two subject groups (Massey & Denton, 1988, p. 287). The interaction index in this category measures the "publicity" of non-residential land uses to residential uses. Lower values of interaction indicate lower exposure. It is necessary to note that exposure and evenness (or diversity) measure different things: exposure measures depend on the relative sizes of the two groups being compared, while evenness measures do not (Massey & Denton, 1988). Third, clustering, which originates in the studies of residential and income segregation, measures the extent to which areal units with different subjects "adjoin one other, or cluster, in space" (Massey & Denton, 1988, p. 293). Clustering considers the spatial arrangement of land uses within neighborhoods.

Among all the above measures of patterns of mixed land uses, entropy is the most prevalent measure. The entropy index is a measure of variation, dispersion, or diversity (Turner et al., 2001). It measures the degree to which land uses are heterogeneously distributed within a neighborhood. A value of 0 indicates homogeneity, wherein all land uses are of one single type; a value of 1 means heterogeneity, wherein area is evenly distributed among all land use categories.[2] Researchers in various fields have implemented this measure in multiple ways to examine the dispersion of land uses. The entropy index incorporates more than two land use types in a single calculation, very conveniently aggregating a measure of land use diversity at various levels. The simplicity in computations of the entropy index makes it desirable.

Given the importance and popularity of the entropy measure in urban studies, the validity of this measure is critical for all empirical studies that use it to examine the associations between built environments and various outcomes. However, in recent years, more and more researchers have found that the Shannon entropy-based land use mix index has many deeply rooted issues that jeopardize its construct validity (Im & Choi, 2019; Manaugh & Kreider, 2013). First of all, entropy measures lack a solid theoretical basis to account for the aspects of land use mix relevant for associations with transportation and health. A second strong criticism of entropy measure is its definition of best composition. The most proper and feasible mixed-use share of a site should be comparable with the share of the regional context instead of an arbitrarily defined equipartition. However, for entropy, the highest index value indicates that every component within it shares an equal proportion. This is an indication of over-emphasis on the evenness. Using empirical statistical methods, Im and Choi (2019) found that a less equally distributed land use mix performed better in an area than the perfectly equally distributed land use mix. Evidently, the fragility of entropy-based land use mix measures may have implications that distort conclusions drawn on associations of land use mix to some dependent variables.

To summarize, measures of land use mix are useful for understanding the patterns of land use distribution. They also enable researchers and practitioners to evaluate the relationship between mixed land uses and individual and community outcomes in disciplines such as transportation, health outcomes, and housing markets. It is tempting to ask which measure is the most appropriate one in evaluating or promoting land use mix by researchers. Obviously, there is no single best measure of land use mix, since each measure captures different dimensions of how land uses are distributed in space. However, our review can provide insights for researchers and practitioners regarding the appropriateness of particular measures for particular purposes.

First, the choice of measure is dependent on the extent to which a measure captures the presence and configuration of land uses in space. For example, is the *pattern* of several land uses more of interest than the mere presence of those uses in the study area? Should the measure account for more than two land use types? Will the index measure what the researcher or practitioner wants to measure? Second, practical considerations should also influence the choice of measure. These include data collection and management, computational burden, and ease of communicability. While some measures require data manipulations that require database programming, others result naturally from a land use cover map. By most accounts, relatively simple measures have been implemented more frequently than complex measures. Of course, this simplicity has tradeoffs and may explain divergent results in various disciplines with respect to the relevance of land use mixes for community and individual outcomes. Finally, and perhaps most importantly, the connection between the measures and the purpose of the investigation should drive the measures selected. In other words, measures should be selected based on the substantive questions driving the inquiry. If the question being asked is about non-motorized travel behavior, then the location of commercial and office land uses relative to residential uses is of paramount interest. A two-land use type measure may suffice. By contrast, if the question motivating the research is the impact of non-residential land uses on property values, then the location of, at least, parks, industrial, and commercial uses relative to residential units should be of concern. It is also tempting to ask what kind of mix of land uses a community should achieve with the help of practitioners. There is no straightforward answer since a good mix of land uses is very context specific.

RESEARCH ON LAND USE MIX AND COMMUNITY OUTCOMES

Land use mix is oftentimes considered as a crucial factor in promoting lively environments as people work, live, play, and perform other activities enabled by the close proximity and interaction of various functions of cities (Jacobs, 1961). Advocates for mixed land uses have argued that these lively environments instill a sense of well-being and are associated with a plethora of individual and social benefits (Yue & Zhu, 2019). Talen (Chapter 7) discusses how urban design principles can help achieve such neighborhoods and the benefit and challenges of implementing these principles.

In this section, I summarize research results on these benefits. In a review, I searched for relevant studies published as articles in peer-reviewed journals. A search of two databases (Web of Science and Scopus) indicates that there is a vast literature examining the relationship between land use mix and individual and community outcomes. Our search query has two parts: the first part included the concept of land use mix, and the second included keywords related to outcomes of interest, for example, transportation (auto ownership, travel behavior), health outcomes (physical activity, obesity), landscape ecology and environmental outcomes (air quality, water quality), housing markets (property values), and urban vibrancy (social activities). The query generated 543 results, of which 87 articles quantitatively analyzed the relationships between land use mix and outcomes.

Land Use Mix and Transportation Outcomes

Many researchers are interested in the potential of land use mix to change people's behavior in favor of more sustainable modes of transportation such as walking, cycling, and using public transit, as opposed to relying on private motorized vehicles (Cervero, 1996). Researchers are also interested in the effects of land use mix on walking and cycling because of the increase in physical activity that is associated with health outcomes (Frank et al., 2005). In a review, I examined the extent of association between land use mix and the following components of transportation: different types of walking such as utilitarian walking, leisure walking, and total walking; bicycling; using public transportation; and total physical activity including walking, biking, jogging, exercising, for example. Welch and Gehrke further discuss the transportation-land use connection in Chapter 10, and Clifton reviews the progress and data on promoting walking in cities over the last several decades in Chapter 9.

Earlier studies investigated the association of land use mix with mode choice from a transportation standpoint (Cervero, 1996; Cervero & Kockelman, 1997). Aided by the increasing abundance of micro-level data that provide a rich empirical basis, the relationship between land use mix and transportation outcomes has received a flurry of attention over the last decade. Having higher mixes of land uses nearby has been positively related to frequency of trips by pedestrian and bicycle modes (Cervero, 1996; Greenwald & Boarnet, 2001; Handy, 1996; Khattak & Rodriguez, 2008; Kitamura et al., 1997) and negatively related to frequency of auto trips (Cervero & Kockelman, 1997). Discrete choice models of travel mode have also shown that high levels of land use mixing in one's home or work neighborhood are related to higher use of walking, bicycling and transit modes (Cervero, 1996; Srinivasan, 2002), although the effect size has been qualified as "fairly marginal" (Cervero & Kockelman, 1997) and "modest" (Cervero & Duncan, 2003). It is necessary to note that positive association between land use mix and use of public transportation is found when land use mix is measured as the proportion of residential area within 400 meters of a convenience retail store. Other measures of land use mix have failed to assert such positive associations between mix and transportation modes. In general, the results for alternative modes of transportation are less robust due to a limited number of studies. Shorter commuting distances (Cervero, 1996) and shorter commuting times (Ewing et al., 2003) have been positively related to mixed land uses. Evidence of associations between mixed land uses and auto ownership is less consistent, with Ewing et al. (2003) finding no relationship and others finding a negative relationship (Cervero, 1996; Hess & Ong, 2002).

Land Use Mix and Health Outcomes

For health-related disciplines, research on land use mix and walking and cycling began to appear in journals of health sciences (Frank et al., 2005; Moudon et al., 2007). This set of studies also focuses on walking and cycling with an emphasis on forms of physical activity. The emergence of ecologic models (Stokols, 1992) has underscored the levels at which multiple factors (personal, interpersonal, community, environment, and policy) can influence individual behavior and health outcomes. As a result, an expanded set of factors, such as neighborhood land use mix, are hypothesized to influence individual behavior (Sallis et al., 1997). As Garfinkel-Castro and Ewing (Chapter 12) point out, critical contemporary issues of public health—physical activity and obesity, traffic accidents, air quality, and mental health—are now recognized as systemically linked to the built environment.

Results have shown positive associations between land use mix and utilitarian walking (Duncan et al., 2010; Kerr et al., 2016). The results for leisure walking are less clear, probably due to the limited number of studies. Bicycling was positively associated with land use mix (Kerr et al., 2016; Van Dyck et al., 2012). For physical activities, the results are equivocal, although land use mixing has been positively associated with length of physical activity time (Cerin et al., 2018; Frank et al., 2005; Hoehner et al., 2005). The emerging evidence with respect to obesity is also equivocal, with studies finding conflicting associations (Frank et al., 2004; Rutt & Coleman, 2005). By contrast, the evidence regarding the relationship between physical activity and the mixing of residential and recreational land uses (such as parks and community centers) more consistently shows a positive association (Giles-Corti et al., 2005; Giles-Corti & Donovan, 2002a, 2002b).

Land Use Mix and Environmental Outcomes

Our review also searched for land use mix and environmental outcomes. In the discipline of landscape ecology, because land uses are intimately associated with ecological consequences, there is an interest in quantifying land uses and potential changes (O'Neill et al., 1988; Turner, 1990). Furthermore, environmental consequences often vary depending on the pattern of uses, the remaining habitat, and the size and proximity of disturbances to sensitive areas (Geoghegan et al., 1997). Thus, quantifying uses relative to each other, their pattern, is essential for monitoring and assessing ecological outcomes.

In this vein, studies have attempted to examine the relationship between land use mix, emissions, and air quality. In general, studies in this area are limited. Although some studies have found that mixed land uses are associated with higher level of emissions (Frank et al., 2000) and poorer air quality (Yuan & Song et al., 2017), others have detected an opposite, negative relationship, indicating mixed land uses are associated with lower levels of emissions and better air quality (Ewing et al., 2003).

Land Use Mix and Housing Market

I also reviewed studies on whether and how land use mixes relate to real estate property markets and individual preferences for housing types. The first assumption is that better land use mix increases the available facilities and public services around the properties, which should be reflected in higher housing prices (Song & Knaap, 2004). Several empirical studies have shown that measures of land use mix between residential and suitable commercial uses generally correlate with high residential land prices (Cervero & Duncan, 2004; Geoghegan et al., 1997; Song & Knaap, 2004).

The second assumption is that the increased interest in mixed-use developments in suburban areas is an indication of changing consumer preferences and the perceived success of these developments by real estate owners, developers, and governing agencies. Real estate developers, owners, and investors have thus asserted that the financial performance and success of mixed-use projects is better than single-use properties. However, in general there is very limited empirical evidence in academic journals to support or disprove this assertion. In related studies, land prices and the mix between residences and open space are generally positively related (Geoghegan, 2002; Irwin, 2002; Irwin & Bockstael, 2001).

Land Use Mix and Vibrancy Outcomes

Although advocates of mixed land uses claim the mix reinforces streets as vital places and instils urban vibrancy, empirical studies along these lines are very rare. Chen et al. (2020) is the only study to test variety and vibrancy. In their study, vibrancy is measured as the number of geo-tagged tweets per person by neighborhood. Variety is defined as a variety of distinct land uses and activities in close proximity to other distinct land uses, measured by the mix of employment types, because employment type relates to the type of land use and the intensity of land use. The study found that mixed land use is positively related to tweets, a proxy of vibrancy.

To summarize, empirical ambiguities remain regarding the relationship between land use mix and community and individual outcomes. The presence of mixed commercial and residential uses of land appears to support non-motorized modes of travel, longer physical activity time, and higher property values. By contrast, the evidence regarding land use mix and obesity and air quality is equivocal. In general, there is a lack of research on land use mix and urban vibrancy. Future studies examining the associations of land use mix with aspects of urban vitality should include true representations of street life and urban vitality.

Although the above summarized ambiguities exist in the relationship between land use mix and community and individual outcomes, there is sufficient evidence establishing land use mix and positive outcomes. In the next section, I turn to discussions on implementation tools for mixed land uses.

SUMMARY ON IMPLEMENTATION TOOLS OF MIXED LAND USES

With research results supporting the potential effects of land use mix in the promotion and sustainment of lively urban areas, the next important task is to inform and support public policies that create vibrant and enriching environments for daily life. In this section, we turn to a review of ways local governments can foster implementation of mixed-use developments, including comprehensive plans and regulatory tools.

Comprehensive Plans

A comprehensive plan is a legal document used by a local government to guide future land uses. It serves as the legal basis for further regulatory ordinances such as zoning, subdivision, and land use codes. I was interested in exploring the extent to which comprehensive plans around the nation have incorporated mixed land use designations. I first obtained about 46 plans for cities with a population greater than a quarter million; sampling was determined by availability of the comprehensive plans. The plans are presented in a variety of formats, and although the time spans covered by each varied, all plans are current at the time of this analysis. I then employed content analysis, a form of quantitative analysis, to systematically and objectively analyze "message" characteristics. In our inquiry, the texts of the comprehensive plans are the analyzed "messages." Each comprehensive plan was loaded into content analysis software as a separate primary document. The format of the comprehensive plans ranged from texts structured with paragraphs and complete sentences to simple bullet point lists. The unit of analysis in content analysis is an identifiable message component such as words, characters, and themes.

Results indicate that two main themes emerge with the "mixed use" code family: "mixed use districts" and "mixed land use designations." These two themes demonstrate the main approaches in the comprehensive plans to promote land use mix.

First, in their land use goals, some plans call for the creation of "mixed use districts." Examples of areas where this approach is applied include undeveloped areas, redeveloped areas, and primarily downtown commercial areas. In some cases, comprehensive plans recommend a change that designates a number of individual parcels as mixed use to provide flexibility so that the market can determine the best combination of uses for the land parcel development. Second, comprehensive plans recommend zoning code amendments to allow for "mixed land use designations." For example, some plans suggest that all residential districts and some commercial zones should be consistent with the "mixed use" designation so that these zones provide flexibility for mixing residential and commercial land uses. This mixed-use designation can be applied to parcels that have been approved for, or are developing as, mixed-use communities. I have observed a great emergence of cities incorporating mixed land use designations into their recently updated comprehensive plans.

Zoning and other Regulatory Tools

Local governments can foster mixed-use development by creating a more accommodating regulatory environment. Addressing regulatory barriers to mixed land use development is therefore a crucial step toward implementation of mixed land uses. Zoning codes, subdivision regulations, land development regulations, and fire and building codes can be re-examined to address regulatory barriers. In addition, permitting, financing, environmental, and political barriers to mixed-use development need to be evaluated and addressed.

In this review, I was mainly interested in knowing whether, for those cities with updated comprehensive plans to increase mixed land uses, their subsequent amendments to zoning ordinances reflect such land use values and goals. Once a jurisdiction updates its comprehensive plan to provide a vision for mixed-use development, the zoning code should be amended within a certain timeframe. I was able to collect about 17 city zoning documents and, using content analysis, investigate the extent to which these zoning ordinances have incorporated mixed land.

As an important mechanism for implementing a comprehensive plan, zoning is a legal device that specifies the types of land uses permitted; the intensity of development; the height, bulk, and placement of buildings; and other conditions deemed necessary to direct development. I was most interested in finding out how mixed-use zoning is accomplished. Several themes emerged from our content analysis of cities' zoning documents: modifying existing zoning district designations to allow mixed land uses, creating new districts specifically designated for mixed-use development, and adopting new zoning code provisions or enhancing existing zoning codes to allow for mixed uses.

Modifying existing zoning districts allows for, rather than requires, a mix (both vertically and on the ground) of commercial and residential uses. The intended physical pattern of mixed development is reminiscent of the design of main streets or downtowns of older cities. Local governments also adopt or amend zoning code provisions to allow for mixed-use development. For example, amended zoning codes might allow for a mix of commercial, residential, and institutional uses within different zoning districts, such as downtown areas, town centers, and commercial zones, with justifications such as reinforcing the historic character of walkable downtowns, strengthening connections between city centers and residential districts, and encouraging a mix of uses to promote walkability and economic vitality. For example, zoning language for a C-2 (downtown commercial) zone encourages a mixed-use pedestrian environment achieved through the use of sidewalks, street trees, public spaces, building massing, signage, land uses, traffic calming, and scale and location of parking, as well as a mix of both residential and nonresidential uses, which include a mix of specialty retail and personal and professional services for both residents and tourists.

In my review, I also found that some communities have turned to form-based codes (FBCs) as a way to regulate the built environment so that mixed uses and walkability are supported (see Talen, Chapter 7, for more on form-based codes). FBCs can be used as a modification or supplement to current Euclidean zoning practices. Geared toward achieving connected, vibrant, and walkable places that allow for a mix of uses, FBCs are a relatively new way of addressing community design and can be added to a city's municipal code using a variety of approaches (Russell, 2004): applying FBCs to a defined geographic area, adding FBCs to portions of zoning or related codes, and/or adopting new land development regulations for the entire municipality. As practitioners design FBCs, one major obstacle is current local zoning ordinances that prohibit both the desired mix of uses and more urban building types. To overcome this, FBCs have to work within the confines of a planned unit development (PUD) ordinance. The drawback of applying the FBCs within the PUD process is that it can be very repetitive, since a new code needs to be written for each new development. Cities can also draft the FBCs into the traditional neighborhood design (TND) or transit-oriented development (TOD) zones. These zones differ from PUDs and can be applied by communities in a wide array of development situations but are still used for specific area plans.

Given the importance of fostering mixed land uses with different planning and regulatory tools, it is startling to notice that there is a paucity of research that examines the efficacy of these tools. Whether these tools work to improve land use mix, and if so, what conditions are indispensable to adopt these tools, remains to be explored.

CONCLUSION

Both researchers and practitioners consider mixed-use development to be a way to rejuvenate communities by creating spaces where a cross-section of a community gathers to work, live, and shop. I reviewed three areas of research in this chapter: land use mix measures, land use mix outcomes of interest to planners and policymakers, and current policy instruments to promote land use mix.

For future research on mixed land uses, I offer the following recommendations. First, when choosing land use mix measures in designing studies on mixed land uses, it is desirable to adopt multiple measures in order to capture different aspects of the construct. When using measures to study associations with outcomes, controlling for regional composition of land uses provides necessary context for interpretation. Second, our review indicates that the presence of mixed uses appears to exhibit some positive individual and community outcomes. For example, mixed land uses support non-motorized modes of travel, longer physical activity time, and higher property values. More studies are warranted on the associations between land use mix and obesity, air quality, and urban vibrancy. Evidently, there is still a vast need for research to establish associations between land use mix and an array of outcomes. Third, future studies need to examine whether these tools are effectively implementing land use mix, and if so, what conditions are indispensable to adopt these policy and regulatory tools.

Although the concept of mixed land uses is in direct contrast to the urban planning paradigms that have dominated for the past century, whereby residential areas are separated from other land uses, planning mixed neighborhoods has gained momentum in recent years with the smart growth regime. The most desired mixed land uses at the neighborhood level include goods and services such as groceries; fresh food and healthcare; mixed housing types of different sizes and levels of affordability; green spaces for everyone to enjoy and for better air quality; and smaller-scale offices and co-working spaces for more people to work close to home. It is necessary to note that since 2020, more cities have been embracing mixed land uses to support a stronger recovery from COVID-19 and foster a more local, healthy, and resilient way of life.

To nurture mixed land uses, planning strategies need to be tailored to a community's culture and circumstances and to respond to specific local needs. First, establishing a comprehensive vision or goal of mixed land uses sets out an essential foundation for subsequent implementation policies and actions. Next, updating the city's zoning and regulations to require properly served uses such as green and open spaces, schools, small healthcare facilities, and essential retail is necessary. At urban core locations, updating zoning codes to promote vertical mixed uses at ground level will help provide spaces for community services. At established suburban locations, encouraging the flexible use of buildings and public space will help neighborhoods retrofit much-needed community services. Mixed uses for buildings, public spaces, and infrastructure can be established at different times of the day and week to serve multiple purposes.

In conclusion, the land use mix, which helps develop both social and functional mix, becomes more relevant than ever as cities work to be more resilient. Such mixing will help to provide more local services, inject vibrancy into local streets, reduce unnecessary long trips, promote health and wellbeing, boost resilience in the face of health and climate shocks, and improve livability.

NOTES

1. Measurement:

$$A_i = \sum_j f(d_{ij})$$

where

A_i = integral accessibility of residential land use (e.g., households or neighborhoods) i to another given non-residential land use (e.g., non-residential land parcels or activity centres) j,

d_{ij} = distance, travel time, or travel cost from residential use i to non-residential use j,

$f(d_{ij})$ = impedance function. The most widely used impedance functions are the inverse power function $(d_{ij} - \beta)$, a negative exponential function $(e - \beta d_{ij})$, or a modified Gaussian function ($(\exp(d_{ij}^2/v))$).

2. The entropy index (Shannon Index) is commonly calculated through the following formula:

$$Entropy = \{-\Sigma_k[(p_i)(\ln p_i)]\} / (\ln k)$$

Examples include:

Measurement 1(E_1): To explore the distribution pattern of households and employment within a neighborhood, the index is implemented in such as way: p_i = population of total land use activities in category i (where the i categories are households, retail employment, office employment, and other employment); and k = 4 (number of land use categories).

Measurement 2(E_2): To examine the distribution pattern of different land uses within a neighborhood, the index spells out that p_i = proportions of each of the six land use types such as single family residential, multi-family residential, commercial, industrial, public institutional and park uses, and s = the number of land uses. In this case, k = 6 (Song & Knaap, 2004).

REFERENCES

Calthorpe, P. (1993). *The next American metropolis: Ecology, community, and the American dream*, New York, NY: Princeton Architectural Press.
Centers for Disease Control and Prevention (2005). *Active community environments*. Retrieved from http://www.cdc.gov/nccdphp/dnpa/aces.htm

Cerin, E., Conway, T. L., Adams, M. A., Barnett, A., Cain, K. L., Owen, N., & Christiansen, L. B. (2018). Objectively-assessed neighbourhood destination accessibility and physical activity in adults from 10 countries: An analysis of moderators and perceptions as mediators. *Social Science & Medicine, 211*(August), 282–293.

Cervero, R. (1996). Mixed land uses and commuting: Evidence from the American Housing Survey. *Transportation Research A, 30*(5), 361–377.

Cervero, R. & Duncan, M. (2003). Walking, bicycling, and urban landscapes: Evidence from the San Francisco Bay area. *American Journal of Public Health, 93*(9), 1478–1483.

Cervero, R. & Duncan, M. (2004). Neighbourhood composition and residential land prices: Does exclusion raise or lower values? *Urban Studies, 41*(2), 299–315.

Cervero, R. & Kockelman, K. (1997). Travel demand and the 3Ds: Density, diversity and design. *Transportation Research D, 2*(3), 199–219.

Chen, Y., Song, Y., & Li, C. (2020). Where do people tweet? The relationship of the built environment to tweeting in Chicago. *Sustainable Cities and Society, 52* (January), 101817.

Congress for the New Urbanism. (1996). *The charter for the new urbanism.* https://www.cnu .org/who-we-are/charter-new-urbanism

Congress for the New Urbanism. (2000). Charter of the new urbanism. *Bulletin of Science, Technology & Society, 20*(4), 339–341.

Downs, A. (2005). Smart growth: Why we discuss it more than we do it. *Journal of the American Planning Association, 71*(4), 367–378.

Duncan, M. J., Winkler, E., Sugiyama, T., Cerin, E., duToit, L., Leslie, E., & Owen, N. (2010). Relationships of land use mix with walking for transport: Do land uses and geographical scale matter? *Journal of Urban Health, 87*(5), 782–795.

Ewing, R. & Cervero, R. (2010). Travel and the built environment. *Journal of the American Planning Association, 76*(3), 265–94.

Ewing, R., Pendall, R., & Chen, D. (2003). Measuring sprawl and its transportation impacts. *Transportation Research Record, 1831*, 175–183.

Frank, L. D., Andresen, M. A., & Schmid, T. L. (2004). Obesity relationships with community design, physical activity, and time spent in cars. *American Journal of Preventive Medicine, 27*(2), 87–96.

Frank, L. D., Schmid, T. L., Sallis, J. F., Chapman, J., & Saelens, B. E. (2005). Linking objectively measured physical activity with objectively measured urban form. *American Journal of Preventive Medicine, 28*(2S2), 117–125.

Frank, L. D., Stone, B., & Bachman, W. (2000). Linking land use with household vehicle emissions in the central Puget Sound: Methodological framework and findings. *Transportation Research Part D: Transport and Environment, 5D*(3), 173–196.

Geoghegan, J. (2002). The value of open spaces in residential land use. *Land Use Policy, 19*(1), 91–98.

Geoghegan, J., Wainger, L.A., & Bockstael, N. E. (1997). Spatial landscape indices in a hedonic framework: An ecological economics analysis using GIS. *Ecological Economics, 23*(3), 251–264.

Giles-Corti, B., Broomhall, M. H., Knuiman, M., Collins, C., Douglas, K., Ng, K., Lange, A., & Donovan, R. J. (2005). Increasing walking: How important is distance to, attractiveness, and size of public open space? *American Journal of Preventive Medicine, 28*(2), Supplement 2, 169–176.

Giles-Corti, B. & Donovan, R. J. (2002a). The relative influence of individual, social and physical environment determinants of physical activity. *Social Science & Medicine, 54*(12), 1793–1812.

Giles-Corti, B. & Donovan, R. J. (2002b). Socioeconomic status differences in recreational physical activity levels and real and perceived access to a supportive physical environment. *Preventive Medicine, 35*(6), 601–611.

Greenwald, M. J. & Boarnet, M. G. (2001). Built environment as determinant of walking behaviour: Analyzing nonwork pedestrian travel in Portland, Oregon. *Transportation Research Record, 1780*, 33–42.

Handy, S. L. (1996). Urban form and pedestrian choices: Study of Austin neighborhoods. *Transportation Research Record, 1552*, 135–144.

Hess, D. B. & Ong, P. M. (2002). Traditional neighborhoods and automobile ownership. *Transportation Research Record, 1805*, 35–44.

Hoehner, C. M., Ramirez, L. K., Elliott, M. B., Handy, S. L., & Brownson, R.C. (2005). Perceived and objective environmental measures and physical activity among urban adults. *American Journal of Preventive Medicine, 28*(2), Supplement 2, 105–116.

Im, H. N. & Choi, C. G. (2019). Measuring pedestrian volume by land use mix: Presenting a new entropy-based index by weighting walking generation units. *Environment and Planning, B, Urban Analytics and City Science*, 2399808318824112.

Irwin, E. G. (2002). The effects of open space on residential property values. *Land Economics, 78*(4), 465–480.

Irwin, E. G. & Bockstael, N. E. (2001). The problem of identifying land use spillovers: Measuring the effects of open space on residential property values. *American Journal of Agricultural Economics, 83*(3), 698–704.

Jacobs, J. (1961). *The death and life of great American cities*. Random House, New York.

Kerr, J., Emond, J. A., Badland, H., Reis, R., Sarmiento, O., Carlson, J., & Sallis, J. F. (2016). Perceived neighborhood environmental attributes associated with walking and cycling for transport among adult residents of 17 cities in 12 countries: The IPEN study. *Environmental Health Perspectives, 124*(3), 290–98.

Khattak, A. & Rodriguez, D. (2008). Travel behaviour in neo-traditional developments: A case study from the U.S.A. *Transportation Research A, Policy and Practice, 39*(6), 481–500.

Kitamura, R., Laidet, L, & Mokhtarian, P. (1997). A micro-analysis of land use and travel in five neighbourhoods in the San Francisco Bay area. *Transportation, 24*, 125–158.

Krizek, K. J. (2003). Operationalizing neighborhood accessibility for land use-travel behavior research and regional modeling. *Journal of Planning Education and Research, 22*(3), 270–287.

Manaugh, K. & Kreider, T. (2013). What is mixed use? Presenting an interaction method for measuring land use mix. *Journal of Transport and Land Use, 6*(1), 63–72.

Massey, D. S. & Denton, N. A. (1988). The dimension of residential segregation. *Social Forces, 67*, 281–315.

McNally, M. G. & Kulkarni, A. (1997). Assessment of influence of land use–transportation system on travel behavior. *Transportation Research Record, 1607*(1), 105–115.

Moudon, A. V., Lee, C., Cheadle, A. D., Garvin, C., Johnson, D. B., Schmid, T. L., & Weathers, R. D. (2007). Attributes of environments supporting walking. *American Journal of Health Promotion, 21*(5), 448–459.

O'Neill, R. V., Krummel, J. R., Gardner, R. H., Sugihara, G., Jackson, B., DeAngelis, D. L., Mime, B. T., Turner, M. G., Zygmut, B., Christensen, S., Dale, V. H. & Graham, R. L. (1988). Indices of landscape pattern. *Landscape Ecology, 1*(3), 153–162.

Pivo, G. (2005). *Creating compact and complete communities: Seven propositions for success*. Case Study. American Institute of Certified Planners. http://www.u.arizona.edu/~gpivo/Practicing%20Planner%20Pub.pdf

Russell, J. (2004). New Urbanist Essentials, Chapter 1 of codifying new urbanism: How to reform municipal land use regulations, *Planning Advisory Service, 526*. Washington, DC: American Planning Association.

Rutt, C. D. & Coleman, K. J. (2005). Examining the relationships among built environment, physical activity, and body mass index in El Paso, TX. *Preventive Medicine, 40*(6), 831–841.

Sallis, J., Johnson, M., Calfas, K., Caparosa, S., & Nichols, J. (1997). Assessing perceived physical environmental variables that may influence physical activity. *Research Quarterly for Exercise and Sport, 68*(4), 345–351.

Shen, Q. (1998). Location characteristics of inner-city neighborhoods and employment accessibility of low-income workers. *Environment and Planning B, 25,* 345–365.

Song, Y. & Knaap, G.-J. (2004). Measuring the effects of mixed land uses on housing values. *Regional Science and Urban Economics, 34*(6), 663–680.

Song, Y. & Sohn, J. (2007). Valuing spatial accessibility to retailing: A case study of the single family housing market in Hillsboro, Oregon. *Journal of Retailing and Consumer Service, 14*(4), 279–288.

Song, Y., Merlin, L., & Rodriguez, D. (2013). The measurement of land use mix: A review and simulation. *Computers, Environment and Urban Systems, 42,* 1–13.

Srinivasan, S. (2002). Quantifying spatial characteristics of cities. *Urban Studies, 39*(11), 2005–2028.

Stokols, D. (1992). Establishing and maintaining healthy environments: Toward a social ecology of health promotion. *American Psychologist, 47*(1), 6–22.

Turner, M. G. (1990). Spatial and temporal analysis of landscape patterns. *Landscape Ecology, 4*(1), 21–30.

Turner, M. G., Gardner, R. H., & O'Neill, R. V. (2001). *Landscape ecology in theory and practice: Pattern and process.* New York: Springer Verlag.

Van Dyck, D., Cerin, E., Conway, T. L., De Bourdeaudhuij, I., Owen, N., Kerr, J., Cardon, G., Frank, L. D., Saelens, B. E., & Sallis, J. F. (2012). Perceived neighborhood environmental attributes associated with adults' transport-related walking and cycling: Findings from the USA, Australia and Belgium. *International Journal of Behavioral Nutrition and Physical Activity, 9*(1), 70.

Weibull, J. W. (1976). An axiomatic approach to the measurement of accessibility. *Regional Science and Urban Economics, 6,* 357–379.

Yuan, M., Song, Y., Huang, Y., Hong, S., & Huang, L. (2017). Exploring the association between urban form and air quality in China. *Journal of Planning Education and Research, 38*(4), 1–14.

Yue, H. & Zhu, X. (2019). Exploring the relationship between urban vitality and street centrality based on social network review data in Wuhan, China. *Sustainability, 11*(16), 4356.

7. The urban design requirements of smart growth

Emily Talen

INTRODUCTION

To some urban designers, smart growth might seem like an exercise in urban pattern manipulation from 30,000 feet up. To some smart growth proponents, urban design might seem like a mere detail, far removed from the weightier concerns of transportation investment or affordable housing policy. In truth, urban design and smart growth are interconnected parts of a sustainable whole—without a close integration, urban design interventions lack context; smart growth policies lack tangibility. The link between urban design and smart growth might be masked by socioeconomic analysis, the rules of bureaucracies, and land use regulation, but many of the elements and forces under the banner of smart growth have profound design consequences—and urban design decisions have a profound impact on our ability to grow smartly.

This chapter lays out the urban design side of the urban design-smart growth nexus, where the smart growth principle of fostering distinctive, attractive communities with a strong sense of place translates, in both practical and normative terms, to the fostering of walkable, compact, diverse neighborhoods. I first review the well-accepted normative principles that are meant to achieve such places, followed by a brief discussion of the importance of nuancing principles by locational context, and the need to consider design process. I next review one of the most important implementation strategies for achieving good urban design—form-based coding. Finally, I summarize the evidence that urban design principles conducive to smart growth offer tangible benefits.

Urban design is about engaging with the physical, material side of cities in a pro-active way—i.e., imagining and seeking to implement alternatives to the urban status quo. Urban design is a normative form of physical planning—"the grounded, tangible, place-bound matter of orchestrating human activity on the land" (Campanella, 2011). "Doing" urban design means trying to shape cities and their component parts in ways that meet social, economic, environmental, or aesthetic objectives. These component parts might be blocks, streets and corridors, public spaces, neighborhoods or districts. Urban design is also about innovation, where innovation means reusing and sustaining what's working and valued, and repurposing what isn't.

It is important to note that urban design can mean a lot of different things and have different motivations. Various strands represent different goals—socialization, excitement, profit, crime reduction, civic pride, health. Urban design might prioritize equalizing access and ensuring closer proximities between people and services, or the primary goal might be to create a "successful" human environment, which often means enhancing the visual, aesthetic experience. Some urban designers are more concerned with the generative processes that create successful environments and "organic wholeness" (Alexander et al., 1987, p. 234) as opposed to prescriptions for end-state forms. Sometimes urban design prioritizes social connection and sense of community. Others are committed to the urban design requirements of sustainability. While all of these design motivations—equality, imageability, vitality, organic wholeness, community, sustainability—factor into smart growth, below I summarize a specific set of normative goals that I believe are most germane to smart growth objectives.

NORMATIVE PRINCIPLES

A number of goals might be attached to designing—or improving the design of—urban places and spaces. Goals might be objective and specific, such as slowing down car traffic, or more subjective and perceptual, like improving "quality of life" or reducing social alienation. It is helpful to think about urban design for smart growth in a normative way—i.e., the health of blocks, neighborhoods, and cities as social units, where the purely aesthetic qualities of streets, open spaces and buildings—although important—are secondary (Talen, 2018). Proposals to connect two spaces, insert a public park, route a path in a certain direction, focus attention on a particular intersection—all of these are supported by an underlying social logic focused on creating healthy neighborhoods and communities. Ideally, an engaged constituency, enabled through a well-crafted planning and design process, comes together to formulate a collective vision, i.e., a physical plan for neighborhood improvement. The end goal is a neighborhood that functions well, accommodates different types of people, promotes a sense of caring about place, and ultimately provides a supportive and inspiring public realm.

Urban design needs to simultaneously support social, environmental, and economic purposes *before* it serves artistic inspiration. In this way, urban design that focuses on helping neighborhoods become better places to live may be much more about instilling time-honored regularities than searching for ways to employ novelty. Design for smart growth is meant to support diverse, sustainable, vibrant, and equitable communities; as such, it is the kind of design that values the common good and the public realm ahead of the bottom line.

Urban design is employed at different scales. At the largest scale, urban design for smart growth means designing entire neighborhoods—the building blocks of the urban pattern. One purpose might be to delineate a set of neighborhoods for a given area. Even if people conduct their lives far outside of a given neighborhood, what happens within local contexts is meaningful. Establishing an overall neighborhood structure is important to urban design because it helps determine what people living in different kinds of neighborhoods have access to in their daily lives. As an ideal, neighborhood structure is based on the walking distance between where people live and the goods and services they need on a daily basis.

From an urban design point of view, the concept of neighborhood has generally varied along three dimensions: size/shape, function, and morphology. Size implies both area (acreage) as well as distance and shape: whether there is a center or an edge, and whether the neighborhood is structured as a circle, square, or polygon. Function has to do with the activities and land uses within the neighborhood. Ideally, the neighborhood is mixed in use, including uses and facilities that serve the everyday life of neighborhood residents: shops, schools, and various types of institutions that serve a local clientele. Morphology refers to the pattern of streets, blocks, lots, and buildings. Such patterns can have a significant effect on neighborhood quality, character, and functionality.

Another large-scale urban design concept relevant to smart growth is connectivity. For smart growth, the idea is generally that more connectivity is better (Hajrasouliha & Yin, 2015). Cities and neighborhoods that maximize connections between people and things are thought to be more vibrant and healthy. Strategies for increasing connectivity are based on the view that the built environment has an effect on constraining or promoting passive contact, an essential aspect of neighborhood-level social interaction (Gehl, 1987). Interaction at this scale is a pedestrian phenomenon dependent on street networks and the social connections that happen as a result of them. Connectivity occurs at multiple scales: regional connections via major transportation routes, neighborhood-level connection via streets and greenways, and block and lot connections via pathways. Connection can involve a linear route or a central place.

At the neighborhood scale, urban design for smart growth may involve centers, edges, mix, and proximity. Neighborhood centers are "centers" in the sense that they provide a common, centrally located destination for surrounding residents. They are a physical articulation of "community"—a tangible, permanent symbol of the common bond that people living in the same neighborhood share. The neighborhood center provides a place for spontaneous interaction, which, potentially, fosters a sense of social connection. In addition, centers may, over time, promote a sense of shared responsibility. Urban design grapples with what centers should consist of, how they should function, and what should be around them.

Edges, like transportation corridors or large parcels, are either non-permeable (acting as barricades and separators) or permeable (acting as seams). Some edges composed of functional space, like commercial areas, have a better chance of serving the function of seam rather than barrier. Urban design strategies might involve integrating either side along an edge, perhaps looking for opportunities to articulate openings and design functional and deliberate pathways that connect to an edge.

In a sprawling suburban world dominated by distance and single use, the need to increase mix (of both land uses as well as people) and proximity (by decreasing the distances between things) are essential urban design strategies. Smart growth aims for neighborhoods that are socially and economically diverse—mixed in income, mixed in use, and actively supportive of places that commingle people of different races, ethnicities, genders, ages, occupations, and households. Urban design for smart growth seeks to foster a close-grained diversity of uses that provides mutual support (Jacobs, 1961).

How might urban design play a role in helping to make neighborhood diversity viable? The list of possible strategies includes: demonstrating how multifamily units can be accommodated in single-family blocks; fostering the necessary linkages between diverse land uses and diverse housing types; creating paths through edges that often disrupt connectivity in highly diverse places; increasing density near public transit in a way that doesn't undermine neighborhood character; demonstrating the value of nonstandard unit types such as courtyard housing, closes, and residential mews; fitting in small businesses and live/work units in neighborhoods that are otherwise entirely residential; fashioning regulatory codes capable of creating a successful land-use mix; softening the impact of big box development in under-invested commercial strips; designing streets that function as collective spaces; and connecting institutions to their surrounding residential fabric. In these ways, urban design addresses the basic requirements of human integration, including the fears that arise from uncomfortable proximities, and the often contentious fitting together of wide-ranging uses. Design is needed not to smooth out every potential conflict, but to help make diversity livable, and even preferable.

Urban design for smart growth is also about decreasing the distances between where people live and work and the goods and services they require for a high quality of life. This is essentially about increasing access, which is a longstanding component of theories about good urban form (see in particular Lynch, 1981, and Jacobs & Appleyard, 1987). Proximity (or access) to facilities, goods, and services is what differentiates urban sprawl from compact city form: development patterns that are low density and scattered necessarily diminish accessibility because facilities tend to be far apart and land uses are segregated.

Other recurrent issues in urban design that are especially relevant to smart growth include density, parking, and traffic. Such issues can be turned into assets rather than problems by applying good design principles. For example, density, if designed right, can be regarded as a community asset. The negative effects of car storage (parking) can also be mitigated (to some extent) with good urban design strategies. And traffic calming design techniques can be used to transform anti-pedestrian corridors into public realm assets.

In all of these ways, urban design for smart growth seeks to mitigate the problem of disconnected, automobile-dependent, environmentally degrading, single-use development. It seeks to change places with a low-quality, poorly conceived public realm into walkable, diverse neighborhoods.

Nuancing Urban Design Principles via the Transect

An essential concept in urban design for smart growth is that urban design principles and strategies (as outlined above) are not meant to be applied in a "one size fits all" manner. Design principles need to be articulated differently depending on the particulars of place.

One useful concept for thinking through this range of articulation is the rural-to-urban transect, an analytical method that organizes the elements of urbanism—building, lot, land use, street, and all of the other physical aspects of the human habitat—in ways that preserve the integrity of different types of urban and rural environments (see Duany & Talen, 2002). These environments vary along a continuum that ranges from less intensity (rural) to high intensity (urban). The idea is that within a transect zone, the various elements of the built environment fit together and cohere. The very definition of sprawl—anti-smart growth—is that urban elements do not cohere well at all. Instead, urban elements are inappropriately located in places at the more rural end of the spectrum, while urban cores are often inappropriately burdened with rural elements.

The transect should be viewed as a way of applying a set of core principles of good urban design to a range of human habitats. The idea that human environments should be walkable, pedestrian-oriented, diverse, and promoting of public space is intrinsic to each type of environment along the transect—but the articulation is different depending on context. This directly addresses the criticism that urban design principles, especially when labeled "new urbanism," are a "one size fits all" approach.

The transect seeks to create an experience of immersion in any type of environment. This is achieved by specifying and arranging the elements that comprise a given environment in a way that is true to locational character—that is, in ways that are expected, given the nature of the place. For example, a farmhouse would not be expected and therefore would not contribute to the immersive quality of an urban core. A high-rise apartment building would not be expected, nor would it contribute to, the immersive quality of a rural environment. Immersive rural environments might consist of wide streets and open swales, while immersive urban environments might consist of formal boulevards and public squares. Based on local vernacular traditions, most elements of the human habitat can be similarly appropriated in such a way that they contribute to, rather than detract from, the immersive character of a given environment.

To aid in the specification of different types of immersive environments, the rural-to-urban continuum is segmented into discrete categories, providing a basis for delineating a range of human habitats that can be coded much like conventional zoning. The translation has mostly been successfully accomplished via form-based coding, the dominant basis of zoning code reform. Not every form-based code is based on transect theory—but most are. A model transect code, known as the "SmartCode," was released in 2003. The code segments the rural-to-urban continuum into discrete categories, and local calibration is used to further specify the urban design qualities of each transect category or zone.[1]

The Urban Design Process

Urban design is never only about end-state blueprints. It also involves a process for getting there. As Herbert Simon (1988, p. 67) observed, "everyone designs who devises courses of action aimed at changing existing situations into preferred ones."

In fact, the design of the process for achieving urban design goals is at least as important as the design of the end state.

One process-oriented approach to urban design is to think about the underlying decision-making that generates certain types of environments. Christopher Alexander has promoted the idea that there are generative "laws" to be discovered that are capable of producing an organic wholeness—cities with "organic, personal, and human character" (Alexander et al., 1987, p. 234). That organic quality defines their success. According to Alexander's theory, growth should be piecemeal, where every increment of building contributes to a larger whole. Rules for incremental change are likely to accommodate finely grained urbanism, as opposed to singularly conceived, monolithic, and segregated urbanism.

Another concept that emphasizes the process of urban design rather than the end product of urban design is placemaking. Placemaking has been described as a user-generated process aimed at enhancing meaning and livability, whereby urban designers facilitate, but residents are the ones "engaged directly in the production of meaningful place" (Cilliers & Timmermans, 2014, p. 414). Whether viewed as the image of the city (Lynch, 1960), the city as a set of sequences (Cullen, 1961), or the idea of instilling "permanence, locus, individuality and memory" (Gosling, 2003, p. 22), placemaking is about promoting exchange, activity, liveliness, happiness and a positive, culturally meaningful experience. Kevin Lynch's (1981) work is an important part of the lineage, as his emphasis on performance criteria such as imageability and legibility are concepts that often factor into placemaking.

As a resident-generated, participatory design approach, placemaking emphasizes the creation of alternatives. Being process-oriented means that there is more than one way of looking at a problem, with more than one solution. It also means that there is value in the process itself—residents coming together, building community, raising awareness of local place-based initiatives, and working together to develop consensus. Creative placemaking, a related term, emphasizes arts and culture in place production (Redaelli, 2018). The focus might be to provide some visual coherence, some framework for making sense of the urban realm, usually by activating a vacant lot, an under-utilized commercial street, or an abandoned building. Cultural sensitivity, whereby place activation pays attention to unique cultural histories and interpretations, is elevated.

IMPLEMENTATION

At some point, urban design principles—ideas, plans and concepts that may or may not have been generated through a placemaking process—require implementation. Implementing urban design principles is achieved by making appropriate investments in public infrastructure (e.g., street calming measures), or by ensuring that the rules that guide private development are supportive of key objectives. The latter involves designing the "operating system" for urban development—i.e., codes and the myriad rules, standards, laws, and incentives needed to achieve ends.

Arguably, the most impactful rules are zoning codes. Conventional zoning has been derided for decades for failing to promote good urban design—and smart growth. Zoning rules create localized effects that, in aggregate, present a significant barrier to the ability of cities to foster places that are walkable, mixed in use, and well-connected.

What traditional zoning does, specifically, that is counter to the promotion of quality urban places can be summarized as follows. First, it promotes a random and disorganized pattern of land use. Over time, zones are modified to fit unique conditions and owner requests, and the pattern of residential zones—especially its relationship to commercial zones—does not follow any particular spatial relationship. Areas might develop as a hodge-podge collection of building types and uses, from corporate office towers to single-family homes.

Second, there has been a gradual expansion of zoning's requirements in terms of unit and lot dimensions. Rules in support of compact development (as opposed to sprawl) would put a maximum—not a minimum—limit on lot size and unit size. Conventional zoning requires the opposite, where low density is ensured through minimum unit size, minimum lot size per unit, and minimum street frontage per unit (thus making units behind the main structure infeasible). In addition, frontyard setbacks eliminate the possibility of additional units on a lot, sideyard requirements eliminate the possibility of rowhouses and duplexes, and sometimes rules require that each unit must have a separate driveway.

Third, it promotes single-use subdivisions—a situation so obviously counter to smart growth that some cities have revised their zoning requirements to eliminate single-family zoning entirely (Kahlenberg, 2019). However, in most areas, zoning still vigorously blocks the mixing of housing types. The most common rules include only one family per lot; no single-family attached housing allowed; all lots must have street frontage, which means bungalow courts, mews, or courtyard housing are prohibited; duplexes on corner lots are not allowed; no density increases on lots adjacent to commercial zones are allowed; and no transitional zones or midblock zoning district lines are allowed, which would rationalize higher densities in locations closer to services.

Finally, zoning plays a role in limiting the degree to which open space can be spatially defined, therefore limiting the ability to create "enclosure"—an essential aspect of walkable streets and compact urban form. Generous setback rules guarantee weak intersections with no spatial definition, and thus no opportunity to create the "outdoor room."

The good news is that there is a significant and growing movement to reform zoning. Mostly this reform is achieved by way of the form-based code (FBC) (Garde & Kim, 2017). FBCs emerged in the 1980s as a way to counter sprawl and implement better design, defined by proponents as codes that "use physical form, rather than separation of land uses, as their organizing principle. They foster predictable results in the built environment and a high quality public realm" (www.formbasedcodes .org). The Governor of Maryland, Parris Glendening, was an early advocate, and held a conference in 1999 on the theme of rehabilitating codes and proposing a "smart growth model ordinance." Since then, FBCs have taken on their own complexity, where cities now merge FBCs with priority areas or overlay zones or create hybrid zones that have some form-based emphasis mixed in with conventional use-based coding.

Because of these variations, it has been difficult to track the progress of form-based coding. The codes may be optional overlays, floating zones, district regulations, or FBC-type requirements that are appended to existing design standards. The codes may by project-specific and apply only to a station area, a central business district, or section of street, or they may apply to a neighborhood, a section of town, or an entire city or region. They may be hybrid codes, in which form-based coding requirements are added to a conventional zoning code.

Despite these complications, it is important to understand how form-based codes help promote good urban design (Talen, 2013). First, FBCs try to reinstate a meaningful spatial pattern of zones either by varying regulations based on locational intensity (transect based codes), or by connecting zones directly to a plan—something most conventional zoning ordinances fail to do. Second, FBCs usually incorporate smaller dimensions than conventional codes. These requirements are keyed to location, where smaller unit sizes, street widths, and lot area requirements are associated with zones "closer in"— i.e., in more urbanized locations. Third, FBCs address homogeneity by aiming for a much greater diversity of land uses within a smaller number of zones. Fourth, FBCs seek to promote connectivity—and therefore mitigate separation—by limiting parking requirements, limiting curb cuts, allowing shared driveways, and requiring that streets, paths, and routes intersect rather than dead-end. Codes might require (rather than suggest) through-block connections, coordinated bike routes, pedestrian crossings, and allowances for future street extensions. Finally, enclosure is a primary concern of form-based coding. FBCs address enclosure by reinstating building lines, prohibiting blank walls and requiring permeability, requiring narrower street widths and shorter turner radii, and regulating public and private frontage. There could be a requirement that garages be set back farther than a house, and that parcels not turn their sides to a main street.

In short, FBCs use zoning to require good urban design. While there are many varieties of FBCs, optimally, they promote compact urban form that encourages pedestrian activity and minimizes environmental degradation. They also encourage social, economic and land use diversity as opposed to homogeneity, connect uses and functions, and promote a quality public realm that provides opportunities for interaction and exchange. FBCs can promote equitable access to goods, services, and facilities. In all of these ways, FBCs advance the key urban design requirements of smart growth (see Song, Chapter 6 for more on FBCs and mixed land uses).

MEASURING THE VALUE OF GOOD URBAN DESIGN

To many planners and urban designers, the advantages of designing cities that are walkable, compact, and diverse seem obvious. But the principles that define good urban design are also grounded in measurable empirical conditions. Of particular interest is research that evaluates how residents who live in places with good urban design are affected. Such places would have services within walking distance of residents, a pedestrian orientation that minimizes car dependence, and a level of density and land use diversity that is higher than low-density suburban areas without these qualities. While not exactly the same as the design parameters outlined above, we can use the measurable conditions of being compact, walkable, and diverse as useful proxies of good design. Research that links compact, walkable, and diverse neighborhoods to their effects on residents has tended to coalesce around three main topics: social relations, health, and safety (Talen & Koschinsky, 2014). Clifton (Chapter 9) further details the research on walkability effects.

To begin with, social relations in compact neighborhoods have been found to foster social interaction, sense of community, and feelings of identity. At the finest scale, William Whyte observed that residents of "ambiguously oriented buildings" tended to be more socially disconnected (Hallman, 1959, p.124). The relationship between density and social interaction is admittedly complicated, however, as studies have shown that density benefits reach certain thresholds or require certain design specifics. For example, Amick and Kviz (1975) found that social interaction was greatly improved in public housing where it consisted of low-rise buildings with high site coverage, as opposed to high-rise buildings with low site coverage.

At the neighborhood scale, a large number of studies have sought to determine the environmental factors associated with social interaction and affective feelings about neighborhood. That resident interaction is affected by spatial organization was advanced by Chicago School sociologists in the 1920s, who observed that contact is maintained by environmental characteristics and ecological explanations, including housing type, density and land use mix (Park et al., 1925). The associations between physical characteristics of neighborhoods and levels of neighboring continue to attract scholarly interest (e.g., Wilkerson et al., 2012; Cabrera & Najarian, 2015).

Comparisons between sustainable neighborhoods (compact, walkable, diverse) and conventional (car-dependent and homogeneous) neighborhoods often find that the former has higher rates of social interaction, sense of community, and stronger place attachment. Urban design can have an effect on constraining or promoting passive contact, and social interaction may ultimately be tied to the amount of passive contact that takes place, especially in sustainable neighborhoods where sidewalks are a prominent feature (Podobnik, 2011). Wood et al. (2010) surveyed residents in Atlanta to find a positive association between sense of community and walkable street design, using the ratio of commercial floor space to land area as a proxy. Some researchers have shown an association between sustainable neighborhoods and higher levels of trust and social engagement (Brown & Cropper, 2001; Leyden, 2003).

Researchers have utilized Robert Putnam's social capital scale (2007) to show the link between the sustainable neighborhood and "higher levels of social capital such as trust among neighbors and participation in community events" (Rogers et al., 2010). Well-designed public space has been shown to have positive effects on social interaction, especially in mixed-income areas (Roberts, 2007). Users tend to utilize public space most often if they can walk to it, i.e., if it is within 3–5 minutes walking distance from their residence or workplace (Kaplan & Kaplan, 1989). Wilkerson et al. (2012) investigated the effect of a number of neighborhood qualities such as sidewalks and graffiti on neighborliness and found a positive link—even when socio-demographics were controlled for—from greater utilization of public space and from greater use of local facilities for shopping. Others have found that the impact of urban design on social cohesion is even higher in high-disadvantaged neighborhoods (Bjornstrom & Ralston, 2014).

Related to these positive outcomes, compact, walkable, diverse neighborhoods are thought to improve health, as Garfinkel-Castro and Ewing discuss further in Chapter 12. A lot of research supports the view that well-designed—i.e., walkable— neighborhoods are likely to result in lower car use; walking is impacted by land use diversity, density, destinations, and intersection design (Ewing & Cervero, 2010). Studies have homed in on specific design features that encourage walking, such as pedestrian-oriented streets and a "well-maintained walking surface" (Pikora et al., 2006). Aspects of the built environment that are "modifiable in the short term," such as access to transit, sidewalks, and car parking availability (Rodríguez et al., 2008, p. 260) have also been shown to impact the degree to which people are willing to walk (Forsyth et al., 2008). Other studies look at specific populations, for example the ability of urban form to influence children walking to school (McMillan, 2005), generally finding that urban form such as intersection density (positively associ-ated) and number of dead-end streets (negatively associated) predict travel mode (Schlossberg et al., 2006). Studies of the effect of urban design on how people travel tend to debate the strength of association: how much compactness and diversity of land use are important for reducing car trips, not *whether* compactness and diversity are important factors. For more on urban design and travel behaviors see Clifton (Chapter 9) and Welch and Gehrke (Chapter 10).

Finally, good urban design can impact safety by (a) making thoroughfares safer for both drivers and pedestrians; and (b) promoting compact urban form, which activates street activity and therefore provides a buffer against crime. See Garfinkel-Castro and Ewing (Chapter 12) for more on urban design and public safety. The linkage between neighborhood design and safety draws from the writings of Jane Jacobs (1961). The basic idea is that active streets with lots of pedestrians encourage "natural surveillance" because residents are more inclined to look out the window. Jacobs introduced the notion of "eyes on the street" (1961), public–private space delineation (supporting unambiguous functionality), and active streets as public safety strategies (Heffernan et al., 2014). Security is also increased by activating "dead" space—unclaimed land for which clear ownership is ambiguous. Jacobs was drawing on evidence that housing that was walled off and abruptly insular, like public housing on superblocks, was unsafe because it did not allow a direct opening or connection to the surrounding neighborhood.

These effects—social interaction, health, and safety—are interconnected. For example, safety is one of the most important variables impacting walking (Alfonzo et al., 2008), and therefore potentially health. Further, an increase in feelings of safety in well-designed neighborhoods has long been believed to have a positive effect on neighboring (Newman, 1972). Social diversity defined by mixed income has been shown to increase feelings of safety among low-income residents who were previously living in concentrated poverty (Briggs et al., 2010).

THE SOCIAL LIMITS OF URBAN DESIGN

Evaluating the worth of urban design principles through a quantitative lens, where the focus is on the measurement of things such as walkability, health, and safety, is one kind of approach to validating the normative urban design principles laid out earlier. But another approach to validation rests on the conceptual argument, especially in relation to social goals. In this vein, one could argue that the principles that define good urban design are based on a historically-rooted understanding of the American settlement experience, in which case urban design principles are rooted in time-honored cultural practices about good city-making. It is a perspective backed by critical writing about the urban experience, with the most recent iterations falling under the headings of smart growth, sustainable development, and new urbanism (e.g., Kunstler, 1996).

But against stated ideals, it has always been necessary to control the temptation to expect too much of a well-designed place. Taken too far, the implementation of urban design principles can seem like an effort to engineer and control society. On the one hand, urban design does impact social and political forms of organization through the design of public spaces, or social equity through the spatial arrangement of public facilities, or social encounters through the design of sidewalks. These connections may seem intuitive, but urban design has to find the right balance in stating its value, contextualizing and nuancing the extent of its impact.

We can take the especially perplexing case of attempting to link physical design to social goals such as "community," "equity," and the "common good," to illustrate the nuances required. The goals of creating a sense of community, fostering social equity, and advancing the "common good" are distinct, and all have been connected to good urban design principles as espoused by new urbanists and smart growth advocates. But the first goal has been especially problematic. One complication is that sense of community can have a *social* component, consisting of various types of social interaction, and an *affective* component, involving a whole range of psychological and emotional responses. Connecting these components to physical design is complicated and sometimes ambiguous, especially since attempts to "build" community through physical design have been linked to social homogeneity and exclusion. However, specific site designs, such as better and more accessible public space, may promote some aspect of social interaction, and social interaction may eventually lead to some dimension of community. Along the way, there are likely to be interactions with other variables and indirect effects that are beyond the control of the urban designer.

Relatively speaking, equity may be a more realistic social goal to achieve via design because it does not depend, as community does, on building social relationships. As it relates to principles of urban design, social equity can be defined in a straightforward way: as the equalization of access to resources. (See Lung-Amam and June-Friesen, Chapter 14, for a broader discussion of equity and planning.) Under this definition, social equity can be directly tied to urban design since design can be said to determine distance and location, and therefore access. Further, three interrelated principles of good urban design impact access: compactness, housing unit mix, and non-car-based transportation. Specifically, urban environments organized around the "5-minute walk" promote accessibility to public goods, services, and facilities because such goods are more likely to be within reach of non-automobile users. There is a recognition that the effect of distance greatly increases for those who do not own a car (i.e., children, the elderly who can no longer drive, and the poor who cannot afford to own a car). Compactness also makes public transit more feasible, and public transit has an effect on accessibility, especially for those who do not drive. A balanced mix of uses (e.g., housing, shopping, work, recreation) within the same neighborhood also improves access by minimizing distances between daily activities. Mixed housing unit types foster diversity and potentially greater equitability of access to resources. Equity is also linked to good urban design when streets are engineered to provide not only for automobiles, but equally for pedestrians and bicycles.

Although not as straightforward as equity, good urban design can be said to support the "common good" as well. One way is the valuation of existing resources, involving, for example, the protection of the environment, preservation of farmland, and historic preservation. The common good might also be linked to the promotion of place-based identity, where good placemaking sustains meaning for inhabitants. Place-based commonality is vital because such an identity promotes a sense of sharing of and belonging to that place, which in turn reinforces commitment, caring, and ownership. And commonality based on place may be an effective antidote to the tendency to seek commonality via social homogeneity. Centrally located public spaces that have been consciously designed and placed for the benefit of local residents contribute to establishing place identity—that is, in fact, their main purpose. Ad hoc focal points and quasi-public spaces do a much less effective job because they are not designed for the purpose of establishing place identity.

In these ways the principles of good urban design can legitimately claim to foster social goals—but limited to spatial equity and place-based notions of the common good rather than feelings about community that require a greater depth of social relationship.

PROGRESS TO DATE

Recognition of the importance of good urban design seemed tangential in the twentieth century, when car-based development in the form of housing subdivisions and shopping malls proliferated and support for investment in urban neighborhoods declined. Whatever recognition there was of the importance of pedestrian-based design had to fight against a suite of anti-smart growth conditions: rising automobile use, expendable income, highway-building, tax subsidies, accelerated depreciation, cheap land, Real Estate Investment Trusts (REITs), conventional zoning and sub-division regulations, production building, and social intolerance. All of these and more created a context in which good urban design—walkability, pedestrianism, compactness, diversity—was lost sight of. The result is that American cities have an urban design problem, with tangible consequences for the American built landscape.

While it seems that these problems are now widely recognized, it is difficult to say whether progress has been made in the effort to build more walkable, compact, diverse neighborhoods. In 2015 we found that only 4 percent of neighborhoods in suburban areas had walk scores of 70 or higher, and only 18 percent of cities and suburbs combined had 70+ walk scores (Koschinsky & Talen, 2015). While walk score is an imperfect measure, the implication of this is that it is highly likely that the majority of Americans live or work in places that are the opposite of well-designed urbanism.

Progress, however, can be found in terms of the shift in cultural understanding and attitude that seems to have occurred. There seems to be widespread agreement that poorly designed cities—sprawl—are a problem, and that there is a need for better design (e.g., Krieger, 2019). Planners and their constituents seem attuned to the important role that design plays in achieving a range of social, environmental, economic, and quality of life goals. There is agreement that we need to reduce energy consumption, "live local," promote walkable access, and build in ways that support transit and other public investments by compacting rather than spreading development. Compact, walkable, diverse urbanism fundamentally conflicts with the scale, pattern, and consumption that accompanies sprawl, mandating a radically different approach to human settlement.

This change in mindset, in turn, is fueling regulatory change—i.e., zoning reform. Smart growth proponents and new urbanists have been particularly vocal about the effect of rules on the built environment, drawing the attention of planners to codes and how they affect urban pattern and form (Hansen, 2014).[2] As of 2019, there were 728 codes, mostly in the United States, that met criteria established by the Form-Based Codes Institute (FBCI), and more than half had been adopted.[3] Whether termed a "form-based code" or not, the emphasis on form, pattern and mixed use pervades all code reform efforts of the last two decades. There are traditional neighborhood development ordinances, mixed-use and live/work codes, TOD ordinances, transit area codes, transect-based codes, smart growth codes, sustainable codes, transit-supportive codes, urbanist codes, and green building codes of various stripes. Groups such as the US Green Building Council (http://www.usgbc.org/) are trying to reform existing codes to be more "sustainable," which, in terms of regulating the built environment, essentially means the elevation of form and pattern over use as a guiding principle. Looking forward, it is the reform of zoning codes that seems to offer the greatest hope for success in promoting good urban design.

CONCLUSION

There are certain tensions involved in the effort to advance good urban design for the achievement of smart growth. One is the potential conflict between normative views of what good urban design is versus open-ended concepts that might prioritize a different sets of ideals. This tension is coming to light under current urban design efforts related to responses to the Covid-19 pandemic and addressing the needs of historically disadvantaged communities.

On certain principles, there is widespread agreement. For example, there is an urgent need to stop harmful infrastructure such as highways running through Black communities. There is also agreement that we need to end exclusionary zoning practices and increase funding for affordable housing, especially in well-served, walkable neighborhoods. Another aspect of urban design with widespread agreement is that meaningful community engagement is essential in any effort to improve design quality. There might even be agreement that investments in the public realm should include long-term anti-displacement and equitable distribution plans, or that public and private investments should be mitigated if they impact affordability.

But on other matters there may be less agreement. Should some activities that impact the public realm prioritize historically disadvantaged or Black communities? Should there be an effort to prioritize investments in neighborhood transit networks over commuter routes that run through Black communities and degrade neighborhood connectivity? And should public realm investment, such as pedestrian upgrades, be undertaken at all when there are more urgent matters of health and safety to attend to?

In the years ahead, many communities will grapple with the degree to which basic social services such as medical care and schools should be funded *before* funding upgrades to the public realm called for by advocates of good urban design. And increasingly, urban design intervention that in a previous era might have been viewed as positive or, at worst, innocuous, will be viewed negatively if it has the effect of increasing inequality.

With increasing understanding that the benefits of well-designed cities and neighborhoods need to be equally shared, this aspiration will continue to be a major challenge as municipalities struggle to find their footing post-Covid-19. Whether these benefits are equitably shared will have a direct bearing on how urban design in a smart growth context is assessed. In some sense, there will be even more attention paid to the fact that affordability in well-designed neighborhoods goes against the basic principles of land economics in the United States. If a neighborhood is walkable and amenity-rich (i.e., well serviced by stores, transit, and schools), demand for such places will quickly escalate housing costs. The laws of supply and demand, together with weak affordable housing subsidies, have ensured a lack of sufficient price point diversity in well-designed places.

Over the past decade, the problem this creates has been playing out dramatically in US cities. There are constant battles over gentrification and displacement, pitting pro-development forces against neighborhood preservationists, "YIMBYs" vs. "NIMBYs." For urban designers working to promote smart growth, this does not mean giving up on the need for good design. But it does mean that good design should not turn a blind eye to its exclusionary effect. The obvious solutions are to grow the supply of walkable, well-designed places, while at the same time adopting mechanisms (such as subsidies) that help a broader segment of the population gain access to quality design.

NOTES

1. Detailed information on the Transect is available on the Center for Applied Transect Studies website: http://www.transect.org/; Full documentation of the SmartCode is available at http://www.smartcodecentral.com.
2. Three publications have documented the rise of form-based codes specifically: *Smart Growth Zoning Codes: A Resource Guide* (Tracy, 2004), *Codifying New Urbanism: How to Reform Municipal Land Development Regulations* (CNU, 2004), and *Form-Based Codes: A Guide for Planners, Urban Designers, Municipalities, and Developers* (Parolek et al., 2008). Morris' *Smart Codes* (2009) documents the way in which codes can be used to implement the goals of smart growth, often by way of a more form-based approach.
3. For details on form-based code progress, see http://www.placemakers.com/how-we -teach/codes-study/.

REFERENCES

Alexander, C., Neis, H., Anninou, A., & King, I. (1987). *A new theory of urban design*. New York: Oxford University Press.

Alfonzo, M., Boarnet, M. G., Day, K., Mcmillan, T., & Anderson, C. L. (2008). The relationship of neighbourhood built environment features and adult parents' walking. *Journal of Urban Design, 13*(1), 29–51. doi:10.1080/13574800701803456

Amick, D. J., & Kviz, F. J. (1975). Social alienation in public housing, *Ekistics, 231*, 118–120.

Bjornstrom, E., & Ralston, M. (2014). Neighborhood built environment, perceived danger, and perceived social cohesion, *Environment and Behavior, 46*(6), 718–744.

Briggs, X. S., Popkin, S. J., & Goering, J. (2010). *Moving to opportunity: The story of an American experiment to fight ghetto poverty*. New York: Oxford University Press.

Brown, B. B., & Cropper, V. L. (2001). New urban and standard suburban subdivisions: Evaluating psychological and social goals. *Journal of the American Planning Association, 67*(4), 402–419. doi:10.1080/01944360108976249

Cabrera, J. F., & Najarian, J. C. (2015). How the built environment shapes spatial bridging ties and social capital. *Environment and Behavior, 47*(3), 239–267. https://doi.org/10.1177/0013916513500275

Campanella, T. (2011). Jane Jacobs and the death and life of American planning. In Page, M. & Mennel, T. (Eds), *Reconsidering Jane Jacobs*. Chicago: Planners Press.

Cilliers, E. J., & Timmermans, W. (2014). The importance of creative participatory planning in the public place-making process. *Environment and Planning B: Planning and Design, 41*(3), 413–429. https://doi.org/10.1068/b39098

Congress for the New Urbanism (CNU). (2004). *Codifying new urbanism: How to reform municipal land development regulations* [Planning advisory service report 526]. American Planning Association.

Cullen, G. (1961). *The concise townscape*. New York: Van Nostrand Reinhold.

Duany, A., & Talen, E. (2002). Transect planning. *Journal of the American Planning Association, 68*(3), 245–266.

Ewing, R., & Cervero, R. (2010). Travel and the built environment. *Journal of the American Planning Association, 76*(3), 265–294. doi:10.1080/01944361003766766

Forsyth, A., Hearst, M., Oakes, J. M., & Schmitz, K. H. (2008). Design and destinations: Factors influencing walking and total physical activity. *Urban Studies, 45*(9), 1973–1996.

Garde, A., & Kim, C. (2017). Form-based codes for zoning reform to promote sustainable development: Insights from cities in Southern California. *Journal of the American Planning Association, 83*(4), 346–364. https://doi.org/10.1080/01944363.2017.1364974

Gehl, J. (1987). *Life between buildings: Using public space.* New York: Van Nostrand Reinhold.

Gosling, D., (2003). *The evolution of American urban design.* West Sussex, UK: Wiley-Academy.

Hajrasouliha, A., & Yin, L. (2015). The impact of street network connectivity on pedestrian volume. *Urban Studies, 52*(13), 2483–2497. https://doi.org/10.1177/0042098014544763

Hallman, H. W. (1959). Citizens and professionals reconsider the neighborhood. *Journal of the American Institute of Planners, 25*(3), 121–127. doi:10.1080/01944365908978319

Hansen, G. H. (2014). Design for healthy communities: The potential of form-based codes to create walkable urban streets. *Journal of Urban Design, 19*(2), 151–170.

Heffernan, E., Heffernan, T., & Pan, W. (2014). The relationship between the quality of active frontages and public perceptions of public spaces. *Urban Design International, 19*(1), 92–102. https://doi.org/10.1057/udi.2013.16

Jacobs, A., & Appleyard, D. (1987). Toward an urban design manifesto. *Journal of the American Planning Association, 53*(1), 112–120.

Jacobs, J. (1961). *The death and life of great American cities.* New York: Vintage Books.

Kahlenberg, R. D. (2019). How Minneapolis ended single-family zoning [Weblog post]. Retrieved from https://tcf.org/content/report/minneapolis-ended-single-family-zoning/

Kaplan, R., & Kaplan, S. (1989). *Experience of nature: A psychological perspective.* New York: Cambridge University Press.

Koschinsky, J., & Talen. E. (2015). From sprawl to walkable: How far is that? In Talen, E. (Ed.), *Fixing sprawl: Addressing seventy years of failed urban form*, Athens, GA: The University of Georgia Press.

Krieger, A. (2019). *City on a hill: Urban idealism in America from the Puritans to the present.* Cambridge, MA: Belknap Press.

Kunstler, J. H. (1996). *Home from nowhere: Remaking our everyday world for the twenty-first century.* New York: Simon & Schuster.

Leyden, K. M. (2003). Social capital and the built environment: The importance of walkable neighborhoods. *American Journal of Public Health, 93*(9), 1546–1551.

Lynch, K. (1960). *The image of the city.* Cambridge, MA: MIT Press.

Lynch, K. (1981). *Good city form.* Cambridge, MA: MIT Press.

McMillan, T. E. (2005). Urban form and a child's trip to school: The current literature and a framework for future research. *Journal of Planning Literature, 19*(4), 440–456. doi:10.1177/0885412204274173

Morris, M. (2009). *Smart codes: Model land-development regulations* [Planning advisory service report 556]. American Planning Association.

Newman, O. (1972). *Defensible space: Crime prevention through urban design.* New York: Collier Books.

Park, R. E., Burgess, E. W., & McKenzie, R. D. (1925). *The city.* Chicago: University of Chicago Press.

Parolek, D. G., Parolek, K., & Crawford, P. C. (2008). *Form-based codes: A guide for planners, urban designers, municipalities, and developers.* J. Wiley & Sons.

Pikora, T. J., Giles-Corti, B., Knuiman, M. W., Bull, F. C., Jamrozik, K., & Donovan, R. O. B. J. (2006). Neighborhood environmental factors correlated with walking near home: Using SPACES. *Medicine and Science in Sports and Exercise*, 38, 708–714. doi:10.1249/01.mss .0000210189.64458.t3

Podobnik, B. (2011). Assessing the social and environmental achievements of new urbanism: Evidence from Portland, Oregon. *Journal of Urbanism: International Research on Placemaking and Urban Sustainability*, 4(2), 105–126. doi:10.1080/17549175.2011 .596271

Putnam, R. D., (2007) E pluribus unum: Diversity and community in the twenty-first century. The 2006 Johan Skytte Prize Lecture. *Scandinavian Political Studies*, 30(2), 137–174.

Redaelli, E. (2018). Creative placemaking and theories of art: Analyzing a place-based NEA policy in Portland, OR. *Cities*, 72(1), 403–410. doi:10.1016/j.cities.2017.10.001

Roberts, M. (2007). Sharing space: Urban design and social mixing in mixed income new communities. *Planning Theory and Practice*, 8(2), 183–204.

Rodríguez, D. A., Aytur, S., Forsyth, A., Oakes, J. M., & Clifton, K. J. (2008). Relation of modifiable neighborhood attributes to walking. *Preventive Medicine*, 47(3), 260–264. doi: 10.1016/j.ypmed.2008.02.028

Rogers, S. H., Halstead, J. M., Gardner, K. H., & Carlson, C. H. (2010). Examining walkability and social capital as indicators of quality of life at the municipal and neighborhood scales. *Applied Research in Quality of Life*, 6(2), 201–213.

Schlossberg, M., Greene, J., Paulsen Phillips, P., Johnson, B., & Parker, B. (2006). School trips: Effects of urban form and distance on travel mode. *Journal of the American Planning Association*, 72(3), 337–346.

Simon, H. A. (1988). The science of design: Creating the artificial. *Design Issues*, 4(1/2), 67–82. https://doi.org/10.2307/1511391

Talen, E. (2013). Zoning for and against sprawl: The case for form-based codes. *Journal of Urban Design*, 18(2), 175–200.

Talen, E. (2018). *Urban design for planners: Tools, techniques and strategies*. Los Angeles: Planetizen Press.

Talen, E., & Koschinsky, J. (2014). Compact, walkable, diverse neighborhoods: Assessing effects on residents. *Housing Policy Debate*, 24(4), 717–750. https://doi.org/10.1080/ 10511482.2014.900102

Tracy, S. (2004). *Smart growth zoning codes: A resource guide*. Local Government Commission.

Wilkerson, A., Carlson, N. E., Yen, I. H., & Michael, Y. L. (2012). Neighborhood physical features and relationships with neighbors: Does positive physical environment increase neighborliness? *Environment and Behavior*, 44(5), 595–615.

Wood L., Frank L. D., & Giles-Corti B. (2010). Sense of community and its relationship with walking and neighborhood design. *Social Science & Medicine*, 70(9), 1381–1390.

8.   Smart growth and housing choice
Casey Dawkins and Jinyhup Kim

INTRODUCTION

Since the early 1990s, smart growth advocates have proposed various land use policy reforms designed to expand housing choice. These reforms come in two flavors. Urban growth boundaries, urban service areas, open space rural zoning, and other *extra-urban* reforms are designed to expand the diversity of urban housing options by shifting housing production from rural to urban areas. Mixed-use zoning, density bonuses, allowances for non-traditional housing types, and other *intra-urban* reforms are designed to relax regulatory restrictions on high-density affordable housing production within urban areas. Both of these reforms seek to expand housing choice by encouraging urban housing options that are more affordable and more diverse by tenure and type.

This chapter reviews recent empirical evidence to assess what is known about the effects of smart growth reforms on housing choice. We begin by exploring the Smart Growth Network's "third principle" of smart growth, which encapsulates the dual aims of promoting housing affordability and enhancing the diversity of housing choices. We operationalize the third principle and examine its embodiment in smart growth policy reforms. Following this introductory discussion, we examine recent evidence linking smart growth policy reforms to housing affordability and housing diversity. The chapter concludes with a discussion of the lessons learned from the research reviewed.

THE THIRD PRINCIPLE OF SMART GROWTH

In 1991, a coalition of urban designers and planners met in the Ahwahnee Hotel in Yosemite National Park to draft one of the early manifestos of smart growth (Landis, 2019). Among the adopted "Ahwahnee Principles" was the statement that "[a] community should contain a diversity of housing types to enable citizens from a wide range of economic levels and age groups to live within its boundaries" (https://www.lgc.org/who-we-are/ahwahnee/principles/). Five years later, the Environmental Protection Agency (EPA) created a partnership of government, business, and civic organizations known as the Smart Growth Network (SGN) to promulgate a similar set of principles. The goal to "[c]reate a range of housing opportunities and choices" was the third principle on the SGN list. Smart Growth America (SGA), an advocacy organization that promotes the adoption of smart growth principles and practices, later adopted this and other SGN principles verbatim (https://smartgrowthamerica .org/our-vision/what-is-smart-growth/).

What does it mean to "expand housing choice?"[1] This aim can be interpreted as a manifestation of the traditional housing policy goal of promoting housing affordability if expanded choice is meant to imply an overall decline in the quality-adjusted price or rent of housing or an increase in the supply of homes affordable to those earning low incomes.[2] Smart growth advocates often supplement this traditional understanding of housing choice with an emphasis on expanding the diversity of housing options by tenure and type. The goal of housing diversity also raises the question of the geographic segregation of housing choices. Housing options may be diverse citywide but homogeneous within neighborhoods if housing options are geographically segregated. If housing options are diverse but segregated, the degree of choice among bundles of housing and neighborhood attributes is more constrained, because fewer neighborhoods provide affordable housing options, particularly if neighborhood amenities and local public goods are funded through local ad valorem taxes that are capitalized into housing prices. Taken together, the third principle can be interpreted in terms of the overarching goal of promoting housing that is more affordable and more diverse at the scale of individual neighborhoods.

To promote the expansion of housing choice, smart growth advocates have tended to emphasize supply-side regulatory reforms over other traditional housing policy tools such as public housing, public subsidies for private sector housing, demand-side rental housing vouchers, or tenant legal protections. The smart growth movement's orientation toward supply-side regulatory reforms can be partially explained by the movement's historical evolution. Many of the policies advanced by smart growth advocates are extensions or modifications of the same regulatory tools that planners have used for generations to shape the location and character of urban development. Smart growth's grandfather, the growth control, was adopted during the 1970s in places such as Petaluma, California, and Ramapo, New York, to limit the amount of growth or link the timing of growth with the provision of infrastructure and services. In response to the criticism that these first-generation growth controls inflated housing prices by constraining housing supply, growth controls and similar policies were rebranded during the 1980s as "growth management" policies. Whereas 1970s-era growth controls often directly limited housing supply without the support of countervailing measures designed to relieve housing price pressures, most growth management policies attempted to mitigate housing price inflation by buttressing growth policy instruments with enhanced comprehensive planning, supported by housing demand projections. As the growth management movement evolved during its third wave into the smart growth movement during the 1990s, advocates called for regulatory reforms designed to promote rather than limit the supply of affordable housing, often collaborating with regionalists and social equity advocates to align smart growth principles with the broader agenda of "equitable" and "fair" growth.

Smart growth advocates emphasize two types of supply-side regulatory reforms. *Extra-urban reforms* include those designed to expand housing choice within urban areas by restricting urban development outside a defined boundary. Extra-urban reforms, often described as "urban containment" policies, include urban growth boundaries, urban service areas, and open-space zoning within rural areas. (See Carruthers, Wei, and Wostenholme, Chapter 3, for more on urban containment, and Hanlon, Chapter 5, for more on infill and redevelopment.) *Intra-urban reforms* include a wide range of zoning and regulatory reforms that are designed to promote a wider range of housing types and styles within urban areas than is normally allowed under traditional single-use, single-family zoning. Examples of intra-urban reforms include reductions in large-lot zoning requirements; allowances for high-density and multi-family housing (particularly near transit and existing developed areas); allowances for smaller non-traditional housing types such as accessory units, efficiency apartments, and manufactured housing; reductions in off-street parking requirements; and inclusionary affordable housing incentives or requirements (Gabbe, 2019). Evidence provided by Pendall et al. (2006) suggests that the adoption of many recent intra-urban reforms coincided with the rise of the smart growth movement. In their nationwide survey of land use practices in the United States, the authors found that between 1994 and 2003, about 10 percent of the local governments surveyed increased maximum residential densities by more than 10 percent.

Although housing policy goals have been elevated to a central platform of the smart growth movement, it remains an open question whether the supply-side instruments of smart growth are the most effective, efficient, and equitable means of expanding housing choice. It is possible that different regulatory reform strategies influence housing choices in very different ways. Whereas most intra-urban reforms are designed to alleviate certain pre-existing regulatory restrictions on housing supply, extra-urban reforms often impose new regulatory constraints on suburban and rural housing supply. Another question is the magnitude of the housing market impact of regulatory reforms and the possible unintended consequences of transitioning from one regulatory regime to another. Critics of supply-side regulatory reforms claim either that regulatory reforms do not go far enough, or worse, they contribute to gentrification and the displacement of low-income households by enabling luxury housing construction within previously supply-constrained areas (Been et al., 2019). In Chapter 13 of this volume, Finio and Knaap discuss how smart growth development approaches may contribute to gentrification.

Preliminary evidence on the third principle of smart growth suggests that the rise of the smart growth movement has not coincided with a nationwide expansion of housing choice. As demonstrated in Table 8.1, the US housing stock has become less diverse and less affordable since the early 1990s, when the smart growth movement first gained momentum. Although homeownership rates have largely tracked the macroeconomic housing cycle, the supply of larger single-family homes has increased since 1990. Housing cost burdens have also risen, particularly for renters. These aggregate trends are revealing but do not provide a full picture of the housing market impacts of smart growth reforms. The next two sections examine recent empirical evidence linking smart growth policy reforms to housing affordability and housing diversity, emphasizing recent studies and those that advance our understand-

Table 8.1   *Selected housing choice indicators, 1980–2019*

Year	% owner-occupied	% single-family detached	% <=1 bedroom	% cost-burdened owners*	% cost-burdened renters*
1980	65.6	63.7	16.4	n/a	n/a
1991	64.2	59.9	15.3	n/a	n/a
2001 (2000 for cost burden)	68.0	61.6	13.2	21.8	34.8
2011 (2010 for cost burden)	66.2	62.7	12.3	28.8	46.0
2019 (2017 for cost burden)	64.0	62.6	12.6	22.5	46.0

Source: American Housing Survey, HUD CHAS (2000, 2010, 2017)
Note: * "% Cost-burdened" refers to the percentage of households spending 30 percent or more of household income on housing costs

ing of the nature and magnitude of the impacts of smart growth regulatory reforms on housing markets.

REGULATORY TAX REFORM AND HOUSING AFFORDABILITY

Most empirical research on the third principle of smart growth examines the link between restrictive land use practices and housing production and/or prices. Unfortunately, few studies have examined the long-term housing market impacts of comprehensive land use reforms designed to alleviate regulatory barriers to housing production. This is partly due to the fact that outside of the recent zoning reforms in Oregon and Minneapolis, comprehensive land use reforms are rare. Since most land use reforms increase rather than decrease the restrictiveness of the local regulatory environment, empirical studies instead tend to take an indirect counterfactual approach, inferring the likely impacts of land use reforms from studies linking regulatory restrictiveness to housing outcomes. One challenge with this strategy is that land use regulations are heterogeneous and cannot be easily categorized along a single dimension such as "regulatory restrictiveness."

Glaeser et al. (2005) propose a novel approach that gets around this problem. The authors calculated the gap between the price of housing and the marginal cost of constructing an additional unit and interpreted this as an estimate of the "regulatory tax" on housing supply. The authors found that the regulatory tax varies substantially across US housing markets, from zero in Birmingham, Detroit, and Houston to 50 percent or more of the house price in constrained markets such as New York and San Francisco. A more recent study that also controls for the effect of land use restrictions on housing demand for a larger number of areas found that land use regulations increase housing costs by about 15 percentage points on average (Albouy & Ehrlich, 2018). Gyourko et al. (2013) reported evidence which suggests that housing supply became more constrained beginning in the 1970s, the decade when residential growth control policies first appeared in many coastal housing markets. Prior to the 1970s, high house prices were accompanied by high levels of residential construction, compared with the post-1970 period, when the opposite trend was observed.

Another approach is to assume that regulatory constraints mimic the effect of binding geographic constraints on the supply of buildable land. Saiz (2010) relied on GIS data to compute natural geographic land supply constraints, defined as the presence of water bodies and slopes in excess of 15 percent, and found that natural land supply constraints inflate housing prices directly by constraining buildable land and indirectly by reducing the responsiveness (elasticity) of housing supply to demand shocks. Saiz (2010) also found that even though regulations have a smaller effect on housing supply elasticity than geographic constraints, geographically constrained areas are more likely to adopt restrictive regulations, which implies that housing supply is doubly constrained in areas where buildable land is scarce.

It is tempting to conclude from the evidence presented by Glaeser et al. (2005) and Saiz (2010) that if land use regulations in the Bay Area were immediately overturned, housing would drop to half its current price, but this is not necessarily true. Even if zoning and other forms of land use regulation constrain housing supply, it is not clear how housing producers would immediately respond to regulatory reforms. Differences between prices and construction costs may persist in the short term if housing supply is slow to adjust to changes in housing demand (Gyourko & Molloy, 2015). Freemark (2020) found that not only does housing supply not adjust in the short term, residential land prices immediately increase following the relaxation of land use restrictions.

Methodological problems also limit our ability to draw definitive policy conclusions from empirical estimates of regulatory tax reform. Existing studies often fail to precisely characterize the local regulatory environment while ignoring its jurisdictional context, employ methods that are incapable of identifying the causal relationship between regulations and housing prices, or ignore the dynamic housing market impacts of regulations. Below, we examine recent studies that attempt to disentangle each of these complexities.

Quantifying Land Use Regulations

Several studies attempt to quantify the actual regulatory environment facing housing producers. A common approach is to rely on composite measures of regulatory restrictiveness such as the Wharton Residential Land Use Regulation Index, which is constructed from 11 different dimensions of the local regulatory environment. This index is described in Gyourko et al. (2008). Others rely on simpler additive measures equal to the sum of the number of land use restrictions in a given jurisdiction (see for example Pollakowski & Wachter, 1990; Levine, 1999; Quigley & Raphael, 2005; Ihlenfeldt, 2007).

One limitation of the composite or aggregate index approach is that housing market agents respond to different types of regulations in different ways. For example, the imposition of a limit on housing construction is a straightforward constraint on new housing supply, but the impact of a new zoning ordinance is more complex because supply constraints may be binding in some submarkets but not others. Furthermore, the housing price effects of submarket constraints depend on the price elasticity of demand for housing within submarkets. Extra-urban policy reforms, which differentiate land supplied for urban versus rural uses, impose an additional supply constraint, the effects of which interact with the constraints imposed by zoning within the contained urban area. It is often difficult to measure regulations in a way that accurately reflects this complexity.

One strategy is to focus on changes in housing outcomes before and after the imposition of a regulation whose restrictions can be exhaustively quantified. McMillen and McDonald (2002) and Zhou et al. (2008) adopted a version of this approach, examining land prices before and after initial adoption and subsequent comprehensive amendment of Chicago's zoning ordinance. McMillen and McDonald (2002) found that Chicago's 1923 hierarchical residential zoning categories increased the value of residentially zoned land relative to commercially zoned land, because residential landowners valued the insurance against future negative externalities. Zhou et al. (2008) found that these effects changed with the adoption of a 1957 amendment that replaced hierarchical zoning with exclusive-use zoning categories. Although the 1957 zoning amendment reduced commercial land owners' option to change land use in the future, the value of land on the border of residential zones jumped following the amendment, because commercial landowners valued the insurance that neighboring properties would not transition to conflicting commercial uses. These findings suggest that intra-urban reforms are likely to affect land and housing prices in complex ways, with the prices of individual residential parcels reflecting the combined influence of the additional uses permitted on owned and adjacent parcels.

A variation on this approach is to exploit cross-sectional variation in housing prices within jurisdictions that have adopted policies hypothesized to have clear spatial impacts. Empirical studies of urban growth boundaries (UGBs) and other extra-urban reforms often adopt a variation on this approach. While several studies have found that land prices are higher inside than outside of UGBs due to constraints on the supply of developable land, higher land prices do not always equate to higher housing prices (Jun, 2006). In a comprehensive review of the housing market effects of growth management policies, Nelson et al. (2002) concluded that UGBs may not inflate housing prices if enough land is provided within the UGB to accommodate population growth. Studies also confirm that the housing price effects of UGBs vary according to the presence or absence of other regulations affecting housing production inside the UGB. For example, Mathur (2014, 2019) found that housing prices are lower inside than outside the King County, Washington, UGB because King County has adopted a variety of complementary zoning and infrastructure provision policies that expand housing supply inside the UGB. (See Chapter 3 for more discussion of urban growth boundaries.)

Another approach is to conduct an exhaustive study of the local regulatory environment within a single metropolitan housing market to identify how regulatory variation influences spatial variation in housing market outcomes. Glaeser et al. (2006b) adopted this approach. The authors assembled a detailed database of zoning codes, subdivision requirements, and environmental regulations governing land use in 187 communities in eastern and central Massachusetts. Precise measures of the local regulatory environment allowed the researchers to draw conclusions that are often not discernable by studies that characterize regulations using additive or composite indices. For example, the authors found that intra-urban reforms that increase the stringency of zoning reduce the level of new housing construction, while intra-urban reforms such as cluster zoning that reduce the stringency of zoning restrictions have a positive impact on new construction. The authors also found that voluntary inclusionary zoning programs that grant density bonuses in exchange for the provision of affordable housing have a large positive impact on housing supply, but the effect is only weakly statistically significant.

Supply versus Demand and Endogenous Land Use Regulations

A lingering question is how to interpret the effects of smart growth policy reforms on housing prices. More restrictive communities may exhibit higher housing prices either because regulations increase the cost of producing housing (a supply-side effect) or because regulations create valued urban amenities for which housing consumers are willing to pay (a demand-side effect). For example, Levine et al. (2005) found that many housing consumers value more dense residential environments, yet in regions such as Atlanta, Georgia, which prohibit such environments through land use restrictions, there is a wedge between housing consumers' stated residential preferences and their actual residential preferences. Smart growth policies respond to this latent demand for density, and housing prices are likely to rise when density is "legalized," because consumers are willing to pay for it. Smart growth reforms may also improve local quality of life by preserving the local property tax base and providing public goods and services more efficiently. Although studies that have quantified the social welfare benefits of land use regulations are rare, Albouy and Ehrlich (2018) concluded that the few studies examining these effects tend to report small social welfare benefits of regulations.

Researchers have adopted a range of strategies to address the joint influence of supply and demand on housing prices. Some turn their attention to housing supply measures, which unambiguously identify whether price increases are associated with an increase or decrease in the quantity of housing units produced. Studies employing this approach tend to conclude that restrictive land use regulations increase housing costs primarily by reducing the number of new housing units constructed (see for example Levine, 1999; Mayer & Somerville, 2000, Pendall, 2000). Another approach is to examine the differential effect of regulations on housing and land prices. If regulations influence housing prices primarily by raising developers' costs and restricting housing supply, this cost should be passed backward to landowners, who would be unable to command a high price for land in more restrictive markets. Ihlanfeldt (2007) employed this approach and found that restrictive land use regulations increase housing prices while reducing land prices.

Others rely on instrumental variables (IV) methods to disentangle the supply-side from demand-side effect of regulations on housing prices. This method relies on variables that are correlated with the explanatory variable (land use regulation) but not correlated with the outcome variable (housing prices) to isolate the causal effect of land use regulations on housing prices. Lin and Wachter (2019) rely on this approach and find that the supply-side regulatory impact on housing prices is much stronger than demand-side amenity effects (4.38 percent versus 0.32 percent of housing prices) in Californian cities that have adopted restrictive land use regulations. Albouy and Ehrlich (2018) adopted a slightly different IV approach for a large number of cities and concluded that households are not more willing to pay to live in areas that have more stringent land use regulations.

A related issue is the reverse causality between land use regulations and housing prices. As Quigley and Rosenthal (2005, p. 69) put it in their review of the evidence, "a statistical association may show regulatory effect or may show that wealthier, more expensive communities have stronger tastes for such regulation." The most common approach to addressing this issue is to rely on instrumental variables that are correlated with the presence of restrictive regulations but are not correlated with housing prices. Studies have relied on various instruments for land use regulation, including lagged jurisdictional, demographic and economic characteristics (see for example Ihlanfeldt, 2007; Schuetz, 2009). Regardless of the instruments chosen, IV estimates of the effect of land use regulations on housing prices tend to be larger than estimates that do not control for the endogeneity of land use regulations (Ihlanfeldt, 2004).

Inter-Jurisdictional Context

Few studies examine how inter-jurisdictional context shapes the impact of land use regulations on the housing market. According to the "monopoly zoning hypothesis," the effect of restrictive land use regulations should be larger within large cities or in regions with few surrounding jurisdictions due to the lack of available substitutes for restricted housing (Thorson, 1996). If housing consumers have choice among communities, housing demand should be more elastic within small communities that have adopted restrictive regulations, dampening the housing price impact within those communities. In hedonic regression models examining the impact of regulations on housing prices in Florida, Ihlanfeldt (2007) found that in counties with a larger number of cities, the effect of land use regulations on housing prices is smaller. Dawkins and Moeckel (2016) relied on an agent-based model to estimate the regional impact of various housing policies designed to promote affordable housing near transit stations. The authors found that region-wide affordability restrictions on new construction have a much larger impact on the sorting of high-income households near transit stations than local restrictions targeted more narrowly to areas around transit stations. (For more on regional approaches to land use, see Chapter 3.)

Another implication of the inter-jurisdictional context of land use regulation is that restrictions in one community may displace housing demand to nearby communities.

Pollakowski and Wachter (1990) and Cho and Linneman (1993) provided early evidence of such inter-jurisdictional spillovers in Montgomery County, Maryland, and Fairfax County, Virginia, respectively. In regression models explaining the probability of development, Landis (2006) found that if a development site is in an area adjacent to a city with a housing unit cap or a UGB, it is more likely to be developed. Evidence of inter-jurisdictional spillovers suggests that the housing price effect of land use regulations is due to supply-side rather than demand-side effects, because housing supply constraints in the restricted jurisdiction are displacing demand to adjacent jurisdictions (Ihlanfeldt, 2004).

Another dimension of inter-jurisdictional context is the level of housing demand within the surrounding metropolitan housing market. In hot markets where housing demand is strong, we would expect regulatory housing supply constraints to have larger impacts on home price inflation. Schuetz et al. (2011) provided evidence supporting this hypothesis. The authors demonstrated that the effects of inclusionary zoning programs on housing prices vary with the level of regional housing price appreciation. During housing market booms, inclusionary zoning increases housing prices, whereas during housing market downturns, inclusionary zoning causes housing prices to decline.

The Long-Run Housing Dynamics of Housing Supply

Most of the studies examined so far rely on cross-sectional evidence to assess the short-term impact of regulations on housing affordability. These impacts may differ over the long-term when we account for the dynamics of housing supply and the cyclical nature of housing markets. Two recent studies find that certain land use restrictions smooth the peaks and troughs of housing cycles, reducing price inflation during boom periods while mitigating foreclosure risk during bust periods. Glasgow et al. (2012) found that city council opposition to growth during the most recent housing boom was negatively related to the number of foreclosures in California cities over the 2008–2009 period. Dawkins et al. (2017) found that inclusionary zoning restrictions which constrain the resale price of homes mediated home price inflation during the most recent housing boom while also slowing housing price deflation during the most recent housing bust.

Other studies support the opposite conclusion, that land use restrictions increase rather than decrease housing market volatility (see Glaeser et al., 2005; Saiz, 2010; Huang & Tang, 2012; Paciorek, 2013; Kok, 2014; and Beracha et al., 2018). In one of the few studies relating zoning restrictiveness, measured in terms of the diversity of housing units allowed by-right under local zoning, to foreclosures, Chakraborty et al. (2013) found that zoning restrictiveness is positively related to the risk of foreclosure.

Land use regulations may also influence housing market dynamics by altering the uncertainty and option value of land for different future uses. If land use ordinances require land to be developed for certain uses or densities that are less than the potential value of uses at a future date, this may have the dual effect of reducing the option value of future uses while also increasing the probability of development at a lower density use in the short term. Cunningham (2007) provided evidence supporting this hypothesis. He found that the imposition of a UGB around Seattle increased the probability of development within the boundary, and once the boundary was in place, price volatility no longer delayed development because the UGB eliminated a principal barrier to investment: uncertainty about optimal future uses.

Assessing the Evidence on Housing Affordability

The bulk of the evidence discussed above concludes that restrictive land use regulations inflate housing prices by increasing the cost of housing production and reducing the elasticity of housing supply. Studies that isolate the impacts of individual regulations suggest that intra-urban reforms, which reduce the restrictiveness of residential zoning within urban areas, expand housing supply and reduce the price of housing, but it is important not to view regulations in isolation, because housing producers face an entire "regulatory regime" that is characterized by a complex mix of incentives and disincentives (Pendall et al., 2006). Evidence suggests that intra-urban reforms that increase housing supply within urban areas mitigate the housing price inflation associated with extra-urban housing supply restrictions. Evidence also suggests that inter-jurisdictional context mediates housing price inflation within restrictive jurisdictions and displaces housing demand to nearby jurisdictions with less restrictive regulations. An implication of this latter finding is that region-wide restrictions on housing supply will have much larger impacts than localized restrictions, particularly during periods of high housing demand.

Some respond to the evidence linking smart growth policies to higher housing prices by pointing out that such evidence merely supports the claim that smart growth policies are doing what they were designed to do: improve communities and enhance quality of life (Dawkins & Nelson, 2002). Albouy and Ehrlich (2018) questioned this assertion. In their review of the empirical evidence, they concluded that the social welfare benefits of restrictive regulations are small in comparison with the welfare losses. Furthermore, even after controlling for demand-side impacts, empirical evidence suggests that restrictive land use regulations inflate housing prices by constraining housing supply.

The long-run dynamics of housing supply under different regulatory regimes is an area worthy of additional research. While the bulk of the evidence suggests that housing supply constraints increase rather than decrease housing market volatility, each of the studies cited above relies on a different measure of regulatory restrictiveness. As suggested by the research of Dawkins et al. (2017), it is possible that policies explicitly targeted to affordable housing goals have dynamic impacts that differ from policies that function primarily through housing supply restrictions.

SMART GROWTH AND THE DIVERSITY OF HOUSING CHOICES

Given that smart growth policies are designed to promote a diversity of housing options at different price ranges, we would expect to find an increase in the cross-sectional dispersion of housing prices since the onset of the smart growth era. Evidence presented by Albouy and Zabek (2016) is consistent with this hypothesis. The authors found that the level of inequality in US housing rents and values has increased since 1970 when residential growth controls were first introduced. By 2012, those with homes valued in the top 20 percent held 50 percent of all home value, a level of housing inequality that had not been observed since the New Deal era. One question is whether this increase in overall inequality is associated with the spatial integration of housing units at different price ranges within neighborhoods, as smart growth advocates would hope, or with the segregation of housing units by type across neighborhoods. Albouy and Zabek (2016) did not directly examine this issue, but they found that most of the rise in housing inequality since 1970 can be accounted for by small-area inequality within, rather than between, metropolitan area commuting zones. The question that remains is whether the increase in metropolitan area housing inequality is driven by inequality within or between neighborhoods.

The most direct way to examine the relationship between housing diversity and the presence or absence of various smart growth policy reforms is to examine the correlation between measures of housing diversity and the presence or absence of smart growth policies. Several papers adopt this approach, relating housing-based measures of urban form such as those developed by Galster et al. (2001) to various indicators of smart growth. For example, Cutsinger et al. (2005) found that density/continuity is higher in metropolitan areas constrained by water or international boundaries.

The problem with the cross-sectional approach is that static comparisons of cities with and without smart growth policies do not provide definitive evidence that smart growth policies cause the observed differences in land use patterns. Two recent studies get around this issue by relating changes in land use patterns to various regulatory and smart growth indicators. Yin and Sun (2007) found that metropolitan areas covered by state growth management programs saw higher percentage increases in population density than areas not governed by such programs. Paulsen (2013) related changes in land use patterns to various state- and metropolitan-level measures of land use regulation and planning. He found that each net new housing unit consumes less land than housing units in weaker planning states or lightly regulated regions. He also found that a stronger state role in managing growth reduces marginal residential land consumption primarily by redirecting growth to already urbanized areas (not by increasing the density of new housing development, per se).

One limitation of these studies is that more densely developed cities are also more likely to adopt smart growth policies. Furthermore, housing takes time to construct, so we would only expect to observe the impact of smart growth policies on urban form after a significant time lag. The most common way to address the second, but not necessarily the first, issue is to examine the flow, rather than the stock, of diverse housing types following the introduction of smart growth policies. The next sub-section examines studies that have adopted variations on this approach.

Diversity through Multifamily Housing Construction

If smart growth reforms are successful in promoting housing diversity, we would expect to observe higher levels of multifamily housing construction in areas that permit a diversity of housing types. Quigley and Raphael (2005) found that the responsiveness of new housing construction to increases in housing demand is weaker in more regulated California cities,[3] relative to less regulated cities, and the difference in responsiveness is greatest for multifamily housing construction, which is often the target of restrictive regulation. One problem with this study is that land use regulations are quantified using indices of regulatory restrictiveness derived from aggregate counts of local land use regulations. This is problematic, because many intra-urban reforms are designed to catalyze rather than constrain multifamily housing construction. For example, studies that examine multifamily construction across larger numbers of metropolitan areas report that local growth management tools (Xing et al., 2006) and urban containment programs (Nelson et al., 2004a) increase rather than decrease multifamily housing construction.

A more promising strategy is to relate multifamily construction to more precise regulatory measures that reflect the time and cost of obtaining approvals for multifamily housing construction. Several recent studies adopting a variation on this approach find that intra-urban reforms such as special permitting processes for multifamily housing (Schuetz, 2009), by-right zoning for high-density housing (Chakraborty et al., 2010), and the absence of voter approvals required for density increases (Jackson, 2016) are associated with an increase in multifamily housing construction. Related evidence was provided by Dong and Gliebe (2012), who found that multifamily housing developers are more likely to select sites for development that have a large supply of vacant, multifamily-zoned land. Shertzer et al. (2018) related historical constraints imposed by Chicago's 1923 zoning ordinance to contemporary land use patterns to discover that multifamily zoning constraints persist over time. Areas zoned in 1923 for multifamily use still had a higher percentage of multifamily units and higher population densities nearly 80 years later.

Diversity through House Size Effects

In addition to influencing the number and spatial distribution of multifamily units, regulations may influence the diversity of housing choices by altering the relative size of newly constructed homes. In more expensive markets, homebuilders may shift up-market in response to more restrictive regulatory environments and construct larger homes than in less-regulated environments. Ihlanfeldt (2007) presented evidence supporting this hypothesis for a sample of homes in Florida. One would expect the house size effects of land use restrictions to vary with the type of policy, but Ihlanfeldt's study relied on an aggregate index of regulatory restrictiveness rather than indicators of specified policies. Other studies examined this issue by isolating the effects of individual policies on home size. Bento et al. (2009) found that, within California, the size of market-rate houses in cities that adopted inclusionary zoning increased more slowly than in cities without such programs. This finding is interesting, because inclusionary zoning programs are often portrayed as a tax on new development. If this is the case, then the evidence presented by Bento et al. (2009) suggests that developers do not respond to inclusionary zoning programs by shifting up-market as in Florida. This finding is likely due to the fact that inclusionary zoning also stimulates multifamily housing construction. Schuetz et al., (2009) found that the impacts of an inclusionary zoning program vary according to whether the inclusionary requirements are mandatory or voluntary. The authors also presented evidence which suggests that voluntary inclusionary zoning programs that grant density bonuses in exchange for affordable units are more likely to stimulate affordable housing production.

Another possible impact of regulatory programs on unit size is through regulations that restrict small "micro-apartment" units. Gabbe (2015) demonstrated how a wide variety of regulatory programs – minimum parking standards, open-space and indoor common-space provisions, unit-mix stipulations, and inclusionary zoning requirements – affect the feasibility of constructing micro-apartments in two prototypical San Francisco buildings.

Diversity through Filtering

According to the filtering hypothesis, in unregulated markets where housing supply is elastic, new construction lowers the price of all housing, because existing homes vacated as high income households move into new homes add to the supply of older homes available to low-income households. Markets characterized by a high degree of filtering should exhibit a diversity of housing units by age and condition. Somerville and Mayer (2003) found that in tightly regulated markets with more inelastic housing supply, affordable homes are more likely to filter up and become unaffordable to those earning low incomes, reducing the diversity of units by age and lowering affordability as a result. Housing may filter up through renovations to the existing stock, overall increases in existing housing prices in the face of supply constraints, or through new construction. Dawkins and Nelson (2003) found that at least a portion of this effect is due to new construction. The authors estimated a regression model for a panel of 293 metropolitan areas over 19 years and found that state growth management programs are associated with a higher share of new residential construction within metropolitan areas' central cities. Hortas-Rico (2015) provided evidence that urban containment programs also create incentives to renovate the existing stock of urban housing, reducing downtown blight.

Schuetz (2019) relied on a unique dataset of building permits for new construction, expansion of existing structures, and renovations to assess how each contributes to housing supply, and in turn, influences home prices. She found that increases in housing values are associated with higher levels of new construction, but only in neighborhoods with less restrictive zoning. She also found that additions and alterations are more prevalent in neighborhoods with more restrictive zoning.

Smart Growth and Residential Sorting

Even if land use policy reforms promote the construction of more multifamily units and a diversity of housing units by size and type, it does not necessarily follow that households earning lower incomes will choose to live in those units. Higher land costs may be passed on to housing consumers, and high-income households may outbid low-income households in neighborhoods offering a diversity of housing styles. Talen (2010) examined a sample of 152 new urbanist projects that aim to promote "affordability by design," primarily by encouraging more densely developed walkable environments and smaller, more compact homes. She found that only 23 percent of the projects included in her sample were affordable to those earning the area median income.

There is some evidence that a nontrivial share of the additional multi-family units permitted in areas with high housing demand will be occupied by high-income households unless additional affordability restrictions are in place. For example, Moos et al. (2018) found that housing in mixed-use zones is less affordable than housing in other areas within Toronto, Canada. Aurand (2010) found that in Portland, Oregon, housing diversity is associated with an increased supply of high-priced units.

These studies seem to imply that new multifamily housing construction fosters the displacement of low-income households, as some affordable housing advocates fear, but this argument ignores the fact that the areas attracting new multifamily investment are often already in high demand regardless of the type of housing built. Boustan et al. (2019) provided evidence that much of the impact of more expensive, high-density condominium construction on housing affordability is due to the development of condos in areas otherwise attractive to high-income households. We can extend the insights of this study to conclude that the reduction in affordability in areas with greater housing diversity may be due not to the presence of housing diversity per se, but to the attractiveness of urban areas where housing happens to be more diverse. This takes us back to the demand side of smart growth. If one of the goals of smart growth is to create valued urban amenities, it will be very difficult to counteract this effect through policies designed to lower the price of housing below what residents are willing to pay. Direct affordability controls are likely the only policy options for retaining affordability in the face of demand-side amenity effects.

Given the possibility of a mismatch between housing diversity and population diversity, several researchers focus instead on the demand side of the housing market to determine how regulations influence the spatial pattern of residential mobility. Several studies find that when land use regulations reduce the elasticity of housing supply, this has the effect of reducing the responsiveness of labor migration to demand shocks. Saks (2008) found that increased labor demand in cities with more restrictive land use regulations dampens new housing construction, increases housing prices, and results in lower levels of employment over the long-term. Glaeser et al. (2006a) found that metropolitan areas with inelastic housing supply have weaker population growth and stronger housing price inflation in response to an increase in labor demand.

Others have examined the relationship between smart growth policies and the demographics of community residents. Levine (1999) found that cities that enacted growth control measures prior to 1990 had higher incomes in 1990. Pendall (2000) examined the effect of five different types of land use controls on jurisdictional racial and ethnic composition. He found that low-density-only zoning reduces rental housing units, which in turn reduces the number of Black and Hispanic residents. Building permit caps had a similar effect on the number of Hispanic residents. Other types of land use regulations (urban growth boundaries, adequate public facilities ordinances, and development moratoria) had limited impacts on housing types or racial/ethnic composition. Resseger (2013) relied on detailed spatial data from Massachusetts to investigate the impact of zoning on sorting patterns by race. He found that census blocks zoned for multifamily housing have higher Black and Hispanic population shares than adjacent blocks zoned for single-family housing.

Others examine the effects of smart growth programs and land use regulation on metropolitan levels of socio-economic segregation. Nelson et al. (2004b) found that while metropolitan areas with strong urban containment programs saw a higher percentage decline in White–Black residential segregation during the 1990s than metropolitan areas without such policies in place, urban containment had no statistically significant effect on segregation between Whites and other races. Rothwell and Massey (2010) found that metropolitan areas with suburbs that restrict the density of residential construction are more segregated on the basis of income than metropolitan areas with suburbs that impose fewer constraints on residential density. Lens and Monkkonen (2016) employed a more recent dataset with a larger sample of metropolitan areas and found that residential density restrictions are associated with the segregation of higher income households but not the poor. Dawkins (2007) found that the presence of an urban containment program is associated with a reduction in nearest-neighbor income clustering.

Locational equilibrium models provide a way of examining residential sorting within a general equilibrium framework that also considers the interaction between migration, local public good provision, and housing markets within a multi-community setting (Epple & Sieg, 1999). Walsh (2007) relied on this approach to estimate the social welfare impacts of a hypothetical urban containment policy in Wake County, North Carolina. He found that while an urban containment policy is effective in increasing urban density, the increased density imposes a net welfare loss on those who do not own their homes. Kulka (2019) relied on a similar procedure to estimate a neighborhood-level discrete choice model using administrative data from North Carolina. Discrete choice models are useful when the outcome variable is defined in terms of two or more discrete alternatives. Simulations from her model suggested that a relaxation of minimum lot sizes from half an acre to a tenth of an acre in high-amenity neighborhoods is associated with a 30 percent decline in average income. In a second analysis that relies on a boundary discontinuity research design, she found that a decrease in the allowable density of one dwelling unit per acre is associated with an increase in average income of 4.5 percent.

Assessing the Evidence on Housing Diversity

Smart growth reforms influence the diversity of housing types by altering the type, size, and age composition of the housing stock. Evidence suggests that intra-urban reforms, which increase the supply of land for multifamily housing, catalyze multi-family housing construction, but the impact on multifamily housing prices is mediated by the demand for this housing type within the larger housing market. Evidence suggests that homebuilders in restrictive markets shift up-market by increasing home sizes in response to restrictive regulations, but additional research is needed that links home sizes to different types of regulatory regimes. Some evidence suggests that in more restrictive housing markets, housing filters down to low-income households more slowly, or filters up, through renovations to the existing stock, more expensive new construction, or increases in the price of existing housing.

Regarding the question of whether increased housing diversity equates to increased population diversity, Pendall (2000) provided the most convincing evidence linking the "chain of exclusion" from regulations to demographic segregation through housing supply restrictions. His evidence is consistent with general equilibrium evidence from Kulka (2019) that equates minimum lot size restrictions to income segregation. Pendall (2000) also found that the effects of regulations vary by type of regulation. Extra-urban reforms such as urban growth boundaries are less exclusionary than direct constraints on new housing construction. This finding is corroborated by evidence presented by Nelson et al. (2004b), who found that urban containment programs slow the segregation of metropolitan areas by race.

Evidence also suggests that efforts to promote housing diversity through regulatory reform are necessary but not sufficient conditions for creating communities that are integrated by income. In areas where the latent demand for diverse housing types and urban amenities is strong, high-income households may be more likely than low-income households to occupy diverse housing environments. Given that one of the goals of smart growth is to create valued urban environments, traditional affordable housing policy tools are needed to preserve household income diversity alongside increases in housing unit diversity within highly valued urban environments. As Lung-Amam and June-Friesen address further in Chapter 14, smart growth development is not necessarily equitable development without such protections.

CONCLUSION

While traditional land use regulations have been shown to inflate the price of housing and limit the diversity of housing options, it is difficult to draw definitive conclusions about the impacts of comprehensive smart growth policy reforms on the housing market, because most smart growth policies are embedded within complex regulatory regimes that simultaneously restrict and expand housing options. Furthermore, affordable housing production incentives such as inclusionary zoning and density bonuses are only effective when the underlying zoning ordinance restricts residential densities. Studies that quantify regulations along a single dimension of "restrictiveness" fail to precisely characterize this complexity. Furthermore, because large-scale reforms of traditional land use regulations are rare, outside of the recent examples of Minneapolis and Oregon, we still know little about what happens following a *change* in the local regulatory regime. Since the adjustment costs of shifting from one regulatory regime to another may outweigh any benefits of a new regulatory approach, additional pre-test/post-test evaluations of policy changes are warranted.

Evidence suggests that extra-urban reforms should not be pursued without close attention to the regulatory environment within the contained urban area. Intra-urban reforms that reduce the stringency of zoning restrictions, reduce the uncertainty surrounding zoning approvals, and expand the supply of land zoned for multifamily housing may expand urban residential land supply and mitigate the effects of extra-urban housing supply restrictions. The combined effect of intra-urban and extra-urban reforms on region-wide housing choice also depends on the level and elasticity of demand for housing within urban and rural submarkets. If the demand for urban housing is relatively more inelastic than the demand for rural housing, and intra-urban reforms reduce urban housing prices by expanding urban residential land supply, the aggregate decline in urban housing prices may outweigh the aggregate increase in rural housing prices, causing housing prices to decline region-wide. Evidence which considers the inter-jurisdictional context of smart growth policy also suggests that region-wide restrictions on housing supply will have much larger housing market impacts than localized restrictions, particularly during periods of strong housing demand.

Our review reaches a conclusion similar to Been et al. (2019), who argue that limitations on housing supply are important – but not the only – barriers facing low-income housing consumers. Land use regulations that restrict the supply of housing add significantly to the cost of housing, particularly in markets with high housing demand, and reforms designed to enhance the affordability and diversity of housing types are an important piece of the puzzle in the smart growth advocates' toolbox. At the same time, even the most laissez faire regulatory environment will not guarantee that diverse populations actually inhabit neighborhoods with an intentionally diverse housing stock. Smart growth policies, when effective, should enhance urban quality of life even if they do not constrain housing supply, and affordability controls and other traditional housing policy tools are necessary complements to supply-side regulatory reforms to ensure that diverse and high-quality urban environments are not exclusively enjoyed by those with the means to afford them (Dawkins, 2017).

NOTES

1.   In this section, we do not differentiate "housing choices" from "housing opportunities." One could argue that housing opportunities are merely potential choices until housing has been purchased or rented, but we avoid this complexity until later in the chapter, when we examine whether choices have been realized by focusing on the spatial pattern of residential sorting.
2.   Following Glaeser and Gyourko (2002), this paper defines unaffordable housing as housing that is expensive relative to the fundamental cost of constructing housing. This definition is different from the traditional definition of housing unaffordability that equates housing prices with the percentage of income spent on housing. As Glaeser and Gyourko (2002) point out, definitions of affordability based on the ratio of income to housing prices are problematic, because they tend to confuse housing affordability problems with the problems of income inequality and poverty. The common standard that housing costs should not exceed 30 percent of a household's income is also arbitrary, ignores income and substitution effects arising from changes in household purchasing power, and tends to ignore the heterogeneity of housing.
3.   The authors rely on regulation data collected from Glickfeld and Levine's (1992) survey of California land use officials.

REFERENCES

Albouy, D., & Ehrlich, G. (2018). Housing productivity and the social cost of land-use restrictions. *Journal of Urban Economics, 107*, 101–120.

Albouy, D., & Zabek, M. (2016). *Housing inequality* (Working Paper 21916). Retrieved from National Bureau of Economic Research: https://www.nber.org/papers/w21916.pdf

American Housing Survey. (1980). AHS 1980 Summary Tables. Retrieved from https://www.census.gov/programs-surveys/ahs/data.html

American Housing Survey. (1991). AHS 1991 Summary Tables. Retrieved from https://www.census.gov/programs-surveys/ahs/data.html

American Housing Survey. (2001). AHS 2001 Summary Tables. Retrieved from https://www.census.gov/programs-surveys/ahs/data.html

American Housing Survey. (2011). AHS 2011 Summary Tables. Retrieved from https://www.census.gov/programs-surveys/ahs/data.html

American Housing Survey. (2019). AHS 2019 Summary Tables. Retrieved from https://www.census.gov/programs-surveys/ahs/data.html

Aurand, A. (2010). Density, housing types and mixed land use: Smart tools for affordable housing? *Urban Studies, 47*(5), 1015–1036.

Been, V., Ellen, I. G., & O'Regan, K. (2019). Supply skepticism: Housing supply and affordability. *Housing Policy Debate, 29*(1), 25–40.

Bento, A., Lowe, S., Knaap, G. J., & Chakraborty, A. (2009). Housing market effects of inclusionary zoning. *Cityscape*, 7–26.

Beracha, E., Gilbert, B. T., Kjorstad, T., & Womack, K. (2018). On the relation between local amenities and house price dynamics. *Real Estate Economics, 46*(3), 612–654.

Boustan, L. P., Margo, R.A., Miller, M. M., Reeves, J. M., & Steil, J. P. (2019). *Does condominium development lead to gentrification?* (Working Paper 26170). Retrieved from National Bureau of Economic Research: https://www.nber.org/papers/w26170

Chakraborty, A., Allred, D., & Boyer, R. H. (2013). Zoning restrictiveness and housing foreclosures: Exploring a new link to the subprime mortgage crisis. *Housing Policy Debate, 23*(2), 431–457.

Chakraborty, A., Knaap, G. J., Nguyen, D., & Shin, J. H. (2010). The effects of high-density zoning on multifamily housing construction in the suburbs of six US metropolitan areas. *Urban Studies, 47*(2), 437–451.

Cho, M., & Linneman, P. (1993). Interjurisdictional spillover effects of land use regulations. *Journal of Housing Research, 4*(1), 131–163.

Cunningham, C. R. (2007). Growth controls, real options, and land development. *The Review of Economics and Statistics, 89*(2), 343–358.

Cutsinger, J., Galster, G., Wolman, H., Hanson, R., & Towns, D. (2005). Verifying the multi-dimensional nature of metropolitan land use: Advancing the understanding and measurement of sprawl. *Journal of Urban Affairs, 27*(3), 235–259.

Dawkins, C. J. (2007). Exploring changes in income clustering and centralization during the 1990s. *Journal of Planning Education and Research, 26*(4), 404–414.

Dawkins, C. J. (2017). Putting equality in place: The normative foundations of geographic equality of opportunity. *Housing Policy Debate, 27*(6), 897–912.

Dawkins, C. J., Jeon, J. S., & Knaap, G. J. (2017). Creating and preserving affordable homeownership opportunities: Does inclusionary zoning make sense? *Journal of Planning Education and Research, 37*(4), 444–456.

Dawkins, C. J., & Moeckel, R. (2016). Transit-induced gentrification: Who will stay, and who will go? *Housing Policy Debate, 26*(4-5), 801–818.

Dawkins, C. J., & Nelson, A. C. (2002). Urban containment policies and housing prices: an international comparison with implications for future research. *Land Use Policy, 19*(1), 1–12.

Dawkins, C. J., & Nelson, A. C. (2003). State growth management programs and central-city revitalization. *Journal of the American Planning Association, 69*(4), 381–396.

Dong, H., & Gliebe, J. (2012). Assessing the impacts of smart growth policies on home developers in a bi-state metropolitan area: Evidence from the Portland metropolitan area. *Urban Studies, 49*(10), 2219–2235.

Epple, D., & Sieg, H. (1999). Estimating equilibrium models of local jurisdictions. *Journal of Political Economy, 107*(4), 645–681.

Freemark, Y. (2020). Upzoning Chicago: Impacts of a zoning reform on property values and housing construction. *Urban Affairs Review, 56*(3), 758–789.

Gabbe, C. J. (2015). Looking through the lens of size: Land use regulations and micro-apartments in San Francisco. *Cityscape, 17*(2), 223–238.

Gabbe, C. J. (2019). Changing residential land use regulations to address high housing prices: Evidence from Los Angeles. *Journal of the American Planning Association, 85*(2), 152–168.

Galster, G., Hanson, R., Ratcliffe, M. R., Wolman, H., Coleman, S., & Freihage, J. (2001). Wrestling sprawl to the ground: Defining and measuring an elusive concept. *Housing Policy Debate, 12*(4), 681–717.

Glaeser, E. L. & Gyourko, J. (2002). *The impact of zoning on housing affordability* (Working Paper 8835). Retrieved from National Bureau of Economic Research: https://www.nber.org/papers/w8835.pdf

Glaeser, E. L., Gyourko, J., & Saks, R. (2005). Why is Manhattan so expensive? Regulation and the rise in housing prices. *Journal of Law and Economics, 48*(2), 331–369.

Glaeser, E. L., Gyourko, J., & Saks, R. E. (2006a). Urban growth and housing supply. *Journal of Economic Geography, 6*(1), 71–89.

Glaeser, E. L., Schuetz, J., & Ward, B. (2006b). *Regulation and the rise of housing prices in Greater Boston.* Retrieved from Harvard University Kennedy School: https://www.hks.harvard.edu/sites/default/files/centers/rappaport/files/regulation_housingprices_1.pdf

Glasgow, G., Lewis, P. G., & Neiman, M. (2012). Local development policies and the foreclosure crisis in California: Can local policies hold back national tides? *Urban Affairs Review, 48*(1), 64–85.

Glickfeld, M., & Levine, N. (1992). *Regional growth and local reaction: The enactment and effects of local growth control and management measures in California.* Cambridge, MA: Lincoln Institute of Land Policy.

Gyourko, J., Mayer, C., & Sinai, T. (2013). Superstar cities. *American Economic Journal: Economic Policy, 5*(4), 167–199.

Gyourko, J., & Molloy, R. (2015). Regulation and housing supply. In *Handbook of regional and urban economics* (Vol. 5, pp. 1289–1337). Amsterdam: Elsevier.

Gyourko, J., Saiz, A., & Summers, A. (2008). A new measure of the local regulatory environment for housing markets: The Wharton Residential Land Use Regulatory Index. *Urban Studies, 45*(3), 693–729.

Hortas-Rico, M. (2015). Sprawl, blight, and the role of urban containment policies: Evidence from U.S. cities. *Journal of Regional Science, 55*(2), 298–323.

Huang, H., & Tang, Y. (2012). Residential land use regulation and the US housing price cycle between 2000 and 2009. *Journal of Urban Economics, 71*(1), 93–99.

Ihlanfeldt, K. R. (2004). Exclusionary land-use regulations within suburban communities: A review of the evidence and policy prescriptions. *Urban Studies, 41*(2), 261–283.

Ihlanfeldt, K. R. (2007). The effect of land use regulation on housing and land prices. *Journal of Urban Economics, 61*(3), 420–435.

Jackson, K. (2016). Do land use regulations stifle residential development? Evidence from California cities. *Journal of Urban Economics, 91*, 45–56.

Jun, M. J. (2006). The effects of Portland's urban growth boundary on housing prices. *Journal of the American Planning Association, 72*(2), 239–243.

Kok, N., Monkkonen, P., & Quigley, J. M. (2014). Land use regulations and the value of land and housing: An intra-metropolitan analysis. *Journal of Urban Economics, 81*, 136–148.

Kulka, A. (2019). *Sorting into neighborhoods: The role of minimum lot sizes* (Working Paper). Retrieved from Department of Economics, University of Wisconsin-Madison: https://cde.wisc.edu/staff/kulka-amrita/

Landis, J. D. (2006). Growth management revisited: Efficacy, price effects, and displacement. *Journal of the American Planning Association, 72*(4), 411–430.

Landis, J. D. (2019). Fifty years of local growth management in America. *Progress in Planning.* Advanced online publication. https://doi.org/10.1016/j.progress.2019.100435

Lens, M. C., & Monkkonen, P. (2016). Do strict land use regulations make metropolitan areas more segregated by income? *Journal of the American Planning Association, 82*(1), 6–21.

Levine, N. (1999). The effects of local growth controls on regional housing production and population redistribution in California. *Urban Studies, 36*(12), 2047–2068.

Levine, J., Inam, A., & Torng, G. W. (2005). A choice-based rationale for land use and transportation alternatives: evidence from Boston and Atlanta. *Journal of Planning Education and Research, 24*(3), 317–330.

Lin, D., & Wachter, S. M. (2019). The effect of land use regulation on housing prices: Theory and evidence from California. Available at SSRN 3363947.

Mathur, S. (2014). Impact of urban growth boundary on housing and land prices: Evidence from King County, Washington. *Housing Studies, 29*(1), 128–148.

Mathur, S. (2019). Impact of an urban growth boundary across the entire house price spectrum: The two-stage quantile spatial regression approach. *Land Use Policy, 80*, 88–94.

Mayer, C. J., & Somerville, C. T. (2000). Land use regulation and new construction. *Regional Science and Urban Economics, 30*(6), 639–662.

McMillen, D. P., & McDonald, J. F. (2002). Land values in a newly zoned city. *Review of Economics and Statistics, 84*(1), 62–72.

Moos, M., Vinodrai, T., Revington, N., & Seasons. M. (2018). Planning for mixed use: Affordable for whom? *Journal of the American Planning Association, 84*(1), 7–20.

Nelson, A. C., Pendall, R., Dawkins, C. J., & Knaap, G. J. (2002). *The link between growth management and housing affordability: The academic evidence.* Retrieved from the Brookings Institution:https://www.brookings.edu/wp-content/uploads/2016/06/growthmang.pdf

Nelson, A. C., Burby, R. J., Dawkins, C. J., Feser, E., Mazilia, E. E., & Quercia, R. (2004a). Urban containment and central city revitalization. *Journal of the American Planning Association, 70*(4), 411–425.

Nelson, A. C., Sanchez, T. W., & Dawkins, C. J. (2004b). The effect of urban containment and mandatory housing elements on racial segregation in US metropolitan areas, 1990–2000. *Journal of Urban Affairs, 26*(3), 339–350.

Paciorek, A. (2013). Supply constraints and housing market dynamics. *Journal of Urban Economics, 77,* 11–26.

Paulsen, K. (2013). The effects of growth management on the spatial extent of urban development, revisited. *Land Economics, 89*(2), 193–210.

Pendall, R. (2000). Local land use regulation and the chain of exclusion. *Journal of the American Planning Association, 66*(2), 125–142.

Pendall, R., Puentes, R., & Martin, J. (2006). *From traditional to reformed: A review of the land use regulations in the nation's 50 largest metropolitan areas.* Retrieved from the Brookings Institution: https://www.brookings.edu/wp-content/uploads/2016/06/20060802_Pendall.pdf

Pollakowski, H. O., & Wachter, S. M. (1990). The effects of land-use constraints on housing prices. *Land Economics, 66*(3), 315–324.

Quigley, J. M., & Raphael, S. (2005). Regulation and the high cost of housing in California. *American Economic Review, 95*(2), 323–328.

Quigley, J. M., & Rosenthal, L. A. (2005). The effects of land use regulation on the price of housing: What do we know? What can we learn? *Cityscape, 8*(1), 69–137.

Resseger, M. (2013). *The impact of land use regulation on racial segregation: Evidence from Massachusetts zoning borders.* Retrieved from Harvard University: https://scholar.harvard.edu/files/resseger/files/resseger_jmp_11_25.pdf

Rothwell, J. T., & Massey, D. S. (2010). Density zoning and class segregation in U.S. metropolitan areas. *Social Science Quarterly, 91*(5), 1123–1143.

Saiz, A. (2010). The geographic determinants of housing supply. *The Quarterly Journal of Economics, 125*(3), 1253–1296.

Saks, R. E. (2008). Job creation and housing construction: Constraints on metropolitan area employment growth. *Journal of Urban Economics, 64*(1), 178–195.

Schuetz, J. (2009). No renters in my suburban backyard: Land use regulation and rental housing. *Journal of Policy Analysis and Management, 28*(2), 296–320.

Schuetz, J. (2019). Teardowns, popups, and renovations: How does housing supply change? *Journal of Regional Science.* Advanced online publication. https://doi.org/10.1111/jors.12470

Schuetz, J., Meltzer, R., & Been, V. (2009). 31 flavors of inclusionary zoning: Comparing policies from San Francisco, Washington, DC, and suburban Boston. *Journal of the American Planning Association, 75*(4), 441–456.

Schuetz, J., Meltzer, R., & Been, V. (2011). Silver bullet or Trojan horse? The effects of inclusionary zoning on local housing markets in the United States. *Urban Studies, 48*(2), 297–329.

Shertzer, A., Twinam, T., & Walsh, R. P. (2018). Zoning and the economic geography of cities. *Journal of Urban Economics, 105,* 20–39.

Somerville, C. T., & Mayer, C. J. (2003). Government regulation and changes in the affordable housing stock. *Economic Policy Review, 9*(2), 18.

Talen, E. (2010). Affordability in new urbanist development: Principle, practice, and strategy. *Journal of Urban Affairs, 32*(4), 489–510.

Thorson, J. A. (1996). An examination of the monopoly zoning hypothesis. *Land Economics*, *72*(1), 43–55.

US Department of Housing and Urban Development's Office of Policy Development and Research. (2000). Comprehensive Housing Affordability Strategy. Retrieved from https://www.huduser.gov/portal/datasets/cp.html#2000

US Department of Housing and Urban Development's Office of Policy Development and Research. (2010). Comprehensive Housing Affordability Strategy. Retrieved from https://www.huduser.gov/portal/datasets/cp.html#2006-2017

US Department of Housing and Urban Development's Office of Policy Development and Research. (2017). Comprehensive Housing Affordability Strategy. Retrieved from https://www.huduser.gov/portal/datasets/cp.html#2006-2017

Walsh, R. (2007). Endogenous open space amenities in a locational equilibrium. *Journal of Urban Economics*, *61*(2), 319–344.

Xing, X., Hartzell, D. J., & Godschalk, D. R. (2006). Land use regulations and housing markets in large metropolitan areas. *Journal of Housing Research*, *15*(1), 55–80.

Yin, M., & Sun, J. (2007). The impacts of state growth management programs on urban sprawl in the 1990s. *Journal of Urban Affairs*, *29*(2), 149–179.

Zhou, J., McMillen, D. P., & McDonald, J. F. (2008). Land values and the 1957 comprehensive amendment to the Chicago zoning ordinance. *Urban Studies*, *45*(8), 1647–1661.

PART IV

SMART GROWTH PRINCIPLES: THE TRANSPORTATION-LAND USE CONNECTION

9. A step ahead for smart growth: creating walkable neighborhoods

Kelly J. Clifton

INTRODUCTION

Walking is a form of locomotion that is inherently human. Thus, the attraction to walking as a phenomenon, a form of transport, a form of exercise, and a way of being in public space is not new. Walking is the foundation for sustainable cities, but it offers more than utilitarian value as a mode of transportation. It contributes to recreation and social vitality, and cities planned with walking at their core are more equitable and accessible across socio-economic and demographic groups. Despite these inherently positive attributes, walking has not always been valued in US cities and has been marginalized in favor of the automobile. However, since the smart growth movement gained recognition over 20 years ago, the interest in walking and other forms of active transportation has increased dramatically across the United States. The smart growth principle "create walkable neighborhoods" has provided an opportunity to address concerns related to health, environment, and quality of life. Driven by advocates, researchers, policymakers, and the public, the walkability movement is rooted in a desire to transform the automobile-centric built environment of North America.

Academic and policy discussions about walking have largely focused on reclaiming those urban environments that were historically designed for walking but transformed to accommodate the automobile; retrofitting suburban environments that largely ignored pedestrians; and incorporating pedestrian mobility into new urban growth from inception. Advocates have placed pressure on federal, state, and local agencies to allocate funding to improve the built environment and support more walking. At the same time, the increased availability of spatially and temporally explicit data on pedestrian travel and the built environment has led to advances in how we characterize the walkability of the built environment, the development of new pedestrian demand models and decision tools, and changes in our fundamental understanding of pedestrian behaviors. Leveraging the increased interest in the redevelopment of cities and consumer preferences for urban living, planners have responded with policy changes that foster the creation of environments to support walking.

This chapter documents the movement to create more walkable communities via a smart growth framework and increase the number and quality of pedestrian trips. I begin with a discussion about what walkability is: How do we define walkable environments and what are the various components of interest to planners? Then,

I review the various tools and strategies that have been developed or evolved in the smart growth era to improve our understanding of walking and the policy interventions needed to improve pedestrian supports. With this era in mind, the chapter then evaluates the progress made in creating walkable environments and the end goal of inducing more walking activity. Finally, I end with a look toward the future and what smart growth research and policy should consider with respect to this essential human form of mobility.

BACKGROUND: RESEARCH ON WALKABLE ENVIRONMENTS

There has been an ongoing debate about defining walkable places across and within the many disciplines that intersect with the built environment. The design of urban spaces to promote walking, human interaction, or even "being" in public space has long been the purview of architecture, landscape architecture, and urban design fields (Ewing & Handy, 2009; Forsyth & Southworth, 2008; Mehta, 2013; Whyte, 1980). In the late 1990s and early 2000s, the health impacts of the transportation system became a driver of research and policy, as Garfinkel-Castro and Ewing detail further in Chapter 12.

Interdisciplinary walking and cycling research surged, fueled by concerns of obesity and other diseases related to the lack of physical activity and funded by the Robert Wood Johnson Foundation, the Centers for Disease Control, and the National Institute of Health (Boarnet et al., 2011; Brownson et al., 2009; Rodriguez et al., 2006; Saelens et al., 2003; Saelens & Handy, 2008). The relationship between the built environment and the use of active transport modes for utilitarian and recreational travel continued to be a key subject of inquiry, but with an expanded interest in children's travel (McDonald, 2008; McMillan, 2007), behavioral change, and the role of attitudes and other psychological and social factors.

From this, a confluence of key environmental concepts and features emerged as important supports for various aspects of walking, including mode, destination, and route. In their seminal work, Cervero and Kockelman (1997) identified density, diversity, and design as fundamental concepts in the relationship between travel mode and the built environment. These were originally described as the 3Ds, but this description has expanded and become more nuanced (Ewing & Cervero, 2010; Handy, 2018). Moudon et al. (2006) operationalized walkability as comprising three elements: origin/destination, area, and route. Similarly, Southworth (2005) identified six attributes of walkability: connectivity, linkages to other modes, fine-grained and varied land use patterns, safety, quality of path, and path context. Alfonzo (2005) expanded these conceptualizations of walkability into a hierarchy, suggesting that elements such as safety, comfort, and pleasure influence decisions to walk only after more basic needs of feasibility and accessibility are met.

The increasing awareness of the ills of the automobile-centric transportation system dominating North American cities led researchers to focus on habits and behavioral change (Bird et al., 2013). Mitigating traffic congestion, negative health and safety outcomes, and environmental concerns would require people to make different decisions about how they travel and where they live. Transportation researchers, drawing on theories of behavioral modification from public health and psychology, aimed to learn from decades of efforts to change smoking, diet, and seatbelt habits through various interventions (Michie et al., 2013). As a result, researchers began to collect information on the perceptions, attitudes, motivations, and beliefs that people possess about walking and relating these to the role of the social and built environment (Handy et al., 2006). As attention turned to the formation of these psychological qualities, researchers focused on the influence that various life experiences might have on the propensity to walk, such as walking to school as a child, the characteristics of a previous residential location, or experiences while on vacation (Jones et al., 2014; Li et al., 2009).

This conceptual and empirical work has identified myriad dimensions of the built environment that are associated with various aspects of walking activity. However, one critique of this work is that the research does not provide practical guidance in a format that could directly inform policy and planning. Talen, in Chapter 7, further discusses the relationship between urban design and walkability, focusing on the implementation strategy of form-based codes. There has also been a long debate about the relative magnitude of the impact urban form has on walking. In fact, scholarly debates about the role of the built environment in shaping travel outcomes continue (see Stevens, 2017 and associated comments). However, despite these ongoing deliberations within academia, the available tools and strategies to plan for walkable communities have increased immensely since the rise of smart growth.

INCREASING WALKABILITY: MEASURES AND TOOLS

The number and sophistication of pedestrian planning tools and planning strategies have expanded greatly, driven by the need to advance the practice of creating walkable communities and, ultimately, to achieve greater levels of walking.

Walkability Measures

Information about street networks and land uses were among the earliest archived digital information available. This provided an opportunity to assess the walkability of places at a variable spatial granularity. For example, Schlossberg (2006) used the TIGER (topologically integrated geographic encoding and referencing) street network files to analyze walkability using geographic information systems (GIS). Measures commonly used today, such as quality of walking environment (often based upon street classification), proximity, and connectivity measures, were developed from these early efforts.

Since then, a host of measures have been developed to capture various facets of the built environment associated with walking, Because of the growth in archived built environment data, standards have been developed to construct various reliable and valid measures using GIS and foster comparative work (Forsyth et al., 2006). These standards continue to evolve today as the availability of such digital information expands. In a review of literature, Lo (2009) identified some common criteria for evaluating walkability, including:

- Presence of continuous and well-maintained sidewalks;
- Universal access characteristics;
- Path directness and street network connectivity;
- Safety of at-grade crossing treatments;
- Absence of heavy and high-speed traffic;
- Pedestrian separation or buffering from traffic;
- Land-use density;
- Building and land-use diversity or mix;
- Street trees and landscaping;
- Visual interest and a sense of place as defined under local conditions; and
- Perceived or actual security.

Despite the increasing detail in archived data, information about the quality of the walking environment at the street level was (and is) not consistently and systematically available, and there is still a need to collect more. Audits of the pedestrian environment were developed for this purpose (Brownson et al., 2004; Pikora et al., 2002). The presence and condition of sidewalks, pedestrian crossing aids, street furniture, and urban design features are just a few examples of the types of information that walkability audits were designed to identify, quantify, and qualify (Day et al., 2006; Moudon & Lee, 2003). Early audit methodologies were pencil-and-paper based and quickly evolved to use computer-aided technology that integrated with GIS frameworks (Clifton et al., 2007; Schlossberg, 2006). Early audit tools were "one-size-fits-all," focusing on objectively measuring the built environment. As the concept evolved, audits were designed to capture the specific needs of various demographic groups (Kealey et al., 2005) or evaluate the subjective interpretations of walkability as part of participatory planning (Schlossberg & Brehm, 2009; Schlossberg et al., 2015). The wealth of data collected from audits has been tested for reliability, validated against behavior, and often scored into an index (Clifton et al., 2007; Kurka et al., 2016; Zhu et al., 2017). Administering audits requires visual inspection and thus remains labor-intensive, even as Google Street View, drones, remote sensing, and other scanning technologies have eased some of the burden (Badland et al., 2010; Clarke et al., 2010; Phillips et al., 2017; Watson, 2020).

These new data raised important questions about how to aggregate this information to characterize the qualities of place. Walkability indices were developed to reduce this often-correlated information into a more manageable score (Frank et al., 2010; McCormack et al., 2006; Pikora et al., 2006). Walkability gained so much currency that a commercial measure WalkScore™ has been used by realtors to rate the pedestrian access for listings. This measure has been linked to higher income areas, economic resilience, and a host of other correlates. However, critics have noted that the score gives weight to destinations desired by wealthier consumers, such as bookstores and coffee shops, and is thus biased in its assessment. As these concepts evolve, walkability indices have responded to the idea that the built environment also provides supports in terms of safety, time, and comfort (Al Shammas & Escobar, 2019).

Measuring Pedestrian Behaviors

Also in the 1990s and 2000s, more attention was given to collecting objective and subjective information on walking behaviors, for utilitarian transportation or recreational activities. Prior to this, most planning tools and thus data collection efforts were solely focused on the use of motorized modes. The smart growth movement and others who were advocating for a return to more human-oriented mobility required data to foster new research, develop policy, and track progress. A combination of advocacy, public initiatives, research, and technology related to walking launched a revolution in the collection of data about pedestrian behaviors. As with the built environment, technology has helped researchers and advocates passively collect data on modes of personal mobility, levels of physical activity, routes, and destinations.

Starting in 2001, the National Household Travel Survey (NHTS) (US DOT, 2001) added questions about the number of walking trips made in the last week and improved administration techniques to help respondents recall short walk trips in their daily travel diaries. In the 2017 NHTS data set (US DOT, 2017), a series of questions about the financial motivations for walking, reasons for not walking, and the amount of walking for exercise were added. Many other household travel surveys administered in the US followed suit. In 2002, the National Survey of Pedestrian and Bicyclist Attitudes and Behaviors (NHTSA & BTS, 2002) was conducted to provide a benchmark of bicycle and pedestrian trips, behaviors, and attitudes. This standardization of surveys and the increased attention to capturing pedestrian behaviors allowed for more comparative research across time and space.

One of the greatest gains in data collection has been the development of pedestrian count programs, which quantify walking on roads, paths, and sidewalks. There are national standards in the procedures used to collect and analyze these data (US DOT, 2016; Ryus et al., 2015a, 2015b, 2017). Further, several states, regions, and cities have issued their own guidance documents (see Nordback et al., 2018 for a list of resources). Automated counting and tracking technology have advanced this practice, given that manual counts are costly and time consuming. However, it is still challenging to capture pedestrian behavior across various environments and the practice still lags behind those programs administered for motorized modes.

Wearable or portable technology has made advances in tracking modes, location/ routes, speeds, physical exertion, time and distance walked, and destinations. With increased emphasis on the health outcomes of non-motorized mode uses, pedestrian researchers have expanded their scope beyond thinking about trips to include the measurement of levels of physical activity using accelerometers. GPS and accelerometers, once burdensome and intrusive, are now mutually incorporated into smart-phones and other portable and wearable devices. To support and motivate behavioral change and habit development, individuals can track their own behaviors – steps, routes, or levels of physical activity. Wearable or portable technology has allowed individuals to track their own movements over the course of the day and gamify walking goals; devices prompt users to increase steps and celebrate when a target number is achieved.

Modeling and Forecasting Tools

With advances in understanding the relationship between walking behaviors, the built environment, and socio-demographic characteristics, the development of tools to predict demand for walking soon followed. There was interest in having models that were sensitive to various smart growth interventions, in order to demonstrate their efficacy for increasing walking and cycling and decreasing automobile use. Such modeling tools include regional travel demand models, which include all (or most) modes, and models specific to pedestrians.

In the 30 years since non-motorized modes first appeared in regional travel models, three-quarters (75 percent) of large Metropolitan Planning Organizations (MPOs) now model non-motorized travel, and over two-thirds (69 percent) of those distinguish walking from bicycling (Singleton et al., 2018). These models are used for long-range planning, allowing regions to analyze various scenarios and projects for their impacts. Models that can forecast walking also have many other applications, such as prioritizing non-motorized infrastructure investments in the short term, and predicting mode shifts and emissions in the long term. The estimates of the number and location of walk trips also provide traffic safety analyses with common measures of risk exposure.

Two recent publications outline advances in non-motorized modeling and provide direction for next steps in the practice. The NCHRP Report 770 (NASEM, 2014) contributes several improvements to pedestrian modeling, including tour and trip generation, mode split, pedestrian-accessibility measures, and enhancements to trip-based models. A follow up project, NCHRP Project 08-36, generated a report that provides an overview of pedestrian demand, factors known to impact walking, a survey of the state of the practice, and directions forward (Rand Corporation, 2019). Despite the incorporation of these modes into models used in practice, improvements are needed in the spatial resolution and details provided about land uses and the network, pedestrian routing, and transferability.

Because models can provide better estimates of the amount of walking (trips, distances, or times), there are attempts to link these demand model outputs to health outcomes (Frank et al., 2006). One approach is to utilize health impact assessments (HIAs), which are evidence-based tools used to evaluate and mitigate the potential health effects of proposed projects and policies. One of the most popular of these HIA tools is the Integrated Transport and Health Impact Model (ITHIM) (Woodcock et al., 2009) which provides relational estimates of the magnitude and direction of potential net health impacts relative to mode shifts. These health impacts are assessed using three exposure pathways: physical activity, air pollution, and traffic injuries and fatalities. ITHIM has been implemented in several communities in the United States (Iroz-Elardo et al., 2014; Maizlish et al., 2013; Whitfield et al., 2017). Despite this progress, utilization of these tools on a broad scale and their impact on planning and project outcomes has been mixed (Cole et al., 2019).

POLICIES AND PROGRAMS

The crux of the smart growth movement around walkability has been a series of policies and programs designed to alter the built environment and curb automobile use in order to support pedestrian activity. Welch and Gehrke (Chapter 10) detail efforts to implement more smart-growth-friendly transportation tools focused on compact growth. A wide range of cities, including Batesville, Arkansas; Milwaukee, Wisconsin; and New York City have implemented various policies and programs to attract and support pedestrians, invigorate commercial corridors, provide safe routes to schools, connect transit, and ultimately create walkable places (see Loh et al., 2019 for a recent summary of examples from across the country). While these policies have many monikers and target different populations or locations, they all fall into the suite of smart growth policies that aim to (a) provide pedestrian infrastructure and supports; (b) increase the density and mix of land uses and increase access to parks, public spaces, and greenspace; and (c) manage overall travel demand to discourage use of the automobile and elevate the pedestrian.

Pedestrian Infrastructure and Supports

The most important advancement for promoting walkable communities is the funding to build infrastructure and other supports. In the early 1990s, Congress passed landmark transportation funding legislation, the Intermodal Surface Transportation Efficiency Act (ISTEA). Signaling the end of the highway-era of transportation investment, this bill responded to communities' demands for more than auto-mobility from their transportation system as well as the lack of funding to continue to support expansion of highways. Of the many innovations in this bill, the availability of federal funds for projects that support non-motorized modes and the recognition that land use planning is a critical link legitimized and promoted walking as an integral part of the transportation system (Lo, 2009). There has been a dramatic increase in federal obligations for pedestrian and bicycle spending. Federal obligations totaled nearly $916 million in 2018, compared with $22 million in 1992 (FHWA, 2018). While this growth is impressive, it still pales in comparison with total transportation spending. For example, between fiscal years 2012 and 2016, federal transportation funds obligated to walking and biking projects equaled nearly $3.8 billion. This represents around 2 percent of obligated federal transportation funding over that period and amounted to $2.36 per capita (League of American Bicyclists, 2018).

Communities have been responding to these funding opportunities by investing in walking infrastructure as part of movements to revitalize urban centers, retrofit suburban neighborhoods, improve public health and safety, and invest in recreational facilities. However, local governments bear most of the responsibility for funding pedestrian infrastructure (Tomer & Kane, 2018).

Despite the increased potential for funding sidewalks, trails, and other pedestrian infrastructure offered by the passage of ISTEA, pedestrian planning tools were initially lacking. Walking was not included as a mode in most regional travel demand models, which are used to forecast future mode choices and evaluate the impacts of new projects (Singleton et al., 2018). Despite all the improvements previously outlined, lack of data about pedestrian behaviors was often cited as hindering the development of these tools. Additionally, information was missing about the built environment at the appropriate scale to understand these behaviors or to assess the walkability of neighborhoods or streets.

Land Use Change

The smart growth era ushered in a new wave of land use strategies intent upon shaping transportation choices, and some communities have become more receptive to these changes than others. Cities have densified as populations have grown and land area has not, particularly in the central cities of regions. Some of this growth has been coordinated and directed with the intent to create more urban infill, vertical and horizontal mixing of land uses, transit-oriented development, and new urbanist communities. All of these land use policies support walking by bringing trip origins closer to potential destinations, thus making walking a viable mode of transport. See Carruthers et al. (Chapter 3) for a broader discussion of contained, compact urban growth, and Hanlon (Chapter 5) for more on the implementation and consequences of infill and redevelopment.

Historically, one of the biggest barriers to changing land use to support walking resided within public planning agencies themselves – the zoning code. The zoning code, particularly R1 zoning, has had the effect of capping densities and segregating, or at least limiting proximity of, different land uses (Levine, 2005; Manville et al., 2020). There is some well documented historical resistance to these densification policies, particularly in wealthy, organized neighborhoods. The public engagement process privileges wealthy homeowners, who often organize to limit higher density development under the auspices of preserving the historic character of their neighborhoods or reducing traffic or parking congestion. This opposition to densification has kept the supply of housing low in walkable neighborhoods, which increases the cost of living (Lens & Monkkonen, 2016; Reeves, 2017).

That said, it is often the wealthy who are benefiting from land use policies that support walking, as low-income neighborhoods with high levels of regional accessibility have been gentrifying and local land development has benefited newcomers' income and tastes. As home values rise with these investments, those with more modest incomes have fewer choices of where to live, and they are often priced out of these walkable neighborhoods. As Finio & Knapp (Chapter 13) and Lung-Amam & June-Friesen (Chapter 14) point out, smart growth efforts have the potential to exacerbate inequalities if affordability protections and equitable development processes are not also put in place.

As a reaction to the issue of housing affordability, policies are being enacted to alleviate this shortage by increasing density. Minnesota and Oregon have passed legislation that permits the development of a wider range of housing options within residential areas. Many areas are experimenting with accessory dwelling units to provide more affordable housing, increase density, and at the same time, provide economic gains for homeowners (Gabbe, 2019).

Just as cities are getting hip to densification and mixed-use policies, technology is undermining the traditional retail structure by moving sales from bricks-and-mortar establishments to online. Thus, many cities that adopted mixed-use zoning have over-built and overestimated the demand for retail space, inadvertently balkanizing existing healthy commercial corridors by diluting the concentration of shopping destinations. Thus, two of the biggest challenges in implementing land use policies for walkability are (a) consideration of equity and affordability, and (b) heading off technological change with the rise of e-commerce.

Transportation Demand Management

Transportation Demand Management (TDM) tools are policies intended to curb the use of the automobile and encourage walking, particularly in places that have benefited from supportive infrastructure and land uses. These policies hinge on their ability to induce behavioral change by sending signals through economic incentives (or disincentives) (Meyer, 1997). Of the triad of policies to support walking discussed here, the least is known about the anticipated response to TDM policies, and the degree to which they are effective in shifting demand to desired modes, alone or in combination with supportive infrastructure and land use.

The TDM policy that has received the most attention of late is managing parking supply, including revising parking requirements for new development, unbundling the cost of parking from housing, and pricing (Shoup, 2005). In concert with this, policies that encourage the use of other modes, such as transit or bicycling, benefit walking by incentivizing use, gamification and rewards, and enhancing the experience. Conventional thinking is that formative years are influential in shaping lifelong behaviors. During the early smart growth era, there was an emphasis on improving the ability for children to walk and bike via the Safe Routes to School Programs (McDonald et al., 2013). These programs included providing the infrastructure discussed above in and around schools, and also a programming component to encourage and support children commuting to school by walking and cycling (Villa-González et al., 2018).

PROGRESS

The smart growth movement has resulted in many physical transformations of our cities, particularly the central cities and surrounding neighborhoods. Walkable neighborhoods are now viewed as desirable places to live, and urban real estate markets have responded to this demand (Handy et al., 2008). Transportation planners have increased tools for considering pedestrian modes in planning and safety analysis, and they know how to leverage funding opportunities to build desired pedestrian infrastructure. Further, ever the fitness obsessives, Americans have embraced wearable technology to monitor their distance or time spent doing physical activity. Given these successes, it may seem that there has been significant progress in improving the environmental and social supports for pedestrians. However, not all communities have realized the same gains in walkability, and the amount of walking that Americans do for transportation and leisure varies across demographics and location. How have our communities fared?

Walkable Neighborhoods

From a planning perspective, there has been a wave of redevelopment and reinvestment in cities during this era of smart growth. Cities across the United States have experienced changes in land use and the built environment as the development community has responded to planning and zoning changes, population growth, and demand for urban living. Permissive zoning policies have realized increases in the density and mix of land uses, often coupled with transit investments. As mentioned earlier, several movements are working to end the dominance of single-family, detached housing by reforming zoning codes to include more inclusive definitions of residential uses (Manville et al., 2020, Wegmann, 2019). There is increasing recognition that current zoning practice increases segregation, prohibits modest density increases, contributes to rising rents, and limits transportation choice.

Residential property values are found to be positively associated with accessibility to walkability and negatively associated with automobile-oriented features (Diao & Ferreira, 2010). There has been much promotion of how resilient walkable neighborhoods were during the 2008 housing crisis and the overall high demand for these neighborhoods on the real estate market. For instance, a study of market values from 2008 to 2012 showed that single-family homes in walkable neighborhoods in Dallas, Texas, held 2.08 percent more value than their non-walkable counterparts (Xu et al., 2018).

These positive changes toward walkability are not without challenges. As several studies have shown, walkable neighborhoods are not accessible to everyone, with gentrification and high housing prices presenting barriers. Riggs (2016) examined neighborhoods in San Francisco and found that those with a higher concentration of Black residents tended to have lower levels of walkability. A study of three different cities indicated significant variability in access to walkable neighborhoods among socially vulnerable groups (older populations, higher poverty rates, more service occupations, lower educational attainment, and a higher proportion of minorities) (Bereitschaft, 2017). Charlotte, a fast-growing, Sunbelt city, had greater inequities in access to walkable areas, while Portland and Pittsburgh exhibited more equitable access across the population. Knight et al. (2018) examined the distribution of walkable neighborhoods in Buffalo, New York, a "shrinking city," and found that walkable block groups were highly clustered in economically stable and gentrifying parts of the city with rising housing values. Black and unemployed residents were more likely to live in areas that scored low on the walkability scale.

Funding pedestrian infrastructure remains a challenge at all levels, from local development fees to federal sources. In requiring mixed uses in multifamily housing, planners' embrace of smart growth tenants may have a perverse effect in some urban neighborhoods, where the supply of retail land uses outpaces the demand. The lack of government intervention to manage, not just plan, for retail may result in oversupply of space allocated to these uses (Gerend & Novak, 2017). The retail landscape is evolving with competition from e-commerce and home delivery services (Grewal et al., 2017). The combined effect of e-commerce and loss of bricks-and-mortar retail is to dilute the concentration of destinations in local commercial districts and limit the diversity, as restaurants, bars, and specialty retail are more prevalent than retail shopping for everyday life. This impacts the types of destinations available in our walkable neighborhoods and ability to walk for various trip purposes.

Suburban neighborhoods have not transformed the character of their urban form at the same pace as those in central cities. The automobile remains the dominant mode of transportation across the American suburbs. This is due in part to the prevalence of low-density zoning and segregated land uses, as well as the difficulty in retrofitting redevelopment there. The ability to walk for utilitarian transportation remains hampered by low-density development patterns, the lack of destinations nearby, land uses that are segregated by the high volume, high speed arterials, and design features that favor the automobile over other modes. Yet, many are walking here, as gentrification and rising rents in central cities and environs have increased the numbers of suburban poor and working class (Benediktsson, 2017). These pedestrian activities are often "invisible trips," as our current data collection methods fail to consider these populations or locations adequately. As a result, pedestrians who are poorer face higher risk of sustaining injuries or deaths (Loukaitou-Sideris et al., 2007).

Walking Behaviors

Despite the interest in walking and the technological advances in data collection, evaluating the amount of walking done for transport or leisure in the United States remains a challenge. Unlike vehicle travel, it is difficult to measure the extent to which smart growth policies have been effective with respect to walking. The most consistent evidence nationwide is from the US Census Journey to Work data. Overall, walk mode share has been in steady decline since the 1960s, where walking accounted for nearly 10 percent of commute trips (US Census Bureau, 1960). In 2018, it amounted to less than 3 percent (US Census Bureau, 2018). However, there is substantial variation in cities, with Boston, San Francisco, Seattle, and Washington, DC, all reporting over 12 percent for 2018.

Other longitudinal examinations of walking trends reveal an uptick in walking in urban areas with supportive infrastructure and land use, though the effect sizes are small. Using household travel surveys, Joh et al. (2015) saw increases in walking mode share and walk trips among areas of Los Angeles from 2001 to 2009, and these increases generally corresponded with increases in population, employment, and transit service densities. In a broader study using the National Household Travel Surveys from 2001 and 2009, Pucher et al. (2011) showed small increases in the average amounts of walking in terms of number of trips, distance walked, and durations. However, gains were not equally distributed across the population, with significant declines in active travel among children, seniors, and women and increases in the prevalence of walking 30 minutes per day for men, the age group 25–64 years, the employed, the well-educated, and people without a car. In a longitudinal study of middle-aged and older adults in the United States, Hirsch et al. (2014) found that higher baseline levels of population density, areas zoned for retail, social destinations, walking destinations, and street connectivity were associated with greater increases in walking for transportation over time. A recent study of 13 metropolitan areas between 2004 and 2016 used repeated counts of pedestrian traffic and saw a 2–3% yearly growth rate in walking among count locations, controlling for other variables (Le et al., 2019). Despite the investments in Safe Routes to Schools programs over this period, the prevalence of children walking to school has remained relatively unchanged since 2004 (Omura et al., 2019).

As walking is on the rise in some areas, so are pedestrian injuries and fatalities. According to the Governors Highway Safety Association (2020), pedestrian fatalities in 2019 were the highest in three decades and have increased 53 percent since 2009. Efforts to increase traffic safety though Vision Zero policies have failed to achieve significant declines in incidents involving pedestrians. While the reasons for this are varied, one possibility is that the improvements in walking conditions are not met with declines in driving. This may be due to planning that creates more walkable neighborhoods through land development but without commensurate infrastructure, safety, and design features, or transportation demand management measures to suppress driving.

Beyond traffic safety, other American health outcomes related to walking are similarly dire. The links between physical activity and positive health outcomes have been long established and were a motivating factor for increasing pedestrian supports. In 1999, US health officials declared the country was experiencing an obesity epidemic, with 30.5 percent of Americans experiencing obesity. Two decades later, 40.2 percent are obese (Hales et al., 2020). Health is complicated and these outcomes may be associated with a variety of personal, behavioral, and community factors. However, it is also a sign that interventions were not successful – either because there was not enough change in the built environment or people did not respond to those changes accordingly.

CONCLUSIONS: LOOKING TO THE FUTURE

Walking is fundamental to the human condition and offers many benefits beyond mobility. Walking continues to be a critical component of a smart growth agenda, but there are new opportunities and concerns as well as persistent issues. Pedestrian safety and equity remain at the forefront of walkability concerns. Climate change was considered when the smart growth era began, but it is now the overarching issue framing much of planning policy, including pedestrian planning.

Although central cities have seen new investments that create the density and a mix of land uses to support walking, those places that rank as highly walkable are some of the most desirable real estate in the country and thus the most expensive. Creating walkable communities that are within financial reach of all is a tremendous equity challenge. Vast inequities still exist.

With automobiles rather than people at the center of our transportation system, communities of color continue to bear the greatest costs in terms of life, injuries and illnesses, as well as lack of local accessibility. Those low-income areas with support-ive land use and infrastructure run the risk of gentrification and no longer remaining affordable for current residents. Persons with physical or mental limitations, whether temporary or permanent, have been largely overlooked in our efforts to increase human-centered mobility. Planning for walkability should consider journeys over their entire course – first and last mile as well as first and last feet. Seamless travel requires navigating both indoor and outdoor spaces.

Technology poses opportunities and threats for walking and pedestrian environ-ments. Artificial intelligence, automated technologies, and wireless communications have ushered in dramatic changes, many that will disrupt transportation and our way of getting around, acquiring goods, and communicating. Included in these new opportunities and concerns are the promise and threats of automated automobility. The development of connected and autonomous vehicle (CAV) technologies is moti-vated by their potential efficiency gains for individuals and society and the safety benefits they offer, including pedestrian safety. But in the planning for CAV adop-tion, pedestrians continue to be considered an obstacle to mobility and not integral to urban transportation options. Just as cities have made great gains in reclaiming urban spaces from the automobile, there is a renewed risk of overfitting the environment to CAVs and eroding walkable environments.

The advances in passive data collection using smartphones have vastly increased the information available for pedestrian trips, including those short access/egress trips. Yet, much of these data are proprietary and not easily accessible to public agencies or researchers. Despite the efforts to collect more information about pedes-trian behaviors, there is a persistent lack of data about the poor, elderly, non-English speakers, children, and people with disabilities. This correlates with their access to and use of smartphones, and the ineffective outreach efforts to include them in household travel surveys. More attention should be given to walking across different population segments with specific needs and capabilities.

Not only are the characteristics of these pedestrians and their trips absent from the models, the environments where they walk and the destinations that they frequent are not represented, and are not often among those considered "walkable" by common measures. Suburban environments still struggle to retrofit neighborhoods and commercial centers designed exclusively for the automobile into more walkable places. Many low-income people and working poor are finding more affordable housing in suburban areas, yet walking many places, including to/from transit stops, in less than ideal conditions. As many are adapting the built environment to deal with changing climate and weather, there are more paths that traverse indoor spaces, which are not captured as routes or reflected in maps.

The number of transportation choices available in the smart growth toolbox is rapidly changing. New (or newly recognized) modes are appearing in cities in large numbers. Cycling was not called out as a specific principle in the original list of smart growth principles, but it was included under the broad principle "provide a variety of transportation choices" (detailed by Welch and Gehrke in Chapter 10). With the vast expansion of cycling infrastructure and bike share systems across American cities and the growth in both recreational and utilitarian cycling, cycling is a viable, sustainable and healthy transportation mode, and thus a critical component of smart growth. Skateboarding, scooters (including electric scooters), and bicycles in various forms (including e-bikes) offer advantages consistent with sustainable objectives. The challenge for policy is to find ways for these to work together to provide a safe, sustainable, equitable, and healthy system of options. Walking should be at the core of these efforts.

As I write this, we are entrenched in the COVID-19 global pandemic, which has resulted in a dramatic disruption of daily life. Many are working from home and walking for leisure and exercise, which has been made more enjoyable due to curbed automobile traffic on local streets. But utilitarian walking has been severely limited by the closure of destinations, some of which will never recover. As communities attempt to reopen and find ways of coping with the virus, many are taking actions to enhance the pedestrian environment by dedicating whole street right-of-way as pedestrian and cycling zones and converting parking spaces to café seating. At the same time, protests of police brutality against Black people were a demonstration of how streets can be recast for civic rights to assembly and protest. Pedestrian activity in the form of organized (and unorganized) protest marches took place on city streets and, in some cases, freeways. Consideration of walking for civic participation is long rooted in civil rights movements but has been lightly treated in the planning literature. These examples provide a look at how smart growth can expand in its next iteration beyond a narrow view of walking and other active modes and the policies that support them.

REFERENCES

Al Shammas T. & Escobar F. (2019). Comfort and time-based walkability index design: A GIS-based proposal. *International Journal of Environmental Research and Public Health*, 16(16), 2850. http://dx.doi.org/10.3390/ijerph16162850

Alfonzo, M. A. (2005). To walk or not to walk? The hierarchy of walking needs. *Environment and Behavior*, 37(6), 808–836. https://doi.org/10.1177/0013916504274016

Badland, H. M., Opit, S., Witten, K., Kearns, R. A., & Mavoa, S. (2010). Can virtual streetscape audits reliably replace physical streetscape audits? *Journal of Urban Health*, 87, 1007–1016. http://dx.doi.org/10.1007/s11524-010-9505-x.

Benediktsson, M. O. (2017). Beyond the sidewalk: Pedestrian risk and material mismatch in the American suburbs. *Mobilities*, 12(1), 76–96. http://dx.doi.org/10.1080/17450101.2015.1019748.

Bereitschaft, B. (2017). Equity in neighbourhood walkability? A comparative analysis of three large U.S. cities. *Local Environment*, 22(7), 859–879. http://dx.doi.org/10.1080/13549839.2017.1297390

Bird, E., Baker, G., Mutrie, N., Ogilvie, D., Sahlqvist, S., & Powell, J. (2013). Behavior change techniques used to promote walking and cycling: A systematic review. *Health Psychology: Official Journal of the Division of Health Psychology*, 32(8). http://dx.doi.org/10.1037/a0032078.

Boarnet, M. G., Forsyth, A., Day, K., & Oakes, J. M. (2011). The street level built environment and physical activity and walking: Results of a predictive validity study for the Irvine-Minnesota Inventory. *Environment and Behavior*, 43,735–775. http://dx.doi.org/10.1177/0013916510379760.

Brownson, R. C., Hoehner, C. M., Brennan, L. K., Cook, R. A., Elliott, M. B., & McMullen, K. M. (2004). Reliability of two instruments for auditing the environment for physical activity. *Journal of Physical Activity and Health*, 1, 189–207.

Brownson, R. C., Hoehner, C. M., Day, K., Forsyth, A., & Sallis, J. F. (2009). Measuring the built environment for physical activity: state of the science. *American Journal of Preventive Medicine*, 36(Suppl 4), 99–123. http://dx.doi.org/10.1016/j.amepre.2009.01.005

Cervero, R. & Kockelman, K. (1997). Travel demand and the 3ds: density, diversity, and design. *Transportation Research Part D: Transport and Environment*, 2(3), 199-219.

Clarke, P., Ailshire, J., Melendez, R., Bader, M., & Morenoff, J. (2010). Using Google Earth to conduct a neighborhood audit: reliability of a virtual audit instrument. *Health Place*, 16, 1224–1229. http://dx.doi.org/10.1016/j.healthplace.2010.08.007.

Clifton, K., Livi Smith, A., & Rodriguez, D. (2007). The development and testing of an audit for the pedestrian environment. *Landscape Urban Plan*, 80, 95–110. http://dx.doi.org/10.1016/j.landurbplan.2006.06.008.

Cole, B. L., MacLeod, K. E., & Spriggs, R. (2019). Health impact assessment of transportation projects and policies: Living up to aims of advancing population health and health equity? *Annual Review of Public Health*, 1(4), 305–318. http://dx.doi.org/10.1146/annurev-publhealth-040617-013836.

Day, K., Boarnet, M., Alfonzo, M., & Forsyth, A. (2006). The Irvine-Minnesota inventory to measure built environments: development. *American Journal of Preventive Medicine*, 30(2), 144–152. http://dx.doi.org/10.1016/j.amepre.2005.09.017.PMID: 16459213

Diao, M. & Ferreira, J. (2010). Residential property values and the built environment. *Transportation Research Record: Journal of the Transportation Research Board*, 2174(1), 138–147.

Ewing, R. & Cervero, R. (2010). Travel and the built environment: A meta-analysis. *Journal of the American Planning Association*. 76(3), 265–294.

Ewing, R. & Handy, S. (2009). Measuring the unmeasurable: urban design qualities related to walkability. *Journal of Urban Design*, 14(1), 65–84. http://dx.doi.org/10.1080/13574800802451155

Federal Highway Administration (FHWA) (2018). *Fiscal management information system*. Washington, DC: Federal Highway Administration, US Department of Transportation.

Forsyth, A., Schmitz, K., Oakes, M., Zimmerman, J., & Koepp, J. (2006). Standards for environmental measurement using GIS: Toward a protocol for protocols. *Journal of Physical Activity & Health*, 3(S1), S241–S257.

Forsyth, A. & Southworth, M. (2008). Cities afoot—Pedestrians, walkability and urban design. *Journal of Urban Design*, 13(1), 1-3. http://dx.doi.org/10.1080/13574800701816896

Frank, L. D., Sallis, J. F, Conway, T. L., Chapman, J. E., Saelens, B. E., & Bachman, W. (2006). Many pathways from land use to health: Associations between neighborhood walkability and active transportation, body mass index, and air quality. *Journal of the American Planning Association*, 72(1), 75–87. http://dx.doi.org/10.1080/01944360608976725

Frank, L. D., Sallis, J. F., Saelens, B. E., Leary. L., Cain, K., Conway, T. L., & Hess, P. M. (2010). The development of a walkability index: application to the Neighborhood Quality of Life Study. *British Journal of Sports Medicine*, 44, 924–933.

Gabbe, C. J. (2019). Changing residential land use regulations to address high housing prices: evidence from Los Angeles. *Journal of the American Planning Association*, 85(2), 152–168.

Gerend, J. & Novak, M. (2017). Planning for retail change: A survey of municipal governments in Washington State. *Planning Practice & Research*, 32(2), 120–131. https://doi-org.proxy.lib.pdx.edu/10.1080/02697459.2016.1222145

Governors Highway Safety Association (2020). Pedestrian traffic fatalities by state: 2019 preliminary data, Washington, DC. https://www.ghsa.org/sites/default/files/2020-02/GHSA-Pedestrian-Spotlight-FINAL-rev2.pdf

Grewal, D., Roggeveen, A., & Nordfalt, J. (2017). The future of retailing. *Journal of Retailing*, 93(1), 1–6.

Hales, C. M., Carrol, M. D., Fryar, C. D., & Ogden, C. L. (2020). Prevalence of obesity among adults and youth: United States, 2017–2018. NCHS Data Brief no 360. Hyattsville, MD: National Center for Health Statistics. https://www.cdc.gov/nchs/data/databriefs/db360-h.pdf

Handy, S. (2018). Enough with the "D's" already — Let's get back to "A". *Transfers*, Spring.

Handy, S., Cao, X., & Mokhtarian, P. (2006). Self-selection in the relationship between the built environment and walking: Empirical evidence from northern California. *Journal of the American Planning Association*, 72(1), 55–74. http://dx.doi.org/10.1080/01944360608976724

Handy, S., Sallis, J. F., Weber, D., Maibach, E., & Hollander, M. (2008). Is support for traditionally designed communities growing? Evidence from two national surveys. *Journal of the American Planning Association*, 74(2), 209–221.

Hirsch, J. A., Moore, K. A., Clarke, P. J., Rodriguez, D. A., Evenson, K. R., Brines, S. J., Zagorski, M. A., & Roux, A. V. D. (2014). Changes in the built environment and changes in the amount of walking over time: longitudinal results from the multi-ethnic study of atherosclerosis. *American. Journal of Epidemiology*, 180, 799–809. https://doi.org/10.1093/aje/kwu218

Iroz-Elardo, N., Hamberg, A., Main, E., Haggerty, B., Early-Alberts, J., & Cude, C. (2014). *Climate smart strategy health impact assessment*. Oregon Health Authority (ed.). Portland, OR.

Joh, K., Chakrabarti, S., Boarnet, M. G., & Woo, A. (2015). The walking renaissance: a longitudinal analysis of walking travel in the greater Los Angeles area, USA. *Sustainability*, 7, 8985–9011. https://doi.org/10.3390/su7078985

Jones, H., Chatterjee, K., & Gray, S. (2014). A biographical approach to studying individual change and continuity in walking and cycling over the life course. *Journal of Transport & Health*, 1(3), 182–189. http://dx.doi.org/10.1016/j.jth.2014.07.004

Knight, J., Weaver, R., & Jones, P. (2018). Walkable and resurgent for whom? The uneven geographies of walkability in Buffalo, NY. *Applied Geography*, 92, 1–11.

Kealey, M., Kruger, J., Hunter, R., Ivey, S., Satariano, W., Bayles, C., Ramirez, B., Bryant, L., Johnson, C., Lee, C., Levinger, D., McTigue, K., Moni, C., Moudon, A.V., Pluto, D., Prohaska, T., Sible, C., Tindal, S., Wilcox, S., Winters, K., Williams, K. (2005). Engaging older adults to be more active where they live: audit tool development. In *Proceedings of the 19th National Conference on Chronic Disease Prevention and Control*. Atlanta, March.

Kurka, J. M., Adams, M. A., Geremia, C., Zhu, W., Cain, K. L., Conway, T. L., & Sallis, J. F. (2016). Comparison of field and online observations for measuring land uses using the Microscale Audit of Pedestrian Streetscapes (MAPS). *Journal of Transport and Health*, 3, 278–286.

Le, H. T. K., Buehler, R., & Hankey, S. (2019). Have walking and bicycling increased in the US? A 13-year longitudinal analysis of traffic counts from 13 metropolitan areas. *Transportation Research Part D: Transport and Environment*, 69, 329–345. https://doi.org/10.1016/j.trd.2019.02.006

League of American Bicyclists (2018). *Bicycling and walking in the United States 2018 benchmarking Report*. Washington, DC: League of American Bicyclists. Available: https://bikeleague.org/benchmarking-report

Lens, M. & Monkkonen, P. (2016). Do strict land use regulations make metropolitan areas more segregated by income? *Journal of the American Planning Association*, 82(1), 6–21. http://dx.doi.org/10.1080/01944363.2015.1111163

Levine, J. (2005). *Zoned out: Regulation, markets, and choices in transportation and metropolitan land use*. Washington, DC: Resources for the Future Press.

Li, K-K., Cardinal, B. J., & Settersten, R. A. (2009). A life-course perspective on physical activity promotion: applications and implications. *Quest*, 61, 336–352

Lo, R. H. (2009). Walkability: what is it? *Journal of Urbanism*, 2(2), 145–166, http://dx.doi.org/10.1080/17549170903092867

Loh, T. H., Leinberger, C. B., & Chafetz, J. (2019). *Foot traffic ahead. Ranking walkable urbanism in America's largest metros 2019*. Washington, DC: The George Washington University School of Business and Smart Growth America.

Loukaitou-Sideris, A., Liggett, R., & Sung, H-G. (2007). Death on the crosswalk: A study of pedestrian-automobile collisions in Los Angeles. *Journal of Planning Education and Research*, 26, 338. http://dx.doi.org/351.10.1177/0739456X06297008

Maizlish, N., Woodcock, J., Co, S., Ostro, B., Fanai, A., & Fairley, D. (2013). Health co-benefits and transportation-related reductions in greenhouse gas emissions in the San Francisco Bay area. *American Journal of Public Health*, 103, 703–709.

Manville M., Monkkonen, P., & Lens, M. (2020). It's time to end single-family zoning. *Journal of the American Planning Association*, 86(1), 106–112. http://dx.doi.org/10.1080/01944363.2019.1651216

McCormack, G. R., Mâsse, L. C., Bulsara, M., Pikora, T. J., & Giles-Corti, B. (2006). Constructing indices representing supportiveness of the physical environment for walking using the Rasch measurement model. *International Journal of Behavioral Nutrition and Physical Activity*, 13(1), 13. http://dx.doi.org/10.1186/1479-5868-3-44

McDonald, N. C. (2008). Children's mode choice for the school trip: the role of distance and school location in walking to school. *Transportation*, 35, 23–35. https://doi.org/10.1007/s11116-007-9135-7

McDonald, N. C., Barth, P. H., & Steiner, R. L. (2013). Assessing the distribution of safe routes to school program funds, 2005-2012. *American Journal of Preventive Medicine*, 45(4), 401e6.

McMillan, T. E. (2007). The relative influence of urban form on a child's travel mode to school. *Transportation Research. Part A – Policy Practice*, 41, 69–79.

Mehta, V. (2013). *The street: a quintessential social public space.* Abingdon, Oxon; New York: Routledge.

Meyer, M. D. (1997). *A toolbox for alleviating congestion and enhancing mobility.* Washington DC: Institute of Transportation Engineers.

Michie, S., Richardson, M., Johnston, M., Abraham, C., Francis, J., Hardeman, W., Eccles, M. P., Cane, J., & Wood, C. E. (2013). The behavior change technique taxonomy (v1) of 93 hierarchically clustered techniques: building an international consensus for the reporting of behavior change interventions. *Annals of Behavioral Medicine*, 46, 81–95.

Moudon, A. V. & Lee, C. (2003). Walking and bicycling: an evaluation of environmental audit instruments. *American Journal of Health Promotion*, 18(1), 21–37. Retrieved from http://www.ncbi.nlm.nih.gov/pubmed/13677960

Moudon, A. V., Lee, C., Cheadle, A. D., Garvin, C., Johnson, D., Schmid, T. L., Weathers, R. D., & Lin, L. (2006). Operational definitions of walkable neighborhood: Theoretical and empirical insights. *Journal of Physical Activity & Health*, 3(s1), S99–S117. https://doi.org/10.1123/jpah.3.s1.s99

National Academies of Sciences, Engineering, and Medicine (NASEM). (2014). *Estimating bicycling and walking for planning and project development: A guidebook.* Washington, DC: The National Academies Press. https://doi.org/10.17226/22330.

National Highway Traffic Safety Administration (NHTSA) & the Bureau of Transportation Statistics (BTS). (2002). *National survey of pedestrian and bicyclist attitudes and behaviors.* Washington, DC. https://www.bts.gov/statistical-products/surveys/national-survey-pedestrian-and-bicyclist-attitudes-and-behaviors-2002

Nordback, K., O'Brien, S., & Blank, K. (2018). *Bicycle and pedestrian count programs: Summary of practice and key resources.* Chapel Hill, NC: Pedestrian and Bicycle Information Center.

Omura, J. D., Hyde, E. T., Watson, K. B., Sliwa, S. A., Fulton, J. E., & Carlson, S. A. (2019). Prevalence of children walking to school and related barriers-United States, 2017. *Preventive Medicine*, 118, 191–195. https://doi.org/10.1016/j.ypmed.2018.10.016

Phillips, C. B., Engelberg, J. K., Geremia, C. M., Zhu, W., Kurka, J., Cain, K. L., Sallis, J. F., Conway, T. L., & Adams, M. A. (2017). Online versus in-person comparison of Microscale Audit of Pedestrian Streetscapes (MAPS) assessments: Reliability of alternate methods. *International Journal of Health Geographics*, 16, 27. http://dx.doi.org/10.1186/s12942-017-0101-0

Pikora, T. J., Bull, F. C. L., Jamrozik, K., Knuiman, M., Giles-Corti, B., & Donovan, R. J. (2002). Developing a reliable audit instrument to measure the physical environment for physical activity. *American Journal of Preventive Medicine*, 23(3), 187–94. http://www.ncbi.nlm.nih.gov/pubmed/12350451

Pikora, T. J., Giles-Corti, B., Knuiman, M. W., Bull, F. C., Jamrozik, K., & Donovan, R. J. (2006). Neighborhood environmental factors correlated with walking near home: Using SPACES. *Medicine & Science in Sports & Exercise*, 38, 708–714.

Pucher, J., Buehler, R., Merom, D., & Bauman, A. (2011). Walking and cycling in the United States, 2001–2009: evidence from the national household travel surveys. *American Journal of Public Health*, 101, S310–S317. https://doi.org/10.2105/AJPH.2010.300067

Rand Corporation. (2019). NCHRP 08-36, Task 141 Evaluation of walk and bicycle demand modeling practice. American Association of State Highway Transportation Officials (AASHTO) Standing Committee on Planning, with funding provided through the National Cooperative Highway Research Program (NCHRP) Project 08- 36. http://onlinepubs.trb.org/onlinepubs/nchrp/docs/NCHRP8-36CTask141FinalReportRSGRAND.pdf

Reeves, R. (2017). *Dream hoarders.* Washington, DC: Brookings Institution.

Riggs, W. (2016). Inclusively walkable: Exploring the equity of walkable housing in the San Francisco Bay Area. *Local Environment*, 21(5), 527–554. https://doi.org/10.1080/13549839.2014.982080

Rodriguez, D. A., Khattak, A. J., & Evenson, K. R. (2006). Can New Urbanism encourage physical activity?: Comparing a New Urbanist neighborhood with conventional suburbs. *Journal of the American Planning Association*, 72 (1), 43–54.

Ryus, P., Butsick, A., Schneider, R., Proulx, F., & Hull, T. (2017). Methods and technologies for pedestrian and bicycle volume data collection: Phase 2: National Cooperative Highway Research Project. http://www.trb.org/Main/Blurbs/175860.aspx

Ryus, P., Ferguson, E., Laustsen, K. M., Schneider, R. J., Proulx, F. R., Hull, T., & Miranda-Moreno, L. (2015a). *NCHRP 797 guidebook on pedestrian and bicycle volume data collection*. Washington, DC: NCHRP. http://www.trb.org/Main/Blurbs/171973.aspx

Ryus, P., Proulx, F. R., Schneider, R. J., Hull, T., & Miranda-Moreno, L. (2015b). NCHRP Web-Only Document 205: Methods and technologies for pedestrian and bicycle volume data collection. Washington, DC: National Cooperative Highway Research Program.

Saelens, B. E. & Handy, S. L. (2008). Built environment correlates of walking: a review. *Medicine & Science in Sports & Exercise*, 40(Supp 7), S550–S556. https://doi.org/10.1249/MSS.0b013e31817c67a4

Saelens, B. E., Sallis, J. F., Black, J. B., & Frank, L. D. (2003). Environmental correlates of walking and cycling: findings from the transportation, urban design, and planning literatures. *Annals of Behavioral Medicine*, 24, 80–91.

Schlossberg, M. (2006). From TIGER to audit instruments: Measuring neighborhood walkability with street data based on geographic information systems. *Transportation Research Record*, 1982(1), 48–56. https://doi.org/10.1177/0361198106198200107

Schlossberg, M. & Brehm, C. (2009). Participatory geographic information systems and active transportation: Collecting data and creating change. *Transportation Research Record*, 2105(1), 83–91. https://doi.org/10.3141/2105-11

Schlossberg, M., Johnson-Shelton, D., Evers, C., & Moreno-Black, G. (2015). Refining the grain: Using resident-based walkability audits to better understand walkable urban form. *Journal of Urbanism: International Research on Placemaking and Urban Sustainability*, 8(3), 260–278. https://doi.org/10.1080/17549175.2014.990915

Shoup, D. (2005). *The high cost of free parking*. Chicago: Planners Press, American Planning Association.

Singleton, P., Totten, J., Orrego, J., Schneider, R., & Clifton, K. (2018). Making strides: State of the practice of pedestrian forecasting in regional travel models. *Transportation Research Record: Journal of the Transportation Research Board*. Washington, DC: Transportation Research Board of the National Academies. https://doi.org/10.1177/0361198118773555

Southworth, M. (2005). Designing the walkable city. *Journal of Urban Planning and Development*, 131(4), 246–257. https://doi.org/10.1061/(ASCE)0733-9488(2005)131:4(246)

Stevens, M. R. (2017). Does compact development make people drive less? *Journal of the American Planning Association*, 83(1), 7–18. https://doi.org/10.1080/01944363.2016.1240044

Tomer, A. & Kane, J. (2018). *Localities will deliver the next wave of transportation investments*. Washington, DC: Brookings Institution. https://www.brookings.edu/research/localities-will-deliver-the-next-wave-of-transportation-investment

US Census Bureau. (1960). *Decennial census of population and housing*. Washington, DC: US Census Bureau.

US Census Bureau. (2018). *2018: American community survey 5-year estimates*. Washington, DC: US Census Bureau.

US Department of Transportation (US DOT), Federal Highway Administration (2001). National household travel survey. https://nhts.ornl.gov

US Department of Transportation (US DOT), Federal Highway Administration (2016). Traffic monitoring guide, Washington DC. https://www.fhwa.dot.gov/policyinformation/tmguide/

US Department of Transportation (US DOT), Federal Highway Administration (2017). National household travel survey. https://nhts.ornl.gov

Villa-González, E., Barranco-Ruiz, Y., Evenson, K. R., & Chillón, P. (2018). Systematic review of interventions for promoting active school transport. *Preventive Medicine*, 111, 115–134. https://doi.org/10.1016/j.ypmed.2018.02.010

Watson, K. B., Whitfield, G. P., Thomas, J. V., Berrigan, D., Fulton, J. E., & Carlson, S. A. (2020). Associations between the National Walkability Index and walking among US adults – National Health Interview Survey 2015. *Preventive Medicine*, 137, 106122. https://doi.org/10.1016/j.ypmed.2020.106122

Wegmann, J. (2019). Death to single-family zoning…and new life to the missing middle. *Journal of the American Planning Association*, 86(1), 113–119. https://doi.org/10.1080/01944363.2019.1651217

Whitfield, G. P., Meehan, L. A., Maizlish, N., & Wendel, A. M. (2017). The integrated transport and health impact modeling tool in Nashville, Tennessee, USA: Implementation steps and lessons learned. *Journal of Transport & Health*, 5, 172–181.

Whyte, W. H. (1980). *The social life of small urban spaces*. Washington, DC: Conservation Foundation.

Woodcock, J., Edwards, P., Tonne, C., Armstrong, B. G., Ashiru, O., Banister, D., Beevers, S., Chalabi, Z., Chowdhury, Z., Cohen, A., Franco, O. H., Haines, A., Hickman, R., Lindsay, G., Mittal, I., Mohan, D., Tiwari, G., Woodward, A., & Roberts, I. (2009). Public health benefits of strategies to reduce greenhouse-gas emissions: urban land transport. *Lancet* (London, UK), 374(9705), 1930–1943. https://doi.org/10.1016/S0140-6736(09)61714-1

Xu, M., Yu, C.-Y., Lee, C., & Frank, L. D. (2018). Single-family housing value resilience of walkable versus unwalkable neighborhoods during a market downturn: Causal evidence and policy implications. *American Journal of Health Promotion*, 32(8), 1714–1722. https://doi.org/10.1177/0890117118768765

Zhu, W., Sun, Y., Kurka, J., Geremia, C., Engelberg, J. K., Cain, K., Conway, T., Sallis, J. F., Hooker, S., & Adams, M. A. (2017). Reliability between online raters with varying familiarities of a region: Microscale Audit of Pedestrian Streetscapes (MAPS). *Landscape and Urban Planning*, 167, 240–248. https://doi.org/10.1016/j.landurbplan.2017.06.014

10. Transportation: a facilitator of and barrier to smart growth

Timothy F. Welch and Steven R. Gehrke

INTRODUCTION: EXPANDING TRANSPORTATION CHOICES

Land use and transportation are inextricably connected. Smart growth policies promote a compact, mixed-use development pattern commonly accepted as a path toward alleviating the ills associated with a past century of automobile dependence. In the American context, the rise of national highway planning efforts during the interwar period of the early twentieth century set the wheels in motion for a dramatic transportation transformation of urban areas that escalated in the coming decades as a result of an expansive and popular national highway program (Boarnet, 2014). Coupled with conventional land use regulations restricting efficient development patterns, the federal focus on highway construction caused a substantial expansion of housing opportunities and commercial activity in outlying suburban areas (Cao & Chatman, 2015; Handy, 2005). The consequences of this unrestricted, low-density growth pattern, which altered urban streets from multimodal avenues into facilitators of fast and efficient automobility, have been far-reaching, spanning each sustainable development component.

Fortunately, in the past two decades, cities have increasingly adopted smart growth policies to help alleviate the environmental, economic, and social consequences brought on by the rise of automobility. The allure of smart growth principles that favor public transportation, multimodal accessibility, and a general shift from an overreliance on the personal automobile for travel provides urban planners, public officials, and transportation advocates with a path forward for lessening the detrimental impacts of sprawl. Many of these effects have resulted from prior transportation policies and city leaders' failure to curb automobility effectively. In this chapter, identifying the many pressing problems attributed to automobile dependence sets the table for a description of key transportation-related efforts where the smart growth movement can best mitigate the automobile's ill effects. Herein, we feature a set of smart growth transportation tools that have opened American streets to more sustainable transportation options and reduced the environmental, economic, and societal consequences of auto-related sprawl.

AUTOMOBILITY AND DIMINISHING TRANSPORTATION CHOICES

Automobility and its Consequences for Sustainability

The reduced competitive nature of more sustainable mobility options and the general decline in multimodal accessibility stemming from the federal highway building period have brought myriad environmental concerns. Due to sprawl, automobility has worsened air quality via increased greenhouse gas emissions as an inherent by-product of internal combustion engine vehicles (Frank & Engelke, 2005). An estimated one-quarter of global carbon dioxide emissions result from the transportation sector, with three-quarters of transportation-related emissions from vehicles crisscrossing our roads (Woodcock et al., 2009). Exposure to such emissions impact individuals in proximity to vehicles, including users of more sustainable travel modes along the same roadways and those who live, work, or play near these auto facilities. Motorists themselves are also subject to higher levels of vehicle-related air pollutants. Exposure to these pollutants is associated with adverse chronic health conditions (Giles-Corti et al., 2016). Other environmental concerns of growing automobility include natural resource consumption and a loss of valuable open spaces resulting from increased car production and road construction, expansion, and maintenance (Laurance et al., 2015). Additionally, externalities related to stormwater runoff and noise pollution result from rising automobile use (Wilson & Chakraborty, 2013).

Beyond environmental degradation, the automobile's predominance has produced profound economic consequences. Commuters who drive incur substantial out-of-pocket expenses related to vehicle ownership, operation, and maintenance. This private cost is in addition to the broader societal costs of reduced travel speeds along heavily trafficked roadways, caused by the commuter's very presence on the roadway (Brueckner, 2000). An ill-advised response to alleviate congestion has been to provide parking space at below-market prices, which subsequently contributes to increased automobile-dependence and limits cities' ability to generate revenue to pay for the public services they are providing motorists (Shoup, 2011). Relatedly, parking construction costs reduce affordable housing supplies because private developers bear this monetary cost, then pass it onto tenants, who must pay for the parking space deeded to their housing unit, regardless of auto ownership status (Howell et al., 2018).

A transportation-land use connection that is synonymous with automobility and sprawl, where reliance on a personal vehicle for day-to-day travel in most places is ubiquitous, has led to a widening gap in mobility and accessibility based on locational features as well as individual-level physical, social, and psychological characteristics (Delbosc & Currie, 2011; Wachs, 2010). The interface of transport and social disadvantage results in transport poverty and inaccessible essential goods and services which, in turn, furthers social inequities and exclusion (Lucas, 2012). Simply put, our sprawling landscapes and declining support of affordable, high-quality public transit services have created an added burden on communities where automobile ownership is now required to ascertain a basic quality-of-life standard. Regrettably, national transportation-related deaths follow positive automobile dependence trends and the provision of a regulated vehicle traffic system (Newman & Kenworthy, 1999). This grim correlation has a disproportionate impact on low-income and minority populations, who are more likely to endure transport poverty and be more susceptible to pedestrian–vehicle crashes than more socioeconomically advantaged communities (Cottrill & Thakuriah, 2010).

Determinants of Automobility

Accordingly, addressing the dominance of automobiles as a primary means of transportation—both in terms of trip mode share and per capita travel—is a central concern of sustainable urban policies (Kenworthy & Laube, 1999). However, enacting policy measures to reduce automobility and encourage more sustainable mode adoption is complicated by many factors supporting automobility. The factors include an individual's physical and psychological motives, activity requirements that motivate travel, and household residential location and lifestyle decisions (Lucas, 2009). Because of these varying factors and federal transportation policies, automobile travel in the United States has continued to escalate over the last half century. From 1969 to 2017, household vehicle miles traveled (VMT) spiraled from 7.76 billion to 2.32 trillion, with more than 9 out of 10 households now owning a private automobile and 35 million American households owning at least two (McGuckin & Fucci, 2018).

Given the sustainability consequences of a current car-dominated landscape in the United States, an obvious need exists to limit how often and far Americans drive (Crane, 2000). Consequently, many cities and states have turned to smart growth initiatives to reduce automobile dependence and mitigate environmental, social, and economic costs. Such initiatives aim to increase population and employment density, promote a mix of land use types, enhance the connectedness of street networks within a neighborhood, or improve local and regional access to destinations, rail stations, or bus stops. Planners have championed these smart growth initiatives as effective methods for cities to overcome inefficient land development patterns, reduce VMT, and facilitate walking and public transit use (Ewing & Cervero, 2010). Although the extent of the relationship between smart growth development and automobility may vary when considering its many determinants (Stevens, 2017), automobility reduction is not achievable without smarter growth (Handy, 2017). An initial goal is to increase a person's access to more sustainable modes of transportation, making driving reductions more feasible and subsequently opening a greater variety of policy options (Zhang, 2007). To turn the tide of automobility, communities must ensure diversity in transportation options by increasing the availability of high-quality public transit services, supporting active travel, and curbing unchecked vehicle access.

SMART GROWTH TRANSPORTATION TOOLS

Over the past 20 years, several programs have emerged under the smart growth umbrella to address a need for better integrating transportation and land use actions, encouraging multi-modalism, and reducing the proliferation of automobile parking.

Non-auto Infrastructure

The connections between smart growth, walkability, and bikeability are supported by a theoretical synergy between the tenets of smart growth and the ascribed benefits of the latter two active transportation modes. Smart growth aims to prevent the patterns of sprawl prevalent in community development throughout the 1900s that continue to prevail in the twenty-first century. Ultimately, to achieve smarter growth and improve the quality of life in cities, innovative development strategies must reduce traffic congestion, increase regional accessibility, and improve air quality. Academic professionals and planning organizations alike view the walkable neighborhood as a cornerstone of the smart growth movement, with less emphasis thus far placed on cycling (American Planning Association, 2012; Litman, 2018, 2019; Zook et al., 2012). The Congress for the New Urbanism similarly touts neighborhood walkability as a vital tool toward improving community development (Poticha, 2000). In Chapter 9, Clifton details the progress made over the last 30 years in promoting walking cities, as well as the research on walkability.

Beyond improvements in personal mobility, walking and cycling are considered means to improve overall health outcomes by increasing physical activity and shifting mode choice away from vehicles (Frank & Engelke, 2001). While Frank and Engelke (2001) did not provide any statistically significant connections between active travel and improved health outcomes, subsequent studies have investigated and substantiated this connection. Data collected on health outcomes at the local, state, and international levels now demonstrate significant relationships between active travel and reductions in obesity and other chronic health outcomes (Lee & Buchner, 2008; Pucher et al., 2010). Garfinkel-Castro and Ewing further discuss the public health benefits of active transportation in Chapter 12.

To further promote active transportation, Atlanta, Georgia, is currently developing one of the nation's most ambitious smart growth projects. Once completed, the Beltline will constitute a 22-mile continuous ring of paved multiuse trails surrounding the city, representing a planned investment of $4.8 billion primarily funded through tax increment financing (Atlanta Beltline, 2020). For a Sunbelt city well known for its auto-centric culture and sprawl (Bullard et al., 2000), the Beltline project marks a reinvestment in the urban core and an attempt to provide sustainable transportation alternatives to automobility.

The benefits of smart growth and its transportation tools that promote walking become more evident when compared with the opposite, unchecked sprawl. Todd Litman (2006) of the Victoria Transport Policy Institute correlated smart growth policies with a set of positive outcomes related to improved walking access to services and public spaces and greater pedestrian network connectivity. In a subsequent study, Litman (2019) found "… smart growth policies that … improve walking, cycling and public transit services tend to increase affordability …" through reductions in housing construction costs and per capita public service expenditures (Goodman, 2019). Additional research has also revealed positive associations between walking and various built environment characteristics considered to be smart growth metrics, including intersection density, land use mixing, and walking proximity to destinations (Ewing & Cervero, 2010; Saelens & Handy, 2008). Walking conditions and outcomes have also improved by enacting other smart growth tenets such as diversifying housing stock, increasing housing density, promoting compact development, and offering more open spaces (Pucher et al., 2010). More recent studies confirm the connection between positive walking outcomes and smart growth practices (Ewing & Hamidi, 2014).

For as many studies that find a relationship between smart growth efforts and positive walking outcomes, a handful of studies still critique these findings. Some scholars believe positive relationships between smart growth factors and walking to be limited due to small sample sizes or an insufficient understanding of the complex relationship between land use and walking (Ewing & Cervero, 2010; Handy, 2005; Saelens & Handy, 2008). Additionally, critiques have highlighted the limitation of these connections to correlations, with little research identifying the causal link between smart growth actions and the shift of travel behavior away from vehicles (Ewing & Cervero, 2010; Handy, 2005). Some of these same researchers have speculated that enacting smart growth strategies has done less to shift travel away from personal vehicle use than it has to facilitate desired walking trips that were previously unfeasible due to physical barriers (Handy, 2005).

While facing complex issues that persistently confront urban revitalization projects, including gentrification and limited affordable housing supply (Powers, 2020), the concept of Atlanta's Beltline and the promise of transportation beyond automobility appears to be overwhelmingly popular. In 2018, with only 30 percent of the trail system completed, the Beltline attracted over two million visitors (Flynn, 2019), making it one of Atlanta's most popular attractions. On any given weekend, portions of the Beltline become so crowded with pedestrians and cyclists that many visitors complain this non-auto infrastructure is too challenging to navigate (Wheatley, 2020). The Beltline's notable successes and failures provide important lessons about the pent-up demand for infrastructure dedicated to more sustainable modes and smarter development patterns.

Transit-oriented Development

Peter Calthorpe coined the concept of transit-oriented development (TOD) over a generation ago in his book, *The Next American Metropolis* (Calthorpe, 1993; Jamme et al., 2019; Renne & Appleyard, 2019; Zhang, 2007). While the definition of the term varies, TOD typically entails creating spatially mixed land uses with considerably high density and urban design features that support non-motorized trips close to the transit station. In this definition are the environmental constructs embodied in the original 3Ds (density, diversity, and design) framework (Cervero & Kockelman, 1997), which has been expanded in subsequent studies to include additional smart growth metrics such as distance to transit, destination accessibility, and transit performance (Chen et al., 2017; Ewing & Cervero, 2010).

The objectives behind making TOD concepts concrete are wide-ranging. They include bolstering transit ridership, addressing negative externalities associated with automobility, expanding tax revenue via increased property values, and enhancing residents' quality of life (Calthorpe, 1993; Cao & Lou, 2018; Crane, 1996). An urban area must have a robust public transit system to orient future development and accomplish these objectives. Past TOD has focused primarily on heavy rail (Loo et al., 2010) and to a lesser extent, light rail systems (Arrington, 2005). TOD can also be successful using high-quality bus rapid transit services, as countries in Latin America have pioneered (Cervero & Dai, 2014). While high-quality transit is a necessary ingredient for successful TOD implementation, land uses that support TOD are also critical to reducing travel by personal automobile.

In Washington, DC, the Columbia Heights neighborhood sought to enact these objectives in developing a successful TOD program around the Washington Metropolitan Area Transit Authority (WMATA) Metro rail station. Faced with a multitude of empty buildings, vacant land, and depressed economic conditions as a result of rioting following the assassination of Martin Luther King, Jr. in April 1968 (Brown, 2017; Green et al., 2017), the 1999 opening of this WMATA Metro station stimulated the revitalization of a walkable neighborhood in the city's midtown, characterized by dense residential construction, retail activity, and historic preservation (Howell, 2017).

Given the intended benefits of TODs, many planning policies have been put in place in the United States and worldwide to operationalize the concept (Cervero, 1998; Zhang, 2007). Concurrently, over the past 25 years, a robust evidence base on this subject has been established and continues to expand. Jamme et al. (2019) found approximately 300 studies or research items on TOD from the United States and Canada alone. Renne and Appleyard (2019, p. 402) noted an exponential increase of annual citations for TOD-related studies over this time, a further testament to the enduring attractiveness of this smart growth concept. Many such studies quantify the impact of living in TOD neighborhoods on travel behavior, revealing that TOD residents tend to drive less than similar residents of non-TOD areas (Cervero & Arrington, 2008; Chen et al., 2017; Griffiths & Curtis, 2017; Kamruzzaman et al., 2015; Nasri & Zhang, 2014; Park et al., 2018). Many studies have also examined the extent to which TOD encourages transit ridership and mode choice (Lindsey et al., 2010; Lund et al., 2004).

In Washington, DC, Columbia Heights experienced strong performance of the Metro heavy rail station, which coincided with an increase in nearby residential property demand and development. This rise in density and mixing of land uses, with one-third of residential land uses classified as medium-high density and 15 percent of the land within one mile of the Columbia Heights station being commercial in 2007

(Hill, 2013), started in 1996 with the DC Redevelopment Land Agency acquiring two large parcels near the planned Metro station (DC Office of Planning, 2004) and continued into 2015 with over 300 new units per 1,000 occupied units constructed in the previous seven years (Schuetz, 2019). For this TOD, there is no mistaking the intrinsic transportation-land use connection.

Recently, there has been growing attention to the social equity aspects of TOD. Scholars and activists have lamented the likely and undesirable scenario by which TODs might displace existing low-income residents due to subsequent increases in land values and rents associated with enhanced transit accessibility. Fortunately, the empirical evidence associating TODs with displacement and gentrification remains limited, with available quantitative studies not necessarily signaling that TODs induce this outcome (Baker & Lee, 2017; Chatman et al., 2019; Dong, 2017). Other studies, primarily using qualitative research methods, offer case-specific analyses indicating how low-income and minority residents cope with neighborhood changes associated with TOD in established communities (Lung-Amam et al., 2019; Sandoval & Herrera, 2015). Finio and Knaap discuss the potential for smart growth efforts to cause gentrification in Chapter 13, and Lung-Amam and June-Friesen argue for more equitable TOD processes in Chapter 14.

While Columbia Heights has, in many ways, served as an exemplar of this smart growth tool, there are sustainability challenges that require attention and action going forward, as other TODs around the country are learning. Foremost, while there has arguably been an achievement in housing stock affordability, the demographic composition of Columbia Heights has changed (Green et al., 2017), with its African American population diminishing by over 20 percent since the Metro station's opening (Howell, 2020).

Complete Streets

Complete Streets (CS) policy has proliferated beyond the transportation planning and urban design sphere, to the extent that the term has become lay vocabulary (Zehngebot & Peiser, 2014). The basic idea of CS stems from the notion that streets should serve a broader set of travel modes beyond the automobile. In this regard, streets must be considered "as places instead of mere transportation links" (Schlossberg et al., 2013). A neighborhood's street network should harmoniously support pedestrians, cyclists, and transit-goers, as well as motorists. While CS interventions are often context-sensitive, the term typically translates to a variety of strategies for urban design and streetscape improvements. These strategies include "ample sidewalks, improved standards for street tree planting and other landscape elements, bike lanes, dedicated bus lanes, comfortable and accessible transit stops, frequent crossing opportunities, median islands, and curb extensions" (Zehngebot & Peiser, 2014). To quantify and inventory such strategies, researchers have developed audit-based assessments for designing CS by incorporating voices from four users: pedestrians, cyclists, transit riders, and motorists (Kingsbury et al., 2011). Other studies have proposed methodologies to quantify how CS' level of service differs from auto-oriented road designs (Elias, 2011).

In Portland, Oregon, the largest urban revitalization initiative in the city's history has taken shape over the past 20 years, with the realization of a new transportation and land development pattern, including CS ideals (De Sousa, 2014). The South Waterfront District, located south of Portland's downtown on a 409-acre former brownfield site that was home to shipbuilding and lumber activity until the decline of these industries in the 1960s (Ramiller, 2019), was planned in 2002 with goals to provide 10,000 jobs, 3,000 homes, and a multimodal transportation system by 2019 (Portland Bureau of Planning, 2002). Building on Portland's tradition of high-quality pedestrian access and imaginative street design elements (Southworth, 2005), the South Waterfront District has emphasized the consideration of design, function, and short- and long-term effectiveness in its street standards and design principles.

Advocates of using CS as a smart growth tool claim the wide-ranging benefits include improved public health and well-being, enhanced traffic safety, and community vibrancy. Due to the multidimensional advantages thought to arise from instituting CS policies and leading interventions, many municipalities in the United States and beyond have sought to implement CS policies, to a varying extent (Gregg & Hess, 2019; Schlossberg et al., 2013).

While CS policy has proliferated, research on the subject remains curiously limited and "thin" (Gregg & Hess, 2019, p. 408). Available studies have shed some light on the quantifiable impact of CS on various travel outcomes. For instance, Brown et al. (2016) used accelerometers to measure walk trips to/from transit stations, non-transit-related walk trips, and cycling trips for residents living near a CS project relative to individuals who reside farther away, and discovered that residents who live near complete streets logged more walking trips than their comparison group. A similar study leveraged before-and-after data in a natural experiment design that confirmed the positive impacts of the CS on observed physical activity (Brown et al., 2015). A study in Lexington, Kentucky, confirmed the smart growth benefits of transforming a two-way street to include CS features (Riggs & Gilderbloom, 2016); road safety improvement was associated with the CS transformation, with increased property values and reduced crime. Another study, employing a randomized experimental design to establish still-stronger causal effects, indicated the economic benefits of CS-oriented streetscape improvements (Gonzalez-Navarro & Quintana-Domeque, 2016).

Today, the realization of Portland's South Waterfront District plan has resulted in a new vibrant neighborhood connected to downtown Portland by the city's streetcar system, to the Oregon Health & Science University atop Marquam Hill by an aerial tram, and to the city's eastside communities by the new multimodal Tilikum Crossing bridge (Sarkheyli & Rafieian, 2018). Portland continues to complete the South Waterfront Greenway as part of a 40-mile Willamette Greenway Trail that will offer a continuous corridor for recreation and active commuting (Lacilla & Ordeig, 2016), advance the Green Loop with pedestrian and bicycle connections between the South Waterfront District and Portland State University campus, and extend current streetcar services to the southern portions of the neighborhood (Portland Bureau of Planning, 2015).

Parking Management

Parking management represents a suite of strategies designed to reduce parking requirements at periods of high demand, limit current parking capacity, and reduce emissions released by idling cars or those circling the block to find parking. Parking management systems are typically designed and implemented at local levels due to the varying effectiveness of context-specific strategies.

Under authority of the Clean Air Act, the Environmental Protection Agency (EPA) has released numerous reports discussing this smart growth tool, connecting smart parking management strategies to reducing emissions and promoting infill and brownfield redevelopment. Since the mid-1970s, the EPA has released several updates aimed at assisting localities in designing parking management systems and developing master parking plans (Dern et al., 1976; Environmental Protection Agency, 1999, 2006; Forinash et al., 2003). Parking management systems, if designed well, have numerous potential benefits, including facility cost savings, improved service quality, flexible facility location and design, additional revenue generation, mobility management support, smart growth facilitation, alternative mode promotion, reduced stormwater management, support for equity objectives, and creation of more livable communities (Litman, 2008). Because of the potential cost savings and quality-of-life improvements associated with parking management, numerous patented parking management systems have arisen in the last two decades (Chen et al., 2013; Clapper, 2000; Howard et al., 2005; Moore, 1998; Rodriguez et al., 2012; Shlomo, 1997). Implemented technologies within parking management systems vary from avant-garde solutions such as radio-frequency identification (RFID) card readers to more traditional solutions, such as license readers and metering.

Although the technologies employed by parking management systems vary considerably, most parking management systems use similar strategies to reduce the parking capacity required. Of these, the most significant reductions come from shared parking, parking regulations, more accurate and flexible standards, parking maximums (as opposed to parking minimums), remote parking, smart growth policies, financial incentives, and unbundling parking from building leases; each with a potential required parking reduction of 10–30 percent (Environmental Protection Agency, 2006; Litman, 2008; Weinberger et al., 2010). In addition to parking requirement reductions, combining these individual strategies within parking master plans can produce more significant reductions. However, some studies indicate parking regulations are not effective without proper enforcement, which can come in the form of traditional enforcement assisted by camera-equipped mobile scanning devices or automated scanning technologies (Weinberger et al., 2010).

San Francisco created an ambitious program to better price on-street parking so as to reduce the demand for parking and encourage alternative modes of travel within the city. The SFpark program started in 2011 as a pilot seeking to demonstrate the feasibility of smarter parking policy. By monitoring the utilization and availability of parking spaces across seven parking management regions, the city dynamically changed the parking price to manage demand (SFMTA, 2014). After this successful pilot program, the San Francisco Municipal Transportation Agency (SFMTA) rolled out the SFpark program across the city to over 28,000 parking meters, to limit parking occupancy to between 60 and 80 percent (Descant, 2018).

SFpark drivers each previously spent nearly 12 minutes simply cruising for available parking spots; with dynamic pricing, the time spent searching for a parking spot was reduced by five minutes (Millard-Ball et al., 2014). Dynamic pricing also had a measurable impact on vehicle miles traveled. With dynamic pricing, drivers traveled 30 percent fewer miles and achieved a similar reduction in greenhouse gas emissions (SFMTA, 2014). Beyond the direct effect on drivers looking for a parking spot, SFpark's dynamic pricing has had a measurable impact on transit ridership and traffic flow. Early estimates of the program's impact on transit ridership show increases in bus ridership of five percent, and as much as 11 percent during peak hours (Krishnamurthy & Ngo, 2020), while lane occupancy fell by five percent. While seemingly small, these figures represent an estimated $34 million in net benefits (Krishnamurthy & Ngo, 2020).

Parking management systems have numerous positive benefits; however, few studies have evaluated the potential negative consequences of parking management systems. Because parking management generally reduces the cost and inconveniences associated with vehicle use, these systems also reduce demand for more sustainable transportation modes, increasing congestion and emissions from vehicles (Weinberger et al., 2010). Parking master plans must connect any parking management strategies with the community's long-range plans to increase accessibility to multimodal transportation, reduce inequities, and discourage conventional development practices that lead to excessive parking.

Before more widely implementing parking management strategies, further research is needed to evaluate potential costs and benefits. However, future smart growth plans for transportation must include a more salient pricing policy. Encouraging smarter growth and more sustainable travel behaviors via pricing will become more possible with the increasing ubiquity of big data sources in urban areas. SFpark is an example of how data availability, combined with better pricing, can lead to more desirable outcomes, particularly in a city's most congested spaces.

Emerging Mobility Options

Access to infrastructure dedicated to sustainable travel options, proximity to rapid transit stations, streets that safely support multiple modes, and parking management strategies are all public policies that can help American cities grow smarter. While examples of policy implementation, which can take a decade or more to reach fruition, are abundant across the country, new technologies can pose a threat to this progress. The rise of ride-hailing services has changed the way people travel in even the densest urban environments over the past decade. Once promising to be a boon for cities seeking to bridge first/last mile gaps in public transit systems, these emerging mobility options are now seen as competing with public transit for ridership and promoting automobility (Gehrke et al., 2019). This replacement of more sustainable travel modes for ride-hailing services also adds congestion, with recent evidence attributing 60 percent of San Francisco's reduced traffic speeds on streets between 2010 and 2016 to new ride-hailing services (Roy, 2019). Further adding to congestion, ride-hailing drivers may spend up to 40 percent of their time on roadways without a passenger in their cars (Brown, 2020).

Just as ride-hailing services are a modernized taxi service, other new mobility options, such as on-demand microtransit, appear little more than iterations of long-established travel modes, infused with new technologies. While microtransit promises to extend "legacy" public transit systems using improved scheduling and routing algorithms, this new demand-responsive mobility option typically serves lower density locations and costs riders more than a public transit trip. Moreover, research suggests that microtransit may in some instances be less efficient than traditional bus services, carrying fewer than half the passengers than a bus over the same period (Higashide, 2019).

Autonomous vehicles (AVs) have been heralded as a transportation revolution for cities that will make more efficient use of existing roads, enhance traffic safety, and reduce or eliminate personal car ownership. However, the implementation of AV technologies and widespread replacement of existing vehicle fleets is years if not decades away, with limited evidence that people will forego personal car ownership. While AVs may improve efficiency and safety, if the current adoption patterns of ride-hailing services offer a glimpse into the future of automobility, then AVs may also threaten to decouple the transportation-land use connection. Drivers will no longer spend their already long commutes navigating roadways but instead participate in new in-vehicle activities that may carry the real estate adage of "drive until you qualify" to entirely new commute lengths.

However, not all technologies are potential problems for smart growth. One oft-cited limitation to broader utilization of public transit is the first/last mile problem. This problem is a gap in high-quality service faced by potential riders between their residence and the closest transit stop or their trip destination and its nearest stop. Recently, shared e-scooters that users rent via smartphone apps have surfaced as a potential technology-based solution to address this important gap. Shared e-scooter services offer the capability to quickly take casual riders to/from their stop at speeds surpassing that of most folks walking. In addition, some urban markets have seen a proliferation in shared e-bike services, following the same dockless approach as e-scooters but offering a potentially faster travel connection. Both e-scooters and e-bikes offer possibilities in extending the range of existing infrastructure without directly competing with existing public transit systems. While questions exist regarding the cost and safety of these options and the longevity of business models, these emerging shared mobility options could breathe new life into current non-auto transportation systems.

CONCLUSION

The rise of automobility in America throughout the twentieth century and its adverse impacts on demand for public transit, walkability, and compact growth, has reshaped our urban landscapes. While the consequences of automobile-oriented development have been dramatic and widespread, optimism remains that the waves of automobile-induced sprawl can be reduced in the coming years. As urban planners continue to develop and adopt new smart growth programs to encourage active transportation, increase transit ridership, and better manage vehicle parking, technology has also facilitated the rise of new mobility alternatives to the personal car. Importantly, the urgency to implement these programs must be matched by their flexibility to meet uncertainty, as the pandemic brought on by COVID-19 has demonstrated. Transit systems that lost riders, services, and revenue due to travel restrictions may take years to bounce back; however, more frequent and reliable services along fewer routes may ultimately best help cities reduce automobility and face the greater challenge of reducing vehicle carbon emissions that contribute to climate change. Together, the continued implementation of the smart growth transportation tools described in this chapter, paired with the prudent integration of emerging mobility options, carries the prospect to offer more people an opportunity to experience life outside of the car and suburbia.

While the transportation policies that have helped to fuel the separation of land uses, lower neighborhood densities, and create disconnected auto-dominated street networks, can still very much be found, there is growing interest in deploying these smart growth tools to reorient cities toward more compact multimodal landscapes. The next twenty years of transportation and land use should offer exciting new possibilities with vast implications for the way our cities will grow.

REFERENCES

American Planning Association. (2012). *APA policy guide on smart growth.* American Planning Association. Retrieved from https://www.planning.org/policy/guides/adopted/smartgrowth.htm

Arrington, G. B. (2005). TOD in the United States: The experience with light rail. In *Transit-Oriented Development – Making it Happen conference*, Fremantle, Australia (pp. 5–8).

Atlanta Beltline. (2020, February 18). *Project funding.* Atlanta Beltline. Retrieved from https://beltline.org/the-project/project-funding

Baker, D. M., & Lee, B. (2017). How does light rail transit (LRT) impact gentrification? Evidence from fourteen U.S. urbanized areas. *Journal of Planning Education and Research*, 0739456X17713619. doi.org/10.1177/0739456X17713619

Boarnet, M. G. (2014). National transportation planning: Lessons from the U.S. Interstate Highways. *Transport Policy, 31*, 73–82. doi.org/10.1016/j.tranpol.2013.11.003

Brown, B. B., Werner, C. M., Tribby, C. P., Miller, H. J., & Smith, K. R. (2015). Transit use, physical activity, and body mass index changes: Objective measures associated with complete street light-rail construction. *American Journal of Public Health*, *105*(7), 1468–1474. https://doi.org/10.2105/AJPH.2015.302561

Brown, B. B., Smith, K. R., Tharp, D., Werner, C. M., Tribby, C. P., Miller, H. J., & Jensen, W. (2016). A complete street intervention for walking to transit, nontransit walking, and bicycling: A quasi-experimental demonstration of increased use. *Journal of Physical Activity and Health*, *13*(11), 1210–1219. doi.org/10.1123/jpah.2016-0066

Brown, E. (2020, February 15). The ride-hail utopia that got stuck in traffic. *The Wall Street Journal*. Retrieved from https://www.wsj.com/articles/the-ride-hail-utopia-that-got-stuck -in-traffic-11581742802

Brown, S. (2017). *Beyond gentrification: Strategies for guiding the conversation and redirecting the outcomes of community transition* (W14-12). Retrieved from Joint Center for Housing Studies of Harvard University website: https://www.jchs.harvard.edu/ research-areas/working-papers/beyond-gentrification-strategies-guiding-conversation-and -redirecting

Brueckner, J. K. (2000). Urban sprawl: Diagnosis and remedies. *International Regional Science Review*, *23*(2), 160–171. doi.org/10.1177/016001700761012710

Bullard, R., Johnson, G. S., & Torres, A. O. (2000). *Sprawl city: Race, politics, and planning in Atlanta*. Washington, DC: Island Press.

Calthorpe, P. (1993). *The next American metropolis: Ecology, community, and the American dream* (3rd edition). New York, NY: Princeton Architectural Press.

Cao, X., & Chatman, D. (2015). How will smart growth land-use policies affect travel? A theoretical discussion on the importance of residential sorting: *Environment and Planning B: Planning and Design*. doi.org/10.1177/0265813515600060

Cao, X., & Lou, S. (2018). When and how much did the Green Line LRT increase single-family housing values in St. Paul, Minnesota? *Journal of Planning Education and Research*, *38*(4), 427–436. doi.org/10.1177/0739456X17707811

Cervero, R. (1998). *The transit metropolis: A global inquiry* (4th ed.). Washington, DC: Island Press.

Cervero, R., & Arrington, G. B. (2008). *Effects of TOD on housing, parking, and travel*. Washington, DC: National Academies Press. doi.org/10.17226/14179

Cervero, R., & Dai, D. (2014). BRT TOD: Leveraging transit oriented development with bus rapid transit investments. *Transport Policy*, *36*, 127–138.

Cervero, R., & Kockelman, K. (1997). Travel demand and the 3Ds: Density, diversity, and design. *Transportation Research Part D: Transport and Environment*, *2*(3), 199–219. doi .org/10.1016/S1361-9209(97)00009-6

Chatman, D. G., Xu, R., Park, J., & Spevack, A. (2019). Does transit-oriented gentrification increase driving? *Journal of Planning Education and Research*, *39*(4), 482–495. doi.org/10 .1177/0739456X19872255

Chen, C.-T., Lin, I.-L., Lee, C.-C., Wu, S.-K., Chen, H.-C., & Wu, S.-W. (2013). *U.S. Patent No. 8502698 B2*. Washington, DC: US Patent and Trademark Office.

Chen, F., Wu, J., Chen, X., & Wang, J. (2017). Vehicle kilometers traveled reduction impacts of transit-oriented development: Evidence from Shanghai City. *Transportation Research Part D: Transport and Environment*, *55*, 227–245. doi.org/10.1016/j.trd.2017.07.006

Clapper, E. O. (2000). *U.S. Patent No. US 6147624*. Washington, DC: US Patent and Trademark Office.

Cottrill, C. D., & Thakuriah, P. V. (2010). Evaluating pedestrian crashes in areas with high low-income or minority populations. *Accident Analysis & Prevention*, *42*(6), 1718–1728. doi.org/10.1016/j.aap.2010.04.012

Crane, R. (1996). On form versus function: Will the new urbanism reduce traffic, or increase it? *Journal of Planning Education and Research*, *15*(2), 117–126. doi.org/10.1177/ 0739456X9601500204

Crane, R. (2000). The influence of urban form on travel: An interpretive review. *Journal of Planning Literature, 15*(1), 3–23.

DC Office of Planning. (2004). *Columbia Heights Public realm framework plan.* Retrieved from https://planning.dc.gov/publication/columbia-heights-public-realm-framework-plan

De Sousa, C. (2014). The greening of urban post-industrial landscapes: Past practices and emerging trends. *Local Environment, 19*(10), 1049–1067. doi.org/10.1080/13549839.2014.886560

Delbosc, A., & Currie, G. (2011). The spatial context of transport disadvantage, social exclusion and well-being. *Journal of Transport Geography, 19*(6), 1130–1137. doi.org/10.1016/j.jtrangeo.2011.04.005

Dern, J., Cole, J., Fallon, B., Heller, J., Hickey, S., Holmes, J., & Sanson, R. (1976). *Parking management strategies for reducing automobile emissions* (EPA-600/5-76-008). Washington, DC: US Environmental Protection Agency, Office of Research and Development.

Descant, S. (2018, January 3). San Francisco rolls out dynamic parking rate model. *Government Technology.* Retrieved from https://www.govtech.com/fs/automation/San-Francisco-Rolls-Out-Dynamic-Parking-Rate-Model.html

Dong, H. (2017). Rail-transit-induced gentrification and the affordability paradox of TOD. *Journal of Transport Geography, 63*, 1–10. doi.org/10.1016/j.jtrangeo.2017.07.001

Elias, A. (2011). Automobile-oriented or complete street?: Pedestrian and bicycle level of service in the new multimodal paradigm. *Transportation Research Record, 2257*(1), 80–86. doi.org/10.3141/2257-09

Environmental Protection Agency. (1999). *Parking alternatives: Making way for urban infill and brownfield redevelopment* (EPA 231-K-99-001). Washington, DC: US Environmental Protection Agency, Office of Research and Development.

Environmental Protection Agency. (2006). *Parking spaces / community places—Finding the balance through smart growth solutions* (EPA 231-K-06-001). Washington, DC: US Environmental Protection Agency, Office of Research and Development.

Ewing, R., & Cervero, R. (2010). Travel and the built environment. *Journal of the American Planning Association, 76*(3), 265–294. doi.org/10.1080/01944361003766766

Ewing, R., & Hamidi, S. (2014). *Measuring sprawl.* Washington, DC: Smart Growth America.

Flynn, K. (2019, February 26). The high stakes of the High Line effect. *Architect.* Retrieved from https://www.architectmagazine.com/aia-architect/aiafeature/the-high-stakes-of-the-high-line-effect_o

Forinash, C. V., Millard-Ball, A., Dougherty, C., & Tumlin, J. (2003, July). *Smart growth alternatives to minimum parking requirements.* In Second Urban Street Symposium: Uptown, Downtown, or Small Town: Designing Urban Streets That Work. Transportation Research Board; Federal Highway Administration; ITE, ITE Traffic Engineer Council, and So Cal ITE; American Society of Civil Engineers; Mack-Blackwell Rural Transportation Study Center; and US Access Board. Retrieved from https://trid.trb.org/view/755617

Frank, L. D., & Engelke, P. O. (2001). The built environment and human activity patterns: Exploring the impacts of urban form on public health. *Journal of Planning Literature, 16*(2), 202–218. doi.org/10.1177/08854120122093339

Frank, L. D., & Engelke, P. (2005). Multiple impacts of the built environment on public health: Walkable places and the exposure to air pollution. *International Regional Science Review.* doi.org/10.1177/0160017604273853

Gehrke, S. R., Felix, A., & Reardon, T. G. (2019). Substitution of ride-hailing services for more sustainable travel options in the greater Boston region. *Transportation Research Record, 2673*(1), 438–446.

Giles-Corti, B., Vernez-Moudon, A., Reis, R., Turrell, G., Dannenberg, A. L., Badland, H., Foster, S., Lowe, M., Sallis, J. F., Stevenson, M., & Owen, N. (2016). City planning and population health: A global challenge. *The Lancet, 388*(10062), 2912–2924. doi.org/10 .1016/S0140-6736(16)30066-6

Gonzalez-Navarro, M., & Quintana-Domeque, C. (2016). Paving streets for the poor: Experimental analysis of infrastructure effects. *Review of Economics and Statistics, 98*(2), 254–267.

Goodman, C. B. (2019). The fiscal impacts of urban sprawl: Evidence from U.S. county areas. *Public Budgeting & Finance, 39*(4), 3–27. doi.org/10.1111/pbaf.12239

Green, R. D., Mulusa, J. K., Byers, A. A., & Parmer, C. (2017). The indirect displacement hypothesis: A case study in Washington, D.C. *The Review of Black Political Economy, 44*(1), 1–22. doi.org/10.1007/s12114-016-9242-9

Gregg, K., & Hess, P. (2019). Complete streets at the municipal level: A review of American municipal complete street policy. *International Journal of Sustainable Transportation, 13*(6), 407–418. doi.org/10.1080/15568318.2018.1476995

Griffiths, B., & Curtis, C. (2017). Effectiveness of transit oriented development in reducing car use: Case study of Subiaco, Western Australia. *Urban Policy and Research, 35*(4), 391–408. doi.org/10.1080/08111146.2017.1311855

Handy, S. (2005). Smart growth and the transportation-land use connection: What does the research tell us? *International Regional Science Review.* doi.org/10.1177/ 0160017604273626

Handy, S. (2017). Thoughts on the meaning of Mark Stevens's meta-analysis. *Journal of the American Planning Association, 83*(1), 26–28.

Higashide, S. (2019). *Better buses, better cities: How to plan, run, and win the fight for effective transit.* Washington, DC: Island Press.

Hill, C. (2013). A geographic analysis of residential land use around Washington D.C. Metro stations. *International Journal of Geographical Information Science, 27*(10).

Howard, C. K., Cayetano, K., & Omojola, O. (2005). *U.S. Patent No. US 6885311 B2.* Washington, DC: US Patent and Trademark Office.

Howell, A., Currans, K., Gehrke, S., Norton, G., & Clifton, K. (2018). Transportation impacts of affordable housing: Informing development review with travel behavior analysis. *Journal of Transport and Land Use, 11*(1). doi.org/10.5198/jtlu.2018.1129

Howell, K. (2017). Building empowerment in market-based redevelopment: Changing paradigms for affordable housing and community development in Washington, DC. *Community Development Journal, 52*(4), 573–590. doi.org/10.1093/cdj/bsv069

Howell, K. (2020). Winning in a "lose-lose" environment of economic development: Housing, community empowerment, and neighborhood redevelopment in the Columbia Heights neighborhood of Washington, DC. *Housing and Society, 47*(1), 22–41. doi.org/10.1080/ 08882746.2019.1697090

Jamme, H.-T., Rodriguez, J., Bahl, D., & Banerjee, T. (2019). A twenty-five-year biography of the TOD concept: From design to policy, planning, and implementation. *Journal of Planning Education and Research, 39*(4), 409–428. doi.org/10.1177/0739456X19882073

Kamruzzaman, Md., Shatu, F. M., Hine, J., & Turrell, G. (2015). Commuting mode choice in transit oriented development: Disentangling the effects of competitive neighbourhoods, travel attitudes, and self-selection. *Transport Policy, 42*, 187–196. doi.org/10.1016/j .tranpol.2015.06.003

Kenworthy, J. R., & Laube, F. B. (1999). Patterns of automobile dependence in cities: An international overview of key physical and economic dimensions with some implications for urban policy. *Transportation Research Part A: Policy and Practice, 33*(7-8), 691–723.

Kingsbury, K. T., Lowry, M. B., & Dixon, M. P. (2011). What makes a "complete street" complete?: A robust definition, given context and public input. *Transportation Research Record, 2245*(1), 103–110. doi.org/10.3141/2245-13

Krishnamurthy, C. K. B., & Ngo, N. S. (2020). The effects of smart-parking on transit and traffic: Evidence from SFpark. *Journal of Environmental Economics and Management, 99.* doi.org/10.1016/j.jeem.2019.102273

Lacilla, E., & Ordeig, J. M. (2016). Waterfront public realm design: Towards a sustainable identity urban projects in Vancouver and Portland. *Journal of Sustainable Development, 9*(2), 169–180. doi.org/10.5539/jsd.v9n2p169

Laurance, W. F., Sloan, S., Weng, L., & Sayer, J. A. (2015). Estimating the environmental costs of Africa's massive "development corridors." *Current Biology, 25*(24), 3202–3208. doi.org/10.1016/j.cub.2015.10.046

Lee, I.-M., & Buchner, D. M. (2008). The importance of walking to public health. *Medicine & Science in Sports & Exercise, 40* (7 Suppl), S512–518. doi.org/10.1249/MSS .0b013e31817c65d0

Lindsey, M., Schofer, J. L., Durango-Cohen, P., & Gray, K. A. (2010). Relationship between proximity to transit and ridership for journey-to-work trips in Chicago. *Transportation Research Part A: Policy and Practice, 44*(9), 697–709. doi.org/10.1016/j.tra.2010.07.003

Litman, T. (2006). *Parking management best practices.* Chicago, IL: Planners Press

Litman, T. (2008). *Recommendations for improving LEED transportation and parking credits.* VTPI. Retrieved from www.vtpi.org/leed_rec.pdf

Litman, T. (2018). *Evaluating criticism of smart growth.* Retrieved from https://www.vtpi.org/ sgcritics.pdf

Litman, T. (2019). *Understanding smart growth savings: Evaluating economic savings and benefits of compact development.* Retrieved from https://www.vtpi.org/sg_save.pdf

Loo, B. P., Chen, C., & Chan, E. T. (2010). Rail-based transit-oriented development: Lessons from New York City and Hong Kong. *Landscape and Urban Planning, 97*(3), 202–212.

Lucas, K. (2009). Actual and perceived car dependence: Likely implications of enforced reductions in car use for livelihood, lifestyles, and well-being. *Transportation Research Record, 2118*(1), 8–15. doi.org/ 10.3141/2118-02

Lucas, K. (2012). Transport and social exclusion: Where are we now? *Transport Policy, 20,* 105–113. doi.org/10.1016/j.tranpol.2012.01.013

Lund, H. M., Cervero, R., & Wilson, R. W. (2004). *Travel characteristics of transit-oriented development in California.* Retrieved from http://www.csupomona.edu/~rwwillson/tod/ Pictures/TOD2.pdf

Lung-Amam, W., Pendall, R., & Knaap, E. (2019). Mi casa no es su casa: The fight for equi-table transit-oriented development in an inner-ring suburb. *Journal of Planning Education and Research, 39*(4), 442–455. doi.org/10.1177/0739456X19878248

McGuckin, N., & Fucci, A. (2018). Summary of travel trends. 2017 National Household Travel Survey (No. ORNL/TM-2004/297, 885762). U.S. Department of Transportation, Federal Highway Administration. doi.org/10.2172/885762.

Millard-Ball, A., Weinberger, R. R., & Hampshire, R. C. (2014). Is the curb 80% full or 20% empty? Assessing the impacts of San Francisco's parking pricing experiment. *Transportation Research Part A: Policy and Practice, 63,* 76–92. doi.org/10.1016/j.tra .2014.02.016

Moore, S. J. (1998). *U.S. Patent No. 5,845,268.* Washington, DC: US Patent and Trademark Office.

Nasri, A., & Zhang, L. (2014). The analysis of transit-oriented development (TOD) in Washington, D.C. and Baltimore metropolitan areas. *Transport Policy, 32,* 172–179. doi .org/10.1016/j.tranpol.2013.12.009

Newman, P., & Kenworthy, J. (1999). Costs of automobile dependence: Global survey of cities. *Transportation Research Record.* doi.org/10.3141/1670-04

Park, K., Ewing, R., Scheer, B. C., & Ara Khan, S. S. (2018). Travel behavior in TODs vs. non-TODs: Using cluster analysis and propensity score matching. *Transportation Research Record,* 0361198118774159. doi.org/10.1177/0361198118774159

Portland Bureau of Planning. (2002). *South waterfront plan*. Portland, OR: City of Portland.

Portland Bureau of Planning. (2015). *Central City 2035: West quadrant plan*. Portland, OR: City of Portland.

Poticha, S. (2000). Smart growth and new urbanism: What's the difference? *Congress for the New Urbanism*. Retrieved from https://www.cnu.org/publicsquare/smart-growth-and-new -urbanism-what%E2%80%99s-difference

Powers, B. (2020, February 18). *Runaway gentrification in the path of Atlanta's BeltLine— CityLab*. CityLab. Retrieved from https://www.citylab.com/equity/2017/11/putting-the -brakes-on-runaway-gentrification-in-atlanta/545555/

Pucher, J., Buehler, R., Bassett, D. R., & Dannenberg, A. L. (2010). Walking and cycling to health: A comparative analysis of city, state, and international data. *American Journal of Public Health, 100*(10), 1986–1992. doi.org/10.2105/AJPH.2009.189324

Ramiller, A. (2019). Establishing the green neighbourhood: Approaches to neighbourhood-scale sustainability certification in Portland, Oregon. *Local Environment, 24*(5), 428–441. doi .org/10.1080/13549839.2019.1585772

Renne, J. L., & Appleyard, B. (2019). Twenty-five years in the making: TOD as a new name for an enduring concept. *Journal of Planning Education and Research, 39*(4), 402–408. doi .org/10.1177/0739456X19885351

Riggs, W., & Gilderbloom, J. (2016). Two-way street conversion: Evidence of increased livability in Louisville. *Journal of Planning Education and Research, 36*(1), 105–118. doi .org/10.1177/0739456X15593147

Rodriguez, J. F., Diaz, E. J., & Cleaver, D. A. (2012). *U.S. Patent No. US20120232965A1*. Washington, DC: U.S. Patent and Trademark Office

Roy, S. (2019). *Quantifying the impact of transportation network companies (TNCs) on traffic congestion in San Francisco* (Doctoral dissertation). Retrieved from https://uknowledge .uky.edu/ce_etds/82

Saelens, B. E., & Handy, S. L. (2008). Built environment correlates of walking: A review. *Medicine and Science in Sports and Exercise, 40*(7 Suppl), S550–S566. doi.org/10.1249/ MSS.0b013e31817c67a4

Sandoval, G. F., & Herrera, R. (2015). Transit-oriented development and equity in Latino neighborhoods: A comparative case study of MacArthur Park (Los Angeles) and Fruitvale (Oakland). *TREC Final Reports*. doi.org/10.15760/trec.58

Sarkheyli, E., & Rafieian, M. (2018). Megaprojects and community participation: South Waterfront project in Portland, Oregon. *Housing and Society, 45*(2), 104–117. doi.org/10 .1080/08882746.2018.1496697

Schlossberg, M., Rowell, J., Amos, D., & Sanford, K. (2013). *Rethinking streets: An evidence-based guide to 25 complete streets transformation*. Retrieved from https://pages .uoregon.edu/schlossb/ftp/RS/RethinkingStreets_All_V2_high_wCover.pdf

Schuetz, J. (2019). Teardowns, popups, and renovations: How does housing supply change? *Journal of Regional Science*. doi.org/10.1111/jors.12470

SFMTA. (2014). *Pilot Project Evaluation: The SFMTA's Evaluation of the Benefits of the SFpark Pilot Project*. Retrieved from https://www.sfmta.com/sites/default/files/reports-and -documents/2018/08/sfpark_pilot_project_evaluation.pdf

Shlomo, Z. (1997). *U.S. Patent No. US 5940481 A*. Washington, DC: US Patent and Trademark Office.

Shoup, D. (2011). *The high cost of free parking, updated edition* (1st ed.). Milton Park, UK: Routledge.

Southworth, M. (2005). Designing the walkable city. *Journal of Urban Planning and Development, 131*(4), 246–257. doi.org/10.1061/(ASCE)0733-9488(2005)131:4(246)

Stevens, M. R. (2017). Does compact development make people drive less? *Journal of the American Planning Association, 83*(1), 7–18.

Wachs, M. (2010). Transportation policy, poverty, and sustainability: History and future. *Transportation Research Record*, *2163*(1), 5–12. /doi.org/10.3141/2163-01

Weinberger, R., Kaehny, J., & Rufo, M. (2010). *U.S. parking policies: An overview of management strategies*. Institute for Transportation and Development Policy. Retrieved from https://www.itdp.org/2010/02/23/u-s-parking-policies-an-overview-of-management-strategies/

Wheatley, T. (2020, February 18). The Atlanta BeltLine's new Westside Trail doesn't feel like its other segments—And that's a good thing. *Atlanta Magazine*. Retrieved from https://www.atlantamagazine.com/list/where-does-atlanta-beltline-go-from-here/westside-trail-doesnt-feel-like-other-segments-good-thing/

Wilson, B., & Chakraborty, A. (2013). The environmental impacts of sprawl: Emergent themes from the past decade of planning research. *Sustainability*, *5*(8), 3302–3327. doi.org/10.3390/su5083302

Woodcock, J., Edwards, P., Tonne, C., Armstrong, B. G., Ashiru, O., Banister, D., Beevers, S., Chalabi, Z., Chowdhury, Z., Cohen, A., Franco, O. H., Haines, A., Hickman, R., Lindsay, G., Mittal, I., Mohan, D., Tiwari, G., Woodward, A., & Roberts, I. (2009). Public health benefits of strategies to reduce greenhouse-gas emissions: Urban land transport. *The Lancet*, *374*(9705), 1930–1943. doi.org/10.1016/S0140-6736(09)61714-1

Zehngebot, C., & Peiser, R. (2014, May). Complete streets come of age: Learning from Boston and other innovators. *American Planning Association*. Retrieved from https://www.planning.org/planning/2014/may/completestreets.htm

Zhang, M. (2007). Chinese edition of transit-oriented development: *Transportation Research Record*. doi.org/10.3141/2038-16

Zook, J. B., Lu, Y., Glanz, K., & Zimring, C. (2012). Design and pedestrianism in a smart growth development. *Environment and Behavior*, *44*(2), 216–234. doi.org/10.1177/0013916511402060

PART V

NEW HORIZONS FOR SMART GROWTH: HEALTH AND EQUITY

11. Planning for opportunity: linking smart growth to public education and workforce development

Ariel H. Bierbaum, Jeffrey M. Vincent, and Jonathan P. Katz

INTRODUCTION

Quality educational opportunities – for both children and adults – are key ingredients for individual and community economic success. "Good schools" are something smart growth proponents point to as an important community element.[1] Schools contribute to fostering "distinctive, attractive communities with a strong sense of place" (Duany et al., 2004). Yet, the planning field has mixed success forging detailed conceptual connections, outlining more pragmatic policy, or designing approaches that link the two. In this chapter, we start from the premise that individual and community success requires that all people have "trajectories of opportunity" – that is, realistic opportunities to access high quality public education and workforce training options (McKoy et al., 2010). Without these options, cycles of poverty and disenfranchisement continue. However, smart growth advocates have largely neglected the challenges of education and workforce training opportunities. Moving forward, the field must better elevate the interconnections between education, schools, and workforce development and smart growth. We present this not as an aspiration or normative ideal, but rather as a principle upon which smart growth advocates and planning professionals can and should build a much-needed body of knowledge.

Smart growth strategies primarily focus on land use and growth management, emphasizing physical, place-based interventions. The education field largely takes a people-based approach, focusing on the development of human capital. The smart growth field has paid less attention to the inequities across metropolitan geographies or the racialized political dimensions of planning, including the unequal provision of public education and workforce development opportunities (Baum, 2004). Yet, decisions about how and where we invest in public education and workforce development – key elements of opportunity structures – are intricately connected to how and where we accommodate "development that serves the economy, the community, and the environment" (Duany et al., 2004; Vincent & McKoy, 2013).

Public education and workforce development have both local place-based and broader spatial dimensions. The place-based dimensions turn our attention to locational specificities bound by jurisdictional lines. These include characteristics of the built environment; demographic attributes of residents in a particular location; and social, political, economic, and institutional relations of those locations. Analyses of spatial dimensions are arguably more abstract, encompass larger scales, focus on mobility across jurisdictional boundaries, and are less contingent on the details of micro-level built environments and social relationships in a particular location. As we will explore further, public schools are physical assets and a key piece of public infrastructure (Vincent, 2006), so their location and condition shape both social interactions and neighborhood conditions. Spatially, public schools and workforce development programs are key elements of a family's "geography of opportunity," which determines the resources and risks to which families have access and exposure (Galster & Killen, 1995).

We begin by describing some commonly held understandings of the nexus between smart growth planning and public education – namely, issues of housing location choice and housing markets, school quality, and segregation. We then move beyond this in two ways. First, we incorporate the often overlooked physical elements of public education and the importance of ensuring learners are in safe, clean, and vibrant school buildings and campuses. Second, we connect the dots between smart growth efforts and workforce development strategies and build out links to a full trajectory of opportunity for young people and adults. Throughout, we point to smart growth's 10 core principles and the ways that public education and workforce development are intertwined with these priorities (see Table 11.1).

METROPOLITAN PATTERNS OF SCHOOL AND HOUSING SEGREGATION

Sprawl – smart growth's key nemesis – is a problem of suburban pulls and urban pushes. Suburban leaders and new development entice people to escape urban "ills." Despite the fact that disrupting this "sprawl system" (Baum, 2004) begs for interventions that address social problems, smart growth historically has focused primarily on issues of housing, retail, transportation, and workplace locations. The reality of the pulls and pushes require a reckoning with the racialized politics of place and, by extension, those of public education.

Since World War II, inequalities in education are largely a function of "the unbalanced qualities of geography, society, and politics" (Katznelson & Weir, 1985, p. 210). Larger forces of industrialization (and de-industrialization), urbanization, immigration, and land use markets drove population and demographic shifts across the country that shaped the regional inequalities we see today. Disinvestment and attendant changes in urban conditions "pushed" while evolving housing policies "pulled" more affluent and white families out of cities and into suburbs. This "pull" of the suburbs was fraught with outright racism – white families with resources fled cities and enrolled their children in all-white suburban school districts. To enshrine this separation, new suburban school districts established policies to demarcate which families could enroll at which schools. As a result, the vast majority of metropolitan areas in the United States have dozens, or sometimes even hundreds, of

Table 11.1   *Smart growth principles and their education–workforce connections*

Smart growth principles	Education–workforce connections
Create a wide range of housing opportunities and choices	• Residential segregation as a driver of school segregation
Mix land uses	• School facilities siting requirements and design • Joint use of school buildings and co-location of community services and programs
Take advantage of compact building design	• School facilities siting requirements and design
Create walkable neighborhoods	• School facilities siting requirements and design • Public school quality and housing location choice • Jobs–housing balance
Foster distinctive, attractive communities with a strong sense of place	• Schools as social infrastructure and community hubs • Joint use of school buildings • School facilities siting requirements and design
Preserve open space, farmland, natural beauty, and critical environmental areas	• School facilities siting requirements
Direct development toward existing communities	• School facilities maintenance, renovation, and new construction decisions • School facility capital funding inequities • School operational funding inequities
Provide in advance a variety of transportation choices	• School travel • Workforce travel • Transportation impacts of school siting and school attendance policies
Make development decisions sustainable, predictable, fair, and cost effective	• School facilities design and construction • School facility capital funding inequities • School funding inequities
Encourage community and stakeholder collaboration in development decisions	• Issues of education as opportunity for parent and youth mobilization • Youth engagement through school curriculum • Stakeholder engagement through workforce development programming

separate and unequal school districts: City school districts rapidly became majority non-white, while suburban school districts became nearly all white.

The increasing suburbanization and "white flight" from urban areas was explicitly funded and enabled by the federal government. New federal highway infrastructure enabled white city workers an easy daily automobile commute to and from the growing suburbs. Private sector lending practices, such as racially restrictive home mortgages, barred non-whites from buying houses in suburban neighborhoods. Combined with local zoning policies that also supported racial segregation, metropolitan patterns of growth, shrinkage, and spatial inequality became locked in (Benjamin, 2012; Jackson, 1987; Massey & Denton, 1993; Rothstein, 2017; Silver, 1997; Sugrue, 2005). Today, segregation and inequality persist across metropolitan areas with concentrations of wealth in some areas and poverty in others (Reardon & Bischoff, 2011).

In 1954, at the height of white flight, the US Supreme Court declared the segregation of schools by race as unconstitutional in its landmark *Brown v. Board of
Education* decision. The Court noted that the problem of school segregation was, at
its root, one of housing segregation, but focused its remedies on schools and established a standard of equality of opportunity in education:

> ...it is doubtful that any child may reasonably be expected to succeed in life if he is denied
> the opportunity of an education. Such an opportunity where the state has undertaken to
> provide it, is a right which must be made available to all on equal terms. (*Brown et al. v.
> Board of Education of Topeka et al.*, 1954)

The Court determined that segregation by race, even if the physical facilities and
other "tangible" factors are equal, deprives children of color equal educational opportunity because racial segregation "generates a feeling of inferiority as to their status
in the community that may affect their hearts and minds in a way unlikely ever to be
undone" (*Brown v. Board*, 1954). The decision's emphasis on equality of *opportunity*
(rather than equality of *outcome*) raises questions about access and the spatial distribution of high-quality education options.

The *Brown* decision also neglected the reality that the "tangible" factors in separate schools were unequal by design. The sprawled patterns of residential segregation
coupled with metropolitan fragmentation into separate school districts catalyzed and
cemented the isolation of central city schools and the communities of color left in
urban areas. Because schools are generally funded by property taxes, the isolation of
lower income people in the city means a lower tax base to fund basic city services and
schools compared with wealthier, whiter, suburbs. (Ayscue & Orfield, 2016; Orfield
et al., 2012; Rothstein, 2014, 2017). (M. Bierbaum, Lewis, and Chapin further
discuss land use and governance structure in Chapter 2.)

Schools are often a reflection of their neighborhood demographics. Neighborhoods
of concentrated poverty are home to schools of concentrated poverty, and in the US,
these patterns of income segregation are often coupled with racial segregation. The
material consequences for individual trajectories of opportunity are severe. Negative
educational outcomes, such as high dropout rates and low test scores, are correlated
with schools of concentrated poverty and those with higher proportions of students
of color (Orfield et al., 2012; Orfield & Lee, 2005; Reardon & Owens, 2014). White
students are the least likely to attend multiracial schools (Orfield & Lee, 2005), and,
inversely, students of color are more likely to attend schools with higher poverty rates
than their white counterparts (Orfield et al., 2012).

Access to schools, workforce training, and jobs are key elements of the geography
of opportunity, and as such are all part of the "bundle of goods" (Tiebout, 1956) that
drive housing location choice and housing markets (Black, 1999; Figlio & Lucas,
2000; Holme, 2002). Home values include some capitalization of school quality, and
studies have found that parents are willing to pay higher house prices and property
taxes for access to high quality schools (Black & Machin, 2011; Nguyen-Hoang
& Yinger, 2011; Ross & Yinger, 1999). Once living in a neighborhood, individual

homeowners near a higher-quality school may invest more in upkeep (Horn, 2015). Studies also suggest that school building investments get capitalized in housing values (Cellini et al., 2010; Goncalves, 2015; Lafortune & Schönholzer, 2018; Neilson & Zimmerman, 2014).

When smart growth proponents call for "a wide range of housing opportunities and choices," they implicate the educational infrastructure that accompanies housing location decisions (Duany et al., 2004).

PUBLIC SCHOOLS AS PHYSICAL AND SOCIO-POLITICAL INFRASTRUCTURE

Public school facilities and campuses are significant place-based public investments of fixed infrastructure in communities and throughout regions (Vincent, 2006). In total, US public schools make up an estimated 2 million acres of land and 7.5 billion gross square feet of buildings – about half the building square footage of the entire commercial building sector in the United States (Filardo, 2008, 2016).

As public infrastructure, K-12 school facilities and grounds affect local and regional communities in many ways. Where new schools get built and decisions about if and when schools close contribute to the character of a community and affect travel patterns to school for children. The visual quality of school buildings signals school and neighborhood quality to current and potential residents. New or well-maintained school facilities can help revitalize distressed neighborhoods (Weiss, 2004). The social activities that occur in and around school buildings can further help build neighborhood social capital and positively affect student achievement (Blank et al., 2003). Investments in the construction and maintenance of school facilities inject money into local economies through job creation and supply purchases (Filardo, 2008). School siting choices are an important element in a sustainable school infrastructure program that support environmental outcomes (Council of Educational Facility Planners International, Inc. & US Environmental Protection Agency, 2004; Ewing & Greene, 2004; Fuller et al., 2009; Hoskens et al., 2004).

Discussion about the physical dimensions of public education – namely the size and location of school campuses – has circulated in smart growth circles for more than 15 years and has deep roots in urban planning history (Hoskens et al., 2004; Vitiello, 2006). Where new schools get built and how they are designed, shape local built environments including walkability, neighborhood character, and development, and also contribute to the regional dynamics of sprawl and growth management (Beaumont & Pianca, 2002; Vincent et al., 2017).

In addition to the aforementioned ways that school locations and quality influence housing markets and home-buying choices, three other key mechanisms of school infrastructure have specific relevance for smart growth: (1) new school locations ("school siting") affect local land development and travel patterns; (2) school facility conditions affect student achievement and overall school quality; and (3) schools act as sites of social connection and political mobilization for local stakeholders.

School Siting, Land Development, and Travel Patterns

State policies and guidelines on the siting and design of new public schools have long been identified by smart growth proponents as prioritizing new school construction that promotes sprawl (Hoskens et al., 2004). In many states, policies encourage or require large school sites, which mean significant land consumption that can contribute to increased reliance on vehicular transportation. Policies such as minimum acreages and facility sizes, types of construction, and permissible reuse can make school construction more difficult in existing communities (Ewing & Greene, 2004; McCann & Beaumont, 2003; McDonald, 2010). Many states' school capital funding formulas privilege new school construction over rehabilitation and renovation of older school buildings. For example, state funding formulas for school construction that require a local funding match privilege better-resourced school districts who can mobilize public support and more easily levy additional assessments for capital projects.

To counter these patterns, environmentalists, public health advocates, and historic preservationists have advocated for the preservation of older school buildings, infill development of new schools, and shared use strategies where school buildings and/ or campuses are jointly used by different organizations for a variety of programs and services (Beaumont & Pianca, 2002; Hoskens et al., 2004; US Environmental Protection Agency, 2003; Vincent, 2014). These approaches to planning, siting, designing, and operating public school buildings reflect smart growth priorities of mixing land uses, promoting compact building design, creating walkable neighborhoods, and preserving open space by directing growth to existing communities (Duany et al., 2004).

These approaches are not new. Historically, normative urban design ideals have placed schools as central features in the physical landscape of neighborhoods (Lawhon, 2009; Mumford, 1938; Vitiello, 2006). Mumford's "integrated city" in the 1930s is the precursor to smart growth's emphasis on a mix of land uses. In the 1920s, Clarence Perry similarly laid out an ideal neighborhood design (called the "neighborhood unit") with the school at the center of a gridded plan along with a church and commercial center (Perry, 1929). Both of these influential early urban designers felt public schools should be physically positioned in the center of neighborhoods. (See Talen, Chapter 7, for more on normative design principles.)

Notably, these normative ideals used school siting as an instrument to organize and differentiate neighborhoods and schools and promoted school segregation. Perry's neighborhood unit assumed racial and class homogeneity (Lawhon, 2009), and decisions of where to build new neighborhood schools explicitly aimed to maintain patterns of racial segregation (Benjamin, 2012; Erickson, 2012; Highsmith & Erickson, 2015). Absent a cogent and explicit critique, smart growth advocates' push for walkable neighborhoods may be used to achieve similar exclusionary aims; indeed, some critics of parallel trends in new urbanism have already levied this claim (Marcuse, 2000; PolicyLink et al., 2013).

School siting matters not only for land use but also transportation. Perry's neighborhood unit plan assumed what we today call active travel to school. He carefully placed a school building "so that a child's walk to school was only about one-quarter of a mile and no more than one-half mile and could be achieved without crossing a major arterial street" (Lawhon, 2009, p. 4). Smart growth still emphasizes walkable neighborhoods, although coupled with "a wide range of housing opportunities and choices," the principles pay much less attention to other services and amenities such as schools. Likewise, smart growth does not explicitly mention – but perhaps implies – attention to schools in its emphasis on "a variety of transportation choices [and] urban and social infrastructure based on population projections." (See Clifton, Chapter 9, for more on walkability.)

Today, distance from home to school affects mode choice and travel time to school, with longer distances resulting in more driving and less biking and walking (Banerjee et al., 2014; McDonald, 2008). More car trips mean fewer health benefits of active travel and more vehicular emissions, which have negative environmental consequences (Krizek et al., 2014; Marshall et al., 2010; Wilson et al., 2007). US Environmental Protection Agency (EPA) researchers found that schools built close to neighborhoods where students live reduce traffic, increase walking and biking by 13 percent, and could create a 15 percent emissions reduction as a result of decreased automobile travel to and from the school site (US EPA, 2003) (Clifton details walkability research in Chapter 9, Welch and Gehrke discuss transportation choice in Chapter 10, and Garfinkel-Castro and Ewing examine the relationship between public health and the built environment in Chapter 12).

Distance to schools has increased in recent years at least in part because of state-level school siting policies that promote sprawled school development (McDonald, 2010). In 2011, the EPA released *School Siting Guidelines* to give local school districts and states guidance on making school siting choices with smart growth priorities in mind (US EPA, 2011). Of course, there are other policies that impact where students attend school. For example, education policies promoting school choice, where families can choose to attend a school outside of their residential neighborhood, have also often led to further distances between home and school. Choice policies allow parents to choose to travel longer distances to access a school that best fits their child's needs (Cookson et al., 2018; Makarewicz, 2013, 2020). A family's decision to take advantage of school choice options is predicated on the ability to physically get to and from school every day. Many students may not be able to take advantage of school choice because their family cannot drive them to and from school every day and/or their neighborhoods lack good public transit infrastructure – a problem perhaps alluded to in smart growth advocates' emphasis on "transportation choices." These conundrums at the nexus of transportation and schools present particularly pressing issues for ensuring both transportation and education equity (Bierbaum et al., 2020).

School Facility Design and Conditions

School districts' investment in building new schools and the operations, maintenance, and modernization of older schools are part and parcel of the "quality" of schools for students, teachers, and staff. However, significant portions of this physical infrastructure of our public school system are aging and in poor condition. Many schools and educational institutions suffer from underinvestment in routine maintenance and have not been modernized in decades, resulting in dangerous conditions such as asbestos, mold, non-potable drinking water, and poor air quality (Barrett et al., 2019; Filardo et al., 2010; Filardo & Vincent, 2017; US Government Accountability Office, 2020; Vincent, 2006). These deficiencies have ramifications for education, health, and community equity.

Studies find significant correlations between poor structural, conditional, and aesthetic attributes of school buildings and negative impacts on adult and student health, teaching and learning, and academic achievement (Allen et al., 2017; Maxwell, 2016; Uline & Tshannen-Moran, 2008). Schools without major maintenance backlogs have higher average daily attendance and lower dropout rates (Branham, 2004). Good facility conditions can also help reduce teacher turnover (Buckley et al., 2005). School buildings in poor conditions are disproportionately found in lower-income communities and communities of color (Alexander & Lewis, n.d.; Office for Civil Rights, 2014). Run-down and worn out public school facility infrastructure still operating through neighborhoods in the United States represent a set of budgetary choices that undermine the smart growth principle to "strengthen and direct development towards existing communities," which Hanlon discusses further in Chapter 5.

Modern, high-quality K-12 physical infrastructure can strengthen schools and communities in many ways, and smart growth priorities that "strengthen and direct development towards existing communities" include school investments that could pay dividends across neighborhoods (Filardo et al., 2018). In places where schools serve as anchor institutions, improvements will strengthen the quality and role of that anchor in revitalization (Khadduri et al., 2003; Patterson & Silverman, 2013, 2014; Varady & Raffel, 1995; Weiss, 2004). Facility modernizing programs increase local property values, boost school enrollments, and help rebuild confidence in struggling school districts (Lafortune & Schönholzer, 2018). For example, a major school renovation program in New Haven, Connecticut, resulted in increased test scores, raised housing values, and increased enrollment (Neilson & Zimmerman, 2014).

School-based Social Capital and Political Mobilization

The physical infrastructure of schools is intricately tied to their socio-political functions. Physical form is a key element in individuals' construction of cognitive maps of their cities and neighborhoods and the cultivation of place attachment (Good, 2016; Witten et al., 2001, 2007). The physical centrality of schools in neighborhoods and to communities often fosters a social centrality. Those early urban designs that placed schools at the center of a neighborhood did so with the intention that schools would be spaces for "social interaction, social activism, and serve as a source of community identification" (Lawhon, 2009, p. 9). Schools also serve other non-educational purposes such as civic spaces or emergency shelter; their placement determines other aspects of planning at the local level, such as emergency preparedness and voting precincts (Dunlop et al., 2014; Vincent, 2006).

When school buildings are used jointly as recreation or community centers, public libraries, health centers, and/or senior centers, they are more than just sites of learning for students; they become an asset for a broader community (Vincent, 2014). Schools serve as "amenities, local resources, and forums for interaction and collective action" in neighborhoods (Joseph & Feldman, 2009, p. 232). Schools "link individuals together in unintended ways that enhance collective oriented tasks" (Sampson, 2011, p. 233) and may promote "child-related social capital" (Nast & Blokland, 2013). These interactions help build trust among school community members and foster a safe, pro-social environment, a sense of belonging, and a communal identity (Kirshner et al., 2010; Witten et al., 2007). In the long run, these interactions also act to build the "distinctive, attractive communities" that smart growth advocates celebrate.

As smart growth advocates "encourage community and stakeholder collaboration in development decisions" (Duany et al., 2004), they may look to involvement in school building and programming decisions and politics. Since at least the early twentieth century, schools have been "important locations in the shaping of American political culture" as sites of political engagement around issues of neighborhood resources, immigrant assimilation, and ethnic and territorial contestation (Katznelson & Weir, 1985, p. 11). In the 1960s and 1970s, many white parents pushed a segregationist agenda, while many disenfranchised groups of people – including poor, Black, working class people and immigrants – mobilized and advocated for desegregation or local community control of schools (Scott, 2011; Stulberg, 2016). More recently, communities have organized at the neighborhood level for school improvements and developed citywide coalitions for education policy changes (Shirley, 1997; Stone, 2001; Warren, 2011). These efforts reveal how issues of public education inspire and motivate local political action and public participation. Incorporating advocacy on school siting, school facilities, and educational infrastructure as part of smart growth activity can broaden the community of stakeholders and activate public engagement in new ways among young people and parents.

WORKFORCE DEVELOPMENT: FOSTERING A PIPELINE BEYOND K-12

Schools and other institutions of education are key components in local and regional workforce development. Beyond their education function for students, school districts are large – sometimes the largest – local employers in a community. Millions of people in the United States are directly employed in primary or secondary education as teachers, administrators, or other staff with diverse levels of skill in building trades, food service, janitorial work, and administrative support (Barrett et al., 2019; Filardo, 2016; Truscott & Truscott, 2005).

School facilities management alone involves thousands of contracts and millions of jobs, which boosts local economies. Collectively, America's school districts spend about $100 billion per year on their facilities – in facility operations, maintenance, repair, renovation, and capital construction activities (Filardo, 2016). For every billion dollars invested in capital construction, there are an estimated 6,664 direct construction jobs, and another 11,121 indirect or induced jobs created (Bivens & Blair, 2016). These contracts and jobs can especially benefit lower-wealth communities, providing an important co-benefit to school facilities improvement.

Less well-recognized is the role that K-12 public education plays as essential infrastructure for workforce development. The public education system has three goals: to integrate students into society and work; to lead towards economic equality by equipping individuals to better participate in the system; and to promote moral and human development (Bowles & Gintis, 1976). Schools are the entry point to workforce training through both skills-building and the "hidden curriculum" that teaches young people about their place in the larger economic system (Bowles & Gintis, 1976). Increasingly, school districts emphasize college and career readiness and offer a full range of options for direct entry into the workforce or into higher education. In particular, career technical education (CTE) provides specialized programming and industry partnerships with specific career sectors (US Department of Education, 2016). For example, a district may partner with a local hospital to offer internships and coursework in healthcare or with a local building trades union to offer the same in construction.

Workforce development efforts beyond K-12 support young people who have been pushed out of the public school system and adults who need additional training to obtain or change jobs (R. L. Jacobs & Hawley, 2009; Lakes, 2008; Myran & Ivery, 2013; Unruh & Dahlk, 2012). Broadly, these efforts require a long-term commitment to train workers, connect workers with employers, and promote economic prosperity for individuals and businesses through ongoing career advancement (Giloth, 2003, 2007; Harrison, 1999; R. L. Jacobs & Hawley, 2009; O'Leary et al., 2004; Schrock, 2014). Workforce development efforts occur through community colleges, local non-profit organizations, and/or regional intermediaries. Community colleges in particular often act as a "nexus" point from which a student is able to find or learn about a job (J. Jacobs & Dougherty, 2006). Community colleges are also place-based institutions (much like K-12 public schools) and often their campuses include employment and other social services, which positively impacts student employment outcomes (Larin et al., 2008; Myran & Ivery, 2013).

A well-trained workforce is the pathway to foster community and regional economic development (Bennett & Giloth, 2007; Chapple, 2005; Harper-Anderson, 2008; Schrock, 2014). Workforce development programs generally have one of three orientations. Some tend to be sector-based, with strong reference to a specific local or regional economy, such as healthcare or technology (Chapple, 2005; Dyjack et al., 2013; Herberg, 2018; Lowe et al., 2011; Nelson & Wolf-Powers, 2010). Others are more people-based, focused on training and job search assistance for workers (Holland, 2017; Schrock, 2015). Still others focus on the labor demand side and emphasize expanded hiring practices for employers, particularly to an unskilled labor pool (Decker, 2011; Jacobson, 2017; Schrock, 2014).

Much like K-12 public education, the landscape of workforce development efforts and intermediary organizations is highly fragmented; the boundaries within which they serve often do not cover the geographies in which people operate (Anglin, 2011; Benner, 2003; Lowe et al., 2011). Workforce investment boards (WIB) define their own catchment areas, usually aligned to regional labor markets. Some programs operate across entire metropolitan areas while other local organizations focus only on single neighborhoods (Decker, 2011; Harper-Anderson, 2008; Lakes, 2008). Workforce intermediary organizations tend to act in sector-based (e.g., information technology, advanced manufacturing, healthcare, etc.) rather than place-based ways (Dyjack et al., 2013; Garmise, 2006; Gasper et al., 2017).

Yet sprawled development, automobile-centric transportation infrastructure, and housing availability and affordability – all concerns of smart growth – are deeply connected to the local and multifaceted nature of job hiring and searching, the accessibility of training programs, and the intersections with extant infrastructure (Bennett & Giloth, 2007; Cervero et al., 2002; Foster-Bey, 2002; Giloth, 2003; Gobillon et al., 2007; Levine, 1998). For example, training programs often do not consider the other barriers that affect the "employability" of jobseekers: social services, housing, and transport (Garmise, 2006; Holland, 2017; Myran & Ivery, 2013). Even access to training programs is dependent on these other systems. Programs in New York City (Leopold et al., 2019), Chicago (Eyster & Nightingale, 2017), Florida, and Colorado (Adams & Gebrekristos, 2018) all combine services such as childcare and housing assistance with training. Anecdotal evidence indicates that the the co-location of social services and better access to transportation, housing, and food security is a boon for jobseekers (Holland, 2017; Kogan et al., 1997; Nguyen et al., 2016; Unruh & Dahlk, 2012).

CONCLUSION: HOW SMART GROWTH CAN SUPPORT TRAJECTORIES OF OPPORTUNITY

In this chapter, we have posited that as the smart growth field looks to the future, it should extend its focus into the fields of education and workforce development. Smart growth interests have natural synergies with the goals of prosperity woven into these disciplines. Place-based and people-based approaches must work in concert to provide trajectories of opportunity for all young people.

The disciplinary separation between education, workforce development, and smart growth planning is wide, no doubt. In fact, it has been designed into the state and local regimes that govern public policy. Few state or federal mandates exist that require school districts and local land use jurisdictions to work together (McKoy et al., 2008). For the most part, local education agencies (e.g., school districts, county offices of education, etc.) are separate jurisdictions with separate authority. They operate with strong local autonomy, and more often act as arms of state, rather than as a part of other local city or county governments. Likewise, workforce development boards operate independently from both local education agencies and other jurisdictions. Sometimes these entities have aligned geographic boundaries, but often they do not. They each face parallel budget processes and constraints. And they work on different time horizons for both capital and programmatic planning.

By and large, education and workforce research and practice rarely interact with traditional smart growth disciplines. As fields, smart growth and education come from very different places. Smart growth proponents largely come out of the design-oriented and growth-management wings of urban planning, focused on the mechanisms that drive and shape physical environments. Smart growth tools and approaches largely aim to manage urban growth and mitigate the negative externalities of sprawled physical development in suburban and exurban areas (Duany et al., 2004). The education and workforce sectors focus on people and, broadly speaking, the fields have been agnostic to place. Yet, as we have highlighted in this chapter, there are overlaps: smart growth advocates have always been concerned with social connections facilitated through particular kinds of design interventions. Likewise, policy questions of education and workforce straddle physical, human, and socio-political domains of growth and development.

The divides in practice and research are not a fait accompli. Rather, our systems and structures of governance enable, facilitate, and perpetuate these silos over time. In communities across the country the links between smart growth planning, workforce development, and public education are palpable to planning practitioners and smart growth advocates. Although formal collaborations may be challenging because of historic policy silos, administrative barriers, and budgetary constraints, local communities are engaged in practices that bridge arenas to foster trajectories of opportunity.[2]

Despite the core connections between metropolitan development and educational opportunities, smart growth advocates have historically taken a fragmentary, and not systemic, approach to analyzing problems of place and education neglected by policymakers. This approach also has not accounted for the planning resources or challenges that smart growth tools provide in efforts to ensure educational equity. For example, desegregation advocates argue for alternative school assignment policies that would foster diverse schools (Orfield & Lee, 2005). These assignment and choice policies disaggregate housing and school locations. In the process, however, they potentially result in longer or further travel patterns, which runs counter to the kinds of reduced travel by automobile for which smart growth planners advocate. Furthermore, the ability to engage in school choice is still constrained by resources; students without reliable access to public transport may not be able to switch schools, or an adult may be forced to drive them. This problem can have negative effects on school attendance and student performance (Blagg et al., 2018; Fan & Das, 2016; Stein & Grigg, 2019), as well as which schools are considered realistically available (Higgs et al., 1997; Mikulecky, 2013).

Alternatively, housing and land use policies could play a larger role in desegregation efforts. Research has found that desegregation is most stable and subsequent academic improvements are largest when desegregation programs are instituted across counties or regions, capturing the full housing market (Orfield et al., 2012; Schwartz, 2010). These findings suggest that regional housing and land use policies, such as inclusionary zoning that requires the construction of affordable housing in urban and suburban areas, would expand access to educational opportunities across a larger geography and diversify schools (Dawkins and Kim, Chapter 8, discuss housing choice and the need for affordability controls).

Smart growth advocates have an opportunity, when considering their policies' socio-economic and cultural implications, to connect education and its delivery, and the concomitant segregation within, to planning and development. Furthermore, smart growth advocates have not fully considered race in their work (Baum, 2004; Gray-O'Connor, 2009), perhaps linked to the fact that urban planners in the United States are disproportionately white (Goetz et al., 2020; Sandercock, 2004). Yet, as scholars have noted, race is deeply present in the development of suburban sprawl in the United States (Lipsitz, 2007; Rothstein, 2014, 2017; Song, 2015; Sugrue, 2005). Considering education's role in these trends not only offers an avenue to push back against sprawl, but against the racial segregation and inequities the sprawl system embodies and enables (Baum, 2004). This push, too, would also work in the specific realms of school facilities themselves.

As smart growth planners consider their priorities over the next decade, they are in a better position to understand the roles that high-quality public schools and workforce development play in realizing equitable and sustainable communities – and the role planning decisions play in contributing to the conditions, quality, and access to K-12 education and workforce training opportunities. Competitive and vibrant metropolitan regions of the future will have high-quality K-12 education systems and workforce development opportunities that attract families, provide robust skill development, and bolster regional economic engines. Our metropolitan regions, however, have been plagued by an uneven distribution of opportunity, which has only worked to fuel disinvestment in older areas and promote sprawl. As Baum (2004) notes, educational opportunities are "quintessential" in this "sprawl system." Smart growth planners will only realize their aspirational visions of equity and sustainable places through a recognition of the mutual dependence and intentional integration with public education and workforce development activities.

NOTES

1. In this review, we focus on public schools, rather than all schools (public, private, parochial). We use the terms "school" and "public school" and "education" and "public education" interchangeably.
2. For examples across the country and more resources on connections between K-12 public education and smart growth planning, see the American Planning Association Public Schools Interest Group: https://www.planning.org/divisions/groups/publicschools/

REFERENCES

Adams, G., & Gebrekristos, S. (2018). *Local Workforce Development Boards and Child Care.* Urban Institute. https://www.urban.org/research/publication/local-workforce-development-boards-and-child-care

Alexander, D., & Lewis, L. (n.d.). *Condition of America's Public School Facilities: 2012-13.* 61.

Allen, J. G., Eitland, E., Klingensmith, L., MacNaughton, P., Cedeno Laurent, J., Spengler, J., & Bernstein, A. (2017). *Foundations for Student Success: How School Buildings Influence Student Health, Thinking and Performance.* The Harvard T.H. Chan School of Public Health. https://schools.forhealth.org/

Anglin, R. (2011). *Promoting Sustainable Local and Community Economic Development.* CRC Press.

Ayscue, J. B., & Orfield, G. (2016). Perpetuating separate and unequal worlds of educational opportunity through district lines: School segregation by race and poverty. In P. Noguera, J. C. Pierce, & R. Ahram (Eds.), *Race, Equity, and Education: Sixty Years from Brown* (pp. 45–74). Springer.

Banerjee, T., Uhm, J., & Bahl, D. (2014). Walking to school: The experience of children in inner city Los Angeles and implications for policy. *Journal of Planning Education and Research, 34*(2), 123–140.

Barrett, P., Treves, A., Shmis, T., Ambasz, D., & Ustinova, M. (2019). *The Impact of School Infrastructure on Learning: A Synthesis of the Evidence.* World Bank.

Baum, H. (2004). Smart growth and school reform: what if we talked about race and took community seriously? *Journal of the American Planning Association, 70*(1), 14–26.

Beaumont, C., & Pianca, E. G. (2002). *Why Johnny Can't Walk to School: Historic Neighborhood Schools in the Age of Sprawl.* National Trust for Historic Preservation.

Benjamin, K. (2012). Suburbanizing Jim Crow: The impact of school policy on residential segregation in Raleigh. *Journal of Urban History, 38*(2), 225–246.

Benner, C. (2003). Labour flexibility and regional development: The role of labour market intermediaries. *Regional Studies, 37*(6–7), 621–633. https://doi.org/10.1080/0034340032000108723

Bennett, M. I., & Giloth, R. P. (2007). Social equity and twenty-first century cities. In M. I. Bennett & R. P. Giloth (Eds.), *Economic Development in American Cities: The Pursuit of an Equity Agenda* (pp. 213–236). State University of New York Press.

Bierbaum, A. H., Karner, A., & Barajas, J. M. (2020). Toward mobility justice: Linking transportation and education equity in the context of school choice. *Journal of the American Planning Association, 87*(2), 1–14. https://doi.org/10.1080/01944363.2020.1803104

Bivens, J., & Blair, H. (2016). *A Public Investment Agenda that Delivers the Goods for American Workers needs to be Long-lived, Broad, and Subject to Democratic Oversight* (p. 19). Economic Policy Institute.

Black, S. E. (1999). Do better schools matter? Parental valuation of elementary education. *The Quarterly Journal of Economics, 114*(2), 577–599. https://doi.org/10.2307/2587017

Black, S. E., & Machin, S. (2011). Chapter 10—Housing valuations of school performance. In S. M. and L. W. Eric A. Hanushek (Ed.), *Handbook of the Economics of Education* (Vol. 3, pp. 485–519). Elsevier.

Blagg, K., Rosenboom, V., & Chingos, M. (2018). *The Extra Mile: Time to School and Student Outcomes in Washington, DC* [Research Report]. Urban Institute. https://www.urban.org/research/publication/extra-mile-time-school-and-student-outcomes-washington-dc

Blank, M. A., Melaville, A., & Shah, B. P. (2003). *Making the Difference: Research and Practice in Community Schools.* Coalition for Community Schools. http://www.communityschools.org/assets/1/Page/CCSFullReport.pdf

Bowles, S., & Gintis, H. (1976). *Schooling in Capitalist America: Educational Reform and the Contradictions of Economic Life.* Basic Books.

Branham, D. (2004). The wise man builds his house upon the rock: The effects of inadequate school building infrastructure on student attendance. *Social Science Quarterly, 85*(5), 1112–1128. https://doi.org/10.1111/j.0038-4941.2004.00266.x

Brown et al. v. Board of Education of Topeka et al., 347 U.S. 483 (United States Supreme Court May 17, 1954).

Buckley, J., Schneider, M., & Shang, Y. (2005). Fix it and they might stay: School facility quality and teacher retention in Washington, D.C. *Teachers College Record, 107*(5), 1107–1123.

Cellini, S. R., Ferreira, F., & Rothstein, J. (2010). The value of school facility investments: Evidence from a dynamic regression discontinuity design. *The Quarterly Journal of Economics, 125*(1), 215–261.

Cervero, R., Sandoval, O., & Landis, J. (2002). Transportation as a stimulus of welfare-to-work: Private versus public mobility. *Journal of Planning Education and Research, 22*(1), 50–63.

Chapple, K. (2005). *Building Institutions from the Region Up: Regional Workforce Development Collaboratives in California* (Working Paper 2005,01). Working Paper. https://www.econstor.eu/handle/10419/39262

Cookson, P. W., Darling-Hammond, L., Rothman, R., & Shields, P. M. (2018). *The Tapestry of American Public Education: How we can Create a System of Schools worth Choosing for All?* Learning Policy Institute. https://learningpolicyinstitute.org/sites/default/files/product -files/Tapestry_American_Public_Education_REPORT.pdf

Council of Educational Facility Planners International, Inc., & US Environmental Protection Agency. (2004). *Schools for Successful Communities: An Element of Smart Growth.* CEFPI. https://www.epa.gov/sites/production/files/2014-02/documents/smartgrowth_schools_pub .pdf

Decker, P. T. (2011). Ten years of the Workforce Investment Act (WIA): Interpreting the research on WIA and related programs. *Journal of Policy Analysis and Management, 30*(4), 906–926.

Duany, A., Speck, J., & Lydon, M. (2004). *The Smart Growth Manual.* McGraw Hill.

Dunlop, A. L., Logue, K. M., & Isakov, A. P. (2014). The engagement of academic institutions in community disaster response: A comparative analysis. *Public Health Reports, 129*, 87–95.

Dyjack, D. T., Botchwey, N., & Marziale, E. (2013). Cross-sectoral workforce development: Examining the intersection of public health and community design. *Journal of Public Health Management and Practice, 19*(1), 97–99.

Erickson, A. T. (2012). Building inequality: the spatial organization of schooling in Nashville, Tennessee, after Brown. *Journal of Urban History, 38*(2), 247–270. https://doi.org/10 .1177/0096144211427115

Ewing, R., & Greene, W. (2004). *Travel and Environmental Implications of School Siting* (No. EPA231-R-03–004). Environmental Protection Agency.

Eyster, L., & Nightingale, D. S. (2017). *Workforce Development and Low-Income Adults and Youth: The Future under the Workforce Innovation and Opportunity Act of 2014.* Urban Institute. https://www.urban.org/sites/default/files/publication/93536/workforce -development-and-low-income-adults_and-youth.pdf

Fan, Y., & Das, K. V. (2016). *Assessing the Impacts of Student Transportation via Transit on Student Attendance and Academic Achievement.* Transportation Research Board 95th Annual Meeting, Washington, D.C.

Figlio, D. N., & Lucas, M. E. (2000). *What's in a Grade? School Report Cards and House Prices* (Working Paper No. 8019). National Bureau of Economic Research. http://www .nber.org/papers/w8019

Filardo, M. (2008). *Good Buildings, Better Schools: An Economic Stimulus Opportunity with Long-term Benefits* (pp. 1–9) [Briefing Paper]. Economic Policy Institute. http://www.gpn .org/bp216/bp216.pdf

Filardo, M. (2016). *State of Our Schools: America's K-12 Facilities* (State of Our Schools, pp. 1–43). 21st Century School Fund, Center for Green Schools. https://kapost-files-prod .s3.amazonaws.com/published/56f02c3d626415b792000008/2016-state-of-our-schools -report.pdf?kui=wo7vkgV0wW0LGSjxek0N5A

Filardo, M., & Vincent, J. M. (2017). *Adequate & Equitable U.S. PK-12 Infrastructure: Priority Actions for Systemic Reform.* 21st Century School Fund.

Filardo, M., Vincent, J. M., Allen, M., & Franklin, J. (2010). *Joint Use of Public Schools: A Framework for a New Social Contract.* Center for Cities and Schools.

Filardo, M., Vincent, J. M., & Sullivan, K. (2018). *Education Equity Requires Modern School Facilities.* BASIC Coalition. https://citiesandschools.berkeley.edu/publications?topic= School+Facilities&pubId=reckCEJXxbgaddJU7

Foster-Bey, J. (2002). *Sprawl, Smart Growth and Economic Opportunity* (Program on Regional Economic Opportunities). Urban Institute.

Fuller, B., McKoy, D. L., Vincent, J. M., & Bierbaum, A. H. (2009). *Smart Schools, Smart Growth: Investing in Education Facilities and Stronger Communities.* Policy Analysis for California Education.

Galster, G. C., & Killen, S. P. (1995). The geography of metropolitan opportunity: A reconnaissance and conceptual framework. *Housing Policy Debate, 6*(1), 7–43.

Garmise, S. (2006). *People and the Competitive Advantage of Place: Building a Workforce for the 21st Century.* Routledge; nlebk. http://search.ebscohost.com/login.aspx?direct=true&db =nlebk&AN=199799&site=ehost-live

Gasper, J. M., Henderson, K. A., & Berman, D. S. (2017). Do sectoral employment programs work? New evidence from New York City's sector-focused career centers. *Industrial Relations: A Journal of Economy and Society, 56*(1), 40–72. https://doi.org/10.1111/irel .12164

Giloth, R. (2003). Introduction: A case for workforce intermediaries. In R. Giloth (Ed.), *Workforce Intermediaries for the 21st Century* (pp. 3–30). Temple University Press.

Giloth, R. (2007). Investing in equity: Targeted economic development for neighborhoods and cities. In M. I. Bennett & R. P. Giloth (Eds.), *Economic Development in American Cities: The Pursuit of an Equity Agenda* (pp. 23–50). State University of New York Press.

Gobillon, L., Selod, H., & Zenou, Y. (2007). The mechanisms of spatial mismatch. *Urban Studies, 44*(12), 2401–2427.

Goetz, E. G., Williams, R. A., & Damiano, A. (2020). Whiteness and urban planning. *Journal of the American Planning Association, 86*(2), 142–156. https://doi.org/10.1080/01944363 .2019.1693907

Goncalves, F. (2015). *The Effects of School Construction on Student and District Outcomes: Evidence from a State-Funded Program in Ohio* (SSRN Scholarly Paper ID 2686828). Social Science Research Network. https://doi.org/10.2139/ssrn.2686828

Good, R. M. (2016). Histories that root us: Neighborhood, place, and the protest of school closures in Philadelphia. *Urban Geography*, 1–23. https://doi.org/10.1080/02723638.2016 .1182286

Gray-O'Connor, J. (2009). Solutions in search of problems: the construction of urban inequality in "smart growth" discourse. *Berkeley Journal of Sociology, 53*, 89–123.

Harper-Anderson, E. (2008). Measuring the connection between workforce development and economic development. *Economic Development Quarterly, 22*(2), 119–135.

Harrison, B. (1999). Workforce development networks: Community based organizations and regional alliances. *Journal of Sociology and Social Welfare, 26*(1), 205.

Herberg, J. (2018). *Skills Brokers in the San Francisco East Bay: Challenges and Opportunities for Creating Equitable Cross-Sector Collaboration through Workforce Intermediaries.* Center for Cities + Schools, University of California.

Higgs, G., Webster, C. J., & White, S. D. (1997). The use of geographical information systems in assessing spatial and socio-economic impacts of parental choice. *Research Papers in Education, 12*(1), 27–48. https://doi.org/10.1080/0267152970120103

Highsmith, A. R., & Erickson, A. T. (2015). Segregation as splitting, segregation as joining: Schools, housing, and the many modes of Jim Crow. *American Journal of Education, 121*(4), 563–595. https://doi.org/10.1086/681942

Holland, B. (2017, May 23). *From Employment to "Employability": A New Way to Look at Workforce Development* [Think Tank]. DC Policy Center. https://www.dcpolicycenter .org/publications/from-employment-to-employability-a-new-way-to-look-at-workforce -development/

Holme, J. J. (2002). Buying homes, buying schools: School choice and the social construction of school quality. *Harvard Educational Review, 72*(2), 177–205.

Horn, K. M. (2015). Can improvements in schools spur neighborhood revitalization? Evidence from building investments. *Regional Science and Urban Economics, 52*, 108–118.

Hoskens, J., Lawrence, B. K., Lee, K., Lyons, J., Stenzler, Y., Susman, M., Torma, T., & Weihs, J. (2004). *Schools for Successful Communities: An Element of Smart Growth.* Council of Educational Facility Planners International. https://www.epa.gov/sites/production/files/ 2014-02/documents/smartgrowth_schools_pub.pdf

Jackson, K. T. (1987). *Crabgrass Frontier: The Suburbanization of the United States* (1st ed.). Oxford University Press, USA.

Jacobs, J., & Dougherty, K. (2006). The uncertain future of the community college workforce development mission. *New Directions for Community Colleges, 136*, 53–62.

Jacobs, R. L., & Hawley, J. D. (2009). The emergence of 'workforce development': Definition, conceptual boundaries and implications. In R. Maclean & D. Wilson (Eds.), *International Handbook of Education for the Changing World of Work: Bridging Academic and Vocational Learning* (pp. 2537–2552). Springer Netherlands. https://doi.org/10.1007/ 978-1-4020-5281-1_167

Jacobson, E. (2017). The workforce investment and opportunity act: New policy developments and persistent issues. *New Directions for Adult and Continuing Education, 2017*(155), 19–27. https://doi.org/10.1002/ace.20237

Joseph, M., & Feldman, J. (2009). Creating and sustaining successful mixed-income communities conceptualizing the role of schools. *Education and Urban Society, 41*(6), 623–652.

Katznelson, I., & Weir, M. (1985). *Schooling for All: Class, Race, and the Decline of the Democratic Ideal.* Basic Books.

Khadduri, J., Turnham, J., Chase, A., & Schwartz, H. (2003). *Case Studies Exploring the Potential Relationship between Schools and Neighborhood Revitalization.* Abt Associates Inc.

Kirshner, B., Gaertner, M., & Pozzoboni, K. (2010). Tracing transitions: the effect of high school closure on displaced students. *Educational Evaluation and Policy Analysis, 32*(3), 407–429.

Kogan, D., Social Policy Research Associates, & United States. (1997). *Creating Workforce Development Systems that Work: A Guide for Practitioners.* Social Policy Research Associates. http://www.ttrc.doleta.gov/onestop/pract.htm

Krizek, K. J., Wilson, E. J., Wilson, R., & Marshall, J. (2014). Transport costs of school choice. In G. K. Ingram & D. A. Kenyon (Eds.), *Education, Land, and Location* (pp. 214–240). Lincoln Institute of Land Policy. http://kevinjkrizek.org/wp-content/uploads/2014/09/08 _ING_00000_CH8_214_240-2.pdf

Lafortune, J., & Schönholzer, D. (2018). *Do School Facilities Matter? Measuring the Effects of Capital Expenditures on Student and Neighborhood Outcomes*. https://www.aeaweb.org/conference/2019/preliminary/paper/2iN6Hbs4

Lakes, R. D. (2008). Rescaling vocational education: Workforce development in a metropolitan region. *The Urban Review, 40*(5), 421–435. https://doi.org/10.1007/s11256-008-0092-z

Larin, K., Mascia, J., Scott, G. A., Morehouse, C., Bradley, K., Stokes, L., McSween, J., Kaufman, S., Mirel, L., Compton, S., & Botsford, J. (2008). *Community Colleges and One-Stop Centers Collaborate to Meet 21st Century Workforce Needs* (GAO-08-547). US Government Accountability Office. https://www.govinfo.gov/content/pkg/GAOREPORTS-GAO-08-547/pdf/GAOREPORTS-GAO-08-547.pdf

Lawhon, L. L. (2009). The neighborhood unit: Physical design or physical determinism? *Journal of Planning History, 8*(2), 111–132.

Leopold, J., Anderson, T., McDaniel, M., Hayes, C., Adeeyo, S., & Pittingolo, R. (2019). *Helping Public Housing Residents Find Jobs and Build Careers: Evaluation Findings from New York City's Jobs-Plus Expansion* (Metropolitan Housing and Communities Policy Center). Urban Institute. https://www.urban.org/research/publication/helping-public-housing-residents-find-jobs-and-build-careers/view/full_report

Levine, J. (1998). Rethinking accessibility and jobs-housing balance. *Journal of the American Planning Association, 64*(2), 133–149.

Lipsitz, G. (2007). The racialization of space and the spatialization of race: Theorizing the hidden architecture of landscape. *Landscape Journal, 26*(1), 10–23.

Lowe, N., Goldstein, H., & Donegan, M. (2011). Patchwork intermediation: Challenges and opportunities for regionally coordinated workforce development. *Economic Development Quarterly, 25*(2), 158–171. https://doi.org/10.1177/0891242410383413

Makarewicz, C. (2013). Vouchers, magnet schools, charter schools, and options. *Transportation Research Record: Journal of the Transportation Research Board, 2327*, 1–8.

Makarewicz, C. (2020). Chapter 16—Balancing education opportunities with sustainable travel and development. In E. Deakin (Ed.), *Transportation, Land Use, and Environmental Planning* (pp. 299–331). Elsevier. https://doi.org/10.1016/B978-0-12-815167-9.00016-5

Marcuse, P. (2000). The new urbanism: The dangers so far. *DisP – The Planning Review, 36*(140), 4–6. https://doi.org/10.1080/02513625.2000.10556727

Marshall, J. D., Wilson, R. D., Meyer, K. L., Rajangam, S. K., McDonald, N. C., & Wilson, E. J. (2010). Vehicle emissions during children's school commuting: Impacts of education policy. *Environmental Science & Technology, 44*(5), 1537–1543.

Massey, D. S., & Denton, N. A. (1993). *American Apartheid: Segregation and the Making of the Underclass*. Harvard University Press.

Maxwell, L. E. (2016). School building condition, social climate, student attendance and academic achievement: A mediation model. *Journal of Environmental Psychology, 46*, 206–216.

McCann, B., & Beaumont, C. (2003, October). Build "smart." *American School Board Journal, 190*(10), 24–26.

McDonald, N. C. (2008). Children's mode choice for the school trip: The role of distance and school location in walking to school. *Transportation, 35*(1), 23–35.

McDonald, N. C. (2010). School siting. *Journal of the American Planning Association, 76*(2), 184–198. https://doi.org/10.1080/01944361003595991

McKoy, D., Vincent, J. M., & Bierbaum, A. H. (2010). *Trajectories of Opportunity for Young Men and Boys of Color: Built Environment and Placemaking Strategies for Creating Equitable, Healthy, and Sustainable Communities*. UC Berkeley: Center for Cities and Schools.

McKoy, D., Vincent, J. M., & Makarewicz, C. (2008). Integrating infrastructure planning: The role of schools. *ACCESS Magazine, 1*(33), 18–26.

Mikulecky, M. T. (2013). *Open Enrollment is on the Menu—But Can You Order It?* Education Commission of the States.

Mumford, L. (1938). *The Culture of Cities*. Harcourt, Brace and Company.

Myran, G., & Ivery, C. R. (2013). The employability gap and the community college role in workforce development. *New Directions for Community Colleges, 162*, 45–53.

Nast, J., & Blokland, T. (2013). Social mix revisited: Neighbourhood institutions as setting for boundary work and social capital. *Sociology*, 1–18.

Neilson, C. A., & Zimmerman, S. D. (2014). The effect of school construction on test scores, school enrollment, and home prices. *Journal of Public Economics, 120*, 18–31. https://doi .org/10.1016/j.jpubeco.2014.08.002

Nelson, M., & Wolf-Powers, L. (2010). Chains and ladders: Exploring the opportunities for workforce development and poverty reduction in the hospital sector. *Economic Development Quarterly, 24*(1), 33–44.

Nguyen, M. T., Rohe, W., Frescoln, K., Webb, M., Donegan, M., & Han, H.-S. (2016). Mobilizing social capital: Which informal and formal supports affect employment outcomes for HOPE VI residents? *Housing Studies, 31*(7), 785–808. WorldCat.org. https://doi .org/10.1080/02673037.2016.1140724

Nguyen-Hoang, P., & Yinger, J. (2011). The capitalization of school quality into house values: A review. *Journal of Housing Economics, 20*(1), 30–48.

Office for Civil Rights. (2014). *Dear Colleague Letter: Resource Comparability*. United States Department of Education. https://www2.ed.gov/about/offices/list/ocr/letters/colleague -resourcecomp-201410.pdf

O'Leary, C. J., Straits, R. A., & Wandner, S. A. (2004). "U.S. job training: Types, participants, and history." In C. J. O'Leary, R. A. Straits, & S. A. Wandner (Eds.), *Job Training Policy in the United States*. W.E. Upjohn Institute for Employment Research.

Orfield, G., Kucsera, J., & Siegel-Hawley, G. (2012). *E Pluribus…Separation: Deepening Double Segregation for More Students*. The Civil Rights Project, University of California – Los Angeles.

Orfield, G., & Lee, C. (2005). *Why Segregation Matters: Poverty and Educational Inequality*. The Civil Rights Project, University of California – Los Angeles.

Patterson, K. L., & Silverman, R. M. (2013). Urban education and neighborhood revitalization. *Journal of Urban Affairs, 35*(1), 1–5. https://doi.org/10.1111/juaf.12006

Patterson, K. L., & Silverman, R. M. (Eds.) (2014). *Schools and Urban Revitalization: Rethinking Institutions and Community Development*. Routledge/Taylor & Francis Group.

Perry, C. (1929). *The Neighborhood Unit*. Reprinted Routledge/Thoemmes, 25–44.

PolicyLink, ChangeLab Solutions, & Safe Routes to School National Partnership. (2013). *Maximizing Walkability, Diversity, and Educational Equity in U.S. Schools*. PolicyLink. https://www.policylink.org/sites/default/files/WALKBILITYANDDIVERSITY_FINAL _AUGUST62013.pdf

Reardon, S. F., & Bischoff, K. (2011). Income inequality and income segregation. *American Journal of Sociology, 116*(4), 1092–1153.

Reardon, S. F., & Owens, A. (2014). 60 years after brown: Trends and consequences of school segregation. *Annual Review of Sociology, 40*(1), 199–218. https://doi.org/10.1146/annurev -soc-071913-043152

Ross, S., & Yinger, J. (1999). Sorting and voting: A review of the literature on urban public finance. In P. Cheshire & E. S. Mills (Eds.), *Handbook of Urban and Regional Economics*, vol. 3 (pp. 2001–2060). North-Holland.

Rothstein, R. (2014). The racial achievement gap, segregated schools, and segregated neighborhoods: A constitutional insult. *Race and Social Problems, 7*(1), 21–30.

Rothstein, R. (2017). *The Color of Law*. W. W. Norton & Company.

Sampson, R. J. (2011). Neighborhood effects, causal mechanisms, and the social structure of the city. In P. Demeulenaere (Ed.), *Analytical Sociology and Social Mechanisms* (pp. 227–249). Cambridge University Press.

Sandercock, L. (2004). Towards a planning imagination for the 21st century. *Journal of the American Planning Association, 70*(2), 133–141. https://doi.org/10.1080/01944360408976368

Schrock, G. (2014). Connecting people and place prosperity: Workforce development and urban planning in scholarship and practice. *Journal of Planning Literature, 29*(3), 257–271.

Schrock, G. (2015). Remains of the progressive city? First source hiring in Portland and Chicago. *Urban Affairs Review, 51*(5), 649–675.

Schwartz, H. (2010). *Housing Policy is School Policy Economically Integrative Housing Promotes Academic Success in Montgomery County, Maryland.* The Century Foundation. http://tcf.org/work/education/detail/housing-policy-is-school-policy

Scott, J. T. (2011). School choice as a civil right: The political construction of a claim and its implications for school desegregation. In E. Frankenberg & E. H. Debray (Eds.), *Integrating Schools in a Changing Society: New Policies and Legal Options for a Multiracial Generation* (pp. 32–52). University of North Carolina Press.

Shirley, D. (1997). *Community Organizing for Urban School Reform* (1st ed.). University of Texas Press.

Silver, C. (1997). Racial origins of zoning in American cities. In J. M. Thomas & M. Ritzdorf (Eds.), *Urban Planning and the African American Community: In the Shadows* (pp. 23–42). Sage Publications.

Song, L. (2015). Race, transformative planning, and the just city. *Planning Theory, 14*(2), 152–173.

Stein, M. L., & Grigg, J. A. (2019). Missing bus, missing school: Establishing the relationship between public transit use and student absenteeism. *American Educational Research Journal.* https://doi.org/10.3102/0002831219833917

Stone, C. N. (2001). Civic capacity and urban education. *Urban Affairs Review, 36*(5), 595–619.

Stulberg, L. M. (2016). Charter schooling, race politics, and an appeal to history. In P. Noguera, J. C. Pierce, & R. Ahram (Eds.), *Race, Equity, and Education: Sixty Years from Brown* (pp. 105–124). Springer.

Sugrue, T. J. (2005). *The Origins of the Urban Crisis: Race and Inequality in Postwar Detroit* (Revised). Princeton University Press.

Tiebout, C. M. (1956). A pure theory of local expenditures. *Journal of Political Economy, 64*(5), 416–424.

Truscott, D. M., & Truscott, S. D. (2005). Differing circumstances, shared challenges: Finding common ground between urban and rural schools. *Phi Delta Kappan, 87*(2), 123–130.

Uline, C. L., & Tshannen-Moran, M. (2008). The walls speak: The interplay of quality ethics, school climate, and student achievement. *Journal of Education Administration, 46*(1), 55–73. https://doi.org/10.1108/09578230810849817

Unruh, R., & Dahlk, K. (2012). *Building Pathways to Employment in America's Cities through Integrated Workforce and Community Development.* National Skills Coalition.

US Department of Education. *Career and Technical Education.* (2016, August 18). [Pamphlets]. https://www2.ed.gov/about/offices/list/ovae/pi/cte/index.html

US Environmental Protection Agency. (2003). *Travel and Environmental Implications of School Siting.* http://www.epa.gov/smartgrowth/pdf/school_travel.pdf

US Environmental Protection Agency. (2011). *School Siting Guidelines.* https://www.epa.gov/sites/default/files/2015-06/documents/school_siting_guidelines-2.pdf

US Government Accountability Office. (2020). *K-12 Education: School Districts Frequently Identified Multiple Building Systems Needing Updates or Replacement. GAO-20-494.* https://www.gao.gov/products/GAO-20-494

Varady, D. P., & Raffel, J. A. (1995). *Selling Cities: Attracting Homebuyers through Schools and Housing Programs*. State University of New York Press.

Vincent, J. M. (2006). Public schools as public infrastructure roles for planning researchers. *Journal of Planning Education and Research, 25*(4), 433–437.

Vincent, J. M. (2014). Joint use of public schools: A framework for promoting healthy communities. *Journal of Planning Education and Research, 34*(2), 153–168. https://doi.org/10.1177/0739456X13513615

Vincent, J. M., & McKoy, D. (2013). *Sustainable Communities Need Opportunity-Rich Schools: A Smart Growth Imperative*. Smart Growth Network.

Vincent, J. M., Miller, R., & Dillon, L. (2017). School siting and walkability: Experience and policy implications in California. *California Journal of Politics and Policy, 9*(3), Article 3. https://doi.org/10.5070/P2cjpp9336923

Vitiello, D. (2006). Re-forming schools and cities: Placing education on the landscape of planning history. *Journal of Planning History, 5*(3), 183–195.

Warren, M. R. (2011). *A Match on Dry Grass: Community Organizing as a Catalyst for School Reform*. Oxford University Press.

Weiss, J. D. (2004). *Public Schools and Economic Development*. Knowledge Works Foundation.

Wilson, E. J., Wilson, R., & Krizek, K. J. (2007). The implications of school choice on travel behavior and environmental emissions. *Transportation Research Part D: Transport and Environment, 12*, 506–518.

Witten, K., McCreanor, T., & Kearns, R. (2007). The place of schools in parents' community belonging. *New Zealand Geographer, 63*(2), 141–148.

Witten, K., McCreanor, T., Kearns, R., & Ramasubramanian, L. (2001). The impacts of a school closure on neighbourhood social cohesion: Narratives from Invercargill, New Zealand. *Health & Place, 7*(4), 307–317.

12. Smart growth and public health: making the connection

Andrea Garfinkel-Castro and Reid Ewing

SMART GROWTH AND PUBLIC HEALTH: WHAT'S THE CONNECTION?

Public health was not mentioned in the 10 original principles of smart growth, yet the goals of public health and smart growth are complementary and interrelated. Historically, public health and planning, both of which emerged during the eighteenth century reform movement, share many objectives, strategies, and standards, including concerns about equitable access to clean air and water, healthy foods, health care, and decent and affordable housing. Many of the urban problems that brought forth these related professions persist, compounded by the addition of contemporary challenges such as auto-centric and obesogenic environments, climate change, gentrification, and pandemics, as well as the growing and justifiable demand for racial equity and justice.

The persistence of our urban challenges suggests that the collaborative efforts of planners and public health officials is needed to achieve the objectives set out over a century ago (Corburn, 2007). No recent challenge has provided better evidence of the relationship between public health outcomes and spatial contexts than the coronavirus pandemic that began in late 2019 (Hamidi et al., 2020). Smart growth and public health advocates can better address such intertwined issues through collaboration, and by smart growth advocates paying more attention to public health. The two fields often work in parallel, but examples of outright collaboration are rare outside the research community. New approaches, enabled by advanced technologies, point to the synergies possible when planners and public health officials work together to better understand the public health impacts of the built environment and, conversely, how we might improve public health through the effects of the built environment. The time is right to make public health a governing principle of smart growth.

This chapter examines the intersection of public health and the built environment. We address four specific dimensions of public health: (1) physical activity and obesity; (2) respiratory ailments; (3) traffic injuries and fatalities; and (4) mental and social health. We organize our discussion of the built environment across three scales: macro (metropolitan), meso (neighborhood), and micro (block). At each scale, we consider the impacts of land use and development patterns on public health and detail the many complex and inextricable relationships between public health and the built environment. These relationships lead to outcomes that vary widely across socio-demographic contexts such as race and income. We close by identifying key limitations of and new directions for practice and research. In particular, we highlight examples of planning and public health collaborations where smart growth is the shared paradigm.

(RE)CONNECTING SMART GROWTH AND PUBLIC HEALTH

Public health and urban planning evolved together in the late eighteenth century to reduce the harmful effects of rapid industrialization and urbanization, particularly infectious diseases. City leaders recognized that poor housing conditions, inadequate sanitation and ventilation, and dangerous working conditions contributed to devastating outbreaks of cholera and typhoid (Frumkin et al., 2004; Corburn, 2007). As these fundamental challenges to health in urban areas diminished in severity, the integration between planning and public health began to dissipate. Public health professions began to focus on the biological determinants of infectious diseases and planners focused on economic development, public infrastructure, and accommodating rapid urban growth. This resulted in an uncoordinated approach to the social determinants of health and the growing health disparities facing the urban poor and people of color.

More recently, however, a reintegration began to occur. Research on the impacts of unchecked growth led to planning paradigms focused on managing the quality of growth rather than just the quantity. Smart growth proponents were among those leading the call for better planning. Around the same time, public health researchers were studying the effects of specific types of spaces (e.g., parks, playgrounds, and trails) and policies such as zoning might have on exercise and leisure activities. Using different measures and approaches, both fields came to roughly the same conclusion: the built environment matters when it comes to public health outcomes.

At the forefront of inspiring this re-connection between the public health and planning fields was the Active Living Research program, an initiative of the Robert Wood Johnson Foundation (RWJF). RWJF had decided to shift its emphasis from tobacco control to physical activity promotion and obesity prevention. It was becoming increasingly apparent to RWJF, along with other experts, that the built environment of the United States had become more and more auto-centric, while levels of physical activity had correspondingly declined, leading to population weight gains. RWJF decided that to counter these health trends, communities needed to be more conducive to physical activity, particularly walking and bicycling (Ewing, 2016).

In the year 2000, experts from public health and planning fields were brought together at the RWJF headquarters in Princeton, New Jersey, to discuss their common concerns and research interests (Ewing, 2016). Participants were amazed at how much the two fields had in common. Planners were researching the effects of development density, land-use diversity, and street design on active modes of transportation, particularly walking and bicycling. Public health professionals were researching the effects of physical activity supports such as parks, trails, and playgrounds on leisure-time physical activity. Yet the two were largely unaware of each other's research activities. Born from this initial meeting were invitations to speak at each other's conferences, joint collaborations on research proposals and studies, and even sabbaticals at each other's institutions. The cross-disciplinary ties were formalized through a new multi-million-dollar program, which required interdisciplinary collaboration. The collaborative efforts of the two professions have produced a vast body of research. A literature review by Mackenbach et al. (2014) found more than 5,500 original articles published in the preceding decade that examined the relationships between built environment characteristics and adult weight status.

This follows a transformation to auto-centricity in the United States that has taken only a century. After millennia of designing and building cities around human- and animal-powered mobility, we now prioritize motorized transport. Vast tracts of low-density new development, facilitated by extensive highway and road systems and mass-produced automobiles, are the foundation of the modern lifestyle (Garfinkel-Castro et al., 2016). However, planning has now come full circle to acknowledge the need for the kind of compact, mixed-use, and walkable environments that characterized the beginning of the twentieth century. Movements such as new urbanism, similar to smart growth in their approaches to the built environment, are among the dominant paradigms for urban planning in the last 30 years (Fainstein, 2021). This has not meant the end of urban sprawl, but attitudes among urban planners have shifted to discourage sprawl (Ewing et al., 2011).

PUBLIC HEALTH AND BUILT ENVIRONMENTS ACROSS FOUR DIMENSIONS AND THREE SCALES

In this section, we focus on four dimensions of public health that researchers and practitioners consider among the most significant today: physical activity and obesity, traffic injuries and fatalities, respiratory ailments, and mental and social health. We consider the impacts of land use and development patterns on these dimensions at three scales—macro (metropolitan), meso (neighborhood), and micro (block)—and synthesize the many complex and inextricable relationships. In addition, certain conditions are best examined at a particular scale. For example, the regional or macro scale is best for observing commuting patterns, whereas the block or micro scale is best for examining how the built environment impacts walkability. As a result, our synthesis of each public health issue focuses on the most relevant scales.

PHYSICAL ACTIVITY AND OBESITY

Of the four health dimensions discussed, obesity is at the forefront of public health concerns. The *obesogenic environment* is the term used to describe a specific social and environmental context attributed to this worldwide epidemic. Key characteristics of the obesogenic environment include limited access to nutrient-rich foods and conditions that discourage active transportation and physical activity. While research shows that newer, low-density suburban neighborhoods are often just as obesogenic as older, high-density urban neighborhoods and inner-ring suburbs, wealthier households are better able to mitigate the unhealthy effects of obesogenic environments. Households in wealthier neighborhoods have better access to healthy foods, can afford to join health clubs, and can live closer to their workplaces, affording them more free time for physical activity. On the other hand, households in lower-income neighborhoods are subject to "deprivation amplification," where a lack of resources compounds the negative effects of the obesogenic environment (Townsend & Lake, 2017, p. 40). We focus here on obesity because the links between sprawl and obesity have proven more apparent than those between sprawl and other health outcomes (see, for example, Ewing et al., 2014).

At the macro or metropolitan scale, the evidence points to a consistent but indirect relationship between regional development patterns and obesity levels. Recent research on regional development patterns shows lower body mass index (BMI) levels in areas that are more compact, thereby contributing to increased life expectancy (Hamidi et al., 2018). Places that have historically supported active transportation, such as the Netherlands, have been notably less impacted by the global obesity epidemic than places where auto dependence has been high for many decades, such as the United States (Swinburn et al., 2011).

At the metropolitan scale, of course, not all locations can be compact and support walking or other forms of active transportation, such as bicycling. Specific contexts vary at the granular level, but the conditions found to support active transportation at the metropolitan scale include higher densities, clustered (or nodal) development, and transit corridors, while impediments at this scale include freeways, wide streets, long block lengths, and large swaths of underdeveloped land and abandoned areas. Creating metropolitan regions with development patterns that are multi-nodal, with nodes designed to support active transportation, has become the dominant paradigm in regional planning (Park et al., 2020).

The relationship between built environment and obesity is complex at the neighborhood scale (Frank et al., 2004, 2006, 2007 and its progeny). Neighborhoods are where we live our lives. Sometimes we live in one neighborhood and work, attend school, have our hair done, or shop in a different one. Researchers have scrutinized what characteristics of a neighborhood lead to or support physical activity. At the neighborhood scale, the built environment is sometimes characterized by five D variables: development density, land use diversity, street design, destination accessibility, and distance to transit (Ewing & Cervero, 2010). Ewing and Cervero found that the combined effect of the five Ds on walk trip frequency was substantial, suggesting that, to the extent that walking translates into lower rates of obesity, better neighborhood design would be linked to better health. However, the relationship is complicated by the possibility of self-selection bias. Compact neighborhoods may lead people to be more physically active and fit, a concept sometimes referred to as environmental determinism. But fit people may also seek out and choose to live in compact neighborhoods where they can more easily be physically active. Recent research by Hamidi and Ewing (2020) tests both theories and finds more evidence to support the latter.

The built environment and obesity are also linked at the neighborhood level in terms of food access. *Food deserts* are neighborhoods served primarily by small grocery stores, convenience stores, and fast-food outlets, all of which lack a variety of fresh foods such as those found in supermarkets. Such deserts, coupled with a lack of walkability, create obesogenic environments. This undesirable combination is ubiquitous, across all types of urban, suburban, and rural landscapes (Swinburn et al., 2011). However, obesogenic environments are particularly detrimental to low-income, transit-dependent households. Hamidi (2020) investigated the association between urban sprawl and the emergence of food deserts at both regional and neighborhood scales and found that urban sprawl, measured via a compactness index, is significantly associated with the likelihood that a census tract is a food desert.

Neighborhood parks can provide important spaces for exercise, especially in places with the above-described health challenges, yet park accessibility is frequently overlooked in underserved neighborhoods. A before-and-after study of park access for a low-income, predominantly African American neighborhood in Columbia, Missouri, showed how increasing access to a park resulted in more people using it. Initially, the park was accessible via one poorly lit footbridge, which did not comply with the Americans with Disabilities Act (ADA), and two far-flung, unmarked intersections. Researchers installed signalized crosswalks across a "five-lane major arterial highway... [with] maximal speeds of 75 mph" (Schultz et al., 2017, p. S96), and park use increased measurably, particularly for women. However, context matters. In a Phoenix, Arizona study, parks with good accessibility were still under-used because of negative perceptions of park safety, particularly in neighborhoods where crime rates were high (Cutts et al., 2009).

Notwithstanding the complexity, research on obesity and the built environment does show one clear finding that is highly relevant to planners and public health officials: diet and exercise programs have minimal impact on curbing levels of obesity, except in places where active transportation is widespread and supported by urban form (Bombak, 2014; Swinburn et al., 2011).

At the block scale, research finds higher rates of obesity in places where sidewalks are poor quality, buildings are architecturally uninteresting, and disorder (e.g., garbage, broken windows, and abandoned cars) is abundant (Boehmer et al., 2007). With original funding from the Robert Wood Johnson Foundation, a series of studies have found higher pedestrian activity in blocks with good urban design qualities (Ameli et al., 2015; Ewing & Clemente, 2013; Ewing et al., 2016a; Hamidi & Moazzeni, 2019; Maxwell, 2016; Park et al., 2019). Talen further discusses the benefits and challenges of implementing smart-growth-friendly urban design principles in Chapter 7. But design qualities alone do not assure walkability. As Jane Jacobs (1961) so keenly observed: "A city sidewalk by itself is nothing. It is an abstraction. It only means something in conjunction with the buildings and other uses that border it..." (p. 29). Jacobs wrote extensively about the "sidewalk ballet" (p. 50)—the ebb and flow of people, as day turns to night, and the different purposes for walking or just being outdoors. She captured the importance of the social environment and people–place synergy, what Rojas (1993) calls "the enacted environment." The enacted environment successfully brings people outdoors, together, repeatedly and regularly and for a variety of practical and recreational purposes. In Chapter 9, Clifton outlines what three decades of research and practice has shown about understanding and promoting walking.

At the block scale, walkability necessarily encompasses more than design qualities and aesthetics, consistent with the smart growth principles of designing places that are walkable, distinctive, and with a strong sense of place. Considering the number of walking travel trips some people must take every day, non-aesthetic concerns are likely primary, including safety, distance, and utility. Theoretical work led by James Rojas (1993, 2017; also see Garfinkel-Castro 2021) points to culturally embedded variations in walking practices, such as the importance to Latinos of street vendors and small retail shops, and shows the need for a broader pedestrian research lens.

Traffic Injuries and Fatalities

Traffic crashes injure and kill drivers, passengers, pedestrians, and cyclists. Road and traffic engineers work hard to strike the balance between keeping traffic moving fast and preventing crashes. The specific environmental conditions most associated with fatal crashes are high-speed arterial roads; high levels of street connectivity resulting in more points of contact among vehicles, pedestrians, and cyclists; strip malls and big box stores; and more vehicle miles traveled (VMTs). At the metropolitan scale, places characterized by sprawl put pedestrians at higher risk. Stoker et al. (2015) suggest that a 1 percent increase in sprawl results in a more than 3.5 percent increase in traffic-related pedestrian fatalities.

Interestingly, it is fatal crashes that show a strong correlation with sprawl. This may be due to the longer driving distances and higher travel speeds in sprawling metropolitan areas (Ewing & Hamidi, 2015). The little empirical evidence available suggests that less severe crashes may be more common in compact areas (Ewing et al., 2016b). Classic fender benders appear to be more prevalent in compact areas, where more frequent cross-streets create more frequent (but low-speed and less injurious) conflicts (Ewing et al., 2016b).

Reducing speeds, lowering the number of miles driven, and increasing visibility for those sharing the road are fundamental approaches to increasing road safety. Metropolitan planning can play a role in addressing these safety factors. Remarkably, societies today have come to accept thousands of road fatalities each year as inevitable. However, research makes clear that the number of crash-related injuries and deaths could be significantly reduced with development that is more compact and transit-oriented. A transit-oriented metropolitan fabric, with nodes that feature a jobs–housing balance and interconnected bike and pedestrian infrastructure, can consequently be a catalyst for more walkable and bikeable environments at the meso and micro scales (Frumkin, 2002).

At the neighborhood scale, meaningful destinations, such as transit stations and shopping, are important for inducing active transportation. Purposeful and safe walking opportunities are especially important for supporting active aging (Michael et al., 2006). But getting people out of cars to walk and be more active depends on whether they perceive neighborhoods to be safe. Traffic speed contributes to this perception, for good reason; vehicle speeds are proven to determine outcomes in vehicle-pedestrian crashes, with the risks for injury and death rising exponentially with higher speeds. For example, in a study of pedestrian risk in Maine, vehicle drivers yielded to pedestrians nearly 100 percent of the time when driving 10 miles per hour or less (Gårder, 2004). The risk to pedestrians of being killed when struck by a vehicle moving below 25 mph is 10 percent; at 33 mph, 50 percent; and at over 40 mph, 75 percent (Tefft, 2013). After falling for several decades, pedestrian injuries and deaths are on the rise again. Worldwide, over 250,000 pedestrians lose their lives each year due to traffic crashes, and many more are seriously injured (WHO, 2013).

A number of factors contribute to overall street safety at the neighborhood scale. Most city streets are designed according to guidelines that favor either vehicle speed and flow or pedestrian safety (Dumbaugh & Li, 2010). Urban designers, planners, and street engineers have approached the problem as binary, with zero sum outcomes. Yet overwhelming evidence shows that drivers, pedestrians, and cyclists benefit from lower vehicle speeds, which reduce impact force, increase reaction time, and increase driver awareness, especially at the neighborhood scale.

At the neighborhood scale, land uses matter. Although commercial uses developed in conventional strip commercial or big box configurations are associated with significant increases in total, injurious and fatal crashes, these same uses are associated with decreases in all three crash types when designed in smaller, pedestrian-oriented configurations that abut the street (Dumbaugh & Li, 2010; Dumbaugh & Rae, 2009). Traditional "main streets," which have buildings that front the street and street amenities for pedestrians, experience significantly fewer crashes and injuries than more conventionally designed arterial streets (Dumbaugh & Gattis, 2005). It nevertheless remains unclear whether such configurations will result in reductions in the number of crashes affecting pedestrians and cyclists, as these uses also tend to encourage higher rates of walking and cycling and may thus lead to increased exposure.

To test this, focusing on pedestrian and bicycle safety, Dumbaugh et al. (2013) included the number of pedestrian-scaled retail uses in a community in their models. While strip commercial uses and big box stores were a risk factor, the pedestrian-scaled variable had a negative, though statistically insignificant, effect on crash incidence, suggesting that road users were modifying their behavior in these environments in a manner that prevented these crashes from occurring. Further, although earlier studies have asserted that population density is a risk factor for pedestrians and cyclists, this study found it to have a weak effect on total pedestrian crashes, and no statistically meaningful effect on pedestrians killed or severely injured, nor on crashes involving cyclists.

Neighborhood traffic-calming measures, such as speed tables and traffic circles, are particularly effective in reducing crash rates (Ewing & Brown, 2009). Some measures just slow traffic, such as speed humps and traffic circles, but others, more common in Europe, such as raised crosswalks and median island narrowings, not only slow traffic but facilitate pedestrian crossings (Ewing, 2008). In general, where pedestrians do not feel protected from harm and traffic, or sheltered from inclement weather, there will be fewer people walking.

At the block scale, the roadway attributes that most affect pedestrians are posted and induced vehicle speeds; quality of pedestrian infrastructure; and, relatedly, visibility. Planners have often prioritized road design that maximizes vehicle flow and speed and reduces delays for drivers. Pedestrians have paid a steep price for this. Slowing the speed of traffic where people and vehicles come into contact, such as through traffic calming, is a proven way to reduce traffic-related injuries and fatalities. Traffic calming can be applied to individual streets as well as entire neighborhoods. However, when applied to individual streets, planners and engineers have to be careful not to simply divert traffic from one local street to another. Some traffic calming measures such as traffic circles appear to divert minimal traffic, while others such as speed humps have much more diversion potential as drivers seek to avoid them (Ewing & Brown, 2009). Additionally, sidewalk quality sometimes varies from one block to another, so adding or completing sidewalks, crosswalks, and other critical pedestrian infrastructure is also key to reducing traffic-related injuries and fatalities.

A lack of basic traffic controls (stop signs and crosswalks) and pedestrian infra-structure (streetlights and benches) often indicates political and financial disinvest-ment in a community. Low-cost measures, such as the use of traffic cones or roadway murals (sometimes called Paint-the-Pavement projects), can be implemented either as a long-term fix or a demonstration of need, but data on their efficacy is mostly anecdotal. Occasionally, one or more households will work together to implement a non-sanctioned traffic calming device, usually after failing to get support from public officials. This approach is called guerilla or tactical urbanism (see Lydon & Garcia, 2015). Community interventions to create traffic calming and improve pedes-trian safety occur block-by-block and are an example of how public health and plan-ning officials can engage with communities to save lives and improve quality-of-life.

Respiratory Ailments

After obesity and traffic accidents, poor outdoor (or ambient) air quality is a major health risk throughout the world. The World Health Organization (WHO) estimates that, in 2016, over four million premature deaths were linked to poor ambient air quality worldwide (WHO, 2018). Vehicle exhaust and fuel burning that provides homes and businesses with heat and energy are two major sources of poor ambient air quality. While issues around air quality are especially complex and intertwined with both political and economic issues, research suggests that smart growth is better poised to address poor air quality than sprawling development. Compact develop-ment is shown to reduce overall VMTs (with caveats), better support mass transit and active transportation, and offer a variety of energy efficiencies (National Research Council, 2009).

Yet solutions that lead to better air quality at the metropolitan scale are surprisingly complex, often involving trade-offs with unclear benefits. Work-related commutes are a major contributor to air pollution, and commutes from low-density suburbs are typically longer and in a low-occupancy car. Replacing a longer commute with a shorter one might seem better, but if the shorter commute is similarly made in a low-occupancy car and includes many stops and starts or is slowed by heavy congestion, there may be no net benefits to air quality. There is even some indication that shorter, car-based commutes in dense urban areas may result in higher levels of air pollution in relationship to the number of VMTs. Equally discouraging is the fact that biofuels may produce air pollutants with risks that are not yet determined (Kaza et al., 2011). Simply reducing VMTs is not enough to improve air quality. Also needed are transit accessibility links between housing and jobs and other essential destinations. Transit accessibility is achieved with rich coverage (route density) and high schedule frequency so that commutes by mass transit and active transportation are comparable in time and effort to those made by car (Thompson et al., 2012).

It is also unclear whether exposure to pollution is greater in high or low-density metropolitan areas. Stone (2008) found that large metropolitan regions ranking high on sprawl experience a greater number of ozone exceedances than more spatially compact metropolitan regions. Importantly, this study controlled for population size, average ozone season temperatures, and regional emissions of nitrogen oxides and volatile organic compounds, suggesting that urban spatial structure may have effects on ozone formation that are independent of its effects on precursor emissions from transportation, industry, and power generation facilities. On the other hand, a follow-up study by Schweitzer and Zhou (2010), while confirming that ozone concentrations are significantly lower in compact regions, also found that human exposure to ozone was higher in these regions because more people live in areas where emissions are concentrated.

At the neighborhood scale, many urban neighborhoods in the United States face dual challenges—close proximity to highways and diesel-spewing buses. During the twentieth century, low-income minority neighborhoods across the United States were repeatedly targeted for highway expansion, resulting in displaced residents, disrupted communities, and degraded environmental qualities. The air quality of inner-city minority communities is often measurably poorer than other parts of the city, accompanied by excessively high rates of asthma for people of color (Sánchez et al., 2003).

The five D variables mentioned above have a direct relationship to vehicle miles traveled (VMT) and hence to vehicle emissions and ambient air quality at the neighborhood scale. Meta analyses have shown that neighborhoods with high densities, good land-use diversity, well-connected streets, good destination accessibility, and short distances to transit generate less VMTs than do sprawling neighborhoods (Ewing & Cervero, 2010; Ewing & Cervero, 2017; Stevens, 2017). Welche and Gehrke further examine the transportation-land use connection and how smart growth tools can reduce automobile dominance in Chapter 10.

Neighborhoods designed with smart growth principles—mixed land uses, walkable streets, and well-developed transit options—can reduce the number of vehicle trips used for short distance travel, leading to less traffic congestion and better air quality. Trip chaining—linking multiple travel needs together in a single trip—also reduces overall VMTs and is more efficient in compact neighborhoods (Ewing et al., 2020). Retrofitting suburbs to be more pedestrian- and transit-friendly is one of the greatest challenges facing planners and urban designers today, owing to the widely held belief among planners that successful transit service depends on high population density. However, a study of bus service in Broward County, Florida, has shown that with good design—high frequency *and* good coverage—buses can effectively serve low-density suburbs, as long as the priority is placed on shortening riders' time in transit (Thompson et al., 2012).

The various health risks for people living near roadways that cause traffic-related air pollution has implications both for overall neighborhood VMTs and for traffic on major roads running through neighborhoods. Liu et al. (2019) performed a meta-analysis of publications containing data on traffic-related air pollutants near roads with distance information on their concentration distribution. Concentration decay rates were calculated for black carbon (BC), carbon monoxide (CO) and nitrogen oxides (NO_2 or NOx) and meta-data analysis on these rates was performed. These analyses showed exponential decay rates of 0.0026, 0.0019, 0.0004, and 0.0027 per meter for BC, CO, NO_2 and NOx, respectively. Using these measurement data-based decay rates, concentrations for BC, CO, NO_2 and NOx over various near-road distances were predicted.

As this suggests, air quality is the consequence of activity at all scales but is experienced directly at the block scale. Researchers are working to better understand the trade-offs between transportation modes, urban form, public health, and air quality, as well as how these intersect with income and race. Another study looking at qualities of walkability in relation to air quality found that locations near (but not at) the urban center were "sweet spots"—the most walkable, with the least polluted air (Marshall et al., 2009). These areas were also scarce and comprised of higher-income households. The least walkable blocks, with the poorest air quality, were "sour spots"—disbursed suburban locations composed of middle-income households.

Low-income and non-White households are most at risk for both exposure to air pollution and chronic respiratory ailments, including asthma. In the United States, Hispanic and African American households are more likely to live in places with poor air quality (Sánchez et al., 2003). According to the Centers for Disease Control and Prevention (2019), asthma is a likely risk factor for COVID-19, implicated in the higher rates of COVID-19 for communities of color, especially Hispanics, African Americans, and American Indians and Alaska Natives (AIAN). AIAN communities are particularly vulnerable to COVID-19, given disproportional rates of comorbid chronic diseases including hypertension, cardiovascular disease, diabetes, cancer, and asthma (Hedgpeth, 2020). Complex modeling can—and should—be used to better understand the trade-offs between public health, community design and development, and environmental justice.

Social and Mental Health

Impacting almost every measure of community health and wellbeing are issues of equity and opportunity. Public outcry about deepening income inequity and systemic racism, seen in the Occupy Wall Street protests and the Black Lives Matter movement, show the urgency of these issues. The concept of individual "upward mobility" captures a number of key quality-of-life issues that contribute to wellbeing, including income growth, racial segregation, income inequality, and quality of education. A recent study suggests that living in a compact region makes upward mobility more likely than living in a sprawling region, in part because access to jobs is not dependent on car ownership (Ewing et al., 2016c).

One regional approach to addressing wellbeing is the Communities of Opportunity framework, which aims to increase resources and opportunity in underserved communities and provide greater access to regionally distributed resources (Kirwan Institute, 2008). Opportunity mapping, a tool that uses key wellbeing and opportunity indicators to apply the opportunity framework to a geographic region, provides maps of equity through opportunity. Smarter planning at the metropolitan scale can bring greater access to opportunity for residents of the entire metropolitan area. Lung-Amam and June-Friesen discuss the potential of a regional approach to addressing equity issues in Chapter 14.

At the neighborhood scale, social capital contributes to wellbeing. Social capital is the networks of relationships among people who live and work in a particular area that enables society to function effectively. Opponents of sprawl have blamed such development patterns for weakening these social networks, but there is a dearth of empirical evidence to support their argument. A study by Nguyen (2010), which examined the relationship between the county sprawl index and social capital factors from the 2000 Social Capital Community Benchmark Survey data, showed that in the United States, urban sprawl may support some types of social capital while negatively impacting the others.

Planners have associated suburbs with social costs in the form of isolation, anxiety, and other negative social emotions (see for example Ewing, 1997). Despite lower rates of crime and far fewer negative environmental hazards, suburbanites have collectively experienced lower levels of trust and civic engagement than urban residents since the early post-war era. This has been attributed variously to long commutes, economic stratification, and socially homogeneous but isolating neighborhoods (Frumkin, 2002). Nonetheless, newer research is finding that suburban contexts do not inherently diminish social connections and overall wellbeing (Morris & Pfeiffer, 2017).

In any setting, isolation and fear—and the resulting poor mental health—are particularly problematic for the elderly. In a study of over 5,600 adults between the ages of 50 and 74, the combination of living in a neighborhood with high crime rates and having low perceptions of safety led to more depression, even after accounting for age, sex, and household income (Wilson-Genderson & Pruchno, 2013). In another, somewhat smaller, study of men and women aged 65 and older, living in walkable neighborhoods reduced the rate of depression among men in the study but not significantly for women (Berke et al., 2007).

CONCLUSION

This chapter explored four measures of public health—physical activity and obesity, traffic injuries and fatalities, respiratory ailments, and social and mental health—and their relationship to the built environment. We addressed this literature at three urban scales— macro/metropolitan, meso/neighborhood, and micro/block—and sought to shed light on these dynamic socio-spatial relationships. We also reflected on how these relationships inform, or are informed by, smart growth principles, finding that a public health principle has a clear place in the smart growth paradigm.

Across the vast literature on the built environment and public health, several limitations are notable. One is the need for more longitudinal studies. Longitudinal studies are particularly well-suited for public health research related to place, given that both public health and built environments tend to evolve slowly. Seeing a public health response to changes in the built environment, such as how asthma rates change where a freeway cuts through a neighborhood, is a long-term endeavor. As community demographics change, we see changes in the built environment as well, but only over time.

Another limitation found in this research is the difficulty distinguishing between self-selection and environmental determinism. This especially impacts work on human behavior in relation to the built environment. One study (Ewing et al., 2016b, that used two different models of analysis, principal component analysis and structural equation modeling) to look at neighborhood qualities and residential preferences, found that both self-selection and environmental determinism were influencing household travel behavior, even though self-selection had a stronger influence.

Complexity emerged as an additional challenge to this research, and to making recommendations from the research. Many single issues become entwined with other issues. For instance, transportation-related air quality studies found that longer commutes in larger, more spread-out regions led to worse air quality, which is linked to respiratory ailments. Longer commutes also increase exposure to traffic collisions, and greater risk of injury or death. On the other hand, shorter commutes in more compact places may result in air quality that is equally poor due to high emissions during stop-and-start traffic, and pedestrians may have higher exposure due to a more walkable environment, leading to as many respiratory ailments as in a more sprawling area (Kaza et al., 2011).

The overwhelming number and range of public health challenges facing the world today suggest that we have much to learn and do to make our cities healthier places to live. The most immediate concerns are infectious diseases and how physical contact and proximity may impact urban form and transportation for the near (and possibly, far) term.[1] More research is also needed on the sociocultural and utilitarian qualities of walkability. Our cities are growing more ethnically and culturally diverse every day. Much of the existing research does not capture the demographic nuances of populations, particularly in terms of culturally-informed practices. Theories and empirical research about cultural-specific urban practices, such as Latino urbanism and immigrant spaces, are relatively new and recent to the literature but shed light on the direction culturally-specific research might take (see for example, Diaz & Torres, 2012; Mukhija & Loukaitou-Sideris, 2014). As planners and public health professionals become more familiar with the cultural component of mobility needs and desires, they could make public space and transportation more welcoming and usable.

Reconnecting planning and public health is urgently needed. The dramatic consequences of the COVID-19 pandemic fall on the heels of an obesity epidemic, which is evidence of historic structural inequities in health and quality-of-life for non-Whites in the United States. Further, the number of annual pedestrian fatalities is on the rise after a two-decade decline, which is ample reason for collaboration across the two disciplines. Movements in this direction can be seen in calls for health impact assessments and consideration of "health in all policy" (American Public Health Association, APHA, n.d.).

However, as our examination of public health across four measures at three urban scales shows, there are no absolute answers to be found. Are compact development patterns that are walkable and mixed-use better or worse than sprawling development patterns that are auto-dependent and zoned for single uses? The answers are mixed. What can be stated definitively is that there is ample evidence for including a public health principle in the smart growth paradigm. This principle should encourage planners to consider public health impacts at all scales of planning and development.

NOTE

1. Recent research on rates of COVID-19 infection and related mortality in 1,000 counties in the United States found that while metropolitan areas with larger populations had higher infection and mortality rates, density at the county level was unrelated to infection rates and actually negatively related to mortality rates, perhaps due to superior health care infrastructure in cities (Hamidi et al., 2020). These results are somewhat counterintuitive, and it is unclear if data alone will be enough to assure people that compact development can provide an attractive quality of life when it comes to disease. More research is needed on risk factors associated with the pandemic.

REFERENCES

Ameli, S. H., Hamidi, S., Garfinkel-Castro, A., & Ewing, R. (2015). Do better urban design qualities lead to more walking in Salt Lake City, Utah? *Journal of Urban Design, 20*(3), 393–410.

American Public Health Association. (n.d.). *Health impact assessment: A tool to benefit health in all policies.* Retrieved from https://www.apha.org/-/media/files/pdf/factsheets/ hiabenefithlth.ashx?la=en&hash=6B2146E596718055C7C33F2B17354CD6D115463E

Berke, E. M., Gottlieb, L. M., Vernez Moudon, A., & Larson, E. G. (2007). Protective association between neighborhood walkability and depression in older men. *Journal of the American Geriatrics Society, 55*(4), 526–533.

Boehmer, T. K., Hoehner, C. M., Deshpande, A. D., Brennan Ramirez, L. K., & Brownson, R. C. (2007). Perceived and observed neighborhood indicators of obesity among urban adults. *International Journal of Obesity, 31*, 968–977.

Bombak, A. (2014). Obesity, health at every size, and public health policy. *American Journal of Public Health, 104*(2), e60–e67.

Centers for Disease Control and Prevention. (2019). *Coronavirus Disease 2019 (COVID-19): People with Moderate to Severe Asthma.* Retrieved from https://www.cdc.gov/cornovirus/ 2019-ncov/need-extra-precautions/asthma

Corburn, J. (2007). Reconnecting with our roots: American urban planning and public health in the twenty-first century. *Urban Affairs Review, 42*(5), 688–713.

Cutts, B. B., Darby, K. J., Boone, C. G., & Brewis, A. (2009). City structure, obesity, and environmental justice: An integrated analysis of physical and social barriers to walkable streets and park access. *Social Science & Medicine, 69*(9), 1314–1322.

Diaz, D. R., & Torres, R. D. (Eds) (2012). *Latino urbanism: The politics of planning, policy, and redevelopment.* New York, NY: New York University Press.

Dumbaugh, E., & Gattis, J. L. (2005). Safe streets, livable streets. *Journal of the American Planning Association, 71*(3), 283–300.

Dumbaugh, E., & Li, W. (2010). Designing for the safety of pedestrians, cyclists, and motorists in the built environment. *Journal of the American Planning Association, 77*(1), 19–31.

Dumbaugh, E., Li, W., & Joh, K. (2013). The built environment and the incidence of pedestrian and cyclist crashes. *Urban Design International, 18*(3), 217–228.

Dumbaugh, E., & Rae, R. (2009). Safe urban form: Revisiting the relationship between community design and traffic safety. *Journal of the American Planning Association, 75*(3), 309–329.

Ewing, R. (1997). Is Los Angeles-style sprawl desirable? *Journal of the American Planning Association, 63*(1), 107–126.

Ewing, R. (2008). Traffic calming in the United States: Are we following Europe's lead? *Urban Design International, 13*(2), 90–104.

Ewing, R. (2016). Active living: A planning subfield comes of age. *Planning, 82*(8), 46–47.

Ewing, R., & Brown, S. (2009). *U.S. traffic calming manual.* New York, NY: Routledge.

Ewing, R., & Cervero, R. (2010). Travel and the built environment: A meta-analysis. *Journal of the American Planning Association, 76*(3), 265–294.

Ewing, R., & Cervero, R. (2017). Does compact development make people drive less? The answer is "yes." *Journal of the American Planning Association, 83*(1), 19–25.

Ewing, R., & Clemente, O. (2013). *Measuring urban design: Metrics for livable places.* Washington, DC: Island Press.

Ewing, R., & Hamidi, S. (2015). Compactness versus sprawl: A review of recent evidence from the United States. *Journal of Planning Literature, 30*(4), 1–20.

Ewing, R., Hajrasouliha, A., Neckerman, K. M., Purciel-Hill, M., & Greene, W. (2016a). Streetscape features related to pedestrian activity. *Journal of Planning Education and Research, 36*(1), 5–15.

Ewing, R., Hamidi, S., & Grace, J. B. (2016b). Urban sprawl as a risk factor in motor vehicle crashes. *Urban Studies, 53*(2), 247–266.

Ewing, R., Hamidi, S., Grace, J. B., & Wei, Y. D. (2016c). Does urban sprawl hold down upward mobility? *Landscape and Urban Planning, 148*, 80–88.

Ewing, R., Meakins G., Bjarnson, G., & Hilton, H. (2011). Transportation and land use. In A. L. Dannenberg, H. Frumkin, & R. J. Jackson (Eds), *Making healthy places* (pp. 149–169). Washington, DC: Island Press.

Ewing, R., Meakins, G., Hamidi, S., & Nelson, A. C. (2014). Relationship between urban sprawl and physical activity, obesity, and morbidity – Update and refinement. *Health & Place, 26*, 118–126.

Ewing, R., Park, K., Sabouri, S., Lyons, T., Kim, K., Choi, D., Daly, K., Etminani Ghasrodashti, R., Kiani, F., Ameli, H., Tian, G., Gaspers, D., & Hersey, J. (2020). *Reducing vehicle miles traveled (VMT), encouraging walk trips, and facilitating efficient trip chains through polycentric development*. National Institute for Transportation and Communities, Transportation Research and Education Center. https://nitc.trec.pdx.edu/research/project/ 1217/Reducing_VMT,_Encouraging_Walk_Trips,_and_Facilitating_Efficient_Trip _Chains_through_Polycentric_Development

Fainstein, S. S. (2021). *Urban planning.* Webpage in Encyclopedia Britannica, Inc. Retrieved from https://www.britannica.com/topic/urban-planning/Changing-objectives

Frank, L. D., Andresen, M. A., & Schmid, T. L. (2004). Obesity relationships with community design, physical activity, and time spent in cars. *American Journal of Preventive Medicine, 27*(2), 87–96.

Frank, L. D., Saelens B., Powell K., & Chapman, J. (2007). Stepping toward causation: Do built environments or neighborhood and travel preferences explain physical activity, driving, and obesity? *Social Science and Medicine, 65*, 1898–1914.

Frank, L. D., Sallis, J. F., Conway, T. L., Chapman, J. E., Saelens, B. E., & Bachman, W. (2006). Many pathways from land use to health: Associations between neighborhood walkability and active transportation, body mass index, and air quality. *Journal of the American Planning Association, 72*(1), 75–87.

Frumkin, H. (2002). Urban sprawl and public health. *Public Health Reports, 117*(May-June), 201–217.

Frumkin, H., Frank, L., & Jackson, R. J. (2004). *Urban sprawl and public health: Designing, planning, and building for healthy communities.* Washington, DC: Island Press.

Gårder, P.E., (2004). The impact of speed and other variables on pedestrian safety in Maine. *Accident Analysis and Prevention, 36*(4), 533–542.

Garfinkel-Castro, A. (2021). Unpacking Latino urbanisms: A four-part thematic framework around culturally relevant responses to structural forces. *Journal of Urbanism: International Research on Placemaking and Urban Sustainability*. doi: 10.1080/17549175.2021.1953111.

Hamidi, S. (2020). Urban sprawl and the emergence of food deserts in the USA. *Urban Studies, 57*(8), 1660–1695.

Hamidi, S., & Ewing, R. (2020). Compact development and BMI for young adults: Environmental determinism or self-selection? *Journal of the American Planning Association, 86*(3), 349–363.

Hamidi, S., Ewing, R., Tatalovich, Z., Grace, J. B., & Berrigan, D. (2018). Associations between urban sprawl and life expectancy in the United States. *International Journal of Environmental Research and Public Health, 15*(861). doi:10.3390/ijerph15050861

Hamidi, S., & Moazzeni, S. (2019). Examining the relationship between urban design qualities and walking behavior: Empirical evidence from Dallas, TX. *Sustainability, 11*(10), 2720.

Hamidi, S., Sabouri, S., & Ewing, R. (2020). Does density aggravate the COVID-19 pandemic? *Journal of the American Planning Association, 86*(4), 495–509.

Hedgpeth, D. (2020). Indian country, where residents suffer disproportionately from disease, is bracing for coronavirus. *The Washington Post*, https://www.washingtonpost.com/climate -environment/2020/04/04/native-american-coronavirus/

Jacobs, J. (1961/1992). *The death and life of great American cities.* New York, NY: Vintage Books.

Kaza, N., Knaap, G.-J., Knaap, I., & Lewis, R. (2011). Peak oil, urban form, and public health: Exploring the connections. *American Journal of Public Health*, *101*(9), 1598–1606.

Kirwan Institute. (2008). *The geography of opportunity: Review of opportunity mapping research initiatives.* The Ohio State University.

Liu, S. V., Chen, F. L., & Xue, J. (2019). A meta-analysis of selected near-road air pollutants based on concentration decay rates. *Heliyon*, *5*(8), e02236.

Lydon, M., & Garcia, A. (2015). *Tactical urbanism: Short-term action for long-term change.* Washington, DC: Island Press.

Mackenbach J. D., Rutter, H., Compernolle, S., Glonti, K., Oppert, J. M., Charreire, H., & Lakerveld, J. (2014). Obesogenic environments: A systematic review of the association between the physical environment and adult weight status, the SPOTLIGHT project. *BMC Public Health*, *14*(1): 233

Marshall, J. D., Brauer, M., & Frank, L. D. (2009). Healthy neighborhoods: Walkability and air pollution. *Environmental Health Perspectives*, *117*(11), 1752–1759.

Maxwell, J. A. (2016). Designing for 'life between buildings': Modeling the relationship between streetscape qualities and pedestrian activity in Glasgow, Scotland (Doctoral dissertation, University of Strathclyde).

Michael, Y. L., Green, M. K., & Farquhar, S. A. (2006). Neighborhood design and active aging. *Health Place*, *12*(4), 734–740.

Morris, E. A., & Pfeiffer, D. (2017). Who really bowls alone? Cities, suburbs, and social time in the United States. *Journal of Planning Education and Research*, *37*(2), 207–222.

Mukhija, V., & Loukaitou-Sideris, A. (Eds) (2014). *The informal American city: Beyond taco trucks and day labor.* Cambridge, MA: The MIT Press.

National Research Council. (2009). *Driving and the built environment: The effects of compact development on motorized travel, energy use, and CO2 emissions – Special Report 298.* Washington, DC: The National Academies Press. Retrieved from doi.org/10.17226/12747

Nguyen, D. (2010). Evidence of the impacts of urban sprawl on social capital. *Environment and Planning B: Planning and Design*, *37*(4), 610–627.

Park, K., Ewing, R., Sabouri, S., Choi, D. A., Hamidi, S., & Tian, G. (2020). Guidelines for a polycentric region to reduce vehicle use and increase walking and transit use. *Journal of the American Planning Association*, 1–14.

Park, K., Ewing, R., Sabouri, S., & Larsen, J. (2019). Street life and the built environment in an auto-oriented US region. *Cities*, *88*, 243–251.

Rojas, J. T. (1993). The enacted environment of East Los Angeles. *Places*, *8*(3), 42–53.

Rojas, J. T. (2017). Latino active transportation: Reinvigorating walking in U.S. suburbs. *StreetsBlog, September 21.*

Sánchez, T. W., Stolz, R., & Ma, J. S. (2003). *Moving to equity: Addressing inequitable effects of transportation policies on minorities.* Cambridge, MA: The Civil Rights Project at Harvard University.

Schultz, C. L., Wilhelm Stanis, S. A., Sayers, S. P., Thombs, L. A., & Thomas, I. M. (2017). A longitudinal examination of improved access on park use and physical activity in a low-income and majority African American neighborhood park. *Preventive Medicine*, *95*(Supplement), S95–S100.

Schweitzer, L., & Zhou, J. (2010). Neighborhood air quality, respiratory health, and vulnerable populations in compact and sprawled regions. *Journal of the American Planning Association*, *76*(3), 363–371.

Stevens, M. R. (2017). Does compact development make people drive less? *Journal of the American Planning Association*, *83*(1), 7–18.

Stoker, P., Garfinkel-Castro, A., Khayesi, M., Odero, W., Mwangi, M. N., Peden, M., & Ewing, R. (2015). Pedestrian safety and the built environment: A review of the risk factors. *Journal of Planning Literature*, *30*(4), 1–16.

Stone, B., Jr. (2008). Urban sprawl and air quality in large US cities. *Journal of Environmental Management, 86*(4), 688–698.

Swinburn, B. A., Sacks, G., Hall, K. D., McPherson, K., Finegood, D. T., Moodie, M. L., & Gortmaker, S. L. (2011). The global obesity pandemic: Shaped by global drivers and local environments. *The Lancet, 378*(9793), 804–814.

Tefft, B. C. (2013). Impact speed and a pedestrian's risk of severe injury or death. *Accident Analysis and Prevention, 50*, 871–878.

Thompson, G., Brown, J., & Bhattacharya, T. (2012). What really matters for increasing transit ridership: Understanding the determinants of transit ridership demand in Broward County, Florida. *Urban Studies, 49*(15), 3327–3345.

Townsend, T., & Lake, A. (2017). Obesogenic environments: Current evidence of the built and food environments. *Perspectives in Public Health, 137*(1), 38–44.

WHO (World Health Organization). (2013). *Pedestrian safety: A road safety manual for decision-makers and practitioners.* Geneva, Switzerland.

WHO (World Health Organization). (2018). *Ambient (outdoor) air pollution.* Webpage. Retrieved from https://www.who.int/news-room/fact-sheets/detail/ambient-(outdoor)-air-quality-and-health

Wilson-Genderson, M., & Pruchno, R. (2013). Effects of neighborhood violence and perceptions of neighborhood safety on depressive symptoms of older adults. *Social Science & Medicine, 85*(201305), 43–49.

13. Smart growth's misbegotten legacy: gentrification

Nicholas Finio and Elijah Knaap

INTRODUCTION: THE RELATIONSHIP BETWEEN SMART GROWTH AND GENTRIFICATION

Academic investigation and debate of gentrification predates the concept of smart growth by decades. British sociologist Ruth Glass coined the term "gentrification" in a socioeconomic assessment of London in the 1960s as the city changed rapidly in its post-war boom period (Glass, 1964). Glass defined gentrification as class transition in neighborhoods, wherein middle class white-collar workers move in and upgrade the residences of departing working class residents. This phenomenon continues today, though the geography of gentrification has expanded dramatically beyond large post-industrial cities to cities of all sizes, and even rural small towns (Brown-Saracino, 2017).

More recently, gentrification has been described as an economic process that "flies in the face of" the dominant form of urban growth in the United States in the post-war era: suburbanization (Griffith, 1995). While central city populations across the country generally decreased from the 1960s through the turn of the millennium, certain neighborhoods in certain cities experienced the redevelopment, reinvestment, and class transition known as gentrification. Concurrently, smart growth and its antecedent policies, such as growth management, and contemporaneous movements, such as new urbanism and sustainability, gained currency in the urban policy arena. These movements and policies were a reaction to the inefficiencies of suburbanization, such as traffic congestion, monotonous architecture, and a loss of green space and ecologically valuable land. Smart growth was also a reaction to the economic decay of once-vibrant urban residential and commercial areas due to decentralization of economic activity and white flight.

Adherents of the smart growth movement believe that strengthening existing communities through economic development can improve metropolitan form and function and manage growth by driving it inward. Arguably, the tenets of smart growth can also catalyze gentrification by stimulating redevelopment in existing areas. Smart growth's articulated principles are silent about the potential consequences of economic growth in existing communities. One primary consequence of gentrification is displacement, which is the forced relocation of incumbent residents—through direct economic displacement, when they can no longer afford to live in the neighborhood; exclusionary displacement, when those who might usually move to the neighborhood no longer can because of reduced or unaffordable housing;

and indirect displacement through social and cultural shifts (Slater, 2009). Cities with smart growth policies therefore must wrestle with the question: do smart growth policies encourage or exacerbate gentrification and its consequences, or can smart growth occur without gentrification?

Over 25 years have passed since smart growth first propagated across the country, and in that time gentrification has also diffused throughout the American metropolitan landscape into more neighborhoods each year (Hwang & Lin, 2016). Policies that support or subsidize infill development have become mainstream, while concerns about gentrification and displacement have risen in tandem. Scholars have begun to critique the relationship between smart growth, which promotes redevelopment and dense urban living, and gentrification. Some argue that "too often, urbanists have prescribed compact development without evaluating the very real consequences of new, dense construction in terms of raising land prices beyond the means of current residents" (Chapple & Loukaitou-Sideris, 2019, p. 3).

In this chapter, we explore the relationship between smart growth and gentrification over the past several decades. First, we explain what we know about gentrification. We then explain why smart growth may cause gentrification. Next, we review an empirical exercise that explained gentrification in US metropolitan areas since the year 1980 and linked that process to smart growth. We discuss the extent to which smart growth caused that gentrification. We explain how smart growth goals can be achieved without exacerbating the negative consequences of gentrification. The final section briefly lays out a twenty-first century vision for smart growth vis-à-vis gentrification.

WHAT DO WE KNOW ABOUT GENTRIFICATION?

Background

When Glass coined the term "gentrification," a new urban middle class was beginning to re-inhabit and invest in working-class neighborhoods in London. Glass purposefully played on the historical term "gentry," which refers to wealthy landowners, in her description and analysis of who was rehabilitating old housing stock, transforming neighborhoods from majority-renter-occupied to majority-owner-occupied, increasing property prices, and displacing working class residents. Beyond detailing the process at the neighborhood level, Glass described gentrification as "an inevitable development, in view of the demographic, economic, and political pressures to which London… has been subjected," forming the crux of her argument that gentrification is a neighborhood process that cannot be attributed to one factor but is instead the result of a complex set of metropolitan interactions (Glass, 1964).

Glass's definition began to enter the urban studies conversation in the United States in the early 1970s, when the growth management movement was nascent, and smart growth was still at least 25 years away. Perhaps best exemplified by the "brownstoning" movement in the Park Slope neighborhood in Brooklyn, New York, the press and the general public became aware of the process of gentrification, which was alternatively termed the "back to the city movement," or "central city revival." Across the country, in cities such as Washington, DC, San Francisco, and Chicago, professionals and bohemians alike were defying the conventional pattern of buying tract houses in the suburbs. They instead sought to rehabilitate and inhabit what they viewed as architecturally valuable, pre-war housing stock in neighborhoods proximate to central business districts (Lipton, 1977).

Gentrification is a form of neighborhood change, and scholarly work on that topic began decades ago with the Chicago School's urban sociology and its study of invasion and succession. According to the Chicago School framework of Park, Burgess, and McKenzie (1925), a neighborhood is a "natural area" that is geographically bounded, has a unique social composition, is a social system that functions as a mechanism of social control, and has ways of life that distinguish it from other areas (Schwirian, 1983). Park and the Chicago School popularized the use of the terms "invasion" and "succession" to describe neighborhood change. Invasion refers to in-movement of newcomers of different social backgrounds into a neighborhood. This can result in a new neighborhood equilibrium, which occurs through a process of succession, by which the original population leaves over time and is replaced by new residents (Park, 1952). Gentrification and displacement can be thought of as this process of succession. The form that neighborhood change takes may be influenced by different social, economic and political dynamics, but 100 years of metropolitan history suggest that neighborhood change in US cities is a constant.

Although early definitions generally focused on gentrification as an isolated process in residential housing markets in certain cities, after the 1980s it became clear that this process was both commonplace and part of a broader cycle of economic and class change in cities across the world. Yet no single definition of gentrification is commonly used in qualitative, case study, and quantitative work; Van Criekingen and Decroly (2003) noted that there was no unanimously approved empirical delimitation of the concept of gentrification 40 years after Glass coined the term. That remains true. For the purposes of this paper, and in line with much of the current scholarship, we define gentrification as an influx of new investment and new residents with higher incomes and educational attainment into a neighborhood (Chapple & Loukaitou-Sideris, 2019).

Measurement

For decades, scholars have used qualitative and quantitative metrics to identify gentrification, track it over time, and measure the consequences of the process. A few key parts of identification and measurement can be distilled by referencing the origins of the term. Glass noted that gentrification occurred in disinvested, central urban areas of London that were largely working class. Over time, these areas experienced both an influx of financial capital—for Glass, investment in existing housing stock—and an influx of new residents of a higher social class. Contemporary empirical studies of gentrification follow this framework by first identifying "gentrifiable" areas, which meet some criteria to be considered disinvested, and then by specifying which of those neighborhoods gentrify over some time period (Galster & Peacock, 1986).

That general framework has been operationalized in dozens of different ways by different researchers. The most common approach is to use quantitative census data at some small level of geographic reference that approximates the neighborhood—e.g., the census tract or block group—to assess socioeconomic and demographic conditions at separate census intervals (Barton, 2016). Mixed methods studies have utilized field surveys of buildings over time to assess physical upgrading, combining that information with census data and/or resident surveys to assess change over time (Hammel & Wyly, 1996; Wyly & Hammel, 1998). More recent work has used video or computer imagery, from services such as Google Street View, to allow large-scale field surveys to be completed remotely (Hwang & Sampson, 2014). Still others have assessed gentrification with parcel-level data from local government sources on building values, renovations, and sales (Helms, 2003). In studies using census data, researchers generally analyze variables such as home prices, income, rent, race, education, occupation, and race, but sometimes also indicators such as poverty, tenure, age, ethnicity, and unemployment. In qualitative work, scholars have referenced city plans, newspaper articles, visual assessments of structures, and the perceptions of residents (Brown-Saracino, 2017). In some qualitative and quantitative work, scholars simply take gentrification as a given in certain areas, referencing other work or their own knowledge of the process locally.

Gentrification researchers have argued that new-build gentrification, or infill on vacant or brownfield lots, is not separable from the upgrading of existing housing as a part of the gentrification process (Davidson & Lees, 2005). Earlier research tried to differentiate the two types of development, but redevelopment generally has been found to occur in tandem with demographic change and upgrades to the existing housing stock. It is possible to imagine a scenario where infill—combined with appropriate policies such as rent control on existing units, inclusionary zoning, or provision of deeply subsidized housing—would result in an influx of capital and physical changes, but not displacement of existing residents. Observing demographic change would depend on the scale of measurement, but in-movement of higher-class individuals coupled with complete stasis in the lower-class population would result in an increase in most socioeconomic indicators such as income or education. That would be defined as gentrification using the metrics most scholars have used.

Research on Causes and Consequences

Decades of research have presented ample evidence that gentrification is caused by a number of factors that operate at the city or regional scale. These factors can be broadly separated into three categories: the demand side, the supply side, and political influence. The demand side evidence has shown how certain groups have been more likely to inhabit central cities as de-industrialization has occurred (Lees et al., 2008). The supply side has emphasized through economic data how certain parcels of land in central cities become undervalued relative to their potential value and eventually experience redevelopment in capitalist land markets (Smith, 1979). Evidence on the political front has shown that city governments themselves are boosters for the gentrification process as they use various policy instruments to encourage new residents and businesses to locate to disinvested areas (Griffith, 1995).

There is also evidence that neighborhood-level factors are related to the process of gentrification. In a review, Brown-Saracino (2017) finds that gentrification's likelihood increases in neighborhoods near cultural amenities, downtown, public transportation, and other gentrifying areas, as well as in neighborhoods with quality housing stock, single family homes, and older buildings. Hwang and Sampson (2014) find that racial demographics matter, as certain neighborhoods that are majority Black are less likely to gentrify than more diverse places, a finding replicated by Timberlake and Johns-Wolfe (2017). Heidkamp and Lucas (2006) surveyed the literature and found that predictors of gentrification at the neighborhood level commonly include rents, home values, household incomes, household size, distance to the Central Business District (CBD), the presence of large institutions providing professional employment, parks, adjacency to already wealthy areas, waterfronts, and education levels. Other research has observed the influence of public policy on gentrification and displacement. The impact of public transportation investments on neighborhoods is well documented, and empirical evidence shows gentrification can be caused by such investment (Zuk et al., 2018). Exploratory models of housing markets show that households bid up the cost of housing near public transportation, potentially causing gentrification (Dawkins & Moeckel, 2016).

Despite "becoming more prevalent in U.S. cities… rigorous research on the extent, causes, and consequences of gentrification remains rare" (Ellen & Ding, 2016). Lees et al. (2008) have observed shifts in research focus: "In more practical terms, the questions have changed: more and more researchers have turned away from questions of *causality* – which almost invariably lead to contests between competing explanations – to examine *consequences*" (Lees et al., 2008 p. 190, emphasis in original). As an example of this, at the metropolitan scale, only a few scholars have attempted to find a link between smart growth policies and neighborhood gentrification. Landis (2015) studied neighborhood upgrading (defined by significant increases in census tract median household income) in a dataset of numerous metropolises and found that the presence of urban containment boundaries was linked to increased neighborhood upgrading. Nelson et al. (2007) studied gentrification (proxied via tenure composition transition from renter to owner) in metropolitan Portland and were unable to causally link the presence of that region's urban growth boundary to gentrification. Those pieces of empirical work embody the scant evidence on those fronts.

Instead, studies of gentrification tend to focus on a persistent debate over displacement, and, further, these studies tend to equate gentrification and displacement (Chapple & Loukaitou-Sideris, 2019). In a review, Brown-Saracino (2017, p. 517) noted gentrification is increasingly viewed in qualitative and micro-level studies as a social problem that is "deeply problematic and consequential for longtime residents." That is only half the debate. In the same review, Brown-Saracino notes that macro-level quantitative analyses offer the viewpoint that gentrification is not as widespread as commonly thought, and further and most importantly, "displacement is far from endemic" (p. 520). This reflects a deeply embedded debate in urban studies, regarding whether gentrification and displacement are inseparable. While some research on the consequences of gentrification is focused on displacement, controversial empirical evidence indicates that low-income residents of gentrifying neighborhoods are not displaced at higher rates than other residents (Delmelle & Nilsson, 2020; Ding et al., 2016; Ellen & O'Regan, 2011; Freeman, 2005). Other evidence has shown that displaced residents are more likely to relocate to disadvantaged areas when they move, and that homeowners are less likely to be displaced than renters (Ding et al., 2016; Martin & Beck, 2018; Newman & Wyly, 2006). Qualitative evidence has shown that long-term residents who are displaced are often negatively psychologically impacted during gentrification processes (Betancur, 2011; Hyra, 2017; Pattillo, 2007), which supports Mindy Fullilove's (2016) thesis on traumatic psychological stress caused by displacement.

As Chapple and Loukaitou-Sideris (2019) explain, displacement may stem from either disinvestment or investment, and, because of this, displacement is not necessarily directly induced by gentrification. However, others scholars, particularly in qualitative research and in critical urban studies, reject the disassociation of gentrification and displacement. Slater (2009) argues that recent research that finds scant evidence of displacement has methodological problems and, further, is far removed from the critical origins of the gentrification debate. For Slater, gentrification has always been linked to inequality and class struggle, and thus displacement.

As our review of gentrification research and perspectives shows, the impact of gentrification on local residents is far from empirically assured. So how does smart growth impact gentrification's trajectory in cities and neighborhoods, and is this impact similarly difficult to assess?

HOW MIGHT SMART GROWTH CAUSE GENTRIFICATION?

Although smart growth has always been a loosely organized movement, its normative goal has been clear. Growth itself is not challenged. Instead, smart growth advocates attempt to achieve a more efficient distribution of growth, with the assumption that the new distribution results in all residents being better off. And that smarter distribution of growth is to be achieved through ten principles, which include the following, relevant to our discussion here:

- Strengthen and direct development toward existing communities
- Mix land uses
- Create walkable neighborhoods
- Foster distinctive, attractive communities with a strong sense of place

These principles all call for physical changes to the built environment, but they do not mention demographic changes. We argue that smart growth tends to foster one type of demographic change that occurs in tandem with physical change: gentrification. Public or private policies and practices that are implemented to advance any of these four principles could contribute to gentrification.

Directing Development toward Existing Communities

Gentrified neighborhoods are, by definition, existing communities—disinvested areas home to residents of lower socioeconomic status. Often, these areas have an older housing stock along with several other characteristics of development in past eras, which to some degree align them with the smart growth principles. These characteristics can include walkable street networks designed before the pre-eminence of the automobile, more variegated residential form and density than suburban tract housing, nearby commercial districts, integration with existing natural features such as bodies of water, and easy access to major institutions such as colleges or hospitals. All of these features have been linked to increased likelihood of gentrification at the neighborhood level (Heidkamp & Lucas, 2006).

The principle of strengthening and directing development toward existing communities offers the clearest potential causal link between smart growth and gentrification. (See Hanlon, Chapter 5, for more on the redevelopment principle and possible consequences.) Ye et al. (2005) and Porter (1999) both note the importance of inner area revitalization and economic development to smart growth. Burchell et al.'s (2000, p. 823) summary of inner area revitalization goals for smart growth policy is as follows:

- Creating and orienting state, federal, regional, nonprofit, and private actions to stimulate and support community and neighborhood revitalization efforts.
- Expanding and evening-out local tax yields through the location of public and private employment to provide funding for new and improved public services.
- Infilling on vacant lands and redeveloping underused and brownfield sites to accommodate future development.
- Restoring and adapting existing structures, neighborhoods, and business areas to more effectively serve market demands.

One part of the phrasing is key: "restoring and adapting ... to *more effectively serve market demands*" (Burchell et al., 2000, emphasis added). Porter (1999) noted that one of the main thrusts of smart growth policy was to revitalize "inner areas," which are urban areas built up in prior eras. Some of these areas had become underpopulated and underutilized by the 1990s when smart growth coalesced as a movement. Through new and re-oriented public and private funding, growth in tax yields, adaptive reuse, and infill and redevelopment, these extant areas could regain economic activity. Ye et al. (2005) note that economic development policies were designed to add housing to city centers that served a range of incomes, along with amenities and employment. These economic development activities in central areas may accelerate gentrification, by increasing land values and rents, bringing in new residents and businesses, and displacing existing ones.

Mixed Land Uses, Walkable Neighborhoods, and a Sense of Place

Smart growth advocates also seek to mix land uses. This principle was a reaction to auto-oriented separation of commercial and residential zones during suburbanization. Mixed uses were much more likely to be present in older neighborhoods; some new urbanist smart growth advocates even sought to create new mixed-use communities from scratch, such as the Kentlands community in suburban Maryland. Such new-build new urbanist communities were not designed to be affordable to lower income groups explicitly, though they did make an effort to include a variety of housing types. See Song (Chapter 6) for more on mixed use development.

Mixing land uses also has the potential to displace. If mixing land uses results in amenities that increase nearby residential land values, lower-income residents may eventually be displaced as housing becomes pricier. From a critical viewpoint, it could be argued that advocacy for infill and mixing land uses has historically been unconcerned, intentionally or unintentionally, with the negative effects on existing populations.

Walkability and a sense of place, which are perhaps inarguably positive attributes of neighborhoods, can also be linked to gentrification. Walkable neighborhoods have been shown to command higher land and housing prices, as increasing shares of higher-income, more highly educated households seek walkable amenities (Li et al., 2015). While sense of place is more intangible, it is similarly a neighborhood amenity that drives up market prices. In seeking to create activated, dense, and busy neighborhood centers, planners may indirectly increase home prices and invite gentrification. See Talen (Chapter 7) for more on urban design and sense of place, and Clifton (Chapter 9) for more on walkability.

The Connection between Displacement and Urban Containment: Empirical Evidence

Gentrification is typically marked by new investment and higher-income, and more highly educated residents in a neighborhood, both of which could be considered evidence of successful inner-area revitalization. But smart growth advocates must wrestle with whether this spurs displacement of existing residents (Chapple & Loukaitou-Sideris, 2019).

The alignment of smart growth goals and gentrification goes beyond economic development and revitalization of inner areas. Controlling the growth of the urban envelope through instruments such as urban growth boundaries, or protective regulations for farmland and ecological areas, may re-direct economic activity inward toward established areas (Nelson et al., 2007), a goal of smart growth. Smart growth advocates have also sought to reduce greenhouse gas emissions and reduce vehicle miles traveled and boost individual and metropolitan wellbeing via investments in public transportation and pedestrian and biking facilities (Ye et al., 2005). This has required increased public investment and transportation funding for public and non-motorized modes, which has also been linked to neighborhood gentrification (Zuk et al., 2018).

In a recent paper (Finio and Knaap, forthcoming), an empirical exercise to examine the link between smart growth and gentrification found that out of 20,647 census tracts eligible to be gentrified in the 100 largest US metropolitan areas, 6,817 (33 percent) gentrified between 1980 and 2000. Between 2000 and 2018, 4,175 out of 23,228 eligible census tracts gentrified (18 percent). This gentrification is generally more prevalent, in terms of shares of eligible places that gentrify, closer to urban cores in these metropolitan areas. Further, in comparing gentrification patterns in Portland, Oregon, and Washington, DC (where containment policies are common) with gentrification patterns in Riverside, California, and Memphis, Tennessee (where containment policies are uncommon) we found that gentrification tends to occur near the central cities of Portland and Washington but near the periphery in Memphis and Riverside.

While not conclusive, these findings suggest that smart growth policies can potentially be a causal factor of gentrification, when it is defined as increases in residents' average income and education and increases to home prices. While these results do not provide direct evidence of displacement, we argue that the smart growth movement did not properly consider the consequences of the gentrification it indirectly advocated for. In the next section, we discuss how smart growth can address this issue.

HOW CAN WE ACHIEVE SMART GROWTH WITHOUT GENTRIFICATION?

Smart growth need not continue to exacerbate the negative consequences of gentrification. A new vision for smart growth requires policies that focus primarily on one multifaceted issue: displacement. Existing residents, unless protected by housing subsidies, strong anti-eviction laws, rent control, permanent affordable housing, and other policies, may be unable to the bear increased rents, prices, and property taxes brought about by gentrification. These residents may be forced to move or be excluded from previously affordable areas. Further, existing residents may own and operate small businesses in gentrifying areas. As rents and incomes rise, these businesses and the residents and culture they support may be displaced as well. If the smart growth movement is willing to accept, prima facie, that residential displacement makes low-income residents worse off, then corrective measures can be taken. As we show in our empirical exercise, central parts of metropolitan areas are experiencing significant gentrification. It is time to act to mitigate displacement and loss of affordable housing.

Many cities are already undertaking these measures, often cast as "anti-displacement" policies (Zuk et al., 2019). Cities are already providing for affordable housing in both time-tested and innovative ways, supporting small businesses, and attempting to preserve local culture through policies that range from strong market regulation, such as rent control, to market-based incentives, such as density bonuses awarded to developers in exchange for construction of affordable housing (Abu-Khalaf, 2018). Additional policies include impact fees charged to developers that are used for community benefit, foreclosure assistance measures, just-cause eviction laws, and legalization of community land trusts. These policies have in some cases been coupled with smart growth policies, such as transportation-oriented development (TOD), which increases housing supply near dense transit nodes. Many new TOD projects now require inclusionary zoning, which preserves a portion of new housing construction for lower income households to both rent and purchase.

As cities have dealt with affordable housing shortages in the wake of gentrification, they have expanded certain programs to increase the supply of affordable housing. For example, the State of Washington requires that public land dispositions are offered via right of first refusal to public agencies that seek to construct affordable housing (Arabo & Leonard, 2018). In a similar effort, Los Angeles's transit agency has an explicit affordability target, such that 35 percent of housing units developed on agency land will be affordable (LACMTA, 2018). Seattle's Sound Transit has a similar program, the "80-80-80" rule, requiring 80 percent of suitable surplus transit property to be held for developers who make 80 percent of units affordable to families or individuals with incomes below 80 percent of median income (City of Seattle, 2015). Inclusionary zoning programs, which apply to all new development projects, have also become popular in the decades since they originated in Montgomery County, Maryland. Inclusionary zoning can be targeted to hold units at very low cost for those most vulnerable to displacement. Developers can recoup the costs of providing affordability through density bonuses, like those offered in Los Angeles and Chicago, which allow developers to build at greater residential densities (City of Chicago, 2018; City of Los Angeles, 2018). Such policies offer a win-win for smart growth and affordable housing proponents. Inclusionary zoning policies can offer units both for rent and for sale, granting homeownership opportunities to low-income residents. See Dawkins and Kim (Chapter 8) for more on smart growth and affordable housing.

In Washington, DC, city leaders have responded to gentrification on multiple fronts. The city's Housing Production Trust Fund has had a strong commitment of $100 million directly from city coffers, funded through real estate transfer taxes and general funds. Such funds, now common across the country, are dedicated sources of revenue for constructing affordable housing, which can be targeted to gentrifying areas. DC also has the Tenant Opportunity to Purchase Act, which offers residents of apartment buildings a chance to collectively purchase their buildings with the right of first refusal when a sale is proposed; this policy has preserved over 1,000 units (City of Washington, DC, 2018). Many other jurisdictions have supported tenants through "just cause eviction" laws, which establish rigorous procedures for landlords to evict tenants, requiring landlords to prove cause. Such policies have been shown to reduce eviction rates (Cuellar, 2019). Such actions are critical in the wake of rampant market-driven eviction in gentrifying areas (Smith and DeFilippis, 1999).

Smart growth can also help reduce the impacts of gentrification by promoting sustainable economic development that supports locally owned small businesses, through policies such as commercial rent control, or urban design that allows for smaller commercial rental units. While some cities have explored the potential for commercial rent control and commercial inclusionary zoning, no policies have been implemented at scale in the United States. Yet small businesses are only one part of a larger cultural environment of schools, public service centers, open spaces, etc., that provide a sense of place. Public non-commercialized space is also a critical part of building inclusive communities, especially in those under gentrification pressure. As neighborhood land values increase under market pressure, space and place for un-monetized community expression must be preserved. Smart growth advocates must advance the inclusion of public and community spaces in planning efforts, in addition to maintenance of affordable commercial rents, in gentrifying areas. Without attention paid to all these aspects of space in areas facing gentrification, existing residents can lose their sense of place.

Land-value capture offers perhaps the most potential to stave off the negative consequences of gentrification. With some exceptions, cities remain hesitant to charge differential taxes on their most expensive land that is ideal for high-rent residential and commercial development. Capturing high land values through tax instruments and reallocating that money to fund public amenities, affordable housing, and other public goods remains an underutilized option in American urban policy. In the coming decades, smart growth advocates who seek more inclusive and equitable redevelopment should include land-value capture, affordable housing preservation and production, small business support, and public space in any and all redevelopment projects.

CONCLUSION

In this chapter we have argued that smart growth policies can be linked to the process of gentrification in US cities. While the rapid spread of gentrification and dramatic price increases for urban residences in some cities would have been hard to predict 20 years ago, some forethought by smart growth advocates about displacement should have been possible. As Atkinson (2002) observed, critiques of gentrification have produced analysis about negative consequences for decades. The original architects of the smart growth movement mostly ignored the potential for smart growth policies to catalyze the negative impacts of gentrification, especially residential displacement. Now many cities are scrambling to implement policies that protect existing residents from displacement and boost housing supply.

As we have shown, gentrification spreads unevenly across metropolitan landscapes in relation to smart growth policies. We have shown that smart growth can be linked to increased home prices and average socioeconomic status in urban core neighborhoods. These areas are often home to sizeable shares of poor and disadvantaged residents, who must contend with increased housing prices brought about by gentrification. Smart growth advocates must recognize the potential for large-scale smart growth policies to increase home prices and potentially cause displacement.

It is possible, however, to achieve the goals of smart growth without gentrification. It will take serious commitments from cities, especially in affordable housing finance and production. Common-sense tools which have worked nationally, such as inclusionary zoning and laws protecting tenants' rights, are the best place to start. The forces of the market, if left unchecked, will result in displacement and replacement of residents in gentrifying neighborhoods.

Smart growth influenced more than two decades of thought and policy about urban revival and sustainable living. As others in this volume have argued, the time for updating smart growth's vision has come. To mitigate gentrification's negative consequences, the smart growth movement must promote both market-based and regulatory measures that preserve and create more affordable residences, protect tenants and incumbent residents, prioritize community space and culture, and support a wide breadth of commercial activity.

REFERENCES

Abu-Khalaf, A. (2018). *Proven local strategies for expanding the supply of affordable homes and addressing cost challenges.* Columbia, MD: Enterprise Community Partners, Inc.

Arabo, F., & Leonard, M. A. (2018, March 23). Affordable housing wins big in Washington State's 2018 legislative session. Retrieved from https://www.enterprisecommunity.org/blog/2018/03/affordable-housing-wins-big-washington-states-2018-legislative-session

Atkinson, R. (2002). Does gentrification help or harm urban neighbourhoods? An assessment of the evidence-base in the context of the new urban agenda. *ESRC Centre for Neighborhood Research*, CNR Summary 5.

Barton, M. (2016). An exploration of the importance of the strategy used to identify gentrification. *Urban Studies 53*(1), 92–111. doi.org/10.1177/0042098014561723

Betancur, J. (2011). Gentrification and community fabric in Chicago. *Urban Studies, 48*(2), 383–406 doi:10.1177/0042098009360680

Brown-Saracino, J. (2017). Explicating divided approaches to gentrification and growing income inequality. *Annual Review of Sociology, 43*, 515–539. doi.org/10.1146/annurev-soc-060116-053427

Burchell, R. W., Listokin, D., & Galley, C. (2000). Smart growth: More than a ghost of urban policy past, less than a bold new horizon. *Housing Policy Debate, 11*(4), 821–879. doi.org/10.1080/10511482.2000.9521390

City of Chicago (2018). Neighborhood opportunity bonus: Leveraging downtown zoning to foster neighborhood development and central area growth. Retrieved from https://www.cityofchicago.org/city/en/depts/dcd/supp_info/realigning-zoning-with-neighborhood-growth.html

City of Los Angeles Department of Planning (2018). Technical clarifications to the transit-oriented communities affordable housing incentive program guidelines (TOC guidelines). Retrieved from https://planning.lacity.org/ordinances/docs/toc/TOCGuidelines.pdf

City of Seattle, WA. (2015). Transit-oriented development strategy system plan, 81 RCW § 81.112.350 (2015).

City of Washington, DC, Department of Housing and Community Development (2018). Tenant opportunity to purchase assistance. Retrieved from https://dhcd.dc.gov/service/tenant-opportunity-purchase-assistance

Chapple, K., & Loukaitou-Sideris, A. (2019). *Transit-oriented displacement or community dividends? Understanding the effects of smarter growth on communities.* Cambridge, MA: MIT Press.

Cuellar, J. (2019). Effect of "just cause" eviction ordinances on eviction in four California cities. *Journal of Public & International Affairs.* Princeton University.

Davidson, M., & Lees, L. (2005). New-build 'gentrification' and London's riverside renaissance. *Environment and Planning A: Economy and Space, 37*(7), 1165–1190. doi.org/10.1068/a3739

Dawkins, C., & Moeckel, R. (2016). Transit-induced gentrification: Who will stay and who will go? *Housing Policy Debate, 26*(4-5), 801–818. doi.org/10.1080/10511482.2016.1138986

Delmelle, E., & Nilsson, I. (2020). New rail transit stations and the out-migration of low-income residents. *Urban Studies, 57*(1), 134–151. doi:10.1177/0042098019836631

Ding, L., Hwang, J., & Divringi, E. (2016). Gentrification and residential mobility in Philadelphia. *Regional Science and Urban Economics, 61*(1), 38–51. doi.org/10.1016/j.regsciurbeco.2016.09.004

Ellen, I.G., & Ding, L. (2016). Advancing our understanding of gentrification. *Cityscape, 18*(3), 3–8.

Ellen, I. G., & O'Regan, K. M. (2011). How low-income neighborhoods change: Entry, exit, and enhancement. *Regional Science and Urban Economics, 41*(2), 89–97. doi: 10.1016/j.regsciurbeco.2010.12.005.

Finio, N., & Knaap, E. (2022, forthcoming). Forthcoming working paper: links between smart growth and gentrification.

Freeman, L. (2005). Displacement or succession? Residential mobility in gentrifying neighborhoods. *Urban Affairs Review, 40*(4), 463–491. doi: 10.1177/1078087404273341

Fullilove, M. (2016). *Root shock: How tearing up city neighborhoods hurts America, and what we can do about it.* New York, NY: NYU Press.

Galster, G., & Peacock, S. (1986). Urban gentrification: Evaluating alternative indicators. *Social Indicators Research, 18*(3), 321–337. doi.org/10.1007/BF00286623

Glass, R. (Ed.) (1964). *London: Aspects of change* (pp. xii–xlii). London: Centre for Urban Studies.

Griffith, A. (1995). Gentrification: Perspectives on the return to the central city. *Journal of Planning Literature, 10*(1), 241–255.

Hammel, D. J., & Wyly, E. K. (1996). A model for identifying gentrified areas with census data. *Urban Geography, 17*(3), 248–268. doi.org/10.2747/0272-3638.17.3.248

Heidkamp, P., & Lucas, S. (2006). Finding the gentrification frontier using census data: The case of Portland, Maine. *Urban Geography, 27*(2), 101–125. doi.org/10.2747/0272-3638.27.2.101

Helms, A. C. (2003). Understanding gentrification: An empirical analysis of the determinants of urban housing renovation. *Journal of Urban Economics, 54*(3), 474–498. doi.org/10.1016/S0094-1190(03)00081-0.

Hyra, D. (2017). *Race, class and politics in the cappuccino city.* Chicago, IL: University of Chicago Press.

Hwang, J., & Lin, J. (2016). What have we learned about the causes of recent gentrification? *Cityscape, 18*(3), 9–26. Retrieved from https://www.jstor.org/stable/26328271

Hwang, J., & Sampson, R. J. (2014). Divergent pathways of gentrification: Racial inequality and the social order of renewal in Chicago neighborhoods. *American Sociological Review, 79*(4), 726–751. doi.org/10.1177/0003122414535774

LACMTA (2018). LACMTA Joint Development Program, Metro.Net, Retrieved from, https://www.metro.net/about/joint_dev_pgm/

Landis, J. (2015). Tracking and explaining neighborhood socioeconomic change in US metropolitan areas between 1990 and 2010. *Housing Policy Debate*, *26*(1), 2–52. doi.org/10.1080/10511482.2014.993677

Lees, L., Slater, S., & Wyly, E. K. (2008). *Gentrification*. New York, NY: Routledge.

Li W., Joh K., Lee C., Kim J.-H., Park H., & Woo A. (2015). Assessing benefits of neighborhood walkability to single-family property values: A spatial hedonic study in Austin, Texas. *Journal of Planning Education and Research*, *35*(4), 471–488. doi:10.1177/0739456X15591055

Lipton, S. G. (1977). Evidence of central city revival. *Journal of the American Institute of Planners*, *43*(2), 136-47.

Martin, I. W., & Beck, K. (2018). Gentrification, property tax limitation, and displacement. *Urban Affairs Review*, *54*(1), 33–73. doi:10.1177/1078087416666959

Nelson, A., Dawkins, C., & Sanchez, T. (2007). *The social impacts of urban containment*. London: Routledge. doi.org/10.4324/9781315552781

Newman, K., & Wyly, E. K. (2006).The right to stay put, revisited: Gentrification and resistance to displacement in New York City. *Urban Studies*, *43*(1), 23–57.

Park, R. E. (1952). *Human communities: The city and human ecology*. Glencoe, IL: The Free Press.

Park, R. E., Burgess, E. W., & McKenzie, R. D. (1925). *The city*. Chicago, IL: University of Chicago Press. Retrieved from: https://www.jstor.org/stable/3004850

Pattillo, M. (2007). *Black on the block: The politics of race and class in the city*. Chicago, IL: University of Chicago Press.

Porter, D. R. (1999). Whither eastward ho! Unpublished paper, *Growth Management Institute*.

Schwirian, K. (1983). Models of Neighborhood Change. *Annual Review of Sociology*, *9*, 83-102. https://doi.org/10.1146/annurev.so.09.080183.000503

Slater, T. (2009). Missing Marcuse: On gentrification and displacement. *City*, *13*(2-3), 292–311. doi.org/10.1080/13604810902982250

Smith, N. (1979). Towards a theory of gentrification: A back to the city movement by capital, not people. *Journal of the American Planning Association*, *45(*4), 538–548. doi.org/10.1080/01944367908977002

Smith, N., and DeFilippis, J. (1999). The reassertion of economics: 1990s gentrification in the Lower East Side. *International Journal of Urban and Regional Research*, *23*(4), 638–653. doi.org/10.1111/1468-2427.00220

Timberlake, J. M., & Johns-Wolfe, E. (2017). Neighborhood ethnoracial composition and gentrification in Chicago and New York, 1980 to 2010. *Urban Affairs Review*, *53*(2), 236–272. doi.org/10.1177/1078087416636483

Van Criekingen, M., & Decroly, J.-M. (2003). Revisiting the diversity of gentrification: Neighbourhood renewal processes in Brussels and Montreal. *Urban Studies*, *40*(12), 2451–2468.

Wyly, E. K., & Hammel, D. (1998). Modeling the context and contingency of gentrification. *Journal of Urban Affairs*, *(20)*3, 303–326. doi.org/10.1111/j.1467-9906.1998.tb00424.x

Ye, L., Mandpe, S., & Meyer, P. B. (2005). What is "smart growth?"—Really? *Journal of Planning Literature*, *19*(3), 301–315. doi.org/10.1177/0885412204271668

Zuk, M., Bierbaum, A., Chapple, K., Gorska, K., & Loukaitou-Sideris, A. (2018). Gentrification, displacement, and the role of public investment. *Journal of Planning Literature*, *33*(1), 31–44. doi.org/10.1177/0885412217716439

Zuk, M., Loukaitou-Sideris, A., & Chapple, K. (2019). Safeguarding against displacement: Stabilizing transit neighborhoods. In K. Chapple & A. Loukaitou-Sideris (Eds), *Transit-oriented displacement or community dividends? Understanding the effects of smarter growth on communities* (pp. 243–266). Cambridge, MA: MIT Press.

14. Growing together or apart? Critical tensions in charting an equitable smart growth future

Willow Lung-Amam and Katy June-Friesen

INTRODUCTION

Urban planners have long argued that strong, vibrant communities require a balance among the "three Es" of sustainability—environment, economics, and equity. While various cities in the United States and around the world have grown more economically robust and environmentally resilient, many have become more unequal. Historically, smart growth has mirrored these trends, focusing principally on the first two Es, with far less attention to the latter. But over the last couple of decades, smart growth has become increasingly concerned with the third E. At the same time, advocates for equitable and inclusive development have become more attuned to the benefits of smart growth. As Robert Bullard (2007) notes, however, these groups still often struggle to recognize their linked fates or work together:

> Generally, people of color and their institutions have not played a visible role in the smart growth and regionalism dialogue. Much of the issue framing has been carried out principally by and for white middle-class leaders and business elites (Bullard, 2007, p. 374).

This chapter examines forces that have brought smart growth and equitable development movements closer together in recent decades and the critical questions and tensions that continue to push them apart. Drawing on established literatures in smart growth, urban planning, and community development, we trace the slow but critical turn in the smart growth movement—from a time when the concerns facing low-income communities of color and other marginalized groups were largely divorced from questions of smart growth to today, when equity concerns are more foregrounded. We focus on the growing regional equity planning movement, an arena in which equitable development and smart growth advocates have forged some common ground, and a promising bridge between these historically fractured fields. However, tensions within the regional equity movement have also threatened the tenuous alliance between smart growth and equitable development advocates. We highlight three key tensions and challenges for this alliance: building regional coalitions and scaling up equitable development policies; prioritizing policies to deconcentrate or invest in poor neighborhoods; and the limits of infill, mixed-use development strategies.

Equity, to be clear, is a topic as sprawling as metropolitan growth itself. It intersects with a range of smart growth issues within and beyond this volume—from climate change and transportation to gentrification, affordable housing, and education. Indeed, the issues of primary concern to smart growth and equitable development advocates are intimately connected (Powell, 2000). We do not purport to do justice to their complex linkages in this chapter. Rather, this chapter charts how advocates and scholars within the smart growth movement—and those who have pushed it from its margins—have come together around a smart *and* equitable regional growth agenda. To continue building this movement, we argue that smart growth and equitable development advocates must bridge their deep and historic divide, address key tensions and challenges, and clarify shared principles to guide an equitable smart growth future.

FROM SMART GROWTH TO EQUITABLE GROWTH

The early smart growth period evidenced the distrust sometimes felt between smart growth and equitable development advocates. Advocates came from different world-views, had different constituents, and used different tools toward different ends. While the former aimed to limit and control metropolitan growth and sprawl, the latter sought to increase opportunities for those living in disadvantaged communities. While they shared some common interests, such as investing in public transportation and existing neighborhoods, their worlds rarely intersected (Bullard, 2007). In recent decades, new bridges have been built. Led largely by community development and equity planners, the emerging regional equity movement has brought attention to these shared concerns (Benner & Pastor, 2019).

Splintered Equitable Development and Smart Growth Movements

When smart growth's guiding principles were established in the 1990s, issues of social and economic equity were not centered. With roots in environmentalism, smart growth focused principally on promoting compact, walkable neighborhoods and preserving open space. Despite calls for community involvement in planning and housing "choices" for all incomes, the ten principles advanced by the Smart Growth Network did not prioritize social, economic, or racial equity. Smart growth policies often gave little attention to their impacts on socially and economically marginalized groups, and many smart growth conversations failed to bring these groups to the table (Bullard, 2007; Glover Blackwell & Fox, 2006). As Angela Glover Blackwell and Radhika Fox (2006) noted, smart growth advocates rarely "led with race and equity" (p. 409). Others argued that race and equity discourses were often not even on the menu (Bullard, 2007; Gearin, 2004; Powell, 1999).

Equitable development advocates critiqued smart growth as too focused on economic competitiveness and environmental sustainability. Without attention to structures that produced inequitable growth and development, they worried that smart growth policies contributed to the production and reproduction of urban inequality, rather than offering solutions (Bullard, 2007; Pastor et al., 2009). Further, smart growth's narrow framing around sprawl and land use controls did not directly address issues of primary concern to marginalized communities (Baum, 2004; Gearin, 2004; Pastor et al., 2009). While sprawl is intimately tied to affordable housing, job and educational access, segregation, and poverty, smart growth advocates seldom made the connections explicit (Bullard et al., 2000; Powell 1999, 2000).

Many equitable development advocates, including equity and advocacy planners, also did not make clear ties between their work and smart growth (Glover Blackwell & Fox, 2006; Powell, 1999). Among equitable development advocates, land use and environmental concerns had long been the domain of environmental justice (EJ). EJ advocates pushed the dominant environmental movement to pay greater attention to those groups and neighborhoods most exposed and vulnerable to toxic and hazardous environments and practices (Bullard, 2007). As Hendricks and Berke point out in Chapter 15 of this book, urban planning has also often failed to recognize the outsized impact of hazards on socially vulnerable groups, and development in vulnerable communities can accelerate hazard risks. Following the pioneering work of Norman Krumholz and Paul Davidoff, equity and advocacy planners often worked to advance the interests of and advocate for marginalized groups in development processes within local communities (Davidoff, 1965; Hexter & Krumholz, 2019). Yet collaboration among smart growth proponents, EJ advocates, and equity planners was rare (Bullard, 2007).

Toward a Regional Equity Movement

By the early 2000s, however, scholars and policy leaders were promoting a regional approach and calling on smart growth and equitable development advocates to foreground the connections between sprawl and urban inequality. Early regional equitable growth advocates, such as Myron Orfield (1997), David Rusk (1993), and john a. powell (1999, 2000) argued that regions were interdependent systems that could not solve problems on their own. While equitable development plans and policies were positively impacting local communities, decades of White flight, municipal fragmentation, and sprawl required a more comprehensive, regional approach. Further, segregation and sprawl were economically, socially, and environmentally costly to entire metropolitan regions (Benner & Pastor, 2019). As Robert Bullard, the so-called "father of environmental justice" argued:

> Because low-income, working-class, and people of color families are disproportionately and adversely affected by the environmental problems resulting from sprawl, it is not difficult to define sprawl as an environmental justice problem, and smart growth and regional equity as the solution (Bullard, 2007, p. 31).

Land use policies, while often established at the local level, impacted entire metropolitan areas. Given inequalities across municipalities, the regional level was where the greatest possibilities for redistributive, equitable planning could be realized (Benner & Pastor, 2019). Smart growth principles and policies, such as transit-oriented and infill development, were useful for addressing regional disparities and directing resources to disinvested communities (Bullard, 2007; Glover Blackwell & Treuhaft, 2008; Pastor et al., 2009).

Seeing the potential for collaboration, EJ leaders Carl Anthony and Robert Bullard, john a. powell, director of the Kirwan Institute for the Study of Race and Ethnicity at Ohio State, and Angela Glover Blackwell, founder of the equitable development non-profit PolicyLink, led a forum on race and regionalism in 2002. This was followed by a roundtable on African Americans and smart growth that highlighted the need to elevate voices of color and power sharing (Nielsen & Parchia, 2004). PolicyLink also convened several national summits on equitable development, social justice, and smart growth in the early 2000s.

Regional equity leaders, including early conveners and others, such as the Funders' Network for Smart Growth, Livable Communities, and the Institute on Metropolitan Opportunity, then began promoting regional equitable growth principles. They argued that the economic and environmental health and prosperity of metropolitan areas depended on and should benefit all communities (Glover Blackwell & Fox, 2006; Bullard, 2007). Regional development processes and plans should ensure meaningful participation, leadership, and political power among diverse voices and communities; focus on people and place; reduce local and regional disparities; and promote equitable, catalytic, and coordinated investments (Glover Blackwell & Treuhaft, 2008).

Regions across the country took up the call, pushing for regional solutions to affordable housing, school quality, transportation, employment access, and other issues (PolicyLink, 2002). Under President Barack Obama, the regional equity movement got a huge boost when the US Department of Housing and Urban Development (HUD) launched its signature initiative, the Sustainable Communities Regional Planning Grant (SCRPG) Program. Between 2010 and 2011, the program awarded more than $240 million to 143 regions and municipalities to promote regional planning, with a focus on equity. It required coordination among cross-sector coalitions of regional stakeholders to produce plans, and it provided a new national database with indicators of regional equity and opportunity to assist this work (Finio et al., 2019). With the presidential election of Donald Trump, federal funding for this and support for the associated Obama-era "affirmatively furthering fair housing" (AFFH) regulations came to an abrupt halt. Many US regions, however, had already begun to take matters into their own hands. From Portland to Minneapolis, regional governments and advocacy groups have brought together diverse residents, for-profits, nonprofits, and governmental agencies to draft regional plans that prioritize equitable and inclusive growth (Finio et al., 2018).

The rise of the regional equity movement has been among the most powerful—though certainly not the only—platform for aligning smart growth and equitable development goals, and identifying common interests. Regional equity plans have pushed equity to the center of debates about land use and growth politics and brought new voices to the smart growth table. But the regional equity movement has also revealed tensions and challenges that raise questions about the continued alignment of equitable and smart growth agendas.

THE REGIONAL EQUITY MOVEMENT: TENSIONS AND CHALLENGES

The bringing together of allied, yet sometimes disparate, movements under the banner of regional equitable growth has been neither a smooth nor complete process. Tensions and challenges have centered on how to effectively scale policy and build regional coalitions; whether to prioritize policies to deconcentrate or invest in disadvantaged neighborhoods; and the limits of infill, mixed-use, and mixed-income development. Fractures among and between smart growth and equitable development advocates on these issues have revealed a regional equity movement still struggling to define itself across its diverse interests.

Building Effective Coalitions to Push Regional and State Policy

A critical challenge for smart growth and equitable development advocates is mobilizing cross-sector coalitions beyond the local level. The smart growth movement has long recognized that growth policy is often most effective at the regional level, yet land-use decisions are controlled locally. In most US metropolitan areas, regional Council of Governments (COGs) and Metropolitan Planning Organizations (MPOs) hold limited policy-making authority. MPOs tend to have more regional decision-making power, given their federally mandated role in transportation planning. But for both, their main functions are often to convene municipal leaders and facilitate data and resource sharing among them. Issues of regional governance have prevented the advancement of regional policies on a number of equitable development issues beyond transportation, particularly affordable housing. While some recent progress has been made in pushing state-level policies, questions remain about how to sustain coalitions across diverse groups and regions and develop the political will needed to push equitable development policy beyond the local scale.

The regional equity movement has broadened the geographic scale of efforts traditionally fought within local municipalities, especially affordable housing, and aligned these battles with smart growth issues, such as transit-oriented development. However, such coalitions have often had only limited success (Zapata & Bates, 2016; Finio et al., 2018). In Baltimore, the Opportunity Coalition came together in 2011 to create a regional plan with $3.5 million in federal SCRPG funds. This was one of the first times that housing advocates sat at the table with regional environmental, transportation, and other smart growth advocates. A key centerpiece of their plan was to build affordable housing in the region's higher-income, more highly educated neighborhoods, which were disproportionately suburban and White (see Figure 14.1). Many hoped that the coalition's promise to work across siloes and political

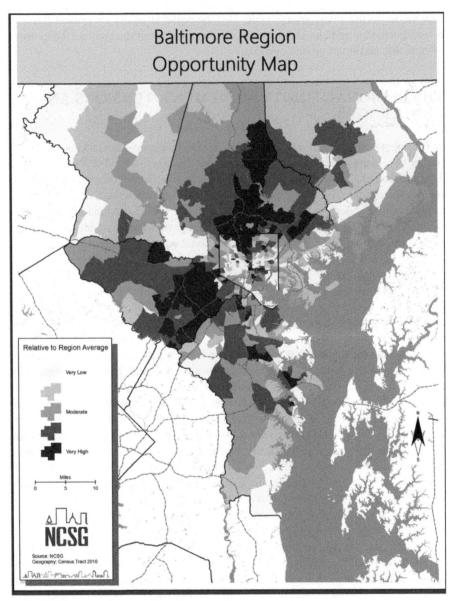

Source: National Center for Smart Growth Research and Education.
Note: The darker shades indicate neighborhoods of "highest opportunity" that were the target of its affordable housing strategies.

Figure 14.1   Opportunity map contained in the Opportunity Coalition's Baltimore Regional Plan for Sustainability Development

boundaries would make inroads into municipalities, such as Baltimore County, whose officials had long resisted subsidized and multifamily housing. However, after five years of planning, the coalition made little progress. A lack of regional governmental authority and local political will, as well as planning silos, left traditional fair housing advocates pushing for change without much support from other coalition members (Finio et al., 2019).

While regional coalitions have often broken down around or failed to make progress on fair housing issues, they have had some state-level victories in recent years. For instance, after Baltimore County failed to pass source-of-income rental discrimination laws, Maryland created statewide restrictions in 2020. In 2019, Oregon passed legislation essentially banning single-family zoning in cities of more than 10,000 people. By 2020, several other states across the United States were considering such bills.[1] A year earlier, both Oregon and California passed state-wide rent control laws, limiting rental increases to an annual state-mandated percentage (Dougherty & Ferré-Sadurní, 2019). These successes suggest the possibilities for smart growth and equitable development advocates to build new alliances and political will at higher scales on issues central to regional equity.

Still, the challenge of sustaining cross-sector coalitions to effect policy change at the regional level remains significant. For instance, in late 2020, California voters failed to pass Proposition 21, which would have allowed cities to enact their own rent control measures on rental housing more than 15 years old, strengthening state-wide protections (Taxin, 2020). Benner and Pastor (2019) argue that getting smart growth, equitable development advocates, and other stakeholders to see their linked fates requires growing a "diverse regional consciousness" with shared knowledge, values, and goals (p. 88). Whether such shared frames are being developed is unclear. To do so, additional state and federal funding is needed to keep regional equity coalitions afloat, as well as stronger regional governance structures to provide the political levers they need to shift long-held metropolitan patterns of racial and economic segregation.

Moving to Opportunity or Improving Opportunities in Place

A long-standing debate among community development and fair housing advocates is whether to prioritize opening up new housing opportunities in advantaged, "high-opportunity" neighborhoods or improve conditions in disadvantaged neighborhoods. The regional equitable growth movement has inherited and enflamed this debate. Regional equity advocates often support neighborhood opportunity policies that some community development advocates argue detract resources away from low-income neighborhoods, while recent demographic shifts between cities and suburbs have further complicated policy solutions. While traditional smart growth advocates have rarely entered into the fray, their participation in regional equity work may require that they do so.

Some urban scholars, planners, and policymakers have long argued that the best way to improve economic mobility for low-income people is to disperse areas of concentrated poverty. Others argue the best way is to improve conditions in low-income neighborhoods. The debate has played out in scholarship on "neighborhood effects," which show that high levels of neighborhood poverty impact residents' economic and social mobility, independent of their individual circumstances (see Galster & Sharkey, 2017 for a review). Community development advocates have challenged some of the underlying principles of this scholarship and prioritized building affordable housing, improving workforce training skills, increasing employment opportunities, and other investments in disadvantaged neighborhoods. Conversely, fair housing and other mobility advocates have pushed for policies to relocate residents to more advantaged, resource-rich neighborhoods. The latter supported major housing policy initiatives, such as the *Gautreaux* program and Moving to Opportunity (MTO), which moved residents receiving federal housing subsidies into higher-income neighborhoods, often in the suburbs (see Goetz & Chapple, 2010 for a review of the debate).

These programs and the recent popularity of neighborhood opportunity frameworks, mapping tools, and data within the regional equity planning movement have rekindled longstanding debates. Efforts to map and measure neighborhood opportunity were made popular by john a. powell in a Baltimore fair housing lawsuit, *Thompson v. HUD.* Powell used multiple indicators of opportunity to illustrate how project-based housing and voucher recipients were disproportionately located in the region's "lowest opportunity" areas. Harvard University's Opportunity Insights project has developed the most popular contemporary iteration of such tools, which show the long-term outcomes for children raised in "high-opportunity neighborhoods" (Chetty et al., 2016). Such efforts reflect neighborhood opportunity as the reigning paradigm in housing policy, or what David Imbroscio (2012) calls a "dispersal consensus" among housing policymakers. In 2016, the federal government launched the Opportunity Project tools and data to help communities comply with new AFFH regulations.[2] Communities and metropolitan regions have also created and deployed their own tools to drive planning and policymaking on transit investments, low-income housing tax credit allocations, and more (Finio et al., 2018).

However, some community development advocates have challenged the "dispersal consensus" upon which these efforts rely. Relocated families have sometimes moved back to their original neighborhoods, and the benefits for adult movers, who sometimes lose social networks and other resources, are not particularly clear (Goetz & Chapple, 2010). Their moves also further destabilize already disadvantaged neighborhoods. Critics have also underscored that how residents define and access opportunities—as well as the "choice sets" they have—vary significantly by race, class, and neighborhood (Lung-Amam et al., 2018).

Regional geographies of opportunity are also changing. For much of the late twentieth century, metropolitan areas were often starkly divided between low-income communities of color in central cities and wealthier White communities in suburbs. Within the past several decades, however, America's racial and economic diversity has shifted. By 2010, a majority of immigrants, racial and ethnic minorities, and people living below the poverty line lived in the suburbs of major metropolitan areas

(Frey, 2011). This demographic shift has underscored that moving out does not mean moving up. While many Black suburbanites live in more racially integrated neighborhoods than their central city counterparts, suburban segregation has widened disparities between low-income suburbs of color and wealthier, White suburbs (Clark, 2007; Farrell, 2016). Many low-income suburbanites struggle to access transportation, social services, and other resources that are important to their economic and social mobility, and are often more plentiful in central cities (Kneebone & Berube, 2013; Allard, 2017).

Smart growth advocates have been largely silent in debates between equitable development advocates on these issues, leading to confusion on their position. Their support for contained growth and infill development suggests a preference for community development strategies, such as building more affordable housing in disadvantaged urban neighborhoods. Yet Smart Growth America and other smart growth advocates also support policies that help people move to "high opportunity" neighborhoods. This may suggest a fracture within the smart growth movement or a middle-ground position. Indeed, many equitable development advocates have argued that choosing between moving-to-opportunity and place-based policies is a false choice between equally valuable strategies (powell, 2000). However, declining federal resources to support affordable housing and community development often forces hard decisions about investments. As partners in the regional equity movement, smart growthers must be invested in the debate to help resolve its critical questions.

Diversity and Density Does Not Equal Equity

A central tenet of smart growth is to limit sprawl and promote dense, mixed-use development in already urbanized areas, particularly around transit. In rapidly growing regions, such strategies can exacerbate existing neighborhood inequalities, promote gentrification, and displace lower-income residents and the businesses and services upon which they rely (see Finio & Knaap, Chapter 13, this book, for more on the relationship between smart growth and gentrification). Increased physical density and diversity does not necessarily lead to more socially diverse, equitable, or inclusive neighborhoods.

In rapidly growing regions, redevelopment tends to increase land and property values and rents (Finio and Knaap, Chapter 13). Existing affordable housing and commercial businesses are often lost through demolition, reinvestment, and tenure conversions (Smith, 1996). This does not just happen because of "natural" market forces. Municipal policies often actively work to attract middle-class residents, consumers, large chain and boutique businesses to historically disinvested neighborhoods (Zukin, 1995; Smith, 1996). Washington, DC, experienced the most "intense gentrification" of any city in the country between 2000 and 2013 (National Community Reinvestment Coalition, 2019). In 2018, activists sued the city, alleging the city's efforts to court "creative class" residents through housing and redevelopment policies discriminated against long-term, lower-income African

American residents.[3] Yet gentrification and displacement are not just urban issues. After decades of disinvestment, population loss, and rising poverty rates, many suburbs close to central cities are now seeing similar changes and anti-displacement activism (Lung-Amam et al., 2018). As Hanlon (Chapter 5, this book) observes, new suburban infill development in older suburbs can make neighborhoods unaffordable for long-time residents. In cities and suburbs, the coronavirus outbreak hit Black and brown neighborhoods particularly hard, putting vulnerable residents and small businesses in gentrifying neighborhoods even further at risk (Federal Reserve Bank of New York, 2020).

Equitable development approaches can combat these trends and complement smart growth strategies by prioritizing the needs of current residents, particularly the most vulnerable (Glover Blackwell & Bell, 2005; Pendall et al., 2005). Successful interventions often occur early and focus on multiple impacts, including the potential displacement of housing, small businesses, cultural amenities, and social services (Cassola, 2019; Hanlon, Chapter 5, this book). Policies to produce and preserve affordable housing and commercial spaces, from rent control to eviction protections, are key (Alvarez et al., 2021). Increasingly, municipalities such as Portland and Seattle have adopted policies that give existing residents preference to relocate to new affordable housing units. Community benefits agreements (CBAs) are also a popular tool for ensuring that new development addresses existing residents' concerns. These legally binding agreements among developers, community-based groups, and local governments can stipulate, for instance, the inclusion of a certain amount of affordable housing or neighborhood amenities. They are generally considered more effective than other tools, such as impact or in-lieu fees, in mitigating the neighborhood impact of development.

Smart growth strategies that promote transit-oriented development (TOD) face similar challenges. As Welch and Gehrke (Chapter 10, this book) note, there is growing attention to equity issues around TOD, particularly when demographic changes follow development. Dense, mixed-use development around fixed-route transit can displace established residents and small businesses (Dawkins & Moeckel, 2016). Yet equitable TOD processes that expand resident input and include strong anti-displacement protections can ensure that marginalized groups, who tend to be most transit-dependent, benefit from new TOD (Pereira et al., 2017). Communities have fought to put plans in place before, during, and after construction to minimize disruptions and leverage new transit investments for community benefit.

In suburban Washington, DC, bi-county coalitions have worked with residents and local government agencies to develop an equitable TOD strategy for Maryland's International Corridor, an area with the state's largest concentration of immigrant and Latinx residents. The development of a new light rail threatens the long-term viability of existing residents and businesses in the corridor (see Figure 14.2). The Purple Line Corridor Coalition, a grasstops organization comprised of organizational and county leaders and run by the University of Maryland's National Center for Smart Growth and the Fair Development Coalition, a grassroots group started by Maryland's largest immigrants' rights group CASA, has helped put in place a number of anti-displacement protections. The coalition's success in promoting new affordable housing investments, housing code regulations, small business technical and impact assistance, and cross-municipal planning highlight the importance of inclusive processes and organizing for equitable TOD outcomes (Lung-Amam et al., 2019).

Source: Willow Lung-Amam.

Figure 14.2   *A typical garden-style apartment complex in Maryland's International Corridor, where many immigrant residents and businesses are threatened with displacement from a new light rail line*

The controversy over a California state bill further underscores the challenges and possibilities of building robust equitable TOD coalitions. Initially proposed by Senator Scott Weiner in 2017 to address the state's affordable housing crises, SB827 sought to pre-empt local zoning regulations on housing construction near transit stations. While the initial bill gained the support of smart growth advocates, it was opposed by many affordable housing advocates, who were concerned that upzoning would accelerate gentrification and displacement (Bliss, 2019). The bill died in its first hearing but was reintroduced in 2019 as SB50 with more tenant protections, including stronger anti-eviction regulations and greater affordable housing set-asides. The revised bill brought together a broader coalition of supporters that included traditional smart growth advocates, such as the National Resources Defense Council, and equitable development advocates, such as the Fair Housing Advocates of Northern California (Bliss, 2019). While the revised bill still split advocates on both sides and failed to pass, the more robust coalition helped the effort gain political traction.

Smart growth efforts also focus on producing mixed-income, mixed-use developments that proponents often cast as diverse and inclusive communities. Yet evidence has frequently shown otherwise. New urbanist developments, for instance, which are designed as walkable, compact neighborhoods with a distinctive sense of place, often lack both economic and racial diversity, and in many places have contributed to rising housing prices (Day, 2003; Markley, 2018). As critics point out, design alone cannot solve racial and socio-economic inequality, and urban form is not a proxy for inclusion. Dawkins and Kim (Chapter 8, this book) explain that housing diversity alone is insufficient for creating or maintaining income diversity in neighborhoods. Unless explicit policies are adopted to create communities for families of diverse income levels, ethnic backgrounds, family compositions, ages, and abilities, racial and economic integration rarely occurs on its own.

Diverse neighborhoods are not, however, necessarily equitable nor sustainable. They include communities experiencing population changes, which are unlikely to remain stably diverse (Kim, 2016). Further, in many mixed-income neighborhoods, residents of different races and classes do not interact, live in the same buildings, or frequent the same businesses. Such micro-segregation is particularly pronounced in gentrifying neighborhoods (Lees, 2008; Tach, 2014). Similar patterns have been noted in HOPE VI redevelopment projects, where public housing has been converted into mixed-income housing that includes new market-rate units (Bolt et al., 2010). Even if low-income residents are not physically displaced, shifts in neighborhood power structures and amenities can lead to cultural and political displacement, as established residents lose a sense of belonging, community, and place (Hyra, 2015). When neighborhood histories, social practices, music, foodways, and gathering places become contested and devalued, residents sometimes leave (Howell, 2015).

Mixed-income, mixed-used neighborhoods, however, offer a vital foundation for more equitable communities to thrive. Smart growth advocates can help ensure that such neighborhoods support equity and inclusion by thinking beyond land use or urban design solutions. Khare and Joseph (2019) encourage planners and policymakers to think about mixed-use *communities* instead of just mixed-use *housing*, arguing for a more holistic focus that includes other vital community elements, such as schools, community gardens, recreation centers, cultural hubs, neighborhood networks, and retail districts. For smart growth advocates, this may mean broadening their concerns and advocacy beyond the typical toolkit.

TOWARD EQUITABLE SMART GROWTH

In 2005, Xavier de Souza Briggs observed that while research on the unhealthy effects of sprawl had grown tremendously, very little of it focused on racial and economic segregation. The rise of the regional equity movement has helped to fill this gap, but many holes remain.

Historically, smart growth advocates rarely foregrounded equity in their principles or included equitable frameworks and protections in their policies. They also often failed to foster inclusive processes in which diverse groups, particularly low-income people of color, helped to define planning strategies and outcomes. In turn, advocates for marginalized groups tended to see smart growth policies as tools of land use control in which they had little power or interest.

Over the past several decades, however, the smart growth movement has put a greater emphasis on social and economic equity. The growth of the regional equity movement has been one result. This movement has, by necessity and design, brought the overlapping interests of these groups closer together. It has educated smart growth advocates about how their policies affect marginalized communities and has shown equitable development advocates the value of smart growth tools and principles. But regional equity coalitions, if they exist at all, are oftentimes still in their generative phase in many metropolitan areas. Many have also struggled to make tangible progress, particularly for the most economically and socially disadvantaged groups. And as these coalitions have come together, old tensions have arisen, and new ones have been born. We conclude with some thoughts on how to sustain this emerging movement and ensure that equitable development and smart growth continue to grow closer together, rather than further apart.

For the two movements to strengthen their collaborative endeavors, there need to be more spaces for truth-telling and healing. Smart growth advocates may need to acknowledge the harm that smart growth policies and practices have sometimes brought to low-income communities, particularly those of color. Equitable development advocates may have to acknowledge their distrust and fears of aligning with the smart growth movement. Some equitable development advocates worry that such alignments will weaken their political power and draw attention away from the critical issues facing marginalized groups (Bullard, 2007; Henig, 2002).

Whether working on policies related to growth boundaries or the transfer-of-development rights, smart growth advocates need to better integrate racial and economic equity frames and think beyond land use. Many of the issues that constrain equitable growth are related to unequal, racialized structures in employment, housing, transportation, and political processes that have attended the country's growth since its founding. Smart growth practitioners can become more aware of the deep, spatialized nature of inequalities and the implications of their decisions by working closely with equitable development advocates, who foreground these frameworks. Working together raises different questions and different solutions. In transportation planning, for example, Baltimore's Opportunity Coalition proposed aligning the transportation needs of low-skilled workers, who largely lived in the central city, with employment opportunities in the suburbs—integrating housing, employment, and transportation planning with an equity focus. In addition to cross-sector coalition-building, smart growth advocates can also draw widely on available equitable development toolkits and data resources to make the case for equitable investments.[4]

To encourage sustainable alliances, regional equity coalitions must recognize what different sides bring to the table and draw on their diverse expertise. Smart growth must be careful not to co-opt nor marginalize the work of fair housing, environmental justice, transportation justice, and other equity-related movements. Likewise, equitable development advocates cannot treat environmental and transportation concerns as appendages to their goals. They must establish shared frameworks, principles, and processes for inclusive conversations that leverage their different assets. They must use their platforms to elevate each other's work and build partnerships that strengthen both. They must look for areas of allied concern as a foundation for shared action.

Too often, however, where equitable development and smart growth advocates have built coalitions around shared regional policy agendas, they have failed to significantly advance equitable policy outcomes. Multiple barriers exist—from a lack of funding, capacity, and policy tools to a lack of political will and authority. These challenges require front-end planning and organizing within and beyond regional planning processes that pull on the skillsets of both groups, as well as a commitment to sustained advocacy. Planning processes must not only define strategies and actions, but also build the political will to achieve them at different scales, from the local to the state level.

The extent to which advocates in these traditionally fractured fields can work across their silos will help to define the next chapter of smart growth. At a time of growing demographic diversity, rising income inequality, and a global climate catastrophe and health crisis, the alignment of these two movements could not be more important. For smart growth to effectively address these issues, equity needs to be intricately woven into smart growth planning principles and action. Indeed, metropolitan growth is not smart unless it supports equitable processes and outcomes. Equitable growth is smart growth, and smart growth is equitable.

NOTES

1. For a review of recent legislation and a critical debate on single-family zoning, see the Viewpoints in the 2020 issue of *Journal of the American Planning Association*, *86*(1).
2. As noted earlier, by mid-2020, the Trump administration was no longer making these tools available and Obama-era AFFH regulations were not being enforced.
3. On the term "creative class," see Florida (2002).
4. Some examples include PolicyLink's All-in-Cities toolkit (allincities.org/toolkit), the National Equity Atlas' strategies for inclusive growth (nationalequityatlas.org), and the Urban Displacement Project's policy toolkit (urbandisplacement.org).

REFERENCES

Allard, S. W. (2017). *Places in need: The changing geography of poverty.* New York: Russell Sage Foundation.
Alvarez, N. T., Andrews, B, & Lung-Amam, W. (August 2021). *Small Business Anti-Displacement Toolkit: A Guide for Small Business Leaders.* College Park MD: Small Business Anti-Displacement Network and National Center for Smart Growth. https://antidisplacement.org/research/brown-papers/

Baum, H. S. (2004). Smart growth and school reform: What if we talked about race and took community seriously? *Journal of the American Planning Association, 70*(1), 14–26.

Benner, C., & Pastor, M. (2019). Can we talk? Conversation, collaboration, and conflict for a just metro. In K. Hexter & N. Krumholz (Eds.), *Advancing equity planning now.* Ithaca, NY: Cornell University Press.

Bliss, L. (2019, April 5). The political battle over California's suburban dream. *City Lab.* https://www.citylab.com/equity/2019/04/california-affordable-housing-bill-sb50-single -family-zoning/586519/

Bolt, G., Phillips, D., & Van Kempen, R. (2010). Housing policy, (de)segregation and social mixing: An international perspective. *Housing Studies, 25*(2), 129–135.

Bullard, R. D. (Ed.) (2007). *Growing smarter: Achieving livable communities, environmental justice, and regional equity.* Cambridge, MA: MIT Press.

Bullard, R. D., Johnson, G. S., & Torres, A. O. (Eds.) (2000). *Sprawl city: Race, politics, and planning in Atlanta.* Washington, DC: Island Press.

Cassola, A. (2019). Promoting mixed-income communities by mitigating displacement: Findings from 80 large U.S. cities. In M. L. Joseph & A. T. Khare (Eds), *What works to promote inclusive, equitable mixed-income communities.* National Initiative on Mixed-Income Communities at Case Western Reserve University. https://case.edu/ socialwork/nimc/resources/what-works-volume/essays

Chetty, R., Hendren, N., & Katz, L. F. (2016). The effects of exposure to better neighborhoods on children: New evidence from the moving to opportunity experiment. *American Economic Review, 106*(4), 855–902.

Clark, W. A. V. (2007). Race, class, and place: Evaluating mobility outcomes for African Americans. *Urban Affairs Review, 42*(3), 295-314.

Davidoff, P. (1965). Advocacy and pluralism in planning. *Journal of the American Institute of Planners, 31*(4), 331–338.

Dawkins, C., & Moeckel, R. (2016). Transit-induced gentrification: Who will stay, and who will go? *Housing Policy Debate, 26*(4-5), 801–818.

Day, K. (2003). New urbanism and the challenges of designing for diversity. *Journal of Planning Education and Research, 23*(1), 83–95.

De Souza Briggs, X. (2005). *The geography of opportunity: Race and housing choice in metropolitan America.* Washington, DC: Brookings Institution Press.

Dougherty, C., & Ferré-Sadurní, L. (2019, September 11). California approves statewide rent control to ease housing crisis. *The New York Times.* https://nyti.ms/34GbDTq

Farrell, C. R. (2016). Immigrant suburbanization and the shifting geographic structure of metropolitan segregation in the United States. *Urban Studies, 53*(1), 57–76.

Federal Reserve Bank of New York. (2020, August). Double jeopardy: Covid-19's concentrated health and wealth effects in black communities. https://www.newyorkfed.org/ medialibrary/media/smallbusiness/DoubleJeopardy_COVID19andBlackOwnedBusinesses

Finio, N., Lung-Amam, W., Knaap, G., Dawkins, C., & Knaap, E. (2019). Metropolitan planning in a vacuum: Lessons on regional equity from Baltimore's Sustainable Communities Initiative. Journal of Urban Affairs. doi:10.1080/07352166.2019.1565822.

Finio, N., Lung-Amam, W., Knaap, G., Dawkins, C., & Wong, B. (2018). *Equity, opportunity, and the regional planning process: Data and mapping in five U.S. metropolitan areas.* College Park, MD: National Center for Smart Growth Research and Education and Enterprise Community Partners.

Florida, R. (2002). *The rise of the creative class: And how it's transforming work, leisure, community and everyday life.* New York, NY: Basic Books.

Frey, W. H. (2011). *Melting pot cities and suburbs: Racial and ethnic change in metro America in the 2000s.* Washington, DC: Brookings Institute.

Galster, G. C., & Sharkey, P. (2017). Spatial foundations of inequality: A conceptual model and empirical overview. *The Russell Sage Foundation Journal of the Social Sciences*, *3*(2), 1–33.

Gearin, E. (2004). Smart growth or smart growth machine? The smart growth movement and its implications. In J. Wolch, M. Pastor & P. Dreier (Eds), *Up against sprawl: Public policy and the making of Southern California* (pp. 279–308). Minneapolis: University of Minneapolis Press.

Glover Blackwell, A., & Bell, J. (2005). Equitable development for a stronger nation: Lessons from the field. In X. De Souza Briggs (Ed.), *The geography of opportunity: Race and housing choice in metropolitan America* (pp. 289–309). Washington, DC: Brookings Institution Press.

Glover Blackwell, A., & Fox, R. K. (2006). Regional equity and smart growth: Opportunities for advancing social and economic justice in America. In D. C. Soule (Ed.), *Urban sprawl: A comprehensive reference guide* (pp. 407–428). Westport, CT: Greenwood Press.

Glover Blackwell, A., & Treuhaft, S. (2008). *Regional equity and the quest for full inclusion*. Policylink.   https://www.policylink.org/resources-tools/regional-equity-and-the-quest-for-full-inclusion

Goetz, E. G., & Chapple, K. (2010). You gotta move: Advancing the debate on the record of dispersal. *Housing Policy Debate*, *20*(2), 209–236.

Henig, J. R. (2002). Equity and the future politics of growth. In G. D. Squires (Ed.), *Urban sprawl: Causes, consequences, and policy responses* (pp. 325–350). Washington, DC: The Urban Institute.

Hexter, K., & Krumholz, N. (Eds) (2019). *Advancing equity planning now*. Ithaca, NY: Cornell University Press.

Howell, K. (2015). "It's complicated…": Long-term residents and their relationships to gentrification in Washington, DC. In D. Hyra and S. Prince (Eds), *Capital dilemma: Growth and inequality in Washington, D.C.* (pp. 255–278). New York: Routledge.

Hyra, D. (2015). The back-to-the-city movement: Neighbourhood redevelopment and processes of political and cultural displacement. *Urban Studies*, *52*(10), 1753–1773.

Imbroscio, D. (2012). Beyond mobility: The limits of liberal urban policy. *Journal of Urban Affairs*, *34*(1), 1–20.

Khare, A., & Joseph, M. L. (2019). Introduction: Prioritizing inclusion and equity. In M. L. Joseph & A. T. Khare (Eds), *What works to promote inclusive, equitable mixed-income communities*. National Initiative on Mixed-Income Communities at Case Western Reserve University. https://case.edu/socialwork/nimc/resources/what-works-volume/essays

Kim, J. (2016). Achieving mixed income communities through infill? The effect of infill housing on neighborhood income diversity. *Journal of Urban Affairs*, *38*(2), 280–297. https://doi.org/10.1111/juaf.12207

Kneebone, E., & Berube, A. (2013). *Confronting suburban poverty*. Washington, DC: Brookings Institution Press.

Lees, L. (2008). Gentrification and social mixing: Towards an inclusive urban renaissance? *Urban Studies*, *45*(12), 2449–2470.

Lung-Amam, W., Knaap, E., Dawkins, C., & Knaap, G. (2018). Opportunity for whom? The diverse definitions of neighborhood opportunity in Baltimore. *City & Community*, *17*(3), 636–657. doi:10.1111/cico.12318

Lung-Amam, W., Pendall, R., & Knaap, E. (2019). Mi casa no es su casa: The fight for equitable transit-oriented development in an inner-ring suburb. *Journal of Planning Education and Research*, *39*(4), 442–455. doi:10.1177/0739456X19878248

Markley, S. (2018). Suburban gentrification? Examining the geographies of new urbanism in Atlanta's inner suburbs. *Urban Geography*, *39*(4), 606–630. doi:10.1080/02723638.2017.1381534

National Community Reinvestment Coalition. (2019). *Shifting neighborhoods: Gentrification and cultural displacement in American cities.* https://ncrc.org/gentrification/

Nielsen, J., & Parchia, M. (2004). *African Americans and smart growth: A joint summary.* Kirwan Institute for the Study of Race and Ethnicity and Institute on Race & Poverty. https://www.racialequitytools.org/resourcefiles/kirwan.pdf

Orfield, M. (1997). *Metropolitics: A regional agenda for community and stability.* Washington, DC: Brookings Institution Press.

Pastor, M., Benner, C., & Matsuoka, M. (2009). *This could be the start of something big: How social movements for regional equity are reshaping metropolitan America.* Ithaca: Cornell University Press.

Pendall, R., Nelson, A. C., Dawkins, C. J., & Knaap, G. J. (2005). Connecting smart growth, housing affordability, and racial equity. In X. De Souza Briggs (Ed.), *The geography of opportunity: Race and housing choice in metropolitan America* (pp. 219–246). Washington, DC: Brookings Institution Press.

Pereira, R., Schwanen, T., & Banister, D. (2017). Distributive justice and equity in transportation. *Transport Reviews, 37*(2), 170-191.

PolicyLink (2002). *Promoting regional equity: A framing paper.* Los Angeles: Lisa Robinson. https://community-wealth.org/sites/clone.community-wealth.org/files/downloads/report-robinson-et-al.pdf

powell, j. a. (1999). Race, poverty, and urban sprawl: Access to opportunities through regional strategies. *Forum for Social Economics, 28*(2), 1–20.

powell, j. a. (2000). Addressing regional dilemmas for minority communities. In B. Katz (Ed.), *Reflections on regionalism* (pp. 218–246). Washington, DC: Brookings Institution.

Rusk, D. (1993). *Cities without suburbs.* Washington, DC: Woodrow Wilson Center Press.

Smith, N. (1996). *The new urban frontier: Gentrification and the revanchist city.* New York: Routledge.

Tach, L. M. (2014). Dynamics of inclusion and exclusion in a racially and economically diverse community. *Cityscape, 16*(3), 13–46.

Taxin, A. (2020, November 3). Proposition 21: California voters reject measure to expand rent control. *The Mercury News.* https://www.mercurynews.com/2020/11/03/california-voters-reject-measure-to-expand-rent-control/

Zapata, M. A., & Bates, L. K. (2017). Equity planning or equitable opportunities? The construction of equity in the HUD Sustainable Communities Regional Planning Grants. *Journal of Planning Education and Research, 37*(4), 1–14.

Zukin, S. (1995). *The cultures of cities.* Cambridge, MA: Blackwell.

PART VI

NEW HORIZONS FOR SMART GROWTH: CLIMATE, ENERGY, AND TECHNOLOGY

15. Community resilience to environmental hazards and climate change: can smart growth make a difference?

Marccus D. Hendricks and Philip R. Berke

INTRODUCTION

Smart growth is a set of principles attempting to improve the efficiency of growth and development patterns as an alternative to conventional sprawl patterns of development (Barbour & Deakin, 2012). Sprawl is distinguished by low density development, homogeneous patterns of land use dominated by spatially segregated large tracts of single-family houses, commercial strip developments, and auto-oriented streets. In contrast, smart growth is characterized by compact forms of urban development that provide higher density, mixed land uses, a range of housing types at different prices, walkable streets, and access to a range of transportation options. Development that reflects these principles is thought to provide a host of economic, social, and environmental benefits. Yet when the principles of smart growth were first articulated, mitigating or adapting to climate change was not among the purported benefits. As awareness of climate change rose during the 1990s and early 2000s, so did recognition that smart growth could address this challenge.

In this chapter, we explore the relationship between smart growth and climate change, including its potential to both mitigate greenhouse gas emissions and to adapt to a changing climate. Climate change adaptation is broadly understood as the steps taken to reduce vulnerability of humans and bult environments to the effects of hazards amplified by climate change, whereas mitigation refers to actions taken to reduce greenhouse gas emissions that contributes to climate change. We begin with a conceptual framing of how specific smart growth principles might serve to advance both mitigation and adaptation. We then review the evidence to support these arguments. We conclude with thoughts about the future of smart growth as a development approach to address climate change in city planning and beyond.

SMART GROWTH IN THE ANTHROPOCENE

Climate change was not a salient issue in the early 1990s when the foundations of smart growth were first established. At the time, climate change was primarily a concern among a small group of scientists and had not been directly tied to development patterns or urban growth. Over time, however, smart growth advocates

Table 15.1   *Smart growth principles and potential benefits in climate change*
                 mitigation and adaptation

Smart growth principles*	Potential benefits in mitigating climate change	Potential benefits in reducing vulnerability
Mix land uses	Mixing uses can bring travel origins and destinations closer together and reduce VMT	Compatible and compact land use decisions can set the stage for incorporating open space within the built environment
Take advantage of compact design	Compact designs can reduce travel and lower energy consumption	Avoid building in hazardous areas
Create a range of housing opportunities and choices	More multifamily and shared wall housing can lower energy consumption	Allows residents across housing types and income groups to benefit from broader resilient community development
Create walkable neighborhoods	Walkable neighborhoods can reduce auto travel and GHG emissions	Enhanced public rights-of-way and streetscapes as well as recreational areas can help to reduce risks (i.e., manage water and heat)
Foster distinctive, attractive communities with a strong sense of place	Distinctive, attractive communities encourage residents from relocating to exurban areas	Creative and attractive public spaces encourage stewardship which is beneficial in maintaining community assets that support mitigation
Preserve open space, farmland, natural beauty, and critical environmental areas	Preserving farm, forest land and open spaces can preserve natural carbon sequestration	Prevents development in hazard-prone areas
Green infrastructure has a variety of benefits including reducing stormwater runoff and in turn reduces flood risks
Protects natural ecosystem services
Direct development toward existing communities	Infill development can mitigate sprawl and reduce VMT	Infill development, particularly in areas that are low-risk can shift development out of sensitive areas
Provide a variety of transportation choices	Travel modes other than the automobile can reduce GHG emissions	Provide more options for emergency evacuation
Make development decisions predictable, fair, and cost effective	Lower cost developments can lower embedded carbon in public infrastructure	Provide an opportunity for everyone to take advantage of mitigation infrastructure toward just transitions
Encourage community and stakeholder collaboration in development decisions	Community and stakeholder engagement enables concerns about climate change to enter debates otherwise dominated by NIMBYism.	Co-development through collaboration allows for participation in hazard identification and adaptive solutions as well as building social capital that has been shown to be critical for community resilience

Note: *Smart Growth America: https://smartgrowthamerica.org/our-vision/what-is-smart-growth/

recognized the potential for smart growth to play an important role in the fight against climate change, first on the mitigation front and more recently on the adaptation front. By 2010, smart growth advocates and the US Environmental Protection Agency Office of Smart Growth began disseminating guidance on how smart growth principles could be effectively used to address climate change (International City/County Management Association, 2010; U.S. EPA, 2010). A guide detailing the potential benefits of smart growth for reducing vulnerability and climate mitigation and adaptation is provided in Table 15.1.

SMART GROWTH AND CLIMATE MITIGATION

Greenhouse gas (GHG) emissions, the principal cause of anthropogenic climate change, come from many sources, but the largest sources include the energy sector, the transportation sector, and the built environment. In the energy sector, the dominant issue concerns the source of fuel used to generate electricity. The less carbon intensive the fuel used to generate electricity, the lower the carbon dioxide (CO_2) emissions. To some extent, this is true in the transportation and building sectors as well. In the transportation sector, significant reductions in greenhouse gases could be achieved by converting the vehicle fleet from gas to electric and in the building sector by similarly converting heating and cooling systems from natural gas to electricity. These fuel-source transitions are beyond the purview of smart growth. But GHG reductions are also possible by changing travel behavior to reduce vehicle miles traveled (VMT), by changing housing preferences to improve the energy profile of the housing stock, and by preserving natural resources that sequester GHG from the atmosphere. Here smart growth has a potentially important role to play.

The Transportation Sector

In the transportation sector, clearly the most effective way smart growth can mitigate climate change is by reducing VMT. Holding fuel technology and fuels sources constant, fewer vehicle miles traveled means lower greenhouse gas emissions. The case for using smart growth principles to mitigate climate change was forcefully made in two Urban Land Institute publications, titled *Growing Cooler* and *Moving Cooler*.

Growing Cooler (Ewing et al., 2007) provided a comprehensive review of studies and concluded that "urban development is both a key contributor to climate change and an essential factor in combating it" (p. 2). *Growing Cooler* recognized that GHG emissions could be reduced in three ways: by enhancing fuel efficiency, by reducing the carbon content of fuels, and by reducing driving or VMT. The case for the latter went as follows: greenhouse gases are produced by driving automobiles; the propensity to drive is higher in built environments characterized by sprawl; and sprawl can be reduced by following smart growth principles, such as providing alternative transportation choices, developing more compactly, mixing uses, and creating more walkable environments. By 2050, *Growing Cooler* suggests, VMT could fall by 30 percent and CO_2 emissions could fall by 7 to 10 percent if smart growth principles are followed. (See Welch and Gehrke, Chapter 10, for more on smart growth and VMT.)

Moving Cooler (Cambridge Systematics, 2009), which builds on the arguments in *Growing Cooler* but with a narrower focus on the transportation sector, addresses a wider range of transportation policy options. These include changes in vehicle technology, fuel technology, travel activity, and vehicle and systems operations. Like *Growing Cooler*, *Moving Cooler* made the forceful argument that by following smart growth principles, including a combination of compact development and investments in transit and other transportation options, greenhouse gases from the transportation sector could be reduced by 9 to 15 percent by 2050.

In 2009, however, the National Academies of Sciences, Engineering, and Medicine (2009) released the report *Driving and the Built Environment: The Effects of Compact Development on Motorized Travel, Energy Use, and CO$_2$ Emissions.* This report acknowledged the proposition that following smart growth principles could reduce greenhouse gas emissions and mitigate climate change. However, it was considerably less sanguine about the potential of smart growth to have a significant impact. More specifically, the NAS concluded that significant increases in compact, mixed-use development could produce at best modest, short-term reductions in energy consumption and CO_2 emissions, though these reductions could grow over time.

The Built Environment Sector

The built environment contributes approximately 12 percent of all greenhouse gas emissions in the United States (US Environmental Protection Agency, 2020). As is the case in the energy and transportation sectors, perhaps the easiest way to reduce GHG emissions in the built environment is by changing heating and cooling fuels from carbon based to renewable fuels. But by building more compactly and with a variety of housing types, it is also possible to reduce GHGs and mitigate climate change (Berill et al., 2021). More specifically, by enhancing building energy efficiency, reducing material use, and reducing the embodied carbon in construction materials, cities can achieve a 44 percent reduction in building- and infrastructure-related emissions between 2017 and 2050, according to a report by the C40 Cities network, consulting firm ARUP, and the University of Leeds (2019).

The Natural Resource Sector

An additional avenue through which smart growth could help mitigate climate change is through natural resource conservation. According to ATTRA Sustainable Agriculture Program (2009), forest and cropland annually sequester approximately 12 percent of US GHG emissions. By building compactly and preserving natural resources, smart growth could help preserve farms and forests that function as carbon sinks through carbon sequestration (National Sustainable Agriculture Coalition, 2019).

The ability of smart growth to mitigate and adapt to climate change has been widely recognized by state and local governments. In the absence of leadership by the federal government, many states and local governments have prepared and adopted aggressive climate action plans. As of 2021, 23 states have fully adopted climate action plans (Center for Climate and Energy Solutions, 2021). Most of these rely heavily on strategies for changing energy sources and reducing the carbon content of existing fuels, but most also include some adoption of smart growth principles to reduce GHG emissions. (See M. Bierbaum, Lewis, and Chapin, Chapter 2, for more on the role of states.)

Wheeler (2008) offered one of the first evaluations of early state and municipal climate action plans and identified several weaknesses: inadequate goals, weak actions, and insufficient institutional and political commitment. Wheeler recommended stronger near-term goals; robust monitoring and progress reporting; a broader range of actions; and changing policies, regulations and incentives to reduce emissions. To meet GHG reduction goals, states have implemented a broad spectrum of policies covering energy efficiency and renewable energy, and many of these climate action plans include GHG reduction strategies related to transportation (Pollak et al., 2011). More recently, Lewis et al. (2018) examined state level approaches to integrating transportation and land use planning to achieve climate goals. They found that states set aggressive targets and identified strategies but fell short on providing funding to implement climate plans or monitor progress towards goals.

SMART GROWTH AND COMMUNITY RESILIENCE

Empirical understandings of smart growth in the context of community resilience to date is scant. The vast majority of research and policy documents are produced by non-peer-reviewed sources. Primary sources include professional practice associations (e.g., American Planning Association, Smart Growth America) and government programs that operate at the national, state, and local levels. This literature primarily deals with smart growth policy initiatives at multiple levels of government, legislative updates by state governments, and guidelines for local planning practice (US EPA 2010, 2014, 2016, 2017).

Very few studies integrate multiple principles of smart growth to examine the impacts of urban developments on hazard vulnerability. A large number of studies examine the impacts of urban development on different types of vulnerability (physical, social, economic, or ecological) for different hazards; however, these studies typically evaluate only one or two principles of smart growth. Consequently, they fail to account for the synergistic qualities and outcomes generated by developments that follow a smart growth development pattern. An example is the evaluation of the links between flood mitigation benefits and individual clusters of developments. Focusing only on the clusters, but failing to examine other principles (e.g., connectedness to existing development and multiple transportation choices) loses many interdependent qualities that generate smart growth impacts. In this case, compared with an interconnected smart growth development pattern, the clustered development could be disconnected and at considerable distance from existing development, and thus more likely to be auto dependent. Greater auto dependence would require more impervious pavement roads, driveways and parking lots to accommodate cars. More pavement increases the intensity of stormwater runoff and flooding, as well as urban heat. Therefore, in this chapter, we focus on research that examines multiple principles of smart growth more comprehensively.

CORE THEMES

Our review of the literature on how smart growth might both mitigate and adapt to climate change revealed three themes in the findings: a synthesis of national and state policy initiatives that link smart growth to hazards and climate change; effects of smart growth on vulnerability; and social disparities and the development paradox.

National and State Programs and Policy

Several influential national and state government programs and policies address the integration of mitigation practices into smart growth. Perhaps the most visible initiative at the national level was the formation of a collaborative partnership by the EPA and the Federal Emergency Management Agency (FEMA). The two agencies work together to help communities hit by disasters rebuild in ways that makes them safer, healthier, and more resilient. The mission of the EPA smart growth office is to promote smart growth while FEMA's mission is to promote hazard mitigation. Specific provisions for sharing resources and staff were formalized in a memorandum of agreement (US EPA, 2016). Despite political headwinds by climate deniers, multiple local and regional initiatives from diverse regions have made considerable progress as a result of the EPA-FEMA partnership. One study, titled "Smart Growth Fixes for Climate Adaptation and Resilience Change," revealed a rich set of best practices on the integration of smart growth principles with hazard mitigation measures, and evidence on how integration can reduce community vulnerability to a range of hazards such as flooding from stormwater runoff, sea level rise, wildfires, and droughts (US EPA, 2017). The National Oceanic and Atmospheric Administration website also documents numerous case studies of best practices focused on the effects of smart growth development patterns in reducing hazards vulnerability (NOAA, 2019).

The potential to incorporate hazard mitigation into smart growth developments can be found in a number of state level efforts. Notably, Smart Growth America (2014), a highly visible national advocacy organization, initiated a State Resilience Program that was a first-of-its-kind initiative. It offered resources, tools, and guidance for state leaders working to build more resilient places and reduce the risk that natural hazards pose to vulnerable populations and local economies, focusing primarily on floods, sea level rise, and drought. Other notable examples include New York's Countywide

Smart Growth/Resiliency Planning Grant program (New York State, 2018), and Idaho's Department of Lands partnership with Idaho Smart Growth (Idaho Smart Growth, 2018).

Smith et al. (2013) examine shared governance arrangements among federal, state, and local governments that link smart growth to hazards. They present alternative arrangements that states can employ to motivate local hazard vulnerability reduction efforts that integrate Smart Growth principles into pre- and post-disaster recovery planning. The authors use a case study of a major flood disaster in Vermont to illustrate how the state government leveraged federal and state aid and regulatory programs to influence local adoption and implementation of land use policies that support smart growth. The case offers a recovery assistance policy framework that includes recommendations for building capacity of disaster-stricken communities to prepare recovery action plans. This involves local efforts to determine community goals for rebuilding; identify recovery funds, regulations and programs; and create inter-organizational coordination arrangements to enable communities to meet locally defined needs and achieve goals.

Effects of Smart Growth on Hazard Vulnerability

As noted, few studies integrate a range of principles to evaluate the influence of smart growth development patterns on hazard vulnerability. Existing findings are uneven in terms of the effects on vulnerability. A study by Deilami and Kamruzzaman (2017) examined the effects of alternative scenarios of land use and development patterns, including smart growth, on urban heat buildup in Brisbane, Australia. The scenarios include, for example, a low-density development scenario, a strip corridor scenario, and a smart growth scenario. The later scenario includes mixed land uses, compact urban design, walkable places, multiple transportation choices, development directed to existing communities (infill), and protected open space. On average, the smart growth policy scenario performed slightly better than the other development scenarios in reducing urban heat buildup.

A team of planning researchers led by the co-author of this chapter explored the potential of new urbanist development projects that incorporate smart growth principles to guide new development away from floodplain hazard areas of development sites (Berke et al., 2009; Song et al., 2009, 2017; Stevens et al., 2010a, 2010b, 2010c). The researchers considered the physical design principles of new urbanism to be consistent with smart growth principles and hypothesized that since smart growth requires high net densities, the new urbanist developments would be more likely to use cluster design, a concept in which urban development is clustered on parts of a development site while the remainder of the site is preserved as open space (Calthorpe, 1993). In addition, the research team expected that high net densities offer more opportunities than conventional development for platting smaller individual lots to accommodate an equivalent number of housing units. The additional area not used would then provide opportunities to preserve more acreage for open space within the development site. The additional open space could yield more area to locate non-structural flood hazard mitigation practices (e.g., constructed ponds and bio-detention basins) and to preserve environmentally sensitive areas (wetlands and riparian stream buffers) that absorb stormwater runoff. Finally, the team expected that avoiding development in hazardous areas (e.g., floodplains) would help project designers reduce the need for onsite structural protection works like stream channel modification (such as widening) or levees.

Using a national sample of new urbanist projects, the team sought to answer the following questions: (1) What percentage of new urbanist projects contain floodplain hazard areas within their boundaries? (2) Do new urbanist projects incorporate more on-site flood mitigation practices than low-density conventional or "sprawl" projects? (3) If there are differences between new urbanist and conventional development projects in the incorporation of mitigation practices, are the differences due to new urbanist design or community technical assistance activities for project designers and contextual factors (socio-economic, prior disaster experience)?

To answer the first question, the team initially identified all new urbanist developments (318) in the United States as of December 2003 and then determined if each project contained floodplain hazard areas. The team found that more than one-third (114) of all the developments were completely or partially in floodplains. These results reveal that a significant percentage of new urbanist developments are not taking advantage of the principles that support avoidance of the floodplain (see Table 15.1). A major concern with these findings is that smart growth developments that are built at higher densities than conventional sprawl could be placing more people, residential and commercial buildings, and infrastructure at risk than conventional lower density sprawl. The issue is exacerbated due to the fact that compact urban developments have been on the rise over the past decade (Barrington-Leigh & Millard-Ball, 2015; Hamidi & Ewing, 2014).

To answer research questions (2) and (3), the team identified a subset of development projects that consisted of 33 matched pairs of new urbanist and conventional developments. It then surveyed the local government planner responsible for reviewing the developments. These planners were asked to provide information about how the developments were designed, including whether each development incorporated four categories of onsite flood hazard mitigation practices. Their responses revealed several key findings in response to question two:

- There is no significant difference between new urbanist and conventional developments in the number of mitigation practices incorporated and the number of environmentally sensitive area protection techniques incorporated, and
- New urbanist developments incorporate more stream channel modification techniques and structural protection techniques than do conventional developments (Berke et al., 2009; Song et al., 2009).

Finally, findings associated with question (3) indicate that new urbanist developments were no more likely than conventional developments to incorporate any of the four categories of flood hazard mitigation techniques when controlling for community assistance activities and contextual factors. Differences in the incorporation of flood hazard mitigation techniques are due to increased levels of local government technical assistance for new urbanist designers compared with conventional subdivisions during the development review process (Stevens et al., 2010a). Technical assistance included: (1) one-on-one assistance meetings; (2) predevelopment conferences; (3) a checklist of items to address in site plans; (4) workshops to explain code provisions; (5) newsletters/bulletins; and (6) audio/video tapes.

Overall, the findings from Australia show tentative promise for mitigating the public health impacts of urban heat buildup. But the findings based on US communities about flood hazards justify concerns raised by hazard planning and policy experts regarding the lack of design standards included in new urbanist design codes (Sun, 2011). These findings cast doubt on the degree to which new urban developments generally associated with smart growth concepts are, in practice, reducing flood risks and protecting environmentally sensitive areas. The limited research to date suggests that the widely publicized models of new urbanist developments from the 1980s through early 2000s that embraced smart growth principles and were designed to address community character, sense of place, and pedestrian movement, were lacking in specific design standards for natural hazard mitigation. This omission has important implications for community resilience to hazards and climate change, because protection from natural hazards should represent a critical component of smart growth.

It is important to note, however, that after the study on flood mitigation was completed, the Congress for the New Urbanism in 2009 changed its new urbanist design codes to reinforce local government floodplain management. The codes now include standards for directing new development away from the floodplain and incorporation of hazard mitigation. However, little is known about the degree to which the changes have motivated improved vulnerability practices.

Social Disparities and the Development Paradox

Urban planning that is focused on vulnerability to hazards and climate change often ignores the uneven impacts of hazards on socially vulnerable populations (Anguelovski et al. 2016; Berke et al. 2019, Carmin & Agyeman, 2011 Hendricks & Van Zandt, 2021). Local regulation, incentivization, and investment in developments that advance smart growth can play an influential role in changing this. Best practices that link smart growth and resilience with social disparities could include the following:

- A community adopts a voluntary land acquisition and buyout policy aimed at relocating poor households in underserved neighborhoods that experience repeated disaster losses;
- poor households are given an opportunity to relocate to a nearby area at a higher elevation and which incorporates smart growth principles;

- an inclusionary regulatory policy requires development projects to include affordable housing, and a municipal bond that provides funds for low-income housing in this area; and
- a sustained engagement program aimed at building the capacity of marginalized populations defined by race, class, and gender directs the design of developments tailored to local needs and values.

However, if well-intentioned policies aimed at addressing inequities fail to account for hazards, these policies can increase the risk of loss for marginalized households and exacerbate inequities. The limited evidence on this issue reveals troubling results. In an update of original work by planning scholar Raymond Burby (2006), the National Research Council (NRC) (2014) examined the impacts of economic development initiatives by urban planners in New Orleans in flood-prone and disadvantaged neighborhoods. The NRC found the tax abatement and capital improvement investments effectively supported economic development and improved public services in the neighborhoods. Yet the policy initiatives did not include provisions to reduce losses from future disaster events. Consistent with Burby's findings, the NRC concluded that urban planning in New Orleans contributed to the catastrophic damage and losses from Hurricane Katrina in disadvantaged neighborhoods. (See Lung-Amam and June-Friesen, Chapter 14, for more on smart growth and equity issues.)

The inverse relationship between social vulnerability and equity policies raises a hazard-related social justice problem that has implications for smart growth. That is, efforts to stimulate redevelopment premised on smart growth principles in socially vulnerable districts may bring unwelcome consequences in the form of a paradox: development could increase risk in hazard-prone areas, and disasters in these areas could severely disrupt progress in development, then that could lock poor neighborhoods into inequity as the hazard threat rises.

The few studies on smart growth and social vulnerability that do exist by Berke et al. (2015, 2019) found that socially vulnerable neighborhoods targeted for smart growth redevelopment projects frequently experience an inverse relationship between the strength of vulnerability reduction policies and the level of social vulnerability. That is, the economic development policy regimes promoting smart growth in several cities—Boston, Massachusetts; Fort Lauderdale, Florida; and Washington, North Carolina—are increasing the risk for socially vulnerable populations. The cities have a well-integrated set of policies that support equity and redevelopment based on smart growth principles, but these same policies do not account for reduction of loss to flood hazards and sea level rise. The housing plans, comprehensive plans, and neighborhood plans, for example, fail to address vulnerability reduction but at the same time emphasize policies that support more affordable housing and promote opportunities for economic development. The implication for emphasizing equity policies but failing to support risk reduction is that plans actively increase the risk of loss in neighborhoods with high levels of social vulnerability, which can disrupt future community health, safety, and well-being.

CONCLUSIONS

Although addressing climate change was not of great concern when the principles of smart growth were first developed, smart growth has now become an important approach to mitigate and adapt to climate change. Although the evidence is somewhat mixed, a consensus has grown that smarter growth can serve to reduce GHG emissions and sequester a portion thereof. For this reason, smart growth principles have become strategies in perhaps every state and metropolitan climate action plan. That said, there remains debate on how far smart growth development can take us toward climate goals, and few would argue that smart growth alone would be sufficient.

On the adaptation front, the hazards research community has given limited attention to producing peer-reviewed publications on the connections between smart growth principles and community resilience to disasters and climate-sensitive hazards. Planning practitioners place far more emphasis on links between smart growth and hazards, focusing primarily on government programs and policy initiatives at the national, state, and local levels.

Nationally, nearly 30 percent of smart growth developments are increasing the vulnerability of people and property due to siting in hazard areas. This trend points to the problem of how urban form principles such as smart growth may intend to reduce flood losses but can actually increase the potential for catastrophe by stimulating development inside the floodplain, a phenomenon referred to as the "safe development paradox" (Stevens et al., 2010b). Essentially, smart growth has the potential to make a difference in risk reduction but only if it is integrated with hazard mitigation and doesn't undermine it. If smart growth undermines hazard mitigation, the exposure of smart growth developments is likely to be exacerbated as climate warming increases the intensity and frequency of coastal hazards affected by the climate (Intergovernmental Panel on Climate Change, 2019). Thus far, evidence suggesting otherwise is almost non-existent; there is little research on the degree to which smart growth creates development patterns that reduce physical risk and disproportionate impact on socially marginalized populations.

RECOMMENDATIONS FOR IMPROVING INTEGRATION OF MITIGATION AND RESILIENCE THINKING INTO SMART GROWTH

Without question, smart growth has the potential to mitigate climate change and enable resilience, but only if embedded within all sectors of related urban planning, including but not limited to land use, infrastructure, environment, and housing. Furthermore, across these sectors, planners and designers must do better at anticipating hazard threats and including hazard mitigation in the plans, regulations, and investments that pursue smart growth. Planners can develop mutually respectful relationships with public and non-profit organizations to better understand their constraints and needs (Hendricks, Newman, Yu, and Horney, 2018). In fact, planners should prioritize and incentivize development proposals that are centered on smart growth principles, particularly ones that are proposed in less risky areas. This approach not only furthers the advancement of smart growth, but also addresses the "safe development paradox," or what Sun (2011) refers to as smart growth in dumb places. More research is needed to evaluate the degree to which smart growth developments are reducing vulnerability across different population groups, especially the poor. Research on other urban and regional planning domains associated with smart growth, such as transportation and market values, has received substantially more attention.

Lastly, at the start of this process, planners must target outreach, programming, funding, and infrastructure for smart growth at members of historically disadvantaged communities and work with those communities to accomplish this (Hendricks et al., 2018). Smart growth has to promote resilience through a justice lens and make difficult choices, balancing the current needs of distressed populations but also accounting for future risk. This is the only way that we can ensure that smart growth lives up to its principled potential.

REFERENCES

ATTRA Sustainable Agriculture Program. (2009). Retrieved from https://www.nrcs.usda .gov/Internet/FSE_DOCUMENTS/nrcs141p2_002437.pdf

Anguelovski, I., Shi, l., Chu, E., Gallagher, D., Goh, K., Lamb, Z., Reeve, K., & Teicher, H. (2016). Equity impacts of urban land use planning for climate adaptation: Critical perspectives from the Global North and South. *Journal of Planning Education and Research, 36*(3), 333–348.

Barbour, E., & Deakin, E. A. (2012). Smart growth planning for climate protection: Evaluating California's Senate Bill 375. *Journal of the American Planning Association, 78*(1), 70–86.

Barrington-Leigh, C., & Millard-Ball, A. (2015). A century of sprawl. *Proceedings of the National Academy of Sciences, 112*(27),8244–8249. doi.org/10.1073/pnas.1504033112

Berill, P., Gillingham, K. T., & Hertwich, E. (2021). Linking housing policy, housing typology, and residential energy demand in the United States. *Environmental Science and Technology.* 10.1021/acs.est.0c05696

Berke, P., Lee, J., Newman, G., Combs, T., Kolosna, C., & Salvesen, D. (2015). Evaluation of networks of plans and vulnerability to hazards and climate change: A resilience scorecard. *Journal of the American Planning* Association, *81*(4), 287–302.

Berke, P., Song, Y., & Stevens, M. (2009). Integrating hazard mitigation into new urban and conventional developments. *Journal of Planning Education and Research, 28*(4), 441–455.

Berke, P., Yu, S., Malecha, M., & Cooper, J. (2019). Plans that disrupt development: Equity policies and social vulnerability in six coastal cities. *Journal of Planning Education and Research* (201907).

Burby, R. (2006). Hurricane Katrina and the paradoxes of government disaster policy: Bringing about wise governmental decisions for hazardous areas. *The Annals of the American Academy of Political and Social Science, 604*(March), 171–191.

Calthorpe, P. (1993). *The next American metropolis: Ecology, community and the American dream.* Princeton, NJ: Princeton Architectural Press.

Cambridge Systematics. (2009). *Moving cooler: An analysis of transportation strategies for reducing greenhouse gas emissions.* Urban Land Institute.

Carmin, J., and Agyeman, J. (Eds.) (2011). *Environmental inequalities beyond borders: Local perspectives on global injustices.* Cambridge, MA: MIT Press.

Center for Climate and Energy Solutions. (2021). *State climate action plans.* Retrieved from https://www.c2es.org/document/climate-action-plans/

Deilami, K., & Kamruzzaman, M. (2017). Modelling the urban heat effect of smart growth policy scenarios in Brisbane. *Land Use Policy, 64,* 38–55.

Ewing, R., Bartholomew, K., Winkelman, S., Walters, J., & Chen, D. (2007). *Growing cooler: The evidence on urban development and climate change.* Chicago: Urban Land Institute.

Hamidi, D., & Ewing, R. (2014). A longitudinal study of changes in urban sprawl between 2000 and 2010 in the United States. *Landscape and Urban Planning, 128.* 72–82. doi.org/10.1016/j.landurbplan.2014.04.021

Hendricks, M. D., Newman, G., Yu, S., & Horney, J. (2018). Leveling the landscape: landscape performance as a green infrastructure evaluation tool for service-learning products. *Landscape journal, 37*(2), 19-39.

Hendricks, M. D., Meyer, M. A., Gharaibeh, N. G., Van Zandt, S., Masterson, J., Cooper Jr, J. T., & Berke, P. (2018). The development of a participatory assessment technique for infrastructure: Neighborhood-level monitoring towards sustainable infrastructure systems. *Sustainable Cities and Society, 38,* 265–274.

Hendricks, M. D., & Van Zandt, S. (2021). Unequal protection revisited: Planning for environmental justice, hazard vulnerability, and critical infrastructure in communities of color. *Environmental justice, 14(*2), 87-97.

Idaho Smart Growth. (2018). *Wildfire planning.* Retrieved from https://www.idahosmartgrowth.org/fire/

Intergovernmental Panel on Climate Change. (2019). *Climate change and land*: An IPCC special report on climate change, desertification, land degradation, sustainable land management, food security, and greenhouse gas fluxes in terrestrial ecosystems: *Summary for policymakers.* Retrieved from https://www.ipcc.ch/report/srccl/

International City/County Management Association. (2010). *Getting smart about climate change.* https://icma.org/sites/default/files/105215_10-159%20Smart%20Growth%20Climate.pdf

Lewis, R., Zako, R., Biddle, A., & Isbell, R. (2018). Reducing greenhouse gas emissions from transportation and land use: Lessons from West Coast states. *Journal of Transport and Land Use, 11*(1), Article 1. doi.org/10.5198/jtlu.2018.1173

National Academies of Sciences, Engineering and Medicine. (2009). *Driving and the built environment: The effects of compact development on motorized travel, energy use, and CO_2 emissions* (special report 298). Retrieved from https://onlinepubs.trb.org/onlinepubs/sr/sr298.pdf

National Oceanic and Atmospheric Administration. (2019). *Coastal and waterfront smart growth.* Retrieved from https://coastalsmartgrowth.noaa.gov/resilience/welcome.html#intergrating

National Research Council. (2014). *Reducing coastal risk on the East and Gulf Coasts.* Washington, DC: The National Academies Press. Retrieved from https://www.nap.edu/catalog/18811/reducing-coastal-risk-on-the-east-and-gulf-coasts

National Sustainable Agriculture Coalition. (2019). *Agriculture and climate change: Policy imperatives and opportunities to help producers meet the challenge.* Retrieved from https://sustainableagriculture.net/wp-content/uploads/2019/11/NSAC-Climate-Change-Policy-Position_paper-112019_WEB.pdf

New York State, Department of State. (2018). Countywide Smart Growth/Resiliency Planning Grant Program. https://dos.ny.gov/nys-smart-growth-program

Pollak, M., Meyer, B., & Wilson, E. (2011). Reducing greenhouse gas emissions: Lessons from state climate action plans. *Energy Policy, 39,* 5429–5439.

Smart Growth America, State Resilience Program. (2014). Resilience summit discusses how states can help vulnerable populations prepare for and recover from disaster. Retrieved from https://smartgrowthamerica.org/resilience-summit-discusses-how-states-can-help -vulnerable-populations-prepare-for-and-recover-from-disaster/

Smith, G., Sandler, D., & Goralnik, M. (2013). Assessing state policy linking disaster recovery, smart growth, and resilience in Vermont following tropical storm Irene. *Vermont Journal of Environmental Law, 15*, 67–102. Retrieved from http://vjel.vermontlaw.edu/ files/2013/11/S

Song, Y., Berke, P. R., & Stevens, M. R. (2009). Smart developments in dangerous locations: A reality check of existing new urbanist developments. *International Journal of Mass Emergencies and Disasters, 27*(1), 1–24.

Song, Y., Stevens, M., Gao, J., Berke, P., & Jen, Y. (2017). An examination of early new urbanist developments in the United States: Where are they located and why? *Cities, 61*, 126–135.

Stevens, M., Berke, P., & Song, Y. (2010a). Creating disaster-resilient communities: Evaluating the promise and performance of new urbanism. *Landscape and Urban Planning, 94*(2), 105–115.

Stevens, M., Song, Y., & Berke, P. (2010b). New urbanist developments in flood-prone areas: Safe development, or safe development paradox? *Natural Hazards, 53*(3), 605–629.

Stevens, M., Berke, P., & Song, Y. (2010c). Compact urban form: Resilient communities or American Pompeii's. In Alverez, M. (Ed.), *Floodplains: physical geography, ecology and societal interactions* (pp. 107–134). New York: Nova Science Publishers.

Sun, L. (2011). Smart growth in dumb places: Sustainability, disasters, and the future of American Cities. *Brigham Young Law Review, 6*(9), 2157–2202.

US Environmental Protection Agency. (2010). *Achieving hazard-resilient coastal & waterfront smart growth.* https://19january2017snapshot.epa.gov/smartgrowth/achieving-hazard -resilient-coastal-waterfront-smart-growth_.html

US Environmental Protection Agency. (2014). *Planning for flood recovery and long-term resilience in Vermont: Smart growth approaches for disaster-resilient communities.* (EPA 231-R-14-003). https://www.adaptationclearinghouse.org/resources/planning-for-flood -recovery-and-long-term-resilience-in-vermont-smart-growth-approaches-for-disaster -resilient-communities.html

US Environmental Protection Agency. (2016). *Memorandum of agreement between the Department of Homeland Security (DHS), Federal Emergency Management Agency, (FEMA) and the Environmental Protection Agency (EPA).* https://www.epa.gov/ smartgrowth/memorandum-agreement-between-department-homeland-security-dhs -federal-emergency

US Environmental Protection Agency. (2017). *Smart growth fixes for climate adaptation and resilience.* Retrieved from https://www.epa.gov/sites/production/files/2017-01/documents/ smart_growth_fixes_climate_adaptation_resilience.pdf

U.S. Environmental Protection Agency. (2020). *Inventory of U.S. greenhouse gases and sinks: 1990-2018.* Retrieved from https://www.epa.gov/ghgemissions/inventory-us-greenhouse -gas-emissions-and-sinks-1990-2018

Wheeler, S. M. (2008). State and municipal climate change plans: The first generation. *Journal of the American Planning Association, 74*(4), 481–496.

16. Tale of two sprawls: energy planning and challenges for smart growth
Jacob Becker and Nikhil Kaza

INTRODUCTION

While the principles of sustainability and resilience have always been embedded in smart growth principles, explicit acknowledgement of energy systems and their planning is surprisingly lacking in the literature (Lindseth, 2004). The compactness of urban form promoted by smart growth dovetails well with energy conservation efforts. Because consumption, conversion, and production of energy and climate change are intrinsically linked, it is time to recognize energy systems as core infrastructure that constrains and directs urban growth rather than as ancillary planning issues handled by private firms, such as utilities.

Many principles of smart growth directly impact or are impacted by energy systems and their transitions. For example, mixing of land uses has implications for microgrids as they rely on renewable energy sources to account for time-of-day demand balancing (Adil & Ko, 2016). New technologies can be used to reinforce smart growth principles (see Godspeed, Chapter 17). Creating walkable neighborhoods directly reduces the number of short trips taken by car and by public transit. Different housing types are shown to have differential energy consumption impacts because of ownership structures and alignment of incentives (Ewing & Rong, 2008). The preservation of farmland and open spaces is as threatened by energy sprawl as it is by urban sprawl (Prados, 2010).

When considering the production end of the energy system, we ought to account for different stages of energy production and the implications on land uses. Kaza and Curtis (2014) identify these stages as (1) primary extraction of fuel; (2) transmission/distribution of fuels or usable energy; (3) siting conversion facilities; and (4) disposal of waste. Different technologies and fuels interact with urban development in different ways. For example, while rooftop solar panels convert their primary fuel into usable energy on-site, biomass must be collected and transported to a centralized facility before it can be converted. Utility-scale renewables are likely to be located far from urban centers on pristine farmland and on ridgelines to maximize fuel extraction. The resulting transmission pipelines and corridors have been a cause of concern for impacting local (including Native American) lands.

On the consumption end, urban form impacts energy demand through type, mix, size, and density of buildings. Furthermore, different climatic zones and behavior patterns necessitate more nuanced approaches to sustainable and resilient urban form. Urban form also impacts transportation energy consumption through trip lengths, volumes, and mode shifts (see Welch & Gehrke, Chapter 10 for more on transportation and smart growth). On the other hand, decarbonization and electrification of public transit systems are likely to be hastened by compact urban form.

Challenges to implementing "sustainable" energy policies primarily stem from institutional and financial barriers. The uncertainty and inconsistency associated with subsidies and tax rebates for renewable energy and electric vehicles have impacted investments in them. Retrofits could lower home energy use but may not pay for themselves over a homeowner's lifetime. The technology exists to build solar panels or wind turbines but installing them at a large scale has a large capital cost. For a grid to run primarily on renewables, large investments in battery storage and grid modernization would be needed. Beyond direct costs, rooftop solar panels can run afoul of aesthetic codes, and land use codes may also not take into account passive climate control. Here, smart growth's emphasis on incentives and regulatory certainty can pay dividends toward decarbonization.

Furthermore, energy planning in the United States has rarely been in the public domain. Electric utilities are required to submit integrated energy management plans to the public utilities commission (PUC). Scenario planning approaches used in the public sector have been pioneered by Royal Dutch Shell, an oil and gas company (Ogilvy, 2002). However, most private sector planning is directed within the firm or externally directed to engage with limited stakeholders, such as the PUCs, and rarely coordinated with other plans such as comprehensive or climate change adaptation plans of municipalities. Because of energy's central role in maintaining economies, it is vital that public planning processes inform energy planning and vice versa. In particular, urban development plans—and by extension, smart growth principles—should explicitly acknowledge the role of energy. Very few of the procedural planning principles have been used in the energy planning realm. It is time to make energy a central component of urban development processes.

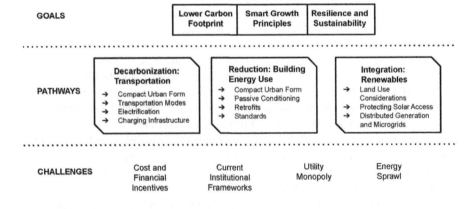

Figure 16.1   *Pathways and challenges for incorporating energy planning principles in smart growth*

We assert that decarbonization can be accomplished without compromising on smart growth principles (see Figure 16.1 for pathways and challenges). Transportation and buildings are responsible for most US energy consumption; compact development can be crucial for lowering the energy intensity of both. Solar energy is the key renewable resource, and land use codes can empower buildings to harvest it for energy and climate control. Renewables, however, may lead to their own land sprawl without guiding codes of their own. Legislative, regulatory, and financial uncertainties can stand in the way of achieving all these goals, making greater regional control necessary.

DECARBONIZATION: TRANSPORTATION

Decarbonization of the transportation system is usually conceptualized along two dimensions: mode substitution and fuel substitution. Different transportation modes have different energy efficiencies. This also holds for fuels used in transportation. In this section, we focus on decarbonization through electrification of the transportation sector. However, we would be remiss if we did not mention the effect of smart growth principles (compactness, diversity of land uses) on mode switching.

Compact Urban Form, Transportation Modes, and Energy Efficiency

The connection between land use and transportation is unassailable. Dense cities, in general, consume less per capita transportation energy (Baker & Steemers, 2003), even though there is some disagreement about the magnitude of this correlation (Echenique et al., 2012; Handy, 2005; TRB & BEES, 2009). In Chapter 10, Welche and Gehrke further detail how compact development enables non-car transportation. However, in the United States in 2017, per-passenger-mile energy consumption of transit motor buses was 7% higher than that of passenger cars (Bureau of Transportation Statistics, 2019). This is largely driven by low load factors of buses in many urban areas (Randolph & Masters, 2008). Compact development, coupled with context sensitive design, can significantly increase the number of people using the transit system.

Shared automobility (for example, ride-hailing services such as Uber and Lyft) poses a peculiar problem for land use patterns. Shared automobility might affect personal vehicle ownership and usage (Hampshire et al., 2018). Yet the deadhead losses (trips without passengers) in these systems are around 42 percent (Henao & Marshall, 2019). This effectively means that these systems are likely to reduce the need for parking but increase congestion on the road because of increases in vehicle miles travelled (Erhardt et al., 2019). Ride-hailing trips are likely to use vehicles that rely on conventional liquid fuels, slowing the adoption of (fully) electric vehicles. Reduced congestion in parking lots is more likely to be offset by congestion on roadways, because of these ride hailing services. The deadhead losses are likely to be lower in denser urban environments. The relationship between autonomous vehicles and parking spaces is further elaborated on by Goodspeed in Chapter 17, but the same logic applies.

Electrification and Charging Infrastructure

In 2018, the transportation sector accounted for 28 percent of the energy consumption in the United States. While 92 percent is derived from petroleum-based liquid fuels, less than 1 percent comes from electricity. Much of the electricity used in transportation is in mass transit systems (US Energy Information Administration, 2019a). With the advances in battery technology, the range anxiety associated with electric vehicles is starting to decrease, spurring increasing adoption. According to some projections, 55 percent of new vehicle sales will be electric by 2040 (Jones et al., 2018). The electrification of personal transport, along with the continuing adoption of electricity for mass transit systems, will impact land use planning processes and smart growth principles.

The key land use issue for the electrification of personal automobiles is the ubiquity of the charging infrastructure. Current refueling efforts with liquid fuels require strategically located gasoline stations in addition to robust transmission and distribution infrastructure associated with petroleum products (e.g. pipelines and tankers). To hasten transportation electrification, similar infrastructure should be created for electricity. While transmission and distribution of electricity are not a major concern in the United States, the location and availability of the charging stations are a key factor in adoption of electric vehicles. Furthermore, because gasoline refueling times are shorter than electric vehicle charging times, the throughput of gasoline stations is higher. Charging infrastructure will thus need to be available at places where vehicles are stationed for a longer duration (parking lots, driveways). Therefore, electrification of personal transport may require a greater number of parking spaces because of higher occupancy rates and lower throughput rates. On the other hand, battery swap or wireless refueling systems will have lower land use impact. Housing type also interacts with adoption of electric vehicles. Households in single family houses with off-street parking are more likely to adopt electric vehicles because of ease of on-site charging infrastructure.

The impact of charging infrastructure on the electrical grid may have diurnal effects. Charging during the day, when "peakers" are operational in producing electricity, is less ideal than charging at night when electrical demand is met by base load power plants. Simulation studies that quantify this total effect of electrification of transport on land use are lacking.

REDUCTION: ENERGY ADDICTION IN BUILDINGS THROUGH SMART POLICIES

Residential and commercial buildings were responsible for 40 percent of all energy consumption in 2018 (US Energy Information Administration, 2019b). Single-family detached homes make up a disproportionate fraction of residential energy use. Residential buildings overall consume 41 percent of energy for space conditioning (Brown & Southworth, 2008). Because energy use is correlated to building size, promoting compact building design through density will lead to energy savings.

Compact Urban Form

The value of density and compact development is discussed in other chapters, but we would be remiss to not touch upon the role density can play in lowering building energy consumption. With increased density comes increased sharing of energy infrastructure and increased viability of district-wide heating and cooling systems (Güneralp et al., 2017). Multifamily units typically are smaller in floor area and share walls, which share space conditioning loads (Ewing & Rong, 2008).

Urban form affects residential energy use primarily by affecting the housing stock and urban heat islands. Areas with constrained land supply (as seen in compact counties) tend to favor more efficient multifamily and attached housing, though the exact mechanism of the effect is unclear (Ewing & Rong, 2008). Urban heat islands are caused by constructed surfaces, lack of plant canopy, vehicle travel, and waste heat from electricity use. The urban heat island creates a greater need for energy consumption in hot seasons. Compact development does increase this heat island; nevertheless, counties with compact development consume less energy than those with sprawling development.

The impact of compact urban form on passive heating and cooling is less clear. Density that does not take into account solar irradiation could lead to a greater need for electric heating or lighting. An analysis of the UK showed that the drawbacks outweigh the benefits for residential development at densities greater than 200 dwellings per hectare (Steemers, 2003). In areas where air conditioning is only required due to building depth, large office or apartment buildings could limit the ability of residents to use natural ventilation and increase the need for air conditioning (Steemers, 2003). This key point will be addressed later: the importance of regional climate and conditions when determining energy use. In areas where natural ventilation is a viable option year-round for cooling, the effect of density on ventilation is a key factor, while in areas where air conditioning is the only means to effectively cool (such as Houston, Texas, where you would be unwise to crack a window to cool down in July) this is not an issue. There is no one size fits all prescription.

Passive Conditioning

While much of the work in passive heating and cooling will be the result of building-specific technologies, shaded and sunlight hours are determined by building orientation and the surrounding landscape. The urban heat island effect can be reduced with greenscape. Deciduous trees provide shade to facades in summer and allow sunlight through in winter (van Esch et al., 2012). Specific setback requirements can encourage or discourage shading. Equator-facing windows and walls give a greater opportunity for passive cooling and heating. Buildings that use passive cooling/heating could have expedited permitting processes. Several American cities have already adopted such guidelines, many of which can be found in the American Planning Association's "Planning and Zoning for Solar Energy" Packet (Planning Advisory Service, 2011). Land use and building guidelines regarding solar access for passive heating can also be applied to distributed solar generation.

Cities that use standard grid layouts with tall buildings flanking a street create an "urban canyon" microclimate, with different wind, temperature, and shading patterns compared with an open area. This usually leads to an increased urban heat island effect, especially for north/south oriented canyons. Wide streets allow for more heat capture in east/west oriented canyons. Therefore, narrow streets are better at mitigating the heat island effect in canyons, and wider east/west oriented streets may help areas hoping to use the canyon's solar gain as passive winter heating. North–south canyons provide more sun in the dead of winter, while east–west canyons provide midday shade on the streets (van Esch et al., 2012). Roof pitch and awning size also play a role in where and to what degree the canyon affects solar access.

Retrofits

At an individual building level, energy efficiency retrofits are one of the simplest methods to reduce energy consumption by targeting space conditioning (Güneralp et al., 2017). These retrofits can be accomplished directly by municipalities and by providing financial incentives to homeowners and businesses. Efficiency doesn't end at the building itself; it includes internal appliances and patterns of use. More efficient refrigerators, light bulbs, washing machines, windows, and more can save 30–75 percent over the standard (Brown & Southworth, 2008). As renewable penetration increases, time-of-use plays a larger role in lowering the carbon footprint of energy consumption, increasing the importance of smart appliances and timed energy use (including EV charging). Attaching a price signal to time-of-day energy use can promote adoption of these technologies and encourage manual smart energy use. There is also a need to electrify heating and cooking systems rather than expand natural gas infrastructure. A recent study shows that methane emissions of four major US cities due to natural gas alone add up to 827,000 tons per year, the same warming effect as 26.5 million tons of CO_2 (Plant et al., 2019).

Setting a Standard for Standards

Green building standards have been used to promote sustainable building and energy efficiency in various places. In the United States, standards such as Leadership in Energy and Environmental Design (LEED) and Energy Star are useful starting points for reducing building energy use. In one study, an average LEED building used 18–39 percent less energy per floor area than an average non-certified building, but the levels of certification are not found to correlate with energy conservation (Newsham et al., 2009). However, another study in New York City found no savings in LEED office buildings and higher energy use in LEED Certified and Silver buildings, even though Energy Star certification showed better energy performance (Scofield, 2013).It should also be noted that while LEED and Energy Star (for residences) are design and building standards, Energy Star for commercial buildings is a performance standard and certification has to be renewed periodically.

The methods to achieve energy efficiency must vary by location. Installing Energy Star air conditioning units in Alaska should not be valued as highly as doing the same in Ecuador. LEED currently uses essentially the same criteria to certify buildings worldwide, with only 3.6 percent of the points value used for assigning a certification reserved for "regional priority." "Energy and atmosphere" is the only category that is directly related to energy consumption, and it only constitutes 31.8 percent of the ranking (Suzer, 2015). If different regions created their own certifications or if existing certifications placed more weight on local environmental concerns, the certifications would have more relevance. In the American Southwest, standards should prioritize water conservation, air conditioning efficiency, building insulation and shade usage, whereas in Sweden standards might value the ability to passively heat the building.

In addition to building scale standards, neighborhood scale standards have also been in play. Prominent among those is LEED for Neighborhood Development (LEED ND), a neighborhood-wide certification given by the US Green Building Council. This standard has similar drawbacks to LEED's building standards due to its similarities. There are valuable considerations in the LEED ND criteria from an energy perspective, such as giving points for heat island reduction, solar orientation, district heating/cooling, and renewable energy production. Regional priorities make up at most four points (of 110) of certification criteria (US Green Building Council, 2014). However, we are unaware of any systematic post-hoc analysis of the actual energy impact of LEED ND certification on communities.

The lack of efficacy of LEED standards highlights the importance of the human factor in energy conservation. A more efficient building could lead to less efficient practices, commonly known as the rebound effect. Without post-construction efficiency metrics and certifications, there is no guarantee of actual reductions in consumption. Repeated energy audits tracking the actual energy use are the best way to truly evaluate the effectiveness of efficiency measures.

This presents an additional marketing challenge over construction certifications: transfer of ownership of buildings does not usually include transfer of conservation practices. To counteract these issues, new building benchmarking and disclosure laws are being adopted in various cities in the United States (Hsu, 2014). These laws are designed to reduce the information gap that limits investments in energy efficiency and conservation. The process of collecting information for disclosure also spurs individual and organizational action (Hsu, 2014). Different policies can be tailored to commercial buildings and multi-family units. Utility-based programs that compare a household's energy consumption to that of their neighbors have been shown to reduce energy consumption (Allcott & Mullainathan, 2010).

We stop short of offering many specific, generalizable recommendations because the ideal guidelines are context sensitive. Street orientation, lot setbacks, density, passive climate control, and canyons all play a role in energy consumption from space conditioning. Most building energy is used for heating and cooling, so controlling how the space interacts with the sun is key to reducing energy use. Beyond temperature, optimizing energy use to coincide with the availability of renewables on the grid will lower energy costs and carbon footprints. Specific policies, guidelines and standards must be context sensitive to be effective at conserving energy.

INTEGRATION: RENEWABLES AND ENERGY SPRAWL

Smart growth grew out of the need to curb sprawling development, as sprawl led to destruction of open space and degradation of environmental quality. Smart growth literature often expounds on the problems caused by urban sprawl, but less is written on the land use impacts of energy infrastructure. Much of the infrastructure required for energy generation and transmission has a large land use footprint, and energy sources that rely on burning fuel have the additional environmental impact of extraction. Renewables may take up vital open space, locations historically used for agriculture and wildlife habitats, without land use regulations. This "energy sprawl" can already be seen in areas that have committed to renewables without a coupled commitment to preserving open space (McDonald et al., 2009). Smart growth principles such as redeveloping areas within the urban core, promoting infill development, and preserving open and natural areas can be applied to the siting of renewable energy generation.

Land Use Considerations

Renewables tend to be less energy dense than conventional fuels. Direct footprints (on unusable land) are approximately 15 square kilometers per terawatt-hour (km^2/TWhr) for solar photovoltaic (PV) energy and closer to 127 km^2/TWhr for wind. A terawatt is 10^{12} Watts; for reference, the United States consumed 29,688 TWhrs of electricity in 2018 (US Energy Information Administration, 2019b). Conventional energy production, on the other hand, has a total footprint of 0.64–8.19 km^2/TWhr on average. Nuclear power has the lowest land use impact of 0.13 km^2/TWhr, though this does not take into account disposal sites (Trainor et al., 2016). One study estimates that decarbonizing conventional energy systems with utility scale renewables in the United States would require 206,000–290,000 km^2 of new land by 2030 (McDonald et al., 2009).

Even more acutely, biomass and biofuel crops have land use requirements far greater than those of any other energy source, requiring an average of 809 km^2/TWhr, more than 53 times that required for solar PV (Trainor et al., 2016). Thus, decarbonization of energy systems requires substantial land use footprint and directly contravenes the compact land use development goals that underlie smart growth principles.

Furthermore, the effect of this decarbonization is geographically differentiated. The American West has both rich energy resources and wild lands important for unique threatened species. Projections put the potential land use footprint at 20.6 million hectares by 2030, primarily in boreal forests, shrublands, and grasslands (Copeland et al., 2011). None of this should be seen as an argument against renewables, as climate change is still the greater threat.

Spain's initial renewable boom, where land use planning and energy planning were detached, provides a useful case study of the pitfalls of rapidly expanding clean energy without considering ancillary impacts. Over 20 gigawatts of solar and wind generation were installed since 1993, enough to power between 3.3 and 6.7 million households. However, these systems were often sited on agricultural land, precipitating the decline of Spanish agriculture (Prados, 2010). These areas also allow renewables to take advantage of the pre-existing irrigation infrastructure, potentially leading to conflicts over water rights. The lack of regulatory clarity in terms of siting has also led to conflicts between local government, regional governments, and environmental groups. Lack of coordinated planning has led to large numbers of small-scale plants, increasing the transmission burden (Prados, 2010). If smart growth principles are not incorporated in energy planning, agricultural land could disappear and water resources could be strained.

Photovoltaic or solar water heaters installed on rooftops and building facades is the gold standard of renewable siting, as there are few, if any, land use impacts. Parking lots and brownfields could also be used as solar farm sites with minimal environmental impacts. Use of these desirable sites could be promoted through the incentives that define smart growth, such as an expedited permitting process. Conversely, planners can also place restrictions on renewable development in floodplains, areas of high biodiversity, areas important for natural beauty, usable farmland, and wildlife corridors. Farmland should not be written off entirely for PV development, and solar panels can provide shade and have a synergistic effect on certain crop yields through agrovoltaics (Dupraz et al., 2011).

Protecting Solar Access

In general, land use plans should consider insolation as a valuable resource. Sunlight can be obstructed by nearby buildings, which increase in number with density. Land use guidelines should consider this effect, and impact fees or PV requirements on the shade-casting building could offset some of the downsides of losing solar resources. Shadows vary by time of year; lands use plans can take this into account based on the local seasonal energy use and generation potential. Care should be afforded to tradeoffs between passive techniques such as mutual shading of buildings and PV generation.

Solar rights can be codified into law as part of property and land use rights (Bronin, 2009). Code could also allow variances for developments which have the capacity to make use of passive heating or solar generation. This would serve to protect and encourage development that can use solar energy or heating. A certain number of unshaded sunlight hours could be guaranteed. Alternatively, protection of solar rights could come in the form of compensation if solar access is impeded.

Many codes fail to assess the impact on extant PV for new construction (Strømann-Andersen & Sattrup, 2011). This is especially important in latitudes far from the equator where shadows are longer. Here again, density can play a negative role in the energy transition by creating shadowy canyons. Buildings with reflective surfaces could increase insolation in dense areas. Planners should consider not only the energy impacts of and on existing building when considering new construction, but also estimate the effects of density on said solar resources (Strømann-Andersen & Sattrup, 2011).

Distributed Generation and Microgrids

The utility of smart growth principles in energy planning is clear: by considering the land use-energy connection, planners can encourage thoughtful siting of renewables while mitigating the impacts on the environment and agricultural lands. Generating electricity within cities as part of mixed-use developments directly protects farmland, open space, and natural areas from being used as utility scale renewable plants. Planners could prioritize smaller scale and brownfield renewables siting and promote decentralized energy systems, such as microgrids.

Studies have shown that many cities could satisfy a significant portion of their energy demand with current rooftop PV technology alone. Oeras, Portugal, and Bardejov, Slovakia, could cover over 60 percent of their energy needs within city PV (Amado & Poggi, 2014; Hofierka & Kaňuk, 2009). Rooftop-only PV could satisfy up to 30 percent of Mumbai, India's, daily demand (Singh & Banerjee, 2015).

Distributed energy systems can involve local generation, distribution, and storage. These systems can be connected into the existing larger grid, or be used to create a semi-independent or completely independent microgrid system. Local control can save energy, because it allows more nuanced decisions on which receptors get high vs. low quality power, as many end uses do not require high quality power with no noise (Marnay et al., 2008). Total possible energy savings through microgrid optimization are estimated to be around 20–30 percent (Guan et al., 2010). Natural disasters can cause traditional grids to go down, causing large scale power outages that can last for weeks. However, microgrids would be able to disconnect from the traditional grid and act autonomously, acting to smooth out issues in the grid or acting completely independently to provide electricity until the macrogrid is restored (Strbac et al., 2015). For example, the Mississippi Baptist Medical Center was able to operate at full service during Hurricane Katrina using its on-site energy generation (Marnay et al., 2008).

The technical details of microgrids are beyond the scope of this chapter, but various models have been developed to optimize PV siting, evaluate the economics of microgrids, determine optimal storage capacity, and create optimal schedules (Chen et al., 2012; Marnay et al., 2008). These models can be used in conjunction with different load profiles implied by different neighborhood land use mix and density to make appropriate design decisions.

Mixing uses can be beneficial to distributed systems by spreading out the timing of peak demands for various uses. At least one study has found load-mixing reduces costs in microgrids (Aldaouab et al., 2017). The size of the mixed-use benefit was found to correlate positively with renewable penetration, as mixing uses decreases the difference between peak load and average consumption, which decreases the cost for utilities.

Technical concerns can be overcome with proper investments and planning, but the current US utility model poses challenges that require policy solutions. Owing to the increased potential for and benefits of distributed energy, electric utilities are no longer a natural monopoly requiring massive economies of scale. In over half of states, consumers do not have a choice between electricity suppliers and are subject to the monopoly of a privately controlled company. In North Carolina, courts upheld regulations on who can sell electricity, preventing an African American church from installing rooftop solar panels and selling their own cheap energy to power the church. Third party solar, and therefore distributed generation without consent of the utilities, is banned in nine states, while 15 states have no clear policy guidelines. Leasing solar panels with a power purchase agreement is allowed in some states, but at rates set by the utility which may not be conducive to installing solar without further grants or tax credits (Gearino, 2018). Utilities lack incentives to build distributed systems or limit greenfield development.

Institutional Challenges to Curbing Energy Sprawl

Smart growth aims to increase community and stakeholder collaboration, remove barriers to urban design innovation, and achieve a greater recognition of regional interdependence and solidarity (Downs, 2001). Regional distributed renewable energy is more amenable to local stakeholder involvement. National and state level bodies such as the Federal Energy Regulatory Commission and Public Utilities Commission regulate much of transmission and distribution infrastructure, leaving local governments little say in energy planning (Goldthau, 2014). Decision-making in centralized systems is often controlled by utilities or requires coordination between utilities and state, local, and federal governments.

Zoning laws, permitting, form-based codes and building regulations also limit the ability to install rooftop PV in many areas. Aesthetic codes in particular can be barriers for rooftop solar, so governments should allow exceptions or alternative compliance provisions for energy generation (White, 2008). Governments could require a percentage of solar-oriented lots in new development, and require variation in lot width to avoid the urban canyon effect (White, 2008). Additional barriers often include requirements for a direct connection from the individual to the grid, limiting the ability of those in the same building who receive separate bills from selling power, and creating legal uncertainty (Moroni et al., 2016).

Distributed systems also lack the standardized funding and investment mechanisms that support utility scale development. Mercurial political support for tax credits has led to uncertainty in how safe clean energy investments are and discouraged large-scale private investment (Sovacool, 2009). Private financing with distributed systems has picked up in recent years, but still falls behind that of utility-scale developments. Homeowners could be given financial incentives to invest in PV, making net metering, tax breaks, or value of solar tariff good incentives (Hess, 2016).

State and local governments have directly financed rooftop solar installations in several states, and partnerships can expedite the process of creating distributed systems (Hess, 2016). Utility-sponsored community-scale solar (such as in Sacramento, California), a system where utilities sponsor distributed solar generation while maintaining control over the electrical system, is another promising model. By letting the utilities maintain control and develop multiple community scale projects, demand can be stabilized across the region in which they operate and the traditional economies of scale and the investor portfolio that utilities rely on can be leveraged. Utilities can also leverage their existing revenue to finance building new solar panels. However, privately owned utilities usually find it more profitable to invest in utility-scale projects (Funkhouser et al., 2015). In order to make sponsored community-scale solar appealing, regulatory incentives would be needed to make rooftops a more alluring option.

Without federal subsidies or an increased cost for fossil fuel electricity, local and state governments can promote solar growth by implementing binding renewable portfolio standards for utilities or by providing subsidies to homeowners. New developments could be given incentives, a hallmark of smart growth, to install rooftop solar. Capital cost is often the largest hurdle to rooftop solar. Local governments and neighborhoods can partner with other entities such as nearby local governments, nonprofits (such as Shine™) or private firms (such as University Park Solar LLC) to tap into existing expertise. These relationships can help leverage potential investors, lessening the major hurdle of covering capital costs (Coughlin et al., 2010). Distributed systems can also benefit from cooperation among municipalities.

Planning at a regional scale may be necessary for smaller communities trying to develop renewable systems (Funkhouser et al., 2015). Along with economic benefits, the more communities involved in a distributed solar project, the more siting options become available. Covering a broader area also increases the reliability and resilience of a solar grid, as energy production will not be at the whim of a single weather system. This is where smart growth's emphasis on innovative design and greater recognition of interdependence overlaps most with energy planning. Regional planning bodies could oversee energy planning in conjunction with coordinating land uses.

CONCLUSIONS

An example of nonprofit sponsored community scale smart growth energy done right is a low-income housing development in Denver, Colorado. First, energy retrofits were done to each of the houses in the program, greatly reducing their overall energy needs. These homes were also smaller than the average American home to begin with, a clear example of energy's synergy with other smart growth principles. Photovoltaic-related job training opportunities were created as part of this project as well. This project required collaboration between several affordable housing nonprofits, the local utility (who provided clean energy incentives and agreed to purchase renewable energy certificates), Denver's Energy Office (who provided a $107,500 grant), the National Renewable Energy Laboratory, and private investors (who would reap tax benefits) (Schwabe, 2012). Another example is University Park Community Solar LLC, a for-profit solar company, owned by those who use the energy, which has installed 22 kW of solar capacity on a local church rooftop. Revenue comes from selling electricity to the grid, renewable energy credits, and tax incentives (Coughlin et al., 2010).

These examples emphasize the key point that smart energy planning requires coordination among different types of actors. Local grants are required as initial capital. Utility, federal, and state programs make renewables more affordable and attractive to investors. These groups and nonprofits can provide the initial capital investment or grant for energy retrofits that pay for themselves over time as well. Renewable energy cannot be made the norm without deliberate, supportive, and coordinated programs and policies. Distributed energy systems are the most effective way to curb energy sprawl, and regional land use guidelines and incentives are crucial to the development of these systems. These should be paired with standards to reduce energy consumption based on the key context-sensitive factors.

Many extant smart growth principles can be used to achieve resilient and sustainable energy systems, which can be used to further justify these principles. However, energy should be explicitly considered part of the mix of land uses for smart growth communities and in comprehensive plans. The potential conflict of renewable energy with preservation of open space, farmland, and natural areas can be mitigated with thoughtful planning. Planners can ensure land use guidelines promote access to solar resources for generation and climate control. Smart growth can incorporate sustainability and resilience by making decarbonization an integral part of its goals.

ACKNOWLEDGMENTS

We wish to thank the editors and Kshitiz Khanal for their insightful comments in pushing us to clarify the argument. Any remaining errors are our responsibility.

REFERENCES

Adil, A., & Ko, Y. (2016). Socio-technical evolution of Decentralized Energy Systems: A critical review and implications for urban planning and policy. *Renewable and Sustainable Energy Reviews, 57,* 1025–1037. https://doi.org/10.1016/j.rser.2015.12.079

Aldaouab, I., Daniels, M., & Hallinan, K. (2017). Microgrid cost optimization for a mixed-use building. *2017 IEEE Texas Power and Energy Conference (TPEC)*, 1–5. https://doi.org/10.1109/TPEC.2017.7868271

Allcott, H., & Mullainathan, S. (2010). Behavior and energy policy. *Science, 327*(5970), 1204–1205. https://doi.org/10.1126/science.1180775

Amado, M., & Poggi, F. (2014). Solar urban planning: A parametric approach. *Energy Procedia, 48*, 1539–1548.

Baker, N., & Steemers, K. (2003). *Energy and Environment in Architecture: A Technical Design Guide*. Taylor & Francis.

Bronin, S. C. (2009). Solar rights. *Boston University Law Review, 89*, 1217.

Brown, M. A., & Southworth, F. (2008). Mitigating climate change through green buildings and smart growth. *Environment and Planning A: Economy and Space, 40*(3), 653–675. https://doi.org/10.1068/a38419

Bureau of Transportation Statistics. (2019). Energy intensity of passenger modes. Retrieved May 18, 2020, from National Transportation Statistics (series) website: https://rosap.ntl.bts.gov/gsearch?collection=dot:35533&type1=mods.title&fedora_terms1=National+Transportation+Statistics

Chen, S. X., Gooi, H. B., & Wang, M. Q. (2012). Sizing of energy storage for microgrids. *IEEE Transactions on Smart Grid, 3*(1), 142–151. https://doi.org/10.1109/TSG.2011.2160745

Copeland, H. E., Pocewicz, A., & Kiesecker, J. M. (2011). Geography of energy development in western North America: Potential impacts on terrestrial ecosystems. In D. E. Naugle (Ed.), *Energy Development and Wildlife Conservation in Western North America* (pp. 7–22). Washington, DC: Island Press/Center for Resource Economics. https://doi.org/10.5822/978-1-61091-022-4_2

Coughlin, J., Grove, J., Irvine, L., Jacobs, J. F., Phillips, S. J., Moynihan, L., & Wiedman, J. (2010). A guide to community solar: Utility, private and non-profit project development. *National Renewable Energy Lab, 56*.

Downs, A. (2001). What does "smart growth" really mean? *Foresight, Kentucky Long-Term Policy Research Center*. Retrieved from http://e-archives.ky.gov/Pubs/LPRC/Vol8no2.pdf

Dupraz, C., Marrou, H., Talbot, G., Dufour, L., Nogier, A., & Ferard, Y. (2011). Combining solar photovoltaic panels and food crops for optimising land use: Towards new agrivoltaic schemes. *Renewable Energy, 36*(10), 2725–2732. https://doi.org/10.1016/j.renene.2011.03.005

Echenique, M. H., Hargreaves, A. J., Mitchell, G., & Namdeo, A. (2012). Growing cities sustainably does urban form really matter? *Journal of the American Planning Association, 78*(2), 121–137. https://doi.org/10.1080/01944363.2012.666731

Erhardt, G. D., Roy, S., Cooper, D., Sana, B., Chen, M., & Castiglione, J. (2019). Do transportation network companies decrease or increase congestion? *Science Advances, 5*(5), eaau2670. https://doi.org/10.1126/sciadv.aau2670

Ewing, R., & Rong, F. (2008). The impact of urban form on U.S. residential energy use. *Housing Policy Debate, 19*(1), 1–30. https://doi.org/10.1080/10511482.2008.9521624

Funkhouser, E., Blackburn, G., Magee, C., & Rai, V. (2015). Business model innovations for deploying distributed generation: The emerging landscape of community solar in the U.S. *Energy Research & Social Science, 10*, 90–101. https://doi.org/10.1016/j.erss.2015.07.004

Gearino, D. (2018, March 14). How solar panels on a church rooftop broke the law in N.C. | InsideClimate News. Retrieved March 3, 2020, from Inside Climate News website: https://insideclimatenews.org/news/14052018/north-carolina-rooftop-solar-panel-laws-duke-utility-monopoly-court-ruling-church-clean-energy

Goldthau, A. (2014). Rethinking the governance of energy infrastructure: Scale, decentralization and polycentrism. *Energy Research & Social Science, 1*, 134–140. https://doi.org/10.1016/j.erss.2014.02.009

Guan, X., Xu, Z., & Jia, Q.-S. (2010). Energy-efficient buildings facilitated by microgrid. *IEEE Transactions on Smart Grid*, *1*(3), 243–252. https://doi.org/10.1109/TSG.2010 .2083705

Güneralp, B., Zhou, Y., Ürge-Vorsatz, D., Gupta, M., Yu, S., Patel, P. L., …, Seto, K. C. (2017). Global scenarios of urban density and its impacts on building energy use through 2050. *Proceedings of the National Academy of Sciences*. https://doi.org/10.1073/pnas .1606035114

Hampshire, R. C., Simek, C., Fabusuyi, T., Di, X., & Chen, X. (2018). *Measuring the Impact of an Unanticipated Suspension of Ride-Sourcing in Austin, Texas.* Presented at the Transportation Research Board 97th Annual Meeting. Transportation Research Board. Retrieved from https://trid.trb.org/view/1495607

Handy, S. (2005). Smart growth and the transportation-land use connection: What does the research tell us? *International Regional Science Review*, *28*(2), 146–167. https://doi.org/10 .1177/0160017604273626

Henao, A., & Marshall, W. E. (2019). The impact of ride-hailing on vehicle miles traveled. *Transportation*, *46*(6), 2173–2194.

Hess, D. J. (2016). The politics of niche-regime conflicts: Distributed solar energy in the United States. *Environmental Innovation and Societal Transitions*, *19*, 42–50. https://doi .org/10.1016/j.eist.2015.09.002

Hofierka, J., & Kaňuk, J. (2009). Assessment of photovoltaic potential in urban areas using open-source solar radiation tools. *Renewable Energy*, *34*(10), 2206–2214.

Hsu, D. (2014). How much information disclosure of building energy performance is necessary? *Energy Policy*, *64*, 263–272. https://doi.org/10.1016/j.enpol.2013.08.094

Jones, P. B., Levy, J., Bosco, J., Howat, J., & Van Alst, J. W. (2018). *The Future of Transportation Electrification: Utility, Industry and Consumer Perspectives* (No. 1464173; p. 1464173). https://doi.org/10.2172/1464173

Kaza, N., & Curtis, M. P. (2014). The land use energy connection. *Journal of Planning Literature*, *29*(4), 355–369.

Lindseth, G. (2004). The Cities for Climate Protection Campaign (CCPC) and the framing of local climate policy. *Local Environment*, *9*(4), 325–336.

Marnay, C., Asano, H., Papathanassiou, S., & Strbac, G. (2008). Policymaking for microgrids. *IEEE Power and Energy Magazine*, *6*(3), 66–77. https://doi.org/10.1109/MPE.2008.918715

McDonald, R. I., Fargione, J., Kiesecker, J., Miller, W. M., & Powell, J. (2009). Energy sprawl or energy efficiency: Climate policy impacts on natural habitat for the United States of America. *PLOS ONE*, *4*(8), e6802. https://doi.org/10.1371/journal.pone.0006802

Moroni, S., Antoniucci, V., & Bisello, A. (2016). Energy sprawl, land taking and distributed generation: Towards a multi-layered density. *Energy Policy*, *98*, 266–273. https://doi.org/ 10.1016/j.enpol.2016.08.040

Newsham, G. R., Mancini, S., & Birt, B. J. (2009). Do LEED-certified buildings save energy? Yes, but…. *Energy and Buildings*, *41*(8), 897–905. https://doi.org/10.1016/j.enbuild.2009 .03.014

Ogilvy, J. A. (2002). *Creating Better Futures: Scenario Planning as a Tool for a Better Tomorrow.* Oxford University Press, USA.

Planning Advisory Service. (2011). *Planning and Zoning for Solar Energy* (No. PAS EIP-30). American Planning Association.

Plant, G., Kort, E. A., Floerchinger, C., Gvakharia, A., Vimont, I., & Sweeney, C. (2019). Large fugitive methane emissions from urban centers along the U.S. east coast. *Geophysical Research Letters*, *46*(14), 8500–8507. https://doi.org/10.1029/2019GL082635

Prados, M.-J. (2010). Renewable energy policy and landscape management in Andalusia, Spain: The facts. *Energy Policy*, *38*(11), 6900–6909. https://doi.org/10.1016/j.enpol.2010 .07.005

Randolph, J., & Masters, G. M. (2008). *Energy for Sustainability: Technology, Planning and Policy*. Washington, DC: Island Press.

Schwabe, P. (2012, June 11). PV for all: Low-income housing residents going solar. Retrieved February 2, 2020, from Rocky Mountain Institute website: https://rmi.org/blog_pv_for_all _low_income_housing_residents_going_solar/

Scofield, J. H. (2013). Efficacy of LEED-certification in reducing energy consumption and greenhouse gas emission for large New York City office buildings. *Energy and Buildings*, *67*, 517–524. https://doi.org/10.1016/j.enbuild.2013.08.032

Singh, R., & Banerjee, R. (2015). Estimation of rooftop solar photovoltaic potential of a city. *Solar Energy*, *115*, 589–602.

Sovacool, B. K. (2009). Rejecting renewables: The socio-technical impediments to renewable electricity in the United States. *Energy Policy*, *37*(11), 4500–4513.

Steemers, K. (2003). Energy and the city: Density, buildings and transport. *Energy and Buildings*, *35*(1), 3–14. https://doi.org/10.1016/S0378-7788(02)00075-0

Strbac, G., Hatziargyriou, N., Lopes, J. P., Moreira, C., Dimeas, A., & Papadaskalopoulos, D. (2015). Microgrids: Enhancing the resilience of the European megagrid. *IEEE Power and Energy Magazine*, *13*(3), 35–43. https://doi.org/10.1109/MPE.2015.2397336

Strømann-Andersen, J., & Sattrup, P. A. (2011). The urban canyon and building energy use: Urban density versus daylight and passive solar gains. *Energy and Buildings*, *43*(8), 2011–2020. https://doi.org/10.1016/j.enbuild.2011.04.007

Suzer, O. (2015). A comparative review of environmental concern prioritization: LEED vs other major certification systems. *Journal of Environmental Management*, *154*, 266–283. https://doi.org/10.1016/j.jenvman.2015.02.029

Trainor, A. M., McDonald, R. I., & Fargione, J. (2016). Energy sprawl is the largest driver of land use change in United States. *PLOS ONE*, *11*(9), e0162269. https://doi.org/10.1371/ journal.pone.0162269

TRB & BEES. (2009). *Driving and the Built Environment: Effects of Compact Development on Motorized Travel, Energy Use, and CO_2 Emissions* (No. Special Report 298). Washington, DC: National Research Council of the National Academies.

US Energy Information Administration. (2019a, May 10). Use of energy for transportation. Retrieved March 3, 2020, from Use of energy explained website: https://www.eia.gov/ energyexplained/use-of-energy/transportation.php

US Energy Information Administration. (2019b, May 14). How much energy is consumed in U.S. residential and commercial buildings? Retrieved February 2, 2020, from https://www .eia.gov/tools/faqs/faq.php?id=86&t=1

US Green Building Council. (2014, June 6). Checklist: LEED v4 for neighborhood development. Retrieved May 19, 2020, from https://www.usgbc.org/resources/leed-v4 -neighborhood-development-checklist

van Esch, M. M. E., Looman, R. H. J., & de Bruin-Hordijk, G. J. (2012). The effects of urban and building design parameters on solar access to the urban canyon and the potential for direct passive solar heating strategies. *Energy and Buildings*, *47*, 189–200. https://doi.org/ 10.1016/j.enbuild.2011.11.042

White, D. (2008). Site design strategies for solar access. *The Rocky Mountain Land Use Institute*, 11.

17. Leveraging the promise of smart cities to advance smart growth
Robert Goodspeed

INTRODUCTION

The proliferation of digital technologies in cities has sparked a growing interest in the concept of "smart cities," the idea that digital information and communication technologies can be used to address urban problems. This chapter discusses the rise and logic of the smart city idea, arguing that it often takes the form of managerial innovations that, although avoiding some of the political conflicts surrounding smart growth policies, raise new political disputes. As a consequence, the smart city and smart growth ideas now coexist as largely separate debates. In response, this chapter argues that smart growth proponents should engage with digital technologies in two areas related to traditional smart growth policy goals: ensure new technologies such as automated vehicles are deployed in ways that pursue smart growth goals, and upgrade professional tools to better monitor and respond to urban change. By launching initiatives in these two areas, practitioners and scholars can show how smart cities technologies can be leveraged to achieve more sustainable, compact urbanism described by the smart growth principles.

BACKGROUND

The concept of smart cities was not included among the original smart growth principles formulated in the mid-1990s as described by Landis (Chapter 1 of this book), since at that time it was only a niche concept which described a vision pursued by a small number of technologically sophisticated world cities (Gibson et al., 1992; Mahizhnan, 1999). Since then, a variety of information and communication technologies (ICTs) have undergone rapid developments, fueling a boom in the idea's popularity starting in the early 2000s (Hollands, 2008). Unlike in the early 1990s, cities today feature ubiquitous internet connectivity, near-universal smartphone ownership, and mature ICTs to collect, store, and process vast amounts of data—even if access to these technologies remains unevenly distributed, even within wealthy cities. A diverse array of stakeholders have coalesced into a smart cities movement, motivated by a shared belief that ICTs may allow cities to make progress on long-standing urban problems and—for technology companies—a desire to unlock a new market. For the private sector, smart cities seem to open up valuable new markets for products; and for city leaders, technological solutions seem to hold exciting new potential ways of achieving goals.

The original smart growth principles reflected concerns about the effects of low-density and auto-oriented urban development. The principles also helped advocates interested in diverse issues see how a holistic perspective on urban growth policy might link their priorities: for example, by protecting habitat by conserving rural lands while redirecting growth pressures to revitalize center cities (Burchell et al., 2000; Landis, Chapter 1). However, Anthony Downs (2005) points out that the policies required to achieve smart growth trigger opposition among various groups, including rural land owners, homeowners, developers, and historic preservationists. Furthermore, given the structure of local government in most of the United States, with important land use authorities lodged among fragmented local governments, implementing smart growth has required state legislative action (for more on smart growth governance, see M. Bierbaum, Lewis & Chapin, Chapter 2). Although some 20 states have adopted some type of smart growth law or program, these vary widely in their scope and effectiveness (DeGrove, 2005). Many states have seen no interest in state smart growth reforms (Boyle & Mohamed, 2007), and some state smart growth policies have been repealed or diluted (Gray, 2007). Since smart growth policies often trigger debates about controversial issues such as the scope of property rights, the importance of environmental conservation, and public transit investments, smart growth has sparked a cottage industry of critics and defenders (Litman, 2018).

In contrast, the term "smart cities" rose to prominence in the wake of the great recession and sparked a different type of political debate. Propelled by significant marketing campaigns by IBM that used the rubrics "smarter cities," and "smarter planet"—partly as a ploy to seek government clients for technology products, beyond their traditional corporate clients (Alizadeh, 2017; Wiig, 2015)—the term has been used to describe a wide range of projects (Neirotti et al., 2014). Hollands (2008) observes the terms "smart growth" and "smart cities" are occasionally conflated and may overlap to a certain degree, but I agree with his judgment that the two terms refer to distinct ideas (Hollands, 2008, pp. 317, note 314). As I will explain further below, the smart city movement lacks the clear definition that smart growth principles provide to the smart growth movement.

CONTEXT AND LOGIC

In its broadest sense, the concept of smart cities refers to the effective use of digital information and communication technologies (ICTs) to address urban problems. Within that general rubric lie myriad contrasting approaches and definitions, and I will highlight three of the most prominent: smart cities as urban cybernetics, smart cities as new urban districts, and smart citizenship.

Smart City Definitions: Urban Cybernetics, New Urban Districts, and Smart Citizenship

The first school of thought under the smart city umbrella has resurrected the logic of cybernetics, primarily conceiving of smart cities as optimizing the efficiency of city systems (Goodspeed, 2015). In this view, problems are resolved primarily through the use of real-time monitoring and control systems, exemplified by Rio de Janeiro's large control center, Centro das Operações do Rio, or the automated control of infrastructure (Gaffney & Robertson, 2018). This approach can therefore refer to any type of city, but imposes a particular logic upon it, emphasizing the benefits of short-term sensing and control operations, often in lieu of longer-term infrastructure or planning interventions.

The second definition equates smart cities with wholesale development (or reinvention) of city districts, exemplified by large-scale real estate projects such as Abu Dhabi's Masdar Smart City (Cugurullo, 2013), South Korea's Songdo (Yigitcanlar & Lee, 2014), or the many proposed smart cities across Africa and India (Datta, 2015a; Greenfield, 2013). The intense debate surrounding the now-cancelled Sidewalk Labs Quayside proposal for Toronto has brought the many dimensions of these projects to light, in that they raise difficult questions about who has oversight and design control, how data will be handled and owned, how privacy will be protected, and the business model for new infrastructural arrangements (Flynn & Valverde, 2019; Wylie, 2018). Commentators such as Townsend (2013) and Greenfield (2013) critique these top-down smart city projects for neglecting the important lesson of modernism that master-planned developments tend to produce inhumane landscapes lacking the vitality and quality of life of conventional urbanism. Detailed analyses have shown the line between marketing language and reality can be murky: One analysis of South Korea's smart cities finds they fail to live up to the promises, functioning as more conventional real estate developments (Yigitcanlar et al., 2019; Yigitcanlar & Lee, 2014). Ayona Datta (2015b) argues India's smart city initiatives constitute a continuation of utopian thinking and have largely failed to result in new urban development. Another problem with master-planned smart districts is the conflict between the long timelines involved for their planning and construction and the short cycle of technology development, which can render planned smart features obsolete even before the projects are complete.

The final definition is not preoccupied with cybernetic control systems or top-down planning, but instead how ICTs may be leveraged to realize new forms of citizenship. As the first two approaches to smart cities have come under criticism, smart citizenship has attracted growing interest as a way of thinking about smart cities that more effectively incorporates consideration of the interests, rights, and voices of city residents themselves (Waal & Dignum, 2017). In countries such as India, where the prevailing smart city discourse has focused on real estate developments, smart citizenship has been proposed as an approach to using ICTs that is centered on the perspectives, priorities, and needs of poor communities, such as participatory mapping projects aimed at improving urban sanitation or pedestrian safety (Sadoway & Shekhar, 2014).

However, the idea of smart citizenship has inherited the legacy of diverse and complex debates about the concept of citizenship itself, which differs across political theories. For example, Cardullo and Kitchin (2019) analyze smart city initiatives in Dublin, Ireland, through the lens of Arnstein's ladder of citizen participation, itself inspired by the theory of participatory democracy. Their case study found that most "citizen-centric" smart city initiatives were based in a "neoliberal conception of citizenship that prioritizes consumption choice" instead of a notion of citizenship from older political theories based on rights and discussion of the common good (Cardullo & Kitchin, 2019, p. 1), which others have called republican citizenship (Zandbergen & Uitermark, 2020).

Instead of focusing on the differences between neoliberal and republican citizenship, Zandbergen and Uitermark (2020) asked whether new technologies are creating new forms of "cybernetic citizenship". As described above, although urban cybernetics can refer to centralized control centers and systems, it can also refer to approaches that rely on citizen participation to crowdsource information and react to real-time information provided via apps and interfaces. MIT's Senseable City Lab has been a proponent of this approach, creating prototypes such as the Copenhagen Wheel, which gives cyclists a boost, while also crowdsourcing urban environmental information (Ratti & Claudel, 2016; Ratti & Townsend, 2011). Zandbergen and Uitermark explored the relationship between cybernetic citizenship—focused on information flows and not broader questions—and republican citizenship, where involvement in smart cities project results in greater political power. Their detailed case study of a project in Amsterdam where residents collected air quality data revealed that participants experienced both forms of citizenship. They conclude that counter to their expectations, neither dominated in practice, and cybernetic citizenship held "seeds of alternative ways of organizing urban life" (Zandbergen & Uitermark, 2020, p. 1745). Therefore it seems clear that smart city technologies are changing the nature of citizenship for city residents in sometimes surprising ways, suggesting this will continue to be an area of experimentation and scholarship.

Smart Cities in Practice

Shifting from these mainly normative paradigms for smart cities, empirical studies of smart city programs and activities have found remarkably diverse practices, many of which fit neither the cybernetic or master-planned categories. Neirotti et al.'s (2014) review of early smart city initiatives found a wide variety of substantive focus areas. Similarly, Ching's (2013) analysis of smart city programs in several cities did not reveal a single ideology guiding them but instead documented an eclectic collection of ideas. Smart city initiatives in cities such as Amsterdam and Vienna have also pursued diverse goals, such as encouraging energy conservation, new mobility, or reducing waste (Fernandez-Anez et al., 2018; van Winden et al., 2016). One common theme in these programs is that the projects involve a collaboration between public and private stakeholders. Therefore, even this diverse set of smart city projects seems to reflect a shared set of assumptions. In an incisive critique, Vanolo (2013) has argued that the adoption of the smart city concept within European Commission funding programs has resulted in the promotion of a certain model of city development characterized by the comparison of cities through urban charts and benchmarking, shifts in discourse about the role of public–private partnerships, and new expectations for citizens. As a result, perhaps smart cities should be seen as a broader conceptual shift in the goal of urban development, which may be realized in different ways in different cities.

Outside of the normative debates outlined above, it has also become apparent that smart cities technologies can be used to implement technically sophisticated totalitarianism. In another article, Vanolo (2016) points out that within utopian, top-down smart cities, citizens are "invisible and silent political subjects" (p. 31). He notes that dystopian smart cities are also possible, cities where citizens are subjugated within a "totalitarian smartness" through ubiquitous tracking and surveillance. The fear that ICTs may be used to create totalitarian states uninterested in democracy or individual rights has a long history in science fiction, such as George Orwell's *1984*, where televisions with video cameras play a key role in facilitating universal surveillance. In recent years it has been creeping into reality. In China, the state has made extensive use of ICTs to monitor the residents of citizens in Xianjiang province, where over 1 million Uighurs and other minorities have been detained in indoctrination camps (Buckley & Mozur, 2019). In democracies, how to manage privacy and prevent surveillance has been a major debate in smart city projects. In one recent example, a smart streetlight project in San Diego, California, sparked controversy and was discontinued when it was revealed it had only been used by the police to investigate crimes, and not to collect traffic data as originally sold (Holder, 2020).

Smart Cities and Smart Growth

Disregarding extreme utopian and dystopian smart cities that fortunately seem unlikely in most places, smart city innovations may have a role to play in achieving normative goals shared by smart growth, focused on fundamental land use and system design considerations. To take transportation as an example, the success of innovations such as real-time transit information, ICT-enabled mobility solutions such as bike sharing, and real-time trip routing show that technologies can play a role in fostering sustainable travel behavior. Although most smart city projects aim at eking out greater efficiency with existing infrastructure instead of more broadly reshaping cities, many believe greater impacts are possible in newly designed city districts.

To conclude this section, although there is no single accepted definition of a smart city, many of the most popular definitions show the importance of complementing smart cities with smart growth concepts. Through a narrow focus on operational issues, cybernetics operates at a different time scale than the long-term land use, transportation, and infrastructure decisions of planning. New urban districts in smart cities may foster a flawed, top-down model of urbanism, ignoring smart growth's focus on the collaborative development of entire regions. Yet smart citizenship highlights the potential for using ICTs to involve citizens in new ways, perhaps complementing the smart growth principle to "encourage community and stakeholder collaboration in development decisions." The next section considers the intersection of these two movements, suggesting four areas where smart growth proponents could build bridges to smart cities ideas without losing sight of smart growth's orientation toward long-term land use and infrastructure decisions.

IMPLEMENTATION AREAS

Most of the 10 principles promoted by smart growth describe long-term land use development priorities, and therefore may seem distinct from smart city technologies such as urban sensors and connected devices (Smart Growth Online, 2019). The principle with the strongest connection to ICTs is probably "provide a variety of transportation choices," due to the importance of ICTs for transit operations and customer service, such as providing real-time arrival times. However, the traditional focus of smart growth supporters has been on the creation and expansion of transit systems. If we adopt the broadest perspective on smart cities and describe them as cities suffused with ICTs and other new technologies, there could be profound—if highly uncertain—consequences for the fundamental issues of land use and urban form at the heart of smart growth principles.

The first publication to consider the intersection between smart growth and smart cities, William J. Mitchell's (2002) chapter in an edited volume on smart growth, "Electronic Cottages, Wired Neighborhoods and Smart Cities," suggests what the impact of new technologies on urban form may be. Admitting there was limited research available on the topic at the time, since "the conditions and systems that concern me are just beginning to emerge" (2002, p. 67), Mitchell speculates about some of the effects digital technologies may have on cities: loosening spatial linkages between places due to telecommuting, more people working outside of traditional workplaces, and changing logistics networks. He offers only a few concrete planning implications related to these speculations, including accommodating live/work units through zoning and redesigning neighborhoods to provide more services for employees who work at home.

One way in which smart city ideas may require modification of the original smart growth principles concerns the ways in which new technology has changed the nature of urbanization (Mitchell, 2002). At the most basic level, this refers to the small but important area of professional practice concerned with equitable access to digital connectivity. In rural areas, this involves broadband planning (McMahon et al., 2012), and in cities can encompass efforts to develop municipally-owned internet service providers, create community-based digital networks, foster digital literacy, and expand access through public kiosks and WiFi (Hovis, 2017). Mitchell speculated that ICTs might spark the need to plan for "electronic cottages" and new forms of "wired neighborhoods," concepts that seem misplaced in a world where every home and every neighborhood has some degree of internet connectivity.

However, shifts in the adoption of urban technology are raising new patterns of transportation and land use that may deserve more nuanced normative principles within a smart growth framework. One notable example has been the rise of app-based ridesourcing services and home-sharing apps such as Airbnb, which facilitate new patterns of using housing and have sparked diverse regulatory approaches based on local housing markets, perceptions of owner rights, and local priorities. Planners can and should create normative principles for the regulations of these services, to ensure their adoption serves the broader urban sustainability goals reflected in the smart growth principles. There is no question that ICTs are resulting in broader changes in the economy and society, including dramatic changes to retailing and wholesaling caused by the growth in e-commerce, and this demands planning responses, including the regulation of app-based home sharing or ridesourcing services. Yet these changes have largely added new issues to the urban planning agenda instead of changing the fundamental form of cities. Broad changes in two areas, only one of which Mitchell identifies, pose the greatest potential to fundamentally alter the structure of urban life: the rise of remote employment and the adoption of automated vehicles.

Today, smart cities and smart growth coexist as generally disconnected concepts for progressive urban reform. Whereas smart growth has developed a reputation as a clearly articulated, yet politically fraught concept, proposed smart city approaches vary. Smart cities concepts have the added benefit of resonating well with the contemporary political climate, which is interested in innovation, entrepreneurship, and private sector innovation. But it is a dangerous mistake for the smart growth community to dismiss smart cities entirely. I argue that both movements will likely coexist in the future, and therefore propose two general areas of implementation activity: ensuring new technologies reinforce smart growth principles, and upgrading professional tools to take advantage of new data and technology.

Ensure Smart City Technologies Reinforce Smart Growth

One important area of implementation for smart growth proponents is to be engaged with the development and application of new technologies to ensure they are used to reinforce—and not undermine—smart growth principles. This section discusses two technological trends that currently have unclear long-term impacts on cities but deserve the close attention of professional urban planners: telecommuting and automated vehicles. In addition, I discuss the issue of equity. Although not included among the original smart growth principles, equity has emerged as a new principle shared among many communities and practitioners, as Lung-Amam and June-Friesen describe in Chapter 14.

Telecommuting

Mitchell (2002) was prescient to identify the development of home-based workers as a potentially significant development for cities. The growth in telecommuting has been a subtle but important shift in many cities, and is perhaps one factor that explains shifting preferences in the real estate market toward more accessible locations. Mitchell correctly observes that home-based workers may appreciate proximity to services and locations for social interaction, which very much aligns with the smart growth principles to mix land uses and create walkable neighborhoods. However, the adoption of telecommuting has persistently lagged behind its proponents' optimistic predictions about how widespread it could become (Streitfeld, 2020).

The COVID-19 pandemic, although still unfolding at the time of this writing, has resulted in the rapid expansion of telecommuting and clarified why this trend may not pose as significant a change as Mitchell expected. First, it has highlighted how a significant portion of the workforce holds jobs which quite simply can't be done at home, including transportation and logistics, manufacturing, retail, and many service sector jobs. Second, among those who have been able to work from home, both employees and employers perceive a mix of benefits and drawbacks, making the long-term trend unclear (Dunn, 2020; Streitfeld, 2020). Although it seems clear COVID-19 may boost telecommuting for an extended period, and therefore may be an important factor for the planning and design of neighborhoods with high densities of home-based workers, it remains to be seen what proportion of the workforce will permanently adopt telecommuting (Khazan, 2020).

Automated vehicle technology

The second area where new digital technologies may have a significant and long-lasting impact on the land use and transportation patterns of cities is the introduction of automated vehicles (AV). The focus of significant investment in recent years, AV technology has sparked speculation about how it may impact cities, with some saying the convenience and ease of AV may result in further decentralization. However, AV development must grapple with a wide range of fundamental uncertainties, such as: whether the technology or regulations will result in vehicles that can travel at all times in all locations or only in more limited ways; whether the vehicles will be privately owned or deployed for ridesharing or transit; whether infrastructure will be redesigned for AV; and how policymakers will choose to regulate and tax the technology (Zmud et al., 2015). As a consequence, a recent review of scenarios about how AV may affect urban form found a wide variety of perspectives (Stead & Vaddadi, 2019). Most of the 13 academic and practitioner scenario studies predicted AV may reduce the need for parking spaces, improve the attractiveness of the urban environment, and allow for more efficient use of transport infrastructure. The studies were inconsistent on perhaps the most important impact, that on the urban form of the city as a whole. This broader impact has been investigated through modeling and simulation studies that seek to capture interactions between transportation and land use systems.

A larger group of studies have investigated how the introduction of AVs will affect general travel behaviors and land use patterns. A review of 37 such studies (Soteropoulos et al., 2019) observed that these studies generally concluded that the adoption of private AV could increase vehicle miles traveled and reduce public transport use, but shared AV could have benefits such as the reduction of parking spaces and total number of vehicles. However, Soteropoulos et al. (2019) point out that all of these results are sensitive to many uncertain assumptions. One careful agent-based simulation analyzing how residential location choice may be affected by the adoption of shared AV illustrates the potential for nuanced effects on land use patterns (Zhang & Guhathakurta, 2018). The simulation shows some households shift further away from employment centers while others may move slightly closer to the center of the city. The continued importance of neighborhood amenities and schools that are present only in particular neighborhoods, partially offset by increased preference for urban areas by certain demographic groups, explains this result. Although Zhang and Guhathakurta's model predicts increased commuting distances, they point out that shared automated vehicles also "can make compact development more appealing by offering more convenient services with less average waiting time in densely developed neighborhoods" (Zhang et al., 2018, p. 12).

One recent project in which a team of University of Maryland researchers constructed sophisticated and detailed scenarios for the Baltimore–Washington region in 2040 illustrates the uncertainty facing all regions (Prospects for Regional Sustainability Tomorrow Project, 2018). The project's "Revenge of the Nerds" scenario featured widespread adoption of AV, which their models predicted would cause further decentralization of housing and jobs, resulting in the greatest losses to forests, farmland, and targeted ecological areas. However, the project also considers three other plausible scenarios, which lack AV, illustrating the possibility for achieving more sustainable outcomes. A major difference between the scenarios is vehicle operating cost—the researchers assume AV will reduce costs by 75% from the baseline, but this can be affected by policies such as tolls and taxes. The conclusion is clear: regional futures remain uncertain, and smart growth proponents should remain engaged in the AV debate to ensure the new technology does not inadvertently undermine longstanding sustainability goals.

Equity

As Lung-Amam and June-Friesen have outlined in Chapter 14, although social equity was not part of the original smart growth principles, it has slowly become more central to the smart growth movement even as many tensions remain within contemporary smart growth coalitions. Therefore, in addition to asking whether smart city technologies may change land use or transportation patterns in undesirable ways, we should also ask whether smart city technologies will hinder—or advance—the emerging smart growth principle of equity, which envisions a just and fair society. Since smart cities technologies are still evolving, practitioners interested in social equity can answer this question by examining two related issues: whether new technologies are accessible to and benefit all urban residents, and whether smart city technologies are designed to meet the specific needs of diverse residents.

The first concern is whether smart city technologies are accessible and valuable to privileged groups. Too often, smart city technologies are deployed only in certain privileged areas, yet present their benefits as being more widely enjoyed. However, even when widely available, app-based systems and interfaces often require people to have smartphones with ample data plans. Online interfaces and services also may not be available to households without modern computers and broadband connections. It has become evident that many broader urban technologies, such as app-based ridesharing services, have been most readily adopted by technologically sophisticated, well-educated residents (Rayle et al., 2016). The heart of this issue is a tension between norms from the private sector, which focuses on a group of users or customers, and the norms of the public sector, which seeks to serve everyone. In one concrete example, Gebresselassie and Sanchez (2018) surveyed transport apps, showing that only a small proportion included universal design and the disability functionality required for apps to reach broad audiences.

Beyond ensuring equitable access to smart city technologies, we should also ask whether smart city technologies are serving the needs of vulnerable communities, such as low-income communities of color. Recent research on this issue explored the needs and perspectives of West Baltimore residents regarding smart city technologies, using focus groups and surveys (Lung-Amam et al., 2019). Researchers found that this community did not perceive some existing smart city technologies—such as connected trash cans and surveillance cameras used by the police—to serve their needs. Instead, they called for smart city initiatives for better WiFi connectivity, job training, and more usable transit. To help ensure that smart city projects result in "equitable, community-centered, and place-based smart city plans and investments," the authors recommend community engagement happens at the initiation of projects (Lung-Amam et al., 2019, p. 1).

As outlined above, the concept of social equity does not figure prominently in most smart city definitions, and this is one area where major tensions may arise between the smart city and smart growth approaches. However, it may also be an area for fruitful collaboration between the two fields, as the smart growth movement can offer equity frameworks, expertise, and community engagement experience to help ground smart city innovations in community needs and help prevent technologies from increasing social inequality.

Upgrade Professional Tools to Better Monitor and Respond to Urban Change

The second general area for implementation is for smart growth proponents to take advantage of new data and technology to upgrade their professional tools so they can better monitor urban changes and respond through planning based on the best quality information and analysis.

Mapping land use change with remote sensing

New technologies allow planning professionals to have unprecedented insight into changes occurring across entire regions. Maps illustrating the expansion of urban areas, and related measures that compare land consumption to population growth, have been central to policy debates about smart growth policies in several states (e.g., Fulton et al., 2001), and figure prominently in important scholarly works such as Barnett & American Planning Association (2007). This author of this chapter vividly recalls former Maryland Governor Parris Glendening giving a lecture featuring maps that illustrated the growth of urbanized land in the state, dramatically showing how suburban development—in bright red—consumed large amounts of land. These maps are readily produced from national datasets such as the National Land Cover Database (NLCD), a longstanding product of the Multi-Resolution Land Characteristics consortium of federal agencies. However, this type of data is not used as widely in planning as it could be. One challenge has been the coarse nature of categorization within the data, which typically classifies all land in metropolitan regions as one of three intensities of "urban" land use. Another reason is the long time-lags associated with NLCD products: at the time of writing, the most recent data available is four years old. Two categories of new data help overcome these problems.

Advancements in the collection, storage, and processing of remotely sensed imagery are revolutionizing the potential of this technology to monitor landscape changes. New techniques, such as random forest models, can derive spatial data about trees, buildings, and roads from aerial images (Gounaridis et al., 2020). Remotely sensed imagery and data are now available at unprecedented temporal resolution, making it possible to rapidly monitor change over large landscapes. For example, the startup company Planet (planet.com) offers daily, high-resolution imagery (3 meter and 72 centimeter resolution) obtained from a fleet of over 120 satellites. Technical advancements in the tools for storing and analyzing the resulting imagery mean it can be more readily converted into useful products, and smart growth advocates could leverage this to identify hotspots of urban growth where targeted and proactive planning or land conservation activities may be needed. Regional planning agencies and university-based research centers should develop rapid response programs to monitor, and publicize, losses to environmentally sensitive lands due to urban development.

Fostering data sharing and urban sensing

Although remotely sensed data will never replace the fine-grain understanding possible from parcel-level administrative datasets, it avoids the data sharing obstacles that face regional planners who must knit together data from dozens, and sometimes hundreds, of local jurisdictions to obtain a regional understanding of development patterns. Remotely sensed data also allows for monitoring in places where administrative datasets are not updated regularly, or contain omissions or errors. One solution to data sharing pursued by Boston's Metropolitan Area Planning Council (MAPC) has been to collect development information through a public website called MassBuilds (massbuilds.com) (Goodspeed et al., 2012). The website allows the public and other key stakeholders, such as municipal staff and other state agencies, to contribute information. Unlike a one-off survey, the website serves as an infrastructure for ongoing data collection activities. All regions could benefit from such a system, which can be readily implemented by leveraging this initial system as well as regional planning and real estate entities, who have a shared interest in seeing a complete picture of development trends.

Many smart city technologies and projects can result in valuable data about emerging urban issues. Ridesharing and urban sensing are two timely examples where this is already starting to occur. Mandated data-sharing between ridesourcing companies and governments in New York, Chicago, Massachusetts and other places has helped planners understand the impact of the ridesourcing in those cities (Berg, 2019). This fine-grain data will help planners understand what policies can encourage ridesourcing trips that have a positive impact on sustainability, such as those that encourage use of transit by providing last-mile connections to stations or provide an emergency ride home, and craft policies to ensure an overall sustainable mix of modes. An interest in urban equity and expanding research documenting the harmful effects of common pollutants has resulted in growing concern about urban air quality. Due to the dynamic and localized nature of air pollution, cities have lacked a detailed understanding of this important issue. The advent of smart city urban sensing projects, such as Chicago's Array of Things (https://arrayofthings.github.io/), are creating urban environmental data on attributes like air quality with unprecedented precision from over 100 locations in Chicago.

Upgrading planning support systems

Finally, an important development within land-use planning in the past two decades is the expanding adoption of planning support systems (PSS) to model and analyze land use patterns at the regional, city, and local scales (Brail, 2008; Geertman et al., 2017; Holway et al., 2012). PSS are often the means through which data are brought into the planning process in a useful way. Knaap and Lewis (2011) observe that GIS data and analysis have played a role in several notable regional plans. These projects have often adopted scenario planning methods (Goodspeed, 2020). Although many of these PSS tools have long histories, often dating back to GIS applications from the 1990s, they are only now entering into wider adoption. The advent of new, web-based geospatial technologies is introducing a new era in PSS, including commercial tools such as UrbanFootprint, which greatly improve practitioner ability to draw on GIS data and model alternative land use patterns (Goodspeed et al., 2017). Shifting to web-based data infrastructures has also allowed planners to more readily analyze and visualize alternative scenarios. Therefore, using these tools provides direct benefits to professional practice by improving the analytical methods and highlighting the concrete benefits of smart growth development. In addition, this technology provides a venue for planners to engage with other professions involved in the smart growth field using the language of data, without sidelining planning's distinctive focus on the long-term consequences of land use and infrastructure decisions. More professionals should adopt web-based scenario planning tools to ensure their plans are accompanied by vivid online maps and persuasive metrics.

CONCLUSION

Smart growth is a progressive reform movement among built environment professionals aimed at creating more sustainable cities, through a primary focus on land use and infrastructure. In contrast, although nominally aiming at some of the same goals, the most popular definitions of smart cities are either focused on short-term operational improvements or long-term but spatially limited utopias. As a result, this chapter has argued that smart growth proponents should engage with smart cities carefully, in ways that do not compromise the focus on traditional smart growth principles. The smart growth community should remain closely engaged with new technologies such as automated vehicles that hold the potential to either reinforce or undermine their principles. In addition, the smart city movement reflects developments in ICTs that planning professionals should move quickly to adopt. As this book points out, the original smart growth principles require some updating to reflect evolving debates about topics such as climate resilience, equity, public health, and energy. The smart growth movement should seek a thoughtful integration of these issues in ways that do not lose focus on the issues that remain the fundamental building blocks for sustainable urbanization.

REFERENCES

Alizadeh, T. (2017). An investigation of IBM's Smarter Cites Challenge: What do participating cities want? *Cities, 63*, 70–80. doi:https://doi.org/10.1016/j.cities.2016.12.009

Barnett, J., & American Planning Association. (2007). *Smart growth in a changing world.* Chicago, IL: American Planning Association.

Berg, N. (2019). Inside the transportation data tug of war. Retrieved from https://theoverheadwire.com/2019/03/inside-the-transportation-data-tug-of-war/

Boyle, R., & Mohamed, R. (2007). State growth management, smart growth and urban containment: A review of the US and a study of the heartland. *Journal of Environmental Planning and Management, 50*(5), 677–697. doi:10.1080/09640560701475337

Brail, R. K. (2008). *Planning support systems for cities and regions.* Cambridge, MA: Lincoln Institute of Land Policy.

Buckley, C., & Mozur, P. (2019, 23 May). How China uses high-tech surveillance to subdue minorities. *The New York Times*, p. A1. Retrieved from https://www.nytimes.com/2019/05/22/world/asia/china-surveillance-xinjiang.html?auth=login-email&login=email

Burchell, R., Listokin, D., & Galley, C. (2000). Smart growth: More than a ghost of urban policy past, less than a bold new horizon. *Housing Policy Debate, 11*(4), 821–879.

Cardullo, P., & Kitchin, R. (2019). Being a 'citizen' in the smart city: Up and down the scaffold of smart citizen participation in Dublin, Ireland. *GeoJournal, 84*(1), 1–13. doi:10.1007/s10708-018-9845-8

Ching, T.-Y. (2013). *Smart cities: Concepts, perceptions and lessons for planners.* (Master in City Planning), MIT, Cambridge.

Cugurullo, F. (2013). How to build a sandcastle: An analysis of the genesis and development of Masdar City. *Journal of Urban Technology, 20*(1), 23–37. doi:10.1080/10630732.2012 .735105

Datta, A. (2015a). A 100 smart cities, a 100 utopias. *Dialogues in Human Geography, 5*(1), 49–53. doi:10.1177/2043820614565750

Datta, A. (2015b). New urban utopias of postcolonial India: 'Entrepreneurial urbanization' in Dholera smart city, Gujarat. *Dialogues in Human Geography, 5*(1), 3–22. doi:10.1177/ 2043820614565748

DeGrove, J. M. (2005). *Planning policy and politics: smart growth and the states.* Cambridge, MA: Lincoln Institute of Land Policy.

Downs, A. (2005). Smart growth: Why we discuss it more than we do it. *Journal of the American Planning Association, 71*(4), 367–378. doi:10.1080/01944360508976707

Dunn, J. (2020). How to work from home alongside your partner without losing it. *The New York Times.* Retrieved from https://www.nytimes.com/2020/03/20/parenting/coronavirus -work-from-home-spouse.html?searchResultPosition=3

Fernandez-Anez, V., Fernández-Güell, J. M., & Giffinger, R. (2018). Smart City implementation and discourses: An integrated conceptual model. The case of Vienna. *Cities, 78,* 4–16. doi:https://doi.org/10.1016/j.cities.2017.12.004

Flynn, A., & Valverde, M. (2019). Planning on the waterfront: Setting the agenda for Toronto's 'smart city' project. *Planning Theory & Practice,* 1–7. doi:10.1080/14649357 .2019.1676566

Fulton, W., Pendall, R., Nguyen, M., & Harrison, A. (2001). *Who sprawls most? How growth patterns differ across the U.S.* Brookings. https://www.brookings.edu/research/who -sprawls-most-how-growth-patterns-differ-across-the-u-s/

Gaffney, C., & Robertson, C. (2018). Smarter than smart: Rio de Janeiro's flawed emergence as a smart city. *Journal of Urban Technology, 25*(3), 47–64. doi:10.1080/10630732.2015 .1102423

Gebresselassie, M., & Sanchez, T. W. (2018). "Smart" tools for socially sustainable transport: A review of mobility apps. *Urban Science, 2*(2), 45.

Geertman, S., Allan, A., Pettit, C. J., & Stillwell, J. (2017). *Planning support science for smarter urban futures.* New York, NY: Springer Berlin Heidelberg.

Gibson, D. V., Kozmetsky, G., & Smilor, R. W. (1992). *The Technopolis phenomenon: Smart cities, fast systems, global networks.* Savage, MD: Rowman & Littlefield Publishers.

Goodspeed, R. (2015). Smart cities: Moving beyond urban cybernetics to tackle wicked problems. *Cambridge Journal of Regions, Economy and Society, 8*(1), 79–92. doi:10.1093/ cjres/rsu013

Goodspeed, R. (2020). *Scenario Planning for Cities and Regions: Managing and Envisioning Uncertain Futures.* Cambridge, Mass.: Lincoln Institute of Land Policy.

Goodspeed, R., Pelzer, P., & Pettit, C. (2017). Planning our future cities: The role computer technologies can play. In T. W. Sanchez (Ed.), *Planning knowledge and research* (pp. 210-225). New York: Routledge.

Goodspeed, R., Spanring, C., & Reardon, T. (2012). Crowdsourcing as data sharing: A regional web-based real estate development database. Paper presented at the *Proceedings of the 6th International Conference on Theory and Practice of Electronic Governance,* Albany, New York, USA.

Gounaridis, D., Newell, J. P., & Goodspeed, R. (2020). The impact of urban sprawl on forest landscapes in Southeast Michigan, 1985–2015. *Landscape Ecology.* doi:10.1007/s10980 -020-01075-9

Gray, R. C. (2007). Ten years of smart growth: A nod to policies past and a prospective glimpse into the future. *Cityscape,* 109–130.

Greenfield, A. (2013). *Against the smart city (The city is here for you to use)* (pp. 153).

Holder, S. (2020, 6 August). In San Diego, 'smart' streetlights spark surveillance reform. *Citylab*.

Hollands, R. G. (2008). Will the real smart city please stand up? *City*, *12*(3), 303–320.

Holway, J., Gabbe, C. J., Hebbert, F., Lally, J., Matthews, R., & Quay, R. (2012). *Opening access to scenario planning tools*. Lincoln Land Institute. https://www.lincolninst.edu/sites/default/files/pubfiles/opening-access-to-scenario-planning-tools-full-v2.pdf

Hovis, J. (2017). CTC President Joanne Hovis testifies before U.S. House Subcommittee: 'Broadband: Deploying America's 21st Century Infrastructure'. Retrieved from https://www.ctcnet.us/blog/ctc-president-joanne-hovis-testifies-before-u-s-house-subcommittee-broadband-deploying-americas-21st-century-infrastructure/

Khazan, O. (2020, May 4). Work from home is here to stay. *The Atlantic*.

Knaap, G.-J., & Lewis, R. (2011). Regional planning for sustainability and the hegemony of metropolitan regionalism. In E. Seltzer & A. Carbonell (Eds), *Regional planning in America: Practice and prospect* (pp. 176–221). Cambridge, MA: Lincoln Institute of Land Policy.

Litman, T. (2018). *Evaluating criticism of smart growth*. Victoria, BC: Victoria Transport Policy Institute.

Lung-Amam, W., Bierbaum, A. H., Parks, S., Knaap, G.-J., Sunderman, G., & Stamm, L. (2019). Toward engaged, equitable, and smart communities: Lessons from West Baltimore. *Housing Policy Debate*, 1–19. doi:10.1080/10511482.2019.1672082

Mahizhnan, A. (1999). Smart cities: The Singapore case. *Cities*, *16*(1), 13-18. doi:http://dx.doi.org/10.1016/S0264-2751(98)00050-X

McMahon, K., Thomas, R. L., & Kaylor, C. (2012). *Planning and broadband: Infrastructure, policy, and sustainability*. (Planning Advisory Service report, no. 569). American Planning Association.

Mitchell, W. J. (2002). Electronic cottages, wired neighborhoods and smart cities. In T. S. Szold & A. Carbonell (Eds), *Smart growth: Form and consequences* (pp. 66–81). Cambridge, MA: Lincoln Institute of Land Policy.

Neirotti, P., De Marco, A., Cagliano, A. C., Mangano, G., & Scorrano, F. (2014). Current trends in Smart City initiatives: Some stylised facts. *Cities*, *38*(0), 25-36. doi:http://dx.doi.org/10.1016/j.cities.2013.12.010

Prospects for Regional Sustainability Tomorrow Project. (2018). *Engaging the future: Baltimore-Washington 2040*. Retrieved from College Park, MD: http://www.umdsmartgrowth.org/wp-content/uploads/2018/04/39317-UMD-Printing-Presto-Long-report-FINAL-1.pdf

Ratti, C., & Claudel, M. (2016). *The city of tomorrow: Sensors, networks, hackers, and the future of urban life*. New Haven; London: Yale University Press.

Ratti, C., & Townsend, A. (2011). The social nexus. *Scientific American*, *305*(3), 42–48. doi:10.1038/Scientificamerican0911-42

Rayle, L., Dai, D., Chan, N., Cervero, R., & Shaheen, S. (2016). Just a better taxi? A survey-based comparison of taxis, transit, and ridesourcing services in San Francisco. *Transport Policy*, *45*, 168–178. doi:10.1016/j.tranpol.2015.10.004

Sadoway, D., & Shekhar, S. (2014). (Re)prioritizing citizens in smart cities governance: Examples of smart citizenship from urban India. *The Journal of Community Informatics*, *10*(3).

Smart Growth Online. (2019). *Smart growth principles*. Retrieved from https://smartgrowth.org/smart-growth-principles/

Soteropoulos, A., Berger, M., & Ciari, F. (2019). Impacts of automated vehicles on travel behaviour and land use: An international review of modelling studies. *Transport Reviews*, *39*(1), 29–49. doi:10.1080/01441647.2018.1523253

Stead, D., & Vaddadi, B. (2019). Automated vehicles and how they may affect urban form: A review of recent scenario studies. *Cities, 92*, 125–133. doi:https://doi.org/10.1016/j.cities .2019.03.020

Streitfeld, D. (2020, 30 June). The long, unhappy history of working from home. *The New York Times*. Retrieved from https://www.nytimes.com/2020/06/29/technology/working -from-home-failure.html?searchResultPosition=6

Townsend, A. M. (2013). *Smart cities: Big data, civic hackers, and the quest for a new utopia.* New York: W.W. Norton & Company.

van Winden, W., Oskam, I., van den Buuse, D., Schrama, W., & van Dijck, E.-J. (2016). *Organising smart city projects: Lessons from Amsterdam.* Amsterdam: Hogeschool van Amsterdam.

Vanolo, A. (2013). Smartmentality: The smart city as disciplinary strategy. *Urban Studies, 51*(5), 883–898. doi:10.1177/0042098013494427

Vanolo, A. (2016). Is there anybody out there? The place and role of citizens in tomorrow's smart cities. *Futures, 82*, 26–36. doi:https://doi.org/10.1016/j.futures.2016.05.010

Waal, M. d., & Dignum, M. (2017). The citizen in the smart city. How the smart city could transform citizenship. *it – Information Technology, 59*(6), 263. doi:https://doi.org/10.1515/ itit-2017-0012

Wiig, A. (2015). IBM's smart city as techno-utopian policy mobility. *City: Analysis of Urban Trends, Culture, Theory, Policy, Action, 19*(2-3).

Wylie, B. (2018). Searching for the smart city's democratic future. *Centre for International Governance Innovation, 13*.

Yigitcanlar, T., Han, H., Kamruzzaman, M., Ioppolo, G., & Sabatini-Marques, J. (2019). The making of smart cities: Are Songdo, Masdar, Amsterdam, San Francisco and Brisbane the best we could build? *Land Use Policy, 88*, 104187. doi:https://doi.org/10.1016/j.landusepol .2019.104187

Yigitcanlar, T., & Lee, S. H. (2014). Korean ubiquitous-eco-city: A smart-sustainable urban form or a branding hoax? *Technological Forecasting and Social Change, 89*, 100-114. doi: 10.1016/j.techfore.2013.08.034

Zandbergen, D., & Uitermark, J. (2020). In search of the smart citizen: Republican and cybernetic citizenship in the smart city. *Urban Studies, 57*(8), 1733–1748. doi:10.1177/ 0042098019847410

Zhang, W., & Guhathakurta, S. (2018). Residential location choice in the era of shared autonomous vehicles. *Journal of Planning Education and Research*. doi:10.1177/ 0739456X18776062

Zhang, W., Guhathakurta, S., & Khalil, E. B. (2018). The impact of private autonomous vehicles on vehicle ownership and unoccupied VMT generation. *Transportation Research Part C: Emerging Technologies, 90*, 156–165. doi:https://doi.org/10.1016/j.trc.2018.03.005

Zmud, J., Tooley, M., Baker, T., & Wagner, J. (2015). *Paths of automated and connected vehicle deployment: Strategic roadmap for state and local transportation agencies.* Retrieved from http://d2dtl5nnlpfr0r.cloudfront.net/tti.tamu.edu/documents/161504-1.pdf

PART VII

UNFINISHED BUSINESS: WHERE DOES SMART GROWTH GO FROM HERE?

18. Toward a "Smart Growth 2.0"

Gerrit-Jan Knaap, Rebecca Lewis, Arnab Chakraborty, and Katy June-Friesen

The previous chapters in this handbook introduced the concept of smart growth and its governance followed by analyses of issues that were and were not addressed by the 10 original principles of smart growth. Authors have offered evidence that smart growth has been the focus of considerable research and has influenced planning practice throughout the United States. In this concluding chapter, we revisit the conditions smart growth was designed to address and the influence of smart growth on planning practice. We discuss the challenges of smart growth implementation, and we offer recommendations for a "smart growth 2.0" going forward.

First, we briefly examine the discourse about smart growth and its principles among the general public, the planning profession, the media, and the academy. Next, we explore the extent to which smart growth principles have become embedded in land use plans and policies. We then present and discuss data on smart growth-related trends at the national level to see if there have been significant changes in the areas smart growth was designed to address. Here we draw on the previous chapters to see what insights may help explain these changes, or lack thereof. Finally, we offer our thoughts on what smart growth has accomplished over the last 25–30 years and where the movement needs to go from here.

THE RISE AND FALL OF SMART GROWTH

Smart growth was conceived as a fresh approach to urban development that sought to change the form and location of growth as an antidote to urban sprawl. The prescription included containing growth within existing urban areas, preserving natural resources, and creating neighborhoods that are mixed use and walkable, with transportation and housing options and a sense of place. As described by Landis (Chapter 1), these principles were promoted by a broad network of mostly Washington-based organizations, supported by the foundation community and promoted nationwide using modern public relations strategies and techniques.

The Smart Growth Movement

Promoters of smart growth included the nation's premier planning organization (American Planning Association), the nation's premier developer organization (Urban Land Institute), the nation's premier real estate organization (National

Association of Realtors), the Clinton–Gore administration, and a broad network of government agencies and professional organizations (Smart Growth Network). As a result, the concept spread quickly. After Maryland Governor Parris Glendening signed the Smart Growth and Neighborhood Conservation Act in 1997, he won prestigious awards and national acclaim (Pelton, 2018). After leaving office, Glendening joined Smart Growth America, a national advocacy organization dedicated solely to the promotion of smart growth principles. Led by Smart Growth America, smart growth advocates produced policy reports, slide shows, websites, videos, talking points, and technical assistance programs, and they organized annual national conferences. Never before had there been such a concerted effort to promote a prescribed approach to land use.

Over the last 25–30 years, however, support for smart growth at the federal level waxed during Democratic administrations and waned during Republican administrations. Smart growth was never an explicit campaign issue in presidential elections, but it was embedded in platforms that addressed transportation, housing, and environmental policy. At the state and local levels, however, the debates were more explicit. Gubernatorial, mayoral, and city council candidates campaigned explicitly on their support for smart growth, or for some other carefully worded agenda—such as balanced, reasonable, or fair growth—that emphasized or de-emphasized certain elements of smart growth. How much smart growth actually became embedded in federal, state, and local policy, however, remains difficult to assess.

Smart Growth as a Topic of Inquiry

Knaap et al. (2021) examined interest in smart growth since the mid-1990s by the general public, the planning profession, and the popular media in a recent working paper. The paper tracked how frequently the term "smart growth" and related terms appeared in Google searches, conference programs of the American Planning Association, requests for information submitted to APA's Planning Advisory Service (PAS),[1] and newspapers from four major metropolitan areas in the United States. In addition to "smart growth," the exercise involved tracking the terminology of related planning paradigms, such as "growth management," "sustainable development," and "new urbanism," as well as terms that represent the principles of smart growth, such as: mixed use, compact development, infill, redevelopment, multi-modal, walkability, and sense of place.

While recognizing that limited insights can be drawn from such word searches, Knaap et al. found that searches for and use of the term smart growth peaked in the late 1990s and early 2000s (see Figure 18.1). Requests for information about smart growth in PAS reports peaked in 1998; the term smart growth appeared most frequently in the APA conference program in 2004; and Google searches for "smart growth" declined after 2004 (the first year information on Google searches is available). Not surprisingly, the largest number of Google searches for smart growth came from Maryland and the District of Columbia, the state leader in smart growth and the home of many development advocacy organizations, respectively. A particularly interesting finding of Knaap et al. is that, over time, as searches for and use of the term "smart growth" declined, searches for and use of terms that reflect smart growth principles remained steady. The number of searches for the terms "infill," "sense of place," "multimodal," and "mixed used" grew to exceed searches for the term "smart growth," especially for "mixed use." These results suggest that while interest in the term smart growth by planning professionals and the general public has dissipated over time, interest in multiple smart growth principles endures.

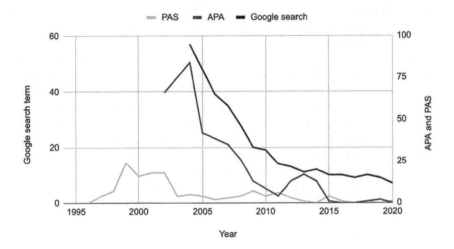

Figure 18.1   Google searches, conference program mentions, and requests for information about "smart growth"

Knaap et al. also explored the appearance of "smart growth" and related terms in four major metropolitan newspapers: *The New York Times, The Washington Post, The Baltimore Sun,* and *The Oregonian* (see Figure 18.2). The term appeared most often in *The Washington Post*, where it peaked in 2002, appearing 260 times over the course of the year, and fell steadily in subsequent years. In all four newspapers, terms that represent smart growth principles—such as "infill," "redevelopment," "walkable," "affordable housing," and "revitalization" generally appeared more frequently than "smart growth," in some cases substantially more. The terms "gentrification" and "public health" increased the most in usage in recent years. Similar to the findings from Google searches, PAS reports, and APA conference programs, the terminology used in news media suggests that while interest in smart growth has dissipated over time, interest in smart growth principles—such as mixed use, compact development, and walkability—endures. Further, the newspaper results reveal a distinct regional variation in the use of "smart growth," with the term more common on the East Coast than the West Coast, and most popular in Washington metropolitan region media.

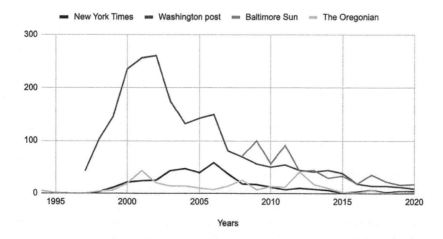

Figure 18.2   *Number of articles in four major metro newspapers that mention "smart growth," 1995–2020*

Peng (2020) explored the prevalence of the term "smart growth" in the academic literature. He found that use of the term grew rapidly after 1996 until about 2008, when the number of publications using the term in academic journals leveled off. The journal that published the most papers on smart growth has always been the *Journal of the American Planning Association*. Peng concludes that smart growth remains a topic of active academic research in a wide variety of disciplinary journals. Most of the papers are published by scholars based in the United States at East Coast and West Coast universities.

These findings suggest that over the last 25–30 years, popular and professional interest in the term "smart growth" has faded, while interest in the terms that reflect principles of smart growth has not. It may be that the general public and professional planners have become so familiar with the term "smart growth" and the concepts it connotes that there is no reason to seek further information about it, and in the case of professional practice, smart growth concepts continue to guide planners' thinking. In the case of the popular press, however, it is more likely that the issues once addressed under the banner of smart growth are now described using other terms, such as urban resilience or sustainable development. While "smart growth" is no longer the contemporary term of art, the issues it connotes remain widely discussed and reported—that is, same wine, new bottles.

That academics continue to use "smart growth" in the titles and keywords of their publications—while professional planners and the public at large seem to have moved on—is interesting. This suggests that the issues under the banner of smart growth continue to elicit inquiry in academic circles, and that academics continue to use the term as a label to describe a planning paradigm.

The Adoption of Smart Growth Principles

It is also difficult to assess the extent to which smart growth principles have influenced the plans and policies of state and local governments. In Chapter 1, Landis suggests that the influence of smart growth can be found in the plans of the 20 fastest growing cities and counties in the United States. He writes that "it would be a mistake to conclude that the smart growth movement has not had a significant impact."

Case studies and examples of tools used to implement smart growth abound. Many of these case studies and examples of "best practice" have been provided by smart growth advocacy organizations, such as Smart Growth America, and the US Environmental Protection Agency. Several academic papers have also explored the adoption of smart growth principles and tools in particular places at particular times. These include Talen and Knaap (2003), who found a lack of smart growth principles in the zoning ordinances of Illinois communities; Ramírez de la Cruz (2009) who, in a survey of land use regulations in Florida from 2002 to 2007, found fewer than one-third of municipalities had any form of growth containment instruments, less than two had density bonus provisions, and less than two "smart growth zoning" tools. Edwards and Haines (2007), in an examination of the comprehensive plans of small local governments in Wisconsin, found little evidence that smart growth principles had been adopted. While these results are disappointing for smart growth advocates, they are not surprising given the dates and locations where these studies were conducted.

The most comprehensive survey of local land use regulations was recently published by the Urban Institute.[2] It contains information about land use regulations by local governments in 1994, 2003, and 2019 for approximately 17,000 jurisdictions in the 50 largest metropolitan areas in the United States. Although the results vary by region and type of jurisdiction, they suggest that between 2003 and 2019, the maximum densities allowed by zoning have not increased, the number of governments with urban growth boundaries or other urban containment tools decreased, and the number of local governments with adequate facilities ordinances decreased. While these results also are disappointing from an advocacy perspective, Pendall et al. (2021), based on a more thorough analysis of these data, draw a more nuanced conclusion:

> Our research reaffirms that the majority-suburban United States has an array of enormously varying localities deploying highly divergent regulatory approaches toward multifamily housing; the trend in zoning from 2003 to 2019 reflects that diversity, defying a simple overarching narrative. But at least two major trends appear to characterize the period. In the first trend, high-density zoning became more common and low-density zoning less so in the most constrained housing markets. ... In the second trend, weaker markets with high levels of Black–White segregation downzoned to [low density zoning] more often than they upzoned from [low density zoning]. (Conclusion section)

Given the mixed results and limitations of these data, Pendall et al.'s findings are far from definitive. A deeper analysis could perhaps unmask significant regional variations between fast and slow growing regions and between progressive and more conservative political culture (see, for example, Richter 2020). But the findings are also far from encouraging.

In Chapter 2, M. Bierbaum, Lewis, and Chapin illustrate how elements of Maryland's smart growth program were adopted by at least eight other states. They conclude that outside of Maryland and Connecticut, state-level smart growth policies were somewhat a "flash in the pan" that faded as new governors took office and attention turned to other topics. Many of the programs have been repealed or disappeared from public view. In some states, such as New York, remnants of smart growth grant programs remain. Other states explicitly rolled back policies during the Tea Party era while some policies suffered from lack of support from new governors and legislatures.

In the 1990s and early 2000s, several scholars produced state-level inventories of smart growth policies adopted by states. Bolen et al. (2002) conducted a detailed state-by-state review of smart-growth-like programs to inform policy makers in California. Wilson and Paterson (2003) examined smart growth and open space policies in a project funded by the Congressional Research Service. DeGrove (2005) wrote several in-depth case studies to document the politics and adoption of smart growth policies in select states. But scholars and other organizations such as the Institute for Business and Home Safety have not produced consistent, updated databases to describe current smart growth policies.

In sum, the extent to which smart growth policies have been embedded in the plans, regulations, and investments by state and local government remains highly uncertain. Research on this question is sparse and dated and not very encouraging. Although Landis found smart growth principles embedded in the plans of the fastest growing cities and counties in the United States, other limited case study research on implementation of smart growth principles at the local level suggests that many local governments did not incorporate smart growth principles in the 1990s. And the recently released data by the Urban Institute suggest not much has changed in US land use regulations since then. Further, as M. Bierbaum et al. (Chapter 2) discuss, there was considerable evidence that states were beginning to adopt or promulgate smart growth principles in the late 1990s and early 2000s, but that momentum waned, and there is little evidence available now to ascertain how much still remains.

HAS PROGRESS BEEN MADE ON THE ISSUES SMART GROWTH WAS DESIGNED TO ADDRESS?

As suggested by many of the previous chapters, smart growth was established as an antidote to urban sprawl, a pejorative term for a particular urban form. Urban form, however, has many dimensions that have been measured at varying scales (Clifton et al., 2008). Here we present and discuss measures of urban form and a few of its consequences at the national level. These measures must be interpreted carefully and with many caveats. National measures cannot reveal differences at the subnational scale. Thus, even if national measures suggest little change has occurred, considerable change might have occurred in some cities, metropolitan areas, or states. What's more, data on national trends offer few insights into the causes of those trends or changes, making it virtually impossible to identify the impacts of smart growth. For these reasons, we make no assertions that these national trends reflect the success or failure of smart growth. In some cases, it is likely that trends would have changed without the adoption of smart growth policies; in other places trends might have changed for reasons that have nothing to do with smart growth; and in still other places improvements could be offset by setbacks in others.

Finally, we fully acknowledge that we offer but a very limited set of indicators that at best provide a partial glimpse at development patterns of recent years. For some smart growth principles, such as "mix land uses" or "foster sense of place", pertinent data just do not exist; in other cases, the data is too limited in time and place. In yet other cases, such as travel behavior or housing markets, the data are extensive but too detailed to report more fully here. In these cases, we intentionally present data on measures, such as vehicle miles traveled and housing affordability, that do not capture important nuances in travel behavior and housing markets but do offer important summary insights.

The Location of Urban Development: Compact Development, Resource Preservation, and Infill

Perhaps the most fundamental tenet of smart growth is that urban development should occur at greater densities than what has occurred in most of the post-war period, preferably within the existing urban envelope, and with minimum loss of farmland, forests, and other natural resources. Unfortunately, over the last two decades at the national level, there is not much evidence of progress in this regard. Urban densities have continued to fall,[3] though more slowly than in previous decades, and farmland has continued to disappear (see Figures 18.3 and 18.4). Infill is more the exception than the rule, as 30 percent of population growth occurred in urbanized areas between 1990 and 2000 but only 17 percent between 2000 and 2010 (Figure 18.5). Acres of forest land, however, have held steady, perhaps even increasing slightly (Figure 18.6). Further, as shown in a working paper by Lewis et al. (2013), between 1990 and 2010, urban density gradients flattened, central city densities fell, only a small share of urban development occurred within existing urban envelopes, and most new development occurred at the urban fringe at very low densities. Similar analyses have not been conducted using 2020 census data, and there is evidence that suggests there are regional exceptions to these trends (Landis, 2017), but at the national level, there is little evidence to suggest that urban growth is being contained or occurring at densities that preserve natural resources. Again, it is important to note that smart growth has never been a policy that was formally or informally adopted at the national level; hence, none of the trends we present represent indicators of the success of smart growth policies. They do, however, suggest that the challenges smart growth was meant to address have not significantly abated at the national level.

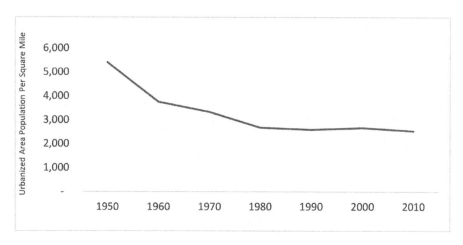

Figure 18.3   Urbanized area population per square mile, 1950–2010

The lack of progress in this area is clearly unfortunate. As discussed by Carruthers, Wei, and Wostenholme (Chapter 3) and by Hanlon (Chapter 5), there is mounting evidence that compact development reduces the cost of public services (if retrofitting is not required) and results in less driving, impervious surface area, and greenhouse gas emissions. Evidence also suggests that containing urban growth can foster urban revitalization, though perhaps at the cost of rising and volatile housing prices.

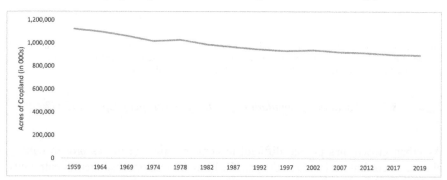

Note: Time periods vary based on the data availability.

Figure 18.4   Acres of farm cropland, 1959–2019

The reasons for this lack of progress in containing and densifying urban growth are not difficult to identify. The Urban Institute data reveal that urban growth boundaries have not become commonplace. Further, according to Carruthers et al. (Chapter 3), urban growth boundaries tend to work best in regional planning frameworks— Oregon having the best-known example. As discussed by M. Bierbaum et al.

(Chapter 2), however, land use policy remains dominated by local governments, which must respond to local political pressures. What's more, at the local level, few urban residents welcome higher densities, especially in their own neighborhoods, and few rural residents like development restrictions, especially on their own property. Hence, except in a few progressive jurisdictions, urban containment has limited political support at the local level. With limited local support, and in the absence of a regional framework, urban growth boundaries, urban service areas, greenbelts, transferable development rights, and tax incentive programs have all had limited trials and even less success at containing urban growth.

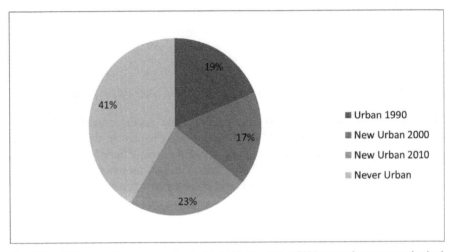

*Note:*Urban 1990 means the area was urbanized in 1990; New Urban 2000 means the area was urbanized between 1990 and 2000; New Urban 2010 means the area was urbanized between 2000 and 2010; and Never Urban means the area was never urbanized, all according the the US Census.

Figure 18.5   Location of population growth by census geography, 1990–2010

As urban growth has proven difficult to contain, urban infill has proven equally elusive, according to Hanlon (Chapter 5). In many metropolitan areas, central city populations have grown substantially (Schuetz & Ring, 2021), stimulated in part by what Carruthers et al. (Chapter 3) call the consumer city. Infill and inner-city revitalization have also been spurred by brownfield redevelopment programs, transit-oriented development initiatives, zoning reforms, and renovation incentives. But barriers to infill development remain formidable. Further, suggests Hanlon (Chapter 5), the suburbanization of poverty, rapid changes in automobile technologies, and the effects of the COVID-19 pandemic could all make urban infill even more difficult in the future. But this remains to be seen.

In addition, as discussed by Newburn, Lynch, and Wang (Chapter 4), much of the containment challenge lies in the exurban fringe, where large-lot development

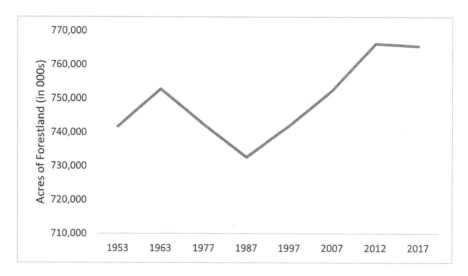

Figure 18.6   *Acres of forestland, 1953–2017. Note that intervals between dates vary*

typically occurs on septic systems, creating landscapes unsuitable for wildlife and badly configured for large scale farming. They further suggest that urban growth boundaries can contain development at moderate suburban densities, but not at very low exurban densities. Incentive instruments such as priority funding areas and tax deferment programs, furthermore, have been even less effective at protecting resource land, while transferable development rights and farmland purchase options tend to leave behind a scattered patchwork of developed and undeveloped properties. Without regulatory restrictions on development on septic systems, they suggest, this kind of urban sprawl will remain difficult to arrest. And in very few places is there adequate political support for such rigid regulatory restrictions.

The Form of Urban Development: Housing Choice, Sense of Place, and Mixed Uses

Trends at the national level suggest that smart growth is not occurring within the urban envelope either. Although there are no data at the national level on mixed-use development, or development with a sense of place, national data on housing affordability, construction type, and household size are not encouraging. Housing became increasingly difficult for low- and moderate-income households to afford (Figure 18.7); that single family housing continues to dominate housing construction (Figure 18.8), even as average household size continues to fall; and average single family home size in square feet continues to rise.

According to Dawkins and Kim (Chapter 8), the smart growth approach to housing choice involves (1) extra-urban reforms, which expand housing choice by, ironically, restricting development outside urban areas; and (2) intra-urban reforms, which provide a wider range of housing types inside urban areas. Consistent with the findings on urban containment, Dawkins and Kim find that extra-urban reforms tend to decrease the supply of land and housing and thus increase their prices. It is puzzling, however, to find that development constraints fail at containing urban growth yet succeed at raising housing prices. Research on intra-urban housing policies also generally finds that land use regulations increase housing prices, decrease housing affordability, and increase the probability of foreclosure. Even policies that are designed to increase the construction of multi-family and affordable housing have been found to have unintended price effects. Inclusionary zoning is explicitly intended to increase the supply of affordable housing, yet it has been found to increase the price of housing that is not price restricted, and shift construction to multifamily units (Bento et al., 2009). New urbanist and other expressly smart growth developments, meanwhile, have been found unaffordable to most low-income households.

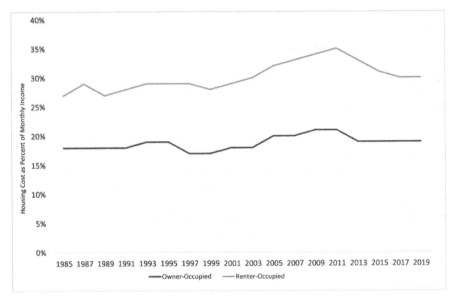

Figure 18.7   *Median housing cost as a percentage of monthly income,*
                  1985–2019

While there are few data on the extent of mixed land use, even at the local level, Song (Chapter 6) demonstrates that land use mix has been an extensive area of research, much of it focused on how to measure land use mix. She finds that it has been measured in many ways, but all measurements show that land use mix helps to reduce driving and, in many cases, increases property values. Further, she notes that form-based zoning codes, planned unit developments, and new urbanist designs

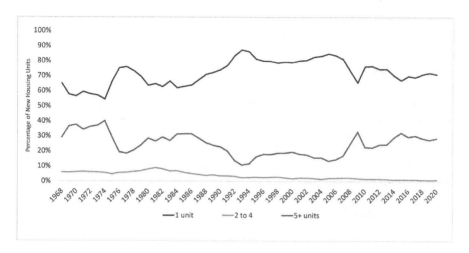

Figure 18.8   Percent of new housing starts by type and share, 1968–2020

foster more land use mixing. The extent to which these have been adopted with favorable results, however, remains unknown.

Similarly unknown is the extent to which the smart growth movement has helped to create distinctive communities with a strong sense of place. Drawing on design principles established long ago, Talen (Chapter 7) identifies normative design principles that should help create a strong sense of place. These include compactness, diversity, enclosure, connectivity and well-defined edges. Form-based codes, she argues, hold the greatest promise for fostering sense of place. Further, she suggests, urban design that follows her normative design principles create value and produce improvements in social relations, health, and safety.

Travel Behavior: Walkability and Transportation Alternatives

The smart growth principles that promote walkability and transportation choice are designed to influence travel behavior primarily by shaping development patterns and public investments in transportation infrastructure. National trends in travel behavior, unfortunately, suggest progress has been slow to nonexistent. After falling during the great recession, vehicle miles traveled (VMT) per capita has again started to rise (Figure 18.9). These patterns in VMT are reflected in travel mode share to work, which remains dominated by the single passenger automobile (Figure 18.10). Transit ridership to work has fallen since the 1970s and has remained stagnant since the 1990s at 5 percent. Not surprisingly, the number of vehicles per household continues to increase, although there has been some increase in households with no automobiles.

The adverse effects of continuing dependence on automobility are thoroughly described by Welch and Gehrke (Chapter 10). Effects include increases in greenhouse gas emissions, air pollution, and water pollution, as well as diminished human health, and more. Considerable research has focused on the determinants of travel mode choice, especially travel by car. While the 5Ds—density, diversity, distance, design, and destination—all seem to have some impact on travel behavior, the effects of density have received the most attention. So much so that a consensus has formed that driving decreases with development density, but not by very much (Stevens, 2017). From a national perspective, however, the point is moot since development densities at the national level continue to fall. Smart growth advocates have sought to decrease dependence on the automobile in a variety of other ways. These include investments in pedestrian and biking infrastructure, transit-oriented development, parking management, and the complete streets design approach. Welch and Gehrke offer evidence to suggest that these strategies can make a difference; but again, at the national scale, the extant changes in urban form are too small to cause significant declines in automobile travel.

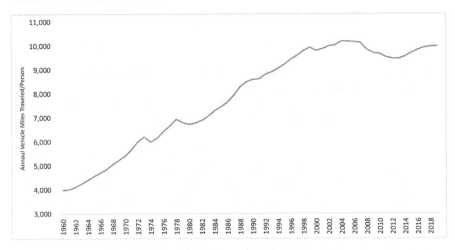

Figure 18.9   Annual vehicle miles traveled per person, 1960–2019

As one of the alternatives to driving, walking suffers from the same conundrum. There is little question that walking has social and health benefits. And as described by Clifton (Chapter 9), considerable research has focused on how to measure the "walkability" of urban environments and which elements of walkability are most effective at getting people to walk. Again, research confirms that walkability can be shaped by the 5Ds, but also that walkable environments produce other favorable outcomes, such as higher and more stable property values over time. However, the evidence seems to suggest that increases in the walkability of urban environments have resulted in more walking in some places and by some demographic groups, but not enough to elicit significant increases in walking at the national scale. Walking as a mode choice to work has decreased since the 1970s and remained stagnant since the 1990s at approximately 3 percent. Pedestrian fatalities decreased from the 1980s

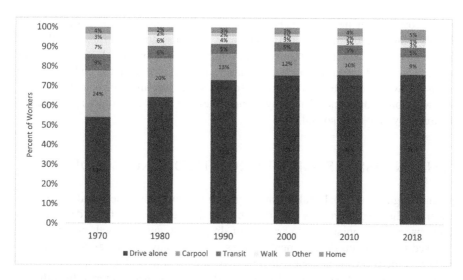

Figure 18.10   Mode of travel to work by percent of workers, 1970–2018

through 2010 but have been rising in recent years, though not to the peak levels of the 1980s (Figure 18.11).

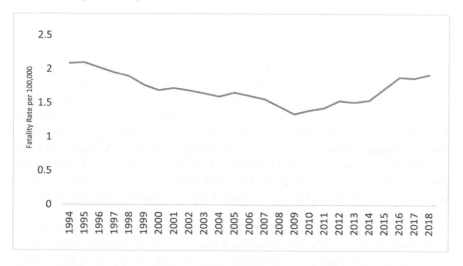

Figure 18.11   Pedestrian fatality rate per 100,000 people, 1994–2018

In sum, while use of the term "smart growth" by the general public and the planning profession has faded, interest in the principles of smart growth have endured—some more so than others. Perhaps more importantly, a large volume of research confirms that the principles have merit. Compact growth, mixed uses, infill development, and resource preservation have important environmental benefits, though in some cases social costs. When measured in Ds, these characteristics also seem to reduce automobility, vehicle miles traveled, and greenhouse gas emissions. Unfortunately, there is little evidence in national measures of development location, development form, or travel behavior that significant progress has been made. We cannot say whether these measures would have been worse if not for the smart growth movement, but we can say with some confidence that many of the issues that smart growth was promoted to address have not been solved.

SALIENT ISSUES SMART GROWTH DID NOT ADDRESS

Even though the original goals of smart growth remain elusive, new challenges have risen in salience and are now inextricable from debates on urban form, development patterns, and the pursuit of smart growth. In general, smart growth principles are focused primarily on development patterns and their environmental consequences, with less focus on social issues such as education, public health, social equity, and gentrification, all of which are closely linked to development patterns. In addition, the original smart growth principles were silent on energy, climate change, and technology. In recent years, many of these issues associated with urban growth have become increasingly relevant and pressing and thus warrant further attention by smart growth advocates.

Education and Public Health

Success in urban containment and revitalization requires strategic investments in public infrastructure such as roads, wastewater services, public transportation, parks, and more. Educational facilities and the services they provide at all levels are among the most fundamental public investments that shape the social dimensions of urban form. Education and workforce training are key to social mobility and thus have profound impacts on who lives where and who gets what. As A. Bierbaum et al. (Chapter 11) suggest, educational institutions have critical impacts on the pattern and the prevalence of social segregation, the spatial structure of neighborhoods, and the landscape of workforce development. They note, "Schools are often a reflection of their neighborhood demographics."

Schools have played a key role in shaping the pattern of racial segregation in US metropolitan areas. Quality educational resources have tended to follow White populations to the suburbs, which further accelerated White flight. School quality is a major factor in household location choice, at least for households with enough income to have such choice. Poorly resourced inner-city schools are barriers that prevent the redirection of growth from the urban periphery to places that are already walkable, mixed use, and served by transit.

In addition, the design and location of school facilities has a major impact on the design and function of neighborhoods. Schools represent a centerpiece of community activity and thus shape travel behavior of not only students but a broad spectrum of community residents. School siting and design can thus serve as an effective instrument for shaping the growth and character of urban neighborhoods.

Like public schools, the efficacy and location of workforce development programs are major determinants of the "geography of opportunity;" where people live shapes their opportunities for quality education, jobs, and other resources. Research has shown the geography of opportunity within metropolitan areas not only has profound impacts on residents' social welfare and social mobility, but can have long-term impacts on the growth and development of metropolitan areas.

The spatial structure of the city, according to Garfinkel-Castro and Ewing (Chapter 12), also has a profound influence on public health through impacts on physical activity, traffic accidents, mental health, and respiratory ailments. The physical activity of urban residents is heavily shaped by the travel behaviors of those residents. Metropolitan areas that encourage automobility in effect discourage active travel modes such as walking and biking. Walking and biking are also influenced by the extent and configuration of public parks, trails, and sidewalks.

Traffic accidents are also shaped by travel behavior. While public investments that create separation between pedestrians and cars can facilitate faster travel speeds, they also produce more fatal traffic accidents, while investments that facilitate more modal integration can have the opposite effect. Urban environments that feature the smart growth principles of density, walkability, and sense of place can also have beneficial impacts on mental health, Garfinkel-Castro and Ewing suggest.. Finally, urban designs that foster less automobility and VMT create less air pollution and help reduce aggregate exposure to air pollutants. Exposure to air pollution is disproportionately borne by low-income residents who live in high-density, high-traffic areas.

Gentrification and Social Equity

Gentrification is an old problem that, as described by Finio and Knaap (Chapter 13), has risen in prominence over the last two decades. Definitions of gentrification vary, but implicit in the root of the expression is the replacement of lower income residents by higher income residents. This can be caused by a variety of factors—changes in government plans or regulations, investments in public infrastructure such as transit or other urban amenities, or the process of neighborhood succession, as described by the urban ecologists of the 1930s (Park, 1936). With reinvestments in city centers creating major changes in many metro areas, housing becoming increasingly unaffordable to lower income residents, and racial segregation on the rise, gentrification has become a pressing public policy concern.

Several principles of smart growth are intended to redirect urban expansion and enhance the physical form and function of inner cities. These include principles that promote urban containment, urban infill, mixed use, walkability and sense of place. If successful, such physical changes are likely to induce social changes that could be described as gentrification. As Finio and Knaap (Chapter 13) suggest, smart growth advocates failed to consider the social consequences of the principles they promoted. This raises two important questions: (1) is it possible to achieve smart growth without instigating social change that increases inequity, and (2) what can be done to mitigate such negative impacts of successful smart growth.

Finio and Knaap make clear that conceptually it is possible to build compact, mixed use, and walkable communities in existing urban areas without displacing existing residents. But it is difficult and unlikely. Further, they demonstrate with data from Washington, DC; Riverside, California; Memphis, Tennessee; and Portland, Oregon, that displacement tends to occur more extensively in metro areas that have adopted smart growth policies than those that have not. Perhaps more importantly, they suggest, smart growth advocates must now promote policies such as inclusionary zoning, right of first refusal, affordable housing tax credits, housing trust funds and more if they are to achieve their smart growth goals but avoid gentrification.

As Lung-Amam and June-Friesen (Chapter 14) make clear, concerns about smart growth policy and urban equity extend beyond the problem of gentrification, especially in the era of Black Lives Matter. For the reasons described above, equitable growth advocates and smart growth advocates have had an uneasy relationship, again partly driven by the separation of the physical and social aspects of urban policy and planning. Whereas early messaging by smart growth advocates focused on environmental preservation and the plight of soccer moms, equitable growth advocates grounded their message in social justice and civil rights. More recently, these agendas have come closer together, particularly during the Obama administration when the US Environmental Protection Agency, the US Department of Housing and Urban Development (HUD), and the US Department of Transportation formed the Partnership for Sustainable Communities.

Under the Partnership for Sustainable Communities, grants were awarded to metropolitan-wide partnerships, often led by metropolitan planning organizations (MPOs). Based on consent decrees that grew out of lawsuits against HUD, as well as a growing body of research that revealed the importance of neighborhood effects, access to opportunity was a key organizing principle of these partnership projects. As described by Lung-Amam and June-Friesen (Chapter 14), grantees created metro-level sustainable community plans designed to ensure that residents of all income levels have legitimate access to opportunity, including jobs, quality education, affordable housing, and more. The implementation success of these plans, however, has been mixed and, in some places, was short lived under the Trump administration (Avin, 2018). However, these planning processes created new partnerships and new approaches to combining smart growth and equity concerns in a sustainable development agenda.

Climate, Energy, and Technology

Climate change was not seen as a critical concern when the smart growth principles were first established in the early 1990s. Yet, as Hendricks and Berke (Chapter 15) describe, many principles of smart growth are germane for the mitigation of, and adaptation to, climate change. Roughly two-thirds of greenhouse gas (GHG) emissions in the United States come from the transportation and built environment sectors. Smart growth principles, research has shown, have the potential to reduce GHG emissions from those sectors. And, as national data show, emissions have been reduced over the years. But it would be hard to assert that smart growth played a significant role in those reductions. Smart growth can reduce emissions by reducing VMT, but VMT has not fallen. Smart growth can reduce emissions through compact development, but growth has not been compact. Smart growth can reduce emissions by preserving farm and forest land, yet only forest land has been preserved. Most of the reductions in emissions have instead come from fuel substitution and technological change. While the Transportation Research Board and the National Research Council (2009) suggest smart growth can play a role in addressing climate change in the future, it will not be a large role because of the barriers to smart growth implementation and the durability of the built environment.

Hendricks and Berke also argue that smart growth is relevant for climate change adaptation, but they reveal how a sample of new urbanist developments failed to incorporate well-known adaptation measures and concentrated growth in climate vulnerable locations. They also suggest smart growth has failed to incorporate rising concerns about environmental justice.

On the energy front, Becker and Kaza (Chapter 16) note that smart growth principles are also silent on issues that pertain to energy conservation, even though many smart growth principles can help minimize energy consumption. Just as compact growth, transportation options, and land preservation can help reduce VMT, these principles can also help reduce energy consumption. National data suggest there is progress in this regard, though changes in technology and enhancements in energy efficiency—not smart growth—are the most likely source.

Becker and Kaza also raise concerns heretofore not widely discussed. Specifically, much of the infrastructure required for energy generation and transmission has a large land footprint. Further, renewables may take up vital open space, locations historically used for agriculture and wildlife habitat. Even more acutely, biomass and biofuel crops have land use requirements far greater than those of any other energy source. Thus, the decarbonization of energy systems requires substantial land consumption and directly contravenes the compact development principle that underlies smart growth.

Furthermore, the decarbonization of energy is geographically differentiated. Geography, geology, and geoclimate all matter. That makes it very difficult to prescribe principles that conserve energy appropriate for all locations. Perhaps the best smart growth principle for energy conservation, therefore, is to tailor energy policies and practices to local built and natural environments.

One way to tailor energy and other urban systems, according to Goodspeed (Chapter 17), is through the adoption of smart cities technologies. "Smart" in this case refers not to the spatial structure of cities and regions but to the use of sensors, data analytics, and communications technologies to enhance the performance of urban systems. Originating in the private sector, and heavily promoted by technology firms, smart cities technologies are less politically controversial but often require substantial investments in hardware, software, consulting expertise, or all three.

When combined, however, their implementation can enhance efficiency in the transportation, energy, communications, public service, residential, commercial, and other urban sectors without land use regulation or changes in development patterns.

Goodspeed also describes, however, how smart cities technologies can help improve the planning process. Using advanced computer models, highly detailed and remotely sensed data, and sophisticated scenario planning techniques, planners can explore alternative futures in new and compelling ways. Such technologies also have the potential to engage citizens in the planning process through real-time and crowd-sourced data collection and digitally enhanced public meetings.

Goodspeed cautions, however, that smart city technologies and smart growth principles do not always align. In the transportation sector, for example, transportation on demand, telecommuting, and automated vehicles all have the potential to reduce congestion and further the efficient use of the transportation infrastructure. At the same time, such technologies also have the potential to reduce the attraction to centralized workplaces, increase congestion, and facilitate greater urban sprawl. To capture the benefits of smart cities technologies while minimizing their costs, Goodspeed suggests, smart growth advocates must find new ways to incorporate rapidly changing technologies within the smart growth paradigm.

THE CHALLENGE OF IMPLEMENTATION

Questions about the validity of smart growth principles and the efficacy of policies to promote them have spurred large volumes of research by academics, legal scholars, and advocacy organizations over the last 25–30 years. Economists found that development constraints and regulations indeed raised land prices and lowered housing affordability, but often varied with local contexts. Engineers found that mixed use, high density urban environments lowered VMT, but not by much. Financial analysts found that compact growth makes it less costly to provide urban public services, but only if retrofitting is not required. Planners found that in states that promoted smart growth, more local governments adopted smart growth policies, although the direction of causation remains in question. As a result, by the second decade of the twenty-first century, a near consensus had formed in the planning community that smart growth was a better approach to urban development than the sprawl pattern of yesteryear. A 2012 paper published in the *Journal of the American Planning Association* that questioned the normative merits of smart growth development was bitterly disputed and became one of the most widely discussed papers in the journal's history (Echenique et al., 2012).

Yet evidence that urban growth in the United States is growing smart is in short supply. Yes, there is evidence that in some metropolitan areas, some parts of central cities have experienced renewal, that mixed-use and mixed-income developments are more common, that street networks in some places are more connected with fewer cul-de-sacs, that town centers create a convivial sense of place, and that acres of land protected from development continue to grow. But as shown in multiple nationwide trends, key urban growth indicators continue to move in the wrong direction. Why has this happened?

In 2005, Anthony Downs (2005) pondered why we discuss smart growth more than we do it. His answers include the following:

- Most Americans are accustomed to sprawl and its consequences, but they are not at all sure what would happen to them under smart growth approaches.
- There is very little willingness by local or state government officials to shift any degree of power over local land use decisions from local to regional or state levels.
- To protect the values of their homes, most homeowners are reluctant to permit into their neighborhoods any housing units that would sell for less than their own homes.
- The relative utility of other modes of travel—such as walking, biking, or transit—as compared with private cars remains exceedingly low for most US residents.
- Shifting new development from an outward-oriented sprawl pattern into a more inward-oriented compact pattern typically increases "red tape" in the development process.
- The compact growth pattern dictated by smart growth principles restricts the ability of rural land-owners to capitalize on further sprawl development.

None of these impediments to smart growth implementation has dissipated over the last 25–30 years, some may have grown in today's hyper-partisan political environment, and rural interests have a disproportionate influence in state government. In addition, the last 25–30 years have brought to the fore new issues tied to the process of urban development that smart growth advocates cannot ignore. The impacts of climate change on communities are more strongly recognized, but the response of national leadership remains inadequate and mired in partisanship. The obesity epidemic marches on, compounded by COVID-19, tying more closely the challenges of public health with those of urban form. Concerns about racial justice exploded following the murder of George Floyd, elevating related concerns that gentrification can exacerbate lack of access to quality education, workforce training, and other opportunities. Finally, rapid changes in technology have created the potential for better planning and analysis but also a deepening digital divide and greater pressures for transportation-driven decentralization.

TOWARD A "SMART GROWTH 2.0"

Although much has been learned about smart growth over the past 25–30 years, the challenges of growing smart have become even more formidable. If the movement for smart growth is to remain viable, it must not only regain momentum for implementing its original—though perhaps revised—principles, but also broaden its scope to meet the critical challenges of the twenty-first century. This will require progress at each and all levels of government.

At the National Level

The start of a new administration is an ideal time to renew a federal commitment to smart growth, either under the same name or a new Biden-era term. Although urban issues were not at the fore in the last presidential campaign—save Trump's intimation that low-income people of color threaten the safety of suburban neighborhoods (Trump & Carson, 2020)—climate and infrastructure were prominent in the Biden platform. Both represent good opportunities to embed and expand principles of smart growth.

At this writing, there is considerable discussion of a large-scale infusion of federal resources toward the expansion and rehabilitation of public infrastructure. Current drafts of the infrastructure bill include significant funding for roads, bridges, airports, shipping terminals, and public transit. Done right, such funding for urban infrastructure could dramatically increase walkability and transportation choice; done wrong, it could cement our dependence on the automobile for the next several generations.

Most fundamentally, funding for infrastructure should support multi-modality. That means a reasonable allocation of funding for pedestrian, bicycle, and transit infrastructure. Further, grants to states for road maintenance and expansion should be conditioned on assurances that impacts will be addressed regarding induced travel, land development, air and water quality, neighborhood preservation, and public health. This is particularly true for infrastructure that supports autonomous vehicles. At the same time, generous support should be provided for building electric vehicle infrastructure. Of course, all these transportation infrastructure initiatives should come with workforce development programs targeted at low-income and minority residents, with the goal of expanding access to opportunity. One way to prevent infrastructure expenditures from causing more harm than good is to enable state and local government to have sufficient time to prioritize and consider the ramifications of alternative spending strategies. Federal spending requirements with short time frames are almost certain to create more damage than progress.

Whether part of an infrastructure package or package of climate initiatives, the federal government should launch new programs that address climate change. Almost any policy that reduces GHG emissions is also likely to promote smart growth. A large volume of research suggests that a carbon tax might have the greatest effect on reducing emissions *and* promoting smart growth, though the politics of passing such a tax are difficult, to say the least. Perhaps more politically feasible is federal funding and technical support for state climate planning. Such statewide or regional plans, as in California, could provide the leverage needed for meaningful progress toward more compact growth and fewer vehicle miles traveled.

On the housing front, HUD must continue its efforts to reduce regulatory barriers to affordable housing. This has been pursued by several administrations without much success. What is needed are not more studies or blue-ribbon commissions.

Instead, what is needed are strong financial commitments for affordable and fair housing. A recommitment to affirmative fair housing has already begun and must continue.[4]

The federal government should also reconsider institutional reform. Coordination among federal agencies is always problematic. The Partnership for Sustainable Communities was a step in the right direction, although far from a smashing success. To enhance the efficacy of the sustainable growth partnership, new partnerships could work to more closely integrate transportation and housing policies and perhaps expand to include the Departments of Health and Human Services, Education, Agriculture and Energy (Urban Institute, 2021).

With these additional agencies on board, a new federal partnership could expand federal support for smart growth to include health, equity, education, climate, and energy. Adding additional agency partners might be less important, however, than changing federal rules that currently impede cooperation and coordination among federal agencies. Perhaps even more effective would be an urban subcabinet that includes an even larger array of federal agencies. The need for a concerted federal approach to cities is currently far beyond the scope or capacity of HUD, and long overdue.

At the State Level

At the state level, it is hard to imagine the revival of a "quiet revolution" in an era when state legislatures are more likely to curtail voting rights than expand the role of state government. But pressures to address climate change, social equity, and housing affordability are mounting, and there are some simple and some difficult things states can do to move toward a "smart growth 2.0."

To begin, states should review the framework that underlies land use planning authority. Many states have a set of goals, principles, or visions that articulate land use planning goals for the state. These may be no more than the "whereas" statements in authorizing legislation or, for example, the more formal goals and guidelines Oregon uses as the basis for state review of local plans. These should be revisited and revised to assure that climate change, social equity, affordable housing, human capital, public health, and urban technology are expressly addressed.

One strategy for reinvigorating smart growth at the state level, however, lies in climate action planning. To date, 33 states have adopted some form of a climate plan.[5] Many of these climate plans include GHG inventories and broad GHG reduction goals. A smaller set include policies to reduce GHG emissions on topics ranging from energy efficiency to VMT. A very small set of states have adopted and implemented funding and regulations to reduce GHG emissions. A few states directly address VMT through encouraging investments in transit, non-motorized transportation, and electric vehicles (e.g., California, Oregon, and Washington). Linking these plans to local land use plans could force or incentivize local governments to adopt plans and regulations that limit GHG emissions though smarter growth strategies, much as criteria air pollutants do for metropolitan planning organizations, and as California currently does for GHG.

States can also revisit education funding formulas to assure a more equitable distribution of state education expenditures. It is well known that reliance on property taxes favors students in more affluent school districts. And the pursuit of high-quality education is what drives many households to the suburbs (Rothbart, 2020).

At the Regional Level

Regions have always been the weakest layer in the marble cake of land use governance, though as M. Bierbaum et al. (Chapter 2) discuss, Metropolitan Planning Organizations (MPOs) rose in prominence during the Obama administration. This should continue. MPOs have played a critical role in transportation planning for many decades, which makes obvious sense. In California, MPOs also play an important role in climate policy, which also makes sense. But for a few exceptions, most MPOs have limited ability to implement their plans or to integrate land use with transportation, housing, and environmental policy at the regional level. Given what we have learned about disparities in access to opportunity, the case for housing policy at the regional level is nearly as compelling as the case for transportation policy at the regional level. Again, California's fair share housing policy offers a useful example, although it has been mired in implementation challenges. Similar policy adoption in other states and regions is unlikely, however, unless such requirements are written into federal infrastructure or climate legislation.

At the Local Level

Most likely, land use planning and many other government policies that shape development patterns will always be most directly addressed at the local level. This is why land use reform is so difficult. Nationally significant change requires action by the thousands of local governments that blanket the nation. There are, of course, many things local governments can do to promote smarter growth. Many if not most of the ideas first suggested in *Getting to Smart Growth* (International City Management Association, 2002) are still quite viable. But there are other more systemic things that can be done.

Zoning reform is perhaps most fundamental. At a minimum, zoning codes should be reviewed to identify changes that would make housing development easier, more diverse, and profitable in the right places. Inclusionary zoning is one increasingly popular instrument, but there are other ways to contain urban growth while facilitating affordable housing within the existing urban footprint. At present there is a growing movement to weaken if not abandon single family zoning. Such strategies allow accessory, townhome, or other medium density housing in some single-family zones. Such a change in single family zoning could significantly reduce regulatory barriers to housing construction and diminish the regulatory foundations of social segregation (Schuetz, 2020). States could also play a leading role in this effort.

More substantial change might include a movement toward form-based codes, which focus less on use and density and more on urban form and design. These kinds of zoning reforms not only have the potential to foster more mixed uses with a strong sense of place, but also represent strategies that can break down barriers to affordable housing and reduce VMT.

But zoning reform alone will not suffice to produce smarter growth. There must also be significant changes in the form and function of transportation systems. Walking, biking, transit, and other forms of micro-mobility will not soon replace the automobile. But electric vehicles (EVs) are very slowly replacing gas-powered vehicles. And through the strategic placement of charging stations and the wise reuse of gas stations, local governments can do much to accelerate this transition. Investments in pedestrian, bicycle, and other forms of micro-mobility are also promising options that have less political opposition and more potential to reduce VMT, as well as produce greater favorable health impacts than continuing investments in new and wider roads.

In addition to facilitating the adoption of EVs, local governments have many other technology options to enhance the performance of local transportation and other urban systems. Smart improvements in environmental, transportation, public service, and educational systems all hold considerable promise for enhancing equity and sustainability at the same time. If the coronavirus pandemic has taught us anything, it is the critical value of broadband access and the effective use of digital technologies. But technology can serve to advance or impede progress toward smarter growth, and the careless adoption of autonomous vehicles in particular could have dramatic effects (National Center for Smart Growth, 2020). How this plays out could have profound impacts of the future of cities in the United States.

Final Thoughts

It is difficult in a single publication to address all the intricacies and impacts of a sweeping 25–30 year movement to reshape development patterns in a nation as large as the United States. Instead, our intent here has been to engage leading scholars on topics that pertain, or should pertain, to smart growth and elicit insights on the state of smart growth knowledge and practice.

We close with the following observations.

Smart growth was conceived in a period of rapid urban growth with the intent to address middle-class concerns about traffic congestion, environmental degradation, property taxes and the banality of suburban sprawl. Building on previous attempts to control the rate and location of growth, smart growth advocates introduced principles to guide the form of growth, promoted the integration of transportation with land use policy, and encouraged the use of incentives over regulation as a means of implementation. Under the leadership of many prominent national organizations and supported by friendly administrations at the national level and in and many states, the concept spread quickly and arguably became the dominant paradigm in planning today. Yet the extent to which these concepts have become embedded in local plans and policies, how well those policies have been implemented, and how effective those policies have been at resolving the nation's land use challenges remains largely unknown and an important topic for future research.

A substantial and compelling body of research on smart growth has largely validated the proposition that smart growth can bring important environmental benefits. Greater urban density and mixed-use development can reduce VMT and mitigate the adverse environmental consequences of the automobile. Natural resource conservation, as a form of green infrastructure, enhances air and water quality and lowers GHG emissions. But resistance to smart growth implementation in most of the United States remains formidable, the environmental benefits are relatively small compared with the burden of implementation, and the impacts on housing affordability and social equity can be adverse. What's more, after 25–30 years of smart growth advocacy, many of the challenges smart growth sought to address remain unresolved, and some—like housing affordability, VMT, and urban containment— have gotten worse. The good news is that research on the efficacy of smart growth has not slowed, and counter to those who argue the virtues of smart growth are now accepted knowledge, the debate continues. For this reason, we argue that the need for continuing, objective research on smart growth is more compelling than ever.

The Biden administration offers new opportunities to further smart growth implementation, if the implementation of the infrastructure bill includes appropriate environmental safeguards and oversight over local implementation. When provided with sufficient incentives from the federal government, state and local governments could well respond accordingly. But no infrastructure or climate bill alone, no matter how large, will solve the institutional challenges to smart growth implementation. We did not, in this volume, directly address the two procedural principles of smart growth—"Make development decisions predictable, fair, and cost effective" and "Ensure community and stakeholder collaboration in development decisions." But we know adherence to these principles alone will not be adequate to overcome the institutional challenges to smart growth implementation; it may in fact make them larger. We leave the challenge of designing effective institutions for smart growth implementation for future work.

Above we have offered recommendations for progress toward smarter growth at the federal, state, and local levels. But a successful "smart growth 2.0" is likely only if it starts where smart growth initially began—among community leaders and a network of professional and advocacy organizations and with the support of the foundation community. Those leaders who successfully raised awareness about the consequences of urban sprawl and offered some simple strategies to address those consequences must now recognize that the original 10 principles were useful in reframing the debate on urban growth but are no longer well suited to address the salient challenges of today.

While the environmental challenges that gave birth to smart growth have not been resolved, social challenges related to public health, education, equity, gentrification, and more have come to the fore. The efficacy of smart growth principles for addressing these challenges remains much more uncertain. This not only creates a need for more empirical research but should cause smart growth advocates to re-examine the principles of smart growth and consider how they can best advance both environmental and social objectives. Whereas the original smart growth agenda introduced principles of urban design, sought to integrate transportation and land use, and featured incentives over the use of regulation, a "smart growth 2.0" must now take bold new steps to prioritize social as well as environmental challenges, assure that new technologies support and enhance more sustainable development patterns, directly mitigate and adapt to climate change, and work to develop more effective and inclusive governance structures for implementation. The time to start is now.

ACKNOWLEDGEMENTS

We thank without implicating John Landis, Uri Avin, Chris Nelson, and Rolf Pendall for their insightful comments on early versions of this chapter.

NOTES

1. The APA planning advisory service provides customized information on selected topics to subscribers of the service on request. See: https://planning.org/pas/reports/
2. See: https://www.urban.org/policy-centers/metropolitan-housing-and-communities-policy-center/projects/zoning-insights-explore-data-national-longitudinal-land-use-survey
3. See Richter (2020) for a contrarian view. Similarly, Nelson (undated), presents evidence to suggest lot sizes in the United States have been falling since 2016.
4. *Washington Post*, June 6, 2021, HUD to reinstate Obama-era fair housing rule gutted under Trump—minus the 'burdensome' reporting requirement.
5. https://www.c2es.org/document/climate-action-plans/

REFERENCES

Avin, U. (2018, January). The impact of the sustainable communities initiative on regional transportation planning. Presented at the 97th Annual Meeting of the Transportation Board, Washington, DC. Retrieved from https://trid.trb.org/View/1495478

Bento, A., Lowe, S., Knaap, G.-J., & Chakraborty, A. (2009). The market effects of inclusionary zoning. *Cityscape*, *11*(2), 7–26.

Bolen, E., Brown, K., Kiernan, D., & Konschnik, K. (2002). Smart growth: A review of programs state by state. *Hastings Environmental Law Journal*, *8*(2), 145–233.

Clifton, K., Ewing, R., Knaap, G.-J., & Song, Y. (2008). Quantitative approaches to urban form: A multidisciplinary review. *Journal of Urbanism*, *1*(1), 17–46.

DeGrove, J. M. (2005). *Planning policy and politics*. Cambridge, MA: Lincoln Institute of Land Policy.

Downs, A. (2005). Smart growth: Why we discuss it more than we do it. *Journal of the American Planning Association*, *71*(4), 367–378. doi:10.1080/01944360508976707

Echenique, M., Hargreaves, A. J., Mitchell, G., & Namdeo, A. (2012). Growing cities sustainably. *Journal of the American Planning Association*, *78*(2), 121–137.

Edwards, M. M. & Haines, A. (2007). Evaluating smart growth: Implications for small communities, *Journal of Planning Education and Research*, *27*(1), 49–64.

International City Management Association. (2002). *Getting to smart growth: 100 policies for implementation*, Washington, DC: ICMA.

Knaap, G.-J., Lewis, R., & Chakraborty, A. (2021). The rise and fall of smart growth (working paper). College Park, MD: National Center for Smart Growth.

Landis, J.D. (2017). The end of sprawl? Not so fast. *Housing Policy Debate*, *27*(5), 659–697.

Lewis, R., Knaap, G.-J., & Schindewolf, J. (2013). The spatial structure of cities in the United States (working paper). Cambridge, MA: Lincoln Institute of Land Policy.

National Center for Smart Growth. (2020). *Smarter roads, smarter cars, smarter growth? Baltimore-Washington 2040.* https://www.umdsmartgrowth.org/wp-content/uploads/2020/07/DRAFT_PRESTOvol2_11012020_2.pdf

Nelson, A. C. (Undated). Residential lot sizes in the United States over time. Unpublished table.

Park, R. (1936). Human ecology. *American Journal of Sociology*, *42*(July), 1–15.

Pelton, T. (2018). *The Chesapeake in focus: Transforming the natural world*. Baltimore, MD: Johns Hopkins University Press.

Pendall, R., Lo, L., & Wegmann, J. (2021). Shifts toward the extremes, *Journal of the American Planning Association*, *88*(1), 55–66.

Peng, Q. (2020). Global trends in smart growth research: A bibliometric analysis (Working paper). National Center for Smart Growth, College Park, MD.

Ramírez de la Cruz, E. E. (2009). Local political institutions and smart growth: An empirical study of the politics of compact development. *Urban Affairs Review*, *45*(2), 218–246. doi: 10.1177/1078087409334309

Richter, R. (2020). Revisiting urban expansion in the continental United States. *Landscape and Urban Planning*, *204*, 1–5.

Rothbart, M. W. (2020). Does school finance reform reduce the race gap in school funding? Education Finance and Policy, *15*(4), 675–707.

Schuetz, J. (2020). To improve housing affordability, we need better alignment of zoning, taxes, and subsidies (Policy report). Retrieved from Brookings Institution website: https://www.brookings.edu/wp-content/uploads/2019/12/Schuetz_Policy2020_BigIdea_Improving-Housing-Afforability.pdf

Schuetz, J. & Ring, M. (2021). The Washington DC region has built too much housing in the wrong places. Retrieved from Brookings Institution website: https://www.brookings.edu/research/the-washington-dc-region-has-built-too-much-housing-in-the-wrong-places/

Stevens, M. R. (2017). Does compact development make people drive less? *Journal of the American Planning Association*, *83*(1), 7–18, doi:10.1080/01944363.2016.1240044

Talen, E. & Knaap, G.-J. (2003). Legalizing smart growth: An empirical study of land use regulation in Illinois. *Journal of Planning Education and Research*, *22*(4), 345–359.

Transportation Research Board and National Research Council. (2009). *Driving and the built environment: The effects of compact development on motorized travel, energy use, and CO_2 emissions* (Special Report 298). Washington, DC: The National Academies Press. doi.org/10.17226/12747.

Trump, D. J. & Carson, B. (2020, August 16). We'll protect America's suburbs. *Wall Street Journal*.

Urban Institute. (2021). Throughout history, the US failed to integrate transportation and land use. It's still hindering policymaking today. https://www.urban.org/urban-wire/throughout-history-us-failed-integrate-transportation-and-land-use-its-still-hindering-policymaking-today

Wilson, R. & Paterson, R. (2003). *Innovative initiatives in growth management and open space preservation: A national study, PRP 145.* Lyndon B. Johnson School of Public Affairs Policy Research Project. https://repositories.lib.utexas.edu/handle/2152/21513

Index

366

Printed and bound by CPI Group (UK) Ltd, Croydon, CR0 4YY

16/04/2025

14658377-0005